Shelter
Women
and
Development

First and Third World Perspectives

Editor
Hemalata C. Dandekar

Shelter
Women
and
Development

First and Third World Perspectives

Proceedings of
an International Conference

College of Architecture
and Urban Planning

The University of Michigan
May 7–9, 1992

Hemalata C. Dandekar *Editor*

George Wahr Publishing Co.
Ann Arbor

George Wahr Publishing Company
304 1/2 South State Street
Ann Arbor, Michigan 48104
Copyright 1993 by George Wahr Publishing Company. All rights reserved.

Printed in the United States of America.

Library of Congress Catalog Number: 93-060832
ISBN: 0-911586-96-2

Book Design: Lynne Buchman

Cover:
Site Plan: Sites and service project in Mogappair, Madras, India.
Photo: Women inhabitants of Mogappair, by Hemalata C. Dandekar.
Elevation: Amandla Crossing, transitional housing for homeless women and children in Edison, NJ,
              by architects Michael Mostoller and Fred Travisano, Princeton, NJ.

Photographs facing theme introductions were taken at the sites and service project in Mogappair, Madras,
India in 1991 by Hemalata C. Dandekar.

Contents

Preface

This collection of papers is an outcome of a conference, entitled *Shelter, Women, and Development: First and Third World Perspectives*, held at the University of Michigan's College of Architecture and Urban Planning, May 5–7, 1992. The organizers (faculty colleagues, graduate students, and I) wanted to underscore the importance of shelter for women's development in a cross-national, multicultural context. We believed that comparisons and contrasts between First and Third World women's realities and their needs for housing, or shelter, as it is referred to in the Third World, might provide new insights into an issue that had received too little attention from policy makers around the world.

Our original plan for this conference was quite modest: to bring together a handful of established researchers who would present their current thoughts on the relationship between housing and women's development. In discussions with students in the architecture and planning programs at the University of Michigan, the idea of putting out a call for papers and soliciting new and ongoing work on this topic began to appear more exciting. It was clear that the literature on the specific topic of shelter and women's development was not extensive and work encompassing First and Third World situations was virtually nonexistent. We issued a call for papers to ascertain the level of interest in the subject. The call was designed to get the attention not just of academics but also of professional practitioners in architecture and urban planning, activists, and those involved in delivery of services to unsheltered women. In addition to papers, visual and project-related contributions were solicited to highlight the shelter-related products of practitioners and artists.[1] This emphasis on the visual and tangible seemed appropriate for a conference on housing to be hosted by a professional school of architecture and planning and convened in a building shared with a school of art.

The seventy or so abstracts and the numerous expressions of interest in the exhibit that we received confirmed that many people are working in various aspects of this topic. They also illustrated (as reflected by the contributions to this volume) the variety and diversity of approaches being taken. In all, over fifty-five presentations were made at the conference. The exhibit included display boards on built projects and organizations, photography, paintings, sculptures, videos, and poetry. These formal presentations and the numerous informal discussions that took place, some into the early hours of the morning, particularly in the campus housing where many participants were lodged, indicated that the conference was an unequivocal success in establishing a dialogue between those working on this topic in the First and Third Worlds. Observing the more than two hundred people involved with the event was gratifying to the organizers. Immediately following the conference several participants reported that they had experienced the gathering as "empowering." They used words such as "inspiring," "exciting," and "important" to describe their involvement. Recent graduates of our program have written to me to say that their work on the conference was the most formative and challenging experience in their years here. From a pedagogic and consciousness-raising perspective, it seems clear that this conference was a significant undertaking. We hope that others like it will follow.

The quantity of presentations and the range and diversity of the case evidence made visible a critical mass of individuals working on this topic. The discussions brought to focus the idea that a gendered approach to the provision of shelter can help to bring about development for women. Besides enhancing our understanding of the substantive and conceptual terrain, they revealed strategies effective in furthering women's development through the provision of appropriate shelter. These proceedings reflect one of the major virtues of this particular conference, the many different perspectives. To acknowledge, indeed to celebrate, the diversity of views expressed at this gathering, this volume presents as many of the contributions as possible, reflecting our continuing commitment to maintain the inclusive nature of the conference. Contrasting and diverse ways of looking and thinking about the topic were given a forum for expression. As a result, the papers included here vary greatly in length, style, and intent. The authors range from entry-level graduate students to distinguished policy makers, professionals, and academics with many years of experience in related work. The consequence is some unevenness in substantive content and the academic apparatus provided in the various papers. Given the scarce resources (financial, time, and person power) available to bring this work to the point of publication, I had little recourse but to publish the papers more or less as the authors had submitted them. Despite the lack of total consistency in format or completeness of the citations, my hope is that this is a stimulating and useful contribution to this subject.

Editing has also been kept to a minimum to maintain the different voices of contributors. Two contributions, both from Africa, have been included, even though the authors were not at the conference. One (Scarnecchia) was unable to attend and the other (Oruwari) was denied a visa to enter the U.S.A. Some significant verbal

presentations, for which written papers were not submitted, were summarized from video recordings by the theme moderators. They have been presented as such under the theme moderators' authorship (Khan by Aliyar, Gillette and Snyder by Bergholz). All the sessions were videotaped to document the event, but there are no plans at present to edit these recordings.

In the interest of sharing information and facilitating networking, the conference program, a list of registered conference participants, and a list of books submitted by publishers and displayed in a book stall in the exhibit have been included in Appendices A, B, and C, respectively. The organizers of this conference believe that the discussion deserves to be continued. We therefore invite another institution to take up this initiative and host a follow-up conference. The information and experience we obtained from our efforts in hosting this conference at the University of Michigan are available to help facilitate such an effort.

Hemalata C. Dandekar
Conference Chair
Ann Arbor, Michigan, May 1993

Note

1 The resulting exhibit took on a life of its own under the able guidance of two members of the architecture faculty, Professors Melissa Harris and Elizabeth Williams. By featuring projects and buildings, the exhibit complemented the conference and provided a unique view of the action and practice component of effort in this arena. The exhibit has been documented and received recognition elsewhere, including prestigious awards from *Interiors* (January, 1993) and the Association of the Collegiate Schools of Architecture. A list of contributors and the titles of their exhibits can be found in the conference program in Appendix A. A monograph documenting the exhibit and making the work accessible to policy makers, practitioners, academics, and designers is currently in progress.

Acknowledgements

The University of Michigan co-sponsored this conference with two bodies of the United Nations: the United Nations Center for Human Settlements [UNCHS (Habitat)], and the United Nations Fund for Women and Development (UNIFEM). Further, UNCHS (Habitat) extended financial support toward the publication of this book. At the University of Michigan, an initial grant from the University Council on International Academic Affairs was followed by commitments from Dean Robert Beckley of the College of Architecture and Urban Planning, which hosted the conference and provided facilities and staff support; the Horace H. Rackham School of Graduate Studies; the Office of the Vice President for Research; the Women's Studies Program; and the Office of the Vice Provost for Minority Affairs.

Ms. Sujata Shetty, a doctoral student in Urban and Regional Planning, was my right hand from the beginning, fundraising, proposal-writing, stage to the closing hours of the conference. Her efforts at making the event work, and her ability to handle stress cheerfully and constructively, were invaluable. The organization of the conference and accompanying exhibit were a collaborative effort that entailed the active involvement of many students and faculty. Too numerous to list here, some are identified under the heading "conference and exhibit organization" in the conference program in Appendix A. The substantive underpinnings of this conference would not have been as robust without these graduate students and faculty who shaped the thematic boundaries and organized the papers that were submitted. This made for cohesion within each theme. One of the blessings of serving as a faculty member for the last fourteen years at the College of Architecture and Urban Planning at the University of Michigan has been the privilege of working with talented and dedicated graduate students who have been drawn here from all over the world. On a research trip to Bombay last November, six months after the conference, I met some of the women who had participated. In various ways they asked, "Where do you get those students? We don't see them here even if they are Indian!" It is these students, their energy and enthusiasm, that made this conference a success. Involvement in this effort is yielding them significant professional and personal benefits, a great source of satisfaction to me.

The monumental tasks of editing, synthesizing, coordinating, standardizing for consistency, retyping, and cajoling, culminating in the publication of this volume, have also been shared. Two friends, Dr. Rudolf B. Schmerl, Director of Research Relations, the University of Hawaii, and Ms. Janet Lineer, Associate Editor in the College of Engineering at the University of Michigan, promised and provided unconditional help in bringing this manuscript to press. I am very grateful to Dr. Schmerl for his untiring devotion to detailed and careful editorial help and amusing, sometimes caustic, but appropriate commentary on each manuscript. Janet Lineer has worked long and hard at the tedious task of typing or retyping, formatting, standardizing, and making this volume as consistent as possible. Dixie Farquharson, academic secretary in the College, helped in this task at critical junctures. William C. Manspeaker, computer consultant in the College, cheerfully and tirelessly transformed the manuscripts received on computer discs from all over the world, of all sizes and formats, using unknown or unspecified software, so that they were accessible on our machines.

Lynne Buchman, a graduate in Graphic Design from the School of Art at the University of Michigan, designed the cover and layout of this book, bringing style and elegance to the final product. Elizabeth Davenport of George Wahr Publishing Co. believed in this work, understood it, and gave it final shape and coherence. The help of these individuals has made these proceedings possible. My daughter Apurva, who is almost three years old now, has lived gracefully for most of her young life with a mother who has at times been distracted by this "Women and Shelter" undertaking. I am grateful to her for her tolerance. I hope that our collective efforts in this conference and with these proceedings will help to facilitate women's access to shelter, and thus to make life for women of Apurva's generation easier and better.

Hemalata C. Dandekar
Ann Arbor, Michigan, May 1993

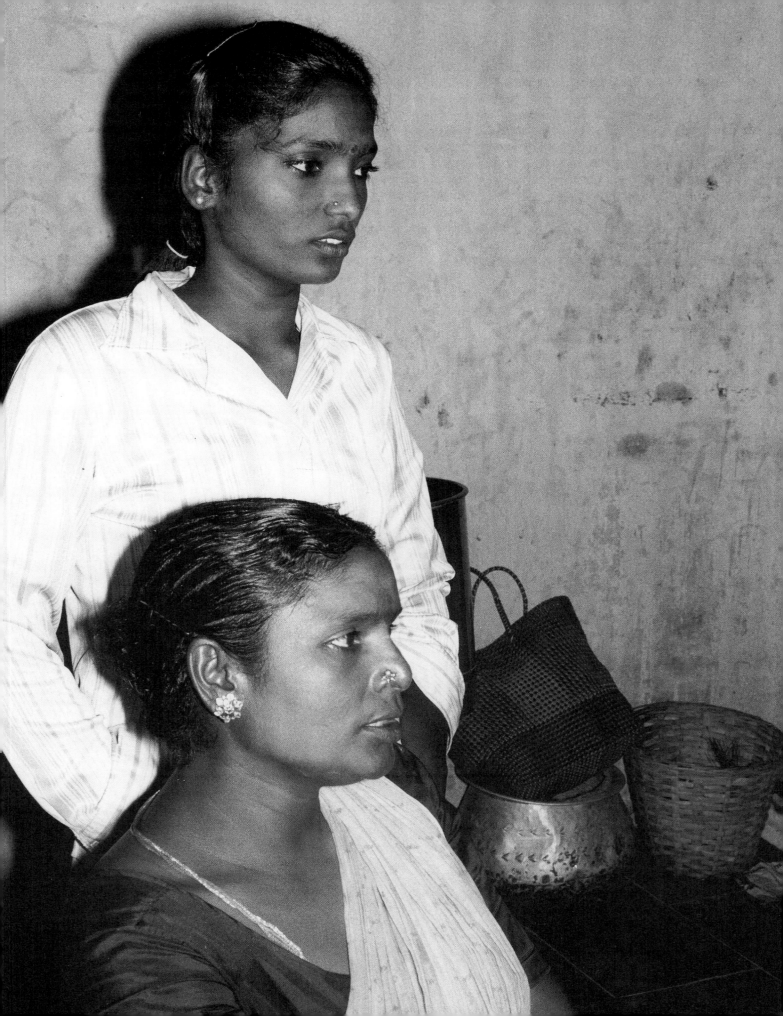

Introduction

Hemalata C. Dandekar

Hemalata C. Dandekar was chair of the University of Michigan international conference, Shelter, Women, and Development: First and Third World Perspectives, hosted at the College of Architecture and Urban Planning, May 7–9, 1992. She is professor in the College and chair of the International Planning and Development concentration in Urban Planning. Her courses include a graduate offering on shelter and physical infrastructure development in the Third World. She has a Bachelor of Architecture, University of Bombay, a Master of Architecture, the University of Michigan, and a Ph.D. in Urban and Regional Planning from the University of California, Los Angeles.

The composition and structure of families have changed dramatically throughout the world in the last five decades. Planned development has followed in the wake of decolonization and independence in much of the Third World. Unleashing the forces of urbanization, modernization, and industrialization, it has served to transform and disrupt the prevailing networks and customs that sustained women in traditional households, irrevocably changing their position and status. In the First World, in countries such as the U.S.A., single-female-headed households have become one of the fastest growing segments of the population. Clearly apparent in various cultures throughout the First and Third Worlds is a fragmentation of the prevailing, traditional, family type.[1] But in the face of these shifts the physical contours of housing and the legal, social, and architectural approaches to housing creation have changed very little. This is a central issue engaging the attention of the authors of these papers.

As the title of this book, *Shelter, Women, and Development: First and Third World[2] Perspectives,* suggests, the papers presented here, which are an outcome of an international conference on this topic, serve to underscore the importance of housing to women's development and to illustrate this in a global, multi-cultural context. They help substantiate the universality of the concern about women's access and relationship to shelter. The term "shelter," rather than housing, has been used in this book, as it often is in Third World countries, to signify not just the physical structure that provides protection, the house as it is recognized in the First World, but also the environment surrounding this structure, including the physical infrastructure, social services, amenities, and other resources available to the residents. Thus the term shelter assumes a truer representation of what constitutes "home" to many, particularly in countries where the physical house itself may only be a tiny, one-room, dilapidated shed of recycled materials. Some papers in this book address the shelter needs of poor women in the First World. They make clear that this definition of home as shelter is pertinent to them too. These papers (Brown and Capponi, Wekerle, du Plessis, Sprague, Peterson) illustrate that the meaning of home, as constituting more than the physical boundaries of a house, holds good for women in the First World too, especially for women who are poor and/or in crisis.

An International Conference on Shelter, Women, and Development

The conference on shelter, women, and development was conceived in early January, 1991, in a conversation with Sujata Shetty, a doctoral student in the Urban Planning Program at Michigan. We were remarking that there appeared to be very little work that concentrated on women's shelter needs, linking this with women's potential for development. Between us we could name three or four books that were significant in the area. As an architect/planner who sometimes works specifically on issues of women's development, I had been interested in this connection for some time. I was exploring some aspects of this topic in pilot research on sites and services projects in Madras and Bombay and in a book on rural women from a village in Maharashtra, India.[3] Sujata and I wondered, who was presently doing work on this topic, and could we bring them to Michigan to obtain an update on the state of the art? Our preliminary review of the literature revealed a small, select number of offerings in First or Third World contexts, very few that juxtaposed the two worlds or offered any theoretical or conceptual framework for understanding the links between shelter, women, and development.[4] It also appeared from the literature review that professionals in practice who were dealing with various aspects of the topic, for instance architects, planners, social workers and lawyers, were talking within their own professions. Clearly we could not address this dearth in conversation about the topic, directly in our own work, but could we, we wondered, stimulate what we perceived to be a much needed conversation between activists, policy makers, professionals, and academics by way of a conference? We discussed this idea with students and faculty around the Michigan campus and there appeared to be a great deal of interest in such a conversation.

Using the seed money we had by this time obtained internally in the University, we expanded our original plans for a small, invited lecture series by experts to an international conference to be hosted in the College of Architecture and Urban Planning at the University of Michigan, May 7–9, 1992. A call for papers was issued. As students and faculty who were primarily involved in the professions of architecture and urban planning, we took shelter as the primary and overarching element in the questions to be addressed. Women's relationship to shelter and its implications for their development were the next order of priority in framing our inquiry. Thus the needed link between the thinking about women as a special group with specific needs for, and relationship

to, shelter was articulated. The objectives of the conference were as follows:

1. To establish that access to shelter is an important component of women's ability to achieve "development"; that housing issues have significant implications for the economic, legal, and social status of women around the world; and that independent access to housing might become particularly important for women in societies where development is carrying societies from the "traditional" to the "modern."

2. To explore whether there is something to be gained from taking a cross-cultural, cross-national, cross-class look at the issues. The underlying expectation was that there are some common attributes which stem from the gender of a person seeking shelter, attributes which transcend the boundaries of culture, nation, and class. It was anticipated that these commonalties would surface, as would the differences which exist, when one compares the issue in First and Third World contexts.

3. To establish a connection between the issue of women and their shelter with the larger discourse on women and their development; to bring to focus the idea that a gendered approach to shelter provision can yield development for women.

4. To achieve not just an enhanced understanding of the links between shelter and women's development but also to identify opportunities for redesigning policy that would achieve greater success in enhancing women's access to shelter and thus facilitate their development. In short, the idea was to talk both about the problems and about creative solutions.

Seven themes related to women's access to housing and the implications of this for women's development were identified through collective deliberation by the organizing committee of students and faculty and publicized in the call for papers. In response to the subject matter addressed in the abstracts that we received, two more themes were added to the list. These nine themes were eventually addressed in some fifty-five presentations at the conference, as follows:

1. Shelter Policy: Implications for Women's Development
2. The Structure of Legal Interventions
3. Shelter and Women in Crisis
4. Women's Participation in the Production of Shelter
5. Shelter and Income Opportunities
6. Women and Shelter-Related Services and Infrastructure
7. Nontraditional Living Arrangements: Beyond the Nuclear Family
8. Design and the Creation of Shelter for Women
9. Shelter Options for Elderly Women

We tried to define the subject matter narrowly in its relationship to the built form. Environmental considerations were limited to physical infrastructure that was shelter-related. Given that large-scale environmental issues were, and continue to be, addressed in other very visible global venues, this delineation made sense to us. Even so, we found that a very large terrain was encompassed in our delineation of themes. To further define the theoretical and substantive boundaries for operational purposes, each theme was reviewed and amplified by graduate student moderators in collaboration with a faculty moderator who assumed oversight responsibility for the theme. The abstracts we received, particularly those that developed gender-based case studies of particular shelter provision efforts, often addressed issues that illustrated several of the nine themes simultaneously. Papers were placed in particular themes on the basis of the original abstracts, sometimes after discussion with the authors. These thematic placements of papers at the conference have been maintained in this book for continuity with the conference and ease of organization.

In the period between acceptance of abstracts by January, 1992, and the conference itself held in May, 1992, student moderators expanded on the thematic boundaries and communicated these to their panelists. These thematic outlines were provided in the conference program (Appendix A) to help situate, for the panelists and the conference attendees, individual papers in a larger context. Following the conference and reflecting on the discussions that occurred during it, overview papers further delineating the thematic areas and framing the issues were written by several of the student moderators. These have been included in these proceedings as the lead paper in each thematic section. Some of these overview papers provide comparisons and contrasts of issues addressed in the papers within that theme. In addition, a brief "road map" to the papers in each theme is provided at the beginning of each, to allow the reader some sense of rationale for the particular sequence.

Nevertheless, the substantive cohesion implied in this thematic organization and the "hard-line" differentiation between themes hold good only to a limited extent. There are many overlaps in the thematic content of individual papers. There are also obvious gaps: important subject areas germane to this topic have not been addressed. For example, the body of literature and work within architecture that addresses the question of appropriate technology, design, and specifications to make construction of shelter more accessible to women

has not been touched upon. Ways to make planning, zoning, and other regulatory mechanisms more friendly to women's aspirations have not been addressed in the context of the First World, where regulation can present major hurdles to innovations in design. But this book was not conceived as a comprehensive, definitive overview of the field. Rather, it is a child of chance and serendipity, a result of more than fifty very diverse perceptions of the topic from a multiplicity of disciplinary viewpoints. This book celebrates this multiplicity of vision, and asks to be accepted for what it is, and what it does do: provide a multifaceted prism for viewing the field. We hope it will succeed in making a contribution and initiate a much needed discourse.

Insights from Multiple Visions

The authors of the papers that follow substantiate, through their many "stories" of women in different parts of the world, that consideration of women's needs for shelter is not just about the problems of poor and homeless women and children in the inner city of North America or the slums and squatter settlements of the Third World. Their work illustrates that this topic is pertinent to more than just such "minority groups." They point out that efforts to bring attention to this issue, which are at times undermined by labeling them a radical feminist effort of little significance to most women, are needed and significant and pertinent to all women around the world, across class, at some time in their life cycle. The papers underscore the point that women's access to shelter and the impact this can have on their own, their children's, and societal development is, and should be, a concern of the majority around the world. Half of the world's population is female and improving women's access to safe and reliable shelter changes the access their children have to safety and security and creates the necessary infrastructure for the development and nurture of a majority of the world's population.

As several of the papers illustrate, policy makers around the world have generally ignored the special issues around women's needs for shelter (see, for example, Shetty and Aliyar, Tinker, Wekerle). If addressed, they are addressed as problems of the minority of women in the world who have been rendered destitute and are alone. The thinking about providing shelter for them is done in a context of providing social welfare and charity (Bhatnagar, du Plessis). But the approach to facilitating the provision of shelter to women needs to be framed not only in social welfare terms, nor just as an issue critical only to a minority group, but also as one which, in various ways, embraces almost all the world's women, over time, across class and cultures, and, insofar as it affects their children, affects a majority of the global population. The authors of these papers are saying, directly and indirectly, that this is an issue which, if addressed effectively, has the potential of empowering groups now vulnerable and needing special consideration, enabling them to become valuable contributors to a nation's development.

The papers in this volume highlight that women in all circumstances, including those in nuclear families, may find themselves equally vulnerable in their entitlement and claim to housing. Women's share in their families' homes are not legally protected in many countries around the world, despite the substantial contributions they may have made to acquiring and maintaining this home (Oruwari, Todes and Walker). Few women have title, sole or jointly with their husbands, to their homes. In addition, in many Western countries where women may enjoy legal title to their property and equal rights with their spouses, mortgages can often last longer than marriages, resulting in an asset difficult to divide when families dissolve. The literature substantiates that, in such circumstances, in the U.S.A., given the differential in earnings of men and women, most women, as the partners, with the lesser earning potential and usually having custody of any children, experience a reduction in the quality of housing they can afford following the divorce (Franck and Ahrentzen, 1989). It is not surprising if, in the Third World where women's *de facto* and *de jure* rights to capital assets such as land and shelter are much weaker (Tinker, Larsson), women who face a broken marriage fear being left destitute and homeless more than anything else (Scarnecchia). If things go awry in the marriage, one of the first thing a woman is threatened with is the loss of her home and the loss of shelter that is her larger sense of home.

Economic stresses in the Third World continue to undermine and destroy traditional social structures for women and their children without replacing them with alternatives. Needing to migrate to the city to survive is often a fact of life for many, especially those on the margins of rural society. In the Third World, urbanization rates have risen dramatically and an increasingly larger percentage of urban dwellers live in shanty towns and squatter settlements. Even in shanty towns, access to housing, although easier than in more formalized housing types, can be difficult for women on their own (Todes and Walker). The lack of housing appropriate to

their situation and needs is a serious burden for women throughout the world. In crisis or in transition, women in a variety of circumstances, abandoned by their partners, widowed, experiencing spousal abuse, addicted to drugs and alcohol, heading single-parent families, impoverished women who are physically or mentally ill, all may require access to a safe and affordable shelter. In the First World homeless shelters can typically become the refuge of women in crisis for some time although the increasing rate of homelessness in women with children is stressing the existing system's ability to provide help (Brown and Capponi). In the Third World, women may face many of the same crises, but shelters to meet their needs are rare, and access to them is so constrained that shelters that exist remain vacant or underutilized. Neela Dabir explains this paradox as stemming from the needs of these institutions to protect themselves from the overwhelming demand for housing in general, shared by many women in societies such as India's where there is an overall and chronic housing shortage.

It would be presumptuous, and probably fruitless, to attempt an overarching summary of the substantive issues which resonate in these papers and which cut across a number of themes. But an exercise in "meta-ethnology" (Nobit and Hare, 1988) identifying from non-comparable, individual renditions of cases described here some observations that seem quite broadly applicable, may be useful in making some larger overview of the arguments made. Given the diversity of styles and content of these papers the exercise is difficult. Readers will develop their own, different, lists of critical issues. But six elements appear to be of great importance across the thematic areas addressed, permeating the discourse at many levels overtly or implicitly. It is very clear as one reads these papers that women, in their need for housing and the relationship of this to their development, should not be considered a homogeneous group. To understand aspects of their condition and need, they must be stratified along criterion that include: whether they are in urban or rural contexts; whether they are from destitute, poor, low, or middle, or upper-income levels; whether they work in the formal or the informal sectors of the economy or are involved solely in domestic, household tasks; and whether they possess through customary or statutory laws the right to ownership of a shelter asset. Given that such categories are applied in examining the problem, the diversity of women's relationship to housing that is revealed includes the effect of the following phenomena:

1. The Fact of a Gender-Neutral Approach to Housing

Several papers refer to the fact that most policy related to housing has been developed so as to be gender-neutral. Shetty and Aliyar highlight the fact that internationally, at the nation-state level, housing policy has given little consideration to gender differences when defining the need for housing. Rather, income has been considered the dominant factor, and policy to facilitate provision of shelter for low- and moderate-income households has been the mainstream effort. In addition, ideas of the nuclear family as the universal norm have permeated all aspects of the shelter-provision system. The cases presented here illustrate that the successful projects which have been identified and described as meeting women's particularized need for shelter have been made to work within the existing policy framework which addresses income and poverty criteria. Some exceptions are identified at the project level (Bhatnagar, Khan) in various countries. Some of the policies that do differentiate along the gender dimension are described as resulting from the influence of some multinational AID institutions. Tinker points out that the role of multinational agencies, relative to shelter, have been similarly gender-neutral with the exception of UNCHS and UNIFEM, which have evolved a specific focus on women and articulated the need to change women's rights to land and housing. UNCHS (Habitat), hand in hand with UNIFEM, has been instrumental in introducing ideas of gender, and the ways to facilitate the inclusion of women into the shelter sector in various countries are discussed (Tinker, Celik). These institutions have attempted to influence the design of World Bank projects on shelter and to infuse them with a gender dimension. But barring such a push from these international agencies, there appears to be very little broad-based impetus toward more gendered shelter policy.

2. The Pervasive Influence of the Nuclear Family and Patriarchal Traditions

Most thinking and analyses about housing appear to have been connected with the norm of the nuclear family in the First World (Gardiner), or nuclear and extended family in the Third World (Scarnecchia, Stucki), as the unit of consideration. In these papers there is much discussion about all the other ways in which other households are formed, are surviving, and making do (Pothukuchi, Varley, Hastings and Yen). There is discourse on the ideology of the nuclear family. It is an ideology which influences the negative manner in which non-conforming households and families are treated by

housing agencies and by the larger society (Sayne). Several factors are described as operative in the persistence of this view of what constitutes the "appropriate" family. They include the institutional, legal structures of a society, the customs and practices that are prevalent, and, significantly, by women's own sense of what is, or is not, accessible or possible for them outside this family norm. Furthermore, women who have fallen out of the structure of a nuclear family and are poor have been perceived as the "undeserving poor" (Gardiner, Sayne). The ideology of "appropriate family" as it is shaped by various forms of patriarchal traditions also continues to surface cross-nationally. These ideas, which are rooted in, and evolved from, the historical needs and mandates of a land based, settled, agrarian, patriarchal society have implications for how women who do not conform to the norm are being differentially treated around the world today *vis à vis* legal rights and entitlement to housing.

3. The Value of Housing as a Productive Good

The consideration of women as producers of income essential for family survival and the importance of shelter in that activity is central to the position taken in some of the papers. Shelter is described as important in income generation and delineated in ways that it cannot be treated, as it conventionally is, as another consumer good. The importance of shelter in women's ability to garner income is based on two facts. One is that in many Third World cultures the societal environment will not allow women a domain outside the domestic one where income may be earned. A home therefore becomes the base where work for cash income, such as sewing, piece work, etc., might occur (Chowdhury, Bhatt). The second is that women working in such ways must continue as the primary child care providers and must carry out their other obligations to their families. If the shelter is not secure or adequate, a number of avenues for augmenting income are denied these women.

4. The Pernicious Effect of Poverty

Issues addressed in a number of these papers are related to the fact that poverty denies a very large group of women access to ownership of shelter and the lack of security of tenure that this implies. The percentage of women in formal sector employment, where wages are higher and more reliable and benefits are generally better, is considerably less than that of men. Poor women by and large do not tend to have formal sector occupations. They are thus less able to buy and own their homes. Poverty severely limits available shelter for women and their children. As potential renters, women with children and without formal sector jobs are perceived as less reliable, at risk, and at the bottom of the landlord's priority list of desirable occupants of available housing. Having to rent, with children, and needing to earn income that is more domestic and shelter-based is double or triple jeopardy for poor women. The physical vulnerability of poor women and their children is alluded to in several papers. Surveys record a high incidence of sexual harassment from landlords or agents of landlords of poor women in housing environments where they feel vulnerable and fear eviction (Novac). The importance of addressing this vulnerability is underscored by data that indicate that in the U.S.A. almost three-quarters of poor, female-headed households rent their shelter.

5. The Need for Appropriate Designs to Satisfy Women's Needs

A series of papers deals with appropriate design, empowering design, and ways to achieve such design. A variety of services beneficial for poor women are discussed — child care, health care, security and income — through the provision of group spaces where certain kinds of activities can occur. Physical design, town planning, and planning regulation changes that can come out of considering women as income producers on the domestic front are suggested. Sex-segregated housing to protect women who feel physically vulnerable is described. Papers commenting on the housing needs of women demonstrate that current zoning is often inimical to the ways in which women earn income, using their homes for cottage industry production, or for provision of services such as child care, or by sub-letting to a tenant who can provide both revenue and security. Needed innovations and changes that can be implemented by the design and planning professions are suggested.

6. The Need to Meet Both Practical and Strategic Development Objectives through Shelter

The papers offering gender-based analyses of shelter suggest that there are structural reasons why women are in a disadvantaged position in society at large and therefore in their access to shelter. They postulate that a developmentally oriented shelter strategy must in the long run change the balance of power between men and women in a society. The SPARC group's work with pavement dwellers (Bapat and Patel) illustrates the type of mobilization that might result in changing power

structures and relationships between men and women. By paying attention to process, to empowerment and mobilization around shelter, these papers delineate an agenda larger than shelter alone, an agenda related to societal structure and changing women's position within it.

As one reads these "stories" and discovers the recurring themes that resonate throughout this book, a compelling argument for paying special attention to women's needs for shelter emerges. Why, one then wonders, have the relevant professions and policy makers been so remiss in identifying women and their needs for shelter as a significant area needing attention? In the wake of radical social changes which have influenced family structures or the dynamics at play within traditional families, housing policy, design, financing, and societal notions of entitlement to shelter have all remained virtually unchanged. In the First World, professions — not only planners and architects but also bankers, lawyers, and policy makers who determine social programs — continue to support the notion that families are made up of two adults raising children in a free-standing home. Most houses, particularly in the First World, have continued to be designed to fit idealized nuclear families, although it is becoming increasingly clear that a significant number of the world's families don't fit this mold (Pothukuchi). Design professionals involved in housing and its environment, such as in the planning of cities, continue to endorse housing that fits the shelter needs of the nuclear family, although such families never existed in some cultures, don't exist any more in others, or exist in some societies for a relatively short period in people's life cycle.

As a result of the professional's monochromatic view of families as nuclear, there is an unrecognized need for alternative kinds of spaces. Single mothers need protected and safe play spaces for their children where child care responsibilities might be shared (Sprague, Wekerle). Women needing to look after children while earning an income need shelter that allows for in-house offices or work spaces where providing value-adding activities, services, or small-scale production is possible and legal (Kusow, Selat, Mahajan, Bhatt). In urban areas any zoning laws and building codes make it difficult for women, even if they have access to housing, to use it in ways that enable them to sustain themselves in their particular situation (Mahajan, Keigher, Hastings and Yen). Religion and customs dictate women's use of home and public spaces (Chowdhury, Scarnecchia) and education and world view influence women's aspirations for housing and what they may plan to do in them

(Adarkar). But the professionals who design and regulate the built environment continue to plan and build homes for family types that are, or are about to become, the minority in some cultures, and in the process render others homeless or vulnerable to predation and homelessness. In addition to the ideological, philosophical, and cultural factors that have been operative in this neglect, and referred to in these papers, there appear to be some established postures within the professions that have contributed to these dilemmas.

The Posture within Shelter-Related Professions

It is useful to understand why, in the professional discourse, the topic of women's need for shelter and the relationship of this to development has been so neglected. Perhaps the oversight stems from the fact that the topic has remained in the peripheral vision of several potential advocate groups. For example, although they have long recognized the importance of housing/shelter to people's sense of well-being and to their social and psychological development, architects and urban planners have been slow in responding to and calling for design change in the face of far-reaching shifts in family structures.

Shelter and Development

In the design professions, John Turner's work (1976) was critical in pointing out the significance of housing to people's development. Turner argued for a design process in which poor families' particular aspirations and needs should help to shape the design of their ideal physical home. But neither he, nor others who have built on his work, have looked at gender in the meaning of housing to people's well-being. Inter- and intra-household differences based on gender have not been a significant factor in the analysis and thus the link between shelter, women, and development have remained understated in the design disciplines

In addition, at the level of national, macro formulation of development strategies, the idea that some component of investment in the housing sector stimulates economic development has only recently gained some currency (Rodwin, 1987). In national policy deliberations, the provision of housing, especially to lower-income groups, has been viewed as primarily an investment in social welfare, and architects and planners have been slow in gathering the information needed to dispel this notion. "Mainstream" economists only tentatively accept that shelter creation and investments in the shelter sector contribute to stimulating economic

production.[5] This has resulted in a paucity of consideration of ways to bring about social and economic development through purposive intervention in the housing sector and even less to doing this with an agenda of facilitating women's development.

In contrast, recent feminist discourse in architecture and urban planning has quite specifically tried to establish the importance of housing/shelter for the well-being of women and their dependent children (Mosher, 1987; Franck and Ahrentzen, 1989; Sprague, 1991). These writers have drawn on the experiences of housing activists, design professionals, and social service providers and on the opinions of individual beneficiaries of these investments. They have succeeded in introducing the notion that gender must be considered in the shelter sector. Advocacy groups in the Third World pressing for shelter as a basic right have included feminists who have introduced the notion that consideration of gender is important in formulating policy about shelter as a basic right. However, these feminists have remained on the margins of advocacy and activism. Consequently, questions of how to bring professional service to focus on gender issues have remained marginal to the mainstream of various relevant professions and to the paradigms of policy makers, although indications that the international shortage of housing is most importantly a woman's problem are substantial.

Women and Development

In the discourse on topics of women and development, too, the contribution that shelter can make in facilitating women's development has received scant attention. In the literature on women and development the significance of home to women is addressed in books as different as *Moscow Women* (Hansson and Linden, 1983) in which Russian women cite the lack of housing as a critical constraint to women's autonomy, and *Women of Tropical Africa* (Paulme, 1963) in which the importance of housing is articulated by women in pastoral societies. In literature and documentation around the world, one finds ordinary women articulate in their rendition of the importance of housing in their lives. Lisa Peattie, elaborating on the various meanings of housing, begins to explain why this might be so. Although Peattie does not herself make a gender analysis she describes a number of attributes of housing that provide benefits particularly important to women, especially poor women, such as security of tenure and ability to involve themselves in income-producing activity.[6]

The stresses on traditional family structures under the impact of development have raised several concerns. The destruction of social structures such as polygamous families in West Africa and joint families in South Asia has removed old supports yet not substituted new ones in women's lives. The feminist, professional community in architecture and urban planning has posited that shelter and development issues are intrinsically linked to gender. However, until recently within the disciplines of architecture and urban planning and in the discourse on women and development, this was not recognized as important. Early works such as Ester Boserup's pathbreaking *Women's Role in Economic Development* (1974) served to "legitimize" the gender and development link. More recent works such as Vandana Shiva's *Staying Alive: Women, Ecology and Development in India* (1989), and Sen and Growen's *Development, Crisis and Alternative Visions* (1987) have served to make some of the connections between the larger physical and environmental domain and a gendered development process. But the link of shelter to development has remained relatively weak.

Shelter, Women, and Development

The need to examine the gender dimension in the shelter sector has been given some visibility in works such as *Women, Human Settlements and Housing* (Moser and Peake, 1987).[7] However, much more remains to be done. By and large, in both developed and developing countries, the thinking about women's needs for housing is subsumed under the generic consideration of the larger societal need for housing. The question of the need and ability to pay for housing is assayed through the stratification on income lines alone. As a result, one observes, and the papers in this volume illustrate, parallels in the problems of women's access to shelter, entitlement, and property rights that stem from the role the State chooses to play and from the postures of the various professionals who are involved. However, the literature specifically addressing the topic of shelter and women in theoretical terms remains quite modest.[8]

Conclusion

To summarize, the nine themes delineated for the discourse at the University of Michigan's International Conference on Shelter, Women, and Development: First and Third World Perspectives, and the conference papers presented in this book, outline an approach to, and rationale for, thinking about shelter, its meaning in women's lives, and the manner of its provision. The case studies presented provide examples of how the

access to shelter, or the lack thereof, and its appropriateness in tangible, physical terms, has significant implications for the well-being and development of women. Access to shelter is a life span issue for women. From childhood through childbearing and in the later phases of a woman's life, appropriate shelter can help provide the security, safety, access, entitlements, power, and resources to enable a woman to maneuver and negotiate a more rewarding life for herself, her children, and family. Although the need for shelter can be, and is, argued to be a basic human need for everyone, a gendered approach such as the one taken in these papers reveals the special concerns and issues that must be addressed if enabling, development-oriented, shelters are to be accesible to women and their dependent children.

Women and their dependent children together constitute a majority of the global population and represent a very large proportion of the global poor. If the premise that development includes the concepts of equity, distribution, and empowerment is accepted, then it is difficult not to pay attention to the contribution that appropriate shelter can make in attaining this objective for this majority. The need to develop a gendered perspective when thinking about shelter policy is underscored. Widespread changes in traditional family structures and the increase in single, female-headed households have raised perplexing questions about the kinds of housing needed, the structures that facilitate access to it, and the relationship of this to the well-being of women and children. The topic of shelter, women, and development therefore promises to be of particular significance for the 1990's and beyond. These papers seek to make a positive contribution in identifying the various parameters of the global need of women for shelter and to finding creative solutions that facilitate women's development.

Notes

[1] As some of the papers in this book attest (Varley, Pothukuchi), it is difficult to get precise figures on the extent of non-traditional, non-nuclear families in the world. Many factors result in the undercounting or under-reporting of such households. For example, in the Third World women who are heading up households because they have been abandoned by their husbands are reluctant to so state as they will lose social status. Long-term migration of men away from their families and the extent that leaves women *de facto* in charge of taking care of their families is another phenomenon about which too little is known. Dwyer and Bruce (1988) claim that up to two-thirds of the Third World households can be considered headed by women. The UNCHS's estimates are that at least one-third of the world's households are headed by women. In the U.S. more than half of the poor households in the country were women alone or women in

female-headed households and 70 percent of these rented their homes (Bishop, Dabir).

[2] The terms First and Third Worlds have been used here although they are ill-defined and furthermore considered to bear a western bias. A three-world classification of countries during the cold war era meant the "First World" of Washington, the "Second World" of Moscow, and the emergence of a Third World attempting to find an alternative path for humanity. This is no longer applicable. I have used the terms First and Third Worlds here as indicating an economic and material reality of nation states, of aggregate affluence versus poverty. The terms are not precise, but they do offer a simple and "imagable" shorthand to very complicated and differentiated economic and social realities throughout the world.

[3] An article describing women's access to the sites and services plots in the projects in Madras and Bombay is in progress. The photographs used in the body of this book and Chapter 30 draw on this work. The book, a follow-up to *Men to Bombay, Women at Home,* (Dandekar 1986), (working title *Where Shall I Go? What Shall I Do? Rural Indian Women Face Development*, CSSEA Publication, the University of Michigan) will be available in late 1993.

[4] Moser and Peake's book (1987) provided the greatest contribution to a theoretical framework, but was based on cases only from the Third World.

[5] L.H. Klassen, J.G.D. Hoogland, and M.J.F. van Pelt discuss the difficulties of distinguishing between the consumption and production aspects of habitat activities in Lloyd Rodwin, ed., *Shelter Settlement and Development.* They argue that judicious habitat investments for shelter for the poor do result in development, especially in a basic needs approach but also to some extent in strategies with rapid economic growth as the primary goal.

[6] Lisa Peattie, in "Housing Policy in Developing Countries: Two Puzzles," in *Third World Development,* Vol. 7, Pergamon Press, 1979, posits a seven-part rationale for the importance of urban housing which includes elements such as the public image of the resident, the right of access to city resources, access to profit through rent or as investment value, and as places of production and exchange.

[7] Moser and Peake posit that, for the investment in shelter to yield development for women, the shelter and the process of its creation must meet both the immediate pragmatic needs of the women as well as what the authors refer to as their strategic needs, which empower women and strengthen their abilities to obtain development for themselves and their families.

[8] There are several publications at the case level such as *Women Block Makers in Kenya,* United Nations Centre for Human Settlements (Habitat):1988 which enumerate success stories and the process aspects of achieving such success (Celik). However much work remains to be addressed. The theoretical discourse on how, where, and why to look at this issue is quite scarce.

References

Boserup, Ester. 1974. *Women's Role in Economic Development.* New York: St. Martin's Press.

Dwyer, Daisy, and Judith Bruce, eds. 1988. *A Home Divided: Women and Income in the Third World.* Stanford: Stanford University Press.

Franck, Karen, and Sherry Ahrentzen, eds. 1989. *New Households, New Housing.* New York: Van Nostrand Reinhold.

Hansson, Carola, and Karin Linden. 1983. *Moscow Women: Thirteen Interviews.* New York: Pantheon Books.

Moser, Caroline and Linda Peake, eds. 1987. *Women, Human Settlements and Housing,* London: Tavistock.

Paulme, Denise. 1963. *Women of Tropical Africa.* Berkeley: University of California Press.

Sen, Gita, and Caren Growen. 1987. *Development, Crisis and Alternative Visions.* New York: Monthly Review Press.

Shiva, Vandana. 1989. *Staying Alive: Women, Ecology, and Development in India.* London: Zed Books.

Rodwin, Lloyd. 1989. *Shelter, Settlement and Development.* Winchester, Mass: Allen & Unwin.

Sprague, Joan Forrester. 1991. *More Than Housing: Lifeboats for Women and Children.* Boston: Butterworth Architecture.

Turner, John F.C., 1976. *Housing by People: Towards Autonomy in Building Environments.* New York: Pantheon Books.

Noblit, George W., and R. Dwight Hare. 1988. *Meta-Ethnography: Synthesizing Qualitative Studies.* Beverly Hills: Sage.

Nelson, Nici. 1979. *Why Has Development Neglected Rural Women?* Oxford: Pergamon Press.

Rogers, Barbara. 1979. *The Domestication of Women: Discrimination in Developing Societies.* London: Tavistock Publications

Waterson, Albert. 1965. *Development Planning: Lessons of Experience,.* Baltimore: The Johns Hopkins Press.

Theme 1
Shelter Policy: Implications for Women's Development

Two assumptions underlie the formulation of existing policy related to shelter around the world. The first is that difficulties in access to shelter affect men and women equally but are differentiated across income lines. This has served to make income the primary, and at times the sole, basis for assessing the housing needs of family units. The second is an all-pervasive notion, particularly emphasized in the First World, that the nuclear family is the norm. This idea persists despite the trend of increasing numbers of non-nuclear and nontraditional households, including those headed by single parents. The papers in this theme have explored the issue from several directions. The first two papers, (Aliyar, Shetty and Tinker) look at existing housing policies around the world and critically examine their genesis, evolution, and impact. Their analysis of housing policies in different countries and review of ideas espoused by major aid institutions shed light on the questions of how far we have come, and how far we have to go, in forging gender-sensitive housing policy. The next two papers are views of an administrator (Bhatnagar) and a policy maker (Khan) from South Asia. They illustrate, through examples of successful interventions in India and Bangladesh, housing projects and policy that incorporate a gender perspective. The importance of the governmental posture in macro policy as it impacts women's access to housing is provided in the empirically based work from South Africa (Todes and Walker). This position is reiterated for the more specific case of housing cooperatives in Zimbabwe (Vakil). A strong case is made for formulating policies geared specifically to the needs of women. Despite this need, poor women in non-nuclear or nontraditional households have been viewed as the "undeserving poor" as Gardiner describes in a historical review of national housing policies in Britain and the United States. Questions remain such as: What should be the aims of gender-sensitive housing policy? Who should frame such policy and how? What is the time frame under which such policy can be made operative? Can these policies be designed to meet strategic and practical gender needs? Novac, in her paper delineating the vulnerability of poor women renting housing in Toronto, argues for gender-sensitive legal interventions in housing, a position that is addressed in more detailed in Theme 2.

Photo: *Hemalata C. Dandekar*

Chapter 1
A Policy Overview

Vinitha Aliyar and Sujata Shetty

Vinitha Aliyar received a Bachelor of Architecture from Madras, India, and a Master of Housing and Interior Design from Virginia Polytechnic Institute. She has worked for numerous architectural firms, both in India and the U.S. She has also held teaching positions at Virginia Polytechnic Institute, Eastern Michigan University, and the University of Michigan. She is currently a doctoral candidate in Architecture at the University of Michigan, Ann Arbor. Her research interests include affordable housing, environment-behavior issues in mass housing, participatory design processes, and the impact of architectural ideology on mass housing efforts.

Sujata Shetty is a student in the Urban and Regional Planning Program at the University of Michigan, studying for a Ph.D. in Urban, Technological, and Environmental Planning. She received a Bachelor of Arts in Architecture in 1988 from the Delhi School of Planning and Architecture and a Master of Urban Planning in 1992 from the University of Michigan. Her areas of interest are in planning for developing countries, the role of women in urbanization and government policies regarding low-income housing.

Two assumptions underlie existing policies related to development and shelter. The first is that the difficulty in access to shelter affects men and women equally. The second is that the nuclear family is the norm and, therefore, the sole social criterion for the creation of policy. Even though these two assumptions have been common to developed and developing nations, in crafting their policies, countries have pursued myriad emphases. The focus in the developed world has been on home ownership, and consequently policies have overwhelmingly aimed at the middle class. In the developing world, housing policies have been intended to meet the tremendous shortage in housing for the urban poor. The housing crisis is perceived as a more visible problem in urban areas and as a result rural housing issues are given secondary importance. Therefore there exists an additional urban-rural dichotomy in Third World countries, one that pervades many domains, housing being one of them.

In the First World, housing issues have shifted from the realm of design implications of the built environment in the home and the city, through women's work and its relationship to home and family (Hayden, 1981; Werkerle *et al.,* 1979; Wright, 1981) to encompass issues that affect housing and women—spousal abuse, substance abuse, homelessness, and new ways in which women are housing themselves (Kozol, 1988; Watson, 1984 & 1988; Austerberry and Watson, 1984). For the most part, the current discourse has concentrated on the issues themselves and has seldom advocated gender-specific housing policies. In the United States, housing policies have aimed at reduction of government spending and have tried to take account of dramatic changes in family structure—the non-traditional family.

Due to the tremendous quantitative shortage in housing in the Third World, there has been work, albeit marginal, on women and housing policy. The corresponding literature on shelter has only recently begun to focus on the special needs of women. Work in this domain has been to "bring to the attention of national governments and international agencies the extent to which women have been 'left out' in housing provision ... the focus has been to show that the specific needs of women have been excluded from current housing policy and programmes" (Moser, 1987: 2–3). Despite numerous publications by the United Nations Center for Human Settlements (UNCHS) on women and human settlements, scant attention has been paid to women's housing needs and ways to meet them. Moser (1987;1989) has proposed a conceptual framework supporting women and shelter policy in the Third World. Most work in the area has been empirical, usually in the form of project evaluations.

Our aim in this paper is to trace the need for gender-specific housing and development policies, both in the First and Third World context. Due to the lethargic and piecemeal manner in which most governments are responding to the need for development strategies and for housing policies, we argue that there is a growing crisis in development (especially in the Third World) and in the housing arena (both First and Third World), with women forming the bulk of the most vulnerable groups. In our paper we have discussed the conceptual and theoretical premises that have spearheaded a rapidly growing interest in gender-sensitive shelter and development issues.

In our discussion we have used gender in the context of overall development as a base for considerations of gender issues in the housing sector. A brief discussion of existing housing policies in Third and First World countries that may possibly be precursors to a more detailed and definitive policy on women and housing has been included. The inherent problems of operating within the parameters of gender-neutral development and shelter policies in developed and developing nations are highlighted.

Underlying Conceptual and Theoretical Framework

The need to gear shelter policy specifically to women has been articulated from an ideological perspective by Moser. Strategic and practical needs and interests have been combined in premises to explain the need for a gender-specific approach to development and, consequently, shelter.

The Concept

Despite the existence of programs dealing with income generation, health care, nutrition, and education for women, these programs have been isolated, rarely an integral part of a more comprehensive gender-sensitive approach to planning or housing. The importance of a gender-driven planning framework, as a specific planning approach that incorporates theoretical feminist concerns, has been articulated by Moser (1989). She posited that it is difficult to incorporate the gender variable into existing planning paradigms. To accommodate the gender variable, a major restructuring of the paradigm shift is in order. As an ideological premise,

this idea has gained currency in academic circles, but is manifested only in a very weak form by governmental and funding agencies.

The argument for specific foci on housing for women was first put forth by Moser (1987; p. 6):

> Men and women play different roles in society with gender differences shaped by ideological, historical, religious, ethnic, cultural and economic determinants. These roles show both similarities and differences across and between classes as well as societies. An understanding of the social construction of gender relations also recognizes that because men and women play different roles in society they often have different needs. Therefore in the examination of gender and human settlements and the planning of housing policy, it becomes important to desegregate within families and communities on the basis of gender.

The literature provides abundant references to women's empowerment via specific examples and case studies. There is no comprehensive work on the status of women's housing issues, whether needs or solutions.

The Theory

Moser juxtaposes Maxine Molyneux's (1985) delineation of strategic and practical gender needs and interests with a definition of women's "triple role." The components of the triad are reproductive work (child bearing and rearing), productive work (agricultural, and in urban areas work in the informal sector), and community management work. Molyneux differentiates between *gender interests*—"those that women or men for that matter, may develop by virtue of their social positioning through gender attributes" (Molyneux, 1985:232), and *gender needs*—the means by which gender interests may be met. *Strategic gender interests and needs* arise out of the societal structure. The gender *interest* arises out of the need for an alternative societal structure that is more equal than the one in place; the gender *needs* are formulated from an analysis of women's subordination to men.

Practical gender interests have less to do with societal structures and are more attuned to the issue of survival. These gender *needs* are formulated from the conditions women face in day-to-day living, given their gender-driven unequal positions in the labor force. Since women are not a homogeneous group, the policies that are formulated to meet women's gender *interests* would necessarily have to be conditioned by the particular socioeconomic, political, and cultural circumstances.

Perhaps the aims of gender-sensitive housing policy are to achieve, in the long run, practical *and* strategic gender interests. It would be easy to believe that an overarching national shelter policy would seek to advance strategic interests, while in its implementation at the grassroots level, it advances women's practical interests. Conversely, the grassroots initiative through meeting practical interests can advance strategic interests. The latter trend has been very recent, as was described in Bangladesh in the comments by Salma Khan. Anna Vakil discussed policy that related to the zonal organization that surrounds the creation of housing in Zimbabwe.

Gender and Development

It is well known that, until recently, discussions on poverty and development assumed that development processes were gender-neutral in their impact. Shelter, usually considered a facet in the development process, was no exception, and housing policy rarely featured a gender variable. Most development policies and projects, housing-related or otherwise, have had severe negative impacts on the survival chances of poor women and their families (Rao *et al.*, 1991). In work conducted in Asia, it was found that women's concerns were given explicit attention only in the family planning, nutrition, and health sections of national development plans. To quote Rao (1991:3):

> The commonly pursued path of economic development primarily follows the profit motive, with development taking place in a socioeconomic context characterized by hierarchies and inequality. This approach had hurt the poor badly ...

Rao goes on to cite Raj Krishna (1983), saying that "a development that hurts the poor will inevitably hurt poor women more." It has been argued that women have not only experienced negative effects of the shift from traditional to "modern" societies through the development process but have also been excluded from the development planning process itself. Housing policy epitomizes this observation perfectly. This is not only because of the income and nuclear family assumptions embedded in policy, referred to earlier, but also because of the gender inequalities within the family structure. Bruce and Dwyer (1988) maintain that gender inequalities in access to control over resources mean that a policy aimed at a family unit will not serve men's and women's distinct self-interests within the family. They have argued that:

Just as men and women differ in their participation in labor markets, in their wage rates and in their prospects, when marriages dissolve through death or separation, men and women also frequently differ with respect to their allocational priorities ... projects are among the primary vehicles used by governments and international agencies to channel resources in the development process. One of the barriers to translating research activity about women into effective and beneficial development programming has been the absence of an adequate analytical framework for integrating women into project realities.

In addition, the feminization of poverty is a common factor across nations. In the developing world it is manifesting itself via increasing numbers of homeless women. The causes are complex, but the fact remains that homeless women are more vulnerable than men in similar circumstances. The safety and security of the woman and, often, her dependent children are primary concerns. Access to physical and social services becomes very important as well.

In the general "development" literature, there has been a shift toward recognizing the role of women not only within the family, but outside it as well. The declaration of the U.N. Decade for Women has symbolized at least an overt acceptance of the importance of women in development. This step forward has been sustained to some extent among international agencies, national agencies, and in academic and intellectual discourse. The Women in Development (WID) approach made popular by United States Agency for International Development (U.S.A.I.D.) was based on the fact that women have so far been an unrecognized resource, and they can make "productive" contributions to development. Unfortunately, with its emphases on economic development, and therefore income generation and anti-poverty thrusts, the WID approach has drawn attention *away* from other equally important aspects of women's development such as housing.

Perhaps the importance of placing women's housing issues in the larger development context of the present comes from the possibility of using shelter as an entry point for development. This viewpoint has been elaborated in Irene Tinker's paper in these proceedings. It has long been recognized that policy rarely recognizes the multiple roles that women play. It is also known that policies are seldom cognizant of the heterogeneity of family structures or the increase in women-headed households. As Dandekar states in the introduction, the housing shortage affects women to a greater degree than men because policy continues to cater to the needs of nuclear families and does not reflect women's special needs.

At this juncture it is important to clarify that we believe that income is an important factor that affects access to housing but it is *not* the only factor. Gender, social status, race, and ethnicity are equally significant issues. Todes and Walker have revealed this in their paper on South Africa, where the latter two factors play particularly seminal roles in influencing housing policies.

The Importance of Focusing on Women and Housing

Over the last decade or so, when most of the literature on women and housing has emerged, several arguments have been put forth for the need for policy makers at national and international levels to focus on specific shelter needs related to women. The arguments often include two key points, as follows.

(1) Dramatic Increase in Women-Headed Households. The increase in the number of women-headed households globally, with and without children, has been dramatic. Although attention has been focused on the plight of urban women, rural women, especially in the developing world, are *de facto* heads of household in the face of widespread male migration to the urban areas.

Speaking of Kenya in particular but making a point perhaps applicable to other nations in the developing world, Nimpuno-Parente (1987) articulated that women's access to housing is determined by their relationship to men even though women often have to engage in paid work because their spouses are unable to support their families single-handedly. The increase in women-headed households is a significant trend that is on the constant increase due to factors such as increasing instability of marriage, unemployment, and in the African case, polygamy, etc. These factors intensify the circumstances that place women in a position where they take wage-earning responsibilities in addition to family responsibilities.

(2) Importance of Housing in Women's Lives. Infrastructure has immediate consequences for women because of their greater domestic responsibilities. Moser (1987) has discussed the importance of focusing specifically on housing and infrastructure in women's lives and how this has been underplayed or largely ignored by those involved in the planning of human settlements.

Particularly because women undertake most of the household duties (cooking, collecting water and fuel, rearing the children), in addition to hard work (in agriculture or in the informal sector), women need to have a greater voice in the creation of their homes. Though rarely considered during the formulation of policy or even during the formulation of specific projects at the local level, women are directly (and often adversely) affected by inappropriate shelter.

As a case in point, in carrying out a government-funded resettlement program in India, the Ahmedabad Study Action Group (ASAG) actively solicited input from women in the beneficiary group. The women participants emphasized the privacy of bathing facilities and the location of cooking facilities, water collection and storage areas, features that particularly affect their lives and which are often ignored by the planners (Singh, 1980).

The Solanda low-income housing project in Ecuador illustrates the importance of "access to housing" not limited merely to the physical structure. The project, funded by U.S.A.I.D., was started in 1982. It targeted 6,000 low-income families for provision of "inexpensive housing, community facilities and planned social programs." Of the heads of households who applied, 175 were women, of whom 89% were single, widowed, or divorced, and 91% of whom did not have enough money for the down payment and as a result did not qualify for the project. Even if the down payment had been reduced by half, 77% of the women would not have qualified (Lycette and Jaramillo, 1984: 25–40). Two possible explanations for the absence of women-directed policies are (1) the lack of resources—women usually comprise the poorer half of the population; and (2) the differential impacts of housing is not given credence by decision makers.

In her paper (included under the infrastructure section) Dandekar elaborates the factors that influence women's access in a World Bank-aided project. In addition to the important factors, information and finance, policies and programs have to deal with women's position in their society. As a group, women tend to be financially poor and worse off than men in terms of literacy, education, and occupational skills, and all this makes it difficult for women to negotiate the bureaucratic and legal red tape that surrounds such projects.

Todes and Walker, in their discussion of three housing subsystems in one South African city, have made access to housing the crux of their argument. Bhatnagar takes a more distant view of one government's attempts to meet the housing needs of women.

Who Should Frame These Policies?

Historically, housing policy has been framed by governments, often in some form of a top-down approach. In recent examples of housing or housing-related policy in Costa Rica, Bangladesh, and India (elaborated elsewhere in these proceedings), the impetus has been from non-governmental organizations working at the grassroots level. In India, Ekta Vihar was a program initiated in part by the government and was the first of its kind that catered specifically to the needs of women. In Costa Rica, grassroots action has culminated in the formulation of a housing program that could possibly serve as a prototypical model for development in general and housing in particular, both in process and product. In Bangladesh, similar efforts have led to changed lending practices whereby housing loans are made either to women alone or to women and men jointly, but never to men alone. This has allowed women to control either half or all of the property.

Role of Multi-national Agencies

Multi-national agencies have often worked with what they perceive to be global problems and trends. While these agencies usually operate within the confines of their own agenda, they sometimes try to influence the host countries where they operate to shift priorities, think differently, identify imminent problems, etc.

Although 1976–1985 was called the United Nations Decade for Women, shelter issues began to receive attention only toward the end of the decade. In 1985, at a conference in Nairobi reviewing the achievements of the Decade for Women, the delegates adopted "the Forward-Looking Strategies for the Advancement of Women" and

> called on governments to integrate women in the formulation of policies, programmes and projects for the provision of basic shelter and infrastructure. To this end, the enrollment of women in architectural, engineering and related fields should be encouraged and qualified women graduates in these fields should be assigned to professional policy and decisions making positions. The shelter and infrastructural needs of women should be assessed and specifically incorporated in housing, community development and slum and squatter projects. Women and women's groups should be participants in and equal

> beneficiaries of housing and infrastructure construction projects. They should be consulted in the choice of design and technology of construction and should be involved in the management and maintenance of the facilities. To this end, women should be provided with construction, maintenance and management skills and should be included in related educational and training programs.

It is interesting to note that, at this stage, the emphasis was on including women rather than shaping policy specific to women's needs. The Global Strategy for Shelter by the Year 2000 which serves as a mandate for the United Nations focuses on achieving adequate shelter for all by the Year 2000.

UNCHS views human settlements as (1) part of an integrated system of human activity, not physical structure alone; (2) an important component of a country's fixed capital assets, one in which investment is rarely wasted; and (3) tied to every aspect of economic and social development. UNCHS also believes that human settlements activity requires a specific focus on women because "... shelter needs of women are still subsumed under those of the family in the majority of countries."

While participation of women is an important factor in UNCHS policy, its more immediate aims are to promote the role of cities in sustainable development, to strengthen urban management, and to implement the Global Strategy for Shelter by the Year 2000. The UNCHS statement issued in 1991 is as follows:

> Women are subject to special constraints in obtaining adequate housing and in participating in human settlements development efforts at all levels. While some of these constraints are the results of *de facto* gender discrimination, others are a result of their severe poverty, their lack of education and their double and triple roles as household workers and workers in the formal and informal sectors of agriculture, industry and commerce. Removing these constraints is important not only because equity in distribution of development benefits is a fundamental principle, but also because increasing numbers of households are either solely or largely supported by women. Depriving women of access to shelter and infrastructure deprives large numbers of families as well. There are concrete and identifiable implications for women in all human settlements and shelter related policies, programmes and projects, whether they deal with the land, finance, building materials, construction technologies, housing or community design. It is necessary therefore, to enhance women's participation in shelter and infrastructure management as contributors and beneficiaries and to put

particular emphasis on the integration of women's activities with all mainstream development activities, on an equal basis with those of me.

The United Nations Development Programme (UNDP) lists "improving women's access to shelter, basic urban services and governmental facilities" as one of the 22 priorities in building and strengthening national capacity (UNDP 1991: 74–75). UNDP's reference to women is in broad general terms, calling for promoting the participation of women in:

1. income generation in the formal and informal sectors;
2. shelter finance and provision, as managers and professionals in the financial, insurance, and real estate fields;
3. basic urban services; and
4. management of municipal governmental and non-governmental agencies (NGOs).

Since 1971, the UNDP has spent more than three billion U.S. dollars on urban projects such as schools, power plants, transportation, and regional planning. It has also provided nearly 250 million U.S. dollars for targeted urban projects—planning, housing, infrastructure and income-generating projects—many executed by UNCHS and other multilateral agencies, seen as catalysts for programs and projects and funded by international agencies like the World Bank, regional development banks, and bilateral donors. Regional development banks such as the African Development Bank, Asian Development Bank, and the Inter-American Development Bank are expected to increase funding for integrated urban projects, regional development, etc.

In the 1990s the UNDP will concentrate on human development and strengthen national and local capabilities to improve the effectiveness of assistance for urban development. It will focus on five aspects that comprise its urban agenda for the '90s, including:

1. alleviation of poverty;
2. provision of infrastructure, shelter, and services for the poor;
3. improvement of urban environments;
4. strengthening of local government and administration; and
5. promotion of the private sector and NGOs.

Participation of women is specifically mentioned in the strategies for dealing with alleviation of poverty, where organization of the poor at community/neighborhood levels and promotion of women's participation are seen as ways to promote job creation, encourage income-

generating activities, and to alleviate poverty through the creation of a strong and stable informal sector.

The World Bank focuses on improving urban productivity, developing effective responses to urban environmental problems, alleviating urban poverty, and expanding urban research. The Bank's urban lending is projected to grow between 1991 and 1993, with the bulk of the money to be allocated for measures representing urban policy reform.

The United Nations Children's Fund (UNICEF) is expected to concentrate on community initiatives to improve the access of the urban poor, especially women and children, to basic urban services. The emphasis on urban issues has been due to rapidly expanding urban populations. However, due to increased migration and diminishing economic opportunities, women face problems in rural areas as well. The rural sector is seldom targeted as an area in its own right. The prevailing approach has tended to target urban problems, implying a hope that rural problems will be addressed by default.

U.S.A.I.D. has concentrated on development projects that foster income generation, agricultural technology, education, health/sanitation, measures, and the like, with not much invested in shelter. The housing guarantee program of U.S.A.I.D. has assisted selected developing countries with financing for low-cost shelter. Gender has not been a factor in its approach. In the 1970s U.S.A.I.D. emphasized infrastructure for the urban poor through sites and services, slum-up gradation programs and guaranteed U.S. private sector loans to developing countries. Since 1962, approximately two billion U.S. dollars have been given in loan guarantees to over 50 countries.

In the mid-1980s the World Bank shifted its emphasis from demonstration projects to establishing national and city level policies that increase the contribution of the urban economy and urban institutions to national development. There has been a shift in the urban sector strategy, reducing the public role in urban service delivery, strengthening maintenance of urban infrastructure, all of which remain completely gender-neutral in focus and approach.

Tinker (in these proceedings) delineates the link between UNCHS and the United Nations Fund for Women and Development (UNIFEM), the two agencies that would be most closely connected with the women-

and-shelter issues in the developing world. Although the aims of these agencies are laudable, there has been no major change in national housing policies, attributed to the fact that the quantitative aspects are so daunting that qualitative aspects such as gender-sensitive policy are sidestepped.

National Housing Policy: Examples from the First and Third World

A cursory examination of housing policies in First and Third World countries points up both commonalities and differences. Most developmental policies in general, and housing policies specifically, consider the nuclear family to be the norm. This pervasive notion is most obvious in housing policies, both in the First and Third World context. Even in industrial countries such as the U.S., the American dream is composed of both parents, the 2.5 children, the family pet, and the home in the suburbs. The major difference between First and Third World housing policies is the way they address the issue of access to housing. In First World countries the aim of the policies has been equal access to housing for both men and women. In Third World countries, the primary objective has been the achievement of financial independence. A desired consequence of the financial stability has been the ability to meet basic needs, including shelter.

The following paragraphs discuss some housing policies in Canada, Australia, and England. Examples from the Third World are discussed in greater detail elsewhere in this volume. Indian policies are included in Bhatnagar's article and Anna Vakil discusses housing issues in Zimbabwe. Even though cross-cultural comparisons of different policies may not be pertinent at the micro-level, at the macro-level they help to identify common themes and trends, and provide valuable lessons that other nations can benefit from.

Canada

Provincial requirements for public housing differ according to region. Source of income is used as a factor to limit access to public housing. Poor women who are on government assistance (dole) are discriminated against. Ontario requires that a mandatory one-year waiting period be established even before a person applies for public housing.

Ontario has initiated a housing program called Program 3000 which funds "second-stage" housing. Second-stage housing is more of a service than a shelter pro-

gram. Battered women and women in crisis situations can use the second-stage housing as a stop-gap shelter arrangement until they find more suitable and permanent forms of shelter. A person can obtain this sort of housing for a limited period for about 6 months to one year. These programs are very selective about the women they accept. The selection process is such that street women, women who are substance abusers, etc., are denied access to these facilities.

The Canada Mortgage and Housing Corporation (CMHC) has a non-profit housing program for low-income individuals and their families. However, the CMHC is reluctant to approve housing programs that target any specific client group, gender-driven or otherwise. They insist on a range of needs and a diverse group of users. The Canadian policy efforts have been toward making housing equally accessible for eligible men and women. No specific provision favors one gender over the other.

Australia

Special programs for housing women were first started in 1978 due to the influx of refugees. These efforts were strengthened with the involvement of the Salvation Army. In 1985 the First National Women's Housing Conference was held in Adelaide. Two years later the Second National Women's Housing Conference was held in Sydney. As a result of these two conferences women's issues were firmly established in the government's agendas and housing policies and programs in New South Wales, South Australia, and Victoria. On a more national level, policies aimed at the reduction and possible elimination of discrimination of access to finance from banks, building societies, and other financial institutions.

In South Australia, special housing programs for single people were established. Single parents with dependent children were given preference. The Home Ownership Made Easier (HOME) scheme was also initiated by the South Australian government. However, this scheme targeted home buyers and had little or no provisions for tenancy, which did not help women who often had renting as the *only* option available to them.

The Victorian Ministry of Housing was influential in affecting housing policies for low-income persons in its area, requiring lenders to take women's future income capacity into consideration when reviewing their applications for loans. As a result of this policy, women who were temporarily unemployed, in crisis situations, between jobs, etc., were able to obtain opportunities to finance housing.

While most of the activity with regard to adapting housing policy to the varied needs of women was concentrated in Southern Australia and nearby provinces, the Northern territories became more stringent in their housing policies. Efforts were made in the Northern territory to maintain and strengthen the notion of the nuclear family. As a case in point, the Federal First Home Owners Scheme in Northern Territory required couples to remain together to sustain a loan. In the event of a break up, neither person's eligibility would be continued.

England

Housing policies have been more concerned with influencing tenure structure. By asserting that owner occupation of the tenure suited most (if not all) people's needs, the fundamental assumption was that the nuclear family is the norm, and what is good for the family is certainly good for women.

Fair rents were abolished by the Housing Act of 1988, and the subsidy structure was changed to encourage the use of private finance, thus reducing the level of direct public subsidy. The 1977 Homeless Persons Housing Act was now incorporated as part of the 1985 Housing Act. As a result, a woman who was considered "vulnerable," i.e., had dependent children or was pregnant, was eligible for some form of public housing. Race and ethnicity are still major concerns in the housing policy debate. (See Todes and Walker's rendition of a similar situation in South Africa.) Gender has not figured in any degree of prominence at the national and regional levels. At the local level, efforts in this directions have been minuscule, and have alleviated problems that women face with regard to shelter only superficially.

Some Concluding Remarks

From existing literature, case studies, anecdotal evidence, and project reports, it is evident that no specific policies exist that address women's needs in development and shelter. Isolated instances of women's housing programs are sporadic, not an inherent part of a national planning strategy. In addition, these minuscule efforts are unable to address effectively what is a global and rapidly exploding problem. Gender-neutral policies are in place due to two fundamental assumptions, namely, that current housing policies affect men and women equally, and that the nuclear family is the norm.

Demographic trends and changing societal patterns have brought these assumptions under increasing scrutiny. Existing shelter and development policies have not been adapted to reflect the dramatic changes that have occurred among the people they affect.

Theoretical arguments that have had their genesis in more encompassing feminist theory and discourse have been used to lobby for gender-sensitive development and shelter policies. Despite the growing acceptance of such views, the conditions of women with regard to development and shelter remain largely unchanged. Tinker particularly mentions how the non-confrontational nature of interventions in the shelter arena can be used to make larger gains—in other words, interventions in the practical domain in order to make gains in the strategic domain.

In addition to gender sensitivity during policy formulation, it is equally imperative that the policies be implemented effectively. A policy is successful only to the degree that it brings about the desired change. Without a "critical mass" of believers in the bureaucracy, policies may be ignored (Everett, 1990). It is our hope that the dissemination of information via the conference and its proceedings will help to establish the required critical mass that will bring about the necessary change, at policy, process, and product levels.

References

Austerberry, H., and Watson, S. (1984). *Women on the margins: a study of single women's housing problems.* London, UK: Housing Research Group, City University.

Boserup, E. (1970). *Women's role in economic development.* London, UK: George Allen and Unwin.

Buvinic, M., Lycette, M., et al. (1983). *Women and poverty in the Third World.* Baltimore: Johns Hopkins.

Everett, J. (1990). *The global empowerment of women.* AWID. Blacksburg, VA: VA Tech.

Forsyth, A. (1985). *Singular women: housing for low income single women without dependents.* Roseville, Australia: Social Impacts Publications.

Hayden, D. (1981). *The grand domestic revolution: a history of feminist designs for American homes, neighborhoods and cities.* Cambridge, MA: The MIT Press.

Hayden, D. (1984). *Redesigning the American dream: the future of housing, work, and family life.* New York, NY: WW Norton and Co.

Kozol, J. (1988). *Rachel and her children: homeless families in America.* New York, NY: Crown Publishing.

Lycette, M., and Jaramillo, C. *Low income housing: a women's perspective.* Washington, D.C.: ICRW.

Molyneux, M. (1985). Women. In Walker, T. (Ed) *Nicaragua: the first 5 years.* New York: Praeger.

Moser, C., and Chant, S. (1985). *The participation of women in low-income projects.* Gender and planning working paper No. 5. London, UK: University College, Development Planning Unit.

Moser, C., and Peake, L. (1987). (Eds.) *Women, human settlements and housing.* London, UK: Tavistock.

Nimpuno-Parente, P. (1987). The struggle for shelter: women in a site and service project in Nairobi, Kenya. In Moser, C., and Peake, L. (Eds.) *Women, human settlements and housing.* London, UK: Tavistock.

Rao, A., Anderson, M., and Overholt, C. A. (1991). *Gender analysis in development planning: a case book.* Connecticut: Kumarian Press.

Redburn, S. F., and Buss, T. F. (1986). *Responding to America's homelessness: public policy alternatives.* New York, NY: Praeger.

Singh, A. M. (1980). *Women in cities: an invisible factor in urban planing in India.* India: The Population Council.

UNCHS. (n.d.) *Women in human settlements and management.* Nairobi, Kenya.

Watson, S. (1984). *Housing and the family: the marginalization of single households in Britain.* Canberra: Urban Research Unit, Australian National University.

Watson, S., and Austerberry, H. (1986). *Housing and homelessness: a feminist perspective.* Boston: Routledge and Kegan Paul.

Werkerle, G., Pearson, R., and Morley, D. (Eds.) (1980). *New Space for women.* Boulder, Colorado: Westview press.

Whitehead, C. M. E., and Cross, D. T. (1991). *Affordable housing in London.* New York, NY: Pergammon Press.

Wright, G. (1981). *Building the dream: a social history of housing in America.* New York, NY: Pantheon Books.

Chapter 2
Global Policies Regarding Shelter for Women: Experiences of the UN Centre for Human Settlements

Irene Tinker

Irene Tinker is a professor in the departments of City and Regional Planning and Women's Studies at the University of California, Berkeley. Throughout her professional career, she has alternated between university teaching and policy-oriented research. Living in Washington, D.C., for three decades, she was founder-president of the Equity Policy Center, and founded the International Center for Research on Women and the Society for International Development's Committee on Women in Development. She is a cofounder of the Wellesley Center for Research on Women, and the Washington Women's Network. She received a doctorate from the London School of Economics in 1954 and completed her undergraduate work at Radcliffe in 1949.

Shelter policy with respect for women marks the culmination of the women in development movement to ensure that development programs and policies recognize and include the differential needs of women. Women's rights to land and housing conflict with customary and family law throughout the world. Urbanization challenges these laws and customs that have their roots in agricultural societies with their emphasis on kinship and extended family; the reformulation of family and household in cities today provides an opportunity to modify these unequal practices on the grounds of both economics and justice.[1]

In the mega-cities of the world, women-headed households are becoming the norm, particularly among the urban poor. This disintegration of the family is not a fact to be celebrated: a woman is forced to work a double day to support and succor her family. Indeed, facilitating the return of men to their household responsibilities is one of the most critical challenges we face today. The answer clearly is not to go back to traditional gender relationships but rather to support greater equity for women. Access to land and housing is fundamental to this re-balancing of gender roles to reflect women's economic and social roles.

Yet nowhere is the move toward equity more difficult than in policies that change women's rights to land and housing. This is an opportune time to insert gender equality into land policies because of changes being made in many countries in the system of land titles and registration. Other elements emphasized in documents about women and shelter (UNCHS 1985, 1989, 1990) encounter less ingrained resistance. Women's access to home financing builds on successful credit programs for micro-enterprise (Tinker, 1989). Greater recognition for women's historic economic activities in and around the house require rethinking contemporary architectural notions of homes (Gurstein, 1991; Kusterer & Vitt, 1991). Improved water supply and sanitation are introduced as health measures regardless of the impact on women's time (Tinker, 1989b): new water points save time but the installation of latrines often takes time for increased carrying of water and cleaning of the site. The tendency to leave decision-making about these crucial services to technicians too often leads to the imposition of "solutions" on the women users. Clearly, if women are to benefit from shelter policies they must be allowed to participate in "all levels of the planning and implementation of human settlements policies and programmes" (UNCHS 1990:3).

My purpose in this paper is, first, to review the policy initiatives of the United Nations Centre for Human Settlements[2] (UNCHS) as they have evolved to include women; second, to identify ways in which international agencies such as UNIFEM might work with local NGOs or women's groups to assist UNCHS to achieve its policies regarding women; and finally, to discuss actual UNCHS programming in three countries of Asia in terms of three major issues: access to land and housing, participation in planning, and the interrelationship between income and housing. Both the policy shift and the subsequent activities UNCHS has undertaken to implement these policies illustrate the symbiotic relationship among the various players in international development: scholars, practitioners, and activists, nudging policy into new areas (Tinker, 1990). Once policies are promulgated, implementing them becomes an even greater challenge. Thus any discussion of policy initiatives must stress both the potentialities and the constraints that such policies face.

UN Programs

UNCHS

The United Nations Centre for Human Settlements was set up as a result of the 1976 international meeting on Habitat: United Nations Conference on Human Settlements, held in Vancouver. This conference had enormous input from non-governmental organizations (NGOs) and advocacy groups concerned with low-cost housing and appropriate technologies meant to alleviate drudgery associated with many survival tasks. Because few national governments or development agencies had placed either human settlements or urban problems high on their agendas, NGO pressure was instrumental in convincing governments to set up a new UN agency. UNCHS was established in 1978 to provide a secretariat for the intergovernmental Commission on Human Settlements; the existing Centre for Housing and Building was placed within UNCHS. In 1981, the Foundation for Human Settlements was created to allow the agency to receive voluntary contributions and so broaden its activities.[3]

Despite the NGO involvement in both the official and unofficial conferences at Vancouver, women's interests in human settlements were not recognized in major conference document (Pietila & Vickers, 1990) although "it called for active participation of women in planning, design and execution of all aspects of human settlements" (UNCHS, 1989:12). Women's specific interests

were overlooked despite efforts of delegates to the World Conference for International Women's Year, held in Mexico City in 1975, who tried to influence the discussions in Vancouver by emphasizing in their World Plan of Action, that because women spend more time than men around their homes, their needs should be featured at the Habitat Conference (Fraser, 1987).

Not until 1985 was the connection between women and shelter strongly detailed in a UN document when the World Conference for the UN Decade for Women, meeting in Nairobi, adopted the Forward-Looking Strategies for the Advancement of Women. Included in this document were two paragraphs calling on governments to "integrate women in the formulation of policies, programmes, and projects for the provision of basic shelter and infrastructure," and declaring that "women and women's groups should be participants in and equal beneficiaries of housing and infrastructure construction projects" (Forward Looking Strategies: para. 209, 210).

These paragraphs did not just happen. Three streams of influence combined to convince both women and UNCHS that the issue of women and shelter must be addressed. These influences came from the United Nations itself, from women in UNCHS, and also from activists working on housing issues in their own countries. Throughout the Decade for Women, the UN had issued directives to all its agencies to integrate women into their programming; increasing pressure was exerted on each agency to produce a report for each Women's Conference. UNCHS submitted a paper for the Mid-Decade Conference in Copenhagen in 1980, but it had no impact on the Programme of Action. In 1984 a focal point for women was created within UNCHS and the assigned officer, Aliye P. Celik, was given oversight of the agency paper on "Women and Human Settlements."[4]

Also produced for the Nairobi meeting was a four page issue of *Bibliographic Notes* on "Women and Shelter." The paucity of references establishes the fact that women and shelter issues had up to that point been given little attention by the women in development community. Studies that focused on women's access to services (Schminck, 1985) or to housing credits (Blayney & Lycette, 1983; Sorock *et al.*, 1984) were all quite recent. Still in preparation was a series of working papers presenting case studies about women and housing and prepared by students in a course under the direction of Caroline Moser at the Development Planning Unit of

University College, London (subsequently published in Moser & Peake, 1987). Because housing was perceived as an urban issue, studies about cities were also included. Papanek wrote one of the first articles detailing women's different experiences in cities (1976). Others were concerned about urban women's need for income and moved beyond earlier studies of women in the marketplace to collect data on women in street foods (Tinker, 1987a; Tinker & Cohen, 1985) and petty trading (Babb, 1982; Singh & de Souza, 1980).

These documents and a draft of suggested paragraphs for inclusion in the Forward Looking Strategies were circulated during the Nairobi meetings both to the official governmental meeting and to the Non-Governmental Organization (NGO) Forum.[5] Anje Wiersinga of the Netherlands organized a workshop at the NGO Forum to discuss shelter issues. She was a member of the Habitat International Coalition (HIC), an umbrella group for NGOs and Community Based Organizations interested in shelter issues that is recognized by and given a position within the UNCHS (Sayne, 1988). This workshop brought together women writing on shelter issues in universities, NGOs, and UNCHS. Their support assisted in getting the paragraphs on housing and infrastructure into the Forward Looking Strategies; their interaction hatched the idea of a women's caucus within HIC. This symbiotic relationship between the women inside UNCHS and those outside, particularly women active in HIC, has propelled women and shelter issues forward in both the governmental and NGO arenas.

Following the Nairobi conference, UNCHS undertook to incorporate women's concerns into its major policy campaign: Global Strategy for Shelter to the Year 2000. Recognizing the limited understanding within the development community of the importance of urban issues and settlement policies in general, and their impact on women in particular, UNCHS convened an international seminar in Vienna in December, 1985, organized jointly with the Division for the Advancement of Women of the Centre for Social and Humanitarian Affairs. The seminar was designed "to familiarize women's organizations with key issues of settlements management" and to ensure that policy-makers were cognizant of "women's perspectives on housing and residential environments" since joint collaborative efforts were necessary to develop realistic national plans of action that would help the agency achieve its goal of "Shelter for All by the Year 2000" (UNCHS, 1990:2).[6] The Vienna Seminar called for five regional seminars to discuss further the key issues of women's access to

housing, land, housing credit, water, and sanitation as well as women's participation in the design and construction of shelter.[7] While the regional seminars were taking place, a special meeting was held to ensure that issues of women and homelessness would be included in the preparations and documentation for the International Year of Shelter for the Homeless, 1987.[8]

The women active in Habitat International Council also pressed their case for greater representation on the Board of Directors and on important sub-committees; they also lobbied for a special working group on women and shelter. At an April, 1987 meeting of the HIC General Assembly, guidelines were adopted that included the eventual goal of equal representation of women and men on the 21 member Board. At its December, 1988, meeting in India the HIC General Assembly accepted the idea of an official Women and Shelter Network (WAS) that could nominate representatives to the Board and major sub-committees (Sayne, 1988). Today the Women and Shelter Network not only has its own newsletter and secretariat in Nairobi headed by Diana Lee-Smith but also has a formal liaison with the UNCHS secretariat. In 1990, the women succeeded in making the UNCHS focal point for women a full time position; the incumbent, Catalina Trujillo, was a founding member of the network (WAS Newsletter 5, August, 1992).

This history exemplifies women's efforts to influence a sector and the male organizations operating within it. Women need their own organizations and offices such as the WAS Network and the UNCHS focal point. Such visible women's groups serve as pressure groups on the male organizations, contact with press and other sectors, and support groups for themselves. But the real power lies in HIC and UNCHS. Women need to be part of the mainstream decision-making within these organizations but well-connected to the women's groups. Women concerned with shelter issues continue to pursue this two-pronged strategy to integrate women's issues into all activities of UNCHS.

This history also illustrates the potentialities of UNCHS itself: seminars and publications to educate both activists and practitioners; consultancies for scholars so that they can present their research findings in a policy, as opposed to an academic, framework; and UN approved consciousness-raising campaigns that set global goals as in the Global Strategy to the Year 2000 and declare years such as *International Year of Shelter for the Homeless, 1987*. Conferences not only facilitate the exchange of information among the committed, but also provide greater access to national policy-makers than is otherwise possible.

These activities also illustrate the constraints that limit UNCHS's impact on national policy. As an international system based on national governments, the UN in its development role is a forum for the exchange of information and discussion of new concepts. The policies emerging from UN agencies are advisory. They frame the debate within countries and provide moral suasion for new approaches. Implementation of new policies are left to existing civil service cadres in each country for whom the new initiatives are too often seen only as an added burden. Hence the growing recognition that national organizations, such as NGOs, community-based organizations (CBOs), and women's groups, have a crucial role in monitoring change and agitating for swifter implementation.

UNIFEM and UNCHS

UNIFEM, the UN Fund for Women, was set up in 1976 "to promote programming for and with women in developing countries and to channel financial and technical resources directly to theses women" (Anderson, 1991:7). Initially, UNIFEM emphasized rural projects revolving around agriculture and micro-enterprise; as more NGOs began working with grassroots women's groups, UNIFEM has increasingly become a point of reference within the UN system for development projects.[9] As part of an exploration of ways to work with poor urban women, UNIFEM and UNCHS discussed a long-term project for "training and capacity-building" for women's groups as well as for non-governmental (NGO) and community-based organizations (CBO) promoting women's access to shelter.

In addition to setting up a network of women's groups, UNCHS sought advice from UNIFEM on how to add income activities for women to their housing projects. As UNCHS began to upgrade urban squatter settlements or provide housing loans for the rural landless, it became clear that, if the families were to continue occupying their improved homes, total family income would have to be increased. Since most housing schemes assume an intact household with the male head already employed, any new income would have to come from women's work.

Because the proposed collaboration with UNCHS represented a departure from previous programming, UNIFEM decided it needed more information on current UNCHS projects before making a decision. I was asked to undertake a joint UNIFEM/UNCHS mission to Indonesia, Bangladesh, and Nepal to assess the extent to which women were already, or could be, included in selected UNCHS projects and to identify opportunities for future cooperation by the two agencies with NGOs, CBOs, and women's groups on activities relating to women and human settlements.[10]

Future Opportunities for UN Programs

Human Settlement Issues

Indonesia, Bangladesh, and Nepal are all in the early stages of developing a national shelter policy. Major international funding agencies such as the World Bank or the Asian Development Bank working in these countries as partners in the UNCHS projects, as well as bilateral agencies involved in related projects, were enthusiastic about the idea that UNIFEM might provide technical assistance on how to include women in their projects. Several offered their own funds to speed up the process. In two instances the project officers had already engaged female consultants to advise their efforts.

Interest was particularly strong concerning urban issues. Rapid population growth and internal migration will propel both Jakarta and Dhaka into the list of cities with over 10 million inhabitants. The rate of urbanization throughout Nepal is overwhelming this previously rural country. Given the pressures of population growth, governments in all three countries are trying to reduce urban migration to major cities. In both Bangladesh and Nepal, the major housing projects are rural and were designed for reconstruction of housing damaged by floods and an earthquake, respectively. In Indonesia by far the largest project focused on urban infrastructure in small towns throughout the archipelago.

Women are seen in official statements in Indonesia and Nepal as mothers and home-makers. Yet studies show that women in these two countries contribute as much as half the income of poor families. In contrast, Bangladesh programs seem to encourage women to increase their economic activity; they also take special note of the poverty of female-headed households. What explains this seeming contradiction? Perhaps the limited traditional roles for women in Bangladesh, perhaps the pervasive influence of national and international NGOs, perhaps the need for all citizens to contribute to national income in such a poor country.

Rights to Land and Housing

Women's rights to own land and a house are recognized by UNCHS as a key issue. Yet in all three countries, as in much of the developing world, the lack of cadastral surveys and clear land rights makes any kind of planning difficult. If women seldom hold title to their urban dwellings, neither do men. Recent studies of urban land policies indicate that only 22% of barrio dwellers in Venezuela owned their land; in Cameroon only 20% of all urban land had been surveyed and titled, a higher figure than the 6% of all lands in the country that are registered (Dowall & Clark, 1991; Farvacque & McAuslan, 1991). In one squatter settlement in San Jose, Costa Rica, the local social workers estimated that 60% of the households were made up of a woman and her children.[11] More common estimates are 40% of all households.

Conflict between tribal or customary laws and modern legal systems adopted in most countries makes urban planning almost impossible. Governments often lack the ability to appropriate land for government buildings, infrastructure systems, or industry, much less for housing. In Port Moresby over 80% of the urban area is held under tribal laws (Tinker, 1989). Indonesia incorporated traditional land tenure systems into a new agrarian law, but adherence to traditional *adat* continues in about one-third of Jakarta (Farvacque & McAuslan, 1991:44).

In Bangladesh, to avoid conflicting claims over land, rural housing schemes require land to be registered before a loan is granted for building on the site. All NGOs administering the loan program require at the least that title is held jointly in the names of husband and wife; the Grameen Bank prefers title in the *woman's own name!* If a woman could not persuade a male relative to sign land over to her, then she was given preferred access to a loan to acquire a land plot; once that loan was repaid, she was then able to receive a loan to build her house.

In contrast, land ownership is not even mentioned in the housing projects in Nepal because of the strength of the customary land tenure system. In Kathmandu, middle-class men often register new homes in their wives' names because customary land inheritance laws prohibit men from exercising any rights over land even when held in their own names.

In Indonesia, although cadastral surveys remain incomplete so that customary rights of kampong dwellers to their land have not been registered, tenure in kampongs and illegal subdivisions is fairly secure. Indonesia's urban policy objectives include provision of land and security of tenure for the poor; women-headed households are listed along with other vulnerable groups as meriting special attention, but policies to implement this aspect have not been promulgated. Two government housing programs for the poor raise a policy issue of entitlement. Kampong upgrading has been an ongoing program in the country; more recently the government has begun building low-rise flats to replace squatters' houses that must be removed for development. Both the improved kampong houses and the flats are rapidly being sold to higher-income groups. Some housing activists argue that the poor should not be allowed to sell their improved homes for a set number of years. Others emphasize that such a sale provides a stake for a poor family to buy rural land to set up a microenterprise. They point out that many poor, especially women, work out of their homes and that the flats made no provision for home-based work.

Work and Housing

Three issues relate to women's work and housing that merit some discussion: the recognition of women's traditional roles in home construction and how these might be enhanced; the recognition of home-based work when planning housing and settlements; and the recognition of food production as an urban occupation.

None of the UNCHS projects reviewed specifically address the question of whether construction of low-income housing could become a possible source of new employment for women. Training women in construction and related skills, from bricklaying to metalworking, that are useful in both squatter housing and in the formal building industry has been introduced by many community groups in other countries (Celik, 1992). However, the programs in Nepal and Bangladesh called for rebuilding traditional homes with certain structural improvements that would make them more durable in future calamities. These projects recognize that while both women and men have some traditional knowledge of home finishing such as weaving grasses for roofing or applying whitewash to walls, the basic structure has usually been constructed by specialized male builders within the community. In fact, in both countries, training for local artisans in new techniques was regarded as the way to ensure improved structures. In Indonesia, one project called for a modern highrise; the low-cost housing project notes the role of informal builders in providing shelter and suggests that lack of credit and insecure tenure, not building skills, are the major problems for the urban poor.

With regard to home-based work, only in the low-cost housing project in Indonesia is there even indirect mention of women's income-earning capacity. Note is taken of a credit program available to family planning acceptors. Reference is made to UNDP's Development of the Role of Women in Small Industry as a prior relevant project. The paper recognizes elsewhere the importance of raising family income to match the rise in housing costs through skill development and provision of facilities to start a micro-business.

Experience with women's income projects varied among the countries. In Indonesia, the concept of *gotong royong,* or working together, continues to influence government thinking. As a result, women's projects have been designed as group activities. Evaluations suggest that such an approach hinders the success of most projects. Adherence to the knitting-and-sewing syndrome in Nepal and Bangladesh has greatly reduced the economic return of women's income activities. In all three countries, NGOs and agencies are experimenting with more adaptive income projects. Small hotels are being promoted in both Indonesia and Nepal through the International Labor Organization (ILO) projects. Making and selling local food products works well in some places, poorly in others. Fresh vegetables and animal products for the urban market have generated significant income. Even weaving and sewing, when combined with well-designed products and prearranged markets, have become a good source of income. Everywhere, small-scale credit for activities of a woman's own choosing apparently produces enhanced income. Typically, there is little exchange of information among groups.

The rapidity of the economic transition influences choices of income activities in all three countries. Indonesia's entry into the world markets as a second round NIC means that many products that women's groups have successfully sold are becoming obsolete as manufacturing expands; much of the experience garnered worldwide is no longer applicable. Bangladesh has recently become a center for the garment industry. Here too the school uniforms and children's clothes that some women's groups make are becoming redundant. This modernizing trend is even observable in Nepal and will certainly affect many economic activities.

Informalization of large industries is leading to greater emphasis on subcontracting. Partly this trend is a reflection of successful vertical integration of firms in Taiwan, where two-thirds of the industry employs five or fewer people, and Japan, where some 60% of all firms employ ten or fewer employees. Much subcontracting is on an individual basis, and pay is by the piece, whether for electronic assembly or toy assembling. There is a positive side to work at home, but there is also possible exploitation. NGOs and women's groups need to monitor conditions of employment. The spatial needs of these women need to be factored into house and neighborhood planning.

Street food vending is a major source of income for women around the world.[12] Scattered evidence indicates that home food production is both a source of family food and a source of income (Tinker, 1992). Cattle are raised in homes in Egypt and their cheese is widely sold. Squatters grow the winged bean in Cebu, Philippines; corn is grown in large concrete containers in the pueblo jovenes outside Lima, Peru; guinea pigs are raised in Oakland, California. In Berkeley a commercial farmer raises lettuce in downtown Berkeley and posts a profit of over $200,000 per year selling to gourmet restaurants. We need more quantitative data on the amount and economic importance of urban and peri-urban food production. Such studies should certainly be part of human settlement planning.

Top-Down Planning

The UNCHS projects under review reflect the host countries' policies toward women and treat them as passive recipients of housing: mothers are seen as needing housing and sanitation in Nepal; women-headed households are mentioned as vulnerable groups in Indonesian housing policy documents and are identified as deserving special consideration in the allocation of sites and service plots in Dhaka. But when the implementation of projects is examined, women are not consulted.

Consider the rural housing schemes undertaken in Bangladesh and Nepal to rebuild but also to upgrade homes destroyed by floods or earthquake. The upgrading consisted first of improved structural details designed to allow new homes to withstand another flood in Bangladesh or more severe earthquakes in Nepal. Secondly, governments in both countries decided to use this opportunity to require that all new/rebuilt houses would be improved by the provision of a latrine; additionally, in Nepal, home builders were to be encouraged to adopt an improved cookstove.

In Bangladesh, the Grameen Bank supplies four reinforced concrete pillars and a sanitary slab as part of the loan package. This slab represented a sixth of the cost of the loan, yet evaluators of the program did not see a single installed latrine (Islam *et al.*, 1989) while I saw one partially built. Remember that rural housing clusters in rural Bangladesh are built on earth islands that rise above the padi fields. During the monsoon, the fields flood to five feet or more; villages move from island to island by boat. The only place for a latrine is to hang off the side of the earth island, exposing the occupant to stares from below and dropping waste where it now goes, on the fields, to be washed away during the floods. The latrine was a water seal type that requires water to flush it. While fetching water is no problem in the rainy season, in the dry season it would require women to fetch buckets of additional water from the one tap in the village, down a steep bank, across fields, and up a steep bank, each way.

In Nepal, home builders willing to construct a latrine were offered a grant in the form of a fiberglass sanitary pad; scrubbing this pad in the usual way soon broke it apart. Again additional water had to be fetched, a chore in the hilly areas. Only in the Tarai, where water is plentiful and the population density much higher, were latrines adopted. A smokeless *chula* cookstove was also to be built into Nepali homes and similar grants offered. The technology for latrines and stoves has not adapted to household needs in the country and has therefore been largely unutilized. Alternative technology that is available in each country was apparently not investigated and no choice was offered.

Two Additional Issues

Absent from discussion of housing is any recognition of the critical needs that single women have for safe and affordable shelter. Hostels for women of various income levels, from factory workers to government clerks, are overcrowded and inadequate to the demand as urban migration accelerates and family support declines. Government policies that view women primarily as housewives obscure this crucial need to build hostels for unmarried women.

The national policies for modernizing transport systems in Indonesia and Bangladesh overlook the contribution of para-transport, particularly the bicycle rickshaw, to women's mobility. Buses not only cannot enter many urban settlements with their tiny uneven pathways, but crowded buses encourage groping and other offensive actions that women, particularly those in semi-seclusion, find especially difficult to deal with.

Conclusion

Pressures from population and urbanization are compelling governments to rationalize their land registration policies by interweaving the traditional customary practices with prevailing western law. Neither of these systems treated women fairly. But changing attitudes toward equity and justice for women and minorities make this an ideal time to intervene in this process of redefining land usage and titles. Further, these changing concepts of justice are reinforced by the practical realization that in a fractured family it is the woman who cares for the children. Even in intact families it is the woman's income that goes primarily for family needs. Clearly, investment in the younger generation requires investment in women, particularly for shelter.

The heavy burdens on women heads of households argue for more home-based work. Crafts and sewing, staples of independent home work, are rapidly becoming obsolete as products of the global factory penetrate poor urban and rural settlements. Informalization of industry is providing more work under contract. NGOs and women's organizations need to monitor working conditions of contract work, whether in Ahmedabad or Los Angeles. For women who prefer to remain self-employed, the street food trade provides a steady income. Home food production certainly provides for the family diet and is likely to become an increasingly important income source.

Top-down planning for shelter, for latrines and cookstoves, for housing design, for neighborhood layout, wastes money and results in unsatisfactory settlements. Greater use of NGOs and women's networks will not only bring to these issues experience and expertise from outside the housing community, but it will also educate these networks to the need for a women's shelter policy. The combined pressure of these groups will cajole government bureaucrats and technicians to listen to the poor urban and rural women and together adapt policies to the local situations.

UNCHS has encompassed all these ideas in its policy agenda. Implementation remains elusive. Its staff continues to lobby other UN agencies such as UNIFEM and UNDP; to seek funds from the World and Regional Banks and bilateral agencies; and to support conferences such as this one in order to convince the development community of the crucial importance of incorporating settlement issues into its programming. There is resistance, perhaps because the magnitude of urban problems is enervating; solutions are not apparent. Bureaucracies find it easier to stay with rural programming even as half of the world's people crowd into urban space. There is much consciousness-raising yet to be done to ensure that women's concerns become part of housing policy.

Conversely, the focus on shelter may provide the women's movement with relatively benign approaches to radical restructuring of gender relationships. To reiterate, shelter policy represents a culmination of women in development policy because it encompasses a broad range of basic women's issues of grave concern to rural and urban women worldwide and combines women's income and nurturing roles, specifically, women's access to land and housing:

> challenges the heart of gender inequality embodied in both customary and modern legal systems of ownership and inheritance that have given men control over these vital assets;

> addresses evolving forms of living arrangements resulting from increased individual mobility and insecure social and family safety nets: shelters for women who are battered, drug dependent, and homeless as well as housing for women who are single, head's of households, and elderly; unites women's roles in production and reproduction by expanding women's opportunities for income in and around the homestead, going beyond crafts to home-based contract and own account work; and finding new markets for production of food, that is growing vegetables and fruits, raising animals, poultry and fish, and preparing street foods; and

> reduces the time women spend on survival tasks through improved infrastructure, namely in the provision of clean water and safe disposal of wastes and through transportation arrangements that encompass safe and convenient access and appropriate transport.

Shelter policy provides a mechanism by which feminist issues can be presented as issues of shelter and so addressed in a relatively non-confrontational manner. Emphasis can be on the need to provide shelter and services to women and their children so that the younger generation does not become a burden in the future. Legal rights for women and minorities can be inserted into the current debate on how to adjust and combine land tenure rights as differentially presented in customary and in modern legal systems.

The women and shelter community, scholars, practitioners, and activists, need to join with UNCHS to ensure that the issue of shelter for women becomes increasingly visible. Internationally, the 1995 UN World Conference for Women scheduled for Beijing, provides an entree into the UN policy process that should not be missed. Nationally, women's organizations concerned with poverty, domestic violence, and the elderly should be recruited to work with women and shelter advocated to focus settlement policies at every level of government on women's differential needs. Such are the possibilities and constraints of global shelter policy as they relate to women.

Notes

1 Jane Jaquette (1990) contributes to our understanding of justice by distinguishing between rights, merit, and need.

2 The UN Centre for Human Settlements adopted the term *Habitat* as its alternate name. Because that name has been appropriated by a variety of NGOs, the UN Centre for Human Settlements tends now only to use UNCHS as a shorter form of its title.

3 In this respect, UNCHS's founding was similar to that of the United Nations Environmental Programme (UNEP) which was set up after the 1972 UN Environment Conference in Stockholm. Both agencies are located in Nairobi; both are very responsive to NGOs; and both receive significant funding from voluntary contributions.

4 Aliye P. Celik had been with UNCHS since 1981 when she was designated head of the focal point while continuing to perform all her original duties as well; she continued to play these dual roles until 1987. Such overload on women in development agencies is typical. She and Ayse Kudat of the UN Centre for Social Development and Humanitarian Affairs prepared the report based on research carried out by Mine Sabunsuoglu and Demetrios Papademetrious. The current focal point officer, Catalina Trujillo, has a full-time appointment.

5 These NGO Fora, which parallel most major UN world conferences, are open to interested citizens while the official UN meeting is restricted to governmental delegations, representatives of international agencies, and the press. At Nairobi, 14,000 women and men attended the NGO Forum compared to the 3,000 persons at the UN Conference. For background on the interrelationships between the NGO activities and the official UN conference of governments at the UN women's conferences, see Tinker and Jaquette, 1986.

6 UN agencies must request approval from the UN General Assembly before they may launch major campaigns such as the Global Strategy for Shelter to the Year 2000 which was adopted as resolution 43/181 on 23 December 1988. Debate in the General Assembly gives further visibility to new policies. Inserting such initiatives in other documents is an additional method of reinforcing new ideas. For example, UNCHS was able to include a paragraph on "sustainable human settlements" in the 1990s Program of Action for the Least Developed Countries (A/46/566). In the International Development Strategy for the Fourth Development Decade (1991–2000) human settlements are included in the section on the "eradication of poverty and hunger" and refer to the need for measures to relieve homelessness (A/C.2/45/L/ 72). Agenda 21, passed at the 1992 UN Conference on Environment

and Development or Earth Summit, included human settlements concerns into the overall sustainable development regime.

7 These seminars were held for Asia and the Pacific in Indonesia, February, 1988; French-speaking Africa in Tunisia, April, 1988; Caribbean in St. Vincent and the Grenadines, June, 1988; English-speaking Africa in Zambia, November, 1988; Latin America in Argentina, March, 1989. The summary report of these seminars, "Toward a Strategy for the Full Participation of Women in All Phases of the UN Global Strategy for Shelter to the Year 2000," UNCHS 1990, was prepared by Caroline Pezzullo. An excellent state-of-the-art document, written by Ayse Kudat, summarizes materials assembled for the seminars (UNCHS, 1989).

8 Three types of shelter situations were discussed: urban poor, rural women, and women living on plantations or work sites. The seminar was held in Harare with funds from the Swedish government (UNCHS, 1990:41).

9 Originally set up as the UN Voluntary Fund for the Decade for Women as the result of a resolution at the UN Conference for International Women's Year in Mexico City, June 1975, the Fund promoted small grants directly to women's groups of poor women. Currently UNIFEM maintains an autonomous association with the United Nations Development Programme and frequently uses its funds as leverage to ensure that women's concerns are "mainstreamed" into major development programs.

10 The official objectives of this joint mission were (1) an assessment of current UNCHS projects in Indonesia, Bangladesh, and Nepal to ascertain the extent to which women are or could be included in all phases of the projects and to investigate obstacles to such participation; (2) the identification of new opportunities for UNIFEM/UNCHS collaboration in working with women's groups, other NGOs, and governments on activities relating to women and human settlements; and (3) the formulation of specific projects or interventions in UNIFEM priority areas of macro policies, data collection, gender training, and institutional strengthening. Visits to the countries took place in December, 1990, and January, 1991.

11 When asked where all the men were, the social worker waved her hands and replied "rotating."

12 Results of an eight country study of street foods, which I directed as president of the Equity Policy Center, found that street food sellers averaged income higher that their country's minimum wage, a wage seldom available to women (Tinker, 1987).

References

Anderson, Mary B., 1991. *Women on the Agenda: UNIFEMS's Experience in Mainstreaming with Women 1985–1990.* New York.

Babb, Florence, "Economic Crisis and the Assault on Marketers in Peru," East Lansing: Michigan State University Working Paper #6 in series on Women in International Development.

Bernstein, Manis D., 1991. *Alternative Approaches to Pollution Control and Waste Management,* Washington, D.C.: Urban Management Program Policy Paper, World Bank.

Blayney, Robert, & Margaret Lycette, 1983. "Improving the Access of Women-Headed Households to Lolanda Housing." Washington, D.C.: International Center for Research on Women.

Bradley, David, Sandy Cairncross, Trudy Harpham, & Carolyn Stephens, 1991. *A Review of Environmental Health Impacts in Developing Countries,* Washington, D.C.: Urban Management Program Policy Paper, World Bank.

Bubel, Anna Z, 1990. *Environmental Sanitation Reviews* No 30, December. Bangkok: Asian Institute of Technology.

Celik, Aliye P., 1992. "Women's Participation in the Production of Shelter," paper read at the Conference on Shelter, Women and Development: First and Third World Perspectives, University of Michigan, May.

Dowall, David, & Giles Clark, 1991. *A Framework for Reforming Urban Land Policies in Developing Countries,* Washington, D.C.: Urban Management Program Policy Paper, World Bank.

Farvacque, Catherine, & Patrick McAuslan, 1991. *Reforming Urban Land Policies and Institutions in Developing Countries,* Washington, D.C.: Urban Management Program Policy Paper, World Bank.

Fraser, Arvonne S., 1987. *The UN Decade for Women: Documents and Dialogue.* Boulder: Westview.

Furedy, Christine, 1990. "Social Aspects of Solid Waste Recovery in Asian Cities," Environmental Sanitation Reviews No. 30, December. Bangkok: Asian Institute of Technology.

Gurstein, Penny. 1991. "The Electronic Cottage: Implications for the Meaning of Home," in volume 26 of the Traditional Dwellings and Settlements Working Paper Series. Berkeley: Center for Environmental Design Research, U. of California.

HIC Women and Shelter Network *Newsletter* #3 August 1991; #5 August 1992.

Hooper, Emma, & Kanta Singh, 1991. "Women and Shelter in Nepal," Report to the Ministry of Housing and Physical Planning, Government of Nepal. Khatmandu. Culpin.

Islam, Nazrul, Amirul Islam Chowdhury, Khadem Ali, 1989. *Evaluation of the Grameen Bank's Rural Housing Programme.* Dhaka: Centre for Urban Studies, U. of Dhaka.

Jaquette, Jane, 1990. "Gender and Justice in Economic Development," in I. Tinker, ed., *Persistent Inequalities: Women and World Development,* New York: Oxford.

Kusterer, Ken, & Loise Vitt. 1991. "Workspace at Home: A Comparative Perspective of First and Third World Environments," in volume 26 of the Traditional Dwellings and Settlements Working Paper Series. Berkeley: Center for Environmental Design Research, U. of California.

Lowe, Marcia D., 1990, *Shaping Cities: The Environmental and Human Dimensions,* Washington, D.C.: Worldwatch Paper #105.

Merrick, Thomas, & Marianne Schminck, 1982. "Women in the Urban Economy in Latin America," in Mayra Buvinic, Margaret Lycette, & William McGreevey, eds., *Women and Poverty in the Third World.* Baltimore: Johns Hopkins.

Milone, Pauline, 1986. *Guidelines for Assessing Gender Issues in Urban Development and Housing Projects,* Manila: Asian Development Bank. Agricultural Cooperative Development International.

_____, 1992. "Kampung Improvement in the Small and Medium Size Cities of Central Java." RURDS (Review of Urban & Rural Development Studies, Tokyo): 5.

Moser, Caroline O. N. & Linda Peake, 1987. *Women, Human Settlements, and Housing,* London: Tavistock.

Papanek, Hanna, 1976. "Women in Cities: Problems and Perspectives," in I. Tinker & Michelle Bo Bramsen, eds., *Women and World Development,* Washington, D.C.: Overseas Development Council; N.Y.: Praeger.

Pietila, Hilkka & Jeanne Vickers, 1990. *Making Women Matter: The Role of the United Nations.* London: Zed.

Sayne, Pamela, 1988. "Theory and Practice of Development Education: A Response to Women and Shelter Provision," unpublished.

Schminck, Marianne, 1985, "The 'Working Group' Approach to Women and Urban Services," *Ekistics* 52/310.

Singh, Andrea Menefee, & Alfred de Souza, 1980. *The Urban Poor: Slum and Pavement Dwellers in Major Cities of India.* New Delhi: Manohar.

Sorock, Margery, Hortense Dicker, Amparo Giralco, & Susan Waltz, 1984. *Women and Shelter,* Washington, D.C.: Office of Housing and Urban Programs, Agency for International Development. Resources for Action.

Tinker, Irene, 1987a. *Street Foods: Testing Assumptions About Informal Sector Activity by Women and Men.* Monograph issue of *Current Sociology* 35/3.

_____, 1987b. "The Real Rural Energy Crisis: Women's Time," *Energy Journal* 8:125–146.

_____, 1989. "Credit for Poor Women: Necessary, But Not Always Sufficient for Change," *Marga* 10/2. Colombo, Sri Lanka.

_____, 1990. "The Making of a Field: Advocates, Practitioners, and Scholars," in I. Tinker, ed., *Persistent Inequalities: Women and World Development,* New York: Oxford.

_____, 1991. "Women's access to housing and work: evaluation of UNCHS programs in Indonesia, Bangladesh, and Nepal," an evaluation for UNIFEM, the United Nations Fund for Women, and HABITAT, the United Nations Centre for Human Settlements, March.

_____, 1992, guest editor, *Hunger Notes* 18/2 on "Urban Food Production: Neglected Resource for Food and Jobs."

Tinker, Irene, & Monique Cohen, 1985. "Street Foods as a Source of Income for Women," *Ekistics* 52/310.

Tinker, Irene, & Jane Jaquette, 1987. "UN Decade for Women: Its Impact and Legacy," *World Development* 15/3: 419–427.

UN Centre for Human Settlements, 1985. *Women and Human Settlements.* Nairobi.
_____, 1989. *Women and Human Settlements Development.* Nairobi.

_____, 1990. *Towards a Strategy for the Full Participation in all Phases of the United Nations Global Strategy for Shelter to the Year 2000.* Nairobi. *Urban Edge* 15/6, 1991.

Chapter 3
Women's Role in Shelter Planning

K. K. Bhatnagar

K. K. Bhatnagar is the chairman and managing director of Housing and Urban Development Corporation, a fully owned Government of India enterprise. He joined the Indian Administrative Service in 1962 and has over thirty years' experience in Public Administration, during which he has been closely involved in regional planning strategies. He was the leader of the Indian delegation to Iran for Cooperation in Development of Fisheries in 1974 and a member of the UNICEF-sponsored study mission on Human Resource Development and Literacy in Indonesia and Thailand in 1981

Contrary to popular belief, every woman is a worker. Her work is multifarious and embraces a multitude of functions of vital social and economic importance. She is a reproducer of the children and a mother, imparting basic skills and knowledge to the future of the country. She is the hub around whom family life revolves. She provides a multitude of services for the well-being of the family. In many cases she contributes directly to the family income. It is this economic contribution that enables the family to survive. Invariably her entire income goes toward this. Women constitute a vital component of human resources and their contribution to development is substantial. It is now generally realized that women can make an active contribution to the development of their communities and that they must be included in all spheres of developmental activities to achieve development objectives.

The condition of poor women and women engaged in the unorganized and self-employed sector in developing countries is quite dismal. Data compiled by various agencies as well as published reports indicate discrimination against and deprivation of women. Life expectancy of women continues to remain lower than men's, the opposite of the case in developed countries. In India, there is a gender imbalance in the sex ratio. This is more pronounced in the rural areas where 70 percent of the population lives. In the urban areas the imbalance is greater in the productive age bracket (20–49 years). Infant mortality rate for females is higher as well. Of late, however, the life expectancy of women in India has risen from 44.7 years to 52.9 years between 1961–71 and 1971–81, respectively. A disturbing factor is the high illiteracy level of women in India, perhaps one of the greatest barriers to their development. It limits their scope of employment, training, utilization of health facilities, access to vital information and services, and exercise of legal and constitutional rights. Although detailed and consistent information on the economic profile of women workers is scant, indications are that the work-force participation rate among women is very low, since most of the female workers are invisible— they are not in the organized sector nor are they enumerated. On the whole, the female work-force participation rate during 1981 was 3.25 times less than that of the males (Census, 1981). At the same time the proportion of women engaged in domestic duties—collecting goods (vegetable, fodder, fuel wood), sewing, tailoring and weaving for household use—is quite high, as can be seen from Tables 1 and 2. Women in low-income communities are not only responsible for economic contribution for the family's survival, but also for a host

Table 1: Percentage of Women Engaged in Household Activities

S. No.	Activities	Rural	Urban
1.	Maintenance of kitchen, garden, orchards, etc.	14.4	4.6
2.	Work in household poultry	14.5	3.9
3.	Work in household dairy	31.8	6.0
4.	Any of 1–3	43.7	11.7
5.	Free collection of fish, small games, etc.	24.1	3.1
6.	Free collection of firewood, cattle feed etc.	43.5	8.0
7.	Any of 1–5	65.1	17.2
8.	Husking paddy	27.6	2.3
9.	Preparation of gur	2.2	0.2
10.	Grinding of food grains	38.8	13.5
11.	Preparation of cow dung cakes	49.9	9.1
12.	Sewing, tailoring	17.4	20.8
13.	Tutoring children	0.4	10.0
14.	Bringing water from outside the household premise	63.0	34.8
15.	Bringing water from outside the village	3.3	–
16.	Percentage of persons engaged in household duties to total persons (5+ years)	42.0	50.5

Source: National Commission on Self-Employed Women and Women in the Informal Sector, 1988.

Table 2: Time Spent by Women on Household Activities

Activity	Hours/day
Fetching water	
Eastern U.P	1.0–3.9
Western U.P.	0.8–3.0
Karnataka	1.0–1.4
Fuel wood gathering	
Himalayan	4.0–7.2
Karnataka	0.4–0.9
Fetching water and fuel wood gathering	
Gujarat - Rajasthan Border	6.0–9.0
Grazing animals	
Western U.P.	0.0–3.0
Karnataka	0.5–1.0
Making dung cakes	
Western U.P.	0.0–0.5

Source: Menaka Roy, Reader on Women & Development, HSMI, New Delhi.

of household functions, thereby increasing their burden and hardship.

Realizing the potential of women and the contribution they can make to social and economic development, the Government of India has initiated a number of steps for their uplift. During 1971, under the aegis of the Ministry of Social Welfare, a Committee on the Status of Women in India (CSWI) was constituted. Its report, "Towards Equality," set out policy recommendations of great importance. This coincided with the declaration of 1975 as the International Women's Year. A series of action/approach papers and reports was produced to operationalize these recommendations between 1976 and 1978. The Sixth Five-Year Plan included a separate Chapter on Women and Development, 1980–85, and the Seventh Plan also emphasizes women's development. A major outcome of the report of the CSWI was the National Plan of Action, 1976, which identified the key areas of focus as well as the guidelines for action on women's development. This led to the establishment of the Women's Welfare and Development Bureau in 1976 under the Ministry of Social Welfare. The main task of the Bureau was to act as a nodal point within the Government of India and coordinate policies, and programs as well as to initiate measures for the development of women. In 1985, the Government established a separate department in the Ministry of Human Resource Development for the development of women and children. In 1987 the Government constituted the National Commission on Self-Employed Women to make a comprehensive study of the working and living conditions of women in poverty. The Commission submitted its report in 1988.

Presently, the Government has about 27 schemes either entirely or predominantly intended to improve the condition of women. These are managed by various departments and ministries. Various programs are being run to benefit women, e.g., Women's Development Corporation, Support to Training and Employment (STEP), Training-cum-Production Centres for Women, Awareness Generation Camps for Rural and Poor Women, Institute for Rehabilitation of Women in Distress, Women's Training Centre, Short Stay Homes for Women and Girls, Voluntary Action Bureau and Family Counseling Centre, Free Legal Aid and Para Legal Training, Working Women's Hostel, etc.

Women's Problems in Housing and Infrastructure

No matter how important women's roles might be, men are the main decision makers in the allocation of family budget and in determining the various priorities of the family. Combining child rearing, housekeeping, income generation, and a subordinate role in budget allocation has several implications for women in terms of their requirements, priorities, and possible contribution towards community development. Planning and development of housing schemes or projects for provision of infrastructure are not sensitive, in general, to their needs and priorities. The draft National Housing Policy (NHP), Government of India, 1990, specially mentions the case of women. The NHP has, in general, addressed the shelter requirements of the disadvantaged in society, including displaced and homeless persons, women in disadvantaged circumstances, etc., and also proposes specific actions on behalf of women: "...women have a vital stake in the management of family affairs and suffer far more from deprived housing conditions and inadequate access to basic services and health care. Adequate attention will be given while devising programmes to meet the specific needs of women in disadvantaged circumstances, including widows and construction workers, in terms of joint or exclusive title, access to credit, home based employ-ment, maternal and child welfare and shelter design and to amend all related laws for this purpose." (NHP, 1990, p. 3)

One of the major problems facing women seeking access to shelter relates to access to land. Land is rarely in the woman's name. Where land or house sites are distributed or where collective tribal land is being privatized, women are losing status because sites are being registered under men's names. Widows, usually without sons, may find it possible to register or list land under their names, but are confronted with complicated procedures of transfer of ownership rights. A widow also finds it next to impossible to retain land in her name for long, due to social and economic constraints.

Women's Needs: Plot Layout and Housing Design

Women's preferences about plot layout, house design or neighborhood improvement are not taken as guides in new housing schemes and slum-up gradation programs. In slum resettlement programs, women suffer most. Apart from numerous problems in a new settlement, they suffer most by losing their source of income. In the Dakshinpuri resettlement colony in Delhi, male employ-ment declined only 5 percent, but an estimated 27 percent of the women had to give up their jobs. Owing to low education levels and socioeconomic status, women face problems in transfer of ownership rights of land and houses.

Women thus face numerous problems which need to be taken care of while formulating housing projects. Notable among them are:

1. Basic facilities such as taps, waste disposal pits, markets, schools, and other public amenities are often far away from the houses. Women have to cover long distances every day to reach these amenities. These should be placed conveniently.
2. Women face privacy and security hazards due to lack of proper bathing and toilet facilities.
3. In new or upgraded housing, the layout or housing design does not take care of their priorities and needs. Designs of kitchen or cooking space, toilets, courtyards, bedrooms or sleeping areas must be sensitive to their needs and priorities.

Women have taken the lead in a number of projects of slum-up gradation, and, working together with the Non-governmental Organizations (NGOs), have been able to mobilize other women in the area and help to create awareness of women issues.

Potentials of Women in Slum-up Gradation

As the primary users, women are more aware of favorable dwelling designs and other aspects related to their living environment, such as location of infrastructural facilities and appropriate plot arrange-ments. With the help of NGOs, women now are increasingly discussing their needs and assessing the lack of basic facilities in their environment. With the support of the NGOs, women leaders collectively formulate their concerns to brief the authorities about their requirements.

Ekta Vihar in Delhi is one such successful project where gender-based housing development has been attempted. In 1989, an NGO mobilized the women to help upgrade the slums. The residents converted themselves into a cooperative society most of whose members were women. The most important innovation in this colony is that rights of ownership of houses rest with the women. Additionally, the women have been provided a loan of Rs.5000 each for construction of a house. Plots have been allotted free of cost. The results of this project are outstanding and the experiment is being replicated in other slums.

Successful projects like Ekta Vihar have made it clear that women possess distinct potentials for contributions to improvement of low-income settlements. In contrast, in conventional housing projects these abilities have not been taken advantage of in either formulation, implementation, or maintenance of the projects.

There is now enough evidence that woman can play an important role in mobilizing financial resources for housing investments. In other words, they contribute substantially in enhancing cost recovery performance in housing projects and preventing men from wasting household assets on relatively unimportant items.

Women's potentials in slum-up gradation can thus be summarized as:

1. Women have concrete ideas about the design of their homes, ideas related to their daily and practical requirements.
2. Women possess strong organizational capacities at the grassroots level.
3. Women possess potentials to contribute to house construction.
4. Women can—with some proper training—easily be involved in the maintenance of the living environment.
5. Women have proven able to protect household assets, even more than men.

Women, Housing, and Employment

An important category of laboring women is home-based workers engaged in a variety of activities like rolling local cigarettes, food processing, garment-making, lace-making, incense-stick and candle-making, weaving and zari working. There is no recognition of such home-based income-generating activities. Many times new housing schemes prohibit the use of the dwelling unit for such purposes. The dwellings' design does not take the spatial requirements of these activities into consideration. Women work in cramped, poorly lighted, and ill-ventilated quarters up to 10 to 15 hours a day. Wherever worksheds or workshops are constructed, they cater mainly to men. Completely isolated from the houses, these worksheds neither have any charm for the women nor provide minimal facilities such as a crèche to take care of infants while the women are working. Wherever cooperatives have been formed, women are seldom taken as members, and even if they get membership they are given unimportant work. For example, among handloom weavers, women are given mainly pre-weaving work, although many are adept at handling the loom.

Housing and Urban Development Corporation (HUDCO) and Women in Development

For quite some time, HUDCO has been actively pursuing a number of programs to sensitize the professionals engaged in the field of housing toward the requirements of poor women and the potential contribution that they can make for the betterment of their communities and neighborhoods.

In 1986, as part of the International Year of Shelter for the Homeless, HUDCO initiated two projects at Delhi as National Site and Shelter Demonstration Projects. Women-headed households were provided shelter in both projects. The communities, along with NGOs, were involved in the schemes right from the beginning in all important decision-making during planning, designing, and implementation. Post-occupancy management, including maintenance of the neighborhoods, is vested with the women. The success of these projects has led to considerable interest in replication in other parts of the country. The case of Ekta Vihar Slum Redevelopment has already been mentioned. This is yet another successful project initiated and supported by HUDCO.

As part of its lending functions, HUDCO has recently introduced financial packages for the construction of condominiums and hostels for working women. For pavement dwellers HUDCO, with the support of the Ministry of Urban Development, has been vigorously pursuing projects of "Night Shelters." These provide a proper shelter for the night, including all basic facilities, to the pavement dweller at a nominal rate. Special attention is paid to the needs of women. In most of these night shelters, health care facilities are made available. Vocational training of poor women is provided during the day. To boost the efforts of environmental improvement of low-income neighborhoods, HUDCO provides support to erect Pay and Use Community Toilets. Women and children have free access to these facilities, whereas men are charged a nominal rate. This is done to encourage and inculcate the habits of cleanliness among women, as it is believed that women are central in creating and propagating mass awareness of cleanliness.

Apart from projects, HUDCO is involved in research and documentation in women-related development issues. There is a dearth of information on these in

India, particularly related to housing. Every year HUDCO encourages and supports young and upcoming professionals to take up research work in key areas of housing and urban development. For this year, HUDCO has identified women and development as the major concern. HUDCO is also engaged in compiling and making available at one place all existing materials on women-related issues in housing. Preparation of training packages and audio-visuals are other important activities. One audio-visual package, "The Neglected Human Factor in Housing," has already been developed with the assistance of the Institute for Housing and Urban Development Studies (IHS), in Rotterdam, The Netherlands. Efforts are underway to develop and conduct a training course on women and housing to sensitize professionals to this area. The Centre for NGOs managed by HUDCO is also engaged in addressing similar problems, along with active support and cooperation from various voluntary organizations.

Chapter 4
Synopsis of Talk by Salma Khan: Housing Policy and Development in Bangladesh

Vinitha Aliyar

Salma Khan is the Division Chief of the National Planning Commission, Government of Bangladesh, and Member, UN Committee for Elimination of Discrimination Against Women (CEDAW). She was an Eisenhower Fellow in 1992. She is an Assistant Professor in the Department of Economics at the University of Cittagong, Bangladesh. She received her M.A. in Economics from the University of Dhaka, Bangladesh and the University of Chicago. She has a diploma in Training Management from the University of Connecticut and studied gender planning at the London University. She just completed her Ph.D. dissertation at the University of Dhaka on the exploitation of the female labor force in garment industries.

Currently a Division Chief of the Planning Commission of Bangladesh and formerly a Joint Chief of the Women's Wing, Ms. Khan has been responsible for the long-term development of perspectives and policies that are specifically geared to women's issues. Ms. Khan was also instrumental in initiating the Women's Wing in the Planning Commission and she facilitated the incorporation of women and development issues in the Fourth Five-Year Plan of Bangladesh.

Affordable housing is a problem of great concern in Bangladesh. Gender-differentiated right to land is the single most important factor affecting gender equality in Bangladesh since, in most cases, the wealth base is composed of land only. Recent studies have pointed up that crisis has additional dimensions for vulnerable groups such as single women and women-headed households. The Urban Studies Unit of Dhaka University investigated the rater deplorable condition of low-income housing in the country. The study found that an average family spends more than 60% of its income for a modest two-room house in Dhaka city. Since such a large percentage is spent on far from satisfactory housing, people seldom have the wherewithall to take care of other equally crucial needs. Persistent poverty and landlessness and the consequent erosion of support of the gamily are making more and more women shelterless. Most of the poor live in thatched houses which can hardly withstand the vicissitudes of nature.

Another study highlighted the plight of one of the most oppressed groups in the country, prostitutes in the red light area of the cities. It was found that such women were constantly harassed, denied housing, or evicted from their dwelling places. A special program of the government specifically focuses on housing issues in disaster-prone areas. Women's housing concerns in areas constantly ravaged by frequent cyclones and floods in the coastal areas is expected to be addressed by this program. Towards evolving an affordable approach to low-income housing, a site and services program has been started with World Bank assistance in coastal areas. A slum upgradation program has also been started in major cities.

The Grameen Bank Project

In 1989, the prestigious Aga Khan International Award for Architecture was bestowed on what appears, at first sight, to be a rather unlikely contestant: a modest two-room house with a sanitary latrine made of wood, bamboo, and tin. The 100 square foot house built on four RCC pillars, costs only US $300.00. This house, the prototype of the housing unit of the Grameen Bank Project in Bangladesh, is the first of its kind to receive such recognition. The Grameen Bank Project has developed a housing project to meet the needs of the landless loanees of the Bank—the Bank loanees constitute those who have no agricultural land but have land only for building a dwelling. The Grameen Bank, which lends money without collateral to landless rural people (92% of whom are women) for income-generation activities, is also providing housing credit under a special scheme of the bank. Already, 150,000 families have built the prototype housing unit with a loan from the Grameen Bank, and their repayment rate is 98%. The Project is meant primarily for lower-income families involved in income-generating activities with Grameen Bank credit. Loans without default payments are considered eligible for the housing loan. About 85% of the beneficiaries at Grameen Bank Credit are women and the rate of repayment of loans is approximately 98%.

This housing project is noteworthy because of its unique eligibility criteria that implicitly favors women. As a case in point, housing loans are granted to single women, women-headed households, or couples. A male loanee cannot apply for these loans without including his wife. Another prerequisite is that the couple have joint title to the land. As a result, many men transfer at least half their land to their wives. Recipients have to adhere to a specific prototype house design developed by the Grameen Bank. An additional stipulation is that the recipients invest sweat equity in constructing their own homes. An informal agreement between loan recipients ensured that the men in the housing project would pitch in to help single women and women-headed households with their housing construction. The Grameen Bank housing project has earned an international reputation and this represents the single largest effort (in volume) to provide affordable housing to very poor people. In addition, this project is the first of its kind to emphasize women's shelter needs.

Women's Participation in Shelter

The need to involve women in shelter resettlements and rehabilitation programs became a critical concern after the flood of 1988, in which the most vulnerable groups were women and children. In severe natural disasters, poor people not only lose their cattle herds and poultry birds but also are left with damaged or destroyed dwellings. In a situation like this, women are found to be providing their labor in repair and maintenance. A survey conducted among the slum dwellers in Dhaka shows that 50% of the labor required for repairing and erecting houses is supplied by women. In rural areas, women traditionally have participated in the repair and maintenance of mud houses. As a consequence of repeated natural calamities and continued poverty, the number of female-headed households is also on the increase, making the shelter needs of women a critical issue. The Task Force, created by the Planning Commission in 1990 to identify major development issues, identified women's shelter needs in disaster prone areas as a priority.

The Task Force developed broad guidelines that targeted the needs of low-income families in general and women in particular. It also advocated changes in construction methods, since houses built using conventional methods could not withstand the onslaught of cyclones and floods causing severe physical devastation. Taking the recommendations of the Task Force as a point of departure, an NGO named Nijira Kodi—"Do it Ourselves"—played a key role in advocating the need for women's participation and input in shelter design.

The NGO mobilized women from disaster-prone areas and numerous workshops were organized with the assistance of UNIFEM, in collaboration with other local agencies. The workshops served as a forum for exchange and discussion about women's shelter concerns, particularly in the disaster-prone areas. Some of the specific shelter-related suggestions proposed by women included the following:

— Houses should have a higher plinth to avoid being inundated during flash floods and cyclones.
— House structures should have adequate wind velocity tolerance.
— Housing units should be designed to accommodate the family's livestock. Almost all families have sheep, cows, or poultry, which often were their only assets and must be protected during floods.
— The public shelters provided by the government needed to have facilities that can accommodate the displaced families' livestock.

The Government of Bangladesh has taken these recommendations quite seriously and has addressed these issues in its recent affordable housing efforts.

The Tikana Housing Program

A much publicized low-cost housing effort of the government was called "Tikana" which means "address." As part of this program, the government helped to form cluster villages composed of 25–50 households, which were situated on reclaimed marshy land. However, this effort was criticized because the houses were provided free of cost. No sweat equity was required and, on the whole, the project was not cost-effective. As a result, such housing efforts were soon abandoned.

Land Pooling and Adjustment Policy

A very innovative policy formulated during the Fourth Five-Year Plan was the Land Pooling and Adjustment Policy. This policy addressed vacant land in the villages and smaller towns which was bought by speculators. The government negotiated with these landowners and promised to provide basic infrastructure such as roads, electricity, etc. In return, the landowners had to give 30% of their land to the Government. This land was to be reallocated to low-income housing projects. So far, such measures have been attempted as pilot projects in ten smaller cities in the country and have achieved a reasonable degree of success.

Urban Housing

Bangladesh's urban housing policies have been largely ineffective in meeting the needs of lower-income families in general and women's specific shelter needs in particular. Affordable housing projects such as "slum upgradation" and "sites and services" have been sporadic and small in scale. To meet the needs of working women, the Ministry of Women's Affairs has built ten Career Women's Hostels in the major cities. These facilities are available only to working women who have to provide proof of employment. The maximum period a woman can stay is three years and children and family members are not allowed. These hostels specifically target single working women. Women-headed households have very few housing options in urban areas.

In sum, Bangladesh's housing policies have been largely ineffective in meeting the great need for housing in lower-income groups. Women and children continue to be the most vulnerable groups. The government has concentrated its efforts in providing appropriate housing in disaster-prone areas. Innovative housing projects such as Grameen Bank Housing Scheme and housing policies such as the Land Pooling and Adjustment Policy have made considerable inroads in making the administration sensitive to women's housing needs. However, the short history of these efforts, coupled with their small scale, has meant that these developments have been rather marginal in addressing the overall shelter needs of women.

Chapter 5
Women and Housing Policy in South Africa: A Discussion of Durban Case Studies

Alison Todes and Norah Walker

Alison Todes is a lecturer in the Department of Town and Regional Planning, and a member of the Built Environment Support Group at the University of Natal, Durban, South Africa. She has a Bachelor of Psychology and a Master of Urban Planning from the University of Cape Town. She worked as a researcher at the Urban Problems Research Unit at the University of Cape Town and at the Built Environment Support Group. Her research work focuses on the urbanization and settlement policy in South Africa, the reorganization of local government in South Africa, housing and upgrading, gender and development, and regional policy. She is the coauthor, with David Dewar and Vanessa Watson, of Regional Development and Settlement Policy, published by Allen and Unwin in 1986.

Norah Walker is a Research Officer and Program Head of Research at the Built Environment Support Group, University of Natal, Durban. She received a Bachelor of Arts in African History and a Master of Urban Planning from the University of Cape Town. She worked as a housing researcher at the Institute for Social Development, University of the Western Cape in Cape Town, and then as a town planner in local government in Cape Town. She received a Master in Housing at the Development Planning Unit, University College, London. She has been involved in upgrading projects in Durban and is currently coordinating a national research project designed to assist the formulation of future housing policy in South Africa.

Within South Africa debate is emerging about the most appropriate form of housing policy. Our paper attempts to stimulate discussion of certain key areas of housing policy from a gender perspective. Our starting point is an analysis and evaluation of women's access to and experience of housing supplied through the major delivery systems that have emerged from past and present housing policies, namely, public housing, housing developed by the private sector, and informal housing.[1]

This focus enables us to comment on the question of competing delivery systems, which has been an important area of debate in South Africa. It also allows us to examine the effect of macro policy on women: too often gender issues are treated as a separate concern, or only at a project level, while the effects of seemingly gender-neutral policy are ignored. This analysis forms the basis for our discussion of some of the issues which should be considered in the formulation of a gender-sensitive housing policy.

As South African housing policies have in the past been formulated on a racial basis, a full understanding of their gendered nature requires an evaluation of the way policies are applied to different races. Our paper focuses, as a start, on policies applied to African people, and to women's experiences of them primarily within three areas in Durban in the Natal Province: public housing (rental and ownership) in Chesterville, private developer-built housing in Umlazi Section Z, Phase 8, and informal housing in Piesang's River, Inanda.[2]

Our paper shows that state housing policy has created sharp divides among different groups of African women, particularly on the basis of class and historical access to urban housing. From a policy perspective, our analysis also highlights the difficulties women confront in the three systems. This points to the complexity of attempting to develop gender-sensitive policy. At a general level, some of the key areas for consideration are the level of service provision; the affordability of housing; the conceptualization of family and household within various aspects of policy; the question of positive discrimination in favor of women; and women's participation in the institutions controlling housing.

Our discussion of both women's experience of housing and of policy must be seen as somewhat tentative and exploratory. We raise questions and issues for debate, but do not attempt to produce answers in policy terms. The evaluation of existing housing systems is based to some extent on preliminary data and, therefore, requires further research. Despite these limitations, our research does raise issues critical to the formulation of a gender-sensitive housing policy.

State Policy and Women's Access to Housing in Durban

African women's present access to, and experience of, housing has been shaped by the way in which housing policy has developed historically, and by the state's changing conception of the African family and women's position in it. In the 1950s and 1960s, the state embarked on a massive public housing program, while removing many existing informal settlements and townships. These public housing schemes became the main form of housing for the African population in Durban, and in other urban centers, until the mid-1970s. By then, the development of public housing schemes had slowed down considerably, and informal settlements became an increasingly important form of housing, particularly in Durban. Today, some 1.7 million people (49% of Durban's population, and more than 60% of its African population) live in these settlements (Tongaat-Hulett, 1989). Although home ownership through the privatization of public housing and private sector development of formal housing has been emphasized as part of state reform in the 1980s, a very small proportion of Durban's African population occupies such housing.

The 1940s and 1950s in Durban saw a rapid growth of the African population, particularly in uncontrolled informal settlements. Cato Manor, close to the center of Durban, was the largest of these settlements. From the earliest years, there were attempts by the municipality—at the time in control of these areas—to remove informal settlements. The development of formal townships, and of stringent rules to regulate them, was a way of strengthening control of the influx as well as a reaction to the social, physical, and political threat represented by informal settlements (Maylam, 1983). The development of Chesterville in 1946, comprising 1,265 two-bedroom houses, was tied to these ends. The shift from informal uncontrolled to formal, regulated housing reduced women's economic and social independence, as Edwards (1988) has shown, in particular through its suppression of informal sector activity.

The provision of public housing on a larger scale and its systems of management and allocation were intimately tied to state attempts to regulate and control the urban African population. From the 1920s, but particularly after the coming to power of the Nationalist Party in 1948, African people in urban areas prescribed for white

occupation were seen as temporary sojourners, whose real homes were in homeland areas. Control of women's movement to town was therefore seen as critical. Housing in prescribed "white" urban areas was developed in these terms: hostels for single men formed an important component of the housing stock, while only people with urban rights could occupy family housing. Many women were excluded on this basis.

Rules governing housing allocation ensured that women's access to housing was almost entirely through men. Women were also constrained by their lack of earning power, and by the Natal Code, in which they were defined as minors, with no contractual powers. In consequence, many single women at the time were forced to make convenience marriages, or to become domestic workers in order to gain access to housing (Eagle, 1987). The development of national regulations for housing allocation in 1968—as part of a process of instituting more stringent control of the influx—did not substantially alter these conditions.

In Durban, African women's access to housing was legally somewhat easier than in many other parts of the country. In contrast to many other major urban centers in South Africa, Durban abuts a homeland area—KwaZulu. Since influx control attempted to dam Africans up in homelands, rather than simply in rural areas, urbanization in homeland urban areas was less rigidly controlled than in prescribed "white" urban areas. Regulations governing the allocation of formal housing and sites in KwaZulu townships were therefore more flexible on the definition of the household head who could qualify for housing, although in practice, Eagle (1987) argues, the definition operated in favor of men, and further that most women were restricted by the Natal Code.

The popular uprisings of the 1970s and early 1980s were partially directed against influx control, and against the conditions under which African people were forced to live in urban areas. Women played a critical role in these struggles, although the gender aspects were rarely articulated. The crisis of the 1970s and 1980s was also underpinned by economic stagnation, in which the limited market and the largely unskilled and therefore unproductive workforce was seen as playing a key role. In response, the Wiehan and Riekert Commissions of 1979 attempted to restructure the African labor force, to segment it into a numerically restricted, but better off, urban African working and middle class (see Hindson, 1987), while imposing firmer controls on the influx of African people without urban rights to prescribed "white" urban areas. The promotion of a "normal" family life for "qualified" African people, with home-owning nuclear families as the bulwark of stability, was very much part of this vision. These shifts were associated with a liberalization of "qualified" women's access to housing. New regulations shifted the definition of the family able to gain access to public housing from men to "qualified" people (who could afford to pay rentals) and their dependents. Similar amendments were made to regulations governing homeland areas. In both cases the effect of the Natal Code was overridden, or fell into disuse (Eagle, 1987).

These emphases were strengthened and taken further in the policy shifts toward self-help housing and the privatization of housing in the 1980s, and in the eventual acceptance of African urbanization and repeal of influx control laws in 1986, following continuing struggles against the state. While the self-help housing policy has had little practical effect in Durban (other than a greater acceptance of the upgrading of informal settlements), privatization has affected housing allocation in a number of ways. Perhaps the most obvious is through the sale of public housing (as for example occurred in Chesterville), and the promotion of privatized housing delivery. The development of Umlazi Section Z in 1988/89 is a product of this process. The promotion of privatized housing was associated with measures which explicitly removed legal constraints on ownership by African women married in terms of customary law (Bekker, 1987). However, it did not entirely remove legal barriers to women's access to home ownership.

Until 1988, women married in terms of community of property were subject to their husbands' marital power, and so could not own property in their own name. Although the law was changed in 1988 to give women equal economic rights in the marriage, it is not retrospective, so women married before this date are still subject to their husbands' marital power (Budlender, 1991). Women married in community of property but separated from their husbands are in a particularly vulnerable position, as their husbands can claim that the property is legally theirs.

Privatization has also affected the way in which public housing is allocated. Regulations in 1986 removed the "person plus dependent" qualification for public housing sales, although it remained for rental housing. But past systems of allocation still affect present access: houses have been sold largely to existing tenants, and in cases of dispute, the bureaucracy intervenes, using the older rules as guidelines. This is not necessarily against

women's interests. One woman told us how her brother attempted to buy the house without her knowledge, but the "office" called her in and told her to buy it instead as she has children.

Privatization has similarly had ambiguous effects on public rental housing. A 1988 act converts existing tenancies to common law leases, makes it possible for non-paying tenants to be evicted, and removes restrictions on who can gain access to housing, theoretically opening up access to such housing. In practice, the older system has been maintained, with some adjustments. As before, houses can effectively be inherited; however, the administration and the family now negotiate who within the family is to "inherit" the lease. Again, the older rules are used as guidelines for the administration: the person must be able to pay the rent, and should have dependents.[3] At one level, therefore, "privatization" in relation to public rental housing shifts the responsibility for allocation from state to family, from bureaucratic rulings to the social relations within households. At another level, however, bureaucratic rulings and definitions of the family continue to influence access, seemingly in a relatively paternalistic way.

Although the legal biases against women have partially been removed, the various biases operating in government regulations, and the failure on the part of the state and the private sector to develop affordable housing, have ensured that the majority of African people in Durban—and particularly women—have had to seek housing in informal settlements. Due to the greater laxity of control, these are generally located in KwaZulu or on land earmarked for transfer to KwaZulu, and held in trust by the South African Development Trust. The Piesang's River informal settlement is one of these areas.

Evaluation of Delivery Systems

How then has this legacy affected the way in which women have gained access to housing, and their experience of it? In this section we evaluate the three types of housing delivery systems: public, private, and informal in Chesterville, Umlazi Section Z, and Piesang's River.

Public Housing

In effect, African women's present access to public housing has been shaped by the way in which housing allocation has occurred historically. Public housing has largely remained within families.[4] Bureaucratic rulings have mainly affected how it is allocated within them. While the sale of houses is likely to change the terms of access for some houses over the longer term, our research in Chesterville suggests that most public houses have been sold to existing occupants, and very few have been resold.

The rules of access used in the 1980s do contain biases against certain categories of women. In contrast to public housing for white, colored and Indian people which was developed as "welfare housing," the rules of access require that lessees have income, and can pay rent.[5] This is likely to affect women more negatively, given their poorer access to employment. The ruling on rents appears to have been applied quite strictly in Chesterville: almost all household heads we interviewed had some form of income, either through pensions or through employment of some sort. Only 6% were unemployed, while 50% were pensioners or received a state grant, and 36% were workers (the rest were teachers, nurses, and informal sector operators). Although unemployment was high (at around a third [37%] of the economically active age group), it tended to occur among non-household heads. As one of our interviewees noted:

It is not difficult [to get a rental house] but sometimes if you are a woman your salary is lesser than a male, so that's when you experience some difficulties (interview with C).

Administrative flexibility in a context of housing shortage can also mean that the personal biases and assumptions of administrators and councilors can influence access to rental housing, with negative consequences for women. Although some felt that

money talks these days (interview with K),

other women argued that

[the] Councilor had an attitude toward women so it was still difficult for women to rent or own houses unless one pleads or bows down to him (interview with MA).

Eagle (1987) argues on the basis of interviews with township managers that in practice married men are favored, where there is a choice. Where married people are the lessees, the lease is almost invariably in the husband's name, placing women in a potentially vulnerable situation. The exception is women who have "inherited" the house from other members of their families, and have later married. In cases of marital dispute, women may be forced out of their homes.

Where husbands die, the system might expose them to competition with sons who may be in a better position to pay. Women living with relatives may be vulnerable to eviction. As one woman living with her nephew said,

I am happy living here but it is better to be independent. I always worry in case my nephew gets married that I might be kicked out (interview with GS).

Despite biases against women in the allocation system, low-income, female-headed households do seem to have been able to gain better access to both rental and ownership housing than might be expected. In the two areas where we were able to gain comprehensive information[6] on the gender of renters, this was certainly the case. In Lamontville, some 26% of houses were rented by women, while 39% of rental housing stock in Chesterville was in women's names.[7,8] An analysis of a sample of 454 sales of public housing in Natal in the 1987–1990 period[9] suggests that 41% was sold to women (primarily widows, and to a lesser extent, unmarried women), while 45% was sold to men. The remaining 14% was sold to couples or to institutional buyers (mainly the South African Transport Services). Given that most owners would previously have been the registered lessees, it is likely that the "person plus dependents" ruling does provide some protection for women-headed households in practice as "she is always with her children" (interview with M).

Women gaining access to housing in this way are not well off. With mean head-of-household incomes of R342[10] per month, an average 2 workers per household, and a mean household size of 9 (compared to 6 for Durban as a whole), the households we interviewed were not very much better off than those in the informal settlement, Piesang's River.[11] In Chesterville, houses are sold at between R1,400 and R2,100.[12] Most owners have bought their houses on a cash basis,[13] although they can be bought at subsidized rates over a thirty-year period, payments in this case being a maximum of R15.84 per month.[14] The cost of buying houses was seen as a barrier by many of the renters we interviewed, particularly when arrears payments of R2,000 to R3,000 were added to the original sale price.[15] A number of these renters, however, intended to buy their houses once they had acquired the money. Although there is some evidence in our survey suggesting that owners are somewhat better off than renters, it is not conclusive: the socio-economic profile of the two groups is similar.[16] For both renters and owners, half of the women heads of households were pensioners earning under R200 per month, and almost none earned over R1,000 per month.

While the "person plus dependent" ruling has allowed low-income women to gain access to public housing, the lack of newly built accommodation and the system of "inheritance" has meant that women heads of household in our survey tended to be older: few are under 40, and half are over 60. Interestingly, single daughters with children, and to a lesser extent, the families of single sons and other relatives were accommodated in many of the households we interviewed. Most households contained at least one subfamily, and there were few simple nuclear families.

The "person plus dependents" ruling does, however, impose a fairly conventional definition of the family. It automatically excludes non-heterosexual relationships, collections of single people, single men and children, dependents who are not sons, daughters or wives, and single people. Emdon (1991), for example, documents a case in 1986 in Soweto in which a woman lost her house on the death of her husband on the grounds that she had no children. The sale of housing has to some extent provided more space in this regard. In our study, in at least one case a widow would have been unable to maintain access to her house under the conditions pertaining to rental. Our analysis of records of sales of public housing also picked up a number of unmarried men who would previously have been unable to gain access to housing.

The policy to sell off public housing does appear to have provided a selected group of women with a space to acquire housing on a more secure basis, and outside of the influence and possible bias of administrators. The relatively high proportion of women buyers may indicate that women have been more keen to buy their houses than men. Reasons cited for purchase generally related to security, and particularly a desire to acquire housing which would provide their children with security. For example, EM bought her house because if she died, her children would be "chased away." Similarly, MC wanted to "leave something for my children when I die." The lower cost of housing in the longer term also emerged as an important issue. The emphasis on security may reflect struggles about the sale of houses whose tenants, if they did not buy them, were threatened with removal. "I had to make sure that I did not lose the house to someone else" (interview with BZ). Single women might have been particularly vulnerable in this process. GH said that she "had to buy the house because there was a threat that I will lose it because I have no husband." It might also reflect women's vulnerability in rental housing more generally. AM, for example, included the fact that she is not married and

needed the security of ownership for her children as part of her reasons for buying her house, while MY argued that "I do not have to worry about getting married as I have my own house."

Women's interest in home ownership can be seen as an extension of their desire to gain access to housing on their own terms, in a context where ownership is presented as one of the few real alternatives. That renting or owning a house in their own names is of significance is not lost on the women we interviewed: most (81%) felt that it gives women greater independence and control over their lives. As MS put it, "you get all the rights which were initially the men's rights." Renting or owning their own home would give women greater control over their home, and over gender relations within it. And as Moser (1992) suggests, men's and women's priorities frequently differ, and it is more often women who take responsibility for housing:

As women, it is us who actually run the house. Men just help here and there, but do not always feel obliged to contribute. So it is better for women to rent or own a house—they become independent, no one can dictate to them (interview with H),

and

Usually men do not contribute—many of them spend all their money in drinking. Sometimes men bring girlfriends home until women are forced to move out. Unless they rent or own housing they will be hassled by men (interview with T).

A few women, however, felt that women were still constrained, and if they were married, "the husband would still make all the major decisions even if the wife owns it (interview with BM).

The sale of housing has allowed a small group of women access to relatively high-quality housing at comparatively low prices. Even so, a number of household heads (and particularly women) did experience financial difficulties as a result of buying their houses, but very few regretted buying. In the longer term, those who have bought are likely to experience windfall profits if they sell, while poor, homeless women will find it very difficult to gain access to this type of housing. The advantages the sale of public rental accommodation presented for women are not easily repeatable.

Conditions for housework appeared to be somewhat better than in the other two settlement types: services were available on the property, and interestingly, there were few instances of a double burden of working and housework in the classic sense. In these large and complex households, containing numbers of unemployed people, housework and child care tended to be shared among the women.[17] Although the quality of houses is better than in informal settlements, it was generally seen as inadequate; houses are old and dilapidated. The small size of the houses (particularly in the context of large households) was also a major source of complaint. Theoretically, informal settlements are more flexible in this regard; however, houses in Piesang's River were in fact much smaller than in Chesterville, and space was again seen as a problem.

Private Sector Housing

Access to housing developed by the private sector developers and utility companies is based on the dictum "you get what you can pay for." Theoretically, it is a system which exhibits no gender bias: the market determines who gets the housing. Nationally determined allocation criteria and inefficient and corrupt local bureaucrats are replaced with estate agents with an interest in selling houses to whomever they can. In theory, the market system does not impose a particular definition of the family, and both single and married people, living in whatever social arrangement, can buy its products. It also offers people a high degree of choice. On closer examination, however, this is not quite the reality. Economic and social considerations tend to undermine the position of women in the private housing market, and influence the composition of households.

The free standing house designed to accommodate the average nuclear family is the only form of housing that has been provided by the private sector developers and most of these houses are in the R 50,000 to R 90,000 price range. As a result, they are beyond the reach of the vast majority of African people, and especially women. This is very clearly illustrated by our analysis of the records of some 1,060 developer-constructed houses in Umlazi, KwaMashu, Lamontville, Klaarwater, and Kwadabeka. Fifteen percent of the houses were owned by women while only 0.4% of the units were owned by the husband and wife. In the older freehold township, Clermont, a larger proportion of the houses is owned by women (25%). A possible reason for this could be that, as in Chesterville, women have inherited the houses from their husbands or family, and further, that houses are generally cheaper than in Umlazi: R 3,000 on average in 1990 (Moonsammy, 1991).

More detailed information was obtained from our survey in Umlazi Section Z (Phase 8). The people who live in Umlazi Section Z are mostly teachers, nurses, police men/women, and clerical workers, and there are, on average, 1.7 workers per household. The average individual and household income was R 1,288 and R 2,502, respectively, while the mean income of women heads of households was R 1,327, some 18% less than that of their male counterparts. Given that the average bond repayment is R 869, housing costs consume a considerable proportion of household incomes.

Approximately 10% of the houses were owned by women, most of whom (55%) qualified for a housing subsidy as teachers and nurses. More generally, the proportion of households relying on subsidies (70%) was far higher than in Chesterville, where very few people had access to subsidies through their employment.[18] Ironically, women's reliance on subsidies forces many of them to remain single, because subsidies are not always available to married women. Further, women married in community of property before 1988 are subject to their husbands' marital power, making it impossible for them to buy property in their own right while they are married. Possibly as a consequence, nearly all the women owners were single. Only one woman was living with her boyfriend. Interestingly, although the majority of women were single, none of them lived on her own, and all the women-headed households comprised a form of extended family. The woman frequently took in parents, siblings, adult children, grandchildren, and other relatives. By contrast 47% of the male-headed households were nuclear families. In male-headed households, no houses were registered in the name of the husband and wife, although a number of the houses had been bought on the basis of the couple's joint income.

The problems owners experienced with their housing related to the difficulties they had in raising the necessary finances, e.g., in raising the deposit (23%) or meeting the lending criteria of the bank (44%). Some were self-employed and could not easily prove what their income was. To quote one of the respondents,

> Raising the deposit was not easy. Qualifying was also problematic because I did not have a profession (interview with VS).

Once they owned their houses, the economic stress of having to meet the monthly repayments was one of their major concerns, and the majority of respondents indicated that they had problems balancing their budget at the end of the month.[19]   This economic stress derives from over-commitment on hire purchase items such as furniture, unforeseen expenditures, and the fact that, because of the unavailability of housing, people have been forced into buying houses they might not otherwise have bought. Rising interest rates and the terms on which banks and building societies lend money were also cited as problems. The terms of financial institutions are far less accommodating than those under the sale of public housing. If borrowers default on their payments for four consecutive months without contacting the lending institutions, the normal practice is foreclosure. Within the area we surveyed there were three houses where this had obviously happened.

From discussions with some of the community members, it seems that the acquisition of housing on the basis of joint income has caused problems in a number of families because the men sometimes fail to contribute their fair share. In one case a married couple who had bought a house on the basis of their joint income started running into financial difficulties. The husband took fright and deserted his wife, leaving her to carry the full burden of repayments on the house. These repayments took up her full salary.

Some very revealing answers to the question, "Do you think it is important for women to own their houses themselves?" were elicited. Those who said "no" lived in the male-headed households and their responses highlighted the weak economic position of women and their implicit acceptance of their subordination to men. In the Chesterville survey, possibly because the rents/ repayments were lower, this was not as apparent.

> [Women] need to depend on someone, those houses are very expensive ... women cannot manage (interview with EG).

> Women cannot afford to live without men, they cannot afford to pay, they need men's decisions and opinions (interview with CM).

The reasons given by those who said yes were similar to those expressed by women in Chesterville:

> You don't have a problem of someone dictating your life. You are immune to the nonsense of worshipping someone because he offers you accommodation (interview with X).

> Husbands sometimes leave us for other women and you have to meet all the expenses yourself (interview with BN).

> Women need to live their own life without dependencies on someone else. If a woman owns a house [she] gets an intellectual freedom. You begin to know things which you did not know, for example, you enter doors of courts preparing for the house ownership (interview with NN).

The above possibly explains why fewer women in woman-headed households (20%) had regrets about buying the house than those in male-headed households (43%).

While women in Umlazi Section Z, no doubt because of their relatively advantaged economic position, had the benefit of labor-saving technology and 25% had servants, conditions of domestic work were not ideal. Women in fact experienced a higher level of double burdening than their counterparts in Chesterville.[20] Households in Umlazi Section Z were generally far smaller than in Chesterville (on average, 5.3 people) and a high proportion of the women in the male-headed households worked (65%). Because the nuclear family was the predominant form of male-headed household and the children in most houses were fairly young, women in these households were not able to derive assistance or support from other women in the household.

The position of women in privatized housing, while different from those in other forms of housing, is not necessarily ideal. The costs of entry into private housing are high and therefore exclusionary. Because the terms on which money is lent are not very accommodating, the financial pressure on households is high, often necessitating that both husband and wife work. The consequences of any drop in income are devastating and if, the house is "repossessed," this can result in long-term exclusion from home ownership.

Informal Housing

Ironically, it is the housing delivery system which is the manifestation of the failure of state housing policy that offers the greatest number of women direct access to housing. It is, however, a system about which we know very little.

As each informal settlement has its own history and set of inter-personal and community dynamics, it is safe to assume that people's access to housing and living conditions vary from settlement to settlement. In some instances it appears that such access has been acquired through informal housing markets and political processes, for example, through evicting landlords, through patronage networks, or through attacking and defeating those who occupy the land. In other instances it is acquired through the illegal invasion of green field sites and persistent battles against eviction by the state or private developers. We know little about the implications of these different forms of acquisition in gender terms, although it can be suggested that the "warlord" forms of control are founded on and do entrench patriarchal social relations (see Beall *et al.*, 1987).

In Piesang's River, an informal settlement in the Inanda Complex, which experienced its most rapid growth between 1985 and 1989, the land was largely acquired in three ways: through illegal subdivision of land and sale by the *de jure* land owner; through its sale by the person who does not own it but has *de facto* control of it; and through the violent eviction of landlords who controlled the rental stock. This form of acquisition appears to have been relatively neutral at least as far as women's access to land is concerned. The majority of the respondents said that they did not experience any problems acquiring the land, and bias against women was not mentioned by those who did experience problems.

This view is supported by the fact that a very large proportion of the houses (40%) are owned by women. This finding compares favorably with surveys conducted in the informal settlements of Umlazi Section D and Nazareth (Black Sash, 1990; BESG, 1990). It is also interesting to note that 33% of the respondents indicated that the house was owned by the husband and wife. This is in contrast to private and particularly council housing schemes where houses tend to be in one person's name, usually the husband's.

A likely explanation for the high incidence of houses owned by women is the relatively easy and low cost of access to land and housing, although this may vary between settlements. The women predominate in the unskilled and semi-skilled occupations and informal sector and earn lower wages than men. The average income of male household heads was R 470 while that of women household heads was R 261. In most instances (57%) Piesang's River households paid less than R100 for the land and 10% paid nothing for the land they lived on. The houses, too, are often relatively cheap to build as they are made of locally available, second-hand, and/or innovative materials such as packing cases and Ijuba boxes.

Although the cost of entry into an informal settlement is lower than for other forms of housing, some aspects of daily living are not necessarily cheaper, and the social costs, especially to women, are higher than other forms of delivery. In this case, because the people of Piesang's River had mounted a campaign against site rent and collected water from communal taps or bought it from water kiosks at a slightly higher rate than the formal township dwellers, their service costs were relatively low. They were certainly better off than some settlements; for example in the Umlazi informal settlements in some cases people were buying water from people living in formal housing schemes at a price 16 times greater than what the sellers were charged (resulting in costs of up to R50 per month). The costs of fuel in informal settlements may be higher than electricity as people have to rely on gas and paraffin, although consumption tends to be lower. Most Piesang's River households interviewed paid less than R20 per month, which was certainly lower than what Chesterville residents paid for electricity. Further, as these settlements are usually on the urban periphery, people have to bear high transport costs.

The social costs of informal settlements derive from the poor quality of housing and the absence of essential services such as water, sewage, roads, and garbage collection. Very few households were satisfied with the quality of their housing. The most common complaints were that "it leaks and is drafty," "it is too small," "it is made of wood and is dangerous to children and burns easily," and "there is too much noise since the houses are joined to one another." When the women were asked what problems they had with their housework, the majority (55%) mentioned water collection. The reasons expressed by two of the respondents are: "I find problems doing my washing as the water is too far," and "my problem is having to leave the baby alone while I go to fetch water — anything could happen to him." In the survey it was found that most households collect water two to three times a day and that 39% of them spend more than half an hour doing so. Discussions with some of the women also revealed that the opening and closing times of the water kiosks made it difficult for households in which all the adults worked to collect water. The lack of safety when going to their pit latrines at night (many are located quite far from their houses) was also raised as a problem in these discussions.

The poor level of service provision in informal settlements affects women severely. In our survey we found that men engaged in housework only when there were no adult or teenage women in the household or when they lived on their own. In a few instances the young men assisted with water collection. The double burdening of women was, however, not as widespread as we had anticipated and very few people were employed to perform household tasks. Child care and water collection were the only functions performed by paid workers, the former being performed by women of all ages and the latter by young boys. Male and female pensioners who lived on their own experienced the greatest difficulty with housework, and most often paid others to collect water. Single people and nuclear households in which the head and spouse worked experienced the highest level of double burdening.

The household structure and high levels of unemployment in most of the other households mitigated against the double burdening of women as other women within these households, particularly those who were students or unemployed, collected water, cooked, cleaned the house, etc. Fifty-two percent of the households comprised some form of extended family, and there was on average only one worker per household. The majority of the households with extended families were headed by women. Twenty-two percent of the households had one or more subfamilies living with them, most commonly, an unmarried daughter and her children. In quite a number of instances, the sub-families comprised the head's unmarried son and his children.

Despite these complex structures, the household sizes were relatively small (average of 5 persons/household), and many families had young children. Seventy-three percent of the residents of Piesang's River were under 30. Possible explanations for this lie in why people moved to Piesang's River. The most common reason given was that they needed to move out of overcrowded housing (often the parents') in the formal townships. Others included the need to move out of tense and conflictual inter-personal and marital situations and the desire of young married couples to acquire a place of their own.

One of the greatest benefits from a woman's perspective is that it is potentially the most flexible and unstructured form of housing delivery. The form of housing can be adapted to the needs of different households and household types, and the house can be expanded when and as people wish. Social and local political considerations do, however, sometimes limit people's ability to do this. Economic constraints and housing densities within the community may restrict the size of the house,

Table 1: Responsibility of Women for Domestic Tasks

Done by	Child care (1)	Housework
Women working outside the home on a regular basis	0%	28%
Women working outside the home on an irregular basis	7%	5%
Women not working elsewhere	71%	52%
Servants, crèche, child minders	22%	0%
Combination (women working outside the home and others, including servants) (2)	0%	15%

NOTES: (1) Excludes households without children
(2) Combination here can refer to a variety of different levels of combining of labor. It may mean that a woman working outside the home does only the cooking, or she may do much more. Although the figure for combination is low for child care, in reality many women look after children when they come home.

insecurity of tenure may reduce people's willingness to spend too much on the house, and in some communities, especially those about to be upgraded, the community or some outside agencies may impose rulings preventing people from expanding their houses.

Concluding Comments: State Housing Policy in the 1980s

We have seen that state housing policy in the 1980s has had a contradictory and uneven effect on women. Policies of privatization have improved the possibility of single, divorced, and/or widowed women getting access to housing, but this is limited to a very small group of women with access to professional jobs or subsidies, able to afford such housing, and to women who, through inheritance from parents or husbands, already had access to state rental housing. While the latter women are not the poorest, their incomes are often very low (no more than pensions), and their households may be very large, with few income earners. Both the "top" of the market, and some of the lowest levels have, therefore, benefited. These women have gained access to relatively good housing, but in many cases the costs of repayments place a financial strain on these households. There are, however, few single women who can afford access to this kind of housing; hence for most women, access depends on being with a male income earner, and this itself may impose certain financial and labor burdens, as we have suggested above.

Privatization, on the other hand, has also meant that the majority of women-headed households (and women within male-headed households) have been forced to live in informal settlements . While it is probably the cheapest form of access to housing, it imposes enormous burdens in terms of housework. This is problematic for all women who are responsible for housework, but especially for those households which are too small or too patriarchal to allow a more equal division of labor.

Reflections on Policy and Policy Implications

How, then, do the above discussions affect consider-ations of policy? How does gender analysis transform policy? In concluding our discussion, it is perhaps useful to highlight some of the key underlying issues which need to be addressed in future policy.

A central point we have made is that, from a gender perspective, different housing systems present different opportunities and constraints. All the systems we have discussed need to be amended in some way if they are to be responsive to women, and to gender concerns more broadly. While some present advantages over others from the perspective of low-income women, none is unambiguously superior. The reality is that all three systems—and others—are likely to coexist in the future.

While private sector housing provides space for a certain category of women, its most serious failing is the cost and type of housing it provides. If private sector housing is to benefit women, it needs to move down market and revise its product mix to suit different kinds of households. State allocation systems potentially allow low-income women better access to housing if these concerns are specifically built into policy, but women can equally be marginalized in public housing. If women are to benefit, their participation in and influence over the institutions controlling housing is critical. This is developed further below.

In the short to medium term, the informal housing delivery system is likely to remain important. Its low entry costs mean that it is likely to be the delivery system through which most women-headed households are housed. The difficulties with informal housing arise from the absence of services, insecure tenure, and from

the forms of social organization which sometimes exist in these areas. The warlord form—common in Durban (although not currently present in Piesang's River)—is often associated with violence, and with patriarchal forms of control.

Attempts to develop informal settlements (through upgrading and other schemes) confront both potential opportunities and constraints from a gender perspective. The project-based approaches (as, for example, directed by NGOs) have possibly the greatest potential to transform women's position by, for example, favoring women's access, tailoring projects to women's needs, and to the needs of particular households, and by building in more developmental aspects (such as training, income-generation, and empowerment more generally) (see Moser and Peake, 1987). However, apart from the problem of replication, where such projects occur in existing settlements, power relations and leadership structures may negate or undermine attempts to empower women, or may place the NGO in conflict with leadership. Further, if not correctly handled, the additional costs incurred by households as a result of the upgrading may place intolerable pressure on them.

A second issue is the importance of lowering the cost of access to housing, and making it more affordable. We have seen that cost has a major impact on the type of housing that women do get access to, and that it has an influence over the kind of households and social arrangements women find themselves in, as well as the social relations within them. Any policy, must, as a starting point, ensure that housing (of whatever form) is supplied on a massive and affordable basis. Given the difficulties poor people, and more particularly women, experience in raising credit from conventional financial institutions, the form and terms on which credit is offered need attention. Community-based loan schemes such as the Thrift Societies in Sri Lanka, the Working Women's Forum in India, and, locally, the Urban Foundation's Group Credit Scheme have improved the access of the poor to credit, and is an approach to housing finance which needs to be introduced on a much wider scale. Whether women-only community loan schemes need to be developed merits further investiga-tion.

Third, a critical area for consideration is the appropriate level of service provision, and how decisions about it are made. At first sight, the most advantageous form of housing for women is formal, full-serviced sites and houses. The quality of services has an obvious impact on the extent and burden of household labor, and also affects health, and thus women's responsibility in this regard (Lastra, 1990). Where women work outside the home, and are responsible for domestic labor within it, poor service levels can exert an intolerable burden on them, as White's (1991) detailed study of Alexandra suggests.

In contexts where these kinds of solutions cannot easily be afforded, however, a high standard of services may not always be the top priority for women, a counter-intuitive position from a professional perspective. The way in which domestic labor is organized and the extent to which women experience a double burden may affect their choices. As we have suggested, the double-burden thesis may be too simplistic to capture the way in which domestic labor is organized. In discussions of the upgrading of Piesang's River, after water (not necessarily on-site) provision, housing was prioritized within the community, and specifically among women. While a basic level of service provision should be treated as a non-negotiable, beyond this, levels of service provision and priorities for expenditure in relation to housing need to be treated in an open and flexible way. Women's opinions must be heard in this process.

Fourth, an important topic of debate in South Africa is whether housing should be seen as a key target for government investment from a macro-economic perspective. A focus on domestic labor reinforces the argument in favor of housing from a gender perspective, since responsibility for domestic work is an important constraint on women's participation and position within the labor force (see Beall *et al.*, 1989), and on their ability to become involved in more remunerative activities. Our finding that the double burden is not as prevalent as is often assumed does not necessarily negate this position. In considering the trade-off with investment in other sectors, what needs to be considered is whether women will in fact benefit through the employment opened up in these sectors. The direct and indirect effects on women's employment of a focus on housing also need to be considered. If preferential investment in housing is to be supported from a gender perspective, then it has to be developed in a way which benefits low-income women, improving their access to housing, employment, and income-earning opportunities.

Fifth, a key area in any housing policy is how the family, household, and its internal social relations are conceptualized. The definitions of what constitutes the family (what is a family, who is part of it, who are "dependents"), who is the household head (and even that

there is necessarily a household head), and how the household economy operates (who earns, who contributes to the household budget, who pays for housing and other household expenditures, how stable the household economy—and the household—is, and so on), all have major implications at a variety of levels. Some of the most obvious are affordability, allocation systems, and subsidy systems, but other issues such as site and house design and size are also affected.

Sixth, a related issue is whether women and women-headed households should be the beneficiaries of positive discrimination and attention in relation to housing, as Machado (1987) and Moser (1985) suggest, or whether, for example, it is enough simply to ensure that the poor have access to housing. A particular issue is women's legal access to housing. In South Africa, women married in community of property are in a vulnerable position in relation to housing. This is an obvious area for intervention.

More difficult perhaps is whether houses or sites should be put in women's names, as Moser (1985) suggests. The women we interviewed were acutely aware of the importance of owning or renting their own home, although some felt that if women were married it would make very little difference to their position. Even within community-based approaches, this is an issue. Cooperative forms of tenure and housing still present the problem, particularly in disputes, of who within a household has rights to land and housing.

Finally, and perhaps most obviously, the critical importance of women's participation in and influence over the institutions affecting housing must be stressed. Without it women will be unable to ensure that their needs are met, either at the level of housing policy as a whole, or in relation to more localized issues such as the practicalities of allocation. This influence needs to extend more broadly than merely to the state and locality: women need to influence the practices of NGOs and civic and community organizations, as these are likely to be an increasingly important sphere in which housing is developed in the future.

For women's organizations to take up the issue of gender and housing, a significant area for development is the levels at which gender issues are most effectively addressed. This is an important area of research as much of the literature on gender and housing focuses on interventions at the project level. The identification of issues which can and should be addressed at different levels of government, and in different institutions, will greatly assist the formulation of a gender-sensitive housing policy.[21]

Notes

[1] State-sponsored site and service schemes and women's hostel accommodation have not been included in the analysis because of their limited occurrence. We have also excluded domestic worker accommodation, and central city accommodation for practical reasons.

[2] The acquisition of housing information on the basis of gender proved more difficult than we had anticipated. Very few state and financial institutions and developers are concerned about the gender of the people occupying or buying houses. Information relating to housing in areas controlled by KwaZulu and the Department of Development Aid proved particularly difficult to obtain as officials from these government bodies did not want to give us access to their records. Our analysis is, therefore, based on information obtained from the Deeds Registry in Pietermaritzburg, a few cooperative township managers and developers, and surveys we conducted. These surveys were conducted in Piesang's River (Soweto), an informal settlement in the Inanda complex; Chesterville, a council housing scheme; and Umlazi Section Z Phase 8, a private housing scheme. The Soweto survey was a general socio-economic survey which included some gender-specific questions and covered 179 households. The Chesterville and Umlazi Section Z Phase 8 surveys were directed at women in single and male-headed households, and samples were relatively small, some 51 and 34 households, respectively. Our surveys in the latter two areas must obviously be seen as exploratory pilot studies raising issues for further investigation. Our conclusions should therefore be seen as tentative, and open to debate.

[3] Manager of Chesterville, personal communication, 16/1/91.

[4] This is borne out in our study of Chesterville: 84% of households interviewed had lived in their house for over a decade, and 69% for over 20 years. Sixty percent of households had "inherited" their house from family, and almost all those who had not were very old, and had lived there for years.

[5] The "ability to pay" requirement in African housing derives historically from attempts to tie influx control to employment, and to keep out those who were unemployed. In more recent times it has been replaced by an emphasis on cost recovery. Notwithstanding these origins, such housing has historically been subsidized.

[6] Unfortunately, despite attempts to acquire more extensive information, township administrators were generally uncooperative, arguing that the information we wanted was "confidential."

[7] On the basis of figures deriving from rental and service charge records for the two townships. In Chesterville, where we were able to test the validity of the records, the actual proportion of women lessees might be slightly higher. In a few cases, the house was in a man's name, but the household head was actually a woman, who had "inherited" the house from her father, husband, or brother. The reverse also occurred, except in far fewer cases.

[8] These differences may reflect variations in the style of administration in the two areas. Alternatively, it may point to circumstances unique to Chesterville, namely, that because of threats of removal, the better-off people and households have tended to move out, and competition for housing has not been as great as elsewhere.

[9] Records prior to this were not available. The figures cover only the areas falling under the Natal Provincial Administration and the South African Development Trust. Our attempts to research the sale of houses in KwaZulu were frustrated by the immense inefficiency of the system in KwaZulu.

[10] $1 = R2.80.

[11] Average head of household incomes were remarkably consistent between male and female heads, and between renters and owners. This may reflect weaknesses in the methodology: women interviewed frequently did not know what their husbands earned, so distorting figures. On the other hand, a large proportion of household heads (48%) were pensioners, accounting for low head-of-household incomes on average. All these households would qualify for subsidized sites under the current Independent Development Trust scheme which offers households earning joint incomes (breadwinner and spouse) of under R1,000 per month a site costing R7,500. The mean household income, at R1,119, was similar to the average for black households in Durban (R1,079), and almost double that of Piesang's River at R577. But if household size is taken into account, the differences are smaller: the per capita income for Chesterville is R131, while that of Piesang's River is R115 per month. The per capita household income for Durban would be R180 per month. Household income per capita was also similar across male- and female-headed households. These figures are used in a purely indicative way; given the sample size it is not considered appropriate to analyze them in detail, or to draw strong conclusions from such an analysis.

[12] Including house and land costs, survey and legal costs, and various discounts in terms of the sale of housing campaign. Prices vary within this range depending on land size, and which of the various discounts are applicable.

[13] There is a cash discount of R464 to encourage buyers to do so.

[14] According to Mr. G. Dibbon, Department of Finance, Natal Provincial Authority, interviewed on 12 December, 1991. In terms of Department of Development Planning Circular No 2 of 1988, repayments over a thirty-year period may be on a sliding scale according to income (starting at 3% or 25 cents per month), to a maximum of the "standard rent," or the payment at an interest rate of 13.5%. All costs referred to in 12 above, other than land costs and a R7 leasehold fee, can be capitalized into the loan amount. Land costs are sometimes included in the loan, but not at subsidized rates. This would push the figure given up slightly.

[15] Arrears payments arise from the rent boycott which had been occurring for some time in the area. Rents are of the order of R35 per month.

[16] Differences between renters and owners occurred mainly at the level of household income, with renters earning R781 and owners R1,304 per month on average. Levels of unemployment were higher among renters, and the numbers of people working per household were lower. Nonetheless, head-of-household incomes were similar. Incomes earned by household members are not necessarily contributed to the household, making household income a poor indicator of affordability. Given the small size of the sample, it is difficult to draw conclusive comparisons between the two.

[17] This point is explored further in Todes and Walker (1992). Some 10% of women experienced a classic double burden, and a further 37% of women working outside the home shared this responsibility with other women in the house.

[18] However, subsidies were built into the rental structure of Chesterville houses, although they are not of the order of the usual employer subsidy, or the first-time home buyers subsidy which was at

the time available for newly built houses. As Parnell (1991) argues, it is primarily the middle classes, whites, and men who have benefited from subsidies.

[19] It was not possible to establish from the responses whether women experienced more problems than men.

[20] Some 32% of women experienced a classic double burden, while a further 26% shared this responsibility with other women in the home.

[21] We wish to acknowledge the University of Natal's New Staff Research Fund for funding part of this research. We would also like to acknowledge the assistance of Dr. Michael Sutcliffe and the following students in the collection and processing of data: Nicola Budd, Yasmin Coovadia, Victor Dlamini, Mpho Hlala, Gugu Hlatshwayo, Elisabeth Lehoko, Princess Mgobhozi, Angel Mzimela, Welile Khuzwayo, and Thandi Sigodi. We would like to thank members of the book committee of the Women and Gender in Southern Africa Conference organizing group for comments on an earlier version of this paper. A version of this paper is to be published in *Urban Forum*.

References

Annecke, W. 1991. "Women, and Natal violence: the costs of the war," Paper presented to the Conference on Women and Gender in Southern Africa, University of Natal, January.

Beall, J., Hassim, S., and A. Todes, 1989. "A Bit on the Side? Gender Struggles in the Politics of Transformation in South Africa," *Feminist Review* 33 , Winter 1989.

Beall, J., Hassim, S., Friedman, M., Posel, R., Stiebel, L. and A. Todes, 1987. "African women in the Durban struggle, 1985–86: Towards a transformation in roles?," in South African Research Services (ed.), *South African Review* 4, Ravan.

Bekker, K. 1987. *A Home of Your Own,* Van Schaik.

Black Sash. 1990. Survey of Umlazi's Section D Squatter Settlement, mss.

Budlender, D. 1991. "Women and the economy," Paper presented the Conference on Women and Gender in Southern Africa, University of Natal, January.

Built Environment Support Group. 1990. Selected Findings of the Socio-economic Survey Conducted in Nazareth, Pinetown, University of Natal, Durban.

Buvinic, M. 1978. "Women's issues in third world poverty: A policy analysis," in Buvinic, M; Lycette, M. and P. McGreevy (Eds), *Women and Poverty in the Third World,* John Hopkins University Press.

Chant, S. and P. Ward, "Family structure and low-income housing policy," in *Third World Planning Review* 9, Number 1, 1987.

Charman, A. 1990. "A response to Albie Sachs. What is the family?" *Agenda* 8, 55–60.

Cole, J. 1986. *Crossroads. The Politics of Reform and Repression 1976–1986,* Ravan.

Eagle, J. 1987. African Women's Access to Housing in the Greater Durban Area, Unpublished MTRP Dissertation, University of Natal, Durban.

Edwards, I. 1988. "Shebeen queens: Illicit liquor and the social structure of drinking dens in Cato Manor," *Agenda* 3.

Emdon, E. 1991. "Urban African Women and Occupational Rights," Urban Forum, ms.

Gwagwa-Ntsaluba, N. 1990. "Women and local government of women in local government?," Paper presented to the ANC Consultative Workshop on Local Government, Johannesburg, October.

Hindson, D. 1987. *Pass Controls and the Urban African Proletariat,* Ravan.

Lastra, L. 1990. "Summary of the study Women and the Urban Crisis'," Paper presented to the Conference on Sustainable Development on an Urbanized Planet?, TRIALOG, Berlin.

Machado, L. 1987. "The problems for women-headed households in a low-income housing programme in Brazil," in Moser, C. and L. Peake (Eds.), *Women, Human Settlements and Housing,* Tavistock Publications, London.

Maylam, P. 1983. "The 'Black Belt': African squatters in Durban 1935-1950," *Canadian Journal of African Studies,* 17 (3), 413–428.

Moonsammy, S. 1991. Local Government and Local Government Finance in KwaZulu and Department of Development Aid Areas, MTRP Dissertation, University of Natal, Durban.

Moser, C. 1992. "Women and self-help housing projects. A conceptual framework for analysis and policy-making," in Mathey, K. (ed.). *Beyond Self-Help Housing,* Mansell, London.

Moser, C. 1985. "Housing policy and women: towards a gender-aware approach," Development Planning Unit Gender and Planning Working Paper 7, University College, London.

Moser, C. and L. Peake. 1987. *Women, Human Settlements and Housing,* Tavistock Publications, London.

Parnell, S. 1991. "Race, class, gender and housing subsidies," *Urban Forum* 2 (1).

Sachs, A. 1990. "The family in a democratic South Africa—Its constitutional position," *Agenda* 8, 40–54.

Sutcliffe, M. 1990. " Baseline Report. Survey of Households in the DFR." Report to the Tongaat Hulett Planning Forum: The Durban Functional Region. Planning for the 21st Century.

Todes, A. and Walker, N. 1992. "Women and housing policy. Analyzing the past, debating the future," Paper presented to the GRUPHEL Workshop, Harare.

Tongaat-Hulett Properties Limited. 1989. The Durban Functional Region—Planning for the 21st century.

Watson, S. and H. Austerberry. 1986. *Housing and Homelessness: A Feminist Perspective,* Routledge and Kegan Paul, London.

Chapter 6
The Contribution of Community-Based Housing Organizations to Women's Shelter and Development: Evidence from Zimbabwe

Anna C. Vakil

Anna C. Vakil received degrees in Canada in Psychology/Sociology and Urban Planning and afterwards worked for three years as an urban planner and consultant in Belize (Central America). She received her Ph.D. in Urban and Regional Planning from the University of Michigan in 1991. Her dissertation focused on community-based development and shelter in Zimbabwe. She will be a faculty member in the Geography/Planning Department at the University of Windsor in the fall of 1993.

Studies in the emergent field of women and housing in low-income countries have for the most part dealt with issues arising from the delivery of housing to individual women-headed households. The research literature addresses questions related to this kind of delivery system, such as design (Sarin, 1991); women's access to land and financing (UNCHS, 1989); household strategies (Rakodi, 1991; Schlyter, 1989 and 1988; Larsson, 1989); self-help (Vance, 1987; Chant, 1987); and the impact of policy on women (Peake, 1987).

Based on some of the findings of a study conducted in 1989–90 on the organizational aspects of five housing co-operatives in Zimbabwe, this paper focuses on the community-based housing organization both as an alternative delivery system in helping to meet women's housing needs and as a tool for women's development. By way of background, some of the essential features of Zimbabwe's culture and history will first be described, as well as the major housing policies which affect women and their families in their search for housing. This will be followed by a brief description of the five case studies.

The paper will review the evidence, based on the research results, for community-based housing organizations as a housing delivery system in Zimbabwe. This will be followed by a discussion of gender issues, involving a description of the differences between two types of community housing organizations, one with an exclusively male membership and the other with a mixed-gender membership. Some of the factors contributing to women's leadership and participation in the mixed-gender organizations will be outlined, followed by a profile of the kinds of Zimbabwean women who are attracted to community housing organizations, their reasons for joining, and what they hope to accomplish.

In concluding, some policy recommendations will be provided that could assist community-based housing organizations to function effectively, meet the shelter needs of their women members, and facilitate the development of women.

Women's Development in Zimbabwe

As is true in many other low-income countries, Zimbabwe is experiencing a dramatic rise in the proportion of women household heads, particularly in urban areas.[1] Typical of the southern Africa region, the majority of urban women in Zimbabwe are relative newcomers to the city, since the colonial powers ensured that most Africans remained in the rural "reserve" areas. Until the escalation of the liberation war in the late 1960s, it was primarily men who lived in the cities, and then only as a cheap temporary source of labor.

At the time of contact with Europeans, women of Shona and Ndebele background (the two major ethnic groups in Zimbabwe) had informal land use rights and limited property rights (Gaidzwana, 1988). With the codification of the traditional or "customary" laws by the Europeans, many of these rights were stripped from them.[2] Before the passing of the Legal Age of Majority Act of 1982, women were considered legal minors, unable to own property or even to cash checks (Ncube, 1987). Following this, the Matrimonial Causes Act of 1985 was passed, entitling women to a share of the matrimonial property upon divorce. This was designed to discourage the common practice of the families of ex-husbands claiming the entire matrimonial property as their own, leaving the newly divorced woman destitute. Despite these changes, however, women's proprietary rights have not since been commonly recognized on a social or administrative level. Almost all municipal authorities, for example, still customarily allocate land title in the husband's name rather than jointly.

One of the more notable aspects of women's development in Zimbabwe can be found in the rural savings clubs, begun in the 1960s, in which groups of people living in the same village or farming area contributed small amounts of money to a fund on a weekly basis. The accumulated savings were often used to buy seed or fertilizer. At the peak of this practice, Chimedza documented an estimated 5,700 clubs operating nationwide, 97% of which were exclusively female in membership (1984:20). Although in decline since the mid-1980s, Bratton claims that it represents "one of the only spontaneous and autonomous grassroots people's movements in Africa" (1990:97).

Housing Policy in Zimbabwe

Since 1985, Zimbabwe has implemented a gender-neutral national housing policy which places priority on facilitating the provision of shelter for the low-income sector of the population, including those families headed by women. Four elements of urban housing policy are relevant to this discussion, as follows.[3]

Granting of Freehold Tenure

After independence, properties which Africans had previously only been able to rent were made available for sale. Added to them were large tracts of municipally owned land which were serviced and divided into lots. These lots were allocated based on eligibility requirements such as age, proof of being the household head, having children under 21, a maximum income, and proof of employment (Government of Zimbabwe, 1989a). Women with unregistered customary marriages, or lacking divorce papers which prove they are the household heads, are typically ineligible. Even those who are eligible, however, have to be placed on long waiting lists with little hope of being allocated a lot in the foreseeable future. In Harare, for example, the waiting list has been longer than 50,000 since the early 1980s.

Minimum Housing Standards

In 1982, the government stipulated that a four-room core (consisting of two bedrooms, living room, kitchen, and bath/shower) was the minimum structure required and that it was to be constructed of modern materials within 18 months of purchase of the lot. As a result of serious shortages of building materials, however, many local authorities have had to extend this time frame. In addition, with the escalation of construction costs, the government itself estimated as early as 1982 that almost one-third of urban households were unable to afford a structure of this size and quality (Government of Zimbabwe, 1982). At the time of the study, (1989–90), the high building standards made home ownership well beyond what most poor families, including those headed by women, could afford.

The Requirement of Aided Self-Help

The government provided assistance with small direct guaranteed loans and made funds available to the building societies, 23% of the revenue from which was to be used for low-income housing loans. The self-help policy necessitates the use of either unpaid labor on the part of the household for the construction of the house, or contracting out for labor. Alternately, the household head can join a housing co-operative which would then be responsible for construction. Women who bear the full responsibility of providing income for the family and caring for children frequently do not have the time or the skills to build their own houses and either cannot afford to hire the labor or foresee difficulties in supervising the work of contractors (Schlyter, 1989:71–76).

The Promotion of Housing Co-operatives

The government pledged to provide assistance in the form of auditing, legal services and training, loans, and surveying services to new housing co-operatives (Government of Zimbabwe, 1989b, 1984). The government has also actively engaged in promoting the formation of housing co-operatives for the employees of large commercial and manufacturing establishments. Probably for this reason, the majority of housing co-operatives operating in Harare at the time of the study were based at private sector companies. Although co-operatives in all sectors have been strongly encouraged on a policy level, the ability to assist them has been limited. Consequently the government has focused on a few sectors, notably fishing and agriculture.

The Five Case Studies

Five housing co-operatives were chosen as case studies, four from Harare, the nation's capital, and one from Bulawayo, the second-largest city. Information was gathered primarily through individual unstructured interviews of members of the co-op's executive committees, participant observation of co-op meetings, and primary and secondary documents. Attempts were made to select organizations representing a range of attributes, including size, age of the co-operative, and gender composition.[4] Since the housing co-operative movement in Zimbabwe was not well established, all the organizations were less than six years old, some having been only recently formed. To shed more light on gender issues, all women in the leadership committees were interviewed (a total of four), and case studies of seven women members from two of the organizations were made as well.

Three of the housing co-operatives were workplace-based: the Cotton Printers Co-operative, composed of workers at a textile processing factory in Bulawayo; Takura Housing Co-operative, based at the National Breweries, a beer-making operation in Harare; and Capri Housing Co-operative, comprised of workers from a Harare-based corporation which manufactures a broad range of household and other appliances. All three organizations were exclusively male, since men have a better chance of being hired in the formal sector and therefore have a greater opportunity to join workplace-based co-ops.

In contrast with the Cotton Printers, Takura, and Capri, the distinguishing features of the remaining two co-operatives are that they are community- rather than workplace-based; and that they have a significant female membership. It is for the latter reason that they will be described in more detail. One of them, Kugarika Kushinga, is an organization based in Mabvuku (previously a black township, now called a "high density area") just outside of Harare, begun in 1986 by members of the local branch of ZANU (the major political party of the country). It has over 2,000 members, one-quarter of them female. In early 1987, the leadership of the co-operative was arrested, an act supposedly masterminded by local ZANU officials who were jealous of the co-op's growing popularity in the neighborhood. At the time of the study, the co-operative had not yet begun building, nor, due to long bureaucratic delays, was it registered with the government. It had nonetheless managed to raise over $Zim 2 million (about $US 1 million).

Tashinga Domestic Co-operative is an organization comprised solely of domestic workers (or house-helpers) living in the affluent Harare area of Mabelreign. (These workers have what is called "tied housing," since their lodgings are directly linked to their employment. If they lose their jobs, they lose their housing as well.) Tashinga was launched in late 1988 by a woman domestic worker, a ZANU party member who immediately established close connections with the Mayor of Harare. Fifty percent of its 375 members are female. Similar to Kugarika Kushinga, it also had not begun construction at the time of the study; nor was it registered, due partly to conflicts among City Councillors (including the Mayor) over whether the co-operative could draw members from particular municipal electoral jurisdictions. At the time of the research, this co-operative had managed to raise over $Zim 200,000 (about $US 100,000 at the time).

The Community-Based Organization as a Housing Delivery System

The study provides some evidence that the co-operatives were potentially viable providers of housing in their ability to generate savings and build affordable houses, but that this was tempered by a restrictive policy environment.

Affordability of Housing to Low-Income Households

Despite the relatively undeveloped nature of the housing co-operative movement in Zimbabwe and the considerable constraints placed on the organizations by the policy environment (described below), those co-ops engaged in construction at the time of the study were able to build at costs comparable or equal to the private and government-sponsored sectors.[5] This implies that if these organizations were provided with more effective direct and indirect assistance, they could contribute significantly to narrowing the shelter gap for low-income households, including those headed by women.

High Savings and Low Default Rates

All five of the co-operatives demonstrated themselves capable of sustaining high savings rates over extended time periods. Interestingly, the two community-based co-ops, whose members' incomes tended to be lower than those of workplace-based co-ops, had higher monthly contribution rates. The members of Tashinga, for example, whose incomes averaged from $114 to $160, contributed $50 a month to the co-operative, over a third of monthly wages. Despite this, the Treasurer of the co-operative reported a low 2.5% default rate over a 14-month period. Kugarika Kushinga's members earned an estimated average of $250 a month, but were expected to contribute $100. Although this represented almost one-half of monthly income for many members, the default rate was only 5% over a two-year period. These findings support the results of research conducted in other parts of the world which demonstrate the ability of poor families to save money.[6]

The Impact of Policy

The research revealed that, commensurate with the findings of other studies (such as those described in Turner, 1988), the policies of local and central government and private financial institutions were a major deterrent of the housing co-operatives' ability to function and build houses for their members. Particular aspects of these policies included delays in registration due to lack of co-operation among various government departments, the lack of recognition of local governments and financial institutions of collective organizations in the allocation of land and financing, time limits on construction, and high building standards.[7]

The All-Male (Workplace) Co-ops vs. Mixed-Gender (Community-Based) Co-ops

The research revealed that there were two major differences between the all-male workplace-based co-operatives, and the mixed-gender community-based co-operatives, one related to the resources available to them, and the other to do with intervention by external political forces.

Resource Inputs

The workplace-based housing co-operatives enjoyed considerable resource inputs from the companies where their members worked. In one case, the Cotton Printers co-operative, the company contributed directly to the co-op, entered a profit-sharing scheme with the co-op (which together provided over half the organization's revenues), guaranteed a loan, paid the bulk of the wages of two co-op employees, and provided legal and auditing services. These and other relative advantages translated into higher revenues and lower fixed costs for the workplace-based co-ops, the members of which tended to have higher incomes in the first place.

External Political Interference

Both Tashinga and Kugarika Kushinga, the two mixed-gender community-based co-operatives, experienced considerable interference by outside political forces, either local politicians or members of the ZANU party machinery. There was almost no evidence of this in the three workplace-based co-operatives.[8] As mentioned above, Tashinga enjoyed close association with the Mayor, but became embroiled in a dispute involving other City Councillors over the geographical area from which it could draw members. In the case of Kugarika Kushinga, the external interference of senior ZANU party members ended in the temporary arrest and detention of the co-operative's leadership. It is possible that the higher female membership in the community-based co-ops may be a factor contributing to the apparent increased vulnerability of these types of organizations (particularly for Tashinga which was led by a woman); but it is also likely that the reason for the external interference by local politicians and ZANU is that, like community-based organizations, they also draw their support from the grassroots. Organizations which enjoy broad support at the community level are therefore seen as a threat.[9]

Women in Housing Co-operatives

The study also investigated women's participation in the two housing co-operatives which had female members, both at the leadership and the membership level. Because of the strong presence of women at co-operative meetings for the two co-ops, seven case studies of female members were undertaken, which revealed the kinds of women who were attracted to joining the housing co-operatives and their reasons for doing so. These factors are further described below:

Female Representation and Participation in Leadership Committees

Kugarika Kushinga, which had a one-quarter female membership, elected two women to the Executive Committee out of a total of ten. Neither of the two women held senior posts (such as Secretary or Treasurer) on this committee. Although the researcher was unable to attend Executive Committee meetings, it was observed during general meetings that the two women Executive Committee members were expected to make logistical arrangements such as refreshments and seating.[10] Although an attempt was made by the Committee to ensure that all members of the Executive participated in leading the discussions at general meetings, this did not appear to extend to the women Executive members.

For Tashinga co-operative, with half its members women, the pattern was different. Although there were only two women out of a total of nine elected onto the Executive Committee, the chair, who was a woman, very much ran things in the co-operative and from interviews of other Executive Committee members, was highly respected for having launched the organization. She had very little formal education, but at 42 was at least five years older than most of the other Executive members. Her age may have added to her legitimacy in the eyes of the other male Executive members.

Attendance and Participation of Women Members at Meetings

While acting as participant-observer of the meetings of Tashinga and Kugarika Kushinga co-operatives, it was noted that women's attendance was consistently higher than that of men. This was particularly striking for Kugarika Kushinga which had only a 25% female membership. (For this reason, until the researcher took a formal count, the co-operative's Executive Committee was under the impression that women outnumbered the men). Higher female attendance was perhaps due to women showing a greater interest than men in shelter-related issues; but in the case of Kugarika Kushinga it could also have been due to male members sending their wives to co-op meetings. Despite high female turnout at meetings, it was the men who tended to dominate Kugarika Kushinga co-operative meetings.[11] This could be due to the pattern set by the Executive Committee,

where female Executive members were seen to be engaged in subordinate tasks. In contrast, women, who comprised the majority of those attending Tashinga co-operative meetings, participated strongly in the discussions,[12] which could have resulted from the strong example set by the Chair who commanded control of all of the meetings.

Women Co-op Members

Seven women members from Tashinga and Kugarika Kushinga were interviewed at length, four from Tashinga and three from Kugarika Kushinga. The women were identified with the help of the four women Executive Committee members of the two co-ops. An attempt was made to interview women who represented the full range of situations and status. Two were divorced; one was living common-law with her children's father (where "lobola" or bridewealth had not been paid); one was widowed; one was single; and two were married.[13] Their incomes ranged from $Zim 130 to $275 per month. They were from 26 to 50 years of age and had from one to four children. Their education ranged from grade four to Form 3 (the equivalent of about US grade 11).

Four of the seven women interviewed had unsuccessfully attempted to apply for lots from the municipal government. Of the remaining two who had applied, one was on the waiting list, and the other's husband was on the list. The four who were not successful revealed that they had been told they were ineligible due to being domestic workers or that their incomes were too low. According to official municipal policy, neither of these was supposed to be sufficient grounds for being rejected. This meant that municipal bureaucrats were discriminating against women applicants in an arbitrary fashion.[14] All the women, whether on the waiting list or not, perceived that the housing co-operative represented their only possibility of attaining a house at some time in their life.

The women consistently stated that they wanted a house both for their children and as security for their old age. Many of the women reported having to leave their children either in the rural areas with grandparents, or (reluctantly) with ex-husbands because they did not have the space to provide for them. In Zimbabwe, women can expect to be taken care of in old age only by male children, since female children, when married, must offer primary allegiance to their husbands' families. Nor can women expect to inherit land from their parents in the rural areas later in life, since only males inherit.

Despite this, some of the women reported working on their parents' farms in the rural areas and almost all sent money intermittently to their parents to help support them. This was reciprocated by their parents who took care of grandchildren for whom there was not enough space in the small living quarters in the city.

Other reasons were expressed by the women for wanting to own their own house. Some were able to grow food for consumption where they were currently living (usually maize), but others were not. Almost all the women had skills to generate other income, such as sewing or crafts, but were unable to pursue them because of lack of capital or insufficient space at home. Lack of time was a problem with others, since many lived far from their place of work and had to spend long hours commuting.

Conclusions

The combined effects of a gender-neutral housing policy that fails to recognize the special needs of women-headed households along with discrimination practiced by lower-level bureaucrats in the allocation of municipal lots have driven women to join housing co-operatives in large numbers in Zimbabwe. This implies that there is a need to revise eligibility policies for the purchase of land so that they take into account the varying marital and family situations of women. It also throws into question the requirement of self-help, since women's dual income-earning and child-rearing responsibilities make it difficult for them either to assemble a house themselves or to hire a builder. Housing co-operatives are therefore seen by women as a way of avoiding this dilemma.

In addition to their attractiveness in assisting women to dodge the inequities and inappropriateness of current housing policies, community-based housing organizations, the research suggests, offer other features to women, such as the ability to generate and sustain high rates of saving and to build houses at a reasonable cost, despite considerable constraints. Effective functioning of the organizations could be facilitated by local governments and private financial institutions adopting policies which recognize collective forms of ownership.

The results also show that the negative effects on women of the gender-neutral nature of housing policy in Zimbabwe are mirrored by policies on housing co-operatives: the promotion of workplace-based co-ops by the government has the consequence of favoring organizations comprised predominantly of men. Although the government has failed to provide significant assistance to either type of housing co-operative, there is a case for recognizing the difference between these two types of organizations and developing special support programs for the community-based co-ops, since they cater heavily to women, are comprised of lower-income people, and have fewer resources available to them.

The evidence of external interference in the community-based co-ops by local politicians and political party officials indicates that these types of organizations need a support structure that could act to reduce their vulnerability to outside manipulation. A strong national-level NGO that provides technical and financial assistance, training, and networking services could contribute toward this.[15]

Although both Tashinga and Kugarika Kushinga were in the early stages of development, there was evidence that women's participation in the organization was related to women's leadership. Female participation and leadership in the co-operative's decisions would be essential in ensuring that future housing solutions are suited to the needs of women-headed households. This implies that training programs need to be developed which are gender-sensitive, encouraging women to take on roles and tasks not traditionally held by them.

Finally, the research suggests that community-based housing organizations, if appropriately developed and supported, could not only improve women's access to housing, but could also act as enabling and empowering mechanisms for helping women to develop their leadership and technical capacities. In this way, community-based housing organizations could constitute an important element in the link between the gender aspects of shelter provision and women's development.

Notes

[1] The government census of 1982 placed the number of women-headed households at 15%. However, it is generally assumed that the real figure is much higher (Schlyter, 1989:27–28; Government of Zimbabwe and Government of Sweden, 1987:20).

[2] Both Jacobs (1989) and Schmidt (1991) argue that there was collusion between European lawmakers and African men who saw the opportunities to be gained from removing certain legal rights from African women.

[3] These are based on the typology used by Mutizwa-Mangiza (1985).

[4] A concerted attempt was made to include at least one all-female housing co-operative; however there were none appropriate for study in the country at the time.

[5] The study results relating to cost comparisons are reported more fully in Vakil (1991:141). The costs for a one- to five-room house for the three co-operatives engaged in construction ranged from $5,000 to $9,720, respectively; for the government-sponsored sector, costs for similar units ranged from $5,087 to $9,818; for the private sector, from $6,600 to $12,800.

[6] See Fugelsang and Chandler (1986) for a description of the most famous example of this, the Grameen Bank, an institution which lends to poor people in Bangladesh.

[7] For a fuller description of the impact of policy on the five housing co-operatives, including an analytical model, see Vakil (1991:192–198).

[8] On one occasion, the Cotton Printers co-operative relied on a ZANU party connection to facilitate its purchase of land. However, this relationship was initiated by the co-operative, not the political official.

[9] See Gilbert and Ward (1984) for a description of similar issues in Latin America.

[10] This tendency of women to take on domestic roles within the organization is confirmed in other studies of women's participation in Zimbabwean co-operatives [see Chinemana (1987); and Smith (1987)].

[11] Despite the high proportion of women attending Kugarika Kushinga co-operative meetings, out of all questions asked by members, less than one-third were posed by women.

[12] Out of a total of 13 questions asked at one Tashinga meeting, for example, 10 were asked by women.

[13] The researcher had initially been led to believe that the two married women were divorced. This is particularly interesting, since in Zimbabwe, it is assumed that the male is the head of the household and would be expected to be the member of the co-operative. In both cases, the women claimed that the future houses would be in their names.

[14] This is corroborated by Schlyter (1989:167).

[15] At this writing, a Canadian NGO, Conseil en development de lodgment communautaire (CDLC), is in the process of establishing the foundations for an organization of this type.

References

Bratton, Michael. "The politics of government-NGO relations in Africa," in *World Development,* 17(4), 1986:42–57.

Chant, Sylvia. "Domestic labour, decision-making and dwelling construction: the experience of women in Queretaro, Mexico," in Moser and Peake (eds.), op. cit., 1987:33–54.

Chimedza, R. "Savings clubs: the mobilization of rural finances in Zimbabe," Geneva: International Labor. Office, Rural Employment Policies Branch, mimeo, 1984.

Chinemana, Frances. *Women and the Co-operative Movement in Zimbabwe.* Harare: GOZ, CUSO and NOVIB, 1987.

Fugelsang, Andreas and Dale Chandler. *Participation as process — what we can learn from Grameen Bank.* Bangladesh. Oslo: NORAD, 1986.

Gaidzwana, R. B. "Women's land rights in Zimbabwe," *Rural and Urban Planning Occasional Paper, No. 13,* Harare: University of Zimbabwe, August, 1988.

Gilbert, Alan and Peter Ward. "Community action by the urban poor: democratic involvement, community self-help or a means of social control?" in *World Development,* 12(8), 1984:769–782.

Government of Zimbabwe. *Urban Housing Policy Implementation Manual.* Harare: GOZ, 1989a.

——. "Draft policy on co-operative development," Harare: mimeo, 1989b.

——. *Government Policy on Co-operative Development.* Harare: GOZ, 1984.

——. *Transitional National Development Plan, Vols. 1 and 2.* Harare: GOZ, 1982.

Government of Zimbabwe and Government of Sweden. *IYSH Women and Shelter Seminar.* Harare: GOZ, 1987.

Jacobs, Susan. "Zimbabwe: state, class and gendered models of land resettlement," in Parpart, Jane and Kathleen Staudt (eds.), *Women and the State in Africa,* Boulder, CO: Rienner, 1988.

Larsson, Anita. *Women householders and housing strategies: the case of Gaborone, Botswana SB: 25.* Gavle: National Swedish Institute for Building Research, 1989.

Moser, Caroline and Linda Peake (eds.). *Women, Human Settlements and Housing.* London: Tavistock, 1987.

Mutizwa-Mangiza, N. D. "A study of low-income housing strategies in Harare with special reference to affordability," *Discussion Paper No. 11,* University of Bradford, June, 1985.

Ncube, Welshman. "Underprivilege and inequality: the matrimonial property rights of women in Zimbabwe," in Armstrong, Alice (ed.), *Women and Law in Southern Africa.* Harare: Zimbabwe Publishing House, 1987:3–34.

Rakodi, Carole. "Women's work or household strategies?", *Environment and Urbanization,* 3(2), October, 1991:39–45.

Sarin, Mahdu. "Improved stoves, women and domestic energy," *Environment and Urbanization,* 3(2), October, 1991:51–56.

Schlyter, Ann. *Women householders and housing strategies: the case of Harare, Zimbabwe SB: 26.* Gavle: National Swedish Institute for Building Research, 1989.

——. *Women householders and housing strategies: the case of George, Zambia SB: 14.* Gavle: National Swedish Institute for Building Research, 1988.

Schmidt, Elizabeth. "Patriarchy, capitalism, and the colonial state in Zimbabwe," *Signs,* 16(4), 1991:732–757.

Smith, Sheila. "Zimbabwean women in co-operatives," in *Journal of Social Development in Africa,* 2(1), 1987:29–48.

Turner, Bertha (ed.). *Building Community: A Third World Case Book.* London: Habitat International Coalition, 1988.

UNCHS. *Women and Human Settlements Development.* Nairobi: HABITAT, 1989.

Vakil, Anna C. "Community-based housing organizations in Third World cities: case studies from Zimbabwe," unpublished Ph.D. dissertation, University of Michigan, 1991.

Vance, Irene. "More than bricks and mortar: women's participation in self-help housing in Managua, Nicaragua," in Moser, Caroline and Linda Peake (eds.), *op. cit.,* 1987:139–165.

Chapter 7
Housing and Gender: Beyond the Public/Private Dichotomy

Patricia Gardiner

Patricia Gardiner is a graduate student in City Planning at San Diego State University. She is Irish, and earned her undergraduate degree in History and Politics at North London Polytechnic in Britain. She has lived in the United States for six years and has worked in a variety of community development jobs, including a period at the San Diego Housing Commission. She worked during the summer of 1988 with the Architects and Planners for Nicaragua (APSNICA), helping to develop a housing plan for the city of Ocotol.

Many of the recent feminist housing analyses in the United States (Sarkissian, 1978; Wekerle & Carter, 1978; Saegert, 1985) have focused on the public/private dichotomy as a way to understand the powerful forces behind suburbanization in the experiences of isolation and loneliness for women in the suburbs. This paper critiques the use of the public/private dichotomy as the primary tool of current feminist housing analysis, because it speaks largely to the housing conditions and experiences of white middle-class women. The shelter experiences of women of color and poor white women historically have not lain in the relative privilege of the suburbs, nor have their lives fallen into a neat public/private dichotomy.

The paper will draw upon the housing experiences of women in public housing in both the United States and Britain, and the work of Mimi Abramovitz in the area of social welfare policy. I will suggest that better insights leading to greater understanding of the housing experiences of poor women and women of color can come from examining how these women are designated as either the "deserving" or "undeserving" poor.

The Public/Private Dichotomy

The public/private dichotomy refers ideologically and historically to the development of a male political community and citizenship, with all its attendant rights, within the public sphere of society. The development of the public sphere, with its exclusion of women, demanded the parallel development of the private sphere of the family and home. The private sphere, without rights of citizenship, became women's place and space. These public and private spheres became mutually reinforcing ideological constructs in spite of their irrelevance to the reality of poor women's lives throughout the industrial age. However, this political and ideological construct was translated into the built form so that public buildings and spaces associated with citizenship and power were male-centered, and the home was considered the woman's realm. The development of the suburbs, with the associated cult of domesticity which idealized women as the center of home and hearth, is an excellent example of the way in which housing reinforced women's subordination in society.

The cult of domesticity idealized women as the center of home and hearth, or to put it more realistically, her primary role in social reproduction. The cult also idealized women's isolation from the public world of the formal economy and political power; it promoted the single-family home as an island of tranquillity; and it reinforced the nuclear family as the primary socializing unit in society. The drive towards suburbanization and the cult of domesticity began in the latter part of the nineteenth century and gained its strongest influence after the second World War. But as writers such as Evelyn Nakano Glen have pointed out, "a definition of womanhood exclusively in terms of domesticity never applied to ethnic women, as it did not to many working-class women." The women referred to by Glen did not have access to the single-family home, either because of low income or discrimination. In addition, they were highly likely to be part of the formal economy, and when the influence of the cult of domesticity had led them to give up work in the formal economy, non-white and poor white women continued their production in the informal economy.

A more useful basis for formulating housing policy for poor and working class women in the United States, and especially female-headed families, is an understanding of how these women are viewed as the "undeserving poor" in our society. This needs to be understood in the context of the role which housing policy plays in strengthening the nuclear family, the cornerstone of a patriarchal society. Mimi Abramovitz's research in social welfare policy is especially valuable in this area.

The "Undeserving" Poor

Abramovitz has shown that, since the Poor Laws of the colonial period, women who have stepped outside of society's narrowly defined role of dependence and nurturing have suffered various levels and forms of opprobrium. This marginalization has been reinforced through social welfare policies used as an instrument of the patriarchal state in regulating the lives of women, and mediating between the demands of patriarchy (i.e., the family ethic) and capitalism (i.e., the work ethic). In her book *Regulating the Lives of Women, Social Welfare Policy from Colonial Times to the Present* Abramovitz has demonstrated that "the rules and regulation of social welfare programs benefit those who live in traditional family structures while penalizing alternative family forms where poor women and women of color tend to predominate."

The deserving female paupers of the colonial period who qualified for aid were widows, the wives of sick, disabled, or temporarily unproductive men, or women who were seen as involuntarily lacking a male bread-winner. They received clothes, firewood, bread, medical care, or possibly a small weekly cash payment. This allowed them to continue both productive and reproduc-

tive tasks in the home, and hold on to colonial society's mark of "a true woman." Undeserving female paupers were single or divorced women, or unwed mothers. They were forced to work in exchange for a place in the poor house, or have their services auctioned off to the highest bidder. With this distinction, colonial poor laws protected the town coffers, as well as the work ethic and the reigning ideology pertaining to women's roles.

With the advent of industrial capitalism and the develop-ment of the focus of production away from the family household and into the public or market sphere, women's roles in the social order became increasingly problematic. Abramovitz points out:

> By the end of the colonial period, capital's need for cheap market labor had combined with the impoverishment of the working class to draw increasingly large numbers of women into the wage labor market. Paradoxically, their entry conflicted with the benefits received by capital from women's unpaid domestic labor. Combined with fewer marriages and more female-headed households, the growing labor force participation of women, which held the possibility of greater economic independence, also contained a challenge to male dominance and patriarchal family patterns.

Social welfare programs have had to deal with these contradictory pulls. They did this largely by channeling "deserving" poor women into the home to devote full time to reproducing and maintaining the labor force, and the "undeserving" poor into the labor market. The development of patriarchal social thought, which held that gender roles were biologically determined rather than socially assigned, helped clarify who was deserv-ing. The emergence of the "cult of domesticity" or "cult of true womanhood," which was to convince women that their place was in the home, rationalized giving working women largely low-paid, low-status jobs.

In 1875 the Wisconsin Supreme Court ruled that "the law of nature destines and qualifies the female sex for the bearing and nurture of the children of our race and for the custody of the homes of the world in love and honor." However, in the same decade nearly 15 percent (1.8 million women) of the adult female population worked for wages—mostly unmarried, widowed, or deserted women. But concerns about working mothers and the quality of the future labor force gave rise to the campaign for Mothers' Pension. The Pension was accorded to those women who were deemed "suitable" to raise their children at home, yet was not enough to substitute for full-time work. Thus the program encour-aged the economic dependence of women on men and defined child-rearing as exclusively women's responsibility. In an address to congress in February, 1909, Theodore Roosevelt reinforced society's identification of the deserving poor. He explained that the proposed Mothers' Pension was for:

> parents of good character suffering from temporary misfortune and above all deserving mothers fairly well able to work but deprived of the support of the normal breadwinner...so that they could maintain suitable homes for the rearing of their children.

The eligibility rules, which varied from state to state, distinguished among women according to their marital status and the Mothers' Pension was largely given to white, widowed women.

During the Depression of the 1930's the growth of female-headed families (3.7 million in 1930) deepened the sense of crisis within the family system. The Aid to Dependent Children (ADC, forerunner to the AFDC) was introduced in 1935 and was purely for the support of children in the care of single mothers. The formula for payment did not include any aid for the mother herself, which was in marked contrast to the pensions for widows of veterans. Both received $18 a month for the first child and $12 for the second, but the veteran's widow received an additional $30 for herself.

The ambivalence about supporting female-headed families was widespread, and by 1940 there were ten states which still had not adopted the program. The program eligibility rules continued to distinguish between the deserving and undeserving women by using the criteria of "suitable homes" established under the Mothers' Pension program. In states where women's low-paid labor was used extensively, rules governing "employable mothers" disqualified able-bodied women with school-age children. This rule was applied especially to Black women. In the late 1930's one southern public assistance field supervisor reported that:

> The number of Negro cases is few due to the unanimous feeling on the part of the staff and board that there are more work opportunities for Negro women and to their intense desire not to interfere with local labor conditions. The attitude that they have always gotten along, and that "all they'll do is have more children" is definite.... There is hesitancy on the part of lay boards to advance too rapidly over the thinking of their own communities, which see no reason why the employable Negro mother should not continue her usual sketchy seasonal labor or indefinite domestic service rather than receive a public assistance grant.

The contradictions for society of women's role in production and reproduction continued through the 1950's. Questions of women's "moral fitness" to receive ADC continued throughout this period, and the "rediscovery" of poverty in the early 1960's fueled concerns about the reproductive capacity of poor families and the role of welfare. As welfare rolls grew, the percentage of AFDC families headed by unwed mothers rose from 21.3 to 28.4 percent. Abramovitz argues that the state perceived that it had failed in "normalizing" the female-headed household by substituting itself for the missing breadwinner and, threatened by the increase in female-headed families, began to treat the entire AFDC case load as "undeserving."

These same designations of "deserving" and "undeserving," and the attempts to support the nuclear family, can been seen clearly in even a cursory examination of public housing policy in the United States.

Public Housing

United States

The public housing program in the 1930's was created to alleviate the poor housing conditions which had led to social unrest, as well as concerns about the inefficiencies of social reproduction. In addition, there was the need to create employment for the millions of unemployed men. But despite the high-minded rhetoric of the 1937 Housing Act which stated as its goal "to provide a decent home and suitable living environment for every American family," it was never the intention of the public housing officials to provide decent housing as a right to all who needed it. Rather, as Rachel Bratt has stated, public housing was for the deserving, temporarily poor, the "submerged middle class." The program therefore targeted those who could not find decent, affordable housing on the private market, but not the so-called unworthy poor and those with no means to pay rent.

And indeed despite the fact that its early tenants were the deserving poor, public housing was designed to be distinctive in appearance from private housing, and thus stigmatized, in order not to become an attractive housing alternative for people. As Gwendolyn Wright noted, public housing was sturdy and functional but also cheap and austere.

In line with its mission of restoring social order, public housing also served to reinforce the primacy of the nuclear family. Most housing authorities accepted what they termed "complete" families, in other words, two parents with several children. Applicants had interviews with social workers, employment verifications, and home visits to ensure that the families conformed to the prevailing norms of the day. These officials would rate both the families, existing living conditions and their readiness to change in their new surroundings, both of which were rated according to middle-class ideas of the way the poor should live. Thus thrift and nuclear family values were supported through design. The design of the apartments contained no storage space as large purchases represented a more comfortable life than the tenants were supposed to enjoy in this transition period. Cupboard doors were left off to encourage neatness.

These early public housing tenants were the deserving poor, the submerged middle class. However, the economic boom of the 1950's saw a change in policy approaches to public housing tenants as the white, working class benefited from the economic upturn and moved out of the public housing and into the suburbs. People on welfare only now became eligible to apply for public housing, and a new kind of tenant emerged, largely African-American families and those on welfare: namely, the undeserving poor, as well as an increasing number of retired people.

Public housing for poor women in the United States in the 1950's and 60's was characterized by large-scale dwellings in the inner cities, in contrast to the suburban lives and experiences of white, middle-class women. Indeed the reality of the lack of state support for low-income housing is brought into stark relief not only by the massive 82 percent cut in the housing budget under the Reagan Administration. It is also illustrated more subtly by the greater allocation of resources, and attention to architectural detail, paid to the deserving poor public housing tenants, namely, the elderly. Senior housing is designed with ramps and safety rails, clinics and community rooms—all features which would also be appropriate to housing for the bulk of the rest of the public housing projects, largely female-headed families.

Britain

In contrast, public housing in Britain, or council housing as it is referred to, is perhaps paradoxically more easily understood within the framework of the public/private dichotomy. However, adding the "deserving/undeserving poor" analysis as a layer of study adds significantly to our understanding of women's housing situation. It is interesting to note that in reviewing the literature on housing in Britain, there is a significant difference

between the analyses by scholars in both countries. While both agree that housing cannot be simply looked at as an issue of shelter, there are certain a priori assumptions in British literature about the universal subordination of women, and the utmost significance of women's contribution to the maintenance and reproduction of the social order (McDowell; Watson). And while it is apparent that feminist housing theory is still in its infancy, as in this country, there is a greater emphasis on understanding the organization and function of women's domestic work in capitalist societies. This is in turn of course related to the social and sexual division of residential space, and the isolation of women in single-family housing. All the feminist scholars in Britain refer to or discuss patriarchy. However, there is little discussion of the centrality of the nuclear family. This is connected to the fact that there are fewer numbers and forms of alternative family structures developing in that society. In the 1980 census figures, 80 percent of all families in Britain were identified as "traditional male-headed family units."

The impetus for building council housing in Britain came in the aftermath of wars, both the First and Second World Wars, which obviously had brought destruction, as well as the rising marriage and birth rates which came after, and the fear of social disorder. The type of housing built after both wars was predominantly single-family housing, on "greenfield" peripheral sites, exacerbating the separation of home and work, and the isolation of women. As Linda McDowell, a British scholar, noted:

> Peripheral location combined with the single family dwellings confirmed the wish not only to preserve the integrity of the nuclear family, but also to keep it as separate as possible from other families and any outside intrusion. During the 1930's flats were commonly regarded, in England and Wales at least, as violating individual privacy. In a debate in the House of Commons in 1938 the member for Argyleshire argued that 'flats are an abomination... never meant for human beings... flats make Communists while cottages make individuals, and incidentally make good Conservatives.'

McDowell pointed out that this nicely combined the desire for privacy with the recognition of the links between housing policy and social quiescence.

Policy makers and local authority officials were not only concerned with strengthening the nuclear family but also ensuring that the mother and homemaker was doing a good job, by distributing leaflets on efficient methods of domestic work and inspecting tenants' homes in unannounced visits. This was part of the legacy of the private charity workers of the late nineteenth century, many of whom believed that any household that violated the prescribed gender division of labor would quickly become a "breeding ground of sin and social disorder." Indeed, the Charity Organization Society of the nineteenth and early twentieth centuries instructed its "friendly visitors" to strengthen "true" home life among the poor, to "dissuade restless wives from seeking outside employment," and to introduce messy housekeepers to the "pleasures of clean, well-ordered homes."

However, it was clear from the housing policies that while poor, white, nuclear families needed to be educated, and were indeed seen as educable, minority and female-headed families did not receive the same attention. Tenants were segregated according to the social norms of the day; thus in Britain, female-headed families and families of color were most likely to receive the poorest dwellings in the lowest status areas. Up until the 1960's, single mothers were included in a housing authority pamphlet entitled "Unsatisfactory Tenants;" and only 24 percent of women with children seeking emergency shelter from spousal abuse were admitted to public housing rolls as officials did not want to encourage the break-up of families.

Clearly, distinctions along the lines of deserving/ undeserving poor were made in the allocation of council housing and the treatment of council house tenants, with female-headed families the obvious designees of the status of "undeserving" poor. And while a feminist analysis of public housing has not yet been carried out, in both Britain and the United States it is clear that, like other welfare programs, the state attempted to use housing policy during the 1940's and 1950's to "normalize" poor families. As the make-up of public housing in the United States changed during the 1960's to include increasing numbers of African-American and female-headed families, the state gave up attempts to enforce middle-class, nuclear family norms and designated all public housing tenants as the "undeserving" poor. Thus the 82 percent cut in low-income housing programs during the Reagan era was implemented without significant protest.

Conclusion

The current focus of feminist housing analyses is on understanding women's housing in terms of the public/ private dichotomy. However, a closer examination of this analysis indicates that it largely excludes non-white and poor white women from its frame of reference.

These women have historically been denied the very status of women (characterized largely in this patriarchal society by the cult of domesticity) which imprisoned white, middle-class women in the spatially distinct private arena of their homes.

As the structure of society changes to include more single-parent families, and as the feminization of poverty becomes a reality for ever-increasing numbers of women, it is important to understand why housing design still reflects the needs of the nuclear family. The work carried out by Abramovitz regarding the way in which poor women are designated either "deserving" or "undeserving" in social welfare policy provides especially valuable insights in this regard, and its relevance becomes immediately apparent when one applies the analysis to public housing.

However, a postmodern understanding of feminism may have much to contribute to the larger discussion of the housing needs of women. Postmodern feminist theorists have pointed out that large-scale theories, what they refer to as "metanarratives," are inappropriate to such heterogeneous and complex modern societies as ours. Theory must be culturally and historically specific and take into account what Linda Nicholson has called "complexly constructed conceptions of social identity." Having said that, I think that one of the most important things we can learn from the recent public housing experiences of poor women in both Britain and the United States is that the state will use housing policy to promote strongly the nuclear family. As we formulate shelter policies for women, we have to recognize that the nuclear family is the cornerstone of patriarchy and non-nuclear family forms are considered a threat to that system. Therefore we must first challenge housing policies specifically, and social policies generally, which denote non-nuclear families as the undeserving poor.

References

Abramovitz, Mimi. *Regulating the Lives of Women, Social Welfare Policy from Colonial Times to the Present.* Boston: South End Press, 1988.

Austerberry, Helen and Sophie Watson. "Women and Housing Policy" in Clare Ungerson, *Women and Social Policy: A Reader.* London: Macmillan Publishing, 1985.

Bratt, Rachel G. "Public Housing: The Controversy and Contribution" in *Critical Perspectives on Housing,* Rachel Bratt, Chester Hartman and Ann Meyerson, eds. Philadelphia: Temple University Press, 1986.

Glen, Evelyn Nakano. "Racial Ethnic Women's Labor: The Intersection of Race, Gender and Class Oppression" in

Review of Radical Political Economics. Vol. 17(3): 86–108 (1985).

Hayden, Delores. *The Grand Domestic Revolution: A History of Feminist Designs for American Homes, Neighborhoods, and Cities.* Massachusetts: MIT Press, 1981.

McDowell, Linda. "City and Home: Urban Housing and the Sexual Division of Space" in Mary Evans and Clare Ungerson, eds. *Sexual Divisions: Patterns and Processes.* London & New York: Tavistock Publications, 1983.

Nicholson, Linda J. ed. *Feminism/Postmodernism.* New York: Routledge, 1990.

Saegert, Susan, Theodore Liebman and R. Alan Melting, "Working Women: The Denver Experience" in Eugenie Ladner Birch, ed. *The Unsheltered Woman: Women and Housing in the 80's.* New Jersey: Center for Urban Policy Research, 1985.

Sarkissian, Wendy, "Planning as if Women Mattered: The Story of Brown Hills." Mimeographed (Berkeley: Department of Landscape Architecture, University of California, 1978).

Ungerson, Clare. *Moving Home.* London: Bell Press, 1971.

Watson, Sophie. "Women and Housing or Feminist Housing Analysis?" in *Housing Studies,* January, 1986.

Wekerle, Gerda and Novia Carter, "Urban Sprawl: The Price Women Pay," *Branching Out* 5, no. 2 (1978).

Wright, Gwendolyn. *Building the Dream: A Social History of Housing in America.* New York: Pantheon Books, 1981.

Chapter 8
Boundary Violations: Sexual Harassment within Tenancy Relations

Sylvia Novac

Sylvia Novac has been consulting on housing policy and research for several years. She has been an active member of the Housing Committee of the National Action committee for the Status of Women in Canada, as well as other women's housing advocacy groups in Toronto. She is a doctoral student at the Ontario Institute for Studies in Education, Department of Sociology in Education.

Housing analyst Sophie Watson has argued that a systematic feminist analysis of housing must investigate those processes within a housing system which serve to produce and reproduce patriarchal relations.[1] Several of these processes can be categorized under the general theme of women's housing security or lack of it. A feminist understanding of security includes the ability to obtain suitable housing and remain in that housing with a feeling of safety.

In fact, the concept of safety is one of our premises for the meaning of home. Women's experiences, however, of feeling safe in their homes takes on a contradictory character. Women are more likely to seek refuge in the home, and to remain there as protection against male aggression in public places. Yet, ironically, women are at even greater risk of sexual violence in their homes. One of the little researched forms of male dominance that affects women's housing security is sexual harassment by landlords, their agents, and neighbor tenants. Awareness and recognition of this problem is partially veiled by the same screen of privacy that shields public acknowledgment of the familial or domestic abuse of women by male intimates, and by the myth of the safe home which parallels the myth of the safe family.

I will briefly outline what we know about the nature and extent of sexual harassment within tenancy relations using preliminary results from a recently conducted multi-method inquiry of women's experiences based on case studies, community-specific small group discussions, and a mail survey of tenant households in Ontario.[2]

Women as Renters

Where housing is treated as a market commodity, as it is in the advanced capitalist state of Canada, the ability to buy or pay becomes a paramount determinant of housing security. Government policies that favor private home ownership have resulted in two-thirds of Canadian households owning the housing they occupy. Of the remaining one-third who rent, women-led households are over-represented and constitute the most housing-disadvantaged groups, particularly as single mothers and single women. Almost two-thirds of women-headed households nation-wide are renters while a similar proportion of all other household types are owners of their housing.[3] This pattern is similar in Canada's largest city, Toronto, where single women are most likely to be renters.

Table 1. Comparison of Housing Tenure Status and Core Housing Need of Wives, Single Mothers, and Lone Women in Toronto[4]

Tenure Status				Core Housing Need (over 30% of income spent on housing)			
	Wives	Single Mothers	Single Women		Wives	Single Mothers	Single Women
Owners	2.8%	44.4%	28%	Owners	10%	20.1%	29.3%
Renters	27.2%	55.6%	2%	Tenants	20.6%	44.4%	4.2%

The increased proportion of women in the labor force over the past few decades has made women somewhat less dependent on familial-mediated housing provision, but they remain significantly disadvantaged in the housing market when they live without male partners (that is, employed men living with women as an economic unit). This relationship is well demonstrated in Table 1, showing statistics on women's tenure status and degree of affordability problems in relation to their family or household status.

Without male partners, and regardless of tenure status, women are much more likely to be paying over 30 percent of their income on housing, compromising their ability to pay for other basic needs. Renters are much more likely than owners to have such affordability problems. With a continuing reduction in low-cost urban housing stock, women are quite likely to have very limited housing options; this is a significant factor in their unequal relationship with landlords, private as well as public.

Sexual Harassment

Within the past two decades Western feminists have publicly challenged a variety of forms of violence against women, including sexual harassment, transforming and reinterpreting what has been considered a private problem into a social issue.[5] The critical work of identifying and labeling the practice as detrimental to women is primarily focused on women's experiences in the workplace, as Catherine MacKinnon states, not because that's where most sexual harassment necessarily occurs nor because it is the only problem women have as workers, but because "the government promises

more."[6] So, too, for renters, does the government promise more; legislation in the Canadian province of Ontario addresses tenants' rights to "quiet and peaceful enjoyment," and to privacy from unwarranted entry. The Human Rights Code expressly prohibits sexual harassment. Reports from legal service providers, however, reveal that women rarely come forward with a complaint of sexual harassment, but rather mention such incidents amid other landlord-tenant problems, most usually when there is already a threat of eviction.

One of the distinctive features of sexual harassment of tenants is the violation of refuge in one's home. I use the theme of boundaries to tie together the personal and spatial aspects of harm inherent in this problem: while sexual harassment in any context is a violation of personal and sexual dignity, autonomy, and safety, sexual harassment of tenants is also a violation of personal space, privacy, and housing security. Our culture's psychic and symbolic association of women—their work and their bodies—with homes and houses combines to create a particularly potent powerlessness which leaves women, in material and psychological terms, nowhere to hide.

Home has been portrayed as a place where one can dream; sexual harassment, especially by men who have keys to your unit, can prevent women's ability to get even a decent night's rest. In cases of severe sexual harassment, constant vigilance causes anxiety and exhaustion. The presence of other household members, especially children, may add to the risk potential. While some male partners or family members will attempt to support a woman who is being harassed, others hold her responsible for the "sexual attention" she receives.

Sexual harassment within tenancy relations has received some notice in the United States in terms of media attention and legal cases,[7] but almost no research.[8] The only previous systematic study of women's experiences is a telephone survey of 297 women tenants conducted by a community-based organization in Montreal.[9] Within the context of women's experiences of discrimination in rental housing, the survey revealed that 12 percent of the respondents had been victims of sexual harassment, coming from landlords or their agents in 77 percent of the cases.[10]

Results from the recently conducted survey of rental households in Ontario[11] show that 16 percent of 352 women report having received "unwanted sexual attention," coming from landlords and their agents in about half the cases. From a series of questions based on a typology of sexual harassing behaviors,[12] 28 percent of respondents had experienced sexual harassment, either as direct targets of the behavior, or as bystanders, or as confidants.[13] From the 141 incident reports, we learn that 58 percent of them were directed at the respondents, 30 percent were witnessed by the respondents, and 12 percent were experienced second-hand through personal disclosures.

Almost half of the perpetrators were landlords or their agents, which means that neighbor tenants are perpetrators much more often than in the Montreal findings. There are two possible explanations for this: first, the low number of incidents from the Montreal study (i.e., N=35) maximizes the error rate; second, the Montreal working-class neighborhoods that were sampled have a predominantly distinctive housing form of three-story walk-ups. It is likely that the inhabitants have fewer neighbor tenants and less contact with them than do women living in the multi-story apartment buildings which house many urban tenants, especially in Toronto, which accounts for about half the rental households in Ontario.

There is a consistent pattern in the research on sexual harassment of an inverse relationship between the severity of the incident and its frequency. In other words, the less severe forms of sexual harassment occur more frequently. The Montreal survey results suggest that the experience for women tenants follows this pattern. In fact, no respondent in that study revealed having experienced assault.[14]

In the Ontario study, the most common form of sexual harassment falls in the category of "degrading remarks,"

reported by 18 percent of the women. Sexual assault, that is sexual touching by threat or use of force, was reported least, by 2.5 percent of respondents, which is consistent with large survey results on workplace sexual harassment.

A summary of the frequency of different forms of behavior follows:

— about 1 in 6 women experienced, at least once, degrading remarks, either against women in general, or against a specific woman, and inappropriate questions or insults;
— about 1 in 10 women have experienced, at least once, indirect suggestions of sex, being "bugged" for dates, pressured for sex, being inappropriately touched, and attempts or threats of physical contact;
— about 1 in 20 women have experienced, at least once, sexual bribery, and exposure to sexual materials (such as pornography); and
— about 1 in 40 women have experienced, at least once, sexual assault (forced sexual contact).

A New York journalist's investigation of the problem of sexual harassment of women tenants, based on interviews with 25 individuals and 50 social service and women's advocacy groups, suggests that women of all age, racial, and income groups were affected, but that low-income women were "hardest hit."[15]

Half of the Ontario survey respondents have serious affordability problems; they pay 30 percent or more of their household income for housing which puts them in "core housing need" according to federal government guidelines. There is no correlation, however, between their level of income and reports of sexual harassment. Women who were born in Canada (as opposed to those born in other countries), and younger women, are both significantly more likely to report sexual harassment.

It has been suggested that two factors—greater economic vulnerability and stereotypes held about women of color—may account for a differential impact of sexual harassment on them, but we are unable to establish this since most of the research on sexual harassment has not asked respondents to indicate their ethnocultural or minority status.[16]

About one-quarter of the Ontario survey respondents are members of visible minority groups in Canada; they were not more likely to report sexual harassment. Community-specific group discussions indicate, however, that the experiences of visible minority women frequently reflect forms of sexual harassment that integrate sexism and racism. For example, Aboriginal women report that landlords and neighbors frequently make unwanted sexual remarks by saying such things as, "I thought all natives shared their women—the Eskimos do, doesn't your band?" In one case, a building superintendent who had just fixed a kitchen light pulled down his pants in the presence of the tenant, a Black woman, and told her to "suck his white cock." In these situations, it is clear that racism is inherent in how women of color are sexually harassed.

The Landlord and Tenant Act in Ontario gives landlords and superintendents the right of access for emergency repairs, and some leases specify further reasons for access. It is not at all unusual for this right to be abused by landlords and superintendents to enter apartments and homes at will. Women who have experienced sexual harassment and repeated illegal entries risk providing grounds for their own eviction if they change the lock and refuse to hand over a key to their abuser. Because of this, legal advocates who specialize in tenant issues advise women in these circumstances to purchase burglar alarms to warn them of illegal entry.

According to the Ontario survey, 29 percent of tenants reported that their unit had been entered by a landlord without the requisite 24 hours notice in writing. There is a significant correlation between those who had experienced illegal entry and those who reported an incident of sexual harassment. While several of the women I personally interviewed were sexually harassed by men who had entered their homes, illegally or otherwise, it is not clear what proportion of sexually harassing behavior occurs in conjunction with illegal entry.

About half of the survey respondents reported that they know about their rights as tenants in terms of discrimination, general harassment, and sexual harassment; and almost two-thirds know about their rights regarding privacy. Knowledge of tenants' rights, including privacy rights, is not a correlate of sexual harassment reports, but experience of discriminatory behavior is.

Women's experiences of discrimination while looking for housing or as a tenant is significantly correlated with their reports of sexual harassment, as is their attitudinal response that women experience more discrimination in housing. Temporal order cannot be established, but unlike knowledge of tenants' rights, knowledge of the law regarding sexual harassment is correlated to reports

of such experiences; this suggests that women learn about their legal rights after experiencing sexual harassment, or that women who are aware of the law are more likely to report incidents of sexual harassment, or some combination of both these processes.

By coincidence the survey was conducted from September to December of 1991, a time period which straddled a televised congressional hearing into allegations of sexual harassment by a Supreme Court judge candidate.[17] The media blitz during the weekend of October 12–15, which heavily penetrated Canadian audiences, resulted in very wide public awareness of the sexual harassment charge. Various outcomes have been proposed for the educational impact on women and men of the explicit description of the sexual harassment and of the treatment of the claimant. About 90 questionnaires received prior to that weekend of non-stop televised hearings were marked for a comparison with those received after any media acknowledgment of the story; there was no significant difference in the reporting rate of sexual harassment before and after the televised hearings. It may be that the media messages were ambivalent with canceled effects, or it may be that such reports do not have a significant impact on women's awareness of sexual harassment or willingness to report it in an anonymous fashion such as through a mail questionnaire.

Women's Responses

The nine women who were interviewed exhibited a range of responses to being sexually harassed. Their responses included ignoring the behavior, telling friends and family, verbal complaints to the superintendent or landlord, formal complaints to legal authorities, and one woman-centered direct action. In several cases, the sexually harassing behavior did not stop as the result of a formal complaint, and appeals to authorities were not effective for the complainants; in fact, the authorities sometimes worsened the experience for the women by ignoring or questioning their interpretation of the events.

Only the woman-centered direct action had satisfactory results for the tenant whose friends confronted the landlord—with her consent, under her control, and in her presence—warning him that they would have to act against him if he repeated his behavior, and that they would tell his wife. The women involved were elated that they had successfully discouraged this man from engaging in further sexually harassing behavior, and that they had accomplished this by themselves.

Formal complaints of sexual harassment in Ontario are directed to the Human Rights Commission whose experience is predominantly with employment-related situations. While a complaint of sexual harassment takes one or more years to process through the Commission, a landlord can fairly easily find grounds and evict a tenant in less than six months. Over the past ten years, 28 accommodation-related complaints of sexual harassment have been filed with the Commission. From nine of these closed files,[18] it is clear that the outcomes for women have not been wildly successful. Minor monetary awards were given to two women for relocation costs. All but one case involved a landlord as perpetrator, most of whom agreed to sign a letter of assurance for the Commission. An assistant superintendent who had sexually harassed several women in the building was fired and evicted along with the superintendent *when it was discovered that they were both in possession of stolen goods belonging to tenants.*

One of the participatory research objectives for the community-specific small discussion groups was to empower the women, through connections with local organizations and provision of seed money, to plan and initiate some form of direct action that they thought would be appropriate for their community. The groups devised various forms of community outreach and education to inform more women of the problem of sexual harassment and of their rights as tenants. For example, a group of Francophone women in Ottawa (the capital city of Canada) attended workshops on popular theater methods, and used their skills to act out vignettes based on their experiences of sexual harassment and their ideas about how women might resist and fight back.

Each of the action projects demonstrates a unique format and method of sharing information and working with women in community-specific ways. While legislative and administrative reform are a fundamental and necessary avenue for change, it is primarily the ongoing struggle of women at the community level that will change everyday oppressive practices and develop women's collective strength to resist exploitative and disrespectful treatment of tenants.

Notes

1 Sophie Watson, "Women and housing or feminist housing analysis?" *Housing Studies* (January 1986):1.

2 The Ontario Women's Directorate with assistance from the Ministry of Housing sponsored and funded this research from July, 1989, to March, 1992. The data were collected throughout this period.

3 Janet McClain with Cassie Doyle, *Women and Housing: Changing Needs and the Failure of Policy* (Ottawa: The Canadian Council on Social Development with James Lorimer & Co., 1984).

4 Gerda Wekerle and Sylvia Novac, *Gender and Housing in Toronto* (Toronto: City of Toronto Women and Work Institute, 1991): 27. The figures are based on an analysis of 1986 Statistics Canada Public Use Sample Tapes, Individual File for women living in the Census Metropolitan Area of Toronto, Ontario.

5 Elaine Weeks, Jacqueline Boles, Albeno Garbin, and John Blount, "The transformation of sexual harassment from a private trouble into a public issue." *Sociological Inquiry* 56, no. 4 (Fall) 1986, p. 432.

6 Catherine MacKinnon, *The Sexual Harassment of Working Women* (New Haven: Yale University Press, 1979): 7.

7 See Annette Fuentes and Madelyn Miller, "Unreasonable access: sexual harassment comes home, *City Limits* 11 (June/July 1986): 16–22; Andrea Boroff Eagan, "The girl in 1-A," *Mademoiselle* (April 1987): 252–255; Janet Bode, "Sex for shelter: when your landlord wants more then the rent," *Glamour* (November 1987): 318 *et passim*): and Jean Franczyk, "No peace at home: sexual harassment surfaces as problem for tenants," *The Chicago Reporter* 17 (July, 1988): 1, 6–7.

8 See Regina Cahan, "Home is no haven: an analysis of sexual harassment in housing," *Wisconsin Law Review* 6 (1987): 1061–1097 for an assessment of the pervasiveness of sexual harassment in housing based on a survey of 150 fair housing agencies.

9 Lyne Bourbonniere, Manon Cote, Jacqueline Desrosiers, and Edith Ouellet, *Discrimination, Harcèlement et Harcèlement Sexuel: Rapport de l'Enquête Femmes et Logement* (Montréal: Comité Logement Rosemont, Front Populaire en Réamènagement Urbain, avril 1986).

10 L. Bourbonniere, M. Cote, J. Desrosiers, E. Ouellet, J. Aubin, and G. Paquin, *Discrimination, Harcèlement et Harcèlement Sexuel* (Montreal: Comité Logement Rosemont, 1986).

11 Questionnaires were mailed to 1,000 randomly selected tenant household addresses. The effective response rate (conservative) was 38 percent. With adjustments for households without women, the response rate is 44 percent. Assuming differential response rates for women and men, the rate may be argued to approach 50 percent.

12 James Gruber, "A typology of personal and environmental sexual harassment: research and policy implications for the 90s," *Sex Roles* (March 1992).

13 Gruber has argued that we have little information on the effects of witnessing sexual harassment, or, I would add, the effects of disclosures from personal friends and family. The broadest net was cast for women who have been affected, especially in recognition of the classic problem of under-reporting in research on sexual harassment.

14 Lyne Bourbonniere *et al.*, ibid.

15 Annette Fuentes and Madelyn Miller, "Unreasonable access: sexual harassment comes home," *City Limits* 11 (June/July 1986).

16 Darlene C. DeFour, "The interface of racism and sexism on college campuses," in Michele A. Paludi (ed.), *Ivory Power: Sexual Harassment on Campus* (New York: State University of New York Press, 1990): 45.

17 Hearings into the appointment of Clarence Thomas came to heightened public attention when Anita Hill claimed that Thomas had sexually harassed her while she had worked for him years earlier.

18 A request to the Human Rights Commission for access to all the relevant closed files resulted in nine records being forwarded more than one year later. The explanation given was that computerized retrieval by complaint type was hampered by system limitations.

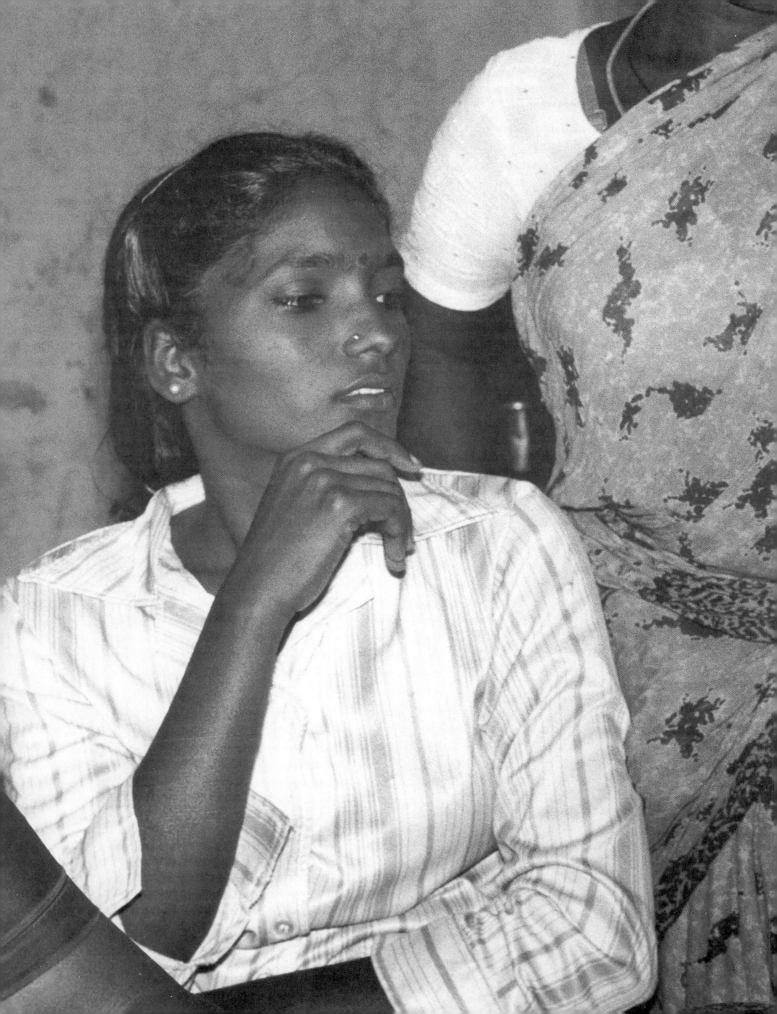

Theme 2
The Structure of Legal Interventions

Laws, whether statutory, customary, or common, have numerous significant implications for women's access to shelter, as addressed in this theme. The papers illustrate, through a historical examination of specific contexts, legacies of the law whereby gender-biased policies are perpetuated. They also suggest some remedies. The first two papers are about prevailing conditions in the United States. The first paper, (Bishop) shows that the current housing shortage in the country is particularly a crisis for poor women, a majority of whom are renters. For this group, gaining access to public or subsidized housing can be critical in preventing homelessness. Bishop's work describes the ways in which women's security in tenure of federally assisted housing can be addressed through passage of appropriate legislation and its aggressive enforcement. The second paper (Dabir) demonstrates this with a description of the positive effects of the Fair Housing Amendments Act of 1988 in mitigating the problems poor women face in gaining access to affordable housing. A conceptual, theoretical position is posited in the third paper (Sayne) in which two ideological ways to view the right to housing— patriarchal and feminist—are discussed. How these ideologies are, or might be, reflected within legal frameworks is discussed in a cross-national context. The next two papers, set in Botswana (Larsson) and Nigeria (Oruwari), highlight the discrimination which are most in need of gender-sensitive reform, and to pinpoint where intervention may be most appropriate and feasible.

Photo: *Hemalata C. Dandekar*

Chapter 9
Federally Assisted Housing:
A Housing Crisis for Poor Women

Catherine M. Bishop

Catherine M. Bishop *received her Bachelor of Arts degree from Skidmore College in 1965 and her Jurisprudence Doctorate from Catholic University Law School in 1973. She is a staff attorney with the National Housing Law Project, a legal services support center where she has written, along with other staff, the practice manual, HUD Housing Programs: Tenants' Rights. She has also written other articles regarding federally assisted housing programs.*

This nation is facing a housing crisis. There is a grave lack of safe, sanitary and decent housing at levels affordable to the poor. In 1989 there were 12 million households that had incomes below the poverty level, which means an income of approximately $10,000 for a family of three.[1] This housing shortage is a particular crisis for poor women. More than half of all poor households in 1989 were women living alone or female-headed households.[2] In 1989, about three-fifths (i.e., 7.5 million) of all poor households were renters. Approximately 70% of the single-parent poor households were renters. In 1989, more than half of the single-parent households (53%) spent more than 30% of income on housing; 31% spent more than 50% of income on housing, lived in substandard housing, or both.[3]

What is Creating the Housing Crisis?

There is a widening gap between the supply and the demand for low-rent housing. Low-rent housing is housing affordable by a poor person paying 30% of income for rent. For example, if net income is $10,000, the affordable rent would be $250 per month (30% of monthly income of $833). In 1970 there were 6.9 million low-income units and 6.4 million low-income renters. In other words, there were more affordable units than poor families. By 1989 there were 9.6 million poor renters, an increase of 3.2 million, but only 5.5 million low-rent units. In 1989, there was an affordable housing gap of 4.1 million units. The gap is probably wider today because of the recession and slow economic recovery.

The Federal Housing Programs Are Not Meeting the Need

The government assists only one-third, or 2.7 million, of the poor-renter households. The remaining 4.8 million poor-renter households paid the full cost of housing without government assistance. Three-fifths of all households in subsidized housing are elderly women or female-headed households.[4] There are estimated to be 1.8 million people on the waiting lists for public and subsidized housing.[5] Federal funding for poor households declined precipitously in the 1980s. From fiscal year 1977 to 1980, HUD made commitments to assist an average of 290,000 families each year. From 1981 to fiscal year 1991 the average number of new commitments fell to 78,000 per year. Had the level of commitment been maintained during the 1980s, some 2.3 million more poor families would be receiving assistance.

The amount of housing benefits provided to poor families should be contrasted with the housing subsidies that primarily benefit the middle and upper income families. In fiscal year 1990, direct federal spending on low-income housing assistance was $18.3 billion. But the tax deductions for mortgage interest and property taxes amounted to $78.4 billion, or more than four times as much. These tax benefits go to the highest-income families. In 1991, some 81% of the tax benefits from mortgage interest went to 20% of the families, those with incomes above $50,000. In addition, the richest 5%—the 4.3 million households with incomes above $100,000—received 31% of the benefits of this deduction.

The Current Stock of Federally Assisted Housing Is Threatened

Currently, 1.3 million families are served by the public housing program. During the 1980s nearly 15,000 units of public housing were lost. In 1987, it was anticipated that as many as 50,000 more units could be lost.[6] In 1990 about 80,000 public housing units across the country were vacant. About two-thirds of these were vacant because of needed rehabilitation.[7]

Prior to 1990 it was anticipated that as many as 300,000 units of federally subsidized housing would be lost through prepayment of the federal mortgages by private owners and cancellation of all federal controls. Congress has addressed this problem.[8] But the Act is estimated to cost $2.9 billion in fiscal year 1993 and similar amounts for the next several years. If the funds are not provided, the federally subsidized private owners will be able to leave the program and displace their tenants. Over 960,000 units of Section 8 housing are also threatened. Similar to the operation of public housing, Section 8 pays the difference between 30% of tenant income and a contract rent for the unit. Contracts for these units are expiring. It will cost nearly $30 billion to renew the contracts for all these units in the next four years.

Women Residents and Applicants for Public and Federally Assisted Housing Face Special Barriers

Women have faced barriers in obtaining admission to federally assisted housing. Housing is not an entitlement program. Not every eligible low-income tenant is entitled to a low-rent unit or housing subsidy. Federally assisted landlords and public housing authorities establish admissions criteria to determine who is eligible

and to screen tenants so as not to admit tenants who will not be able to comply with the obligations of tenancy. Some PHAs and federally assisted landlords have interpreted their obligation to screen tenants in a manner that denies housing to certain classes of women. These PHAs and landlords have adopted admissions criteria that have nothing to do with whether the family or individual will fulfill the obligations of tenancy. Instead, the criteria are based upon the individual's status. For example, PHAs and federally assisted landlords have excluded families because the head of household was an unwed mother,[9] a battered spouse,[10] not a member of a two-parent household,[11] or had not established a residence separate from the current family member whom she wished to leave.[12]

Many women have successfully challenged such admission policies. The successful cases have been those that attacked established policies of the PHA or landlord which sought to exclude a certain class of applicants. One of the first public housing admissions cases involved a challenge to the automatic exclusion of unwed mothers from housing run by the Housing Authority of Little Rock.[13] The court proscribed the automatic exclusion of unwed mothers, describing the policy as "drastic beyond reasonable necessity." In the court's eyes the policy possessed the fatal flaws of inflexibility and general disharmony with the spirit and aims of the low-rent housing program. In so finding the court explained that the prohibition was absolute, making no distinction between the unwed mother with one child and the unwed mother with ten children. Shortly after the decision in *Thomas*, HUD issued a directive which prohibited a PHA from establishing policies which automatically deny admission to a particular class, such as unmarried mothers.[14]

Despite this directive, nearly fifteen years later the New York City Housing Authority was sued by a number of applicants including a battered woman who wanted admission to public housing but was being denied it because she had not established a residency independent from the batterer and lived independently for six months.[15] This minimum duration-of-family composition policy was also found to be illegal. The *James* court relied upon the decision in *Thomas* and the regulations to strike down the policy because it created an absolute category and denied housing to everyone who fell into the category without allowing for a fuller investigation to determine the individual circumstances of the applicant. Thus, the lesson of this case is that, despite clearly enunciated regulations, the tenant had to resort to litigation to obtain admission. Undoubtedly similar policies in effect that adversely affect women in particular have not been challenged, and prevent women from obtaining the affordable housing that they desire.

The more difficult case is that of the battered spouse who was denied a unit because the PHA director feared for her safety if she were to be admitted to the public housing unit.[16] The relevant facts in this case are that the applicant was residing in temporary housing owned by the public housing authority that was leased to a battered women's shelter. The aggressor was at the time of the assault staying with friends or one of his two sisters who also lived in the project. The batterer damaged PHA property at the time of the assault. The applicant filed and obtained a protective order after the assault at the project. Criminal charges were not pursued because she did not receive notice of the hearing. Later the applicant filed criminal charges against the batterer on a subsequent assault for which he served 10 days. The mother of the applicant was a long-time employee of the PHA, and she told the director that she feared for her daughter's life if she were admitted to the project.

The court in upholding the denial of admission found that the PHA had not acted in an arbitrary or capricious manner. The opinion of the court is, however, wrong. It is arbitrary and capricious to deny admission to an applicant based upon the acts of a third party over whom the applicant had no control, especially since she took all reasonable steps to prevent the recurrence. The reason that this case is more difficult is because it provides the appearance of an individualized determination, but fails to focus on the policy of excluding an individual based upon the acts of a third party over whom the tenants had no control. The court also noted but failed to weigh the changed circumstances (i.e., the actions that the applicant took to prevent the recurrence) which indicate the probability of future favorable conduct.[17] Finally, it is likely that this opinion would not be followed today because a person who lives with an individual who engages in physical violence is considered involuntarily displaced and is afforded a priority for admissions to public housing and Section 8.[18] This priority policy could be used to overcome the PHA's policy based upon a claim of fear for the safety of the applicant and should aid in convincing a court or PHA that excluding a tenant on this basis is arbitrary.

Women also face barriers in maintaining the federally assisted housing at affordable rental levels. Most low-income tenants residing in federally assisted housing pay a rent set at 30% of adjusted income. Because rent is a function of income, the definition of income is very

important. Family income is defined to include all income anticipated in the next 12 months. Child support payments are considered to be income. Women are often charged more for rent because child support payments are included in income, whether the woman receives the payment or not. Those tenants who have challenged the practice have been successful in getting the landlords to exclude this income.[19] But the problem will undoubtedly recur because PHAs and federally assisted landlords are instructed to include the child support and alimony and to exclude it (in the case of several programs) only if the tenant reports that it has not been received and has taken steps to collect the money, including filing a court action or with the appropriate agencies. There is no basis for requiring tenants to take steps to collect child support payments or pay an excessive rent, but the HUD policy has not been changed.[20] In addition, there is no directive explaining to the PHAs and federally assisted landlords that child support is notoriously an unreliable source of income for poor women, so that care should be used to anticipate it realistically.

Women are also harmed by a related policy that includes that child support payments in the income of the payer, even though the payer does not receive the income because it is deducted from payer income through garnishment.[21] Such a policy discourages the payer, generally the man, from earning income and thereby increasing the child support payment: his rent, based upon 30% of his income, will include the payment and thus exceed ability to pay.

Both of these issues, including income, for purposes of establishing rent, money not actually received, and a deduction for payments made for child or spousal support, have been addressed in legislation.[22] But these legislative changes were made subject to appropriation acts and Congress has not taken the necessary next step in an appropriations act.

Women also face eviction for reasons that impact adversely upon them because they are women. Women are often faced with eviction for the acts of guest or other third parties and for allegations that they have boyfriends living in their apartments. In federally assisted housing, tenants can be evicted only for good cause. The case law is still developing to define the permissible grounds for eviction. But good cause is generally defined to mean that there must be a serious or repeated violation of the lease or local law. Using this standard, women whom the PHAs have sought to evict because they were assaulted and battered on the premises have argued that there were no grounds for eviction because the disturbance was a one-time event that did not seriously disturb other tenants.[23]

In situations involving the acts of other third parties, women and others have successfully argued that they should not be evicted for the acts of parties over whom they have no control or for acts of which they have no knowledge. Thus a woman has successfully argued that she should not be evicted because a brother brought a gun into the apartment without the tenant's knowledge.[24] In another case, a woman's tenancy was threatened by a fight between a boyfriend and ex-spouse and subsequent property damage by the then ex-boyfriend and assault by the ex-spouse. But because the tenant could not have known that the fight would happen, and took steps to keep the ex-spouse off the premises, she retained her tenancy.[25]

A change in circumstances or responsible reaction to an unanticipated event are also arguments that women have used successfully. For example, women have argued that they reported the assault of the batterer to the police, or that they have obtained a restraining order to keep the aggressive individual away from the unit, or have excluded the offending family member from the household.

When the project owner or PHA is seeking to evict a woman because her boyfriend is allegedly living with her, the arguments made by the woman to retain her tenancy are different. In some cases the woman is in a Catch-22 situation. She wants the man on the lease but the landlord will not permit it, and upon being informed of the tenant's desire the landlord seeks to evict her. In these cases the woman argues that the landlord's action to deny her request for a lease change is arbitrary. The issues become more complicated when the individual that the woman wants to add to the lease has a criminal record. But some tenant organizations have been able to negotiate with the landlord. The tenant has to demonstrate changed circumstances that will portend the boyfriend's or spouse's favorable future behavior.

When the man is merely visiting, tenants have successfully argued that PHAs and federally assisted landlords cannot impose standards of morality upon the tenant if the tenant's conduct is not interfering with others tenants' use and enjoyment of the property. This argument is most successful when the boyfriend who sleeps over at a woman's apartment has another fixed place of residence.[26] The woman has a more difficult argument when the boyfriend has no other fixed place of

residency but still is not living with her. Nevertheless, some courts have been sympathetic to the woman's position and have focused the inquiry on whether the facts demonstrate that the man was actually living in the unit or was just visiting.[27]

Conclusion and Recommendations

The issues facing women applying for or residing in federally assisted housing are varied. The most significant problem, however, is the critical lack of affordable units. This lack is most emphasized by the statistic that one-third of the homeless population is women with children. The issues involving a woman's security in tenure in federally assisted housing can be addressed through legislation and aggressive enforcement of tenant's rights. Some recommendations for action are:

— Expand the public housing program and continue to fund the Section 8 Certificate program so that more families are served.

— Increase the operating subsidies for public housing so that the vacant units can be rehabilitated and returned to the market and the occupied units can be adequately maintained. Also, fully fund the flexible subsidy program so that federally subsidized, privately owned housing can be fixed up.

— Monitor compliance with the current requirement that for every public housing unit sold or demolished another is built.[28]

— Demand adequate funding of the prepayment program for the federally subsidized projects.

— Demand adequate funding for the extension of the expiring Section 8 contracts.

— Urge that the tax deduction that a family can take for mortgage interest and taxes be changed (by either capping it, changing the deduction to a credit, or eliminating the deduction for a second home) and that any savings be earmarked specifically for low-income housing.[29]

— Amend the Public Housing and Section 8 statute to provide that "no tenant or household member shall be evicted for activities of others if he or she did not know about these activities or did not consent to them."

— Implement the statutory provisions (1) defining income that states that "any amounts not actually received by the family may not be considered as income"[30] and permitting (2) the deduction of $550 for each dependent, (3) the $550 deduction for payments made for child or spousal support, (4) the deduction of medical expenses for non-elderly families and the deduction of 10% of earned income.[31]

— Limit project owners and PHAs admissions criteria to consideration of only (1) the applicant's history of meeting financial obligations including rent, (2) any history of the applicant's family causing a disturbance to neighbors or destruction of property, (3) any history of criminal activity, and (4) any prior evictions. Any information should be considered only to the extent that it provides a sound basis for predicting the applicant's likelihood of defaulting on his or her obligations as a tenant. Consideration must also begiven to the time, nature, and extent of the applicant's conduct and any other factors which might indicate a reasonable probability of favorable future conduct.

Notes

[1] Unless otherwise noted, the statistics cited in this paper are from Lazere, Edward B., *A Place to Call Home; The Low Income Housing Crisis Continues,* Center on Budget and Policy Priorities (Wash. D.C. 1991).

[2] Of the 4.5 million poor people who lived alone 73% were women, two-thirds of which were elderly. Nearly one-half of the 7.9 million poor households of two or more were female-headed.

[3] In 1989, 62 percent of the poor elderly households were homeowners. But they too bore a heavy cost of housing. Approximately 68 percent of the poor elderly spent at least 30 percent of their income on housing and 41 percent spent at least half of their income on housing.

[4] *Unlocking the Door: An Action Program for Meeting the Housing Needs of Women,* Women and Housing Task Force, National Low Income Housing Coalition (March 1991).

[5] These figures are not completely reflective of the need. The waiting lists may contain duplicate names as some people apply for several types of housing. But many PHAs and project owners have closed their waiting lists, so that no new families can apply.

[6] National Housing L. Project, *Public Housing in Peril,* Berkeley: National Housing Law Project, 1990.

[7] There is more than likely an overlap between the units projected for demolition and the number of vacant units. These two figures were obtained from different reports.

[8] 12 U.S.C. § 12,713.

[9] *James v. Housing Auth.,* 282 F. Supp. 575 (E.D. Ark. 1967).

[10] *Ullom v. Housing Auth.,* No 82-0085-W (N.D. W. Va. June 21, 1983).

[11] *Hoskie v. Housing Auth.,* No. N 78-17 (D. Conn. consent decree filed Oct. 27, 1983), 17 *Clearinghouse Rev.* 1,240 (No 23,499, Mar. 1984).

[12] *James v. New York City Hous. Auth.,* 622 F. Supp. 1356 (S.D.N.Y. 1985).

[13] *Thomas v. Housing Auth.,* 282 F. Supp 575 (E.D. Ark. 1967).

[14] 24 C.F.R. § 960.204 (1991).

[15] *James v. Housing Auth.,* 282 F. Supp. 575 (E.D. Ark. 1967).

[16] *Ullom v. Housing Auth.,* CA No 82-0085-W (N.D. W.Va. June 21, 1983).

[17] 24 C.F.R. § 960.205(d) (1991) (the criteria for selecting applicants shall include consideration of other mitigation information if adverse information is received).

[18] See, e.g., 24 C.F.R. § 960.211(d)(2) (1991).

[19] See, e.g., Letter from Kirk L. Gray, HUD Regional Director, Office of Public Housing (Region III), to Tony Sade, Legal Aid Society of Charleston, West Virginia (Sept. 1985) (in income determination calculations, when there is a verifiable pattern of nonpayment of child support, PHA should consider the *actual* documented pattern of payments, not the payments ordered by the court); *Johnson v. United States Dept. of Agriculture,* 734 F.2d 774 (11th Cir. 1984) (FmHA case involving, *inter alia,* challenge to policy of including as income all court-ordered support payments: court stated that FmHA will have to prove reasonableness of this income calculation.

[20] Compare Hemekes v. Plourde, No. SKO-90-FE-84 (D. Me. Apr. 17, 1991) (only income received is counted towards rent calculations; failure of tenant to attempt to collect child support due but not paid is not 'grounds for eviction for nonpayment of rent in Section 8 new construction unit, despite HUD Occupancy Requirements of Subsidized Multifamily Housing Programs 4350.3, through CHG-20 (Nov. 1981–Jan. 1992), ¶ 3–6), CHG-1 (Mar. 1985).

[21] *Lorain Metropolitan Housing Auth. v. Cajka,* No. 88 CVG 1065 (Ohio Mun. Ct., Lorain Cnty., Feb. 6, 1989) (Clearinghouse No. 44,256) (child support payments are not income for the payor).

[22] 42 U.S.C. § 1437a(b)(4) and (5).

[23] *Moundsville Hous. Auth. v. Porter,* 370 S.E.2d 341 (W.Va. 1988) (beating of tenant by boyfriend was not good cause to evict even though tenant did not take steps before the assault to exclude him from household); *Heartland Realty Management, Inc. v. Case,* CV-90-04160 (Idaho 3rd Dist. Crt., Canyon Cnty., Finding of Fact Conclusions of Law & Order, Dec. 28, 1990) (Clearinghouse No. 46,512) (no good cause for parties and domestic violence because other tenants had similar parties and only proof of disturbance of other tenants due to domestic violence was that police were called).

[24] *Chicago Hous. Auth. v. Rose,* 148 Ill. Dec. 534, 560 N.E.2d 1131 (Ill. App., 1st Dist. 1990) (guns in apartment without tenant's knowledge are not grounds for eviction).

[25] *Peabody Properties v. Donnelly,* No. 18066 (Mass. Super. Ct. Apr. 26, 1985), *aff'd,* 22 Mass. App. 1101 (1986).

[26] See, e.g., *Messiah Baptist Hous. Dev. Fund v. Rosser,* 400 N.Y.S.2d 306 (1977).

[27] *Kurdi v. DuPage Cnty. Hous. Auth.,* 161 Ill. App.3d 988, 514 N.E.2d 802 (1987) (reversing trial court approval of Section 8 termination decision based on alleged unauthorized occupant because the decision was based on hearsay and against "manifest weight of evidence").

[28] 42 U.S.C. § 1437p.

[29] In California it is estimated that if the mortgage interest deduction was capped at $70,000, it would save $60 million.

[30] 42 U.S.C. § 1437a(b)(4).

[31] 42 U.S.C. § 1437a(b)(5).

Chapter 10
The Fair Housing Amendments Act of 1988: Creating New Housing Opportunities for Women

Surabhi Dabir

Surabhi Dabir is the Senior Reference Specialist for the HUD Fair Housing Information Clearinghouse and is the contributing author for the Clearinghouse newsletter, Fair Housing Update. She has a Bachelor of Architecture from the University of Bombay and a Master of Urban Planning from the University of Michigan. She is an active member of the National Women and Housing Task Force, and the Education and Training committee of the Interagency Fair Housing Coordinating Group in Rockville, Maryland. She is also the coeditor of the newsletter published by the Organization of Pan Asian American Women.

Women and their children are the group most affected by the housing crisis. Few single mothers are homeowners; most rent their homes, paying a substantial percentage of their income for housing. Women of color bear a disproportionate burden of poverty and housing needs. This burden is made heavier by discrimination; women who maintain families face discrimination because of sex, marital status, income source, and the presence of children. While it is difficult to totally change discriminatory behavior, it is possible to reduce its incidence by making it illegal. Victims have to be educated about their rights, and perpetrators of discriminatory practices have to be punished by levying severe monetary penalties.

The adoption of the Fair Housing Amendments Act of 1988 has demonstrated that developing and enforcing enabling legislation can address and mitigate the problems faced by women in gaining access to safe, decent, affordable housing of their choice. This paper discusses provisions under the Fair Housing Amendments Act of 1988 and their implications for women seeking housing. What the law does and does not do is reviewed, followed by a summary of the nature and extent of progress made in eliminating discriminatory housing practices against women. In conclusion, an analysis of the obstacles that remain is presented, with recommendations for overcoming them, so that the Fair Housing Law can indeed remove some of the obstacles now impeding women who seek housing.

A Profile of the Problem

Alice and her two children, Tom and Sally, are escaping an abusive family situation. Alice is determined to make things work. She has a job and a few good friends to support her. Once she finds an apartment to rent, she can get on with her life, raise her children, and put the past behind her. She stays with friends temporarily, doubling up while she hunts for her apartment with optimism. But everywhere she goes she finds doors slammed in her face.

> We have no apartments for you. We rent only to young, single people. You will feel out of place here.

> This is an adults only community. We don't allow children under 18 years of age to live here.

> You will have to rent a three-bedroom apartment. We cannot allow your son and daughter to share a bedroom. Can you afford that?

The rents here are probably too high for a single mother like you but I'm sure we can work out an arrangement, honey.

Hope turns to despair as Alice finds herself moving further and further away from her chosen area of residence, resigned to accept a long commute to her job, to change her children's school, and to move away from the support of her friends. Perhaps her story will end in a homeless shelter, or worse, on the street. Alice's story illustrates the problems faced by countless women in the United States. According to the National Coalition against Domestic Violence, one out of three women will experience domestic violence in her lifetime. The latest nationwide statistics report that approximately 374,000 women and their children are given emergency housing in 1,200 shelters annually, and approximately 150,000 are turned away for lack of room. These numbers are increasing. A Ford Foundation report claims that 50 percent of all homeless women and children in this country are fleeing domestic violence.

The lack of adequate affordable housing and federal assistance for low-income persons affects women in poverty more severely than any other group. Their predicament is exacerbated by widespread discrimination against families with children, and by numerous other forms of housing discrimination faced by women. *Female Headed Households*, a report published by the Office of Policy Development and Research (Limmer:1978), documented statistics on the housing problems faced specifically by women and children in poverty. According to the report, women heads-of-household and their children lived disproportionately in substandard housing and paid a higher percentage of their incomes for housing compared with the national average. If a woman was black, Hispanic, or headed a large family, she was more likely to be poorly housed. Other studies and research in conjunction with lobbying by housing advocacy groups finally led to the amendment of the Fair Housing Act to prohibit discrimination against families with children.

Despite this, the significance of change in family life and the prevalence of women-maintained households are not yet an integral part of public consciousness. Single mothers are still regarded as a deviation from the family norm, societal liabilities instead of assets. This is because most are poor and have limited access to opportunities for self-sufficiency. The following section describes the problems women continue to face and discusses the complexity of associated issues.

Diminishing Stock of Affordable Housing

Affordability of housing is a growing problem. While housing-related costs have risen significantly, the supply of low-cost rental housing is disappearing. In 1970, there were 9.7 million units that rented for $250 or less (30 percent of a $10,000 annual income). By 1985, that number had dropped precipitously to 7.9 million (National Low Income Housing Coalition, 1990). There are now more than two low-income households for each affordable unit in the inventory. Affordable housing for the poor has decreased by 19 percent between 1978 and 1985 (U.S. Bureau of the Census et al., 1989). Though the homeless are the most visible manifestation of the affordable housing crisis, much of the problem remains hidden and undocumented. Many households are paying more than 50 percent of their income for rent or doubling up with other families to stay housed (Dolbeare, 1990). Today, nationally, one out of five single mothers is living doubled up, a step away from homelessness (Pearce, 1990).

Growth in Households of Women and Children in Poverty

In the last quarter century, the number of poor households headed by women has doubled, with increases of roughly 100,000 each year (Pearce, 1990). According to a study conducted by the National Women in Housing Task Force, more than two-thirds of all poor renter households with children are maintained by women. Conservative census figures report that in 1988, single mothers supported 23.7 percent of all families with children under 18 (U.S. Bureau of the Census, 1989). More recent statistics cite the number of single-mother households as 8.8 million (Pearce, 1990). Poverty is the norm for women-maintained renter families with children; with a poverty rate of 58 percent in 1986, they were more than three times as likely as other renter families to be poor. Sixty percent of these poor women-maintained families with children were living in unsubsidized, private sector units.

Women in poverty are not a homogenous group. This makes understanding the complexities of their problems even more difficult. Some women are the sole support of their children through choice or as a result of the death of a spouse, separation, or divorce. Many have been victims of abuse, violence, or incest. Influenced by family, partners, peers, or the pain of their circumstance, some single mothers have backgrounds of substance abuse (Sprague, 1991). Furthermore, this group is composed of homeless women, battered women, displaced homemakers, rural women, elderly women, women in public housing and other groups of women with special needs, each having distinctive circumstances and problems with no one clear solution.

Single-women-maintained families with children are often invisible, doubling and tripling up with other families, living in abandoned housing, old cars, and even chicken coops and campsites. Many single mothers, particularly those who are homeless, are virtually alone in the world. In a research study, most homeless women cited their social worker or their children as their only supportive relationship (Bassuk et al., 1987). According to the National Coalition for the Homeless, both census and poverty figures record only those who have addresses. Single-mother households, therefore, are counted only if they have a home or if they are not sharing homes with relatives, in which instance they are counted as part of the relative's family. A single mother does not report that she is homeless unless this qualifies her for housing because without adequate housing she risks losing her children to foster care. Homeless women whose children are in foster care are recorded as homeless single women. The Coalition estimates that single mothers and children comprise 40 percent of the homeless population and are cited as the fastest growing subgroup of the homeless. Based on the number of women who live doubled up and the fact that many homeless single-mother households are not included in any count, approximately 3 million women and close to 5 million of their children may need housing and services to bring stability to their lives (Sprague, 1991).

Cracks in Federal Assistance Approaches

Although HUD provides subsidies to over 4.3 million households, this is only one-third of those in need (Zigas:1990). While the number of households subsidized today is a substantial increase over the number helped in 1980, housing assistance has not kept pace with the growth of the problem.

There is a widespread misconception that if women could manage to get off welfare and acquire jobs, their housing problems would disappear. Many women who have difficulties in finding affordable housing already have jobs; employment has not solved their housing problems. A full-time minimum wage job pays less than $7,000 a year. At 30 percent of income for shelter, this provides no more than $175 monthly for housing costs, far less than the amount usually needed (National

Women and Housing Task Force, 1991). In addition, in about 32 states, the maximum public assistance cash benefit for a family of three is below 50 percent of poverty level (Shapiro and Greenstein, 1988). To compound matters, the average waiting period for most assisted housing is 22 months.

Problems Compounded by Discrimination

Women-maintained families face discrimination because of sex, race, marital status, and income source. In addition, they have had to contend with limited housing options because of widespread discrimination against children in rental housing. In 1980, HUD released a nationwide survey showing that 25 percent of all rental units excluded children; another 50 percent of the units limited families' access by imposing restrictions on the age, number, and sex of children. Of the families that were interviewed in the survey, 50 percent had recently experienced difficulty in finding housing because of exclusionary policies and 20 percent were living in less desirable housing because of these policies. Other studies of local housing markets have confirmed that child discrimination is widespread in numerous states across the nation (Morales, 1988).

The nationwide emergence of housing discrimination against children is related to long-term demographic trends. The number of households in the United States has grown much faster than the population because of the higher proportion of single-person households (and childless couples). This significant increase in smaller households adversely affects housing opportunities for families with children in two ways, by increasing the demand for housing, and increasing the number of childless (and therefore preferred) adults competing for it.

A study of the racial composition of single-women-maintained families indicates that discrimination against children falls with particular severity on Hispanic and Black households. Four-fifths of Hispanic women householders have children, as do four-fifths of Black women householders, compared to three-fifths of all female householders (Women and Housing Task Force, 1991). Other factors that have a discriminatory impact on the housing opportunities available to women include sexual harassment in housing, prejudiced advertising, zoning regulations that prevent the building of group homes for women such as homes for battered women, and discriminatory practices in the sale, rental, and financing of housing.

The Response

One approach to combating the problems enumerated so far is the adoption of appropriate legislation and enforcement mechanisms at the federal level. In response to what had become a growing problem, the Fair Housing Amendments Act of 1988 addressed the issue of discrimination faced by women seeking housing. It is one example of enabling legislation that improves women's access to available, affordable housing. Through enforcement, education, and outreach, the law provides victims with information about their rights. In the event of discrimination, the victim has recourse to monetary and compensatory remedies. Together, this results in increasing housing opportunities for women. This legislation, though not drafted only with women in mind, has a profound impact on the particular situation of women. It addresses the concerns of women seeking shelter, whether as single parents or, more generally as individuals seeking housing that is safe and responsive to their needs.

An Overview of the Fair Housing Amendments Act of 1988: One Step In the Right Direction

"The Fair Housing Amendments Act of 1988" (Public Law 100430) was passed by the 100th Congress on September 13, 1988. The Act, effective on March 12, 1989, was the result of more than ten years of congressional effort to amend the 1968 Fair Housing Act. The Amendments added handicap and familial status to the classes protected from discrimination and expanded the enforcement powers of the Departments of Housing and Urban Development, and of Justice. The Fair Housing Act specifically prohibits discrimination in the sale or rental of dwellings; in residential real estate-related transactions; and in the provision of services and facilities in association with such activities on the basis of race, color, religion, sex, disability, familial status, or national origin.

Overall, the Fair Housing Amendments Act expands protection under the law to families with children and persons with disabilities, creates additional administrative remedies and enforcement mechanisms for housing discrimination, prohibits discrimination in all kinds of residential financing, and imposes stiff civil penalties for violations. The new Act also requires reasonable modification of dwellings to accommodate persons with disabilities, and that the design and construction of certain new multifamily dwellings scheduled for first occupancy after March 13, 1991, meet stipulated adaptability and accessibility requirements. Highlights

of the stronger enforcement provisions of the 1988 Amendments include the following:

— The Act extends the time for filing a complaint from 180 days after the alleged discriminatory act occurred to one year after the discriminatory act occurred or terminated.
— It empowers the HUD Secretary to investigate complaints of interference, coercion, or intimidation filed by any person exercising a fair housing right.
— The HUD Secretary is authorized to initiate an investigation of housing practices without a complaint and to file a complaint.
— The Attorney General is entrusted with the power to seek prompt judicial action on behalf of a complainant, when authorized by the HUD Secretary.
— Finally, the Act sets stringent time frames for HUD investigation and resolution of complaints.

These administrative and judicial processes are significant because they provide victims of discrimination with an avenue of redress other than private litigation when HUD's conciliation efforts fail.

The U.S. Department of Housing and Urban Development anticipates the new regulatory structure established by the Act to lead to more aggressive enforcement of the Act. The increase in the number of complaints and resulting conciliations experienced since the legislation is expected to lead to greater compliance, particularly in the new protected categories of persons with disabilities and families with children. Current provisions of the Act prohibit the following discriminatory practices:

— Refusing to sell, rent, negotiate for, "or otherwise make unavailable or deny" a dwelling;
— Discrimination in the "terms, conditions, or privileges of a sale or rental" of a dwelling or in the "provision of services or facilities in connection therewith";
— Making or publishing any discriminatory statement in regard to a sale or a rental;
— Misrepresenting the availability of a dwelling;
— Inducing a person to sell or rent any dwelling by representations about the presence of members of a protected class in the neighborhood; and
— Discriminating in access to real estate services.

The law also adds a new section prohibiting discrimination in residential real estate transactions and in the terms or conditions of such transactions. These transactions include the making of loans for the purchase of a dwelling, the making of loans secured by residential units, and the "selling, brokering, or appraising of residential real property."

Historically, to encourage compliance by the private sector, HUD has relied upon Voluntary Affirmative Marketing Agreements (VAMA's) with national organizations representing components of the housing industry. With respect to the Fair Housing Act, HUD has signed voluntary agreements with the National Association of Home Builders, the National Association of Real Estate License Law Officials, National Association of Realtors, National Association of Real Estate Brokers, and the National Apartment Association. The goal is for individuals of similar income levels in the same housing market area to have similar choices in housing regardless of race, color, religion, sex, national origin, familial status, or disability. By signing the VAMA's, these groups agreed to promote equal opportunity in the sale, rental, and financing of housing; to institutionalize affirmative marketing principles in their day-to-day operations; and to encourage their state and local affiliates to sign and implement similar agreements at the state and local levels.

What the Law Does: Implications for Women in Search of Housing

Discrimination against Families with Children

Families with children have more difficulties finding and remaining in suitable housing than families without them. Until recently, many families had no remedy against the property owner who denied housing on the grounds of an adult-only policy, overly restrictive occupancy standards, or other age-restrictive practices. The recently enacted federal law, however, provides significant new remedies for discrimination against families with children, and thus creates new housing opportunities for families.

In 1980 approximately three-fourths of the nation's housing supply was unavailable to families with children because of various policies and procedures in effect, according to an estimate by the U.S. Department of Housing and Urban Development. Discriminatory policies were implemented through "excess person" surcharges, a "no kids" rule, larger than usual security or damage deposit requirements, noise regulations, or limiting use of certain facilities and services to adults. The Fair Housing Amendments Act now prohibits discrimination based on familial status. This provision by definition covers households in which a minor (a person under 18) is domiciled with:

— a parent,
— a person having legal custody of the minor, or
— a designee of the parent or person having legal custody of a minor child.

The definition of familial status also includes pregnant women and those in the process of securing legal custody of a minor child. The protected class thus includes virtually all households with children. The impact of the new law is most significant in the 34 states that do not have fair housing protection for families with children. Although there were 16 states that did already have such protection, the federal law is stronger than most of these states' nondiscrimination laws, so families in these states benefit as well (Morales, 1988). Under the Amendments, families with children have the same rights as other protected groups.

— Families with children have the right to live on any floor of a high-rise building;
— Owners and managers are not permitted to preclude families with children from living in a dwelling of their choice under the pretext of implementing stringent "occupancy codes and standards";
— Mobile home parks are covered by the Fair Housing Act and specifically by the familial status provisions; and
— Facilities segregated by familial status, i.e., with "adult only" and family sections, are unlawful.

More subtle forms of discrimination are also unlawful. For example, housing complexes commonly restrict families with children to certain buildings, floors, or units. In many cases, families with children are relegated to the least desirable units in a complex. The practice of segregating units by age or family status is essentially a refusal to sell or rent because a family with children is barred from certain units. Another common barrier to families' obtaining the housing they desire is overly restrictive occupancy standards. Property owners frequently exclude families with children from units by unduly restricting the number of occupants to a unit. Families can combat this by taking one of two approaches: they can show that the occupancy standards are intentionally designed to exclude families with children, or if they cannot prove intentional discrimination, they should be able to rely on statistical proof that overly restrictive occupancy standards have a disparate impact because they exclude a greater proportion of households with children than childless households. Several courts have held that policies having a disparate impact constitute unlawful discrimination under the Fair Housing Act.

Zoning and Group Homes

State governments and local planning and zoning boards will have to examine their local requirements closely to ensure that their codes comply with the new fair housing amendments. Some jurisdictions have taken a proactive stance and have already reviewed their own ordinances. Cambridge, Massachusetts, for example, has eliminated the requirement for a special-use permit for group homes, as well as its space requirement and density restrictions. The State of Michigan will no longer alert local agencies and neighborhood organizations to plans to open group homes nearby. Kansas has expanded its State authority over local zoning. In fact, the only thing a jurisdiction can legally regulate now, relative to group homes, is the number of occupants, and even these must reflect public health and safety concerns.

Current regulations and zoning ordinances are formulated on the premise of someone's home being separate from work. Typically the regulations limit some residential areas to single-family houses and may further limit the number of unrelated persons that can occupy these houses. The Fair Housing Amendments prevent communities from instituting such exclusionary zoning practices. They represent the first step toward helping to formalize the sort of housing Joan Forrester Sprague describes in her book *More Than Housing: Lifeboats for Women and Children.* (Lifeboat housing encompasses a wide realm of housing choices that take into account the specific needs of women. It includes newly constructed as well as rehabilitated housing, transitional and permanent housing, providing for sharing space, child care, and social support services when necessary.)

Sexual Harassment in Housing

Sexual harassment is a criminal violation of federal and state law. It is a federal offense for someone willfully to intimidate, coerce, or interfere with any person either orally, in writing, or by other means, in connection with a residential real estate-related transaction. This includes many forms of sexual harassment, ranging from the landlord or agent (superintendent, maintenance worker, rental manager, etc.) making sexual comments or innuendoes, to actual physical assault.

Sexual harassment in housing is a new, largely unlitigated area. It is believed to be both widespread and unreported. Its victims often endure a cross

between employment discrimination and domestic violence, feeling they have no safe haven from the perpetrator. Single mothers in poverty are particularly vulnerable to landlords or apartment managers who inflict sexual extortion. When faced with the threat of eviction, most mothers tend to cling to their homes. Now the Amendments offer legal recourse to victims of this type of harassment, shifting the power balance significantly, and enabling single women and mothers to gain more control over their living situations.

Discriminatory Residential Lending Practices

Discrimination in financing of real estate-related transactions (sales, home improvement, capital construction) is now prohibited by the Fair Housing Amendments Act. Most home purchases require some form of financing from the seller, from a bank or savings and loan, or from a commercial mortgage company. The new law expands the types of financing covered to include activities relating to the purchase of loans, transactions involving the secondary mortgage market incorporating the purchase and pooling of mortgage loans and the terms and conditions of the sale of securities issued on the basis of such loans. Prohibited activities also include discrimination in the servicing of such mortgages. Typically, it has always been more difficult for women to secure real estate financing and obtain mortgages, particularly on a single income. The new law offers some measure of relief from the subtle discriminatory practices that have pervaded this arena.

Education and Outreach Initiative

Under the federal Fair Housing Initiatives Program (FHIP), HUD is authorized to make grants to, or enter into cooperative agreements with State or local government agencies, public or private nonprofit organizations, or other institutions that are administering programs to help eliminate discriminatory housing practices. The Education and Outreach component of FHIP provides funding for the purpose of developing, implementing, or coordinating education and outreach programs designed to inform the public of their rights under the fair housing law. Funded activities include the development of national, regional, and local media campaigns, and other special efforts to educate the general public and members of the housing industry about their fair housing rights and obligations.

A National Media Campaign funded under FHIP and coordinated by the National Fair Housing Alliance, an umbrella organization of 60 private, nonprofit fair housing agencies, was launched in 1991 to instruct the public about fair housing issues. One of the foci of the campaign was to generate an awareness about the new protected category of families with children and about sexual harassment in housing. Women as the casualties of discriminatory housing practices can seek justice only if they are aware of their rights and the remedies available to them by law. Education and outreach efforts serve the important function of "getting the message out." Knowledge about the new law empowers people, alerts them to subtle forms of discrimination, and enables them to seek justice.

What the Law Does Not Do

Exemptions for Housing Older Persons

The Fair Housing Amendments Act does not outlaw housing specifically designed for older persons. In establishing the protection for families with children, Congress and the civil rights community agreed that senior citizens have legitimate needs for specialized housing, and the Act clearly exempts housing for older persons from the "familial status" provision. Certain housing for older persons may exclude children, but must first demonstrate that it meets the special needs of older Americans. Housing may qualify for the "older persons" exemption if it meets one of several criteria:

— It is provided under a state or federal program specifically designed and operated to assist older persons; or
— It is intended for and occupied solely by persons 62 and over; or 80 percent of the units are occupied by at least one person 55 years of age or older, and it provides significant facilities and services for older persons, and it publishes and adheres to policies and procedures that demonstrate its intent to provide housing for persons over 55.

Fair housing advocates claim that these exemptions have to some extent resulted in a scramble by current adult-only communities to satisfy the requirements of housing for older persons, especially the 55-and-over criteria, in order to preclude the entry of families with children into the adult housing communities.

The Fair Housing Amendments Act does not require evictions of current residents of adult communities. The Act includes a transition provision intended to prevent the eviction of current residents of housing facilities that now exclude children and intend to continue to do so under one of the provisions of the older persons housing exemption. Current residents of such housing need not be counted toward qualification under the 62 and over,

or 55 and over, exemptions, provided that new residents meet the relevant age restrictions and that other relevant criteria are also met. Fair housing advocates are worried that, even though the law prohibits such actions, landlords of 55-and-over communities have sought to terminate the tenancies of families with children by requiring compliance with the adult-only rule. According to Christopher Brancart, a fair housing attorney from California, it is not unusual for landlords to defend familial status cases with the argument that current adult tenants are exempt from new 55-and-over rules, but that children must go (Brancart, 1991). This has the effect of evicting families, because parents are extremely unlikely to send their children away in order to remain in an apartment or a mobile home.

Legitimate Regulations Still Applicable

The Fair Housing Amendments will not force landlords or owners to rent or sell to families who are unsuitable residents for other legitimate reasons. The Act does not alter existing landlord-tenant laws that allow landlords, managers, and owners to refuse or evict residents on legitimate grounds: bad credit history, lease violations, or disruptive behavior, provided these criteria are equally applied to a childless resident as they are to a "family with children."

This stipulation has the effect of licensing landlords to reject applicants on the grounds of poor or inadequate credit history, according to fair housing advocates. Single-women-maintained families are particularly affected by these criteria. Traditionally, single women often have poorly established credit ratings. Frequently, the income of a single-parent does not meet the income criteria based on unit size, as established by landlords. And, paradoxically, acceptable unit size for a family is determined by number of occupants. So, the larger the family maintained by a single woman, the less likely it is that she will be able to find suitable housing. In addition, the prohibition of familial status discrimination does not preclude the construction of apartment buildings with small units, such as efficiencies.

Reasonable Occupancy Standards Allowed

The Fair Housing Amendments Act specifically states that "reasonable occupancy standards," which govern the number of persons that may occupy a unit, will not be affected. HUD General Counsel Francis Keating (Keating, 1991) has attempted to clarify HUD's position on occupancy standards and policies; owners and managers may develop and implement reasonable

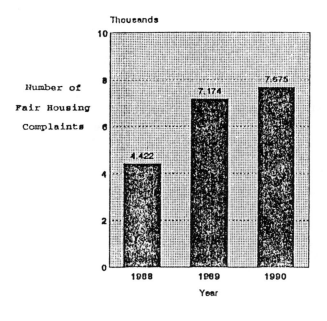

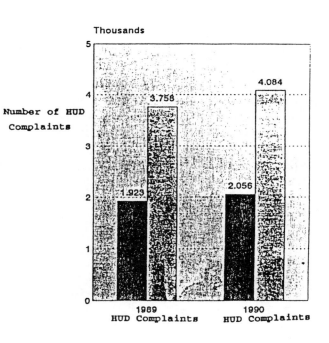

Fig. 1: Increase in Annual Fair Housing Complaints.

Fig. 2: Basis of HUD Complaints.

occupancy requirements based on factors such as the number and size of sleeping areas or bedrooms and the overall size of the dwelling unit. In the event of a complaint alleging discrimination on the basis of familial status, HUD will carefully examine any such nongovernmental restriction to determine whether it operates unreasonably to limit or exclude families with children. When HUD reviews occupancy cases, it will consider several criteria to determine whether an occupancy policy is reasonable or not:

— Size and number of bedrooms
— Size of unit
— Configuration of unit
— Age of children
— Other physical limitations of housing
— State and local law

In addition, other factors, such as discriminatory rules about the use of common facilities, and enforcement of occupancy policies only against families with children, will be examined to determine whether an occupancy policy is discriminatory (an occupancy policy that limits the number of children per unit is likely to be deemed discriminatory as opposed to one that limits the number of people per unit).

Fair housing advocates expect this position to have a disproportionate impact on single-women-maintained families; a mother with three children may find herself

unable to rent a two-bedroom apartment due to occupancy standards that stipulate a two-person-per-bedroom maximum. Lisa Mihaly of the Children's Defense Fund fears that HUD investigators, rather than using the Keating clarifications as guidance for evaluating evidence, will use the two-per-bedroom limit as a definitive test, and a shortcut to disposing of cases. Numerous advocacy groups, including the National Council of La Raza and the NAACP Legal Defense Fund, are seeking further clarifications of the allowable occupancy standards.

The Nature and Extent of Progress Made in Eliminating Discriminatory Housing Practices against Women and Children

"Enforcing fair housing for all, equally the same for everybody everywhere is our goal," HUD's Assistant Secretary for Fair Housing and Equal Opportunity Gordon Mansfield has said (Mansfield, 1990). In working toward this goal, HUD has achieved many milestones since the passage of the Fair Housing Amendments Act of 1988. Accomplishments under the Act are reported to Congress annually. The data presented are taken from "The State of Fair Housing, Report to the Congress Pursuant to Section 808(e)(2) of the Fair Housing Act, 1989 and 1990" (Fig. 1).

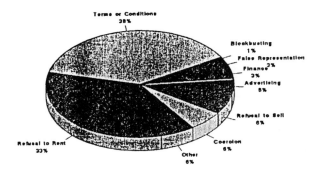

Fig. 3: Overview of Issues Raised by Complainants
in Post-Act 1989.

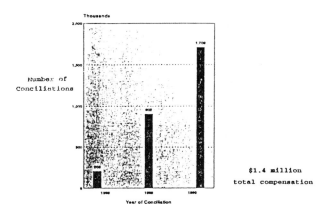

Fig. 4: HUD Conciliations.

Summary of Achievements

Increase in Annual Fair Housing Complaints

Since its passage, the Fair Housing Amendments Act
has had a profound impact on the receipt and processing
of fair housing complaints. HUD complaints more than
tripled from the previous year. In part, the increase was
due to the new prohibitions against familial status and
handicap discrimination.

A record 7,675 Fair Housing complaints were filed with
HUD and State and local agencies in 1990, exceeding
the number filed in 1989, also a record, by more than
500.

Familial Status as Basis of Discrimination

After the Amendments took effect, more than half of the
HUD complaints alleged discrimination on the basis of
familial status (Fig. 2).

Four-fifths of all HUD complaints in post-Act 1989
alleged only one basis of the discrimination, while the
remainder were filed on multiple bases. Most of the
single-basis complaints were familial status complaints
and included the following:

— Challenges to housing providers' claims to exemptions as
  housing for older persons.
— Occupancy limits applied to children but not adults.
— Refusal to rent to families with children under a certain
  age.
— Exclusion of children from services provided to adults.

To facilitate resolution of the growing volume of
complaints, HUD signed a total of 34 contracts with
State and local agencies for investigating familial status

and handicap discrimination complaints. These contracts have greatly expanded HUD's resources for
processing complaints. Sex discrimination accounted
for about 15 percent of all allegations by 1990, including
allegations of:

— Sexual harassment
— Differential terms and conditions
— Refusal to approve a mortgage application

Complaints alleging coercion, intimidation, threats, or
interference with fair housing rights more than doubled
by 1990, reflecting a growing public awareness regarding HUD's jurisdiction to handle these complaints
(Fig. 3).

Effective Processing of HUD Complaints

The 1988 Amendments also had a significant impact on
the processing of HUD complaints. The new law
resulted in:

— A great increase in the number of investigations and
  successful conciliations.
— Substantially more relief for complainants through
  conciliation agreements.

In 1990 HUD successfully conciliated 1,709 complaints.
Thus, conciliations grew from an average of 17 a month
prior to passage of the Act to 142 a month in 1990. For
the first three months of 1991, HUD reports processing
586 complaints (Prentice Hall, 1992). The enforcement
authority vested in HUD by the 1988 Amendments has
been an important factor in amplifying HUD's ability to
achieve successful conciliations (Fig. 4).

After passage of the Amendments Act, the total value of successful conciliations increased six times. This increase was due to :

— Growth in the number of effective conciliations.
— Escalation in the amount of each conciliation (an average of $500 more per conciliation than such amounts prior to the passage of the 1988 Amendments).

HUD obtained over $14 million in relief for conciliations in 1990—and complainants secured housing in nearly 30 percent of all conciliated cases.

A notable occurrence was that HUD and the Department of Justice obtained prompt judicial action for complainants eight times in 1989. Six of these instances were related to complaints based on familial status, while two were based on race. The first temporary restraining order (TRO) that HUD obtained under the Fair Housing Amendments Act illustrates the effectiveness of the new mechanisms of prompt judicial relief: the TRO was obtained on behalf of a family of four that had located a vacant apartment uniquely suited to its needs. The apartment had enough bedrooms, the location would enable the children to continue attending desirable schools, the rent was affordable. However, while attempting to rent the apartment, the family was told that the apartment was unavailable to families with children. When contacted by HUD, the owner refused to keep the apartment available until this issue was resolved, and further, the owner refused to process the family's application. HUD authorized the Attorney General to issue a TRO. Later, the respondents settled the case, as a result of which the family was able to move into the apartment. The family was also awarded three months' free rent. This example also illustrates that the Fair Housing Amendment Act has dramatically improved HUD's ability to conciliate disputes successfully, to obtain the respondent's agreement to take action that protects both the interests of the complainant and others who may be similarly situated, and the public, and is acceptable to both the complainant and to HUD.

Reasonable Cause Determinations

Complaints that are not conciliated are investigated by HUD, which then makes a "cause" or "no reasonable cause" determination based on whether the findings indicate that discrimination has or has not occurred. Only a few cases in which the Act has been violated are likely to reach the stage of a HUD determination, since many respondents are willing to conciliate disputes prior to a formal HUD finding. In 1990, HUD made "cause" determinations in 81 cases which were distributed across the nation. They covered a broad range of activities. Almost 75 percent of all charges alleged familial status discrimination.

Administrative Law Judge Hearings and Civil Enforcement

Subsequent to a charge of "reasonable cause for discrimination" being issued by HUD's Office of General Counsel, the discrimination case can be heard by an Administrative Law Judge (ALJ), or before a U.S. District Court Judge. Administrative Law Judges, just like the district court judges, can, in the event of a Fair Housing Act violation, order the respondent to provide relief including:

— Compensation for actual damages, including pain, humiliation, and suffering.
— Injunctive relief, such as making housing available to the aggrieved persons.
— In addition, if appropriate, attorneys' fees and other equitable relief and civil penalties, as high as $50,000 in a single case, can also be recovered.

An Administrative Law Judge cannot impose punitive damages.
In 1990, administrative law judges found Fair Housing Act violations in twelve of the thirteen cases tried. They awarded a total of $33,079 in damages to aggrieved persons and assessed $18,000 in civil penalties. Interestingly, nine of the twelve cases were against one mobile home park and resulted in a single decision, which awarded the complainants a total of $9,988 in damages and assessed the park $2,000 in civil penalties. The judge found that the park failed to demonstrate that it qualified as housing for older persons and that, therefore, by excluding children it violated the Fair Housing Act. In addition to the foregoing procedures, the 1988 Act continues to permit enforcement by direct civil action filed by the aggrieved party. The statute of limitations on such direct action has been extended to two years. A previous cap of $1,000 on punitive damages in such actions has been eliminated.

In all, HUD, the Department of Justice, and State and local agencies obtained more than $25 million in settlements, damages, and penalties—a testimony to the effectiveness of the Fair Housing Amendments Act of 1988.

Other Activities

The Department of Justice defended the Government in two lawsuits challenging the constitutionality of the Act's familial status provisions and HUD's implementing regulations. Thus, overall, through the first quarter of 1991, HUD continues to make a significant contribution in the struggle to achieve fair housing for all. The successes detailed above are indicators of the strides made in addressing equal housing opportunity for women seeking safe, decent, and affordable housing of their choice.

Comments from the Fair Housing Advocate Community

The generally skeptical fair housing advocate community acknowledges the positive contribution of the Fair Housing Amendments Act of 1988. According to the advocates, single women, especially single minority women, who are often single parents too, face the most obstacles of finding safe, affordable housing. They also face tremendous discrimination and harassment. A large number of all fair housing complaints are from this group.

Where enforcement is undertaken by private centers of fair housing, where a network of these centers exists, there has been a dramatic impact on housing discrimination. For example, in cities where fair housing advocates are active, 99 percent of the newspapers do not accept advertisements that specify "no children." In another instance, the effectiveness of the new Amendments is evinced by examples such as a case in Toledo, Ohio, recently settled by private fair housing groups for $20,000.

In some cases, ensuring equal opportunity in housing is merely a matter of educating the community about the letter and spirit of the law. Once educated, most housing providers are eager to comply with the law. Others who would find ways to circumvent it hesitate to do so once they are aware of the legal recourse open to potential victims. So, in effect, the very presence of an active network of private, nonprofit fair housing groups within a locality serves as a deterrent.

Success Stories

Measuring the extent of the progress made or measuring the impact of legislation requires one to identify parameters with which to evaluate success. Looking at the big picture involves accumulating data and statistics

to determine the extent of progress. At the micro level, however, it is the actual instances where provisions under the new law have made a real difference in people's lives that offer heartening evidence of the positive impact of enabling legislation.

Landlord Delores Rollhaus refused to rent her house in Wright City, Missouri, to Lisa M. Soliz and her daughter. Rollhaus told Soliz that she preferred to rent her house to a single man and not to a single mother. She also expressed concern about the ability of a woman to care for her property. Rollhaus made similar remarks to a single mother with three children who subsequently inquired about the house at Soliz's request.

The HUD Administrative Law Judge presiding over the case ruled that the landlord did not give Soliz legitimate reasons for rejecting her application. In addition, the landlord did not ascertain whether Soliz's acquaintance had a job or could afford the rent before refusing her tenancy. Rollhaus was ordered to pay the complainant Soliz $2,860 in compensatory damages and a civil penalty of $3,000 *[HUD v Rollhaus, HUDALJ No 07-90-0309-1, (HUD Office of Administrative Law Judges, 12/9/91)] (Fair Housing-Fair Lending, 1992).*

Numerous other similar cases have been resolved both through the district courts and through the HUD complaint processing system.

Another story that stands out as unique, and whose ultimate resolution is particularly rewarding, is the Fairfield North case *(Fiedler v Dana Properties, No S 89-1396 LKK (ED CA); US v Dana Properties, No S 90-0254 LKK (ED CA), 1/27/92).* This story highlights a problem that had received little attention from courts and public agencies until now: sexual harassment in housing.

Owners of the Fairfield apartment complex have agreed to settle the two sexual harassment suits—one filed by a group of female tenants and the other initiated by the Department of Justice—for a total of more than $165 million in damages, attorneys' fees, costs, and penalties. These lawsuits have resulted in the largest recorded settlement in a sexual harassment and housing discrimination case.

The episode was one of a two-year litany of unmitigated harassment that an apartment manager named Skinner inflicted on more than 15 women and their children at the Fairfield North Housing complex. Skinner ran the complex like a fiefdom, physically threatening the women, stealing their welfare checks, and ordering them to pose in lingerie for photographs and watch pornographic films with him. During his tenure, the women claim Skinner molested them, and threatened them with guns. He entered their apartments when they were sleeping or in the shower, tampered with their mail, intercepting food stamps and child-care aid. This often resulted in bureaucratic tie-ups that in some cases resulted in the termination of the women's aid. Skinner routinely threatened the women with removal of their children by reporting them to child protection services and preyed upon their fear of homelessness. He threw some of them out on the street, loudly making an example of them, the women affirmed. The worst part, many women said, was constantly worrying about not having a roof over their heads.

At Fairfield North, where 20 percent of the tenants live in subsidized apartments, many single mothers had fallen into poverty because they were deserted or battered. Indeed it seemed to them that Skinner solicited their tenancy exactly because they were so vulnerable.

Justice did not come easily to these women. They had to undertake an unrelenting quest, seeking assistance from numerous social service, and legal aid-type organizations before they found the lawyers who finally defended their case. Several parties have now settled their claims with individual settlements ranging from $3,000 to $60,000. In addition, the defendants have been ordered to pay $688,000 in lawyers' fees and expenses with a 20 multiplier for the attorneys' fees. The consent decree with the Justice Department requires the defendants to pay $45,000 in civil penalties and to take affirmative steps to prevent fair housing violations from occurring in the future, in addition to individual damages. The *Los Angeles Times* reported that Skinner himself was in jail awaiting trial on rape charges made by a Fairfield North tenant and her sister.

Levy and Oppenheimer (1992), whose law firm is representing some of the women and children, claim such problems are pervasive among low-income, single-women-maintained families. The right to be free of perpetual harassment in housing is a civil right, and needs to be recognized as one, say the lawyers.

The most significant victory as a result of this case is the ultimate empowerment of the women victims. The women have now formed a group, WRATH: "Women Refusing to Accept Tenant Harassment." Their goal is

to collect nationwide data about sexual harassment in housing and assist other women in situations like theirs.

The Skinner case illustrates the problems faced by numerous single women, problems compounded by the women's lack of awareness regarding their rights and regarding remedies available under the law to victims of discrimination. The law is new. Much confusion and uncertainty still exists about what is allowed, what is prohibited, and what remedies one can obtain for a victim. As case law develops, new interpretations will be made which will help clarify some of the regulations and iron out the controversies. (Information on this case was compiled from newspaper articles, *Fair Housing-Fair-Lending*, 1992, and conversations with attorneys Levy and Oppenheimer [1992].)

The Obstacles That Remain

HUD's record of enforcing the Fair Housing Act is reviewed periodically by the Administrative Conference of the United States, an independent federal agency that issues recommendations on administrative practices. Private fair housing groups and fair housing advocates also observe HUD's performance and monitor the impact of the law. While HUD has made efforts to enforce the mandate of fair housing for all, some inadequacies and problems remain. The impact of administrative and enforcement problems is intensified when the victims of discrimination are not aware of their rights and the provisions of the law. Unfortunately, these circumstances make women, especially single mothers, easy targets for housing discrimination.

A brief analysis of the obstacles to be overcome to enhance fair housing compliance is presented in this section. Information on these obstacles has been compiled primarily through interviews with advocates from private fair housing groups.

Problems with Enforcement

Despite the new option for a hearing before an Administrative Law Judge that is available to victims of housing discrimination, the parties in many fair housing cases continue to choose to resolve their disputes in federal court. HUD's Assistant Secretary for Fair Housing and Equal Opportunity Gordon Mansfield attributes this to the differences in remedies available under both systems. Congress needs to equalize these to address this issue.

As case law develops, oversight in previously processed cases is revealed. For example, a child of a complainant may be omitted from the action, precluding the award of damages. The child in a family subjected to discriminatory behavior is equally a victim. As precedent is established, it is expected that victims of discrimination will obtain fuller remedies.

Shanna Smith (1992), Director of the National Fair Housing Alliance in Washington, D.C., points out that low settlements result in the devaluing of people's pain and suffering as a result of discrimination. The impact is particularly severe when one considers the background of the individual who is discriminated against. In many instances the person is escaping an abusive situation. A high penalty for discriminatory activities serves as a greater deterrent.

Administrative Delays

As a result of the addition of the new categories, families with children and people with disabilities, to the protected classes, the Fair Housing Amendments Act has generated a tremendous volume of cases for HUD to process. As a result, HUD has to cope with a backlog of cases and has to allocate its limited resources to handle them as well as new cases.

Given the magnitude of complaints and its limited resources, HUD is having difficulty meeting the 100-day statutory deadline for completing complaint investigations. There needs to be a sense of urgency in responding to discrimination complaints, particularly when dealing with families with children. For many victims, a quick response may mean the difference between being sheltered or being homeless.

The Administrative Conference of the United States has asked HUD to encourage the use of alternative dispute resolution, and to ensure that its processes are perceived as working fairly *(Fair Housing-Fair Lending, 1992)*.

New Regulations

The newness of the Fair Housing Amendments Act has meant that regulations and operating procedures governing many existing programs either do not reflect the law or do not conform to the legislation. Conflicting regulations result in confusion among housing providers and disparate treatment for the program participants. An example of this problem is the existence of widely differing occupancy standards, in the absence of federal standards, promulgated by landlords, apartment manag-

ers, and even public housing authorities. According to some intake regulations followed by housing authorities, children of the opposite sex cannot share a bedroom. Therefore, a mother with a son and daughter would be required to rent a three-bedroom apartment. This puts obvious undue hardship on these families. Rules and regulations for various HUD programs need to be updated to ensure compliance with the new federal fair housing mandate.

In an attempt to clarify HUD's position on occupancy standards, General Counsel Keating circulated a public memorandum which had the effect of ratifying unreasonable occupancy limits, according to fair housing advocates. As a result of discussions with private fair housing groups such as the National Fair Housing Alliance, National Council for La Raza, Children's Defense Fund, the NAACP Legal Defense Fund, and others, General Counsel Keating further clarified HUD's position through a second memorandum: generally a standard of two persons per bedroom is considered acceptable, if applied across the board, and if it proves reasonable in context.

Growth in Subtle Discrimination

In response to questions about whether the letter and spirit of the fair housing law have changed rental and sales practices, fair housing advocates have a mixed reaction. Often housing providers, on learning the requirements of the new law, are eager to comply and have readily changed their previous practices. Others are determined to circumvent the law. In such instances people refine their discriminatory practices and indulge in more subtle forms of discrimination. If you are not suspicious, you may believe there is a genuinely valid reason for the refusal to rent, and not register a complaint. For example, in the rental of units, reasons for refusal such as credit inadequacies, or "other people ahead of you," or simply a delay in processing of an application, may appear legitimate. Often the individual wanting to rent a unit is considering a couple of different alternatives, and does not always have the patience to wait, and ends up accepting another unit. The delay method, according to fair housing advocates, is the best way to deter single-parent families who usually need housing urgently.

Lack of Research

Changes in the extent of discrimination against families with children since the Amendments Act went into effect have not been well documented. No baseline study, against which the impact of the prohibition of discrimination against families with children could be measured, has been done. The HUD-sponsored Housing Discrimination Studies did not address this category at all, but concentrated instead on race cases. As a result, no primary data exist against which to measure the impact of the Amendments conclusively, particularly when looking at women's access to housing.

Conclusions and Recommendations

Overall, the Fair Housing Amendments Act has made a significant contribution to providing equal housing opportunity for all groups of people. The following recommendations are intended to address the problems discussed and improve the impact of the law on expanding housing opportunities for women.

Cooperation between HUD and Private Groups

The most important factors requiring attention are the current enforcement procedures. Due to the volume of complaints pouring in, it is necessary to expand available investigation and complaint processing resources. Increased cooperation between private fair housing enforcement groups and HUD would facilitate improved testing and complaint investigations at the local level. This would reduce HUD's case load, and further the cause of fair housing for all.

Special consideration should be given to developing mechanisms to respond promptly to complaints where issues of the safety and well-being of women and children is involved. Lengthy processing procedures are neither appropriate nor practical.

At present HUD enters into voluntary agreements with the real estate industry and public housing authorities to encourage voluntary compliance with the fair housing law. Encouraging voluntary agreements by more housing industry groups, perhaps including non-profit housing providers, would have the effect of delegating authority to encourage compliance. In addition, it would enable HUD to monitor compliance with the law by efficient allocation of resources.

Expansion of the Education and Outreach Programs

Education and outreach programs such as the Fair Housing Initiatives Program (FHIP) should be reauthorized by Congress in full. Results of the evaluation of the current program should be incorporated in improving

outreach activities. Educating women about their rights under the Fair Housing Act will alert them to subtle and sophisticated forms of discrimination. In this regard, the real impact of the National Media Campaign, funded by the FHIP program, should also be measured, particularly for the extent of discrimination against women.

The National Media Campaign funded by HUD helped to expand considerably the awareness among victims of housing discrimination. HUD currently sponsors seminars on accessibility to inform all interested parties about the provisions under the new Fair Housing Accessibility Guidelines. Similar seminars on the familial status provision would ameliorate ignorance about the subject.

In an effort to enhance education and outreach activities, HUD created the Fair Housing Information Clearinghouse. The Clearinghouse is a repository of various fair housing materials and resources and should be more widely publicized. Information from the Clearinghouse serves to educate and assist fair housing professionals. In addition, the Clearinghouse can be used as a hub for communication and interaction between the various players involved with fair housing activities. This will prevent duplication of efforts and generate a lively forum for exchange of information and ideas.

Responsive Legislation and Regulation

This paper examines the Fair Housing Act within the context of how it affects women in search of housing. It is necessary to study other legislation similarly, though such legislation was not specifically drafted with women's issues in mind, to determine how it affects women and affects their ability to live and work in an independent fashion.

The National Women and Housing Task Force has compiled a rudimentary list in the document: *Unlocking the Door: An Action Program for Meeting the Housing Needs of Women, 1991*. The National Women and Housing Task Force is a group composed of various housing organizations and individuals that provides information on the nature of the housing crisis as it affects women and generates policy recommendations to the public, policy makers, and Congress. The task force has studied the problem of women and housing in depth, particularly the housing problems of single women and of women raising families alone. The group's conclusions are presented in the report mentioned above and were presented to national policy makers and President Bush in 1989.

Unlocking the Door documents the need for housing advocacy for women. This need must be put on the agenda of national and local policy makers and lobbying organizations. Policies responsive to the needs of women seeking housing will assist in mitigating homelessness among single women and their children.

In addition to policy and legislation, it is necessary to develop significant regulatory guidance for the enforcement of HUD's housing programs in general and the fair housing law in particular. Since the passage of the Fair Housing Amendments Act, HUD has promulgated numerous decisions on an *ad hoc* basis, concerning the scope of the Amendments and the prohibitions against discrimination on the basis of familial status and disability. It would be beneficial to compile these decrees and regulations governing other HUD-administered housing programs in a technical guidance manual. Such a manual would serve to iron out discrepancies between HUD's various housing regulations. It will also serve as an up-to-date reference source, provide clear direction to enforcers of fair housing, and facilitate the compilation of all of HUD's various recent clarifications of the implementation of the Fair Housing Amendments Act of 1988.

In order to empower women, it is essential to ensure that they have access to safe, decent, affordable housing in the location of their choice. The alternative is an inordinate cost to society for a vast population of deprived and dependent women and children. Discrimination against women and children frustrates attempts by single women to take control of their lives—especially when the women are escaping backgrounds of abuse and domestic violence.

Women's need to house themselves, and often their children, is integral to their finding employment and leading self-sufficient lives. The Fair Housing Amendments Act of 1988 is an example of how responsive legislation developed by Congress can begin to address some of the problems faced by women in their attempts to obtain housing. It allows women to pursue housing of their choice that is responsive to their distinctive needs, and empowers them, when denied the opportunity they seek, to obtain redress. Legislation alone cannot, however, resolve all the problems. It needs to be combined with implementing regulations, publicity, and diligent enforcement.

Finally, it is only when the special needs of women are recognized as vital, and are placed on the agenda of national and local policy makers, that new housing opportunities for women will evolve.

Note

I wish to thank Nina Corin, Manager of the Fair Housing Information Clearinghouse and other colleagues at Aspen Systems Corporation for their encouragement and assistance.

References

Annual Report to Congress: Civil Rights Data on HUD Program Applicants and Beneficiaries. Washington, DC: U.S. Department of Housing and Urban Development, 1990.

Annual Report to Congress: Civil Rights Data on HUD Program Applicants and Beneficiaries. Washington, DC: U.S. Department of Housing and Urban Development, 1989.

Aoki, Keith. *Recent Developments—Fair Housing Amendments Act of 1988.* 24 Harvard Civil Rights—Civil Liberties Law Review 249, Harvard University, 1989.

Bassuk, Ellen and Lenore Rubin. *Homeless Children: A Neglected Population.* American Journal of Orthopsychiatry 57, April 1987 quoted in Sprague, Joan Forrester. *More Than Housing: Lifeboats for Women and Children.* Boston: Butterworth-Heinemann, 1991.

Brancart, Christopher. 1991. Personal communication with author at the National Fair Housing Alliance Annual Conference. Washington, D.C.

Cooper, Candy J. *Unprecedented Court Victory for Harassed Women.* San Francisco Examiner, July 7, 21, and 30, 1991.

Dolbeare, Cushing N. *Out of Reach—Why Everyday People Can't Find Affordable Housing.* Washington, DC: Low Income Housing Information Service, 1990.

Fair Housing Amendments Act of 1988, Pub.L. No. 100-430, 102 Stat. 1619 as amended; U.S.C. Title 42 §§ 3601–3616, signed September 13, 1988.

Fair Housing—It's Your Right. Washington, DC: U.S. Department of Housing and Urban Development, 1990.

Keating, Francis. *HUD Internal Memorandum.* Washington, D.C.: U.S. Department of Housing and Urban Development, 1991.

Levy and Oppenheimer. Personal telephone communications with author. February, 1992.

Limmer, Ruth. *How Well Are We Housed: Female Headed Household.* Washington, D.C.: U.S. Department of Housing and Urban Development. 1978.

Martin, Nina. *Harassment Victims Complain of a Torn and Tattered Legal Safety Net.* San Francisco Daily Journal, July 10, 1983.

Mansfield, Gordon. Plenary speech at the National FHAP Policy Conference. Dallas, Texas: 1990.

Mihaly, Lisa. *Housing Discrimination Against Families with Children.* Washington, DC: Trends, 1990.

Morales, James. *Creating New Housing Opportunities for Families with Children.* Clearinghouse Review, 1988.

Moy, Catherine. *Skinner Accusers Hoping for a Trial.* Daily Republic, August 13, 1991.

Pearce, Diana. *The Feminization of Poverty: A Second Look.* Unpublished paper presented at the American Sociological Association Meeting, August, 1990, quoted in Sprague, Joan Forrester. *More Than Housing: Lifeboats for Women and Children.* Boston: Butterworth-Heinemann, 1991.

Shapiro, Isaac and Robert Greenstein. *Holes in the Safety Nets, Poverty Programs and Policies in the States, National Overview.* Washington, DC: Center on Budget and Policy Priorities, 1988, quoted in Sprague, Joan Forrester. *More Than Housing: Lifeboats for Women and Children.* Boston: Butterworth-Heinemann, 1991.

Sidel, Ruth. *Women and Children Last: The Plight of Poor Women in Affluent America.* New York: Penguin Books, 1987.

Smith, Shanna. Personal communication. Washington, D.C., March, 1992.

Sprague, Joan Forrester. *More Than Housing: Lifeboats for Women and Children.* Boston: Butterworth-Heinemann, 1991. *The State of Fair Housing: Report to the Congress Pursuant to Section 808(e)(2) of the Fair Housing Act.* Washington, DC: U.S. Department of Housing and Urban Development, 1989.

The State of Fair Housing: Report to the Congress Pursuant to Section 808(e)(2) of the Fair Housing Act. Washington, DC: U.S. Department of Housing and Urban Development, 1990.

Tribune News Services. *Rape Charge.* Oakland Tribunal, July 31, 1991

Fair Housing Amendments Act of 1988: A Selected Resource Guide. Washington, DC: U.S. Department of Housing and Urban Development, 1991.

Fair Housing–Fair Lending. (Monthly Bulletin). Englewood: Prentice Hall Law and Business, 1991 and 1992.

U.S. Bureau of the Census and Department of Housing and Urban Development. American Housing Survey for the United States in 1987. Washington, DC: U.S. Department of Commerce, Bureau of the Census, 1989.

U.S. Bureau of the Census. *Studies in Marriage and the family.* Washington, DC: U.S. Department of Commerce, Bureau of the Census, 1989a quoted in Sprague, Joan Forrester. *More Than Housing: Lifeboats for Women and Children.* Boston: Butterworth-Heinemann, 1991.

Women and Housing Task Force. *Unlocking the Door: An Action Program for Meeting the Housing Needs of Women.* Washington, DC: National Low Income Housing Coalition, 1991.

Yates, Larry. *Low Income Housing in America. Washington, DC: Low Income Housing Information Service, 1990.*

Zigas, Barry. 1990. *Roundup.* Washngton, D.C.: Low Income Housing Information Services.

Chapter 11

Ideology as Law: Is There Room for Difference in the Right to Housing?

Pamela L. Sayne

Pamela L. Sayne *has worked as a community organizer, educator, researcher, administrator, and activist for housing and community development since the early 1970s. Her critical approach has benefited from the diverse backgrounds and viewpoints of the community members with whom she has worked in Canada, the United States, and Mali, West Africa. She is a member of a Right to Housing Committee in Toronto. As the North American representative to the Habitat International Coalition Women and Shelter Group, she has participated in several regional and interregional housing studies and strategy sessions. She coedited the Fall 1990 edition of* Canadian Woman Studies *on Women and Housing. She is completing a doctoral thesis entitled, "Women's Knowledge as Power in the Political Economy of Housing," in the Adult Education Department at the Ontario Institute for Studies in Education.*

The many ways in which the "right to housing" are understood play a large role in defining how and for whom housing is provided in everyday life. The concept of a "right to housing" is socially learned, and both shapes and is shaped by ideologies about how a particular society functions. For example, ideologies of race, gender, sexual orientation, and class influence where people live within cities and often the quality of shelter to which they have access. The right to housing therefore has many interpretations revealed in social stratifications. These interpretations are specific to the ideological beliefs and socio-political context reflected in housing-related law, policies, programs, and regulations of a community or society;[1] and through law, policies, programs and regulations, ideological beliefs are constantly being revised or refined.

In this paper I am going to discuss two ideological ways to view the right to housing—patriarchal and feminist—and how these ideologies are or might be reflected within legal frameworks. My approach is not that of a legal expert but rather that of an activist in housing and in local and international development. Therefore, to illustrate my argument, I will draw from First and Third World communities as well as U.N. Conventions to show how the right to housing is shaped and expressed as a cultural ideology and how the right to housing is or is not entrenched in the law.

Development Ideology and the Right to Housing

I will begin by borrowing a framework that has evolved through feminist critiques of "development" models. One development model is patriarchal capitalism with its underlying value assumptions of uniformity, distancing, and hierarchical, linear growth. The second is a feminist model with underlying value assumptions of diversity, proximity, and reciprocal interactions or cyclical change.[2] However, the debate between patriarchal and feminist approaches does not take place in a pure or abstract form, but in the real world of contradiction, dialectic, and praxis. Conceptions of the "right to housing" are thus constantly shifting with changes in social context and perspective. However, social practice lends more or less support either to a patriarchal world view or to a feminist one and so can be roughly categorized.

For example, the ways in which a "right to housing" may be understood will be different from the perspective of healthy subsistence economies, which depend on diversity of production, proximity of production/ consumption, and an economy of interdependent cyclical growth, compared to the perspective of modernized industrialized cities, which encourage uniformity of production, distancing of producers/consumers, and an economy of linear growth. Not only are different traditional frameworks involved but, under patriarchal dominance, incompatible values and ways of seeing our earth. These contradictory perspectives are evident in the social and economic fabric which shapes the identity and behavior of peoples and in various methods of governing.[3]

Thus, an indigenous community, based on a local subsistence economy, is more likely to regard adequate housing as interdependent with the earth's renewable natural resources, not as a structure that separates people and their activities from the natural elements. From this viewpoint, a threat to renewable resources by the market economy is also a threat to one's housing, which is shaped by interdependence with the natural environment.[4] Dr. David Suzuki cites a native in Canada who emphasized that when a people's livelihood, based upon living interdependently with nature, is destroyed, "we will be like everybody else."[5] The right to housing thus reflects a nation's values, distinct social identity, and diverse ways of living that are holistic, recognizing interdependence with natural resources and the local environment.

In contrast, the right to housing is understood much differently in man-built urbanized environments. Though housing is recognized as meaning more than just a roof over one's head, housing programs are often reductionist in approach, emphasizing, for example, the number of units built. Concerns such as safety, security, employment, work, and community relationships, or the relationship to the natural environment are often considered to be secondary or separate components (if they are considered at all) in the hierarchical provision of housing needs.

Poor communities, which are marginalized from the centers of wealth and power generated by the inequities of a market economy, receive substantially less support to meet comprehensive social and economic needs than communities which are central to the wealth and power of the market economy.[6] The primary focus of state housing initiatives is often, at best, on the number of units existing relative to those required for a population. But all too commonly, the political will to fulfill housing needs is based upon capital-centered market indicators. Poor communities are colonized, through power

inequities in the market economy, into using reductionist models in their struggle to obtain housing and to avoid further marginalization. Political movements and communities advocating housing rights thus are often advocating a right to a form of housing wherein livelihood, community identity and governance, safety, security, and maintenance of natural resources are not well integrated. Within the patriarchal model, poor communities and groups are set up to compete against each other for limited and inadequate access to minimal resources.

Reductionist government housing programs and policies often erode housing rights and the dignity of specific groups and communities. This is exemplified by the history of Bleeker Street in Toronto. A vibrant inner-city community in Toronto was destroyed by evicting residents, tearing down homes, and rebuilding for different residents, providing profits for the developer. Development programs and policies which were thought to exist to serve community members and support community infrastructures were manipulated and used to destroy the neighborhood which people called home.[7] Capitalist venturers were the primary benefactors at the cost of safety, security, and community relationships of the neighborhood.

Another example of such colonization was observable in a relocation project in the late 1960s. A native housing relocation project in Elliot Lake, Ontario, was intended to improve living conditions in the community. Instead, the project demonstrated the cultural arrogance of western modernization models of development. Westernized patriarchal housing design, planning, and social structures were unquestioned in the implementation of the housing project.[8] Indigenous people's livelihood, identity, and community structures were ignored and devalued through "development" based upon western modernization models.

Gender Ideology and the Right to Housing

Gender bias in the housing development programs and policies of market economies erodes the dignity and livelihood of women particularly. Women have traditionally been disadvantaged by the patriarchal ideologies of private ownership of property. Private home ownership ideology is an expression of patriarchal relations that have historically rendered women subordinate to and dependent on men for their housing rights. That is to say, men are the primary producers/owners/ controllers of housing and related resources and industries, while women are the users and caretakers.

Men, through private ownership, control of decision making, and paid employment in the housing industry, gain autonomous economic power and access to credit, while women, as the primary users and caretakers of housing, receive little autonomous social or economic security from their activities and do not gain access to credit. Hence, the subordination of women is enforced through the privatization of the housing industry.[9] Similarly, social and economic disparities between women and men are exacerbated through the social engineering expressed through housing programs and policies.[10] The engendered dualism (autonomous man and dependent woman) of the housing industry fosters institutionalized sexism. Heterosexual relations and patriarchal family structures become coercive "options" for women who must meet their basic housing needs.

Simply to encourage private home ownership "for women too," without addressing other systemic inequities, is not a very progressive or particularly feminist response to a patriarchal ideology of housing provision (Sayne, 1990). As Maria Mies has pointed out:

> ... the feminist movement ... does not want to replace one (male) power elite by another (female) power elite, but ... wants to build a non-hierarchical, non-centralized society where no elite lives on exploitation and dominance over others (1986, 37).

Women encountering the lack of adequate housing in Bombay have expressed a similar perspective:

> As patriarchy derives its strength from private property, our struggle for shelter for women will necessarily be in direct opposition to the present socio-economic system (Shelter, 1987).

The above examples have illustrated how the right to housing is conceived within various social contexts based upon gender and other ideologies of exclusion, and how sexism, racism, classism, and heterosexism are colonizing practices entrenching a hierarchy of rights. The right to housing thus becomes competitive; and competing rights to private property are weighed in the practice of law. This reductionist socio-economic housing system, carried out through the practice of law, does not allow for consideration of the social context, or for other interpretations of governing. Rather, competing rights in the liberal western legal system demand hierarchical systems of exploitation and colonization. This may prove to be legal, but it does not recognize basic human rights.

Kathleen Lahey observed that "historically, men appear in law as subjects and women as subject matter" (1989,101). The problems of women as the subject matter of the law as opposed to women's experiences being central to the law have been acknowledged in the writings of numerous feminist commentators from several countries (MacKinnon, 1987; Razack, 1991; Maboreke, 1990; Hellum, 1990; Lahey, 1989; Canadian Advisory Council on the Status of Women, 1989; Burrows, 1986; Taub and Schneider, 1990; Olson, 1990; Crenshaw, 1990; Stewart and Armstrong, 1990). Maria Mies has argued that in patriarchal society male purpose has been the accumulation of property, and women are considered to be men's property (1986, 64–65). I would also argue that those who own private property (primarily men) become the subjects of the law and those who do not own property are objectified by the law (primarily women).

United Nations' Ideology and Women's Right to Housing

United Nations Conventions serve as cases in point, and this has universal implications for women's legal status. The language used clearly reflects the notion of women as the subject matter of law, and patriarchal legal constructs are clearly identifiable. For instance, Article 25 of the United Nations Universal Declaration of Human Rights of 1948 states:

> Everyone has the right to a standard of living adequate for the health and well-being of himself and of his family, including food, clothing, *housing* [emphasis added] and medical care and necessary social services, and the right to security in the event of unemployment, sickness, disability, widowhood, old age or other lack of livelihood in circumstances beyond his control.[11]

The notion of "universality" in this document clearly applies to the male gender, while women's rights are not directly expressed but are subsumed under men's. Similarly, the United Nations International Covenant on Economic, Social, and Cultural Rights, Article 11 (adopted in 1966 and entering into force in 1976), states:

> The States Parties to the present Covenant recognize the right of everyone to an adequate standard of living for himself and his family, including adequate food, clothing and *housing,* [emphasis added] and to the continuous improvement of living conditions.[12]

In the limited patriarchal legal imagination of "covenants," all women are invisible but assumed to cohabit with "himself and his family"—which would come as a great surprise to most lesbians. In 1987, the U.N. International Year for Shelter for the Homeless, Riane Eisler summed up the continual conflict between language and experience as follows:

> Human rights have traditionally been defined as "men's inalienable right to life, liberty, and property." The term "men" has sometimes been said to include women. But this has not been reflected in human rights theory or in its application....
>
> Modern theories of "human rights" have historically developed in two separate theoretical strains. Leading philosophers writing on the "rights of man" ... specifically articulated a double standard of thought.... Women, on the other hand, were defined not as individuals but as members of men's households and thus, along with their offspring, under male control.[13]

Women's invisibility is reflected in the gender-biased wording of these international documents which are meant to guarantee the right to shelter/housing. "Men" does not include women. Therefore, any serious attempt at securing housing rights for women, by governing bodies or advocacy groups alike, must include inclusive language and must recognize that women are not universally members of men's households.

However, reclaiming legal language is only the necessary beginning to claiming women's experience as central to legal discourse. As the legal system is an unavoidable area of practice for feminist social transformation, we must ask what feminism has done to create alternative visions and strategies within the legal system. Does feminism suggest an alternative to the failure of nation states and the United Nations to address the growing housing crisis effectively? How would a feminist analysis of international law and State obligations address the right to housing? Lahey argues that "a feminist theory of women and law... is about the ways in which law reflects and reinforces the social, economic, and political structures that surround subject women in liberal patriarchy" (1989, 102). She challenges concepts of private property which have historically been embedded within sexism, colonialism, and other systems of exploitation.

Feminist Ideology and Approaches to Legalize the Right to Housing

A feminist approach to law is evolving which demands attention to inequity in legal discourse and begins with women's lived reality instead of with the law.[14] This approach has been termed "Women's Law" by Mary Maboreke in Zimbabwe. Its aim "... is to expose the (usually hidden) law-sex connections, and since this relationship does not usually become apparent until the practical effects of the rule have been observed, it is necessary to follow the law into the world of women's real lives" (1990, 2).[15]

Women's subordinate legal situations and lived realities in various countries are diverse. In *Perspectives on Research Methodology,* which discusses women and the law in southern Africa (Hellum, 1990), the situation of women as a group is contextualized in changing customary and civil law. This text addresses the dilemma that occurs when women's realities are separated (or distanced) from legal governance:

> We feel that using a perspective which looks at the whole woman, and starts with her needs and her lived experiences, is particularly important in our societies where the formal law is largely unknown and *distanced* from the majority of the people" (p. ii; my emphasis).

Anne Hellum has described women's experience in the Scandinavian countries, modern western welfare states, where long-standing "gender neutral law often discriminated against women" (1990, 93). In the practice of Women's Law, she has stated, "... it was ... necessary to start out with women's reality instead of the law." Hellum continues:

> In women's law in Norway, legal advice was developed as a research method which enabled us to gather empirical data about women's lives. Legal advice cases have, combined with an open and qualitative approach, provided information and helped us to understand discrepancies between law and practice from women's perspectives (1990, 93).

A methodology of Women's Law is clearly evident in the feminist movement in Canada (Razack, 1991). Razack describes the practice by feminist lawyers and activists of working with women's community participation in reshaping the law. Through consulting women's communities, our experience becomes central to the practice of litigation and the development of law, and each case is contextualized to account for women's differences.

This approach is essential to the development of legal arguments for sexual equality, since the context of each case identifies inequities based upon subordination and disempowerment, which in turn challenges inequities based upon hierarchies of power and privilege embedded in racism, class, and other differences. The concept and practice of hierarchical relations are being replaced by a feminist practice with an ideology that encourages an holistic, interdependent social order. An interdependent social order can take into account diversity and proximity, and can challenge the conceptualization and practice of competitive rights claims within the legal framework. It is an alternative to either/or arguments embedded in reductionist, dualist legal thought.

In Canada, the political opportunity to introduce women's realities as different from men's, and to gain legal recognition for women's specificity has been sought by feminists shaping and using the Canadian Charter of Rights and Freedoms. However, very few legal actions using U.N. legal instruments (to which Canada is a signatory) and/or Sections 15 and 28—the equality clauses—of the Canadian Charter of Rights and Freedoms have been linked to women's right to housing in Canada. Canada has demonstrated a commitment to concerns about equality in the Canadian Charter of Rights and Freedoms, which states:

Every individual is equal before and under the law and has the right to the equal protection and equal benefit of the law without discrimination and, in particular, without discrimination based on race, national or ethnic origin, color, religion, sex, age or mental or physical disability. (2) Subsection (1) does not preclude any law, program or activity that has as its object the amelioration of conditions of disadvantaged individuals or groups including those that are disadvantaged because of race, national or ethnic origin, color, religion, sex, age or mental or physical disability. (Section 15).

Notwithstanding anything in this Charter, the rights and freedoms referred to in it are guaranteed equally to male and female persons.(Section 28)

Participants in the 1987 Canadian conference to observe the International Year of Shelter for the Homeless referred to the potential use of the Charter:[16]

Although the Charter governs National Housing Acts and all federal and provincial housing authorities, [Lynda] Gehrke [observed], "... There is very little litigation around issues of housing in the Canadian Charter." Further, if the right to shelter is recognized, what limitations might be placed on those rights? Do government budgets represent reasonable limits? Will the courts subject policy decisions regarding the allocation of resources to scrutiny? "I believe that argument could be made, ... [but] whether it is accepted or not remains to be seen" (quoted in New Partnerships, 1988, 33–34).

In Canada, arguments for women's access to housing are often built upon claims of discrimination based on source of income, age, and family status rather than on a right to housing. The right to safe, secure, and affordable housing, addressing the failings of socio-economic structures, has not yet developed into a strong legal argument. Thus, claims of social, economic, or cultural inequalities have not been well integrated into our legal system. Although Canada has ratified U.N. proclamations on the right to housing, most notably the International Covenant for Social, Economic and Cultural Rights, a right to housing has not yet been incorporated into the Canadian Charter of Rights or into legal arguments.

A recent federal budget terminated the Economic Council of Canada and the Law Reform Commission of Canada, which were established in part "to determine where law may be "discriminatory or protective" of women's rights; [and] to investigate the problems associated with the relationship between the law and the role, status and material circumstances of women" (Status of Women, 1987). This again was a step backward for women's right to housing in Canada. It also is a clear illustration of the government's undermining of both the 1979 U.N. Convention on the Elimination of All Forms of Discrimination against Women[17] and the 1985 Nairobi Forward Looking Strategy, to which Canada has made an international commitment.

Nevertheless, as access to safe, secure, and affordable housing continues to erode in Canada, a grassroots momentum is building for the incorporation of a right to housing within a Canadian Social Charter. Without more political pressure, it seems unlikely that housing rights in a Charter will reflect women's lived realities. This will require a human rights legal framework that addresses the systematic discrimination against disadvantaged and subordinant groups as opposed to a continuation of competitive rights claims common in private property debates.

The question remains, Is a male-centered and male-dominated legal system even capable of ensuring the equality rights of women through the Canadian Charter of Rights? The record to date is not promising. From 1985 to September, 1989, of the 44 cases brought to court regarding sex discrimination, only 9 were on behalf of women, while 35 were on behalf of men (Courts, 1989). As Kathleen Lahey has observed:

Unless Canadian judges move decisively to reject this so-called neutral and principled approach to equality, it will soon become virtually impossible to argue that the Charter is designed to eliminate the social, economic, or legal causes of actual inequality (quoted in Brodsky and Shelagh, 1989, 201).

In spite of the increasing lack of secure, safe, and affordable housing for women and children, relatively few Supreme Court cases regarding housing have used equality arguments under the Charter of Rights. In the few cases that have used equality arguments, the results have been problematic for women. For example, in Hseun v. Mah [(1986), 7 B.C.L.R. (sd) 21], the argument against adult-only apartment buildings was lost in the courts and the trend of developers to promote adult-only buildings continues. This trend works against single women more than single men since women represent a larger number of single-parent households. Several other decisions in Newfoundland[18] found that public housing projects could remain exempt from the Provincial Landlord Tenant Act. Since women and children make up the majority of public housing tenants (a form of tenure which provides no long-term social or economic security), these decisions denied women and children protection from eviction without due process.

In comparison, the U.S. legal system has evolved as "an active promoter of socially desirable goals and conduct (i.e., capitalist economic growth)" (Kairys, 1982, 16). The U.S. has ratified the International Convention on Civil and Political Rights, which favors private property claims, but not the International Covenant on Economic, Social and Cultural Rights, which favors collective rights claims.[19] The U.S. position historically accords privileges to individual private property rights, fueling individual rights claims to compete in a system of patriarchal capitalist economic growth. This is at the expense of those who, due to belief systems, world view, abilities, or lack of resources, may not choose to participate in competitive rights claims. As such, they are thereby politically disempowered and subordinated in a capitalist economic growth system. In short, they are colonized. This legal practice reinforces the private property rights of individuals, thereby re-enforcing existing socio-economic disparities. This practice runs counter to basic American "ideals" since all men are not born equal, and also counters all-women-are-equal-to-men claims. Libertarian principles in recent U.S. law deny the inherent class, race, and gender inequities within the American social fabric (Kairys, 1990). David Kairys, in *The Politics of Law: A Progressive Critique* (1982), discusses how under American democracy

any person who differed from the majority—by ancestry, religion, appearance, or disagreement with majority positions—was suspect and blamed for social problems, which usually took the heaviest toll on them. The goal was to eliminate *difference*. ... [G]overnment, including courts, offered no protection" (p.147; my emphasis).

It is not surprising, then, that while the U.S. has ratified the Covenant on Civil and Political Rights, it has never ratified the Covenant on Social, Economic and Cultural Rights. Through collective class-action suits in the U.S., the National Association for the Advancement of Colored People has been successful in challenging development practices that, for example, reduced the number of moderate-income housing units built.[20] Such victories are vital to serve immediate needs and encourage social mobilization and awareness of how racism is reproduced in housing provision. However, these initiatives may remain within the liberal legal framework if the development model[21] itself does not change in the U.S. Economic, social, and political inequities of the patriarchal capitalist development model require a change in the notion of liberal legal solutions.

Diane Polan, a U.S. lawyer, has challenged the sex equality claim addressing women's issues in litigation and lobbying because this gives

"tacit approval to the basic social order, ... giving up ... [a] more radical challenge to society." She argues that "... litigation ... can only be effective ... [when] ... undertaken in the context of broader economic, social and cultural changes" (cited in Kairys, 1990, 461–462).

However, with the failure to pass the Equal Rights Amendment and the U.S. refusal to ratify the U.N. Convention on the Elimination of All Forms of Discrimination against Women, it is clear that not even a liberal approach to sex equality is well supported in U.S. national and international law.

Razack (1991,14–16) cautions against a legal approach to rights claims that does not acknowledge "a theory of difference" relating to the diversity of women as a group and as members of different and varied communities. Unless women's differing situations are contextualized and understood as interdependent within various communities, there is little chance that rights claims can move beyond the present liberal dualist framework of patriarchy. Such dualist hierarchical frameworks encourage competitive legal claims where one's gain is another's loss. This competitive framework is so pervasive in the legal system that it becomes difficult to see other options. As Razack asks, is it likely that challenges within the present liberal legal system can contribute to radical change in society without challenging the dominant western "pedagogy of truth, language, knowledge, and power" forming the legal system? She cites the arguments of feminist theorists such as Shelly Gavigan, Mary O'Brien, and Sheila McIntyre, who see the law not as an unchanging monolith but as having "transformative potential" (1991:26).

I suggest that Women's Law is challenging the pedagogy of truth, language, knowledge, and power. As Anne Hellum points out:

> Women's law does not deal or look at law the way it was practiced traditionally, or by traditional types of scholars. The trend has been to deal with the lives of women and their references/practices, with the aim of constructing a new legal framework and legal concept covering the experiences/ practices of women (May 1990, 43).

Summary

This paper has explored how differing conceptions of the right to housing play a large role in shaping how and for whom housing is actually provided. The legal framework for both the United Nations, and for nation states, reflects the ideology of patriarchal capitalism. It embodies social and economic practices of distancing through dualist relationships, sameness through non-contextualized equality, and social hierarchies through competitive rights. Hierarchies enforce inequities based on sex, race, and class differences. These practices are historically rooted in western patriarchal capitalism which upholds the profit-driven, linear, market economy as equally feasible for all. Women have traditionally been marginalized by or excluded from the profit-oriented market economy in modernized societies, restricting the right to housing and related human needs.

In conclusion, there has been little room for difference in patriarchal ideology as law. However, feminist legal practitioners are attempting to create room for difference, specifically for women and feminine values of non-competing rights claims. This is being accomplished through women's community consultation, education, research, and activism, to illuminate the social, economic, and political disparities enforced through legal practices. Not until social, economic, and political conditions are considered in law can the system of hierarchical competitive rights be transformed.

Development that promotes the right to housing will then be supported in the legal practice of justice. The question of contributing to a radical change in law continues to be debated where theory and practice for social change meet; and it is not surprising that women are creating the political spaces for these changes.

Notes

[1] For examples of this point see Stone, 1985, pp. 126–127 and Kanes Weisman, 1992.

[2] These value assumptions in development models are illuminated in such works as Mies, 1987; Kneen, 1989; Shiva, 1989, 1991; Sen and Grown, 1987; Waring, 1988.

[3] The differences between patriarchal capitalist approaches to housing and the environment and more feminist ones are increasingly being illuminated in the literature critiquing development. See, for example, Marie Wadden, *Nitassinan: The Innu Struggle to Reclaim Their Homeland* (Vancouver: Douglas & McIntyre Ltd., 1991); Vandana Shiva, *The Violence of the Green Revolution* (London: Zed Book Ltd., 1991) and *Staying Alive* (London: Zed Book Ltd.,1989).

[4] From the exploitation of natural resources such as minerals and forests to the structuring of cheap human labor systems, not one global region has not experienced the massive loss of homes and a way of life due to mega-modernization development projects imposed from outside the community.

[5] Cited by Dr. David Suzuki at *The Earth Spirit Festival* at Harbourfront, Toronto, July 5, 1991.

[6] One example of this is provided by Marilyn Waring, who has pointed out that the U.S. government spent more on military housing than on social housing for its citizens (Waring, 1988, pp.169–170).

[7] This event is documented in *Bleeker Street,* available through the Toronto Public Library, 1974.

[8] This practice of colonizing the social values, structures, and way of life of indigenous peoples is clearly, though unintentionally, documented in the film *Elliot Lake,* available from the National Film Board archives upon special request.

[9] This example of institutionalized sexism can also be observed as institutionalized racism as specific groups have been marginalized from private home ownership projects and access to credit programs.

[10] For regional examples of this bias, see *Canadian Woman Studies.* 11 (2) (Fall 1990) and the case studies from poor countries in Caroline Moser and Linda Peake, eds., *Women, Human Settlements and Housing* (London: Tavistock Publications, 1987).

[11] United Nations, *Human Rights, A Compilation of International Instruments* (New York: United Nations Publication, 1983), p. 5.

[12] Ibid. p.5.

[13] Riane Eisler, "Human Rights: Toward an Integrated Theory for Action," *Human Rights Quarterly,* 9 (December, 1987): pp. 287–289.

14 This is discussed by Anne Hellum, "Legal Advice as a Research Method: The Case of Women's Law in Norway and Its Relevance for the Women and Law in Southern Africa Research Project," pp. 91–114. Cited in *Perspectives on Research Methodology* (Harare: Women and Law Southern Africa Research Project, December 1990) and in Sherene Razack's *Canadian Feminism and the Law* (Toronto: Second Story Press, 1991).

15 The methodology of Women's Law is more fully described in the works of M. Maboreke (1990) and Anne Hellum (1990).

16 Lynda Gehrke is the former senior staff lawyer for Jane-Finch Community Legal Services, Toronto, and a researcher specializing in the Canadian Charter of Rights and Freedoms as applied to housing.

17 In 1981, the Convention on the Elimination of All Forms of Discrimination against Women came into force and was ratified by 112 countries by December 1, 1991. About fifty-six countries have not ratified the Convention, including the United States.

18 These cases can be found in court reports (1987), 62 Nfld. & P.E.I.R. 287; (1987), 62 Nfld. & P.E.I.R. 269; (1986), 59 Nfld. & P.E.I.R. 275.

19 For a more in-depth discussion on these two U.N. Conventions, see "Poverty Stops Equality/Equality Stops Poverty," pp. 7–11, by Havi Echenberg and Bruce Porter in *Canadian Women Studies,* 11 (2) 1990.

20 Leslie Kanes Wiesman, *Discrimination by Design: A Feminist Critique of the Man-Made Environment,* Chicago: University of Illinois Press, 1992, pp.134–137.

21 Development models in richer countries often avoid critique in international dialogues. It is important to recognize the development models used in "First World" countries as they may reproduce and maintain a "Third World" within.

References

Anglophone African Women and Shelter Seminar. Harare: Author's personal notes, April 1991.

Canada. *Canadian Charter of Rights and Freedoms.* Ottawa: 1981.

Canada. Status of Women. *Fact Sheets Nairobi Forward-Looking Strategies for the Advancement of Women: Issues and The Canadian Situation.* February 1987.

Bleeker Street. Documentary. Toronto Public Library. Red Redsern, 1974.

Boserup, Ester. *Woman's Role in Economic Development.* New York: St. Martin's Press, 1970.

Brodsky, Gwen, and Shelagh Day. *Canadian Charter Equality Rights for Women: One Step Forward or Two Steps Back?* Ottawa: Canadian Advisory Council on the Status of Women, 1989.

Burrows, Noreen. "International Law and Human Rights: the Case of Women's Rights." In *Human Rights from Rhetoric to Reality,* pp. 80–97. Edited by Tom Campbell, David Goldberg, Sheila Mclean and Tom Mullen. Oxford: Basil Blackwell, 1986.

Crenshaw, Kimberle. "A Black Feminist Critique of Antidiscrimination Law and Politics." p. 195. In *The Politics of Law: A Progressive Critique,* David Kairys, ed. New York: Pantheon Books, 1990.

Eisler, Raine. "Human Rights: Toward an Integrated Theory for Action." *Human Rights Quarterly* 9 (December, 1987): 287-289.

Elliot Lake. Documentary. National Film Board of Canada, 1967.

Global Report on Human Settlements—1986. United Nations Centre for Human Settlements (Habitat). New York: Oxford Press, 1987.

"Courts need new view of sex bias, council says." *Globe and Mail,* September 29, 1989 , A3.

Hellum, Anne, ed. *Women, Law and Development: Report from a Seminar.* Oslo: Division of North/South University Cooperation, University of Oslo, 1990.

Hellum, Anne, ed. *Perspectives on Research Methodology.* Harare: Women and Law in Southern Africa Research Project, December 1990.

IYSH Women and Shelter Seminar: Seminar Report Harare: Ministry of Community Development and Women's Affairs, et al., 1987.

Hellum, Anne, "Legal Advice as a Research Method: The Case of Women's Law in Norway and its Relevance for the Women and Law in Southern Africa Research Project," pp. 91–114. In *Perspectives on Research Methodology* Hellum, Anne, ed. Harare: Women and Law Southern Africa Research Project, December 1990.

Kanes Weisman, Leslie. *Discrimination by Design: A Feminist Critique of the Man-Made Environment.* Chicago: University of Illinois Press, 1992.

Lahey, Kathleen A. "Celebration and Struggle: Feminism and Law." *Feminism: From Pressure To Politics.* Ed. Angela Miles and Geraldine Finn. Montreal: Black Rose Books, 1989.99–122.

Lang-Runtz, Heather, and Ahern C. Doyne, eds. *New Partnerships - Building For The Future.* Proceedings of Canadian Conference to Observe the International Year of Shelter for the Homeless, September 13–16, 1987. Ottawa: Canadian Association of Housing and Renewal Officials, 1988.

Maboreke, Maria. "Introducing Women's Law." pp. 1–6. In *The Legal Situation of Women in Southern Africa.* Julie Stewart and Alice Armstrong. eds. Harare: University of Zimbabwe Publications, 1990.

MacKinnon, Catharine A. *Feminism Unmodified.* Cambridge: Harvard University Press, 1987.

Mies, Maria. *Patriarchy and Accumulation on a World Scale*. London: Zed Books, 1986.

Mohanty, Chandra Talpade, Ann Russo, and Lourdes Torres, eds. *Third World Women and the Politics of Feminism*. Bloomington: Indiana University Press, 1991.

Moser, Caroline, and Peake, L., eds. *Women, Human Settlements and Housing*. London: Tavistock Publications, 1987.

Olsen, Frances. "The Sex of Law." In *The Politics of Law: A Progressive Critique*, pp. 453. Edited by David Kairys. New York: Pantheon Books, 1990.

Razack, Sherene. *Canadian Feminism and the Law*. Toronto: Second Story Press, 1991.

Sayne, Pamela, and Judith Bell, eds. Women and Housing [Special issue] *Canadian Women Studies* 11.2 (Fall 1990).

Sayne, Pamela. "Food For Thought: Making Women Visible." *Environments and Urbanization*. 3.2 (October 1991): 46–50.

Sayne, Pamela. "Housing Language, Housing Reality?" *Canadian Woman Studies* 11.2 (Fall 1990):6.a)

Sayne, Pamela. "Up Against the Wall: a feminist approach to housing." Unpublished paper, 1990.

Sen, Gita, and Caren Grown. *Development, Crisis and Alternative Visions*. New York: Monthly Review Press, 1987.

Schabas, William. *International Human Rights Law in the Canadian Charter: A Manual for the Practitioner*. Carswell publishing, 1991.

Shelter For Us. Bombay: Bombay Women and Shelter Group, 1987.

Shiva, Vandana. *The Violence of the Green Revolution*. London: Zed Book Ltd., 1991.

Shiva, Vandana. *Staying Alive*. London: Zed Books, 1989.

Status of Women Canada. *Nairobi Forward-Looking Strategies for the Advancement of Women: Issues and the Canadian Situation*. Ottawa: Status of Women Canada, 1987.

Stewart, Julie, and Alice Armstrong, eds. *The Legal Situation of Women in Southern Africa*. Harare: University of Zimbabwe Publications, 1990.

Stone, John. *Racial Conflict in Contemporary Society*. Cambridge, Mass.: Harvard University Press, 1985.

Suzuki, David. *The Earth Spirit Festival* at Harbourfront, Toronto, July 5, 1991.

Taub, Nadine, and Elizabeth M. Schneider. "Women's Subordination and the Role of Law." In *The Politics of Law: A Progressive Critique*, pp. 151. David Kairys. ed. New York: Pantheon Books, 1990.

Wadden, Maria. *Nitassinan: The Innu Struggle to Reclaim Their Homeland*. Vancouver: Douglas & McIntyre Ltd., 1991.

United Nations. *Global Report on Human Settlements, 1986*. New York: Oxford University Press, 1987.

United Nations. *Human Rights: A Compilation of International Instruments*, New York: United Nations, 1983.

Waring, Marilyn. *If Women Counted*. New York: Harper and Row, 1988.

Chapter 12
The Importance of Housing in the Lives of Women: The Case of Botswana

Anita Larsson

Anita Larsson is a researcher at the National Swedish Institute for Building Research in Lund, Sweden. She was trained as an architect/ town planner and has a Ph.D. in Architecture. After working for about fifteen years as a town planner for Swedish municipalities as well as for the government of Botswana, she started her research on housing in Botswana, with a focus on the transition from traditional to modern housing and its consequences for low-income people, especially for women. Currently, she is studying low-cost housing, urbanization, changes in everyday life, and government housing policies in Botswana from the perspective of the government and the household.

In my studies of the transformation of urban and rural low-cost housing in Botswana not only the important role of women in providing houses and creating homes, but also the importance of housing in the lives of women has become more and more obvious.[1] Today three important roles of housing can be identified:

— the dwelling is the place for women's domestic work;
— the dwelling offers long- and short-term security for women as householders; and
— the dwelling contributes to strengthen women's identity in their roles as mothers and often also as a wives.

For an understanding of the importance of housing for women in today's society one has to have in mind women's attachment to houses and housing in the Tswana society[2], a fact I will return to. According to the thorough records of Schapera (1984), the houses, in line with traditional household utensils and furniture, were regarded as the belongings of women and under their control and supervision. Although the plot was allocated to the husband in his position as the head of the family, Tswana houses were referred to by the name of the wife occupying them. As the houses and the yard served as the physical environment for the woman's care of the family, she was the head of these houses. In addition, women played and play an important role in house building.

The paper will discuss and analyze the three roles of housing in relation to low-income women. In the final section some suggestions for developing existing housing policies as a part of gender policies away from discrimination and subordination of women are outlined.

The three roles are by no means separate from each other. On the contrary, they often support each other. For instance, if a dwelling supports a woman in her daily domestic chores, her identity as a housekeeper and good wife is strengthened. I will nonetheless discuss the three roles one by one.

The Dwelling as the Place for Domestic Work

When housing in relation to women is the topic, practical aspects such as how well or poorly the kitchen functions, if the floors are easily cleaned and if there is enough storage space for clothes and china often come to one's mind first, at least for Western women. As the person responsible for household work, a woman may raise a number of demands that the dwelling may fulfill or not. What is the situation in this respect for low-income households in villages and towns in Botswana?

The Village Dwelling

Urbanization is a late phenomenon in Botswana, and consequently most people have gained, and still gain, their first experiences of housing in a Tswana dwelling in the village, that is, in the type of dwelling rooted in Tswana culture and society. The Tswana dwelling of today, though simple in many ways, has some important qualities of utility. The most evident ones are access to sufficient space and the differentiation of the use of space.

A Tswana dwelling is made up of the houses *and* the surrounding yard, enclosed by a fence (Fig. 1). The houses, generally two to four in number, are constructed from mud, wood, and grass, that is, from materials which can be collected in or around the village. Daily activities take place both indoors and outdoors. While indoor space is mainly for sleeping purposes, for storage of personal belongings, and for providing privacy, the outdoor space is used for a number of activities. There may be special constructions for different activities or just an area set aside for a specific purpose. There are special enclosures in which food is cooked on an open fire and household utensils stored. Visitors are often received at the inner courtyard or lolwapa.

As necessary building materials are at hand without cost, at least in principle, a new house can be built whenever another room is needed, for instance, when children reach their teens (Tswana rules require boys and girls to sleep apart). Overcrowding and conflicting uses of the same space are thus not likely to occur in such a dwelling.

In contrast, daily household work is rather inconvenient. Firewood is still the most important fuel for cooking. It has to be collected, today often from far away. Also, water has to be fetched, but today most people have a communal standpipe within 400 meters. Due to lack of cold-storage facilities, fresh food, if included in a meal, has to be bought just before preparing. A lot of work takes place on the ground. The hearth is on the ground and there hardly ever is a counter for doing the dishes or washing clothes.

The Modern Low-Cost Dwelling

The main policy for housing the urban population in Botswana, like many developing countries, is home-ownership. Self-help projects have been set up to encourage people to build their own dwellings. In such projects low-income people are supported through the

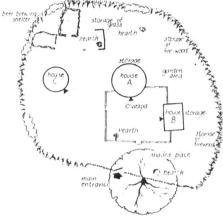

Fig. 1: In the Tswana dwelling both indoor and outdoor space is used for daily household activities. Drawing by Viera Larsson.

supply of building materials loans on favorable terms, technical advice and the supply of standard house plans. The first house to be built is a two-roomed one. Later it is extended by more rooms, or an additional multi-roomed house is constructed (Fig. 2).

In urban low-cost housing areas the infrastructure services are not significantly different from those in rural areas. Water has to be fetched, though the distance to the standpipe is shorter. Firewood can no longer be collected within a reasonable distance. Instead it is either bought or replaced by paraffin or gas. As in the village, lack of electricity prevents most people from having a cool storage space for fresh food. The use of gas or paraffin for cooking requires the stove to be indoors. But generally people cannot afford to set aside a special room only as a kitchen. Instead the stove has to be placed in the corner of a room used for many other purposes. Sinks for washing clothes and dishes are consequently lacking.

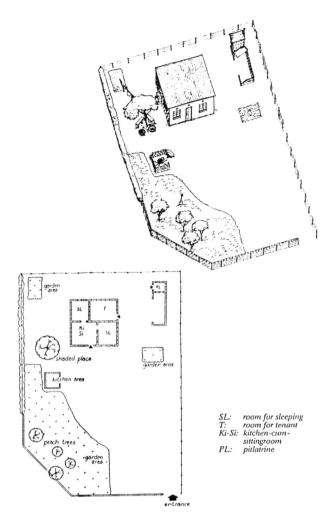

SL: room for sleeping
T: room for tenant
Ki-Si: kitchen-cum-
       sittingroom
PL: pitlatrine

Fig. 2: A modern dwelling in an urban self-help housing areas. One room is let to tenants.

Urbanization and modernization of housing have thus entailed few improvements in facilities making household work more convenient for low-income women. At the same time they have experienced deterioration in access to indoor space. In urban self-help housing areas only so-called modern materials are allowed to be used. For many people such materials mean considerable economic sacrifice and only two or three rooms can be built. In addition, the use of space has changed in the process of modernization and urbanization in conflicting ways: the need for indoor space has increased. For instance, the stove moves indoors due to new types of fuel. The risk of theft in towns requires that many bulky items have to be stored indoors, at least at night. New, modern ways of entertaining visitors indoors, or at least the desire for modern living-room furniture, raises the demand for indoor space. The important quality of

utility, expressed in sufficient indoor space for the family's different needs, including privacy, is thus missing in the modern low-cost dwelling. The traditional rules for arranging sleeping quarters at night can seldom be maintained (Fig. 3).

Sufficient space and adequate facilities for household work are both important qualities of the dwelling when women carry out household chores and take care of the family. Lack of such qualities were, however, not very explicitly expressed by the women in my fieldwork. Most people, whether men or women, who have built a modern house in an urban self-help housing area are proud of their achievements. They seldom see the above conflict between qualities of utility and a modernization of housing as mainly limited to a change of building materials. Complaints were instead generally expressed when I asked more specific questions like "are you satisfied with the arrangements for cooking?" or "are you satisfied with the way you can arrange sleeping quarters?" Then many women answered me with "No, we are overcrowded," "We need more space," or "I would like a proper kitchen."

One woman, an exception in her ability to verbalize her experiences, expressed the difficulties of living in a modern two-room dwelling in town in this way:

> We are crowded here, we sleep on top of our food. When I cook during rainy days it is terrible, my eyes get sore from the smoke, and the clothes in the wardrobe get smoky. At night we have to move around things to get space for sleeping. A traditional village dwelling is better, it is how we are born. In the village we have a fire-house for cooking and other houses for sleeping. Here it is more awkward than at home in the village.

Modernization and Improvements of Housing

Why has the modernization of housing not yielded any important improvements of dwellings in amenities to carry out household work and space for the family's different needs? The existence of a domestic sphere for women and a public sphere for men in Tswana society,[3] the clear division between them, and changes that have occurred as a result of the introduction of the cash economy offer some understanding.

The domestic sphere of Tswana society includes all types of work somehow related to the care of the family. It includes most duties needed for the preparation and cooking of food, such as fetching water and firewood, making beer, tilling the fields and collecting the harvest.

a piece of furniture
bedding in a bed
bedding on the floor

Fig. 3: This figure illustrates sleeping arrangements at night in two "furnished" houses. The house to the left is inhabited by eleven people. Husband (H), wife (W), and a four-year-old daughter (D) sleep in the bedroom in beds; four females and a young male share another room, three of them sleeping on the floor; and three young males sleep on the floor in the living room. In the house to the right a female householder (FH) sleeps in one room together with four small children. Three grown-up daughters sleep on the floor in a room used during the day as a kitchen. GD=granddaughter, S=son, GS=grandson, FR=female relative. Drawing by Viera Larsson.

It also includes building houses and being in charge of them. All those responsibilities are assigned to women in their role as wives. In rural areas these duties of women are still much alive while the roles assigned to men in Tswana society have changed considerably.

The public sphere of Tswana society was concerned with political and judicial decisions made by men only. It was characterized by its hierarchical organization, where the rank of the individuals was based on both heritage and individual achievements. One important means to express rank for men was through the number of cattle they owned.

When labor migration to South Africa started, it was the men who went away to earn cash. Cash earnings allowed them to buy not only food and other necessities, but also different objects such as furniture and to some extent building materials. The replacement of the subsistence economy by the cash economy and the subsequent introduction of modern building materials eventually entailed important changes concerning both the responsibility for housing and the qualities of utility. As modern materials are purchased and the husband earns money more often than the wife, the provision of modern housing has become the concern of the husband. It has meant a transfer of housing from the sphere of women to that of men. In the public sphere of men, the modern house, as a symbol of status and achievement, is of significance in a way corresponding to cattle. Much of women's experiences and knowledge of how to provide a dwelling for the family's needs has been lost in the transfer. The new role of houses as symbols of

status has overruled the role of houses as the place of living for the family. Modern housing has become synonymous with modern-looking houses through the use of modern materials.

The Importance of Housing for Unmarried Women

The few comments by women concerning functional and practical aspects of the dwelling were significant for both married women and single women who headed their own households in Gaborone, the capital. Women householders emphasized the second role of housing. The fact that dwellings provide long-term and short-term security by far overshadowed its practical aspects. Why are these characteristics of the dwelling so important to the single women in town?

The question is partly answered by looking at the background of the single women in Gaborone. That the number of households headed by women, not only in Botswana and Southern Africa but in the whole world, is increasing is widely recognized. The proportion of women-headed households in Gaborone is estimated at 45% (Botswana Government, 1988). The large majority are *de facto* heads of households. As a rule they are unmarried but may also be divorced or widowed. A small proportion are *de facto* heads of households, that is, they take the responsibility to head the household while the husband is away for a longer period, perhaps to work in South Africa.

Women Town-Migrants

The reason for coming to town stated in my interviews was mostly "to look for a job." Some who had arrived in town during periods of drought expressed themselves more dramatically, e.g., "I was running away from hunger" or "I was starving, life was too heavy on me." These types of answers fit well into women's migration patterns that emerge from different studies of rural women and women as migrants (for instance Izzard, 1982). Judging from such studies, a certain group of rural women exists who are more or less pushed away to town to make their living. For this group the traditional family network with its obligations no longer works. Although rural women have been in the role of house-holders (being widows, divorced, or unwed mothers) since the thirties, they have as a rule belonged to a wider network that could support them. It included men who in their capacity as fathers, brothers, uncles, or adult sons were supposed to help the women both economi-cally and practically (for instance, by ploughing the fields) according to traditional norms. When such norms are no longer as valid as before, a number of fairly young unwed mothers are left without support and are unable to survive on arable farming only. As possibilities for women to earn cash are almost non-existent in rural areas, there remains little for this group to do but to go to town and look for a job.

It is this group of women without supporting men that we are likely to find in urban low-cost housing areas, as squatters, as tenants of single rooms, or among plot-holders in self-help housing areas. We may also find them as domestic servants in high-cost areas or temporarily accommodated in others' households. What is important to bear in mind is that, when these women arrive in town, they have no reason to expect much support from relatives, especially not from male ones. If such support had existed the women might have remained in the rural areas. On the contrary, many of these women have aged parents to look after and send money back to. In return, the parents may take care of the women's children until the women have managed to create a platform for life in town.

"A Place of My Own"

My interviews revealed that not only to get a job and an income but also the need to get a "place of my own" are of outstanding importance while securing a platform for the urban life. The importance of earnings are obvious. Cash is needed for the support of children to replace the self-subsistence economy that has failed. Any place to stay provides a shelter to sleep, rest, and store one's personal belongings. Only a house of one's own, however, makes it possible for the woman to run her own household, that is, to become the head of the household. To achieve such a house is a lengthy and tiresome struggle for the women. Nonetheless, a housing trajectory can be traced from the life stories of women town-migrants.

Most women, like other town-migrants, have to be accommodated by relatives or friends upon their arrival in town. Thereby they become dependent on others. This situation is always experienced as temporary and insecure and consequently the women try to find a more secure and less dependent type of accommodation. Some women find a room to rent after they get a job and an income. This is, however, a costly type of dwelling and although the women are heading their own households they may be restricted by the landlord in different

ways. For instance, they may not be allowed to have their children around. Other women get jobs as domestic servants and in that way also a place to live. The domestic quarters are experienced by most women very much in the same way as the rented room. In addition, it is a very insecure type of housing: if the woman loses her employment, she also loses her dwelling.

To get away from the less secure types of housing, many women aim at building a house of their own in a self-help housing area. Women are thus well represented among plot-holders in such areas. According to the 1981 Census and other surveys, the average proportion of women plot-holders is roughly one-third, that is, close to the proportion of women-headed households in towns at the time of these surveys (Botswana Government, 1982 and 1985).

Such a house offers both short-term and long-term security, and it contributes to stability in women's often insecure urban life. It offers short-time security in the sense that temporary lack of a job or money does not force the women to leave their houses. The monthly cost of a house in a self-help housing area (including service levy and repayment of building material loan) is about half of that for renting one single room. In addition, one or two rooms in the house can be let and contribute to the income of the household. It is also a place where self-employment activities can be carried out when other ways of cash earnings are insufficient. And it is a place where the women can have their children around, to raise and enjoy—a desire expressed by most women.

Having a house of one's own offers long-term security in the sense that it provides a place to live in during old age, when no longer working; or to hand over to children so that they may get a fair chance to earn enough cash to support their mother on her return to the home village. Many women expressed a desire for such a return. If the children fail to get jobs in town, there will still be the possibility of getting money through letting rooms in the town house.

Migrating to town and having one's own house are thus important factors of women's survival strategies, and they are closely linked to each other. The house is, however, not just a means of survival. It also offers possibilities to live an urban life under the control of the women themselves and with human dignity. The house is both a means and an end.

Women's Commitment to Housing

My research concerning the role of housing in women's survival strategies has so far only included women householders. Does the dwelling of married couples fulfill the same role for married women? Answers from married women indicate that this is not necessarily the case. Women's subordinated position in marriage may result in a different relationship to housing than that illustrated by the unmarried women. To assume that husband and wife have the same relationship to their joint dwelling is probably a mistake, as suggested by research in Sweden (Bjork, 1989). What the situation in a country like Botswana looks like can be found out only if the gender perspective is brought into housing research.

An indication of a different relationship between housing on the one hand and men and women, respectively, as householders on the other hand is offered by data from an evaluation of the self-help housing projects in Botswana.[4] It showed that women-headed households earned less than men-headed households, which remained true even when the size of the household was taken into consideration. Despite these differences, the women-headed households had invested the same amount of money and built the same number of rooms for the family. When relating the income to the number of rooms in the house of each household, the survey showed that among households earning sufficient money to have a small surplus for investments, women householders had built more rooms than men householders. Notable also is that women householders were more concerned about paying back building material loans, especially among the households with very low incomes.

Women's Experience of Constraints

The above data support the consistent impression gained from interviews: women householders are sincere in their endeavor to get a house of their own despite having small incomes and many responsibilities. In this process the women experience a number of constraints. Governmental rules and regulations pertaining to assistance given low-income people do not, however, seem to discriminate against single women in any serious way. The constraints are instead related to the situations women confront, e.g., women-headed households are more often among the poor ones, women householders have the sole responsibility of child-rearing, bread-winning, and domestic work, etc. During my fieldwork a number of women pointed out that housing improvements had been postponed because much money was spent on secondary school fees. The abolition of school fees in 1988 was consequently a great relief to many women householders.

The constraints are also related to women's general subordination in society. Women get little practical support from the agencies of self-help housing. (Instead, I have come across some cases of counter-actions.) Women may also be cheated by the local builders employed for building the houses.

The most severe cases of discrimination are to be found in relation to marriage laws and their effect on property such as housing. Women who are divorced, widowed, or "live in separation" as well as married women are discriminated against concerning houses in such laws. Both customary and common law of Botswana are rather complicated and few people understand all the implications of them, both before conflicts in the marriage arise and when problems have to be sorted out. The essence of the law is that a modern urban house is generally under the husband's marital power. Thus a wife cannot prevent a husband from selling the house.

The fact that many women, when they have passed the age of thirty, are reluctant to marry, has been observed by many researchers (such as Gulbrandsen, 1986; Izzard, 1982). Single women, in contrast to married women, do not suffer from the legal constraints related to property. They manage their own property, including the house, and they can own their own business, and buy goods on credit. A married women can do that only if special precautions have been taken at the time of marriage. Under such circumstances, and having in mind that it was long ago that an unwed mother was stigmatized, it is perhaps no surprise that single women aim at becoming plot-holders in self-help housing areas. The very large number of unmarried women living in their own houses can perhaps be interpreted as the result of a very conscious strategy: to run their lives through the support of "my own house" rather than through the unsure support of a husband.

The Role of Housing in Strengthening Women's Identity

From the above it is evident that a dwelling of one's own is important not only for unmarried women's survival in town but also for supporting their identity as independent women and when fulfilling the role as mothers. Such a woman's own house makes her the householder and allows her to take care of the children herself. But the importance of dwellings for women can be seen not only for unmarried but also for married women in modern urban Tswana society.

Women as Heads of Houses and House Builders

I have previously pointed out the existence of a domestic sphere of women in Tswana society and women's close attachment to housing. The duties assigned to a wife were all related to the care of her family in a wide sense. They included her supervision and building of houses, and her role as the head of the house.
A number of records clearly show that women have long been involved in house building. According to the records by visitors to different Tswana societies during the beginning of the nineteenth century, women did all work related to house-building at that time. They cut the trees and collected grass and mud. They also built the walls, raised the roof structure, and put on the grass (Lichtenstein, 1930 and 1973; Burchell, 1953).

Around the middle of the last century men gradually took over the work to cut wood for the roof structure and to raise it. In connection with labor migration to South Africa, men picked up a new way of thatching from the Boer. This type of thatching, in which a stronger type of grass is used, provides a more solid and durable roof in comparison with the only previous method. Since the beginning of this century, Boer thatching is the work of local craftsmen. The older way of thatching is still practiced and today referred to as the traditional way. It has remained the duty of women, like all work carried out in mud. Although men carried out some duties of house building, Schapera in several of his records from around 1930 clearly points out that women held the responsibility to build houses and that men assisted the women in their work.

The duty as both head and builder of houses assigned to women formed the background, and still does, of the important role houses play in creating married women's identity and confidence in Tswana society. This became very evident in my work documenting Tswana houses in the early eighties. It was the wives of the households who told the story of how, when, and why the houses had been built. They also told how space was used indoors and outdoors and about different physical arrangements in the yard. The interviews all revealed a great degree of pride and confidence in the responsibility for these tasks and in the ability to handle them.

Women's Creativity

I also found that the active role of women in Tswana house building allowed them to develop their creativity, especially when decorating the houses and designing the walls of the lolwapa. Different clays were collected at different places to make a number of colors of the plastering possible. Since the plastering was often redone yearly, the color and the patterns of Tswana houses changed at regular intervals. Lolwapa walls were often redecorated shortly before wedding festivals. It was the pride of the women to have a nice lolwapa wall and women would compete by giving new shapes and ornaments to the walls.

These recent experiences fit very well with nineteenth century records and Schapera's writings. For instance, Burchell, after his visit to the Batlhaping[5] in 1812, wrote that the house of the chief's uncle "was also of the largest size; a circumstance to be ascribed perhaps more to the architectural talents of his wife, than to his own rank or situation in society" (1953, p. 367). Around 1930 Brown found that "some women show great skill in the ornamentation of the walls and many of them are expert potters" (1926, p. Sl) and Schapera noted that "women smeared on the mural decorations which were the pride of every self-respecting house-wife" (1967, p. 14).

Modern Houses and Women's Identity

The responsibility of providing decent housing and a home for the family together with the confidence derived from such tasks are also to be found in urban low-cost areas. The commitment to house the family properly, which I found among the women householders in Gaborone, can be regarded as an indication of the survival of women's traditional duties of providing shelter, although the setting had totally changed.

The creativity that women can develop when actually building Tswana houses has, however, apparently been lost in the process of housing modernization. Only once in a while may one see a colored concrete wall with patterns similar to what can be found in the villages, or a low lolwapa-like wall around a terrace in urban housing areas. Women feel that building in modern materials is a task that can be carried out only by men. This fact, together with the government's decree that only modern materials are to be used in most towns, has meant that women do not develop their skills and creativity in connection with modern housing. Instead they have been deprived of the confidence derived from their active participation in house building.

The modern house in town contributes to the identity of women in a different way. Migration to town is necessary for many women and in that perspective the achievement of a modern house, although not modern in the sense that it has amenities to make household work more convenient, is an indication of having become a town-dweller. The modern house as a symbol and visible token of modern urban life confirms a woman's success both as a town migrant and a modern person. Instead of decorating the houses as such, attention is devoted to the interior. If the women can afford it, they buy furniture of modern design and put decorations of different types up on the walls.

Summary and Policy Implications

I have so far tried to show how housing plays several important roles in the lives of women. These roles have changed over time. The transformation is linked to the modernization of housing and of society. I will summarize these changes and indicate their implications for the development of housing policies in relation to gender.

Housing has always been important for the support of a women's identity as mother and housewife. In Tswana society this role of housing in Botswana is strongly linked to the domestic sphere of women and all the duties inherent in the sphere. The wife was both the builder and caretaker of houses. The role of housing as a means for the wife in Tswana society to express pride, confidence and creativity has, however, not been carried over into modern society. To build houses in modern materials has instead become the concern of men. In the process of housing modernization, married women have been deprived of their traditional duty to provide shelter for the family. Their most important role today in relation to housing is to carry out the daily household work.

For today's women householders, the situation is different. The role of housing most explicitly expressed in the interviews with such women was that housing was a prerequisite to and a means for running their own households and their lives. An overall modernization of society has allowed such women to become heads of households. The importance of housing is strongly linked to their arrival in town alone in order to support their children. A house of her own supports a woman in her more or less conscious efforts away from a general

situation of discrimination and subordination. If the words of the women are taken as indicators, such a role of housing is by far more important than simply meeting practical needs for shelter. Single women who build modern houses gain and retain their identity, both as modern people and as those responsible for providing shelter to the family.

Married women in the urban setting do not have the same relationship to housing as single women. In contrast, in case of a legal divorce or just a separation, they experience a number of constraints created by the existing marriage laws.

Housing Modernization and the Domestication of Women

Women's traditional knowledge and experiences have thus not been considered as resources in the development of housing after Independence. As in many other cases in developing countries, the government's plans to develop a certain sector have not taken into consideration women and their important traditional roles. Instead, overall changes of society have contributed to what has been called the domestication of women. Rogers (1980) argues that women are generally losers in projects to promote development. Instead of being allowed to participate, they are confined, or domesticated, to the unpaid domestic sector separated from the modern one. This is true for agriculture in many African countries, including Botswana. It is true for housing in Botswana, and perhaps in many countries in the Third World. Housing has become part of the modern sector, and thus housing modernization has deprived women from participation in the development of the modern sector.

Modernization of housing has meant lack of improvements, and even deteriorations in the dwelling's use values. There have been few improvements for women when carrying out their daily household chores of cooking, washing, and cleaning. Instead, women often experience shortage of indoor space and lack of privacy. Women are, however, reluctant to raise claims concerning the practical qualities of a dwelling. This reluctance, I feel, should not be taken as a token of women's satisfaction with existing space and amenities for household work. Factors such as the subordinated position of women, both in the modern and traditional Tswana society, women being used for a great number of labor-intensive tasks in the domestic sphere, and men's important role in modern housing offer important explanations of the present situation. Instead of accepting the course of events as natural, I feel that dwellings, whether in low-, medium-, or high-cost areas, should be improved in this respect. The improvement of qualities of utility in low-cost housing is indeed a little explored area within the field of housing. But to adjust the level of standards to what people can afford will require various means.

A Housing Modernization to Support Women

A way to overcome the shortcomings that so far have been linked to housing modernization is to identify and recognize fully the important role of housing in the lives of women and the important role of women in Tswana housing. One way of doing that would be to aim at a legal position of the dwelling they live in together. Another way would be to allow women to play a more significant role in the development of housing policies.

According to present Botswana law, a wife has a say over the house if the wife is the owner according to the deeds register, only if she and her husband are married *out* of community of property *and* the marital power of the husband has been excluded through a prenuptial agreement. This possibility has meaning only for women who have enough income or capital to allow them to live economically independently of their husbands. That is seldom the case, and especially not for low-income women.

A first step to improve the situation of low-income women would be to register both husband and wife as plot-holders (holders of certificate of rights) in the self-help housing areas. Presently only the head of the household, that is, the husband in a married couple, can be recognized as the formal plot-holder. The plot could instead be registered in the name of both husband and wife and both could be required to give their consent before the house can be sold. While the woman in such cases may be put under pressure to sell, she is neverthe-less given a chance to prevent the sale, if she feels it is necessary.

If the spouses are separated, the main constraints today are not so much the existing laws but the difficulties involved in getting a legal divorce at the High Court. Money and legal assistance are necessary but not available prerequisites for low-income people. If the couple has been married in community of property, the woman will get half of the value of their joint property, including the house in the self-help area. Thus a legal

divorce, after a separation, may make a great difference for her. Many women, however, have to leave the house and other properties in connection with a separation and then start a new life from scratch.

Women householders' economic situation is further weakened by the difficulties unmarried or separated women experience trying to get child maintenance from the father of the children through a verdict at the Magistrate's Court. The experience of many women is that their cases never come up for a hearing in court. They seem to be stuck at the end of the list. Information and legal assistance directed specifically to low-income women in the self-help housing areas would be of great help for many.

Women can also play a more important role in the development of housing policies at different levels in the administration if training and recruitment specifically directed to them are introduced. For instance:

— at the local offices of the self-help agencies: women can be encouraged, even purposely selected, to become technical officers and other types of supporting staff;

— at Town Councils: women can be encouraged to become architects or building engineers involved in tasks such as the design of low-cost dwellings, the development of standard house-types, and the development of building regulations; and

— at the Ministry of Local Government and Lands (respon-sible for housing) and at the Botswana Housing Corpora-tion: women can purposely be selected to handle housing matters as senior officers.

Women's role as housekeepers, which makes them more concerned about qualities of utility of the dwelling, is one important argument in favor of such changes. Another is that women technical officers are likely to be better at understanding and supporting women who want to get help and advice from the branch offices of the self-help agencies. A conscious concentration on women in the running of the self-help agencies would benefit all women somehow involved in house-building in low-cost housing areas. These changes would also mean that women are offered more types of employment opportunities on the labor market. The outcome of the housing transformation, instead of enforcing the domestication of women, would be to give women more opportunities to participate in housing as a part of the modern sector.

Notes

[1] My studies of housing in Botswana are presented in four reports: Anita Larsson and Viera Larsson (1984), Anita Larsson (1988, 1989, 1990). This article is based on all four reports.

[2] The Tswana are one of the major sub-groups of the Southern Bantu cultures. Today there are about one million Tswana people living in Botswana (total population of around 1,200,000) and another million living in South Africa, mainly in the so-called homeland Bophuthatswana.

[3] I use the concepts "domestic and public spheres" in line with their interpretation by Rosaldo (1974). For a detailed elaboration of their meaning in the Tswana society, see Larsson (1990).

[4] The evaluation is presented in Botswana Government (1985) but not in relation to male vs. female householders. The collected material included, however, information on the sex of householders and thus the information could be analyzed accordingly. For more details, see Larsson (1988).

[5] One of the major sub-groups of the Tswana, who lived in the northern part of South Africa at the time of the arrival of Europeans.

References

Bjork, Mia. (1989) *Min tid ar din* ("My time is yours."). Arbetsfördelningen mellan könen ur ett boendeperspektiv. M:30. Gavle, Sweden: the National Swedish Institute for Building Research.

Botswana Government (1982). *Summary Statistics on Small Areas.* Central Statistics Office, Ministry of Finance and Development Planning. Gaborone: Government Printer.

Botswana Government (1985). *An Evaluation of the Self-Help Housing Agencies.* Ministry of Local Government and Lands.

Botswana Government (1988). *Household Income and Expenditure Survey: 1985/86.* Gaborone: Government Printer.

Brown, J. Tom (1926). *Among the Bantu Nomads: a Record of Forty Years spent among the Bechuana.* London: Seeley Service.

Burchell, William J. (1953). *Travels in the Interior of Southern Africa.* Vol 2. London: The B Batchworth Press.

Gulbrandsen, Omulf (1986). "To marry or not to marry. Marital strategies and sexual relations in a Tswana society." *Scandinavian Journal,* 51 (1-2): 7-28.

Izzard, Wendy (1982). *Rural-Urban Migration in a Developing Country: The Case of Women Migrants in Botswana.* Oxford University: Ph.D. thesis.

Larsson, Anita (1988). *From Outdoor to Indoor Living. The transition from traditional to modern low-cost housing in Botswana.* Report R:44 1988. University of Lund: Department of Building Functions Analysis.

Larsson, Anita and Larsson, Viera (1984). *Traditional Tswana Housing. A study in four villages in eastern Botswana.* Stockholm: Swedish Council for Building Research. Document D7:1984.

Larsson, Anita (1989). *Women Householders and Housing Strategies. The Case of Gaborone. Botswana.* SB:25. Gavle: The National Swedish Institute for Building Research.

Larsson, Anita (1990). *Modern Houses for Modern Life. The Transformation of Housing in Botswana.* Report Rl:1990. University of Lund: Department of Building Function Analysis.

Lichtenstein, Harry (1930). *Travels in Southern Africa. Vol. 2.* Cape Town: The Van Riebeeck Society.

Lichtenstein, Harry (1973). *Foundation of the Cape. About the Bechuanas.* Cape Town: A.A. Balkema.

Rogers, Barbara (1980). *The Domestication of Women. Discrimination in Developing Societies.* London: Tavistock Publications.

Rosaldo, Michelle Zimbalist (1974). "Woman, Culture, and Society: A Theoretical Overview." In: Rosaldo, Michelle Zimbalist and Lamphere, Louise (eds), *Woman Culture and Society.* California: Stanford University Press.

Schapera, Isaac (1967). "The Old Bantu Culture." In I. Schapera (ed), *Western Civilization and the Natives of South Africa.* London: Routledge & Kegan Paul Ltd.

Schapera, Isaac (1984). *A Handbook of Tswana Law and Custom.* London: Frank Cass and Company Limited.

Chapter 13
The Invisible Contribution of Married Women in Housing Finance and Its Legal Implications: A Case Study from Port Harcourt, Nigeria

Yomi Oruwari

Yomi Oruwari is an architect and urban designer. She is a lecturer at the Department of Architecture, Rivers State University of Science and Technology, Port Harcourt, Nigeria.

The importance of housing finance to the provision of urban shelter in Nigeria is undeniable. This in itself emphasizes the seriousness of the problems militating against the involvement of married women in housing finance in Nigeria, even though female recipients of mortgage loans have been more responsible about repaying their debts than male recipients, and a greater proportion of male recipients are defaulters (Moser and Chant, 1985). The paper discusses the legal implications of home ownership in Nigeria and how they affect the participation of married women in housing finance. Focusing on educated married women in Port Harcourt and their invisible contribution, the discussion includes the unfairness of the laws of ownership and inheritance. It offers a different perception of the role of women in the development of human settlements.

Generally, studies of women are of poor rural women, because it is assumed that urban women are more enlightened and therefore do not need assistance. Married women have not been conceptualized as comprising a group in need of special attention, especially in housing studies. In developing countries, housing finance studies that focused on women have concentrated on the difficulties female-headed households have in mobilizing resources and more specifically on their limited accessibility to housing loans and their repayment behavior (Schlyter, 1988; Mose and Peak, 1987). But there are indications that educated married women in urban areas are suffering from principally three main oppressions they encounter in their homes: oppression because they are women; oppression because they are educated and if given the opportunity they can assert their rights; and oppression because of the oppressive nature of traditional values and customs that they cannot do anything about individually.

Detailed information will be presented concerning twenty married women who have attained the highest level of competence in their chosen fields of occupation, are either in monogamous or polygamous homes, and whose husbands have built or bought houses and their involvement in the financing of such buildings. The women live in Port Harcourt, the capital of Rivers State and the fourth major industrial city in the country. Interviews of five married men who have built houses were also conducted.

The problems of women's involvement in housing finance are not restricted to Nigeria. They have been and are being experienced in other developing countries. They reflect the erroneous assumptions that all families conform to the Western nuclear model and that spouses everywhere pool their resources for the welfare of everyone in the household. These assumptions ignore the extended family system of Nigerian society. Nevertheless, they permeate housing policies and programs in Nigeria. Thus the programs have been directed at heads of households, invariably men. Women's programs are few and far between, although it has already been acknowledged that women are a little over half of Nigeria's population.

Research Methods

This paper is based on structured personal interviews. Although the age of the household was not a criterion, it turned out that none of the respondents had been married for less than ten years. The number of women to be interviewed was not decided in advance although we tried to vary their professions as much as possible. The interviews were continued until it was realized that new interviews would not add important information to our understanding of the problem under investigation. In all, twenty women were interviewed, as were five men, to get their opinions of their wives' involvement in housing finance.

To derive a better understanding of the problem, the following questions were posed:

1. What has been the contribution of women to the building or acquisition of houses by their husbands?
2. What are the current marital laws and their gender implications as they relate to housing?
3. What are the constraints limiting the participation of married women in housing finance?

These questions guided the preparations for the interviews. The different attitudes of monogamous and polygamous households, the different cultural values existing in the country, and the different attitudes of the Moslem and Christian religions were recognized.

The Role of Women in Housing Finance

Some basic social assumptions are common to all the different cultural systems of Nigeria. These are:

1. Social and economic stability depends on men being made primarily responsible for maintenance of their families.
2. Cultural family laws create unequal responsibilities for maintenance and therefore permit unequal distribution of family assets.

Thus traditionally, it is the duty of the man to provide his wife with a place to live. However, this view is inconsistent with reality.

The following family circumstances are presented to give a more dynamic picture of the role of women in housing provision in general and in housing finance in particular. They will also highlight the contributions, both visible and invisible, made by the women and their feelings about how their contributions are appreciated by both their husbands and the state. Inferences from these recordings will inform the summary at the end of the paper.

Indirect Contributions

Generally, the women not only contributed directly by giving money to their husbands but also indirectly by assisting in running the home, especially during the construction period.

Caroline has been married for twelve years. Her husband has just finished building his house. Although she did not contribute directly, she knows that she contributed a lot by encouraging him to start building incrementally since they got married; during the construction, subsidizing the feeding allowance he gave her and/or doing without it when he did not give any; lending him money and foregoing the feeding allowance in any month he repays the loan; emotionally, by advising him; and morally, by encouraging him. When she asked her husband why her name was not included in the title to the property, he said there was no need to worry because what belongs to him belongs to her. The question is, "If it belongs to us, why is my name not on the title deed? Seeing my name on it makes all the difference." She knows that in case of divorce, she has to pack up and move out. Her consolation is that her children will inherit his properties, for no Nigerian man forgets his children. That is why as far as she is concerned any marriage without children is no marriage and of course she is his only wife (on paper). She cannot fight the issue on her own because the problem stems from the marital and traditional laws: women are not expected to own anything. However, women's organized conferences, talks, etc., have been opening everyone's eyes to the shortcomings of our cultural laws (e.g., women are gradually inheriting land). Another problem is that the battle for women in developing countries is fought more by women in the developed world. She does not keep a joint account with her husband because in our society a husband and wife face different pressures from their extended families, the only sources of welfare. She also sincerely believes that a women should be individuated in the control of the resources she creates.

Monica has been married for forty years by the common law with six children. When her husband was building the house twenty years ago, he consulted her. She assisted in paying the monthly mortgage, although he was the only person that signed the loan's papers. She also gave him money to buy building materials. It never occurred to her to ask whether her name was on the title to the property or to ask for the receipts of purchases she paid for. On hindsight, she knows that, had she asked, he would have insinuated that she did not trust him or asked whether she wanted to kill him. After the building was completed, she encouraged him to leave the civil service and set up a business of his own. During the teething period, she was practically financing the household alone. Fortunately, the business flourished. Then her husband took a younger wife by customary law and has practically abandoned her. When she consulted a lawyer, she was told that it would be difficult to contest the house since there is no proof of her involvement in the building, and furthermore she would not like to embarrass her children by taking their father to court. The only regret she has is that, instead of assisting her husband to build his house, she should have expended her energies to build a house of her own.

The Effect of Customary Laws

In some cultures, marriages cannot be dissolved.

Ester has been married for twenty-five years with five children. The husband consulted her when he was going to start the building. The title deed bears his name alone. She does not have a house of her own since she cannot afford to buy land in the open market. She was denied access to crown land which is given on a lease basis because her husband had already been given his. She did not play any role during construction because her husband did not consult her. She claimed that her type of marriage gave her confidence that all is not lost. "You are his property, although there can be separation, there can be no divorce even though he can marry more wives." She explained that it is not that the educated women are sleeping, but according to her, "When the people that take decisions are men—what do you expect?" For example, she is a member of the Women and Development Organization. They organize lectures and talks to enlighten the women. They know that there

cannot be meaningful changes until a lot of women get to positions of power. She does not keep a joint account with her husband. He discouraged the idea. She knows that our men are generally insincere and unfaithful to their wives all around.

Influence of Polygamy and Religion

In Moslem marriages, the wife is encouraged to own her own property. In a polygamous home, the economic tie between the husband and wife is very loose.

Sadia, who has been married for fifteen years, is the second wife in a polygamous Muslim family. The husband informed her when he was going to start the building. Although she did not contribute to the building, she consciously made less demands on him during the period. She knows that she does not have any stake in the house. However, her children have rights equal to those of the other wife's children. She knows her name was not on the deed of the house, but she did not expect it to be. In case of divorce, she does not expect to contest the house. "How can I, when I know that there is no law to back me? I would be crazy to take a housing loan with him to build a house. If I am able to take a loan, it will be for my own house." As far as she is concerned, the efforts of the women's commission is a lost cause. "Who is going to judge the cases? Is it not male judges, who invariably will be in the same circumstances like my husband?"

The Strong Cultural Influence

The marriage is influenced by the culture whether it is contracted under common law, Islamic law, or customary law.

Linda, who has been married for eighteen years, contributed financially to the building of the house, although only the husband's name is on the deed to the property. She contributed because they share their resources together, although they do not have a joint account. She said that her husband is more understanding than most, because in her culture, the man has rights over everything, including the wife's salary. For example, her friend is having a lot of problems with her husband: he insists that she gives him her pay, from which he doles out what she will spend according to his decisions. Her husband made all the decisions about the housing loan and its disbursement, but she monitors the repayment because she does not like owing money, and she knows that her husband can be extremely careless. What baffles her is that men cleverly forget that according to the same custom, tradition, and culture, the man is expected to take care of the household and build houses for his wives.

Influence of the Extended Family System

Because of insecurity in the household, spouses keep close ties with their first families to which they fulfill economic commitments.

Hope, who has been married for thirteen years, informed her husband about the house when it was up for sale since she works in the building section of the ministry in charge. She knows that her name is not on the lease because her husband is fond of telling her to move out of his house any time there is a misunderstanding. "If my name is there, he will not do so." She has no house of her own but she contributed to the building of her parents' house because she knows they can never reject her. She is aware of her rights and does not push for them just to keep peace in the home. If she raises the issue of inclusion of her name in the deed, it will trigger anger and bitterness on his part. "It is the fault of our social system which gives the man the freedom to do whatever he likes and the wife either takes it or ships-out." Educated women are the most prepared to subjugate their rights to the requirements of society, to subordination of women to their husbands' whims and caprices, so as to keep their marriages.

Influence of Diverse Upbringing

Because of diverse upbringing by different cultures, customs, religions, etc., most married couples view their homes differently.

Beauty has been married for ten years. She did not contribute anything because she did not know that her husband was building a house. She learned of it by accident through a friend. When she confronted him, she was told that it was meant to be a surprise. Automatically, she assumed his name alone will be on the title to the property. She does not have any stake in the property and in case of divorce, she does not expect any benefit from it. She feels that this is because the orientation of a home is not in her household. It has to do with the different background of both of them. According to her, a man from a polygamous home, although married by the common law, does not know how to make a home with a woman. All he knows is that his father and mother lead separate lives and that is what he brings into his own married life. She knows that the level of awareness of women is very low and

that they should be educated about owning houses of their own without depending on their husbands.

Professional Influence

From their experiences of the few cases that get to the law courts, some of the women are insisting on their rights.

Janette has been married for ten years. She keeps a joint account with her husband and he consulted her before buying the land and building the house. Initially in their married life, the husband's name was on their possessions, e.g., furniture, cars, etc., but with her experiences in the law courts as a lawyer, she had to change things. This is why she insisted that her name should also be on the deed of the house. The reason is that the extended family members can be very troublesome, especially within her own traditions. She said that, generally, Nigerians have a superstitious phobia about writing wills and that women are fond of blindly trusting their husbands. They built the house through their joint resources and took a loan together from their bankers. Because of the confidence he gave her, she decided he should control the disbursement of the money to the workers. She could not see married women taking active part in housing finance except for direct enactments and judges are becoming more accommodating to the needs of women. She thinks that women should be more vocal and active in demanding their rights, educating the nation, and demanding actions, although there is the problem of intimidation both at home and in society.

The Men's View on the Issues

The views of some men were sought and reported, to balance the presentation.

James has been married for eleven years. He told his wife that he had bought land after the fact, and he did not consult her before he started the building, although she knew about it as the work progressed. He behaved in this fashion because he knows that she does not want to contribute to anything in the household although she earns as much as he does. Since he was spending his money, he did not need her consent. Of course the title to the property is in his name alone because whatever he has belongs to him and his children. He does not think that the house belongs to the two of them because she is always resisting contributing so, in case of separation, she has to move out of his house. He feels that contribution to housing finance in whatever form should be voluntary, and it is the materialistic nature of women, especially the married ones, that is the major block to their better treatment by their husbands. He thinks that for women to be able to assist in housing, they must change their attitudes, and that if a wife is cooperative, a man does not need the law to tell him to include her name in the title to the property.

John, who has been married for seventeen years, has seven children. He is proud to admit that he has a very close relationship with his wife. He discusses everything he does with her, although they do not keep a joint account. After he has praised her with all the superlatives, it is surprising that his name is the only one on the title to the deed to the house. His explanation is that there is no need to put her name on it since she belongs to him; it is contrary to our culture; and as far as his inheritance is concerned, she is number one although he has not made a will. He admitted that his wife played a very important role in the building of the house by contributing financially and morally, and by giving him encouragement. He never contemplates divorce, because as Christians they cannot divorce. He knows that, if they have problems, prayers will solve them.

The Problem of Marital Laws in Nigeria

The problem with marital laws stems from the infusion of the common law instituted by the former colonial administrators into the existing customary laws. Thus, in contrast to the Europeans' one-system law, Nigeria operates three systems: common law, customary law, and Islamic law. The common law has remained at the state of English common law when women were classified with children and lunatics. This has resulted in confusion, with the result that women are unable to take their husbands to court for most of the offenses the men get away with. The revised constitution of 1949 declares that there is no child that is illegitimate; thus men now openly commit bigamy. If women take their husbands to court for bigamy, very few marriages by the common law will be left in the country. Also, women have realized the futility of embarking on prosecution for bigamy, because the judge, who invariably is a man, will in most cases be guilty of the same offense. In customary and Islamic law, a man can have more than one wife.

In Nigeria, in case of rights intervivos, it seems that in every type of marriage the husband has automatic right to the wife's property, but the wife has no such reciprocal right to her husband's property. According to the common law, all and any property of the wife brought to the marriage or acquired while she is married belongs to both of them, unless the wife clearly manifests a contrary intention. The same is not true of the husband's property. Even when she has contributed, she must be able to show concrete evidence of her contributions.

No system of customary law gives the wife any right to inherit her husband's property. It does not recognize monetary or non-monetary contributions by the wife either to the marriage or to the purchase of matrimonial assets as constituting a claim to an equitable interest in any of the properties owned by the husband. Although Islamic law generally encourages the principle of separate properties, the same principle as that of the customary law applies. In both customary and Islamic law, as observed by Akande (1979), the wife is herself a property of the husband. Therefore, whatever she acquires in marriage is a property of the husband.

In all systems, a divorced wife must vacate the premises since her right to remain depends on her continued marriage to the husband. She has no claim to the property. With regard to inheritance, a wife has no succession rights to her husband's estate, irrespective of her contributions toward the acquisition of the property. At the same time, a woman cannot acquire or hold an interest in property which her husband built in the village, even if she contributed to the cost of its building.

Findings and Implications for Women's Involvement in Housing Finance

1. The social and cultural norms in Nigeria have very strong effects on the behavior of spouses irrespective of the type of marriage contracted.

2. Married women's potentials in mobilizing resources, especially for housing finance, disbursing same, and making sure that mortgages are paid regularly, have not been utilized because of the identified constraints of marital laws existing in the country.

3. A woman's effective possession of the resources she produces or earned within the household is determined by her relative power via-à-vis her husband's, whereas the husband's control of the resource she creates depends on him. In most of the customs existing in the country, she does not have any rights.

4. A long habit of not thinking a thing wrong gives it a superficial appearance of being right, especially when it is a custom with a religious foundation that has always favored a dominant group. There must, therefore, be planned interventions as distinct from autonomous

processes of social change. And, as argued by Lele (1986), it is by changing the mix of legal institutions, education, and economic incentives, that public policy over time will make a significant difference to social choices affecting female members of traditional households.

5. Two concepts of sharing in households have emerged: total sharing and partial sharing of resources between spouses. Policies must recognize the two concepts for them to be effective. Partial sharing gives the wife room to have her own investments irrespective of the contributions she makes toward the husband's invesments. Laws are needed to back up her ownership. In the case of total sharing, the study has shown that the family set-up is not conducive for it to be effective.

To utilize the potentials of about half of the population, policies must recognize that there are different actors in the household and, therefore, must be directed at individuals in the households rather than households themselves.

When a house is being built, the spouses do not antici-pate future separation. As argued by Lord Denning (1980), if the whole of the husband and wife's resources are expended for their joint benefits, then the product should belong to them jointly. This is the crux of the problem — the inequitable distribution of household benefits. It is only when married women know that they have a stake in the properties that they will be willing to assist in their financing and execution.

We can argue that policies should move in this direction, but we must recognize that, because of tradition and culture, the task will be formidable. What we need, first, are judges who are forward-looking activists, who recognize that women are persons and not things as already stated in the Nigerian constitution.

At present no organizations give credit specifically to women for housing in Nigeria. It is necessary to recognize that women can own houses of their own, even when they are married. It is surprising that, although women use housing more than men, they participate less than men in the execution of the projects. The men conveniently refuse to recognize their invisible contribution through subsidizing other household expenses. It is not possible to correct this imbalance found to exist in property right bias between husband and wife without legislation (Lord Denning, 1980).

But when legislation is needed to correct injustices passed down through tradition and custom, then it is society, epitomized by the judiciary, that has to decide to rid itself of this injustice. Only when women know that they have a right to what they earn, have a right to the houses they build with their husbands, that they will willingly assist in acquiring housing for their house-holds. But tradition is a matter of process, and ridding it of negative influences will also have to go through stages.

Summary

It would be difficult and pretentious to end this paper with a conclusion since the lessons of how to finance the provision of shelter are still being assimilated and absorbed. Some of the issues are becoming clearer. There is a growing awareness of the need to seek pragmatic solutions to the problems that arise, to listen and learn from the people themselves about their experiences and what must be done to maximize their involvement in acquiring and using available resources. Since the problem has strong cultural connotations, global generalizations cannot be made.

The country's marital laws, especially regarding property and ownership, are the major constraints on married women's involvement in housing finance. But the resource women represent cannot be useful until society is ready to recognize its importance and there-fore changes its retrogressive attitude to women. At the same, time women's organizations should not relent in their efforts to educate the populace through lectures, conferences, and research of this nature so as to direct the attention of men to the benefits and the importance of participation of married women in housing finance and to the interrelated problems that face women in the urban environment.

References

Akande, J. (1979), *Law and Status of Women in Nigeria.* Addis Abada: Economic Commission for Africa.

Denning, Lord (1980), *The Due Process of Law.* London: Butterworths Publishing Company.

Federal Ministry of Works and Housing (1979), *The National Housing Policy for Nigeria*, Lagos.

Federal Republic of Nigeria (1985), *Report of the Special Committee on New National Housing Policy.* Lagos.

Federal Republic of Nigeria (1989), *The Revised Constitution..* Lagos.

Jones, C.J. (1981), "Women's Legal Access to Land," in B.C. Lewis (ed.), *Invisible Farmers: Women and the Crisis in*

Agriculture. Washington, D.C.: Women in Development, A.I.D.

Lele, Uma (1986), "Women and Structural Transformation," *Economic Development and Structural Change, 34,* No. 2.

Moser, C., and L. Peake (1987), *Women, Human Settlements and Housing.* London: Tavistock Publications.

Moser, Caroline O.N., and Sylvia H. Chant (1985), "The role of women in the execution of low income housing projects training module." D.P.U. Gender Planning Working Paper 4 No. 6, London.

Okocha, Hopelinda (1991), "The Concept of Justice and Equality for Nigerian Women: Fact or Fiction." An unpublished Bachelor of Law project at Rivers State University of Science and Technology, Port Harcourt, Nigeria.

Peltenbert, Monique (1990), "Women and low income housing finance: towards a research programme." A paper presented at Seminar on Gender and Housing. Lund: The National Swedish Institute for Building Research.

Pittin, Renee (1984), "Documentation and Analysis of the Invisible Work of Invisible Women: A Nigerian Case Study." *International Labour Review, 123,* No. 4, July–August.

Rakodi, Carole (1991), "Women's work or household strategies." *Environment and Urbanisation, 3,* No. 2, October.

Schlyter, Ann (1988), *Women householders and housing strategies: the case of George, Zambia.* Galvle: The National Swedish Institute for Building Research. SB: 14.

Schylter, Ann (1990), "Women in Harare: Gender Aspects of Urban-Rural Interactions," in: Jonathan Baker (ed.), *Small Town Africa.* Uppsala: The Scandinavian Institute of African Studies.

Tym, Roger (1984), "Finance and Affordability," in: G.K. Payne (ed.), *Low Income Housing in the Developing World.* New York: John Wiley and Sons Ltd.

Urban Edge, 12, No. 1 (1988), "Making Development Work for Urban Women."

Whitehead, Ann (1981), "I'm hungry, mum: The Politics of Domestic Budgeting," in: Kate Young, *et al.* (eds.), *Of Marriage and the Market.* London: CSE Books.

Theme 3
Shelter and Women in Crisis

The absence of appropriate housing options plays a key role in the situation of many women in crisis. Women experiencing spousal abuse, women addicted to drugs or alcohol, women abandoned by their partners, and impoverished women who are physically or mentally ill all may require immediate access to a safe, affordable shelter. Shelter alone, however, is inadequate to assist such women in resolving their crises. The necessity of coordinating affordable shelter with appropriate social services creates a unique challenge to practitioners in both fields. The papers in this theme investigate ways in which organizations from both the First and Third World have met this challenge. The societal and economic causes leading to homelessness and the special crises of homeless women in First and Third World countries are compared in the first paper (Bergholz). The second paper delineates the mismatch between the needs of women in crisis in Bombay and services and facilities offered by the existing shelter homes. Dabir suggests needed organizational changes. The next two papers describe efforts to house women with specific vulner-abilities—women with AIDS (Cameron and Lee) and chemical addiction (Snyder). The last three papers describe innovations to create new housing units which are suitable for women in crisis. Gillette discusses the creation of affordable housing by nonprofit organiza-tions to counteract the increasing homelessness of women. Some illustrations of this approach are pro-vided in the two papers which follow. Brown and Capponi share the lessons obtained from their experi-ence of housing homeless women in Toronto. Peterson describes the issues which surface when transitional housing for women is developed by various grassroots, women-led groups in Boston. The underlying objective is empowerment of women through their involvement in creating housing, an objective which is addressed at length in Theme 4. The papers in this theme serve to focus attention on the spectrum of needs of women in crisis. They provide an opportunity to learn from the experience of practitioners active in this area and to reach some general conclusions about the approach and process that is needed to address the housing needs of women in crisis.

Photo: *Hemalata C. Dandekar*

Chapter 14
Women and Crisis: An Overview of Homelessness in the First and Third World

Margrit Bergholz

Margrit Bergholz *is a master's student in the Department of City and Regional Planning at the University of North Carolina at Chapel Hill. She has extensive professional experience in affordable housing development and finance, having worked for the cities of Philadelphia and Fremont, California; the County of Los Angeles; and several nonprofit organizations.*

Homelessness in some form exists in every society. However, substantial differences exist between First and Third World countries in such basic aspects of homelessness as its definition, its genesis, and the percentages of populations affected. Paradoxically, the causes and problems of homelessness among women show a striking consistency across cultures. Writing in reference to Southeast Asia, J.D. Conroy (1987:100) observes:

> Disadvantages affecting access to shelter which women face today in Third World Countries are generally quite familiar to observers from industrial societies. Few are so derived from particular cultural and religious situations as to be unique.... [D]ifferences between societies are more a matter of degree than of kind, and it is more helpful to conceive of the status of women as varying along a continuum, rather than as dichotomized between "advanced" industrial and poor "developing" countries.

Still, to fully understand the condition of homeless women, it is necessary to comprehend the causes of homelessness in a developing or developed society as well as the common situations shared by women everywhere.

Throughout this paper, the consideration of homelessness in the First World will be restricted to the situation in the United States, unique among developed countries. Much of the housing stock in other areas of the First World, specifically Western Europe, is socialized: built, subsidized, and maintained by government-sponsored authorities. Homeless persons are given preference in obtaining these units, so long-term homelessness of the kind found in the United States does not exist for all practical purposes (Huttman, 1991, Great Britain Commission for Racial Equality, 1988).

Homelessness in the Third World

Defining the Problem

In Third World countries, the problems of homelessness are inseparable from the problems of substandard housing. A person sleeping in a cardboard box on the sidewalks of New York is immediately recognized as homeless, but a person living in a hut made of cardboard and flattened tin cans beside the road in Africa will usually be considered a squatter or slum dweller. The differences in identification seem to arise from the proportion of the population affected. Although the definitions and methods chosen to estimate the size of the homeless population have become political issues subject to considerable debate in the United States, most researchers agree the size of the homeless population is somewhere between 0.10 and 0.25 percent of the total population (Cordray and Pion, 1991).

In Third World countries definitions of homelessness have not been a subject of debate, but the problems of inadequate housing are widespread and severe however they are measured. The World Bank estimates that from 20 to 40 percent of households in the Third World are squatters, living on land which neither they nor, if they rent, their landlord owns (Conroy, 1987). A 1985 survey in Bangkok found similar conditions, with almost 20 percent of the city's population living in squatter settlements (Shahand *et al.,* 1986). The Director of the United Nations International Year for Shelter for the Homeless estimated that one-quarter of the world's population lives in inadequate, unhealthy, or disaster-prone housing (Smith, 1988); and the United Nations Commission for Human Settlements (UNCHS) found that in Third World cities a majority of households cannot afford the cheapest legal housing plot, let alone the cheapest legal housing structure (Conroy, 1987).

Structural Factors Which Promote Homelessness

The most commonly cited structural causes of homelessness in the Third World are quite different from those in the United States. These include economic restructuring, rapid urbanization driven by migration from rural areas, governmental budget constraints, and changes from traditional to formal land ownership systems. All these are highly interrelated and arise from the ongoing transition from indigenous to industrialized economies.

In rural areas, changes in technology and types of crops grown have drastically reduced the need for agricultural labor (Conroy, 1987). These changes have been promoted both by internal pressures to modernize agricultural techniques and by external forces. Since most Third World countries are debtors to First World countries or multinational organizations such as the World Bank, they must produce goods which generate foreign currency to repay their debts. This has led to an abandonment of traditional subsistence farming of Third World agriculture in favor of efficiently produced cash crops, displacing large numbers of agricultural laborers (Ahmed, 1985). The consequences include massive migrations to urban areas and a general increase in absolute poverty, defined as an income insufficient to purchase basic food requirements, combined with a shift

of the locus of poverty from rural to urban areas (Conroy, 1987).

Such a rapid increase in the poor population of urban areas makes inadequate housing and homelessness inevitable. Calcutta's population, for example, grew 348 percent over the last 20 years, from 3.1 million in 1970 to 10.8 million in 1990, and a study of 10,000 homeless pavement dwellers in the city found that over 98 percent were migrants (Mukherjee, 1975). In addition, urban poverty is more likely to result in homelessness. While it needs to be recognized that rural homelessness and poverty are significant problems (Parvathamma, 1987), generally it has been argued that in rural areas the poor can construct adequate shelter from native materials using traditional building methods (Conroy, 1987).

The need to generate foreign currency to service foreign debts not only drives agricultural production, but prevents Third World countries from investing in non-revenue generating endeavors such as housing. This lack of funds for housing programs causes aid providers to concentrate on housing schemes which recover their cost. Such schemes, however, cannot provide assistance to the poorest 10 to 15 percent of the population (Conroy, 1987). Political instability in much of the Third World also leads countries to focus available revenues on military expenditures over housing and other social programs. Sivard estimated that during 1980 the three largest budgetary expenditures in Third World countries were military ($117 million), education ($105 million), and health programs ($41 million) (in Ahmed, 1985).

The absence of well-structured land ownership systems and the process of creating them is another factor which can contribute to homelessness. Third World governments need accurate systems of land ownership to generate the tax revenue necessary to sustain services. Creation of universal land ownership could also work to end the insecure tenure of squatters promoting self-help improvement in slum dwellings (Prapapat, 1984, Conroy, 1987). Setting up formal land ownership systems does seem to benefit the majority of slum dwellers, but is often detrimental to the poorest segments of society. Examples of this can be seen in India, where the process of registering land ownership is complex and dominated by corrupt local committees inimical to the interest of the poor (Parvathamma, 1985); and in Indonesia, where the poorest of slum dwellers have built structures on land unsuitable for housing and are subject to programs such as transmigrations or forced repatriation (Conroy, 1987). Another negative outcome of formalizing land ownership can result if the society lacks other stable investment opportunities. Excessive investment in land for speculative purpose may ensue, creating inefficient land uses. Speculation is blamed for the situation in Bombay where 50,000 acres of land within the city remain vacant while 3.5 million persons are squatters or homeless (Conroy, 1987).

Is Slum Housing Necessarily Bad?

It was noted earlier that definitions of homelessness are not subject to debate in the Third World because it is universally acknowledged that squatting and slum conditions are widespread. But whether such conditions can or should be remedied is indeed controversial. On the one hand, experience with housing development projects caused foreign aid groups to became disaffected from the goal of high-standard housing. Reasons for this included the huge subsidies necessary to construct and maintain such housing, the small proportion of the population which could be served, and the success of higher income groups in securing this housing over the poor population for whom it was intended. Currently, aid providers tend to favor less expensive programs which can benefit more people and promote private investment such as sites and services housing, slum upgrading, and infrastructure improvements (Conroy, 1987).

On the other hand, the argument is made that slum housing is only inadequate in comparison with normative standards imported from First World countries. In a paper for the International Workshop on Housing for Third World countries, John Ondongo examined research on the ills supposedly cultivated by slums such as poor health, criminal behavior, political radicalism, and psychological distress from overcrowding. He found that none of these ills was linked specifically to housing except for problems from overcrowding, and these occurred only between non-relatives in multi-story buildings. Ondongo concluded that a critical deficiency in studies of slum conditions was that the slum dwellers' opinions of their housing were not considered (Ondongo, 1979). In a later study of Bangkok, researchers did survey slum residents' opinions of their housing and found ownership was so strongly linked to satisfaction that, no matter how low the housing quality, slum dwellers were satisfied with their housing if they owned it (Shahand *et al.,* 1986).

Homelessness in the United States

A Changing and Growing Homeless Population

Although the proportion of homeless persons in the United States is small compared to the Third World, homelessness has recently become a concern due to increasing numbers and a changing character of the homeless population. Since the industrial revolution, there has been a population of transient male workers and male alcoholics who congregated in "skid row" areas of American cities. These areas contained single-room occupancy (SRO) hotels to house a poor and unstable population. The number of men seeking SRO rooms increased and decreased with economic cycles while the number of available rooms stayed constant. When demand exceeded supply, men slept on the streets in these areas or found a bed in Salvation Army missions (Lang, 1989).

During the 1980s, the number of homeless persons increased and significant numbers of women and children entered the ranks of the homeless for the first time. While some researchers see this as ultimate proof of the bankruptcy of a capitalist system which provides housing as a commodity (Marcuse, 1989; Lang, 1989), most believe the change arises from a combination of governmental policy decisions and social and economic trends. These influences resulted in decreasing numbers of units of low-cost housing while poverty increased for the poorest segment of the population.

The United States experienced an unusually long period of economic growth and prosperity from 1945 through the 1960s. During this period, demand for skid row housing fell and projects to redevelop central cities became popular. Consequently, large numbers of SRO hotels were demolished. In Seattle, 15,000 SRO units were demolished between 1960 and 1981, and in Chicago 18,000 units, almost half of the total number, were lost between 1973 and 1984 (Ringheim, 1990). In addition to this loss of privately owned low-cost housing, the federal government decreased its role as a low-cost housing provider. In 1981, $31 billion was allocated for all low-income housing programs at the federal level. By 1987 this amount had fallen to under $8 billion dollars (Ringheim, 1990).

Starting in the 1980s, economic changes and decreasing welfare benefits worsened the situation of the poorest Americans. While the number of poor persons remained stable, they became poorer: the amount of the nation's aggregate income shared by the poorest one-fifth of the nation is only 4.6 percent, a thirty-year low (Ringheim, 1990). This segment of the population became poorer for several reasons, including the loss of well-paying manufacturing jobs to Third World countries. Jobs now available for low-skill workers are in the low-paying service sector.

Another reason is that welfare payments have been cut throughout the country. Many states have instituted welfare reforms, eliminating payments to "able-bodied" men and single women. The country's largest welfare program, Aid to Families with Dependent Children (AFDC), also reduced benefits. Between 1970 and 1987, indexed for inflation, maximum AFDC benefits fell 40 percent in 10 states and fell 25 percent in 25 states, with only 3 states maintaining 1970 levels of payments (Ringheim, 1990). The increase in people who are able to afford only the least expensive housing, coupled with a decrease in the supply of that housing, has created pressures to increase the price of low-cost housing. In her study *At Risk of Homelessness,* Karin Ringheim found there was an increase in the number of renters with incomes below 125 percent of the poverty line in all the cities she studied and all cities also experienced rent increases greater than the rate of inflation (Ringheim, 1990). This situation is blamed for increasing the number of householders who cannot find any affordable unit and who therefore become homeless.

Structural Causes versus Individual Responsibility

While most researchers focus on structural problems when explaining increasing the numbers of the homeless, the federal government, under the administrations of Presidents Reagan and Bush, has blamed the personal problems of the homeless themselves. In 1984, President Reagan even stated that homeless persons sleeping on the streets in American cities were doing so by choice. This stance is used to justify the government's lack of spending on social programs. Unlike Third World countries, the United States arguably has the resources to end most homelessness if this were the government's priority. However, these administrations have concentrated on spending for the military and programs benefiting higher income groups. For example, in 1988 the amount of tax deductions given to homeowners was four times larger than all federal spending on low-income housing (Ringheim, 1990).

Many homeless persons do have personal problems. The pertinent question is whether these problems are the only cause of their homelessness, or whether the personal problems simply make them more vulnerable to larger influences. The two most commonly cited problems which might cause a person to become homeless are mental illness and substance abuse. Due to advances in drugs which control psychological illness, many persons with mental illness are no longer institutionalized. Between 1950 and 1982 the number of patients in mental institutions fell from 588,922 to 125,200 (Ringheim, 1990). Patients who no longer needed to be institutionalized were supposed to be cared for in a system of half-way houses which has, for the most part, not materialized. A survey of shelter and soup kitchen users found that 19 percent had been hospitalized in a mental institution (Cohen and Burt, 1989). Extrapolating from the research available, Ringheim estimated that at most 20 percent of the current homeless population would have been institutionalized in the past (Ringheim, 1990). The same survey of shelter and soup kitchen users found that 33 percent had been treated for substance abuse.

Most researchers dispute the premise that either substance abuse or mental illness can be the primary cause of homelessness. They point out the relatively small proportion of the homeless who are mentally ill and that mental illness is no more prevalent in society than it ever has been; yet homelessness has increased. In the case of substance abuse, it is pointed out that higher-income substance abusers generally do not become homeless and, while it appears that the incidence of substance abuse among the homeless is somewhat higher than among the general population, in the absence of evidence to the contrary, a reasonable hypothesis is that this has occurred as a result of being homeless rather than precipitating the condition (Ringheim, 1990). Ultimately, service providers point out that a residence is a prerequisite to resolving whatever problems a homeless person might have (Burt and Cohen, 1989, Lang, 1989). Ringheim (1990:28) concludes:

> In the case of the homeless who are mentally ill, retarded, disabled, substance abusers, or have AIDS, housing alone is clearly not enough. But many shelter operators and transitional housing experts maintain that efforts to treat, rehabilitate, and employ the homeless must be preceded by a stabilized home environment. The trauma of being homeless and living in the stressful environment of a group

shelter presents, for many, too great an obstacle to learning new skills or coping mechanisms.

Women and Homelessness

Women face a special vulnerability to homelessness and special problems when they are homeless. Most elements which contribute to women's particular situation are shared by women in the First and Third World. These include lower levels of education and training in job skills; segregation of women into lower-paid work in the formal labor market; child-rearing responsibilities which constrain women to work in the informal market; women's vulnerability to physical and sexual abuse; absence of affordable child care; and diminished access to credit (Ali, 1975, Conroy, 1987, Cohen and Burt, 1989). Women in the Third World suffer additional vulnerability because they experience inferior legal and, political rights (Ali, 1975, Conroy, 1987). They may also experience greater inequality in education: a 1980 study in Thailand found women comprised almost 70 percent of illiterates (Shahand *et al.*, 1986). In the United States women with children are affected by a premium paid for children in rental housing. Ringheim (1990) found that households with children paid more for rent, holding size, quality, and other factors constant.

The problems faced by women have become increasingly important due to a rising proportion of female-headed households throughout the world. UNCHS estimated in 1986 that 30 percent of the world's households are headed by females (Smith, 1988). Women earn less than men in all societies. In the United States women work in lower paying jobs; in the Third World, women may be paid less for exactly the same work. Parvathamma (1987) found on average women laborers earned 6 rupees for the same work for which men were paid 8 rupees. As a result, female-headed households comprise a disproportionate segment of the poor population. Forty-six percent of all poor families in the United States were headed by females in 1982, although such families comprised only 15.5 percent of the total (Wilson, 1987).

The growing number of female-headed households is cited as the cause of increasing numbers of homeless women and children. While not much longitudinal information is available about the demographics of the homeless population in the United States, historically the homeless population has been composed largely of adult males. In New York City the number of homeless children in shelters quadrupled between 1982 and 1987;

overwhelmingly, they were members of female-headed families (Ringheim, 1990). A national survey of the homeless found that 20 percent of homeless adults were women: 9 percent of the total were single women, 9 percent were women with children and 2 percent were women accompanied by another relative (Cohen and Burt, 1989). Women also comprise a significant proportion of the homeless in the Third World. A study of 34,316 homeless persons in Calcutta found that 43 percent of the adults were women. Although women were not identified as female-headed in the overall survey, in detailed interviews of 101 homeless households, 34 percent were headed by females (Mukherjee, 1975).

The Cohen and Burt survey found significant differences in characteristics among the homeless between men, single women, and women with children. The most striking of these were in patterns of institutionalization and service use. Homeless men are much more likely to have a history of incarceration or hospitalization for mental disorders or substance abuse. Fully 74 percent of single men had been institutionalized for at least one of these, while 45 percent of single women and only 20 percent of women with children had such a history. Women were much more likely than men to find lodging in a homeless shelter. The survey found that 70 percent of homeless women with children spent all of the last 7 nights in a shelter, compared with 53 percent of single women and 29 percent of single men (Burt and Cohen, 1989).

The lower wages earned by women and concomitant difficulty which women face in supporting a family often constrain women from leaving a male supporter. Women in abusive situations, however, may find the worst economic circumstances better than living with their partners. It is estimated that, in the United States, three to four million women are battered a year and approximately one million women a year seek medical assistance for injuries caused by battering (Diehm and Ross, 1988) A study of battered women in Texas found that 53 percent left the relationship. The problems of battered women, and their likelihood of becoming homeless, have been increasingly recognized in the United States, and the number of shelters serving them has grown to over 1,200 (Diehm and Ross, 1988). In the survey of households in Calcutta, 18 percent of the homeless women had become homeless because they left an abusive situation (Mukherjee, 1975).

In the Third World, women face other situations which might result in homelessness. In many cultures, women historically have not inherited land equally or at all, but traditional family arrangements have provided support for unmarried or widowed women (Hoshen, 1988a). The development process tends to break down traditional family structures and, as discussed above, to foster formalized land ownership. Women may lose the right to use land through the priorities given in registering ownership. Land is often registered only in the name of the husband, which can make it impossible for the wife to claim her rights in the case of divorce or death of her spouse (Smith, 1988). Also, when ownership is registered, the rights of widows may not be recognized; a study of Indian land reforms found that families who lost their land under a registration scheme were primarily non-cultivators and widows (Parvathamma, 1987).

Women in the Third World have suffered disproportionately in the change from subsistence farming to cash crops. After studying women's labor force participation in rural, urban, and transitional economies, Ester Boserup concludes the change from a traditional to a modern economy widens the knowledge and training gap between men and women (in Rihani, 1978). Sen and Grown (1987) note the development process generally reduces the access of the poor to resources and Elise Boulding (in Rihani, 1978) notes that, as societies modernize, women are left with subsistence tasks while men enter the market economy.

Third World governments also have tended to channel aid toward men. Men receive priority for assistance in government-sponsored affordable housing projects (Smith, 1988). Households are given assistance through the male head which is not always effective in helping women and children, Schrijvers (1984) found that only 35 percent of the net income of male farmers benefited the rest of the household. The increase in farming cash crops also hurts women. In Africa, food production has been decreasing for 10 years because women subsistence farmers have been pushed off the land. Men get technical aid, modern tools, fertilizers, and credit from the government. Women are denied services by government extension offices and are forced to work for their male relatives without pay, which has increased poverty among women and children (Ahmed, 1985, Hoshen, 1988a).

Much of the vulnerability of women to homelessness is the result of discrimination. Various racial and ethnic groups also experience discrimination and are also vulnerable to homelessness. Women who are members of minority groups will therefore find themselves particularly vulnerable to homelessness. Parvathamma (1987) notes that, in India, although poverty is the main cause of homelessness, discrimination plays a role since untouchables and scheduled castes are allowed to build houses only in overcrowded ghettos. In his survey of 2,924 homeless persons he found that 45 percent were members of scheduled caste groups. Cohen and Burt (1989) found that 83 percent of homeless women with children and 59 percent of homeless single women were non-white, compared with 22.5 percent of the United States population.

Conclusions

In a great many instances, homelessness is attributable to the economic and social structure of society. These factors are notably different in the First and Third Worlds. In the Third World, the process of developing modern economies creates many of the structural causes of homelessness. In the United States, governmental policies of housing and welfare contribute substantially to the problem, while a restructuring economy, which is increasing impoverishment in the poorest segment of society, also plays a role. In all cultures minority groups are more likely to become homeless.

The problems of women relating to homelessness are often similar in First and Third World societies. The growth of female-headed households, the discrimination and resulting poverty these households experience, the limitations imposed by child-rearing responsibilities, and women's vulnerability to abuse put women at greater risk of homelessness.

In both the First and Third World, any attempt to reduce homelessness needs to address the structural causes at the root of homelessness in general. However, correcting structural causes of general homelessness will not help all people who are especially susceptible to homelessness. Women will still be more vulnerable to homelessness, along with other groups such as minorities, the mentally disabled, or substance abusers. Policy makers should not ignore areas where women's needs fall outside the general causes of homelessness, such as laws regarding spousal abuse. Practitioners also must tailor programs to meet the needs of different groups. Many practitioners already do so. The papers which follow in this section describe the experiences of some practitioners who are offering services to such groups as battered women, chemically dependent women, women with AIDS, and women refugees.

References

Ahmed, Iftikhar. 1985. Rural women and technical change: Theory, empirical analysis and operational projects. *Labour and Society, 10,* 3: 289–306.

Ali, Parveen Shaukat. 1975. *Women in the Third World: A Comprehensive Bibliography with an Introductory Essay.* Zaildar Park, Ichbra-Lahore: Progressive Publishers.

Birch, Eugenie Ladner. 1985. "The Unsheltered Woman: Definition and Needs." In *The Unsheltered Woman: Women and Housing in the 80s,* edited by Eugenie Ladner Birch. Rutgers: Center for Urban Policy Research.

Burt, Martha R., and Barbara E. Cohen. 1989. Differences among Homeless Single Women, Women with Children and Single Men. *Social Problems. 36* (5): 508–524.

Conroy, John D. 1987. *Shelter for the Homeless: Asian-Pacific Needs and Australian Responses.* Australian Council for Overseas Aid, Development Dossier No. 22.

Cordray, David S., and Georgine M Pion. 1991. What's Behind the Numbers? Definitional Issues in Counting the Homeless. *Housing Policy Debate. 2* (3) 587–616.

Diehm, Cynthia, and Margo Ross. 1988. "Battered Women." In: *The American Woman 1988-89: A Status Report,* edited by Sara E. Rix. New York: W.W. Norton and Company.

Fenton, Thomas P., and Mary J. Heffron, eds. 1987. *Women in the Third World: A Directory of Resources.* Maryknoll, New York: Orbis Books.

Fuentes, Annette, and Madelyn Miller. 1988. "Unreasonable access: sexual harassment comes home." In: *Women, Housing and Community,* edited by Willem Van Vliet. Aldershot: Avebury.

Great Britain Commission for Racial Equality. 1988. *Homelessness and Discrimination: Report of a formal investigation by the Commission for Racial Equality into the allocation of housing by the London Borough of Tower Hamlets.* London: Commission for Racial Equality.

Hoshen, Fran. 1988. "Women and Property." In: *Women, Housing and Community,* edited by Willem Van Vliet. Aldershot: Avebury.

Hoshen, Fran. 1988b. "Women, urbanization and shelter." In: *Women, Housing and Community,* edited by Willem Van Vliet. Aldershot: Avebury.

Huttman, Elizabeth D. 1991. "Housing Segregation in Western Europe: An Introduction." In *Urban Housing Segregation of Minorities in Western Europe and the United States* edited by Elizabeth D. Huttman, coedited by Wim Blauw and Juliet Saltman. Durham: Duke University Press.

Lang, Michael H. 1989. *Homelessness Amid Affluence: Structure and Paradox in the American Political Economy.* New York: Praeger Publishers.

Lindsay, Beverly. 1980. *Comparative Perspectives on Third World Development.* New York: Praeger Publishers.

Marcuse, Peter. 1989. "The Pitfalls of Specialism: Special Groups and the General Problem of Housing." In: *Housing Issues of the 1990's,* edited by Sara Rosenberry and Chester Hartman. New York: Praeger Publishers.

Mukherjee, Sudhendu. 1975. *Under the shadow of the metropolis: they are citizens too: a report on the survey of 10,000 pavement-dwellers in Calcutta, September 1973–March 1974.* Calcutta: Calcutta Metropolitan Development Authority, Calcutta Metropolitan Planning Organization.

Odongo, John. 1979. "Housing deficit in Cities of the Third World: fact or fiction?" In *Housing in Third World Countries: Perspectives on Policy and Practice,* issued by the International Workshop on Housing in Third World Countries, edited by Hamish S. Murison and John P. Lea. London: The MacMillan Press Ltd.

Parvathamma, C. 1987. *Housing, Rural Poor, and Their Living Conditions.* Delhi, India: Gian Publishing House.

Prapapat, Niyom. 1984. "Facts and Figures of Slum Eviction in Bangkok 1983." Paper presented at the seminar, "The Right to Stay: The Poor, The Land and The Law in Asian Cities." Bangkok, Thailand.

Pryor, Robin. 1979. "Migration patterns and housing needs in Southeast Asia." In: *Housing in Third World Countries: Perspectives on Policy and Practice,* issued by the International Workshop on Housing in Third World Countries, edited by Hamish S. Murison and John P. Lea. London: The MacMillan Press Ltd.

Rihani, May. 1978. *Development as if women mattered: an annotated bibliography with a third world focus.* New TransCentury Foundation.

Ringheim, Karin. 1990. *At Risk of Homelessness: The Roles of Income and Rent.* New York: Praeger Publishers.

Schrijvers, Joke. 1984. Blueprint for Undernutrition: An Example from Sri Lanka. *Sociologia Ruralis. 25* (3/4) 255–273.

Sen, Gita, and Caren Grown. 1987. *Development, Crises, and Alternative Visions: Third World Women's Perspectives.* New York: Monthly Review Press.

Shahand, Assadullah, Marcia Arvisu Tekie, and Karl E. Weber, with Helen Veldman-Montagu, Chuthathip Phosuphab, and Zilla C. Phoathivongsacharn. 1986. *The Role of Women in Slum Improvement: A Comparative Study of Squatter Settlements at Klong Toey and Wat Yai Sri Suphan in Bangkok, Thailand.* Studies on Human Settlements Development in Asia HSD Research Report No. 10. Bangkok: Division of Human Settlements Development, Asian Institute of Technology.

Smith, Diana Lee. 1988. "Women and habitat: Nairobi 1985." In *Women, Housing and Community,* edited by Willem Van Vliet. Aldershot: Avebury.

Stone, Madeleine R. 1988. "The plight of homeless women." In *Women, Housing and Community,* edited by Willem Van Vliet. Aldershot: Avebury.

United Nations Center for Human Settlements. 1981. *The Residential Circumstances of the Urban Poor in Developing Countries.* New York: Praeger Publishers.

Waltz, Susan E. 1988. "Women's housing needs in the Arab cultural context of Tunisia." In *Women, Housing and Community*, edited by Willem Van Vliet. Aldershot: Avebury.

Wilson, William Julius. 1987. *The Truly Disadvantaged: The Inner City, the Underclass and Public Policy.* Chicago: University of Chicago Press.

Chapter 15
Shelter Homes: A Need to Develop a New Approach for Women in Familial Distress

Neela Dabir

Neela Ashok Dabir *received her Bachelor of Education and her Master of Social Work from the University of Bombay and is registered for a Ph.D. in the S.N.D.T. University of Bombay. She has been a training and revaluation coordinator in the child sponsorship project of CASP-PLAN, which involves 2,100 families. She was a research officer in the study of Shraddhanand Mahilashram, a well-known shelter home in Bombay, for thirty months. She has been the coordinating officer in Shraddhanand Mahilashram since July 1991 and is president of a voluntary organization, MUKTA, which is mainly involved in organizing income-generating activities for women.*

Women in India are always viewed as dependent creatures with hardly any right over the family property. Very few women in India can claim to possess a shelter of their own. In many situations, a woman is forced to leave her house because of the familial conflicts. If she is denied support by relatives and friends, she has to seek admission in one of the Shelter Homes to overcome the crisis.

In India, Shelter Homes for women in crisis have a long history. The first Shelter Home for women in crisis was started in the state of Maharashtra in 1868. There are now 25 different organizations in Bombay actively involved in helping women in distress. These organizations can be classified into two groups:

1. The Shelter Homes managed by different voluntary bodies or religious trusts and the Homes run by the Government.
2. The support cells or counseling centers managed by different autonomous women's groups.

The majority of Shelter Homes have a long tradition and are equipped with spacious buildings, open spaces to build additional structures, and the necessary infrastructure to accommodate large numbers of women. In most of these Homes, more than 50% of the seats are always available. In contrast to this, the support cells are of recent origin and do not have shelter facilities. They are trying to set up new Homes for the women who approach them for help. This paper tries to highlight the existing rules and regulations for admission to these Homes and ways to utilize the available resources more effectively and meet the needs of women in distress in the present social system. A more liberal approach is needed to help women in crisis. They should be treated as responsible adults who need a little support and guidance to cope with their situation.

Background

In Indian culture, a woman is always viewed as a dependent creature from her childhood to old age. She is supposed to be protected by her father or brother in childhood, by her husband after marriage, and by her son during old age or widowhood. Traditionally, Indian women, by and large, did not have property rights. Now, even after legal reforms in this direction, very few women get a share in the family property. As a result, only a small percentage of Indian women can claim to possess a shelter of their own. Usually, a woman is supposed to be living in her father's, brother's, or husband's house. Unfortunately, many women themselves have a similar perception, irrespective of their significant contributions to the family income. Many situations force a woman to leave home: family conflicts, marital conflicts, personal problems, or physical and mental torture. It is quite common that women are driven out of the house at odd hours.

The problems of Indian women should be viewed within their cultural context. The class and caste structure in Indian society has a great influence over the status of women. Formerly, the higher the caste, the more restrictions or sanctions on women. Among women of higher castes, a married woman had the highest social status as compared to the unmarried woman or a widow. Her status was enhanced further by giving birth to a male child. When society changed from a matrilineal system to a patriarchal one, the only purpose of a woman's life was to reproduce. To control this process of reproduction, more and more sanctions were laid on her, especially in the higher castes. She was denied the opportunity to receive a formal education. The age at marriage for a woman decreased progressively and a stage came when the parents of a girl child started to get her married in the cradle! The parents were supposed to arrange the marriage of their daughter before she reached menstruation. The religious scriptures considered a father sinful if he failed to get his daughter married before her puberty. However, a bridegroom could be any age. Polygamy and remarriage of a widower were socially accepted practices. The network of health services being very poor, the mortality rate, in general, was very high. Because of epidemics and high rates of child mortality, many girls and boys lost their spouses at a very early age. The boy could easily remarry but no new marriage was possible for a widow, irrespective of her age. The percentage of women dying during child birth was quite high. The widower, in such cases, had no alternative but to marry a very young girl. Because of the large age difference among such couples, the percentage of widows in the younger age group increased considerably. All these factors put together gave rise to an alarmingly high percentage of child widows in India. A close look at Table 1 will give us a fair idea of the intensity of the problem.

A widow had no status in society. She was considered to be most inauspicious and was not allowed to participate in social or religious functions. Young widows were often forced into embarrassing situations because of sexual abuse and illegitimate pregnancies. Many cases of suicides and infanticides were reported during the first half of the nineteenth century. This was the major social problem in those days. The first Shelter Home for women in distress was started in 1868 by

Table 1: Distribution by age of Hindu widowers and widows in India in the year 1988

Age	Hindu widowers	Hindu widows
Below 10	21,000	63,000
10–19	173,000	486,000
20–29	539,000	1,571,000
30–39	786,000	2,797,000
40–60	1,744,000	7,007,000
Above 60	1,133,000	4,177,000

Based on reports of the 1891 census, it was estimated that in the Brahmin community (highest caste among Hindus), more than 33% of women were widows and about one-third of them were child widows (Source: Renade Pratibha, Stree Prashnanchi Charcha, 1991, p. 172).

Mahatma Jyotiba Phule, a great social reformer, in the city of Poona in the state of Maharashtra. The main purpose of this Home was to give shelter to the widows for delivery. It also offered a facility for children abandoned in the Home. The first Shelter Home was closed within a few days, but it was indeed a very progressive step toward helping women in distress. Within a few years, many such Homes were started by different religious groups as well as by social reformers. These Homes were situated at places of pilgrimage or in big cities. Widows or deserted women used to take shelter in a Home where they did not have to disclose their identity.

Shelter Homes for women in distress thus have a long history. They responded to the needs of women by giving them shelter during crisis and saved the lives of many women who otherwise could have been ostracized. With the spread of education and the introduction of various social reforms, the status of women of the higher castes improved considerably. The incidence of child widows, polygamy, and desertion by husbands decreased markedly. But the lower castes, in the process of upward social mobility, started introducing more and more restrictions on their women. The communities which readily accepted divorce and remarriage for widows and divorcees have now started to become more rigid in these matters. The 1981 census report (Census of India, 1981, Series-I, India, Part II special, Office of the Registrar General and Census Commission for India, pp. 15 and 23) shows that the sex ratio in India is progressively decreasing and there is still a very high percentage of illiteracy among women—only 24.8% of women are literate as compared to 46.9% of men. The enrollment of women in vocational and professional courses continues to be very low. Although women are making some entry into various professions, they are generally confined to teacher's training courses and nursing. Poor women are invisible workers. The 1981 census report shows the workforce participation rate among females as just 14% (main workers) as compared to 51.6% among males. An overwhelming proportion of women (i.e., 93% or more) are engaged in the unorganized, informal sector mainly as self-employed wage earners, non-wage earners, or casual workers. Thus, most women in India have hardly any possibility of owning a house or having enough resources to stay independent if they lose family support. The need to have Shelter Homes for women in familial distress and also for destitute, orphaned women still exists. It is possible that Shelter Homes may need to offer a different set of services to these women. The next section reviews services offered by various Shelter Homes in Bombay, the needs of women approaching them for help, and different alternatives that can be considered to fulfill these needs.

Organizations for Women in Distress

More than 25 different organizations are actively involved in Bombay in helping women in distress. These organizations may be broadly classified into two groups:

1. The Shelter Homes managed by different voluntary bodies or religious trusts and the Homes run by the Government.

    The majority of Shelter Homes were set up more than 50 years ago and possess wide experience in this field. Some of these homes offer packages of services for women in distress, women from different age groups with different needs. Some homes have a limited scope of activities. In spite of their long-established reputation, some of these Homes have experienced a decrease in the number of women inmates from the age group 18 to 60 years during recent years. The demand for admission to old-age homes is ever increasing. In most Shelter Homes for women, more than 50% of the spaces are always available. Some of these Shelter Homes have spacious buildings, open spaces to build additional structures, and all the necessary infrastructure to accommodate many more women.

2. The support cells or counseling centers managed by different autonomous women's groups or women's organizations.

    The support cells are of relatively recent origin, having been established during the last 10 to 15 years. Most of these cells are managed by active workers from the feminist movement. These support cells do not have residential facilities for women. Many of them do not even have a proper office of their own. They offer pre-and post-marital counseling. The number of women approaching these cells is increasing day by day. Many times it becomes necessary to make arrangements for shelter for the clients. Having no residential facilities, the support cells have to refer such cases to local Shelter Homes. They face some difficulties in making such arrangements. Some workers from the support cells feel that the inability to make proper arrangements for shelter for their clients is a major hurdle in their work. Many support cells are approaching the Government for grants to build their own Homes. In a city like Bombay, with its high land and construction costs, it is not so easy to build a new structure having all the basic infrastructure.

The situation of shelter facilities for women in familial distress is thus paradoxical: on the one hand, the existing Shelter Homes have more than 50% vacancies and these resources are underutilized; on the other hand, the support cells are struggling hard to collect the necessary resources to establish new Shelter Homes. Is there no need for such services because of the changes in the social status of women? Or are there some drawbacks to the nature of the services offered by these Homes? The women who are usually in need of shelter may be grouped as follows:

1. Women with marital problems:
    (a) Unemployed women,
    (b) Working women, and
    (c) Working or unemployed women leaving home with children.
2. Unwed mothers.
3. Mentally disturbed women.
4. Women in need of permanent shelter:
    (a) Middle-aged, single women, and
    (b) Aged women.

I will not include the shelter-related needs of aged women in this discussion. Their problems are different from the other groups and the majority of old-age homes are fully occupied, with long waiting lists. Table 2 presents data on policies and services of different Shelter Homes in Bombay.

A Review of the Admission Policies of Different Shelter Homes in Bombay

A close look at the admission policies of Shelter Homes makes it clear that a large number of women do not become eligible for admission in these homes because of set rules. Only two institutions admit working women. A women engaged in a low-paid job cannot stay in the

Table 2: Policies for admission to and services offered by the shelter homes in Bombay

Name	Admission Policies	Services Offered
1. Sukh Shanti	Any woman in distress along w/her children under 6, and unwed mothers.	Vocational training above the age of marital counseling. Facility to go out and work inexceptional cases.
2. Asha Sadan	Children under 6, women between 14–20, & unwed mothers.	Work center & vocational training.
3. Govt Reception Center	Any woman between 18–40 & unwed mothers.	Rehabilitation through marriage or counseling.
4. Shishu Bhavan	Only unwed mothers	
5. Shraddhanan Mahila Ashram	Women from any age, boys under 6, & unwed mothers	Vocational training, work center, marriage counseling, facility to keep boys under 6 & girls any age along with mother.
6. St. Catherine's Home	Girls under 18 & unwed mothers	Vocational training & educational facilities for girls
7. Bapnu Ghar	Women with marital problems only	Marital counseling, hostel for working women having income below Rs 1500/-p.m, facility to keep children under 6 along with mothers
8. Haji Allarkha Sonawala Andh	Any blind, retarded, handicappedwomen above 16	All medical facilities with the help of local Municipal Hospital
9. YWCA Working Women's Hostel	Two beds in each of 4 hostels for hostels for women in distress	Temporary shelter until she gets a job or other arrangement for long-term shelter could be made
10. Bal Anand	Only unwed mothers	
11. Bal Asha	Only unwed mothers	
12. Salvation Army	Girls under 18 & unwed mothers	Education for girls
13. Manav Seva Sangh	Girls under 6, women with children under 6 if they are willing to work in the institution	Employment for the women & shelter for her children

Working Women's Hostel. She has to leave her job if she wishes to stay in a Shelter Home. Shelter Homes do not want to take the risk of sending women out to work. Because of a few negative experiences in the past, most Shelter Homes segregate women from the outside world. Some Shelter Homes are planning to set up a hostel for women from the lower-income group where there will be a crèche in the same premises. Then the women can stay with their children. One such hostel recently started. But they are not ready to mix working and unemployed women.

The Working Women's Hostel is mainly for women earning more than Rs.800/- p.m. With the exception of two hostels which recently opened, these hostels are fully occupied and do not have the capability of admit-ting children. Thus, it is not easy to get immediate admission in one of these hostels for a working woman in distress, especially if she is from the lower-income group.

No institutions, except the Government Reception Centers, are ready to admit rescue cases (women rescued from brothels). The living conditions and the treatment of the inmates in the Government Reception Centers impel most of the women to try to leave within a few days after admission.

Nine different institutions shelter unwed mothers. Of these, five have restricted their admission of women to unwed mothers. During the last few years, very few unwed mothers have come to them for shelter and delivery. They often receive calls from the Private or Municipal Nursing homes to collect the new-born babies. Most of them are now engaged in providing for the welfare of destitute and orphaned children, including adoption.

In one institution, services are restricted to married women with familial distress. They concentrate on marriage counseling and legal aid and also offer premarital counseling. Three institutions admit any woman in distress, irrespective of her age and marital status, but do not offer systematic marriage counseling or legal aid.

No home wants to admit and treat V.D., T. B., and leprosy cases. Patients with an advanced stage of such diseases require hospitalization but, once they are non-infectious, can be admitted in Shelter Homes. However, such cases are usually rejected by everyone—family members as well as institutions for women.

There is only one institution for blind and disabled destitute women and it is usually fully occupied. Most institutions are not equipped to deal with mentally disturbed women. Sometimes, these women are in a disturbed state of mind because of familial problems. There are two groups in such cases. Some women need special care and treatment but, for some, a few days of institutionalization works as therapy. Because of a stay in Shelter Homes for a few days, the woman gets some time to reflect on her problem and is able to make up her mind about her future. In such cases, all that is needed is a separation from the family for a few days.

Very few institutions admit women with their children. In some Homes, a woman is allowed to stay with her children under 6. Many times, the child stays in the same institution but away from the mother. Thus, existing Shelter Homes cater mainly to either destitute and orphaned girls or destitute women above the age of 60. Almost twelve institutions give shelter to old and infirm women above the age of 60.

From discussions with committee members, social workers, and others working with women in distress, it was evident that the present situation needs review and appropriate changes need to be made. Before we proceed to the suggestions for change, let us also have a look at the practical problems faced by women coming for shelter and the staff members of shelter homes, as well as the support cells.

Problematic Experiences of Women after Admission to Shelter Homes

Many educated women do not want to apply for admission to Shelter Homes because of the social stigma. When they finally agree to stay there, they are often quite apprehensive about their stay in the institution. If a woman is admitted to a Shelter Home, her familial problem is no longer private. Other people then come into the picture. It is very difficult for the woman to accept such a situation. The atmosphere inside Shelter Homes is such that many women face the problems of adjustment. The way food is served or the remarks by staff members and other inmates are sometimes quite insulting. Such negative experiences result in leaving the Home within a few days.

It appears that Shelter Homes and support cells differ in the approaches toward the causes of distress within families. The Committee members of the Shelter Homes have a certain ideology of "family" as an institution. They consider it to be very "sacred" and, hence, that it should not be broken if at all possible. The woman having a familial problem is considered a deviant, if not a fallen woman. The rehabilitation of such a woman within the family is the best solution. After counseling of her husband and other family members, she is sent back to her family. Very rarely is she encouraged to seek legal remedy. There is a kind of patronizing attitude toward the inmates. An out-of-wedlock pregnancy is considered a "social offense." Since the man cannot be traced in most of these cases, the woman has to suffer alone. In some institutions, the woman admitted for delivery has to pay some amount for her stay in the institution. This money has to be paid as a "Token Fine" for her social offense. Shelter Homes are usually influenced by religious philosophy.

Support cells have emerged as a part of the women's movement. Their approaches toward the causes of distress are different. They do not want to condemn the woman because she violated so-called social norms. They believe in programs that can help women to know their rights and gain strength to protest injustice. A woman in familial distress should be helped to make a decision for her future and then guided accordingly. Because of the differences in the perceptions of the two types of organizations, sometimes there are problems, e.g., a woman decides to leave home after a long struggle and is not in a position to accept reconciliation. When such a case is referred by the support cell to the

Shelter Home, the woman does not receive the necessary support. The woman sometimes has to agree to reconciliation because of the pressures put on her by the staff members of the Shelter Home. If the woman faces problems after going back to her husband, she loses faith in counseling. Or if she does not want to compromise, she leaves the Home within a few days.

Women admitted to Shelter Homes are often refused the freedom to leave the institution, to try to face their problems in their own way and to come back if they fail to do so. In some institutions, when a woman leaves the institution on her own, she has to sign a written statement that she is fully aware of the policy that, after leaving the institution, she will not be readmitted. This policy also applies to women who are married through the institution and face marital problems afterwards. The reason cited for such a policy is to prevent the women from leaving and coming back every now and then, and so the inmates do not develop the erroneous belief that they have the freedom to come back to the institution for any petty reason.

Once the woman is admitted to a Shelter Home, she should not remain idle for more than a week. The institution should be in a position to offer her some occupation where she can engage herself for a minimum number of hours a day. The institution should have some activities which can accommodate women with different educational backgrounds and aptitudes. It often happens that the lack of occupation makes her feel more depressed and she does not have the patience to wait until necessary action can be taken on the problem which caused her to enter the Home.

There is a lack of proper communication between staff members of the support cells and Shelter Homes. Whenever a woman approaches any support cell for help, a social worker or counselor tries to find out all the details about her problem. If the woman needs Shelter facilities, she is referred to a Shelter Home or is helped to secure admission to a Shelter Home. Afterwards, if there is very little dialogue between the counselor from the support cell and that of the Shelter Home, the woman has to face another round of investigations. In some cases, the woman in familial distress is treated so that she leaves the Shelter Home within a few days. In some cases, the support cells fail to keep in touch with the woman after her admission in the Shelter Home, which causes inconvenience for staff members as well as the woman. In places like Working Women's Hostels where there is a facility to admit a few cases of women in distress, the staff is not trained to deal with

such cases. The referring organization is expected to do the necessary follow-up in these cases. When such a follow-up is not done, there are problems.

Suggestions for Better Utilization of Existing Shelter Home Facilities

From the review of the situation presented so far, we may state that the existing Shelter Homes already possess the basic resources such as building, staff, funds, and other infrastructure. All these facilities are under-utilized at present and may remain so if proper policy changes are not implemented. There is also a possibility that some of them may change the focus of their activities to some other target group and utilize existing infra-structures, such as buildings, for them. At the same time, the shelter-related needs of women with familial distress will keep on increasing. A few suggestions for better utilization of existing Shelter Homes follow:

1. The Shelter Homes should review their admission policies and rules in the context of the changing needs of women and move towards a more open institutional framework to expand the scope of their work.

2. There is a need to have proper communication between the Shelter Homes and support cells. Any case referred by the support cell to the Shelter Home should be discussed properly and a joint decision for further action should be made. In the absence of such an understanding, the woman gets confused due to the contradictory messages she receives.

3. The support cells should prepare the woman for admission to a Shelter Home. She should have some information regarding life in a Shelter Home. It will help her to adjust in the home after admission.

4. Many women are mentally disturbed because of their familial problems. Instead of refusing to admit such cases, the institutions should have the facilities for proper medical treatment. They should have one or two rooms for the isolation of difficult cases.

5. The Shelter Homes should admit working women. They may be housed along with the other inmates or in a separate room if necessary. Similarly, the admission of women with their children will be of great help. With the proper understanding of the nearby schools, the problem of school-going children could be overcome and the children could be admitted to the hostels in due course. Liaison with the hostels should be maintained.

6. There is a need to develop an institutional framework in which the inmates will be treated as responsible adults, free to make decisions, after providing them with the necessary guidance. Women should feel confident that they can ask

for support if they face problems after leaving the institution. In the case of genuine problems, a woman should get at least one or two chances to come back for help.

Suggestions for Alternate Institutional Frameworks

1. Groups of women with familial problems and the need for shelter can stay together and manage their day-to-day living through assistance received from the Government. Such an arrangement should be for a fixed duration.

2. The institution may have separate rooms to permit a woman to occupy one room with her children, like a hostel for women and children together. (It is reported that such an arrangement has been tried in Haryana.)

3. The institution should have a vocational training center on the campus where, along with the inmates, other women can also enroll for the training courses. If the institution becomes a multipurpose center for women, it will help to lessen the segregation between the inmates and outside women.

4. The Government should have a special scheme for those who do not want to stay in a Shelter Home and need to have a permanent shelter. It could be in the form of financial aid to buy an accommodation or some reservations in the housing colonies for single women.

5. The institutions should offer a package of services to women with familial distress. The woman should have a choice of appropriate programs as needed. The package should include the following: counseling center with legal aid facilities, different types of vocational training programs, income generation, activities in which many women can be accommodated after a short period of training, the ability of working in the income-generation project for single women who would like to stay independent or in a group of single women and be self-reliant after the initial support.

These suggestions are based on the understanding that women in familial distress should be viewed as victims of the prevailing social conditions, not as fallen women. They should be treated as responsible adults who need a little support and guidance to cope with their situation. Unless the existing Shelter Homes recognize women in this light, they will not be in a position to help them.

Chapter 16
Housing for Women with AIDS

Theresa Cameron and Yul Lee

Theresa Cameron *is currently visiting assistant professor at Cornell University, Department of City and Regional Planning. She received her Master of Urban Planning from the University of Michigan and her Doctorate of Design from Harvard University in 1991. She also has ten years of experience as a planner in the private and public sector. Her research interests are housing for special needs populations, urban land-use, and community and economic development.*

Yuk Lee *is professor in the College of Architecture and Planning, University of Colorado at Denver. Formerly, he was Director of the Urban and Regional Planning Program and Associate Dean. He received his Master of Architecture from the University of Cincinnati and his Ph.D. from Ohio State University. His research interests are in urban land-use, transportation planning, and location analysis.*

AIDS in the U.S. has been stereotyped as a "gay man's disease." Despite the best efforts of many people, American society as a whole still is not adequately prepared to respond to the housing needs of women with AIDS. In fact, the provision of appropriate housing facilities for the AIDS patients in general, and for women with AIDS (WWA) in particular, has long been ignored. The purposes of this study are to provide evidence to support the hypothesis that WWA have housing needs that are different from those of men with AIDS (MWA), and to suggest means for designing housing facilities for WWA. Ten current AIDS housing facilities across the U.S. are analyzed for such purposes.

Housing needs for WWA do not seem to present any major problems at this point. According to the Center for Disease Control, in 1991, women in the United States who were tested HIV-positive made up 9.8% of the total AIDS population in this country. The relatively small number of WWA at this point might well be the reason why most residential care facilities in the U.S. have been developed primarily for single men. However, some researchers believe that women constitute the fastest growing group among people with AIDS (Shayne and Kaplan, 1991, p. 21). The increasing seriousness of AIDS for women is abundantly illustrated by the following statistics. In New York City, AIDS was the leading cause of death for women between 25 to 34 in 1987 (Koonin *et al.*, 1989, p. 1306). In the U.S., the number of cases of AIDS diagnosed in women of color 18 to 44 years old increased 29% from 1988 to 1989, as compared to an increase of 18% in men in the same age group (Kent, 1991, p. 1442). Furthermore, AIDS was one of the five leading causes of death among women in 1990 (Chu *et al.*, 1990, pp. 225–229). Therefore, it seems reasonable to expect that housing needs for WWA will soon become critical and even unmanageable.

In developing appropriate housing facilities for WWA, it would be beneficial to understand the nature of care for AIDS patients. A number of problems can be readily identified regarding the provision of care (Cameron, 1992, pp. 9–14). The first problem relates to the fact that many current and former IV drug users who have AIDS are often difficult to manage medically. They frequently miss medical appointments, do not always take medication as prescribed, and fail to follow through with social service appointments for government benefits. It is difficult to keep these people stable in their homes and therefore they present a tremendous challenge to health care providers.

The second problem is the objection of communities to AIDS facilities. Many people are still afraid of AIDS patients. Indeed, the "Not In My Back Yard" mentality is widespread, and people in general react negatively when housing for AIDS patients is proposed in their neighborhoods. A specific concern is that this type of residential care facility may decrease the value of their property. Also, some communities believe that crime, noise, and traffic in the neighborhood will increase significantly.

Another problem regarding the provision of care for AIDS patients involves its cost. The reliability and consistency of information about the costs of treatment of AIDS patients is limited. For example, on the average, hospital costs per day in New York City in 1987 were $500. Intensive care or care for a patient with AIDS can drive the costs to $1,500 (Smith, 1987, p. 28). It has been estimated that the costs of health care for an AIDS patient from diagnosis to death are about $50,000 (Bartlett, 1987, p. 3). On the other hand, researchers at New England Deaconess Hospital in 1986 suggested that the cost for hospital care alone is around $147,000 per patient. The prevailing view regarding AIDS health care costs is that "nobody knows what private insurers are paying," because these companies do not always disclose what they are paying for hospital care (Brunetta, 1988, p. 7). The few estimates available do not include ancillary or community-based home care services. Also, these figures are just for inpatient medical care and do not reflect the estimated cost of outpatient visits and prescription drugs that almost all AIDS patients require.

Barriers in Housing Women with AIDS

A number of problems are readily identifiable regarding housing WWA. A major problem is that many of these women are incapable of taking proper care of themselves. Many of these women are drug users and often have severed their ties with their families. Furthermore, a disproportionately higher number of WWA are from Black and Hispanic families. In 1991, Black and Hispanic women made up a disproportionately high percentage of WWA, accounting for 52.4% and 20.4%, respectively (HIV/AIDS Surveillance Report, 1991). However, according to recent U.S. population statistics, Black women accounted for only approximately 14.7% of the U.S. female population, while Hispanic women were only 7% (Shayne and Kaplan, 1991, p. 22). Also, many WWA are of childbearing age, many are single heads of their households of families with children,

many are poor and some are engaged in prostitution (Shayne and Kaplan, 1991).

At least three groups of characteristics set WWA apart from their male counterparts. The differences might help to explain why WWA have housing needs different from those of male AIDS patients. These are biological, socioeconomic, and epidemiological characteristics. First, according to one study, between 80% of the AIDS cases reported among adult women have been diagnosed among women of reproductive age, 15 to 44 years old (Koonin et al., 1989, p. 1306), and obviously only women can bear children.

Second, as mentioned earlier, a disproportionately high number of women with AIDS are poor and are ethnic minorities. According to Shayne and Kaplan, about 73% of mothers with children who have AIDS are recipients of public assistance. The few that were employed were earning an average annual income of about $10,000 (no specific dates were provided for these statistics in the study but the implication was that these statistics were prior to 1987) (Shayne and Kaplan, 1991, p. 29). Although these characteristics may rot distinguish female from male AIDS patients, they are associated with such distinctions. WWA are often subject to abandonment and discrimination by friends and family (Shayne and Kaplan, 1991, p. 28), and a higher proportion of women contracted the AIDS virus through intravenous drug use than their male counterparts. Between August, 1990, and July, 1991, 48% of WWA had contracted the disease as the result of IV drug use, in contrast to only 21% of the MWA (HIV/AIDS Surveillance Report, 1991).

Third, a major epidemiological characteristic that sets WWA apart from their male counterparts is that women function as the receptacle of the spread of AIDS. By citing statistics from the Center for Disease Control and several other studies, Shayne and Kaplan point out that about 30% of WWA have been infected through heterosexual sex, in contrast to only 2% of male AIDS patients. This is probably because there are many more men infected with HIV than women (Shayne and Kaplan, 1991, p. 25). Therefore women are more likely to encounter an infected man than the reverse. Another epidemiological characteristic is that WWA can pass the virus on to unborn children. Many HIV-infected women often remain undiagnosed until the onset of AIDS or until a prenatally infected child becomes ill (Kent, 1991, p. 1442). In fact, women infected with the HIV have been the major source of infection of infants with

AIDS (Shayne and Kaplan, 1991, p. 28). Finally, women with AIDS typically are sicker than their male counterparts, and as a result, WWA do not live as long as MWA (Bakeman et al., 1986; Shaw, 1987). In fact, the average life span for WWA is seven months; for MWA it is two years (Kent, 1991, p. 1442).

Methodology

A list of housing services for women with AIDS has been obtained from the National AIDS clearinghouse through the U.S. Department of Health and Human Services. It contains information about services offered to persons with AIDS in over 100 facilities throughout the United States. Ten of these residential care facilities were identified for this study, chosen as providing long-term care for WWA, in operation for over 18 months, and offering comprehensive services.

To obtain information regarding WWA from these facilities, a questionnaire was developed and sent to the selected AIDS residential care facilities. Telephone interviews with the administrators of these facilities would be conducted several days later. The questions were designed to obtain information regarding the age distribution, ethnic mix, and length of stay of the patients, the building design, type of medical facilities, nature of over-night accommodation for family members and "significant others,"[1] type of social and medical services offered, reasons for patients' stay in facility, and differences in caring for women with AIDS and men with AIDS. We report here on two of the ten facilities, Bailey House in New York City and Shanti Project in San Francisco.

Case Study Analysis

Bailey House, New York City

According to the documents provided by AIDS Re-source Center, Inc., Bailey House opened in December, 1986, to provide supportive housing for approximately 44 homeless persons with AIDS (PWA). It is operated by AIDS Resource Center Inc., and is located in Greenwich Village, New York City. The geographic area served by Bailey House includes the five NYC boroughs. Bailey House is not a medical care facility, nursing home, hospice, nor a care giver of the last resort. It is a supportive residence for persons with AIDS. It provides referrals for medical, mental health, and substance abuse care. Also, Bailey House provides for its residents medical monitoring, counsels residents about issues related to having AIDS, works with families, provides recreation, and offers pastoral care and housekeeping services.

Every resident has his or her own room, private bath, television, telephone, and small refrigerator. Three meals a day are served in the dining room, and snacks are available between meals. Residents are allowed to come and go as they wish, and are permitted to receive guests. Each bedroom has a lock, and residents are encouraged to decorate and personalize their rooms. Overnight guests for both women and men are allowed at Bailey House. Children may stay overnight with their parents, with a limit of two per parent per night. All visitors must pay for their meals. However, no more than four children are allowed in the building on any one night. Each child may visit up to two nights each week. Cots are placed in a resident's room for overnight guests.

All Bailey House residents are referred to the facility by the Case Management Unit of the city's Division of AIDS Services (DAS). Most are referred to DAS by hospital discharge units while others may come through such other channels as the YMCA and YWCA. For admission to Bailey House, applicants must be diag-nosed with AIDS. Also, they must be homeless, eligible for public assistance and Social Security Insurance or disability, and be ambulatory.

Bailey House's operations are primarily funded by New York City, which receives about 50% reimbursement from the state Department of Social Services. Other funding sources include the federal Ryan White Act, the residents' entitlement checks, the state Division of Substance Abuse, and private fund-raising activities. Each resident of Bailey House is required to pay $364 per month for rent, food, and care.

When Bailey House was first opened, a few residents came from mainstream backgrounds, such as gay artists or waiters, who became impoverished once they became sick. The majority, however, have lived on the streets or in unstable environments for a number of years. Many of the women residents have children. Fourteen percent of the Bailey House resident AIDS patients since 1986 have been female. Of the female population, 65% has been Black, 19% Hispanic, and 15% White. Further-more, most of the women have been substance users (i.e., intravenous drug users) and some have been the sexual partners of men at risk. At the time the question-naire was administered (March 31, 1992), 49 AIDS patients resided at Bailey House, including four women (two Hispanic and two Black). All four females were over 30 but had not reached their fortieth birthdays.

The major reasons for the care of WWA in Bailey House are that many of its women residents have medical, mental health, economic, prostitution, and substance abuse problems that preceded their diagnosis with AIDS. As for the length of stay for AIDS patients, Bailey House does not keep separate statistics for men and women residents. In general, residents have lived at Bailey House from eleven days to more than two and one-half years as of March, 1992. Ten of the residents have lived there for more than two years. Twelve residents died within their first month at Bailey House. Currently, the WWA and MWA at Bailey House have been there from 3 to 9 months and from 4 to 36 months, respectively. Many residents chose Bailey House because its social services and housing are affordable and comprehensive. Other male residents are street people who do not have any housing options other then Bailey House.

Eighty-six percent of the Bailey House resident AIDS patients since 1986 have been male. Of the male population, 55% have been Black, 25% Hispanic, and 20% White. The male population has been evenly divided between one-time intravenous drug users and gay men, with about 5% overlap of the two. At the time of our study, there were 24 male residents between 30 and 39 years of age; 15 between 40 and 49 years of age; and 6 over 49. There are 16 Black, 14 Hispanic, and 15 White residents.

Responding to the important questions of whether caring for MWA differs from caring for WWA and whether WWA actually have different housing needs, the Bailey House administration points out that gay men may have different housing needs from those of their female counterparts, especially if WWA were heterosexual or IV drug users. Gay men may simply want to associate with other gay men. On the other hand, the administration also points out that WWA might have housing needs different from those of their male counterparts.

As previously indicated, women are usually sicker then their male counterparts. This would lead to a need for more medical services. If more medical equipment is required, more storage and bedroom space would be needed to house the additional equipment. Women with AIDS who have children or who are pregnant may require additional living quarters for themselves and their children. Women with AIDS often feel uncomfort-

able living with homosexual men with AIDS. House staff suggest that because the majority of the residents are gay males, it may be difficult for a woman resident to personalize the space she shares with other residents.

Shanti Project, San Francisco

Prior to caring for persons with AIDS, the Shanti Project was a facility for seriously ill patients. In 1984, the Shanti Project started offering residential care solely to persons with AIDS. Currently, Shanti Project leases 17 apartments, two 24-hour hospice care facilities, and one single-family residence. These facilities are located throughout the City and County of San Francisco. Among them is a single-family residence specifically for WWA, opened in September, 1990. It is a two-story building located in Noe Valley. The geographic area served by Shanti Project includes the entire Bay area.

Similar to Bailey House, the Shanti Project's congregate living program is a supportive residence for persons with AIDS, and does not provide medical care or nursing care services. Case management and visiting nurse services are provided on a contract-out basis. Each flat is assigned a case manager. Residents can receive referrals for medical, mental health, and substance abuse care. In the two 24-hour care facilities, medical monitoring by a nurse is also provided on the premises. Residents in all the Project facilities are counseled on issues related to AIDS.

In the single-family residence every woman has her own room but shares such other facilities as bathroom, television, telephone, and refrigerator. Residents buy their own food. Meals can be shared or prepared separately by residents. Also, residents are allowed to come and go as they wish, and are permitted to entertain guests. WWA in the single-family residence are encouraged to decorate and personalize their bedrooms. Overnight guests of WWA are allowed at the Noe Valley residence. "Significant others" may stay overnight with their partners, with a limit of five overnight stays per month. Children cannot stay overnight in the building, but are not limited in the number of visits. Overnight guests must sleep in a resident's room. All visitors must pay for their meals.

Potential residents for Shanti Project are identified through city and county social service agencies. Some are referred by hospital discharge units while others may come through other channels. For example, WWA living in a family setting no longer comfortable may be encouraged by the social worker to seek placement in

Shanti Project. For admission to Shanti Project, applicants must be HIV-positive or diagnosed with AIDS. Also, they must be eligible for public assistance and Social Security Insurance or disability payments, and be ambulatory. Ellen Hardtke, Residence Program Director, notes that potential residents must also be cooperating in their care for medical, mental health, and substance abuse needs at the time of admission. Furthermore, residents must be amenable to a culturally diverse setting.

Shanti Project's operation is primarily funded by the City and County of San Francisco, which receives about 40% reimbursement and donations. Other funding sources include the federal Ryan White Act, the residents' entitlement checks, and private fund-raising activities. Each resident is charged 25% of her or his income for rent and other services.

According to the information provided by the Shanti Project administration, since 1984, the Project has served over 10,000 AIDS patients. Among them, less than 5% of the resident AIDS patients has been female. Of the female population, 70% has been Black, 15% Hispanic, 5% White, and less than 1% Asian/Pacific Islander. Some of the women have been substance users, and some have been the sexual partners of men at risk. At the time the questionnaire was administered (April 1, 1992), three WWA lived at the single-family house in Noe Valley: one Black, one White, and one Asian/Pacific Islander. The women came from middle-class backgrounds: they became poor once they became sick. None of the women has children. Two are under 30 and one is over 40.

In general, WWA have lived at the Noe Valley residence from six months to more than two years, averaging one year. On the other hand, MWA in Shanti Project stay an average of 14 months. The longest stay for MWA is approximately three years and the shortest, one month. A number of male residents died during their first month at Shanti Project's congregate living program. The length of stay has been increasing for both men and women because of proactive medical treatments, early HIV testing, and outreach counseling.

Like the WWA in New York's Bailey House, many women residents in Shanti have medical, mental health, economic, and substance abuse problems that preceded their diagnosis with AIDS. The Shanti administration points out that, because there are considerably fewer women with AIDS, most facilities in the U.S., and in San Francisco, are for MWA; only a few are for both

WWA and MWA. There is a significant lack of affordable housing in the San Francisco Bay Area. Therefore WWA who are unemployed have few housing options. Additionally, these women often lack emotional and financial support from family members and, as a result, do not have family members or friends willing to provide housing for them.

Among the MWA in Shanti, a number have medical, mental health, economic, and substance abuse problems that preceded their diagnosis with AIDS. Although there are considerably more residential care facilities for MWA, only a few of them have the experience and level of social services provided by Shanti Project's congregate living program to persons with AIDS. Like the WWA, many of these men also lack emotional and financial support from family members and "significant others." Thus MWA do not have family or friends willing or able to provide the level of support that would be necessary to keep them at home.

The same perception also exists among the Shanti Project administration that gay men might have housing needs different from those of their female counterparts, especially if the women are heterosexual and/or IV drug users. Furthermore, staff at the Noe Valley residence believe that WWA have housing needs different from those of their male counterparts. Not surprisingly, though, the same reasons are cited by the Noe Valley staff. These include the fact that WWA are usually sicker than MWA and, therefore, need more medical services and more space; WWA often have children or are pregnant; and that WWA might not feel comfortable with homosexual men with AIDS.

Recommendations

The essential questions posed by this study are: Do women with AIDS have housing needs that differ from those of their male counterparts? And if so, how can we provide housing facilities that are more conducive to caring for them? It would be inappropriate to provide a definitive answer to these questions on the basis of only two of the ten selected facilities, i.e., results at this writing are too preliminary to justify conclusions. However, some of the differences between WWA and MWA identified in this study are established biological and medical facts. Furthermore, we have found that, with the majority of WWA being heterosexual, they in general feel uncomfortable and some have even expressed a concern for safety (for their children, relatives, and themselves) in being housed in the same facility with mostly gay men with AIDS. Similar perceptions regarding housing needs for WWA have been expressed by the personnel of Bailey House and Shanti Project, two of the largest AIDS care organizations in the U.S. The hypothesis that WWA have different housing needs thus seems reasonable at this point.

We recommend a range of housing options for WWA and their families. These housing options, each equipped with different social and medical services, must be able to address the needs of single WWA as well as WWA with families. We advocate a continuum of housing options for WWA in different stages of the illness.

WWA in the early or in non-acute stages of the illness can live relatively independently. As the illness progresses, the women may need housing options with more services that can best be provided in a residential care facility which has a stronger medical component. WWA in the later stages of the illness may need palliative care in the form of in-home or residential hospice care. To meet the housing needs of WWA, two different design options emerged from the information obtained. In one option, a woman would be moved to the facility that could best address her medical, social, and daily living needs. In other words, WWA in different stages of the disease should be cared for in a separate housing and health care facility. As noted earlier, WWA are generally sicker than their male counterparts; thus they may need to reside in a residential care facility located in a one-story building. Because they are much sicker when they seek medical intervention, they may need larger bedrooms to accommodate the medical equipment used to sustain their lives.

In the second housing option, comprehensive health care and social service programs are to be provided within one single facility. In a single residence all WWA's daily needs could be cared for in the same structure. Thus, services would be delivered to WWA and their children regardless of their HIV status. The structure could contain several floors. Every floor could be geared for single WWA or for WWA with families. These residential care facilities could also be divided according to medical status or a combination of the two. All activities would be accommodated on the premises: offices would be provided for the unit for such services as counseling, medical, physical therapy, housekeeping, day care, and legal services. There could be communal areas centrally located throughout the building for recreational space, reading, and an outdoor area. Communal space could be used by any family.

In summary, information from two major AIDS care organizations lends support to the argument that WWA have housing needs different from those of their male counterparts. Two housing options are posed in the study to meet the specific needs. Clearly, a more definitive answer and appropriate housing designs for WWA would require the analysis of more AIDS care facilities.

Note

[1] This term is used to describe arrangement between two individuals who are not legally married but as a practice maintain a living arrangement very similar to married couples. In San Francisco and Seattle the arrangement is recognized by law.

References

A Families USA Foundation Report (October 1990). *EMERGENCY: Rising Health Costs in America.* Families USA Foundation, 1334 G. Street, NW, Washington, D.C. 20005.

Altman, D. (1986). *AIDS in the Mind of America.* First Edition. Garden City, NY: Anchor Press.

Altman, I., and Chemers, M. (1980). *Culture and Environment.* Monterey, CA: Brooks/Cole.

Arno, P.S. (1986). "The Nonprofit Sector's Response to the AIDS Epidemic: Community-based Services in San Francisco." *American Journal of Public Health, 76:* 1325–1330.

Arno, P.S. and R.G. Hughes (1987). "Local Policy Responses to the AIDS Epidemic: New York and San Francisco." *New York State Journal of Medicine, 87:* 264–272.

Bakeman, R. and J.R. Lamb (1986). "AIDS Rick Group Profiles in Whites and Members of Minority Groups." *The New England Journal of Medicine. 315:* 191–192.

Bartlett, John M.D. (June 1987). "Planning Ahead." *AIDS Patient Care,* 3–5.

Barreto, Felix R. (1988). "Developing a Community-Based Housing Plan for People with AIDS: A Case Study of Dallas County, with Preliminary Findings of a National Survey of AIDS Housing Service Providers." Paper presented at the 1988 meetings of the Association of Collegiate Schools of Planning, Buffalo.

Beatrice, D.F. (1981). "Case Management: A Policy Option for Long-term Care System." In *Reforming the Long-term Care System,* ed. by J.J. Callahan and S.S. Wallack. Walthem, MA.: University Health Policy Consortium.

Brandt, A. M. (December 1986). "AIDS: From Social History to Social Policy." *Law, Medicine and Health Care.* 5–6: 231–242.

Bruininks, R., F. Hauber and M. Kudla (1980). "National Survey of Community Residential Facilities: A Profile of Facilities and Residents in 1977." *American Journal of Mental Deficiency*, No. 84.

Brunetta, Leslie (February, 1988). "Paying the Bills." *AIDS Patient Care*, 7–9.

Butler, L.H. and P.W. Newacheck (1981). "Health and Social Factors Relevant to Long-Term Care Policy." In *Policy Options in Long-term Care*, eds. J. Meltzer, F. Farrow, and H. Richman, pp. 38–75. Chicago: University of Chicago Press.

Cameron, T. (1992). *Community Homecare For AIDS Patients.* Working paper.

Chu, Sy., Buehler, J.W., Berkelman, R.L., "The Impact of the Human Immunodeficiency Virus Epidemic on Mortality in Women of Reproductive Age in the United States." *JAMA*, 1990, 264: 225–229.

Droste, T. (1987). "Going Home to Die: Developing Home Health Care Services For AIDS Patients." *Hospitals.* 8: 54–58.

Frackelmann, K. (1985). "State Officials Desperate for Facilities Homes Willing to Admit AIDS Victims." *Modern Healthcare.* 9: 48.

Ginsburg, P.B., and D.M. Koretz (1983) "Bed Availability and Hospital Utilization: Estimates of the 'Roemer Effect." *Health Care Financing Review.* 5: 87–92.

Green, J., M. Singer, N. Winfeld, K. Schulman, and L. Passman (1987). "Projecting the Impact of AIDS on Hospitals." *Health Affairs.* 6: 19–31.

Greer, D.S., V. Mor, J.N. Moris, S. Sherwood, D. Kidder, and H. Birnbaum (1986). "An Alternative in Terminal Care: Results of the National Hospice Study." *Journal of Chronic Disease.* 39: 9–26.

HIV/AIDS Surveillance Report (June 1991). Published by the Division of HIV/AIDS, Center for Infection Disease Control, Atlanta, GA 30333.

Hughes, A., *et al.* (1987). *AIDS Home Care and Hospice Manual.* San Francisco: Visiting Nurses Association, 1987.

Kent, Michael (May 16, 1991). "Women and AIDS." *The New England Journal Of Medicine.* 326: 1442

Koonin, L., Ellerbrock, T.V., Atrash, H.K., Hague, C.J., Harris, M.A., Chaukin, W., Parker, A.L., Alpin, G.J. (March 3,1989). "Pregnancy-Associated Deaths Due to AIDS in the United States." *JAMA, 261*, No. 9, 1306–1309.

Landesman, M.D., Sheldon, H., Minkoff, Howard L., Willoughby, Ann (March 3, 1989). "HIV Disease in Reproductive Age Women: A Problem of the Present." *JAMA, 261*(9): 1326–1327.

Mosson, W. (1987). *An Analysis of Community Reaction to the SRO Project.* Master of Social Work thesis. Ann Arbor: The University of Michigan.

Shaw, S. (1987). "Wretched of the Earth." *New Statesman.* 3/30: 19–20.

Shayne, V., and Kaplan, B. (1991). "Double Victims: Poor Women and AIDS." *Women and Health.* 17(1): 21–37.

Smith, Andre M. (June 1987). "Alternatives in AIDS Homecare." *AIDS Patient Care.* 28–32.

Chapter 17
Synopsis of Talk by Sara Snyder, Grateful Home

Margrit Bergholz

Sara J. Snyder, *executive director of Grateful Home, Inc., is the director of one of the oldest treatment programs for women in the state of Michigan. She is a certified addiction counselor (CAC), and has an Associate Degree in Mental Health. She has worked in the field of chemical dependency for sixteen years and has been the director at Grateful Home for six years. Previous positions include crisis counselor at the NSO Walk-in Center, substance abuse counselor at Columbia Hospital, counselor at Women in Transition (domestic violence shelter), therapist at Marion Manor Medical Center, and at Interim House/Women and Children's Chemical Dependency Program.*

Ms. Snyder has been director of the Grateful Home Non-profit Corporation for 6 1/2 years. She is also an alumna of the program, having graduated in 1974. At that time, Grateful Home was the only treatment program for indigent, chemically addicted women in Michigan. The other program for women was at Brighton Hospital and was open only to women who had good medical insurance.

Grateful Home, at 30 years, is the oldest program serving chemically addicted women in Michigan. For its first 24 years, however, it was only a half-way house, providing food and a bed. For 4 1/2 years after Ms. Snyder became executive director, she worked to make the kind of social services and counseling available she would have liked to have had when she was a resident there. In addition to adding support services to Grateful Home, Ms. Snyder had two primary goals to improve the program. The first was to increase its size. There are at least 500 chemically addicted women in Detroit, at any given time, in need of shelter. Yet Grateful Home had only nine beds available. The second goal was to create a system to help women in the program regain custody of their children.

For the last year and a half, Ms. Snyder and other formerly chemically addicted women have worked on the Dreamweaver Power Project. This project began when Ms. Snyder learned, at a community meeting, that the Archdiocese of Detroit had offered the land and buildings of the closed St. Bernard parish to the Society of St. Vincent de Paul for one dollar. Ms. Snyder learned the site was well located to serve their client base. The site was central to the 48213, 48214, and 48215 zip codes, the most service-deprived areas in Michigan. The land comprised an entire city block with four large buildings: a four-story former elementary school, a two-story former convent, a nine-bedroom former rectory, and a church, in addition to a playground and a parking lot.

Because Grateful Home was not a Catholic organization, however, the real estate office of the archdiocese wanted market rate for its purchase, which was $250,000. Grateful Home could not afford that purchase price, but Ms. Snyder went to the Bishop of Detroit with a description of the services Grateful Home offered and $34.50 which had been collected from current clients in the program. The Bishop agreed to sell the site to Grateful Homes for the $34.50, but the real estate office, which was responsible for selling numerous closed parishes in Detroit, was afraid that, if they gave such an advantageous price to Grateful Home, other non-profit organizations would expect similar prices. During these negotiations, the Junior League of Detroit, which was working with Grateful Home on another project, learned of Grateful Home's interest in the site and committed itself to funding for the purchase of the property. The property was ultimately purchased for $125,000.

Once Grateful Home occupied the property, they realized that the 35,000 square feet of floor space on the site was far more than their program could utilize. Ms. Snyder, therefore, proposed to her board that they lease some of the space available to other non-profits. At this point, six non-profits are renting space on the site. The non-profits chosen provide services needed by Grateful Home clients. Their lease agreement requires that they provide free services to Grateful Home residents, in exchange for discounted lease rates, and to provide services in a way which conforms with the Grateful Home philosophy, namely, they emphasize empower-ment, bonding, and a family-style environment for their clients. The non-profits operating on site are:

— St. Vincent de Paul Food Bank
— Women and Community Services (Job Bank)
— Detroit City School G.E.D. Program
— Drama Therapy
— Bon Secours Health Clinic
— Life Directions (Teen Outreach)
— Black Family Development

All these groups provide services to the general commu-nity as well as to residents at Grateful Home. In addition to these social services, the former convent is being operated as a child care center.

While the Dreamweaver project was being developed, the Governor of Michigan cut General Assistance (GA) welfare payments to 83,000 people in Michigan. To help meet the needs of the numerous women who became homeless because of the cuts in GA, Grateful Home converted the church on the Dreamweaver site into a 60-bed emergency shelter. In operating the emergency shelter, Grateful Home found that 90% of the women housed there were eligible for their substance abuse program, and the shelter has become a major source of women who enter that program. The rectory is being used as a post-treatment transitional living center for women after they graduate from the residential care program, which is still housed at its original site on East Grand Boulevard.

Although the state pays for only 90 days of treatment for the substance abuse program, Grateful Home allows

clients to stay as long as they need to. Ms. Snyder believes it is important in a successful substance abuse program to remove the roadblocks of transportation and child care from treatment. The Grateful Home programs provide all the social services the women in the sub-stance abuse program need on one site, along with child care.

Chapter 18
Synopsis of Talk by Robert Gillett, Legal Services of Southeastern Michigan

Margrit Bergholz

Robert Gillett *is an attorney and the executive director of Legal Services of Southeastern Michigan. As an attorney, he has specialized in housing law, including eviction and foreclosure prevention issues and low-income housing developmetn issues. He is a 1978 graduate of the University of Michigan Law School, and has practiced as a public interest lawyer in Michigan since his graduation. Legal Services of Southeastern Michigan is one of over 300 local non-profit organizations providing free legal services to low-income persons in civil legal cases. Established in 1966, L.S.S.E.M. provides services primarily in the areas of housing law, public benefits law, and family law.*

Mr. Gillett is an attorney with Legal Services of Southeastern Michigan, specializing in housing issues. He presented a discussion of what he sees as developments and current trends in affordable housing for women. Mr. Gillett works with women facing homelessness and with community groups which provide housing. Legal Services helps prevent homelessness in three broad ways:

— In eviction and foreclosure prevention, by representing the tenants or owners.
— In domestic violence situations, by getting restraining orders to give women physical security and by gaining women the right for exclusive use of the marital home.
— In public assistance cases, by representing clients against the federal or state government, to maintain income for housing and other basic needs.

The work Mr. Gillett does with affordable housing developers is more in the nature of solutions to homelessness.

Women and children in the United States have a higher incidence of poverty and extreme poverty than other sectors of the population. The federal Department of Housing and Urban Development (HUD) defines poverty as below 50% of median income, which means, for Washtenaw County, Michigan, a family of four with an income of less than $22,500 a year, and provides statistics on poverty by that definition. The clients Mr. Gillett sees are generally recipients of welfare, either Aid to Families with Dependent Children (AFDC), which provides about $4,800 a year to a family of three (this income is 12% of area median), or General Assistance (GA), which provides about $2,400 a year to a single person (this income is 6% of area median).

Since the beginning of the Reagan Administration in 1981, no new affordable housing has been developed. Before 1980, some federal housing programs had aimed at housing very low-income persons, and some new programs have begun very recently to address this issue again. Mr. Gillett believes that this lack of new afford-able housing has been the major cause of the increase in homelessness over the past ten years. For a significant sub-group of the homeless, the deinstitutionalization of mental patients has caused homelessness, but he thinks economic reasons are far more important than deinstitutionalization. A contributing economic cause is the freezing of welfare benefits since 1980, which has resulted in relative reductions in benefits. In 1980, the housing portion of an AFDC grant in Washtenaw County was $175 per month. Today, this is still the housing portion of the grant, even though it would be impossible to find an apartment for that rental rate.

The recent (October 1991) cut-off of GA payments to 83,000 people in Michigan was presented by the Governor and portrayed in the press as something which would affect only young, able-bodied black men living in the City of Detroit. This is not the case, and the reductions have affected a significant number of women. In fact, 40-45% of the GA caseload was female and the average age of recipients was over 40. A state assessment of GA recipients found that 82% of recipients were unemployable or functionally unemployable.

Ten years ago in the Midwest, homelessness among women and children was almost unknown. Now it is a significant problem. Family Emergency Shelters in Washtenaw County, which have 35 beds, experience demands for at least 200 beds at any time. This increase in homelessness has not come from social trends or sociology but has been the result of deliberate government policy.

In working with female clients who face homelessness, Mr. Gillett believes it is important to recognize the importance of the home to women's sense of security. The school schedule, proximity of churches, doctors, services, and membership in a particular community network are very important to most women psychologically and socially. When women are threatened with homelessness, they suffer emotionally and psychologically and it is important to deal with these personal issues, as well as the housing issue, through counseling or support.

Mr. Gillett urges housing professionals not to neglect the prevention of homelessness when dealing with housing problems. It is much less expensive, more humane, and more what the women want—to provide assistance which will keep them from becoming homeless in the first place.

Since the government has given up its role in providing affordable housing for more than a decade, many social service providers have stepped in to try to develop new, affordable housing. These groups usually do so because they see a lack of housing as a major problem facing their clients, but the change from providing social services to developing housing is difficult and raises many issues which these groups must grapple with. It is a positive trend that non-profits are becoming increasingly involved in providing affordable housing. Now that the HOME program was passed in 1991, some

federal funds are available and even more groups should be entering the field.

When service groups begin to develop housing, they must deal with issues of housing finance, design, and legal structure of ownership and finance, which are often completely new to them. When they get over the hurdles of developing housing, then the groups have to decide who will manage the housing and how it will be done. Many groups oriented to providing services to their clients have a hard time becoming landlords and dealing with issues of rent collection and evictions. The groups have to decide if they should manage the housing themselves and, if they do, whether it should be managed by a separate section or integrated into the service section of the organization.

Community service organizations usually have to start with small developments. To help groups in developing housing, a trend toward consortia is developing. Instead of 15 groups having to learn housing finance in order to create 50 units, only one group will become expert in finance and then provide that service to the others.

Even though the federal government has created an affordable housing program recently, the level of funding is nowhere near the need. In the late 1960's and early 1970's, more than 1,500 units of affordable housing were built around Ann Arbor through the federal government's 236 and 221 mortgage insurance programs. The need for affordable housing in Ann Arbor is now greater than it was during that period. To build 1,500 units today would require over $60,000,000 in subsidies, but the amount available to Ann Arbor this year is under $1,000,000.

Mr. Gillett sees the trend toward the development of affordable housing by non-profit organizations as positive. He sees the field of developing affordable housing today as very experimental, where groups are trying new solutions and creating new models. He thinks non-profits and government should keep this in mind when evaluating programs and stay flexible and keep adjusting programs to improve them. He feels that a significant increase in federal funding for very low-income housing is necessary to move communities from small, experimental developments to larger developments that can address the tremendous housing need.

Chapter 19
Housing Homeless Women in Toronto

Joyce Brown and Diana Capponi

Joyce Brown *has been a shelter worker for fourteen years. In addition to counselling and shelter work, she is involved in housing and mental health issues with various community boards and committees. She has a Master of Social Work from Carleton University. She is currently working in an Environmental Studies Program and focusing on women's issues, homelessness, and international development.*

Diana Capponi *has been a housing worker for seven years. She has previously been involved in the mental health field and criminal justice systems. She currently serves on many committees and community boards on issues related to women's issues, mental health, and housing.*

The situation of the homeless has steadily worsened in Toronto over the past decade. Metropolitan Toronto is a city with a current population of nearly three million. Estimates of the number of homeless people in Toronto now range from 15,000 to 20,000. This article will take a brief look at the reasons women become homeless and at some of the housing which has been built by the nonprofit housing sector in an attempt to address the needs of the homeless. It examines how the needs of homeless women differ from homeless men and how their housing needs may differ.

The information is based on several years' work in an emergency shelter for women; on work in the housing field; on feedback from the women who have been housed; and on 23 interviews with founders and early staff of nine nonprofit housing projects in Toronto. It is part of an ongoing research project which will analyze the effectiveness of various approaches to providing housing. Although numerous definitions of homelessness have been put forward, the focus for this discussion is on those women who have frequently used the hostel system, have resided on the street, or have been in contact with social service agencies because of continuing housing problems.

How Women Become Homeless

Women arrive in the shelter system for a number of reasons. For some the cause is primarily economic—high rents, low income, and a great scarcity of affordable housing. Others are fleeing abuse either by a partner or parents. In the past few years an increasing number of refugees have arrived at women's shelters—particularly from Ethiopia and Somalia. Still others have come through the mental health system and ended up on the street. For many it is a combination of factors, but the majority will have experienced abuse at some point in their lives. In this they may not be different from the population of women at large, but their difficulties are compounded by poverty and lack of affordable housing.

An American researcher, Maxine Harris, interviewed a number of homeless women in the U.S. for her book *Sisters of the Shadow*. She states that

> perhaps the most startling psychological characteristic of many homeless women is their profound sense of alienation. Many of the women interviewed had lost large portions of their own life stories. They either could not remember things that had happened to them or had dissociated

themselves from particularly painful elements of their personal histories.... [A]lienation from self is not the only recurring theme in the psychological profiles of homeless women. Equally important is the almost pervasive history of abuse. Many of these women were victims of child abuse, of incest within their home, of abuse by spouses, and once they became homeless, of physical abuse and rape on the streets.

These findings coincide with the experiences of people who work with the homeless population in Toronto. A former worker at a project known as Streetcity stated that nearly all the women living there had histories of abuse and the large majority of them had a history in the mental health system or current mental health problems.

Men, on the other hand (perhaps also victims of child-hood abuse, although this is not documented as clearly as for women), arrive on the street by a different route. They are commonly seen to go through a cycle of lost jobs and alcoholism. They are far more likely to encounter the criminal justice system and be labeled by it. Thus, often it is women who have been institutional-ized by the mental health system and men who have been incarcerated who end up on the streets. Although the majority of women in hostels do not have connec-tions with men in the hostel system, housing developers put these two groups together when developing projects. This has become a major topic of debate in women's services in Toronto: Should these two populations be housed together when their histories and issues are so different?

Traditional Response to Homelessness

Hostels have been the traditional institutional response to homelessness in Canada. Local governments, religious institutions, and nonprofit organizations have all sought to serve this population by providing hostels of various types. Men's and women's hostels have approached the issue from a different philosophical basis and their history of providing service to men and women is also distinctly different. Hostels for men were developed in the late 1800s in response to a growing migrant work force of single males moving from farms into the cities for work. Dormitory style accommoda-tion was provided by the churches for men who were between jobs or suffering from illness. Only the most basic necessities were provided and this tradition has continued to the present day.

Women have traditionally been more bound by familial ties and less likely to live alone. It is only recently, with the growing awareness of the needs of abused women, street youth, and the deinstitutionalization of women from mental health facilities, that the need for shelters for women has been recognized. In the l970s and 1980s several shelters for women were opened in Toronto and the surrounding area. A number of these were based on feminist principles and one of their basic goals was to empower women. The shelters were usually situated in large houses and services such as supportive counseling, child care, and referrals were provided. The feminist shelters are generally more wholistic in their approach to providing service than men's shelters, and create a supportive atmosphere rather than providing only a bed and food.

In the early 1980s the issue of homelessness came to be recognized as an urgent problem by both the municipal and provincial governments. As a result of the policy of deinstitutionalization, thousands of people who had spent years in psychiatric facilities were released into the community. Community services for this population were extremely limited and many ended up on the street or in rundown boarding homes. In response to this crisis, the provincial government funded a number of nonprofit agencies to open group homes. In spite of this effort, a large number of psychiatric survivors remained homeless due to the stringent admission criteria of the group homes and their emphasis on communal living, a situation many did not desire. To maintain their housing, people were required to attend programs. To a certain degree they continue to be perceived as ill. Other factors such as the gentrification of downtown Toronto and the subsequent loss of hundreds of rooming houses, and skyrocketing rents contributed to a massive increase in the homeless population.

The Non-profit Response

In 1983, Homes First Society opened 90 Shuter Street, the first building to provide affordable housing for singles with low income. It was seen as the "wedge" which forced the provincial Ministry of Housing to acknowledge that affordable housing should be available to people based on income, not on a special need or disability. It was also a relatively inexpensive method to providing housing. 90 Shuter is shared housing, based on the rooming house model. It is a ten-story high-rise which houses 77 people in apartments shared by groups of four or five.

Homes First was the first nonprofit to introduce "facilitative management," a method which promotes the development of community spirit withiñ a project and facilitates people working through issues and coming to a resolution regarding factors pertinent to the running of the building. Facilitative managers are meant to promote community living rather than to assist people with individual problems. Emphasis is placed on the separation of housing and support services. However, in the absence of adequate support services, facilitative managers face a difficult role when they are unable to provide individual support.

It is important that support services be separate from housing, that tenants be clear about their rights and that the role of the housing management is clear. Too often the support needs of people determine their housing or make them ineligible for it. What has become evident is that for many the provision of housing is not enough. Once people have settled, perhaps for the first time in years, other issues often come up such as memories of childhood sexual abuse, addiction problems, and the need for training and employment programs. The lack of support services for women becomes overwhelmingly apparent when women are housed.

Since 1983 a number of nonprofit housing developers have built a variety of housing projects of both shared housing and self-contained units. These have ranged from refurbishing an old post office warehouse to encompass a "72-unit town," which is set up with streets and stores within the warehouse, to traditional apartment units. Rather than discuss the particulars of the various projects, the focus of this paper is on some of the issues that have arisen during the development process and since the buildings have opened: on elements which seem to work well and which don't. This is not to suggest specific answers but rather to highlight some of the issues which require careful thought and planning before a project is built.

The areas we will focus on are:

— Community development and community participation
— Project size
— Shared versus self-contained units
— Tenant selection
— Tenant mix
— Safety issues and violence
— Women's housing needs

Community Development and Community Participation

Several of the projects in Toronto employed community development staff prior to the opening of the housing. The extent of the community development process varied from holding a few community information sessions to a series of in-depth meetings in which potential residents worked through a number of issues regarding grievances, security and procedures for residents meetings. Those projects which had the opportunity to have several community meetings, to have tenants get to know one another beforehand and to make decisions regarding rules and policies seemed to have a smoother transition period once the project opened. For others, the initial six months were often chaotic with frequent altercations between residents and a general lack of security for everyone. Staff spoke of being afraid while on the job and unclear about their roles and responsibilities. The tenants were similarly confused. Sometimes it was only when the situations became extremely volatile that the tenants came together as a group to set their own rules and procedures. Often women were not brought into the development process until later. This exacerbated any power differentials between the male and female tenants, since men were more comfortable in speaking up at meetings and used to being in control on the street.

For some women the process of community development was intimidating and required attendance at meetings, which made the housing unattainable. For someone who is homeless, the wait for housing may seem endless when the need is immediate, and the prospect of interviews and meetings may be too threatening.

Project Size

In general, smaller projects seem to run more smoothly. It is difficult to specify an optimum number of units, but projects with fewer than twenty units were most content with their size and those with over 70 units felt that their size was a problem.

Shared versus Self-Contained Units

The large congregate living projects in Toronto are based on the rooming-house model and are a form of high-rise rooming house. This model is most familiar to men and has been developed by the men's shelter network. The overwhelming majority of women express a need for self-contained units. Again, shared accommodation is seen to work best with smaller projects and for women when they do not see it as permanent housing.

Tenant Selection

The projects in Toronto select their tenants through a variety of methods. In shared units, tenants make the final selection of who will move in when a vacancy arises. In buildings where the units are self-contained, this is usually decided by the housing provider based on factors of income or referrals from support agencies. Some housing providers have screened out people who they feel will require too much support, while others have focused exclusively on those who have been denied housing for many years.

Tenant Mix

Tenant selection and tenant mix are closely related. Several staff have suggested that a community mixed in age, family size, and background provides more balance and a wider range of views. Having criteria which specify a wide mix resolves some of the dilemmas of tenant selection.

The government of Ontario is moving more toward projects which also reflect a mix of income. While this is a commendable goal, the urgent housing needs of the homeless must not be lost in an attempt to provide a mixed community.

Safety Issues and Violence

One might suppose that violence would be more frequent in shared units due to the increased contact and possibility for conflict, but this has not been borne out by experience. Violence in the various projects has come primarily from two sources: violent male partners and incidents related to drug trafficking.

In many of the projects the initial six months were tumultuous. Many projects did not have procedures and policies in place. Neither tenants nor staff knew how to handle incidents of violence, verbal abuse, and discrimination. By the time procedures were established and some evictions had taken place, other residents had begun to leave because they couldn't tolerate the environment and were too frightened or intimidated to speak out against the perpetrators of the violence. Women were usually the ones to leave for this reason. Women were also sometimes forced to leave because of a violent male partner.

While some housing providers see this initial settling-in period as inevitable, others see it as unnecessary and ultimately unfair to the tenants. A thorough community development process seems to make the settling-in period smoother.

Women's Housing Needs

There appears to be a need for affirmative action projects for homeless women, in which they would be the population first consulted regarding a new project. It would then be their decision whether to have a women's-only project, or to have a mixed one in which they would determine the mix (perhaps greater than 50% women). They could also then choose the population of men they wished to have housed with them and whether the tenants would be referred from a hostel, community center, or another group.

The possibility of involving women first would empower women. It would offset the street code of men making decisions for women who are not accustomed to this role. If the women were the first involved in a project, a more equitable division of power might evolve at later stages.

Questions For New Housing Projects

Learning from the experiences described in this paper, we have developed the following list of issues which need to be addressed to ensure a successful project.

1. How to balance the usefulness of community development with the needs of women who are not able or willing to participate in such a process?
2. What style of management is to be used?
3. How to balance security of tenure with the needs of other residents if accommodation is shared?
4. What is a healthy mix in size of unit and tenants?
5. What support services can be provided?
6. What responsibility do housing providers have for safety?
7. Who can't be housed?

References

Alternative Housing Subcommittee. City of Toronto. "Off the Streets: A Case for Long-Term Housing." 1985.

Daly, Gerald. *A Comparative Assessment of Programs Dealing with the Homeless Population in the United States, Canada, and Britain.* Faculty of Environmental Studies. York University.

Gerstein, Reva. "Final Report of the Mayor's Action Task Force on Discharged Psychiatric Patients." Toronto: Office of the Mayor. 1984.

Goering, Paula *et al.* "Gender Differences Among Clients of a Case Management Program for the Homeless." The Clarke Institute.

Hamdi, Nabeel. *Housing Without Houses.* Van Nostrand Rheinhold. 1990.

Harman, Lesley D. *When A Hostel Becomes A Home.* Garamond Press. 1989.

Harris, Maxine. *Sisters of the Shadow.* Norman: University of Oklahoma Press. 1991.

Hirsch, Kathleen. *Songs from the Alley.* Ticknor & Fields. 1989 .

"Homeless, not Helpless." Report of the Homeless Persons Outreach Project. Healthy City Office. 1990.

Leavitt, Jacqueline, and Susan Saegert. *From Abandonment to Hope.* New York: Columbia University Press. 1990.

"National Action Plan on Housing and Homelessness." Big City Mayor's Caucus. Montreal. 1991.

"Nellie's Housing Research." 1988. (unpublished document)

The Phillips Group. "An Evaluation of Streetcity," Final Report. Toronto 1992.

"Planning for Social Housing: A report by the City of Toronto's Planning Advisory Committee to the Ministry of Housing." 1991.

Ross, Aileen. *The Lost and the Lonely: Homeless Women in Montreal.* Montreal: McGill University Printing Service. 1982.

Rowe, Stacey. *Social Networks in Time and Space: The Case of Homeless Women in Skid Row, Los Angeles.* Los Angeles Homelessness Project. 1988.

The S.D.P. "Hostels and Homelessness." 1983.

The S.D.P. "The Case for Long-Term, Supportive Housing." 1983.

The S.D.P. "From Homelessness to Home, A Case for Facilitative Management." 1987.

Sprague, Joan. *More than Housing: Lifeboats for Women and Children.* Butterworth-Heinemann. 1991.

Van Vliet, Willem, ed. *Women, Housing and Community.* Gower Publishing Company. 1988.

Watson, Sophie. *Housing and Homelessness: A Feminist Perspective.* Routledge and Kegan Paul. 1986.

Wekerle, Gerda, and Barbara Muirhead. *Canadian Women's Housing Projects.* Faculty of Environmental Studies, York University. 1991.

Chapter 20
Wings, KaFanm, Re-Vision House: Case Studies of Transitional Housing for Women

Lynn Peterson

Lynn Peterson has experience in planning and direct social services. She was an assistant planner for the Boston Public Facilities Department. As congregate housing coordinator for elder services of the Merrimack Valley, she managed two congregate homes. She initiated a program for orphans in a community-based home in Cartago, Costa Rica. At the Women's Institute, Ms. Peterson is responsible for projects with Casa Myrna, Re-Vision House, Sojourner, WIHC, WINGS, and Women, Inc. She holds a Bachelor of Arts in Human Services from Northeastern and a Master of Arts in Urban Policy from Tufts University.

The Women's Institute for Housing and Economic Development is based in Boston, Massachusetts. Its role is to support grassroots groups and social service agencies with hands-on technical assistance that can help make their vision a reality. Our approach is flexible, depending on the client's needs. We can act as project manager for an entire development project or offer shorter-term consultation on specific areas. Either way, we build the internal capacity of organizations to own and manage real estate. Our clients range from large, well-established social service agencies to newly formed, grassroots groups working with the homeless, single mothers, battered women, older women, teen parents, refugees and immigrants, women recovering from substance abuse, people with AIDS, and women in prison. In the last year, 70% of our projects were created and run by women; 70% were managed by people of color. All our projects benefit low-income women and their families.

The Development Process of Women's Grassroots Groups

Many of the organizations that the Women's Institute works with are formed by low- income women with a vision of creating housing for a specific population. Some of the women are driven by their own life experiences and others by the problems that plague their environment. For example, a personal history of substance abuse, physical or sexual abuse, teen pregnancy, or immigration motivates some women to help others with similar needs. Either they want to emulate and improve upon a program they benefited from or they wish to create a program that will fill a gap they identify in services or housing. They often create organizations specifically to achieve the kind of housing they desire. These organizations may have ancillary activities, but initially development is their prime focus. In essence, each of these projects is an economic development project. Women without incomes or with low incomes come together, and by creating a non-profit organization, employ themselves and others. They are learning business development and management skills. They are taking their leadership abilities to new heights—initially as advocates and activists and eventually as board members, executive directors, or program coordinators. The creation of the program and its success validate their advocacy work.

With new groups, the housing development process occurs simultaneously with organizational development. The group may be filing for incorporation at the same time it is creating its program. The process is very often slow, at least slower than private development, due to a number of factors:

— management issues
— internal conflict
— complicated lives as low-income women—frequent health and family issues
— trust of "outsiders" who want to help has to be developed
— the group must be marketed to funders, city agencies, etc., and confidence in their ability to develop and operate the program has to be cultivated
— the internal capacity of the group has to grow so that it can manage the program successfully

A typical development process by a grassroots organization begins with a leader, or visionary. The leader may recruit others who share a common goal. Although a small core group will coalesce, the leader will be driving the project. A group may take its idea directly to the Women's Institute because it is aware of our involvement in other community projects, or it may go to the city or a bank, who in turn refer it to us. We meet with the group and learn about its vision, current activities, organizational structure, strengths, and weaknesses. We explain the development process and different options. If there is a mutual consent that we will work together, a contract and statement of and scope of services are drawn up. Very often a group has no funds to pay us. We decide if it will become an "early stage assistance project" where we provide free up-front services, and then help to raise funds to cover our services.

Our services include all aspects of real estate development, such as site selection, feasibility analysis, financial packaging, and project coordination, and program development services, such as developing the service component, negotiating contracts, incorporation, and personnel and management issues. We assist groups with developing written materials about their organization, with marketing their program to sponsors, and with negotiations. Depending on their interest in understanding the technical aspects of real estate development, we train groups in this area. We provide information such as where to find funding and how to put a proposal together, which is critical to their ongoing success, and we make referrals to other organizations that offer complementary forms of assistance. In this paper, three case studies are described to illustrate the issues faced by women's groups seeking to shelter themselves and the services needed to facilitate their attaining this objective.

Re-Vision House, Inc.

In December, 1989, Yvonne Miller-Booker, a woman active in her community, approached the Women's Institute for Housing and Economic Development with the idea to develop Re-Vision House, a transitional program for homeless, teenage mothers and their infants because of the lack of housing and support services available to this population. With seed money from the Clipper Ship Foundation, Ms. Miller-Booker hired the Women's Institute to secure funds for both the acquisition of the site and the supportive services. A proposal was developed in response to a Request for Proposals for state-assisted shelters. Since Re-Vision House was not yet its own organization, Ms. Miller-Booker convinced a tenant activist organization to take the project under its wings, with the intention that the program would eventually become an independent agency. The rigorous RFP process forced the founder to think about the minute details of the program. Although the State of Massachusetts did not fund the program, subsequent proposals were developed and sent to the federal government.

In October, 1990, the Re-Vision House, Inc., program was awarded $200,000 from the Department of Health and Human Services in Washington, D.C. An additional grant from the Boston *Globe* Foundation was also awarded. The federal and private grants became an impetus for local support. Media publicity and an attentive city government also contributed to the realization of the program.

About the time of the awards, newspapers were reporting alarming rates of infant mortality in Boston, particularly among minority families. St. Margaret's Hospital in Dorchester, a neighborhood with a large poor and minority population, was proposing to move to Brighton to merge with St. Elizabeth's Hospital. This outraged the residents of Dorchester, who claimed that the health care resources in the inner city were already limited, although Boston has seven teaching hospitals. Mayor Flynn, responding to the recent reports of high rates of infant mortality and homelessness among minority families in Boston's neighborhoods, initiated a hospital linkage program requiring hospitals to contribute funds and services to the local health centers and transitional programs. Re-Vision House, Inc. became the first recipient of the Hospital Linkage program, with Boston City Hospital as the linked institution. Boston City Hospital contributed $40,000 toward the operating costs as well as pre-natal and pediatric services to the residents.

The Public Facilities Department assisted the organization with locating the current site, a newly renovated triple-decker that was previously a city-owned vacant building. The Home Builders Institute, a construction training program sponsored by the National Association of Home Builders, renovated the building and then leased it to Re-Vision House, Inc. A low-interest loan from the city and a grant from the Neighborhood Housing Trust Fund enabled Re-Vision House, Inc., to purchase the building in November, 1991. Re-Vision House, Inc., became its own non-profit organization in June, 1991, at which time it opened its doors to its first residents.

Documentation of Need

Re-Vision House serves very poor young women, many of them from poor families and broken homes. A recent report by the Boston Foundation, *In the Midst of Plenty: A Profile of Boston and Its Poor,* provided the following statistics: the poverty rate among Hispanics in Boston is 46% and 23% among Blacks. The percentage of single-parent families below the poverty line is higher: 79% of Hispanic and 35% of Black single-parent families live on or below the poverty line. Young mothers (under the age of 25) earn, on the average, $6,000 per year. This reflects mostly AFDC payments, which provide only 73% of the poverty level.

According to a joint report by the Citizen's Housing and Planning Association and the Alliance for Young Families, there are 7,000 teenage households in Massachusetts, and 2,100 are in need of housing. In a survey of shelter providers across the state, 75% of them said they were unable to serve homeless pregnant and parenting teens. In 1988, 630 pregnant and parenting teens were turned away from shelters due to lack of space. The sixteen transitional shelters across the state have been overwhelmed with requests for assistance and turn away 2–3 teen households weekly. Only 5% of the teen households requiring transitional housing are served. The report stressed that more transitional housing programs are needed urgently. Teen parents have an especially difficult time obtaining access to permanent housing for two main reasons. First, they have such low incomes, depending largely on government payments (AFDC), that they cannot afford most rents. Waiting lists for subsidized housing in he greater Boston area span five years. Second, teenage-headed

families face discrimination when trying to obtain permanent housing.

Client recruitment for Re-Vision House is through the Department of Social Services, the Department of Public Welfare, social service providers, and emergency shelters who have teen families not ready to move into permanent housing. At this writing 147 Boston families are in shelters and over 100 in hotels and motels each night. The Re-Vision House program is a substantially better alternative to emergency husing since it provides comprehensive services and allows young mothers and their children to remain in the residence for a minimum of nine months and up to two years. Families can stay in emergency shelters only for up to 90 days, which is not sufficient time for young mothers to get adequate pre-natal care, and comprehensive services before and after the birth of their children.

Teen mothers are selected for the program on the basis of objective criteria developed by Re-Vision House staff and Advisory Board. Criteria include homeless status, pregnancy or parenting status, and age (17-21). Since Re-Vision House is a voluntary program, the residents must acknowledge their need for assistance, be motivated, and interested in participating in the program. The teen mothers are interviewed by the Director and Assistant Director at which time the house rules and expectations are reviewed. The young women must agree to abide by the rules and to follow the program.

Program Design

This program is designed for ten pregnant and parenting teens who are homeless and in need of shelter as well as counseling, drug and alcohol treatment—prevention services, parenting training, job training, and education. Re-Vision House is an innovative and critical program in a community plagued with interrelated social and economic problems such as high unemployment, a growing number of teenage parents, drug abuse, violence, poverty, infant mortality, and homelessness.

Re-Vision House takes a preventative approach to ensure healthy deliveries by offering on-site substance abuse treatment and training in parenting, child development, and nutrition. The young mothers also learn life skills such as budgeting, meal preparation, and stress management. Each resident works individually with a counselor who assists her in developing a plan for her activities while at the residence. This plan includes phased goals and strategies to meet those goals. Residents are referred to services in the community. Residents must commit themselves to sobriety, develop goal-oriented contracts, participate in education and employment training, and uphold the rules of the house as a condition of their stay. Linkages with community social services, hospitals, and specialized health care programs enhance the program services. This helps increase the possibility for success after families are placed in their own apartments.

The model that has been created is a tiered system. The program is divided into three phases, each lasting a minimum of three months. The completion of Phase III will signal a resident's readiness to leave Re-Vision House. It is recognized that completion of each phase will vary in time for each resident due to individual needs. Each phase is constructed to meet general levels of responsibility, emotional growth, and technical skills. An Individual Development Plan is devised by the staff with each resident. The goals for Phase I are developed and the counselor helps the resident in locating assistance to meet those goals. A set of activities will be outlined to reach the stated goals. The initial phase is focused on a healthy delivery and includes health care, drug treatment, and parenting skills. The second phase may focus on education and job readiness training, and the final phase will involve securing permanent housing and employment.

Success

Re-Vision House, Inc., has been open for almost one year now and has already proven to be a success. All the babies were born healthy and are doing well. The mothers are all in school or working and one is in college. Two more young women will be attending community college in the fall. Re-Vision House will be holding a graduation this month for the two young mothers who have completed the program and will be moving into their own subsidized apartments. They will continue to participate in the support groups and staff will follow them up for at least one year. Re-Vision House staff have learned that in order for teens and their babies to thrive and become independent members of society and good parents, they need a tremendous amount of support, guidance, and instruction. Staff have also observed that many teenage parents do not have an immediate or extended family that has the capacity to assist them in this process, either financially or emotionally. Many of the young parents referred to this program will have received inadequate parenting themselves and therefore need positive role modeling.

Re-Vision House is now planning its second development —a twelve-unit permanent housing complex for families leaving the transitional program. Here, families will reside in individual apartments and receive case management services.

Women's Institute for New Growth and Support, Inc.

Incorporated in 1989, The Women's Institute for New Growth and Support (WINGS) is a dynamic organization led by women of color recovering from addiction. It was founded by a group of women of color frustrated with a social service system that was failing to meet their needs as women, as homeless individuals, and as people in recovery. Meeting on a daily basis in a Roxbury apartment, five recovering women began discussing ways to address the needs of other recovering women for affordable housing, assistance with re-entry into the workplace, and family reunification. After reaching out to the Roxbury community and gaining its support, they formed WINGS. Its mission is to empower recovering women by developing their leadership and life skills, advocating changes in the current legal and service delivery systems, and building a drug-free community.

The organization operates a Resource and Referral Center at 22 Elm Hill Avenue, Roxbury, a newly renovated building owned by the Action for Boston Community Development. The Center's staff advocate and the Director of WINGS provide information and referral concerning education, employment, housing, and legal services for women in recovery. Board members, staff, and volunteers reach out to individuals in recovery by attending Narcotics Anonymous and Alcoholics Anonymous meetings throughout Roxbury and Dorchester. At this writing, WINGS is developing lodging for an underserved and often ignored population—women in recovery whose children are in the care of others.

In 1987, several founding members of WINGS organized a sit-in at 9 Valentine Street, a vacant city-owned building in Roxbury, to demonstrate the need for housing for homeless individuals in recovery. Three years later, the City of Boston granted WINGS the same building to develop a "Living and Learning Center" for recovering women. WINGS' goal is to create an environment conducive to maintaining the residents' sobriety and building their capacities as parents, wage earners, and peer supports to other women in recovery.

Savina Martin, the vibrant and articulate founder of WINGS, was once homeless herself. Her own experience, as well as her compelling vision of the relationship between homelessness, drug abuse, racism, and sexism has made her a powerful and recognized spokesperson for adequate services and systemic change.

The Living and Learning Center will provide a drug- and alcohol-free residence for seven women who are moving from a therapeutic community or transitional housing program and need a safe, affordable place to live while stabilizing their lives. Women will work toward reuniting with their children in foster care. An advocate will assist residents in obtaining education, employment and training, and health services. In addition, residents will meet weekly to facilitate peer support. WINGS' long-term vision is to convert the abandoned building and vacant lots around the Valentine Street site into affordable housing and build a community of recovering people and their families. The Women's Institute is providing WINGS with technical assistance and has assisted WINGS with obtaining funding from CEDAC, the Boston *Globe* Foundation and the Public Facilities Department and Section 8 certificates from HUD. Additional funds are still required for the development of the Living and Learning Center, and to support the on-going and critical work of WINGS, Inc.

Activities

WINGS is engaged in a number of activities to assist women in recovery, support family reunification, and achieve its long-term goal of creating a drug-free community.

1. *Providing direct advocacy and outreach to women in recovery.* WINGS began operating a Resource and Referral Center in the Dudley Square area of Roxbury in August, 1990. Recovering women receive information and referral regarding education, health, employment and training, housing, and legal services available. In addition, the Center's advocate, Director, and Board conduct vigorous outreach at AA/NA meetings held daily in Roxbury, Dorchester, and Mattapan.

2. *Initiating and facilitating support groups in collaboration with other community groups.* WINGS, in collaboration with Peaceful Movement, facilitates a support group of women in recovery living in Orchard Park public housing development. Recently, WINGS has launched a second support group which will meet weekly at Dudley Square Library and which it hopes will draw participation from a more diverse group of women in the Roxbury area.

3. *Conducting empowerment sessions for youths, women in prison, and other groups.* In cooperation with People to People, WINGS recently gave a presentation for women at the Massachusetts Correctional Institute at Framingham. The presentation focused on ways recovering women in prison can organize themselves to improve the quality of their lives and increase their options upon release.

4. *Educating the public and the social service community about the needs of women in recovery and homeless women through legislative advocacy and public speaking engagements.* In the spring of 1992, WINGS actively lobbied to amend legislative bills H.3417 and H.3045, which involve expanding access to treatment services. WINGS has advocated that resources currently spent on incarceration could be better utilized to create a open system of "treatment on demand" for women in need of services.

5. *Developing a lodging house in the Highland Park area in Roxbury for homeless women completing detox treatment and/or transitional housing programs and who need an affordable, sober residence and access to services.*

Documentation of Need

Every night in the Roxbury, Dorchester, and Mattapan communities, about 500 recovering men and women gather in church basements and community centers to attend support groups. Approximately 300 of these recovering individuals are women. Before WINGS' efforts at outreach and "street advocacy," AA/NA meetings sometimes provided the only support for recovering women's continued sobriety. While detox centers and short-term transitional programs are critical as a first step for recovering women, these programs do not address other central issues in a recovering individual's life—the need for affordable housing, economic support, employment and training services, and a living environment supportive of continued sobriety. Without programs which address these issues, recovering women have little hope of staying "clean."

Homeless Women in Recovery

The number of homeless women in Boston who need safe, drug-free housing is great. According to the 1990 Census of the homeless published by the City of Boston, there were approximately 3,500 homeless individuals in the city. Of the 3,500, 50% were reportedly substance abusers. Fourteen percent of the 3,500 individuals are single women, which means that 490 homeless single women were counted in the survey. Homeless single women, who are not elderly or disabled and do not have children or custody of their children, are ineligible for public assistance and public housing. Homeless women in recovery, therefore, have almost no affordable housing options. At this writing there are two transitional residence and two half-way houses open to recovering women in Roxbury and Dorchester. However, these programs cannot accommodate the number of recovering women referred to them. Women denied access to such programs are faced with the choice of entering homeless shelters or returning to the streets. Without affordable, drug-free housing they are completely at risk of abusing alcohol or other drugs again.

WINGS' experience in outreach to homeless women in recovery has shown that, for many, a place to sleep and access to local AA/NA meetings may not be enough. Many women need information to obtain access to adult literacy and GED programs, job training, and peer support. Of the 21,074 women treated for substance abuse statewide in FY 1989, two-thirds were unemployed and 40% had no health insurance. According to a 1990 report (A Profile of Women Admitted to Substance Abuse Treatment in FY 89, Health and Addictions Research, Inc.), one-third of the women treated state-wide in publicly supported in-patient and out-patient programs did not have a high school diploma.

Mothers in Recovery

Although there are a number of grassroots organizations in the Roxbury area working on behalf of recovering individuals, WINGS is the only organization that represents recovering mothers whose children are in the custody of the state. A large percentage of women in recovery are parents. According to a study conducted by Nardon and Steriti (1990), 60% of the 21,074 women admitted to publicly funded treatment programs in Massachusetts have children. Of the mothers who were patients in these programs (12,644), approximately 55% of these women (7,143) did not have their children living with them at the time of admittance. Some of these children are living with relatives. Some women lose custody of their children to the state Department of Social Services (DSS) due to their substance abuse. Others voluntarily relinquish custody to enter treatment programs. According to DPH statistics, approximately 1,500 women in publicly funded treatment programs stated that they had been involved with DSS at some time.

Women who have lost their children to the custody of the state are particularly vulnerable when they leave treatment programs, both economically and emotionally. Ineligible to obtain housing subsidies and AFDC

benefits, many women find it difficult to regain the custody of their children and to re-establish control over their lives. DSS requires that recovering parents remain drug-free for a specified period, and have permanent housing and a means to support themselves before their children can be returned to them. A supportive, drug-free environment is vital for women to achieve the emotional and economic stability necessary to reunite with their children. WINGS decided to develop its "Living and Learning Center" for such women because of their service needs as well as their potential for recovery with adequate support systems.

Some Process Issues

When WINGS, Inc., came to the Women's Institute, its staff and board had very strong feelings about community control and wished to be developers of not only 9 Valentine Street, but of the block itself. They did recognize that they needed assistance with real estate development and requested assistance from the Women's Institute. Originally, they felt they could do some of the project management and would eventually own and operate the building. As time progressed and the development had its ups and downs, interest on the part of the one paid staff person and the volunteer board waned. Many of the tasks and decisions became mundane. While the project manager has strengths in public speaking and advocacy, managing details was not her strength. The Women's Institute then took on more of the project manager's role.

As WINGS began to grow and develop its resources as an agency, the project received less and less attention. Soon, the Women's Institute was in an uncomfortable position of trying to balance empowerment and control of the organization with moving the project forward. The illness of the project manager brought the whole project to a halt. The founder/
Executive Director/project manager was performing several roles simultaneously which resulted in strain on the heart. Her decision to pull back from her workload created a crisis in the organization because the agency was being run as a one-woman show. The board consulted with the Women's Institute, and together we made several suggestions for restructuring the agency and regaining control of the building development.

First, several new board members were recruited, including an architect and a non-profit real estate developer. Second, an advisory committee of the board was established including these two women, a WINGS founder, and another board member. This committee would meet at least once a month in the beginning and then almost weekly, to address all the building concerns. This would "free up" the regular board meetings for other business. WINGS has goals other than real estate development which need addressing and which were competing with the Living and Learning Center for time and human resources. Third, WINGS began to re-examine its various functions and to prioritize what should be done. In the past, the women had overextended themselves, which in the long run was unproductive.

Several issues, such as who will manage the property, still need to be addressed. Originally, WINGS assumed that this function would be its responsibility, but later considered hiring an outside firm. WINGS members are learning that control does not necessarily mean doing it all yourself. That approach has served only to frustrate and burn out board members. As the board members recognize where their strengths are and what tasks they choose to perform, there is a new openness to inviting "outsiders" to participate in the project.

WINGS is in a transition period and is learning how to operate as an agency. At the same time it is providing direct services at the Resource and Referral Center and is developing the Living and Learning Center. In the meantime, the Resource and Referral Center recently received two large grants and services there will continue. A new support group is being planned. There is still much to do by the way of program planning, management, and ongoing fundraising.

Ka Fanm, Inc.

Ka Fanm, Inc., is an organization of Haitian women dedicated to the support and the empowerment of women living in the Boston area with primary focus on the development of housing and services for Haitian families. Ka Fanm's English translation is Home for Haitian Women in Massachusetts, Inc., but its name is a Creole expression for "the condition of women's lives." The Board of Directors of this non-profit corporation is represented by core members of the Association of Haitian Women in Boston, AFAB, a Creole expression for "welcoming." Besides their anger at and their frustration with the system, the five women who form Ka Fanm's board have a lot in common. They all have gone through the process of empowering themselves. They are all professional women who already have, or are working toward, an advanced degree. They also share an impressive record of constant and consistent service of the Haitian communities where they have

been living since their arrival in this country. Viewed in the context of the structurally male-oriented and male-dominated Haitian society, Ka Fanm's dynamic and driven organizing is more than just a beneficial grassroots organization's initiative; it represents a significant breakthrough for Haitian women living in the Boston area. It brings the missing female leadership to an immigrant community whose predominantly male leadership has too often failed to recognize women's basic rights or to address women's issues.

According to the Boston *Globe,* there are about 50,000 Haitians living in the Boston area. However, Haitians living in this area report that the number is even greater. As an immigrant group, Haitians have a unique cultural heritage which intensifies the difficulty of adjustment to and integration into the American system. The Haitian community relies on very traditional values to structure its society. Sacredness of family, the love of children, and respect for the wisdom of the elderly prevails across the spectrum of a historically rigid class system. Their culture is African and French with a most recent American influence. It is overall a very paternalistic society designed by and for men.

Half of the Haitians living in the Boston area are women who do not have anywhere to go for support and understanding. They need decent affordable housing, ESL classes, child care, basic health care and orientation to the system, domestic violence counseling, job training, and other basic services and commodities. Most of all, they need organizations which can understand their needs and address them. Since 1988, AFAB/Ka Fanm members have been providing a broad range of volunteer services to the Haitian community. These services include a support group for women, ESL classes for adults, a cultural and recreational program for adolescents, as well as other much needed educational and support services.

Ka Fanm, Inc., envisions a joint venture with the Women's Institute to develop a housing program to meet the growing need of homeless Haitians and their families. Ka Fanm has identified a site which is central to the Haitian community. It is a building located at 580 Blue Hill with six 2- and 3-bedroom apartments and a large basement. The initial concept of the project combines permanent and rental units with project space in the basement. Two of the six apartments would be rented to Section 8 certificates holders, while two others would be marketed to working Haitian families in need of affordable housing. The remaining two units would be shared by homeless families with subsidy from the

Department of Public Welfare. If necessary, the project could be supported by the income generated by six Section 8 apartments.

This project is in the early stages of development. With the assistance of the Women's Institute, the organization has recently filed for incorporation. A site has been identified and the Women's Institute is in the initial stages of site evaluation.

Some Reflections

Many grassroots organizations face common dilemmas:

1. Founders syndrome—where the visionary wants full control of the project.
2. Leadership issues—internal conflict due to control and decision-making issues.
3. Organizational management—groups are learning the mechanics of running a non-profit organization, which includes board process and development, financial systems, personnel issues, etc. For many of our clients this is the first formal structure they have participated in and all the systems were new.
4. Advocate position vs. working within the system—most of our client groups are activists used to an adversarial role with the city and other major institutions. It is sometimes a conflicting role to obtain support from a former adversary and then have to follow its lead.
5. Institutionalizing systems—moving from an informal to a formal structure, becoming business-like, and following procedures can also feel counter to how a group wants to operate. However, when funds are received, and audits are required, it becomes necessary to follow systems.
6. Tendency to employ themselves—the programs tend to be economic development projects as well, because the founders very often are low-income, un- or underemployed people who need work. They tend to create programs to employ themselves. There are positive and negative aspects to it. Board members vying for staff positions and a narrow look at the potential hiring pool are two problems.

These tensions have to be dealt with for the organization and the project to succeed. Discussing these issues in a direct manner with the client groups has proved to work best. The Women's Institute refers the groups to other technical assistance providers that offer training in organizational development, which can be very helpful if a trusted trainer can be found.

The Women's Institute has tried to balance the client group's need for control with their need for assistance.

Our definition of empowerment is a flexible one, determined by the organization itself. Originally, we placed a great deal of the responsibility on the organizations themselves to follow through in a number of areas. We painstakingly taught them the fundamentals of real estate development. Some groups wanted this responsibility and information and others did not. In many cases this need for information sharing has slowed the process and it has had positive and negative results. With Re-Vision House, the founder wanted to learn real estate development and had plans for future projects. She absorbed what she learned and is applying it to a second project. In the case of WINGS, the founders originally wanted to learn real estate development and control all aspects of it. They soon learned that it was in conflict with their other goals and that there are many areas that could be shared. On the other hand, the women of Ka Fanm from the beginning decided that they do not want to be real estate developers. The Women's Institute will be a co-developer of the project to share the risk and it will eventually be turned over to Ka Fanm. Unlike Re-Vision House, Ka Fanm sees development only as a means to an end. The women are more concerned with the final product than with controlling the steps along the way. We have decided that empowerment can be achieved in many different ways depending on a group's capacity and interest in becoming housing developers.

Theme 4
Women's Participation in the Production of Shelter

The level of women's current involvement in the production of shelter serves as one indicator of their access to shelter and the extent to which attaining shelter can help bring about women's development. Recognizing the importance of shelter in their lives, women throughout the world are increasingly involved in various aspects of housing production. The papers in this theme reveal the current level of women's participation in shelter production in various parts of the world and provide examples of what could be possible in the future. A perspective that weaves through all of the papers in this theme is that participation in housing production is an empowering activity for women. In addition to yielding a product that has an immediate material benefit, secure shelter, it makes the actors more confident and able to bring about development for themselves. In the first paper, Basolo and Morlan examine three types of successful women's participation in shelter production in the First World. They delineate the similarities and contrasts with the Third World in the socioeconomic, political, and personal dimensions. In the second paper, Wekerle provides an overview of projects in a First World country, Canada, where women's groups have created housing tailored to their needs. These new housing alternatives offer lessons for appropriate design, organization, and support services. The next three papers address this topic from a Third World perspective. Bapat and Patel posit, from their success in organizing women pavement dwellers in Bombay to act to secure shelter, the attributes of a participatory process that can yield a changed self-image and thus empower even the most economically vulnerable group. Women's participation in the informal and formal sectors of the construction industry in different Third World countries and the types of support, technological or organizational, which are needed if women are to become active in the production of shelter are identified by Celik. May and May conclude with a case study from Jamaica which illustrates the need for including women in the design process. These papers reveal the commonalities in women's participation in housing production. These success stories make clear that, given the characteristics of the women involved, the structures of the organizations they form, and the products they attain, the most strategic outcome of women's activity in shelter production may be the empowerment of participating women.

Photo: *Hemalata C. Dandekar*

Chapter 21
Women and the Production of Housing: An Overview

Victoria Basolo and Michelle Morlan

M. Victoria Basolo *is a doctoral student in the Department of City and Regional Planning at the University of North Carolina at Chapel Hill. Her research interests include housing policy and urban politics.*

Michelle Morlan *received joint master's degrees in Social Work and Urban Planning from the University of Michigan, Ann Arbor. She works as a legislative aide for State Representative Alex Santiago of Hawaii.*

The involvement of women in the development of housing is increasing throughout the world. Housing activism by women is related to the shedding of traditional constraints on women and is, in some cases, a reflection of changing societal structures and social norms. In both First and Third World countries, the number of female-headed households is on the rise. This emergent family structure calls for a rethinking of traditional housing. The role women play in the design and production of housing projects continues to grow. Women have established non-profit corporations to design and build shelters which are responsive to the special needs of women and their families, or to provide technical assistance to developers of such housing for women. Professional women, including architects, planners, businesswomen, and educators have mobilized to increase the awareness of women and housing-related issues. In addition, women in local communities have joined to enlarge their role in every aspect of the decision-making process in their communities, including the production of housing.

The efforts of women to produce and sustain shelter reflect the importance of housing in their lives. Whether the context is a rural Third World village or the heart of a First World city, women share this basic need. Clearly, the need for shelter is not restricted to women; however, cultural forces create circumstances for women that require special attention to their housing needs. With these forces as a backdrop, this paper will explore the impetus for women's production of shelter, examine the methods women are using to develop adequate housing, and discuss the different types of housing or product created by women in both the First and Third Worlds.

Background

Historically, women have held a secondary position to men. In the ground-breaking feminist work, *The Second Sex,* Simone de Beauvoir describes this relationship. She writes: "woman has always been man's dependent, if not his slave; the two sexes have never shared the world in equality ... even today woman is heavily handicapped ..."

(Beauvoir, 1953, p. xviii). Although these words were written over forty years ago during a time when denial of property rights and exclusion from participation in national and community governance was the status quo for women throughout much of the world, this sentiment supports the feminist argument of the present.

Table 1: Female-headed Households in the U.S., 1970–1990

	Number of Households (in 1000s)	Percent of Total Households
1960	4,507	10.0%
1970	5,591	10.8%
1980	8,705	14.6%

Source: United States Bureau of the Census, Statistical Abstract of the U.S., *1991.*

Table 2: Female-Headed Households—Selected Latin American Countries

	Average Percent of Total Households
1950	17.8%
1960	17.9%
1970	17.2%

Statistics for Costa Rica, Nicaragua, Panama, Argentina, Chile and Mexico (Leitinger, 1981).

Throughout the world, the status of women remains secondary to that of men in almost every context of daily life. The struggle for fundamental rights, such as voting and property ownership, was fought and won in most western countries during the last century. However, women are by no means equal to men in these countries. The notion of economic justice, that is, equal pay for equal work, continues to be a rallying point for feminist activists (Eichler, 1980). Equal access to positions of authority from corporate offices to political chambers to community and family circles is also an important objective of the women's movement. In a similar vein, women in developing nations continue to struggle under an overtly inequitable system. In these countries, progress toward equality of basic and equal human rights is often hampered by societal norms, religious beliefs, and legal structures which limit the actions and potential of women.

Despite the many differences between First and Third World contexts, the central importance of shelter, and the need for decision-making power in the production of shelter, have been exemplified by women's actions throughout the world. In some countries, for example Saudi Arabia, women architects have begun to participate in the design process despite cultural restrictions which deny them access to much decision-making power. In less restrictive societies such as Canada, women have organized and gained control of their housing through cooperative ownership (Wekerle, 1988). The objective of these efforts is the same: to increase women's participation in the design and production of housing. The creation of housing that serves the needs of women is implicit in this goal.

The creation of housing specifically for women is a fairly recent phenomenon, at least in the sense of addressing a broad range of needs. Although women's residence hotels could be found in large western cities seventy years ago, these rooming houses generally were reserved for single women without children. Their purpose was to provide security for women and to protect their virtue, as reflected by the signs stating "no men allowed" egregiously posted in the lobbies of the hotels. Clearly, this housing served a limited number of women. The development of housing for women today must address more than just security issues, although security remains a major concern; it must begin with an understanding of changing family structures, economic constraints, and aspects of design.

Households in both the First and Third Worlds reflect changes in traditional family structure. The increase in female-headed households in the United States is shown in Table 1. The presence of a large number of female-headed households is not unique to the United States by any means. Indeed, in many countries, demographic figures suggest the need for a redefinition of family. Table 2 shows figures on female-headed households in selected Third World countries.

Female-headed households include single women, young and old, and women with children. Priorities in housing features may not be the same for each subgroup of women-headed households. For example, community play areas visible from dwelling units may be very important to women with children (Trejos, 1991), while single, elderly women may prefer accommodations with shared kitchen and recreational facilities.

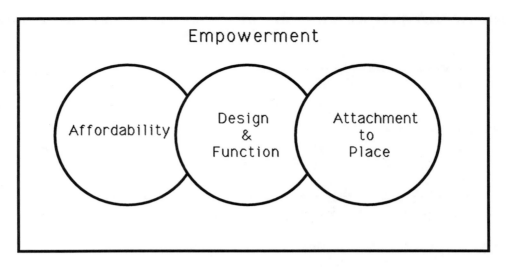

Fig. 1: Reason for the Production of Housing for Women.

At the same time, because they are all women, there tend to be commonalties among subgroups. In almost every region of the world, female-headed households suffer economic hardships. Women's financial resources are limited for several reasons. As mentioned above, women tend to earn less than men, both generally and for equal work. To confound matters, in some countries women receive little, if any, of the family estate when their husbands or other family members die. Likewise, divorced women are often left with few financial resources or skills to offer in the formal employment sector. In many cases, whether a woman is widowed, divorced or never married, children are involved, creating additional financial burdens for the household.

Women design and create housing for several reasons, presented graphically in Figure 1. The diagram illustrates the importance of empowerment. It is the issue of empowerment, whether an objective of production or a by-product of the process, which envelops the entire diagram. Within this envelope, there are three less abstract elements presented as interlocking rings. First, and most basic, is the need for affordable housing. Women in both First and Third World countries tend to make much less than men and often are responsible financially for one or more children (Sprague, 1991; Machado, 1987); these conditions contribute to the prevalence of poor, female-headed households throughout the world. Second, overlapping the affordability issue, is a need for functional housing. For the most part, traditional housing design has ignored the special needs of women for community space and surprisingly, in many instances, ignored security needs as well (Brion

and Tinker, 1980). Third, overlapping design concerns is the psychological aspect of women's attachment to place. There is evidence that women tend to be more attached to their homes and invest more of themselves in the decoration and atmosphere of the home (Saegert, 1989).

Women's housing concerns are complex. In reality, even when developed by women, housing production may not incorporate all the important considerations into the planning process. The cultural context, as well as the lifestage and family structure of the woman, suggest different responses to shelter needs. For this reason, as well as others, efforts aimed at the design and production of housing for women by women tend to be initiated at the local or community level. In the Third World, these efforts are often prompted by a lack of alternatives offered by governmental or other sources (OAS, 1985).

Participation in the Process

A local response to women's housing allows the development of appropriate shelter and facilitates the participation of women in the process. It has been argued that involvement in housing decisions, both production and management, not only empowers individuals, but that exclusion from the process threatens personal fulfillment (Turner, 1976). The self-build process of housing occurs for many reasons according to John Turner, a proponent of self-help housing. Turner characterizes two types of self-builders: bridgeheaders, or those who need mobility to maximize employment opportunities, and consoli-

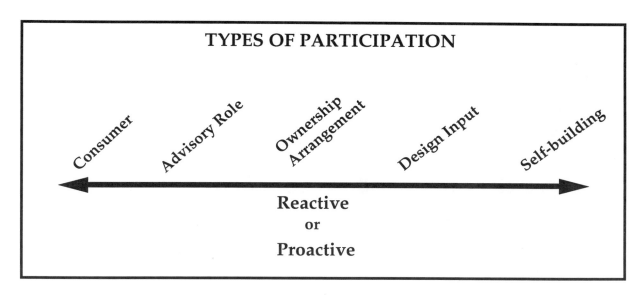

TYPES OF PARTICIPATION

Consumer   Advisory Role   Ownership Arrangement   Design Input   Self-building

Reactive
or
Proactive

Fig. 2: Types of Women's Participation in Housing.

dators, who place greater emphasis on stability of tenure to meet increasing expectations of the future. Additionally, Turner articulates several advantages of self-built housing such as physical and financial flexibility, greater independence in choices of location, and the stimulation of social development.

The enhancement of social development underscores the importance to women of participation in the housing production process. In almost every example of participation, whether it is simply providing input (proactive or reactive) on design issues, arranging to gain ownership or control, or actually constructing units, a common sense of empowerment can be found.

Several forms which women's participation in housing may take are examined herein and differentiated along a continuum of participation. This continuum (Figure 2) stresses the importance of the process rather than its end product. In other words, participation as a means of empowerment is the central focus of the following discussion.

Of course, it is helpful to examine the various contexts from which examples of women's participation in housing production are drawn. In some instances, women gain ownership and control of housing by using existing bureaucratic and legal structures. This approach tends to focus on transfer of ownership as opposed to design and construction of housing. In other examples women are on new ground, in control of almost every aspect of the process. These examples vary from country to country and reflect the cultural

environment; that is, the political, legal, economic, and religious contexts. However, one cannot always assume that more participation in the process automatically means more empowerment or greater accomplishments. It is our opinion that the examples of participation cited here do reflect gains in empowerment for women.

First World Experiences

The participation of women in the production of housing in the First World generally takes three forms. First, women sometimes play an advisory role to governmental agencies concerned with housing. Second, women produce housing directly through a takeover of existing buildings and conversion to resident management or cooperative ownership and through development of new structures with various ownership schemes. Third, non-profit organizations created by women develop new housing or rehabilitate older buildings for occupation by families. Typically, this latter form serves female-headed households. These three forms are complemented by the efforts of women architects, planners, academics, and businesswomen who, through research or service to non-profits, use their professional skills to facilitate the production of housing for women.

All three forms of participation contribute to an expansion of the awareness of women's housing needs. The advisory role provides an opportunity for women of all income levels and social circumstances to participate in the housing development process. In some situations, a woman or group of women may informally address housing needs by confronting their political representatives. Informal channels of communication include phone calls and letter writing to government officials and appearances at public meetings. Although recommendations by these informal advisors are unsolicited, this type of activity serves two purposes. It draws the attention of decision-makers to the housing concerns of women. In addition, participation in the political process can empower women and may foster stronger, more formal women's organizations.

Formal housing advisory roles for women exist in some developed countries. In the Netherlands, for example, locally based women's committees specifically concerned with the housing needs of women have existed for several decades. Although these committees represent a formal structure with ostensible influence on government housing policy and development, their role to date has been more reactive than proactive. In other words, the government bureaucracy often seeks the advice of the committees after housing is built and experiencing some type of problem (Penrose, 1987).

Women in the advisory role frequently experience political resistance and bureaucratic barriers. Specific policies and programmatic measures directed at women's housing needs may be responsive only, and implementation can be protracted. For this reason, many women utilize existing government programs not directly designed with women in mind, or they bypass the bureaucratic maze entirely to solve their immediate housing concerns.

In a rational bureaucratic and political environment, government policies and programs identify an issue and design measures targeted at achievement of objectives. Although a specific objective may be addressed, it is common for government policies and programs to provide unforeseen advantages (or disadvantages). Two examples, one from the United States and the other from Canada, illustrate this phenomenon in relation to the production of housing for women.

In New York City, the economic distress of the 1980's resulted in the abandonment of residential buildings by landlords. Tax defaults associated with landlord abandonment were common and, as a result, the City acquired a surfeit of abandoned structures. The onus of property management, as well as reduced tax revenues, prompted the City to design and implement a slew of new housing programs. These programs resulted in the conversion of some of the buildings to tenant management or a change to tenant cooperative ownership. In

both the rental and ownership scenarios, women took a leadership role in the organization of their buildings (Saegert, 1989). Although the objectives of the City officials did not include improvement of housing conditions for women specifically, the women used the programs to that end.

The development of women's cooperatives in Canada possesses elements of all three forms of participation as described above. Women developed housing cooperatives through local non-profit organizations by taking advantage of an existing government program. The federal non-profit program provides financial assistance for the development of cooperatives in Canada. The program began in the late 1970's with the objective of changing official policy concerning public housing development; in other words, non-profit cooperatives were intended to supplant the traditional public housing approach to sheltering low-income households (Wekerle and Simon, 1986). The targets for assistance were not necessarily women. Nonetheless, Canadian women often chose this type of alternative to conventional ownership and housing. Canadian women took their desire for cooperative living with a women's perspective one step further. Women entered the political process directly with the help of legal advisors and gained authority to develop women-only cooperatives (Wekerle and Novac, 1989). This accomplishment makes the Canadian experience different from the American model of cooperative formation.

The formation of cooperatives is an increasingly popular alternative to traditional housing arrangements for women. The creation of cooperatives, however, does not necessarily involve government housing programs implemented in a rational, structured environment. In fact, cooperative development may result in response to housing crises. In England, changes in the law and the long waiting period for public housing forced some women to look for housing alternatives. While many of these women were accustomed to squatting or other transitional shelter situations, they desired more stable housing. The Seagull Housing Cooperative provided these once powerless women with a permanent home born of their own effort (Brion and Tinker, 1980).

A crisis situation prompted residents of a multi-family building in East Orange, New Jersey, to take control of the structure and initiate formation of a limited-equity cooperative. Landlord neglect resulted in general deterioration of the building and broken water pipes, coupled with lack of heat , at one point threatened the health and safety of the occupants. The tenants, mostly low-income women with children, convinced the landlord to relinquish ownership. Although these tenants possessed limited resources, their tenacity paid off. They made repairs, paid off back taxes, and now own and manage their building (McAuley Institute, 1989).

The role of a non-profit organization varies, depending on the circumstances. The non-profit may be a legal vehicle designed to protect the underlying individuals from litigation or personal financial exposure. At times, a non-profit apparatus may be required to attain certain government funding. However, some non-profits are organized to plan and implement full-scale housing development or rehabilitation projects. It is this latter type of non-profit organization to which we will now turn.

The creation of a non-profit housing corporation is a sizable task. In addition to a background in housing development, negotiation and business management skills are essential, not to mention the ability to work with local government officials and staff. In the U.S., community non-profit housing developers exist in many cities and rural areas. Non-profit housing developers concerned with women's needs, however, are not as prevalent. Still, there is a growing network of women-oriented, non-profit housing developers scattered across the country.

The first non-profit development corporation founded by women appeared in Providence, Rhode Island, in 1975. Aptly named the Women's Development Corporation (WDC), this organization seeks "to promote developments which best serve(s) women." (Women's Development Corporation informational packet). To date, WDC has completed, or is in the process of completing, rehabilitation or construction of almost 300 units of affordable housing. Generally, WDC combines funding from a complex web of sources, including local sources. While not immediately accepted by local and state officials, WDC earned the respect of most naysayers and today is the largest developer of low-income housing in Rhode Island (Foster, 1990). The Women's Institute for Housing and Economic Development (Women's Institute) was created by female professionals concerned with the needs of low-income women. For the past eleven years, this non-profit organization has provided invaluable technical assistance to community groups. Project design and advice on development financing are just two of the crucial services provided to local housing groups by the Women's Institute (Peterson).

Non-profit organizations specifically addressing women's housing needs are also found in Cincinnati, New York City, Washington, D.C., and other cities throughout the country. It is important to note that many of these organizations, large and small alike, were established by women in the design, law, and finance fields. For example, the founders of WDC included female architects and planners. The contribution of these women professionals should not be understated. Through participatory activities such as surveys, these professional women encourage other women, often low-income, seemingly powerless women, to enter the housing development process. The result is empowerment for both the participant and professional.

Third World Experiences

Examples of Third World women's participation in housing production span the entire range of the participation continuum. In some countries, women experience oppressive conditions which place distinct limits on their activities. Religious laws that require gender segregation and, hence, discrimination often translate into highly limited roles for women in society. In other countries, women's participation in production occurs on a non-professional level. In such countries, poverty is generally widespread, rural rather than urban living is most pre-

valent, and the phenomenon of self-building is considered the norm. Where this occurs, women can be found building their own homes (usually from indigenous materials) and are often relied upon to provide at least half of a family's income. Such conditions, in addition to more instances of female-headed households in these countries, make for a more central role for women at the family and community levels. Their motivation to become active in the process can be attributed to the centrality of home in their lives, as well as their need for housing design and function which fits with the demands placed on them, such as supporting a family. In these cases, there exist few alternatives to self-built homes and women must take the initiative to meet their own needs.

In Costa Rica, where high urbanization rates over the last two decades have created extreme crises in housing and infrastructure, women have successfully organized to demand better living conditions. In many low-income areas near the capital city of San Jose, women have come together to protest the severe housing conditions which they and their families endure. In a neighborhood called Santo Domingo, these women demonstrated in the streets of San Jose, participated in hunger strikes, and approached public officials with their demands for affordable and appropriate shelter. These efforts led to the forming of the Heredia Housing Cooperative (Trejos, 1991). Supported by the Feminist Center for Information and Action (CEFEMINA), their protests also gained national attention and prompted the government to answer their call. These women argued that the few government-sponsored housing projects that had been built were nothing short of disastrous, and that housing programs must better address their specific concerns. They proposed that instead of building massive and costly projects without consulting future residents, the government should support local production efforts by the women themselves. The women felt that this alternative would ensure that their needs were addressed, and in a more efficient manner.

The government reluctantly consented and the results have been extraordinary. The Heredia Housing Cooperative has become a successful community planning and design model, which addresses issues of housing production, community design and the provision of community facilities. The original process of organizing for social action has evolved into a self-governing community structure in which women hold over 80% of the leadership positions. The results of greater empowerment can be seen on a personal as well as interpersonal level as these women have broadened their scope of participation from the family to community level. This case represents the response of one group of women to government inaction in housing provision. In many Third World countries, however, the effects of such inaction are replaced by action of the wrong kind. Programs which force inappropriate, minimum-grade housing projects can be seen everywhere, and often ignore all aspects of user concerns.

In Kingston , Jamaica, where many international aid organizations direct development programs, an attempt to provide such shelter prompted the organization of single mothers to protest what they viewed as yet another outside solution to their housing needs (May and May). This response was motivated not only by issues of affordability, design, and attachment to location, but also by the use of inappropriate building technology in the construction of these houses. As in the case of the Heredia Housing Cooperative, this reactionary organizing process has led to the creation of new roles for women in the community. May and May observe that women have expanded their participation to the level of

community leaders in what was previously a male-dominated system.

Bapat and Patel in their work in Bombay, India, emphasize that the decision-making process of women in low-income and squatter settlements are based on the day-to-day experiences in these women's lives (Bapat and Patel). The process is rooted in the struggle for survival within a system which oppresses and exploits these women. This reality has implications for housing development policy in Third World countries. Clearly, participation in the decision-making process empowers women and may also provide the most informed and best solutions to their shelter needs.

The Housing Product

The housing created by First and Third World women reflects the needs and often the priorities of these women. In the most basic case, mere shelter is the goal of the women. However, most of the housing development addresses more than just basic shelter needs. As discussed earlier in this paper, women produce housing for many reasons. Design and function, affordability and attachment to place, both home and community, are the primary reasons women develop their own housing. One or all of these elements, as well as the overall sense of empowerment, are present in every housing production effort by women.

First World Experiences

Women produce housing opportunities in a variety of ways. The context of the production effort colors the end product. For example, political and legal constraints, as well as financial resources, represent some of the contextual factors shaping the final housing product. Cooperatives appear to be a viable housing product for women in the First World. Although traditional western views stress ownership of single-family detached homes, this position presupposes certain family structures and income levels. Clearly, the needs of all women are not addressed with the "traditional" product. Cooperatives represent a different model of tenure and meet many of the immediate housing needs of women. The cooperative arrangement provides affordability, management control, and community support for the women residents (Wekerle and Simon, 1986). Cooperatives may include design elements specifically targeted at women. However, cooperative design, especially in terms of conversion of an existing building, may be severely constrained. Without question, new construction or extensive rehabilitation provide the biggest opportunity to address design elements that are sensitive to women's needs.

New construction and large-scale rehabilitation of housing for women produce many housing types. Basic shelters, transitional housing, rental housing, and ownership housing present an opportunity for design and development for and by women. For over a decade, female architects and planners have worked actively to advocate housing designs sensitive to the needs of women (Sprague, 1991). Today, examples of housing built for women attest to the perseverance of these professional women. There are numerous examples of housing developed or redeveloped with women in mind. Typically, this housing is multi-family development with some aspect of shared space; it can be transitional in nature or more permanent, as in ownership or rental housing. As described in a previous section, non-profits, often run by women, develop the housing. Although there are many variants of the production model, an existing project can serve to illustrate a typical type of housing developed for women.

The Eden Housing Corporation, a non-profit housing developer in the San Francisco Bay Area, built a multi-family residential project with female-headed house-holds in mind. The architect wanted to embrace some of the traditional features of single-family homes, while creating a sense of neighborhood or community. The project reflects these goals. All homes have a separate front entrance and resemble single-family houses in appearance. Clusters of five homes encircle a paved, fenced courtyard. The courtyard serves as a play area, as well as a central area for adults to interact; therefore, security and neighborhood are facilitated by the design (Ho, 1992). Also important, the units are considered affordable by local market standards.

The housing product developed by women for women may take many forms. The alternatives reflect the different cul-tural contexts or personal circumstances of women. While housing for women must acknowledge the diversity among women, it must also address the needs common to women. Whether as individual issues or in combination, afford-ability, security, as well as the role of women as caregivers seem to be a few of the recurrent concerns of women. Advocates and producers of housing for women must rec-ognize the variety of women's housing needs and continue to question conventional design and development wisdom in order to provide the best product for their clients.

Third World Experience in Production

The participation of women in the production of housing in Third World countries yields a wide variety of products. Where women's roles in society are severely limited by political, legal, or religious constraints, these products may take the form of increased participation and influence in a male-dominated process. In this case, greater empowerment can be seen as an outcome of the process of participation. In other contexts, where women have greater freedom in society, the process of participation has also produced a change in traditional roles for women in their daily lives. The forming of a housing production collective which can sustain itself offers greater opportunities, both physical and non-physical, to the women involved. This illustrates the many development possibilities present when such activities are supported.

In Costa Rica, where the Heredia Housing Cooperative organized to provide for its members' own housing needs, over 300 units of new housing have been built since 1986. In addition, the women have designed community open spaces and facilities and planned their own neighborhood to meet specific concerns for safety, functional design, and community environment. Houses arranged around common play areas, few major streets, large community meeting spaces, and preservation and conservation of the natural environment are a few of the design elements which these women have implemented. In addition, the structure of the planning process for new development in the community is intended to facilitate the involvement and active participation of newcomers. This popular housing project has been recognized by the government as an efficient (and preferred) alternative to government-produced housing in Costa Rica.

Results from other countries, while not always produc-ing housing, have nonetheless suggested the future possibilities for women's involvement in the production of shelter. The emphasis on appropriate building technologies, those which are both easy to use and provide safe, sound products (May, 1992), as well as the attention to the specific concerns of the sub-group of women involved, are only a few of the many advantages to supporting the housing production efforts of women in Third World countries.

Summary and Recommendations

Women have made great strides in the development of housing to meet their needs. Still, institutional barriers and traditional views continue to impede housing production by and for women. Some of these obstacles are shared by women in both the First and Third World, while others may be unique to a particular culture or more pronounced in certain countries or regions of the world. However, regardless of the context, the responses of women faced with inadequate housing provision indicate both a willingness and an ability to meet their own needs. The examples identified in this paper indicate the advantages of women's involvement in the production of housing. Also, these experiences suggest the need for further private and public support to facilitate women's efforts. Given these observations, the following recommendations are made for consideration by policy makers, design professionals, activists, and academics:

1. Those involved in design should re-evaluate and rethink traditional and existing designs in terms of the needs of women.

2. National governments and international aid institutions should support community-based and non-profit efforts to produce housing sensitive to the needs of women.

3. National governments should review existing laws that may preclude housing developments designed for women and occupied solely by women and/or their families.

4. Local public agencies should support community non-profit developers through flexibility of local building and development codes and, when possible, provide financial assistance to housing developments for women.

5. Women as consumers of housing must be brought into the early phases of the development process to increase the designers' and developers' awareness of the diversity of needs.

6. The efforts of women at the village and community level to address their housing needs should be supported as a healthy, empowering, and effective method of producing appropriate housing.

7. Governments should support the development and use of building materials which facilitate women's ability to play a central role in the production of housing.

References

Barfield, Deborah. 1991. "Affordable Housing Program Launched." *Providence Journal Bulletin.* March 21.

Beauvoir, Simone de, 1953. *The Second Sex.* New York: Bantam Books.

Breed, Donald D. 1990. "Survey of Women's Wants Led to House Design." *Providence Journal Bulletin.* September 9.

Breitbart, Myrna Marguiles. 1990. "Quality Housing for Women and Children." *Canadian Woman Studies* 11, No. 2, 19–24.

Brion, Marion, and Anthea Tinker. 1980. *Women in Housing: Access and Influence.* London: Housing Centre Trust.

Eichler, Margrit. 1980. *The Double Standard.* New York: St. Martin's Press.

Foster, Catherine. 1990. "Female Solutions to Housing Need." *The Christian Science Monitor.* November 6.

Ho, Mui. 1992. Personal Correspondence with V. Basolo, March 16.

Leitinger, Ilse A. 1981. "The Changing Role of Women in Latin America. A Descriptive and Theoretical Analysis of Six Countries, 1950–1970." Dissertation, University of Denver.

Machado, Leda M.V. 1987. "The Problems for Women-headed Households in a Low-income Housing Programme in Brazil." In *Women, Human Settlements, and Housing,* Caroline Moser and Linda Peake eds. London: Tavistock Publications.

May, Ann H., and David K. May. 1992. "The Planning of a Squatters' Community in Kingston, Jamaica: User Involvement, Housing Types, and Site Planning." Unpublished abstract submitted to Shelter Women & Development: First and Third World Perspectives Conference held in May, 1992.

McAuley Institute. 1989. "Against All Odds: Women Facing Community Challenges." *Shelterforce.* Oct/Nov/Dec.

Organization of American States Inter-American Commission of Women. 1985. *Status of Women in the Americas at the End of the Decade of Women (1976–1985).* Series: Studies No. 14, Washington, D.C. General Secretariat OAS,

Penrose, Jan. 1987. "Women and the Man-made Environment: The Dutch Experience." *Women and Environments,* Vol. 9, No.1.

Saegert, Susan. 1989. "Unlikely Leaders, Extreme Circumstances: Older Black Women Building Community Households." *American Journal of Community Psychology* 17, No. 3.

Sprague, Joan Forrester. 1991. *More Than Housing: Lifeboats for Women and Children.* Boston: Butterworth Architecture.

Sprague, Joan Forrester. 1989. "Two Cases of Transitional Housing Development in Boston." In *New Households New Housing,* Karen A. Franck and Sherry Ahrentzen, eds. New York: Van Nostrand Reinhold.

Trejos, Marta. 1991. In a speech delivered to the ECO'92 Public Forum, Amsterdam, RAI. May 10th.

Turner, John F.C. 1976. *Housing By People.* New York: Pantheon Books.

United States Bureau of Census. 1991. *Statistical Abstract of the U.S.: 1991* (111th Ed.). Washington, D.C., p. 45, Table No. 56.

Wekerle, Gerda. 1980. "Canadian Women's Housing Cooperatives: Case Studies in Physical and Social Innovation." In *New Space for Women,* Gerda Wekerle, Rebecca Peterson, and David Morley, eds. Boulder: Westview Press.

Wekerle, Gerda. 1988. *Women's Housing Projects in Eight Canadian Cities.* Ottawa: Canada Mortgage and Housing Corporation, April.

Wekerle, Gerda, and Novac, Sylvia. 1989. "Developing Two Women's Cooperatives." In *New Households New Housing,* Karen A. Franck and Sherry Ahrentzen, eds. New York: Van Nostrand Reinhold.

Wekerle, Gerda, and Simon, Joan. 1986. "Housing Alternatives for Women: The Canadian Experience." *Urban Resources* 3, No. 2, Winter.

Chapter 22
Responding to Diversity: Housing Developed by and for Women

Gerda R. Wekerle

Gerda R. Wekerle *is a professor in the Faculty of Environmental Studies, York University, Toronto, Canada. Her research focuses on gender and cities. She is coeditor of* New Space for Women *and has published widely on gender and politics and safer cities programs. In the housing field, her research has evaluated high density living arrangements, gentrification, and open space standards in new downtown neighborhoods. She has documented a wide range of housing projects in Canadian cities and is currently working on books related to housing and inequality and women's restructuring of the Canadian welfare state.*

In the last ten years, there has been an unprecedented increase in housing projects in Canada specifically targeted for and developed by women. Women's groups have emerged as new actors in the housing system, developing non-profit housing to fill gaps in both shelter and service provision. Direct service providers, housing advocacy groups, and women's community groups have become developers of permanent, affordable housing for women. In the process, they have pioneered new models to go beyond shelter which include child care, life skills training, and participatory housing management. In Canada, women's housing projects are characterized by diversity: several are designed for teenage mothers and their children; single parents have developed non-profit housing projects across the country; lesbians have developed their own non-profit housing co-operatives; women over the age of forty in four cities have developed non-profit housing co-operatives that will allow them to age in place. Immigrant, visible minority and aboriginal women have developed housing that responds to their unique cultural needs.

In my research, I have identified 56 housing projects across Canada, representing more than 1,500 housing units developed and controlled by women. I estimate that there are a total of between 75 and 100 such projects. During the period 1985–86, architect Joan Simon and I conducted in-depth case studies of ten women's housing projects in Victoria and Vancouver, British Columbia; Regina and Moose Jaw, Saskatchewan; Toronto, Ontario; Quebec, Quebec; Halifax, Nova Scotia; and St. John's, Newfoundland. We interviewed people who had been involved in the initial development of each project, including board members, community representatives, and housing offices. We interviewed current residents and managers of the housing to determine how a project was managed and its special features. We hired local interviewers to conduct in-depth, two-hour interviews with residents about their experience of living in the housing. In the summer of 1991, I completed a telephone survey of an additional 46 women's housing projects across Canada.

There are three kinds of women's housing projects that have developed in Canada:

1. Second-stage housing, transitional housing, or next step housing has a limited stay of a few months to a year and is directed to abused women and their children. This housing often includes enhanced services such as

counseling, child care, or job upgrading opportunities. Second-stage housing has generally been developed by women's shelters.

2. There are non-profit women's housing projects developed by existing community and women's service organizations such as the Young Women's Christian Association (YWCA) or local groups such as the Young Mothers Support Group for teenage mothers in Toronto. In these cases, the non-profit community organization owns and manages the housing and residents are tenants.

3. Non-profit housing co-operatives have been developed by groups of women and are controlled and managed by the residents that live there.

This paper addresses only the permanent housing projects developed as non-profit, or non-profit housing co-operatives. While the early projects were fairly small, averaging about 30 units, the trend is to larger projects with higher capital costs. For example, projects now under development will cost $17 million for a 114-unit project and $12.5 million for 42 units. Housing developed by women was initially made possible by federal and provincial funding programs encouraging community groups to become the developers and providers of non-profit housing. There was federal sponsorship of these programs from the mid-seventies to the mid-eighties when the federal government devolved substantial responsibility for non-profit housing delivery to the provinces. Certain provincial governments, for example Ontario's, have set up provincial housing programs to fund non-profit housing. In the 1992 federal budget, the government eliminated the federal commitment to the non-profit housing co-operative program. Although women's groups have utilized existing federal and provincial housing programs, no housing program has been directly developed for women, although the federal government funds a small initiative to build next-step, second-stage housing for battered women and their children.

Growth in Canadian Women's Housing Projects in the Last Decade

There are four fundamental reasons for the upsurge of women's housing projects in the last decade:

1. Continuing systemic discrimination against women within the housing system;
2. Family and household changes that have increased the number of women in need of housing;
3. Shifts in the women's movement that have made housing a priority for action and advocacy;

4. Changes in the relations between women's advocacy groups and the state housing sector.

The Fate of Women within the Housing System

Within the system that develops, builds, allocates, and manages housing, issues of race, class, and gender interact so that women are among the most disadvantaged group . Housing inequalities are deeply gendered within Canadian society. During the eighties, changes in the Canadian housing system and women's continued and increasing poverty have interacted to put women at even further disadvantage. Women have been kept out of home ownership by low incomes in a country where more than two-thirds of households are homeowners. Women relied on subsidized housing due to inadequate incomes. Among women-led households, two-thirds were renters; among other households, two-thirds were homeowners. Home ownership rates for women doubled after they were 65, when they often inherited a house (McClain and Doyle, 1984). Women who owned their own houses had less available income to support them and were more reliant on government transfer payments and pension funds to pay housing costs (McClain and Doyle, 1984).

In Canada, women were disproportionately dependent on housing in the social housing sector: public housing, municipal and non-profit housing, and non-profit cooperative housing projects. Across the country, more than two-thirds of all families who were renting in public housing were women-headed. Women who were heads of single-parent households were the majority of applicants for social housing and the majority of families on waiting lists (Canada Mortgage and Housing Corporation, 1990). Because they were predominantly renters in the eighties, women were the hardest hit by inflation in housing costs in cities with growth economies. In rental markets in cities across Canada, they were squeezed out by higher income tenants. Women were subjected to sexist discrimination in obtaining housing, including discrimination against single parents, social assistance recipients, and single women in housing markets characterized by scarcity.

Family and Household Changes Have Increased the Numbers of Women in Acute Housing Need.

During the eighties, there was an increase in women-headed households, many of them poor. There were increases in the number of single parents, elderly women living alone, and single women living alone younger than 65 (Statistics Canada, 1986). The fastest growing group of the homeless were mothers with young children. In the last 20 years, the greatest increase in core housing need, i.e., households paying more than 30% of income on shelter and living in overcrowded and inadequate housing, has been among non-senior households and single parents. These households generally had only one adult wage earner. The majority were female-headed with the head of household earning on an average only two-thirds of the average male wage (Canada Mortgage and Housing Corporation, 1991).

Canadian Women's Movement Makes Housing a Priority

The Canadian women's movement has not traditionally viewed housing as a core issue for advocacy. This has recently changed as housing is linked to other forms of systemic discrimination against women. At the national level, the National Action Committee on the Status of Women has established a Housing Committee, developed housing policy statements, and published a housing newsletter. The federal Advisory Council on the Status of Women has recently funded research on the housing needs of immigrant and minority women and the impact of housing policies on women. At the provincial level, the Ontario Women's Directorate is funding a long-term participatory research project on the sexual harassment of women tenants. At the local level, new groups have formed across the country that focus specifically on women's housing needs, women and homelessness, and women and housing design.

Traditional women's organizations, such as the YWCA, have made the provision of women's housing a priority. In some cases, women's service organizations have redirected their efforts from direct service provision to the development and management of permanent housing as they find that women they serve cannot survive without secure affordable housing. For example, an organization that provides referrals and parenting skills to teenage mothers has developed permanent housing. Shelters for women have expanded their mandate from the provision of temporary shelter to either second-stage or permanent housing. All these initiatives have increased the numbers of women who know something about housing, whether as architects, planners, housing activists within co-op or tenant organizations, or within local women's groups or housing consumers. In this way, the resources available to women's movement groups around housing have increased.

Starting as early as 1972, groups of community women have developed non-profit housing cooperatives directed specifically at women. Since the early 80's, the number of housing projects targeted to women have accelerated. Initially, these were developed by well-educated, middle-class, predominantly white women in larger cities. As more women's housing cooperatives were developed, the diversity of women's co-op housing groups has also increased. Now we have co-ops being developed by Filipino nannies, minority and immigrant women, aboriginal women, francophone women, older women, and even the International Ladies Garment Workers Union. Women's housing cooperatives are being built in smaller centers, suburban areas, and the Canadian North.

Women's Advocacy Groups and the State Housing Sector

Women have been largely invisible in state housing policy in Canada. Women's housing projects have developed at the margins of the housing system within the small under-funded, non-profit housing sector. Although upward of 1,500 housing units have been developed by women for women, this does not imply that there is a housing policy that is deliberately supportive of women or particularly friendly to women. Women have seized the initiative and made sure that they received a fair share of existing programs. But we also have to acknowledge the role that workers in the state sector have played in making women's projects possible.

Within the state housing sector, federal and provincial housing ministries and planning and housing departments at the municipal level are important in providing either supportive or unsupportive environments for the development of women's housing. Feminists within state housing organizations at all levels identified with women's projects and provided assistance. Projects were often pushed or championed by one person. These women became a resource to feminist organizations. Often, where a women's housing project was considered a novelty, if not an aberration, it was important to its success that bureaucrats within the housing system had ties to the women's movement, and thus were aware of successful models elsewhere. These alliances and networks between women working in the state housing sector and women in community organizations have often been critical to the fruition of women's housing developments.

A New Approach to Housing

Women's groups have pioneered new housing environments to meet the diversity of women's housing needs.

Fig. 1: Entrance to YMCA housing in Toronto (1989).

Fig. 2: Office on ground floor overlooks entrance. YMCA housing Toronto.

This housing includes services that go beyond shelter to include child care, life skills training, and opportunities for residents to learn housing management skills. The projects represent grassroots responses to the diversity of women's housing needs, often providing housing for doubly disadvantaged women: teenage mothers, older women, immigrant and minority women, lesbians, and single parents.

Housing Developed by Non-Profit Groups

Among traditional women's organizations, the Young Women's Christian Association (YWCA) has been involved in housing Canadian women for the past century. Initially the YWCA's provided housing for single working women moving to cities. Then, the local YWCA organizations in cities began providing emergency shelters to women. The next phase was to develop permanent housing for women and children. In the province of Ontario, permanent housing has been developed by the YWCA in Toronto, Oshawa, Peterborough, and other cities. Typically, the local YWCA chapter has established a housing committee composed of staff of the YWCA, community representatives, and potential residents of the housing. They contracted with a resource group, a non-profit consulting group, to help them obtain public funding from the state housing sector, assist in negotiating the approval process, identify potential sites, help find an architect, and generally teach them the various stages involved in developing a successful housing project. Funds for non-profit housing are strictly limited in relation to the costs

of housing, and housing sponsors find such limits affecting their choice of site (due to high land costs in the major centers) and also the design, space per unit, and the amenities that can be provided.

The YWCA of Metropolitan Toronto completed a 77-unit, 5-story housing project in 1989 at a cost of $6,350,000 (Figure 1). They hired a woman architect, Ellen Allen of Allen, Ensslen, Barrett Architects, who worked with them to incorporate features that were a priority, including office space on the ground floor that would overlook entrances and the playground to provide better security (Figure 2). There is a lounge with kitchen, community room, and rooms for counseling and referrals on the ground level. The laundry room is at ground level and overlooks the playground. Enclosed sun rooms or balconies are provided for each unit. The housing is designed for low-income, difficult-to-house women with and without children. A full-time housing manager and three community workers provide referrals, counseling, and programs for children. Tenants are actively involved in hiring staff and in managing the building. Residency is limited to women and their children.

In 1990, the Oshawa YWCA opened its permanent housing for women. This is a 40-unit building constructed at a cost of $14 million. It is a four-story apartment building which includes both one- and two-story units. The YWCA owned an emergency hostel on a large site in the downtown area close to services, schools, and transportation. The new housing was built on the site. Special attention was paid to security features, including a secure entrance system, unobstructed sight lines to the emergency housing with 24-hour staff, and locating common areas in high-visibility locations on the first floor. The laundry room is located at the front entrance overlooking the playground. A full-time housing manager and staff provide support groups and parent-child activities. These are funded by "Enhanced Management Program" funds from the provincial government which was convinced that a high percentage of special-needs residents required more management time. Residents were involved initially in programming for the building, especially in making suggestions about the kitchens in units. Residents are also involved in planning programs for the 60 children who live in the building and in setting policy for the building. Residents are limited to women only, including women in temporary housing who need support services, abused women and those with psychiatric problems, female-led families and single women. Eighty percent of the units are subsidized.

In 1991, the Peterborough YWCA constructed its 40-unit, $4.5 million dollar project as a suburban community located in a cul-de-sac adjacent to luxury condominiums and single family homes. It was completed in 1991 and differs from the typical suburban subdivision in its mix of townhouses and stacked townhouses, the playground in the central court, and its self-standing community service building that houses offices, a community room, community kitchen, food co-op, and a laundromat. It is adjacent to a community college, new suburban shopping plaza, and seven-acre park. Since the housing is for women leaving abusive relationships, only women can be tenants. All but two units are subsidized. There is an on-site housing manager funded by the Ontario Ministry of Housing and two community development and youth workers funded by the Ontario Ministry of Community and Social Services.

Community groups that serve women have also expanded their mandate to include housing in recent years. Jessie's Non-Profit Homes in Toronto was sponsored by Jessie's Center for Teenagers, an organization that has provided services to teenage parents for many years. This group experienced major difficulties in obtaining permanent, adequate, and affordable housing. The non-profit organization designed a building that would serve a multi-purpose. The first two floors would provide a new and expanded community center; the top four floors would provide 16 units of non-profit housing. They chose a downtown site, close to public transportation and services and hired an internationally known architect, Jack Diamond, to design their building. The community center provides counseling and referral services, a school room for young mothers, a free store for clothing, medical offices for visiting doctors and

nurses, and a nursery for 20 children. The housing units are two- and three-bedroom units. They share a meeting room and children's playroom on the roof and a roof garden that goes all the way around the building and provides a view of the lake and the downtown. The housing is managed by a non-profit housing society that manages other housing in the community and is run by a board which includes residents and the staff of Jessie's.

Women's Non-Profit Housing Cooperatives

Across Canada, more than 60,000 units of non-profit cooperative housing have been built over the past two decades. Among these are housing cooperatives developed by women for women. The process has been similar to that of non-profit groups wishing to develop non-profit housing for women. The difference is that *ad hoc* groups of women from the community have been able to incorporate as non-profit housing co-operatives and obtain state funding for a housing project that they will jointly own and manage. Because this is a non-profit program, co-op membership fees are nominal (often $25), and the resident does not have to invest any capital, but there is also no "profit" or capital gain when the resident leaves the housing. An initial co-op board is set up which is involved in all stages of the development process, including the choice of site, choosing the architect, and working with the architect and builder to determine the final housing design. Most non-profit housing co-operatives are self-managed by the residents.

One of the first non-profit, women-initiated housing co-operatives in Canada was Grandir en Ville in Quebec City, developed in 1981. A group of women who were single parents organized to stop the demolition of a large convent complex in the financial district of the city which was owned by the provincial government. They convinced the province to use the 300-year-old stone buildings for cooperative housing, and six co-ops were planned for the site. Grandir en Ville is one of these with 30 units, a roof garden, and children's playroom (Figure 3). A child care center and grocery store is shared with the other co-ops on the site. This is not a project only for women, as the initial founders of the project determined to maintain a household mix by establishing a quota system for different types of households. Rents are low compared with market rents and the location in the center of the city is unsurpassed (Figure 4).

The Constance Hamilton Co-op in Toronto was opened for occupancy in 1982. Its founding board consisted of professional women in the community who wanted to

Fig. 3: View of converted chapel, Grandir en Ville, Quebec City.

Fig. 4: Street view of Rental Units, Grandir en Ville, Quebec City.

create permanent housing for women only. There are 30 units and a six-bedroom transitional housing unit for women who have been in shelters. Women were involved in the design process, working with architect Joan Simon to develop housing that would respond to a range of needs. There are seven different unit designs. There is a shared courtyard and the co-op is part of a larger neighborhood of other non-profit, cooperative housing projects. The housing co-op is managed by the residents who have established committees for social activities, maintenance and policy (Figures 5 and 6).

The Women's Community Co-operative in Hamilton, Ontario was completed in 1988. It is a six-story brick building with 47 units located in a suburban neighbor-

hood adjacent to a regional shopping mall. The architect was Ellen Allen. The objective was to provide housing for women aged 40-59 at the time of application—women who were not well served by existing housing in either the social housing sector or in the private market. Eighty percent of the units are subsidized. Committees of residents are responsible for maintenance, interviewing applicants, and organizing social events. This co-op provides residents with extensive informal social support networks and services that include regular communal meals, buying trips, and outings.

Ujama Housing Cooperative in Scarborough, Ontario, a suburb of Metropolitan Toronto, will be completed in 1992. The architect is also Ellen Allen. This is a project

Fig. 5: Constance Hamilton Co-op. Toronto (1982).

Fig. 6: Constance Hamilton Co-op. Toronto (1982). Entry Detail.

of 56 units in a five-story apartment building. Eighty percent of the units will be subsidized and the housing is for women of color who will be responsible for self-managing the housing project.

What Issues Are Raised by the Experience of Women's Housing Projects?

The experience of women's housing groups in Canada have much to teach women interested in providing housing for women in other countries.

Innovative Funding Strategies

To get housing built, women have come up with an assortment of arrangements far from standard in the housing field. They have forged alliances between human service providers and housing providers to invent new funding mechanisms to pay for support services for residents. Because women's groups are unfamiliar with the housing field, they are also unaware that housing agencies and social service agencies do not generally speak to one another. They have insisted that services are needed and received exceptions to the rules in demonstration projects where housing agencies and social service agencies work together. These have become significant models for other housing agencies. One group established an agreement between a women's service organization and a public housing authority to lease housing to the group for $1 a year. Some groups have developed scattered-site housing with housing workers from the agency providing support services to residents. One group mortgaged a member's house to come up with the initial capital to buy a building.

Combining Housing and Services

Non-profit housing providers, especially those serving homeless men, argue that shelter should not be tied to service. But women's providers argue that women's needs might differ from homeless men or other groups. When residents are single parents, teenage mothers, abused women, or older women, it is unrealistic to assume that they have the time and the mobility to obtain needed services wherever they may be located in the community. Services for these groups are more appropriately located on site as long as residents have the option to use them or not.

Shift From Advocacy to Housing Provider

In the eighties, small women's organizations began to use their limited resources to develop and manage permanent housing. Often this replaced their former activities of writing briefs to government, lobbying for change, or organizing their constituencies for political action . In this way, governments that do not respond to women's housing needs co-opt community women's groups and deflect them from their role of criticizing and prodding governments. When groups shift to providing housing, they compete with other groups for scarce resources instead of building coalitions. This means that instead of communicating with one another, each group competes for the small pool of available funds and housing.

Women's Groups as Landlords

Women's groups that develop and then manage housing become landlords and this can be a drain on a organization's resources and staff for decades. These organizations must now continue to concern themselves with upkeep of the housing and its management. Many of the women's groups that have developed permanent housing are committed to some form of facilitative management whereby residents and the organizational sponsor co-manage the building, and residents are integrally involved in policy making and in key decisions that affect their day-to-day lives. Non-profit housing organizations providing housing for women tend to fall between the housing system and the movement. Frequently, they are not connected to the formal housing system nor are they linked to other housing groups across the country. Their connections are to the women's movement where housing is still largely marginalized. Women's non-profit housing providers may become isolated in these circumstances.

Non-Profit Housing Co-operatives Developed by Women: Housing for Women Only

In Canada, some non-profit housing providers and non-profit housing cooperatives limit tenants to women only, often because women have been at risk from male partners and women need time and space to heal and develop their own sense of self-esteem and community. In some cases, women prefer the sense of community possible in an all-women's environment. This has raised problems, including how this affects male children: are they members of the housing cooperative? And what happens when a woman develops a relationship with a male partner? The terms of the tenancy are tied to family status, in this case. The question often arises whether women's housing creates ghettoes or whether it provides a positive alternative for those women who value housing defined and controlled by women.

Retaining a Women's Community

The goal of some women's housing projects is housing as a base for community building. There is a concern about what will happen over time as initial founders move on. Does the project maintain its unique culture and identity or does it become just another place to live? When funding does not permit services or space to provide opportunities for community to develop, it is difficult to develop a sense of community; but funding constraints often support shelter to the exclusion of other spaces.

Conclusions

Women's housing projects have given women the opportunity to become active agents within a housing system that excludes them as developers, builders, managers, or owners of housing. Across Canada, women's groups and individual women have become empowered by this experience—creating affordable, secure housing that meets their needs. For these women, developing housing is not a mysterious or specialized process but within the capabilities of most women.

Women's active involvement in the housing system has created a new model of empowerment rather than the conventional image of women's victimization by the housing system. Across Canada, women have learned the lesson that if some women have been able to do it, others can as well. They have learned that women can take charge, learn new skills, and infiltrate a non-traditional field for women. The idea that women can control and manage their own housing has been powerful in consciousness-raising and in giving women the courage to demand greater control over their own housing environments in other sectors of the housing system.

Women's housing projects have generated new housing alternatives: new ways of putting together housing and services; attention to community; an emphasis on facilitative management where residents are integrally involved. Women have rejected the notion that housing is a commodity and have focused on what it can do in women's lives by supporting the development of greater self-esteem and providing a secure base for growth.

Women have taken a holistic view of the housing system, insisting that social services be linked with housing, and that housing become a priority for women's movement groups.

Finally, the Canadian women's housing projects are linked to international movements to empower women through control of housing both in other industrialized countries and in developing countries. The Canadian projects are examples of self-help housing that is self-managed and linked to other women's self-help housing initiatives throughout the world.

These initiatives have met with substantial success. Within very limited budgets, women have done what women always do—made do, scrounged, persevered. They've set up new housing that had never been done before in their communities. They've learned to play the housing system and did not take "no" for an answer from housing bureaucrats. They've come up with innovative funding options and demonstrated that combining housing and services makes good sense for families in need. Best of all, women will control this housing for a long time and be an inspiration to all women who want to control their own housing environment rather than be dictated to by a housing industry for whom housing is primarily a commodity rather than a place to create a home.

References

Canada Mortgage and Housing Corporation. *Evaluation of the Public Housing Program.* Ottawa: Program Evaluation Division, 1990.

Canada Mortgage and Housing Corporation. *Core Housing Need in Canada.* Ottawa: CMHC,1991.

McClain, Janet, with Cassie Doyle. *Women and Housing: Changing Needs and the Failure of Policy.* Toronto: James Lorimer and Company, 1984.

Statistics Canada. *Census of Canada.* Ottawa: Statistics Canada, 1986.

Wekerle, Gerda R., and Sylvia Novac. *Gender and Housing in Toronto.* Toronto: Equal Opportunity Division, City of Toronto, 1991.

Wekerle, Gerda R., and Barbara Muirhead. *Canadian Women's Housing Projects.* Ottawa: Canada Mortgage and Housing Corporation, 1991.

Wekerle, Gerda R. *Women's Housing Projects in Eight Canadian Cities.* Ottawa: Canada Mortgage and Housing Corporation, 1988.

Chapter 23
Beating a Path: Towards Defining Women's Participation

Meera Bapat and Sheela Patel

Meera Bapat received her Bachelor of Architecture, University of Bombay, and a Ph.D. in Development Planning, London. She has published papers on shelter issues, the urban labor market, health and environment, and jurisprudence regarding allocation of urban space. Important assignments include membership on Government of India Planning Commission committees to set up the Seventh and Eighth Five-Year Plans, participation in research programs established by the United Nations Research Institute for Social Development, and consulting work for Oxfam.

Sheela Patel is director and founding member of the Society for Promotion of Area Resource Centers (SPARC), an organization which works as a partner rather than a patron with communities and organizations of the poor in India. Her work with SPARC was recognized with a fifth annual IYSH Award at a ceremony in Tokyo, Japan, on the occasion of World HABITAT Day 1992. She is involved in community organization activities within squatter communities in India.

This paper is based on the experience of community organization work that SPARC (the Society for Promotion of Area Resource Centers) has been involved with since its formation in 1984.

Starting with the most vulnerable, isolated, and deprived among the urban poor, SPARC has developed a popular education program that attempts to reorganize marginalized communities. It instills women's central participation and collective leadership as central features and addresses not only the question of women's subordination but also of the marginalized position of the communities. The approach develops from needs and aspirations of such groups, especially women, leading to the self-discovery of their capacity to analyze, challenge, and transform their reality. It is concerned with developing critical consciousness among these groups and with building their skills which lead to assertive and confident practices and formulating strategies that contribute to changing their marginalized position.

In the case of pavement dwellers with whom SPARC began to work in 1984, the popular education program began with the lack of secure shelter, regarded by the pavement dwellers as their most pressing and crucial problem. A shelter training program evolved as a result. The communities endorsed women as main participants to spearhead the training and subsequent action. The paper documents, as an illustration, the first cycle of the training program as it evolved. It records the way in which this training is utilized, first to secure women's central participation and then to sustain it by developing their skills to gather, analyze, and systematize information and use it for collective decision-making. The last section illustrates how the strategy devised by SPARC attempts to integrate women's empowerment with fulfillment of urgent needs of their families and communities, and how it is harnessed to resolve immediate problems and address long-term goals.

The Context

SPARC is a voluntary organization (or a non-government organization—NGO) based in Bombay in western India (the metropolis had a population of more than 12 million in 1991). SPARC's founders are professionals in social work, social activism, social sciences, and related research. To work toward equity and social justice, they felt a need to set up an organization which aligned as a partner rather than as a patron of marginalized communities and organizations of the poor. To fulfill its aspirations, SPARC has set up resource centers in areas geographically accessible to the groups that need them. In such centers, people find information, interact with their neighbors and others in similar situations as themselves, develop skills, and learn to represent themselves. In such resource centers, management is gradually transferred to the communities that use them.

SPARC has two partner organizations: Mahila Milan (MM) and the National Slum Dwellers Federation (NSDF). Mahila Milan (MM) was formed in 1987 initially as an organization of women who live on pavements and who trained themselves with the help of SPARC to lobby for their rights, among which is access to secure shelter. The organization has developed strategies to ensure that the women are supported by the entire community of which they are a part. Women are encouraged to work not only within their own community but also with women from other communities to help them to take on similar initiatives. In the process, they gather strength as the membership of their collective grows.

The National Slum Dwellers Federation (NSDF) had been in existence for several years prior to becoming a partner of SPARC and had worked sporadically on issues concerning slum dwellers. After SPARC conducted an enumeration of pavement dwellers in 1985, NSDF, attracted to the use of an information base to mobilize people, began to interact with SPARC. NSDF has member federations in Bombay and in other cities in India.[1]

SPARC began its work with women from families living in hovels on pavements in Bombay. It saw pavement dwellers as the most deprived and isolated among the urban poor and those who have fewest organizational and political skills. Women among them, as compared to women from poor households, are greater sufferers in the struggle for survival because of their added vulnerability arising from the ever-present threat of demolition of their dwellings. By starting with the most vulnerable, SPARC believes it is developing an alternative generally relevant to the problems it wishes to address: if it proves relevant to the most marginalized, it can be adapted to the less deprived because of its built-in flexibility.

When SPARC began its work, the organization had a philosophy of work but did not have a set course of action or a methodology. As its involvement in its work grew, it formulated its approach almost intuitively. So far this work has little to show in concrete results or gains, but the process it has set in motion, we believe, is

a contribution toward changing the marginalized position of disadvantaged groups and, in particular, of women.

Reviewing Approaches to Women's Development

This experience needs to be viewed against the background of approaches used for achieving women's development and strategies adopted for countering their subordination, especially since 1975 when the United Nations' Decade for Women began.[2] "The almost uniform conclusion of the International Women's Decade research is that, with a few exceptions, relative access to economic resources, incomes, and employment has worsened, their burdens of work have increased, and their relative and even absolute health, nutritional and educational status has declined!"[3] What is significant is that this decline in women's situations has taken place in spite of all the information, publicity, and pressures surrounding women in the last two decades or so.

Policy approaches that have been successively adopted in an attempt to change women's status have been described as welfare, equity, anti-poverty, efficiency, and empowerment.[4] Each approach was born out of an understanding of its time of women's roles in development. These approaches have been operationalized not singly but in combination. Most of these approaches, however, have failed to address the fundamental problems that women suffer from.

To analyze why women's status has altered little, a distinction needs to be made between the "condition" and "position" of women.[5] A woman's condition means the material state that she finds herself in (e.g., poverty, lack of education, burden of work, lack of access to credit or technology, etc.). Her "position" means her social and economic standing relative to men.

The condition of women is the subject of much of development literature on women and a major part of development concerns centers on finding ways of improving women's condition by targeting ameliorative resources to them rather than by radically changing underlying structures. The emphasis on women's condition has two consequences. Firstly, there has been a tendency to emphasize women's practical and day-to-day needs—giving greater access to credit, special training schemes, etc. Secondly, the approach makes it difficult for structural issues concerning women's position to be raised. It inhibits posing the question of whether women's condition is related to their structural position and/or whether any serious and sustainable improvement in their condition is possible without structural changes. As a result, while women's needs as mothers, producers, etc., are highlighted, their interests as women are not.[6]

When discussing women's needs, it is essential to differentiate between "the needs of women as occupiers of particular social roles and interests of women as a social category with unequal access to socially-valued resources (both economic and social) and political power."[7] This differentiation has been further developed as practical needs and strategic interests.[8] "Examples of practical gender needs derive from the necessity of fulfilling particular roles allocated to them by the division of labor; e.g., care of children, maintenance of the house, care of the elderly, servicing of family and community.... Strategic gender interests arise from women's growing recognition that the age-old structures of male dominance and privileges are not sacrosanct, but social impositions [and] are, as such, amenable to change."[9]

The approach to the development of women that is concerned centrally with the position of women and their strategic interests is the "empowerment" approach. Strategic interests are defined on the basis of an analysis of gender subordination and a formulation of a vision of alternative gender relations. It is clear that if women are to attain justice in society, it will be necessary to transform the structures of subordination: i.e., changes are required in laws, civil codes, property rights, labor codes, and social and legal institutions that underwrite male control and privileges. The empowerment approach, however, recognizes the limitations of top-down government efforts to meet strategic gender interests. Even when these strategies are adopted, to implement them, sustained efforts in the form of political mobilization, consciousness raising, and popular education are required. The empowerment approach uses practical gender needs on which to build a secure support base and as means through which more strategic interests may be reached.

Popular education is regarded by adherents of the empowerment approach as an important component of a strategy that challenges gender subordination. Popular education "is concerned with developing critical consciousness amongst the marginalized groups, with strengthening behaviors and attitudes which lead to more confident and assertive practices and to formulating strategies to contribute to the changing of their marginalized position."[10]

The approach develops from the needs and aspirations of the marginalized groups and leads to the self-discovery among the people of their own capacities to analyze, challenge, and transform their own reality.

Why Focus on Women Pavement Dwellers?

In the work done by SPARC, as now seen with hind-sight, the element of popular education which attempts to address the situation of women's subordination evolved as a critical component. The group arrived at its methodology of work not from studying any manuals or handbooks on the subject but from their commitment to take, as the starting point, needs and aspirations of marginalized groups as defined by the groups themselves. The workers in SPARC were acutely conscious of not imposing their own values, attitudes, and ideas on the people and communities they worked with.

The focus on women pavement dwellers arose from the experience of some of the individual members of SPARC of earlier work with such committees.[11] It had shown them clearly that these women, on the one hand, have to face extremely hostile and difficult situations, but on the other, are a key to the survival of their families and communities. They not only nurture and create the physical and psychological space for fulfilling family needs but also create the community's survival system based on mutual support which is so essential for getting by in a highly competitive and alienating environment of the city. They manage resources in such a way as to ensure their conservation and equitable distribution. And yet, their contribution to the building, consolidation, and development of their settlements remains unacknowledged. Women do not give any credit to themselves for their own contribution either. They are never consulted in formulating interventions (by NGOs or government agencies). To address the needs and aspirations of marginalized groups, however, those who face crises and devise survival strategies (i.e., women) must play a central role in decision making, in designing strategies, and in implementing them. Hence, SPARC focuses on women. This is a means of acknowledging existing processes and building upon them.

Therefore, right from the start in SPARC's work, central participation of women is a critical component of a gender-sensitive community organization. It attempts to achieve this by facilitating the renegotiating of men-and-women relationships within their families, communities, and federations to achieve the goal of equity.

Reorganization of Communities and Gender Sensitivity

A Changing Self-Image of Women

The reorganization of groups to be gender-sensitive must occur in large enough numbers of communities to provide the environment in which new relationships can not only sustain themselves but also get reproduced. Popular education becomes a critical tool to create the new environment. Popular education programs with women ensure that both women themselves and communities constantly acknowledge women's central role in the process of change. In the popular education programs, as the first step toward self-discovery by women, SPARC initiates individual introspection by women into their past. Women are encouraged to share their experiences, starting from childhood. This narration includes events, views, feelings, opinions, and much reflection. The listener (catalyst) is not passive but demands accountability from the speaker to ensure that socially and self-promoted myths do not intervene.

It is not that the women do not talk about their lives or know about each other's histories. What is different in this new narration is the value that is ascribed to that experience. It no longer remains an isolated, individual experience; instead, it is linked to critical milestones in the settlement's history. This ensures that, in the future, women's role and contribution to making decisions on issues that affect the settlement/community can no longer be marginalized. This introspection enables women to see themselves as agents of change. It reveals to them that this experience is a process of their own creation and worthy of becoming a reference point in discussions.

The next step in the process of self-discovery is to move from individual stories to group histories. Small groups of women are assisted to discuss, collectively, their experiences and issues related to themselves. When women know about each other's life histories, it is easier to refer to individual incidents in group meetings and discussions. In such discussions, the role of the catalyst is to help women form a collective experience and then build on it.

In subsequent discussions, men as well as women participate. At this point, the catalyst supports men to narrate their life history as they perceive it, and then to integrate it with women's experience to build the entire community's history. From this point onward, any discussion on the past experience refers to what women

and men have contributed to the settlement/community history. This is one of the most difficult stages and marks a watershed in the process. In this process of reorganizing the community's history, the question of who in the community is to spearhead desired changes is debated continuously. There is an agreement that it should be those who build and consolidate the settlement, face crises, and solve problems. Invariably, on these criteria women are endorsed to work as agents of change.

The process is difficult and drawn out because it challenges existing leadership patterns and upsets existing power equations within the community. Women generally avoid confrontations over this matter. They cajole, connive, and even maneuver situations to gradually develop a working relationship with men in the community. The catalyst helps by providing the women space to use their newly found knowledge to facilitate changes in their community in a manner and at a pace that they can cope with and make use of. In such an environment, the women that SPARC has worked with have clearly displayed their desire to play crucial roles in decision-making. They have demonstrated that it is possible to develop strategies to set in motion a process leading to the transformation of their situation of subordination within their families and communities.

This experience is significant in itself, especially in light of the recognition by the international women's movement that there has been little success in effectively challenging gender subordination. An important reason identified for this is the perceived lack of acceptable alternatives which do not entail intolerably high costs.[12] The experience of oppression and subordination that women may suffer is mediated by experiences which may lead many women to conclude that their situation cannot be changed or that attempting to change it will worsen their existing situation which they have learned to cope with. This belief may not only deter women from taking action to change their situation but may even lead certain categories of women to support the structures and institutions of male domination. In SPARC's work, the transformation of women's situation of subordination is linked to improved life for the entire community and, therefore, is accepted by men and the community as a whole.

The scope provided in the approach devised by SPARC to transcend women's anxiety about the cost of challenging their existing situation has proved to be a crucial feature. After the alliance with Mahila Milan was initiated, men and women whose roles were reorganized through this process began to participate as partners with SPARC. Mahila Milan and NSDF are more effective in this process since they demonstrate to the communities benefits of this rearrangement; and when men discuss this transformation, it is even more effective. This is the point after which SPARC no longer plays the role of a catalyst, but hands that responsibility over to members of MM and NSDF. They reproduce the process that they have been through with other communities that join the federation.

Establishing Collective Leadership

A critical part of the popular education strategy devised by SPARC is the upgrading of information levels of all members of communities. This is essential for facilitating their participation in the process of mobilization and for establishing collective decision-making. It is also crucial for enabling the communities to demand accountability from the collective leadership. Building people's capabilities to examine and systematize their knowledge, and to use it to advance their collective cause, is central to community organization initiated by SPARC. This is contrary to the traditional pattern of community structures in poorer settlements in which leaders are often brokers of (political) patronage. They prop up their own position as leaders by exploiting their access to information or knowledge (of the working of government agencies, banks, welfare schemes, etc.). They thrive in a situation where people in the community are not exposed to the working of such institutions and, therefore, lack the confidence to seek information themselves. The community leaders use this situation for obtaining gains for themselves. They are, therefore, not interested in changing this situation by building people's capabilities to take on such tasks. In the popular education and community organization strategy devised by SPARC, these traditional leaders usually get sidelined and replaced by a responsive collective leadership.

Popular Education Using Question of Shelter

Women living on pavements express as their first priority the need for secure shelter, mainly for the sake of their children. Owing to this consideration, SPARC evolved its popular education program around the question of shelter.

Shelter is the most critical question for pavement dwellers. Their lives are fraught with an acute sense of insecurity arising from repeated demolitions by authori-

ties of their shelter and consequent loss of belongings. Demolitions rarely achieve the objective of clearing pavements, for their residents almost always manage to return to the same location and erect their shelter all over again. Demolitions, however, not only deplete the meager asset base of these families but also torment and terrorize them. They are made to feel powerless and begin to regard their situation as hopeless. Apathy sets in as a result. The trauma, anguish, and rage felt on account of demolitions give way to passive acceptance of the situation. The psychological damage caused by demolitions is severe and difficult to remedy. Apathy and the feeling of powerlessness incapacitate people and make them incapable of participating in a process leading to a change in their situation. This is even more true for women in such groups. This poses a big challenge for devising strategies that will change this situation of inaction. In this environment, identifying shelters as a focal point of intervention and women as agents of change is a strategic choice made by SPARC.

In mid-1985, SPARC conducted an enumeration of pavement dwellers (a people's census).[13] It revealed that nearly 6,000 families (27,000 people) lived on pavements in just one district (ward) and four arterial roads in Bombay. The enumeration was conducted as much as a strategy to mobilize the people as to generate information about them (which was scanty), to create public opinion against mass demolition, and to deter the local authority from taking such a drastic action.[14] The objective was to bring into focus the reality that a problem of such a magnitude and complexity could not be solved by demolishing huts and evicting the people.

Tension and anxiety mounted as the day after which demolitions were expected to begin drew closer. To the relief of pavement dwellers and their supporters, however, mass demolitions did not occur (this was as much due to intensive mobilizing of pavement dwellers by various organizations as to a play of diverse forces in local politics). But the event brought the extent of their vulnerability home to pavement dwellers. Women began to ask how long they would go on accepting such a precarious existence and whether their children's children too would be born on pavements. Not only was their situation desperate—the poverty, hand-to-mouth existence, isolation, and hopelessness—but difficulties seemed insurmountable and no solution was in sight.

The threat of imminent demolition after the Supreme Court judgment provided the critical historical moment for building an alliance between SPARC and pavement dwellers. SPARC felt that the apathy of pavement dwellers could be turned into a positive force, galvanizing the people into action, provided they:

1. Developed a vision of an alternative: the people needed to develop an alternative, working toward which would provide the motivation to shed apathy and take action.
2. Conducted organized action: a large enough number of people needed to believe that change was possible.
3. Built stamina and capacity for sustained action: they needed to develop stamina and capacity for a long, drawn-out process of negotiations and lobbying to legitimize and institutionalize the change they desired and demanded.

The impending threat of mass demolitions and anxiety caused by it provided the impetus to focus on the question of shelter. The enumeration of pavement dwellers and subsequent discussions of its findings with the people had created the background for conducting a training program which explored possible ways of changing the prevailing situation.[15]

Essential features of this training can be described as:

1. a. With the community concerned and its leadership, organization of existing knowledge, information, and practices that the people have used in working out their shelter strategies.

   b. Examination of this information to understand the circumstances in which the strategies have evolved and to analyze their advantages and drawbacks.

2. a. Identification of areas where changes are needed and articulation of why these changes are essential.

   b. Identification of the various actors involved, other than the community itself, to identify the required skills and resources and who can contribute to them.

   c. Development of the required skills within the community to undertake the process leading to the desired change.

3. Having developed this understanding, development of skills to articulate the alternative to people within the community, to other communities in a similar situation, and to outsiders (professionals, citizenry, and government officials).

Integral to this training must be sustained community mobilization essential for carrying on the action through a drawn-out process before the alternative can be achieved. Therefore, this training process ensures as outcomes (1) a clear understanding of aspirations; (2) a statement of how the community proposes to achieve them; (3) development of insights into internal and external factors that will lead to achieving the alterna-

tive; and (4) recognition that structural changes are needed to resolve most critical problems of the poor. The outcome of this training program becomes the foundation for community action.

The decision to treat this training process as an educational component of community mobilization was somewhat intuitive. On hindsight, its rationale can be described thus: to enable poor communities, especially women among them, to work with SPARC as partners in building an alternative; a reorganization of the communities' way of functioning must form an essential feature of this process. A sustainable change is not possible without such a reorganization.

A critical part of the training is to upgrade the information level of the entire community, for without this all its members are not in a position to participate in the mobilization process. Community members (not SPARC) then develop criteria for selecting leaders. This ensures that the leaders are accountable to the community. Members of SPARC discuss, argue, and negotiate with the people regarding each other's ideas on leadership and the final concept emerges out of a consensus. Creating processes which allow negotiations to occur in order to arrive at a consensus are as much a part of the training as building actual skills.[16] Group discussions are a mechanism used for arriving at a consensus. The entire community (i.e., men and women) participates in these discussions.

In the process of transformation, the twin factors of women's central participation and collective decision-making, once endorsed by the community, become the most important aspects of the organization process. Some groups and individuals in the community (e.g., the traditional male leaders) may continue to deride these features. Rather than exclude the traditional leaders for their derogatory behavior, the process of debate and discussion challenges their views until an internal consensus is reached. Once women's participation in creating alternative shelter emerges, the basis for a collective leadership has been established.

Shelter Training Program

To explain the shelter training program in practice, it is useful to describe the first cycle of the training that SPARC and women pavement dwellers developed in 1986–87. In the specific case of pavement dwellers, public meetings were arranged to discuss impending demolitions and to work out strategies to avert or deal with them. Women's participation, in case such an eventuality occurred, was linked to the "NEED" rather than to a "RIGHT" by emphasizing that the question of shelter concerned women the most, since it was they who made a pavement dwelling (or any dwelling) a home. Further, a crisis such as a demolition was faced generally by women since men were at work when it occurred. After a series of meetings, men accepted that women would be the spearheads of the training program. This position was publicly ratified. The key role given to women put them in a position of responsibility which they were willing to shoulder. Any fears, anxieties, and doubts that this responsibility created among women were openly discussed so that they did not act as deterrents to their participation. The group took the responsibility of coping with the work collectively.

The first training program was conducted for 600 women participants. Men also participated sporadically. It was undertaken in an atmosphere conducive and congenial to participation by women and the community. Days, timing, and the agenda of the meetings were flexible and organized by women. Members of SPARC made sure that all critical issues were discussed, however difficult some of them were. They were dealt with by the community in a manner and at a pace that they could handle. The informal atmosphere in which the training took place made women feel at ease. The training used language, form, and manner that made sure that the participants were not intimidated. They were, in fact, put in a position of advantage because the discussion began from a narration of their experiences.

Several questions were discussed in the training program. For example, since the demolition of dwellings was a major concern for pavement dwellers, a detailed discussion of this problem was included in the training. During these discussions, women made analytical observations on a number of issues related to demolitions (e.g., which settlements had to face demolition squads more frequently than others, why it was necessary to build huts using materials that could be dismantled quickly, costs involved in maintaining such structures, the loss of belongings, including food and stored grains confiscated during demolitions and consequent hardships suffered, violence during demolitions). Attention of the participants was drawn to the distinction between demolition (i.e., destruction of dwellings) and eviction (i.e., preventing people from occupying the pavement). This distinction helped them to differentiate between their inability to save their homes and their strength in resisting being evicted altogether from the pavement. The group then listed all the actors involved in the drama. This led to an explora-

tion of possible alternative responses to impending demolitions.

It became clear in these discussions that these families did not wish to reside on pavements. They were willing to move to alternative sites in the city to attain secure shelter. Until this alternative could be realized, which the participants recognized would be a very long process, it was essential to devise ways of minimizing the psychological and economic damage caused by demolition of shelter. Several steps were planned to deal with such an eventuality (and were subsequently executed). Women delegates visited the municipal ward office and the local police station and demanded and obtained clear information about the stipulated procedure to be followed during demolitions. It became clear to them, for example, that the presence of the police was as much to protect the people as to effect violence-free demolitions. This information was passed on to all members of the community to be made use of when required.

A "battle plan" was drawn up to face demolitions collectively, with residents of neighboring settlements coming to assist (e.g., in dismantling huts to prevent the ignominy and indignity of hacking of dwellings by the demolition squad, providing food to the affected families on the day their homes are demolished). This plan is now routinely practiced when facing demolitions. This has helped break the feeling of isolation and to create a feeling of solidarity among pavement dwellers.

The next stage was to develop alternative shelters. The crucial issue here related to the availability of land. Pavement and slum dwellers have repeatedly been told by local and housing authorities that no land is available in Bombay where they can be accommodated. This is not true, and to demonstrate this, vacant stretches of land were located (on the Development Plan of the city, from information received from slum dwellers living in other areas, from professionals in the relevant departments of the state government). Visits were arranged to inspect these sites. The training program included the gathering of information, checking its validity, and arranging visits so that each member of the community saw the vacant land. For many, especially women, this was their first visit to another area of the city using public transport. The site visits provided an opportunity for the people to interact with other communities and this strengthened networking. Having established that vacant land exists in Bombay, the next complex question that needed to be thrashed out was why it was not officially available to the poor. This discussion illustrated how people began to grasp that their deprivation was a result of a number of external forces. It made them aware of the magnitude of change required to fulfill their aspirations for secure shelter.

By now, people felt comfortable as members of large groups. But for everyone to try to participate in everything would have been unwieldy and unrealistic. Not everyone had the time or the capability for doing various concrete tasks that needed to be done. By this time, a stage had been reached at which some of the participants had shown the qualities of prime movers and leaders. The group, in turn, was by now seeking representatives for doing future work, and a process of identifying collective leadership began. Essentially, leaders were to be those who could share, nurture, support, and assist those who sought to do the work rather than to wield power—those who wished to contribute their efforts and found time to do what needed to be done.

One woman was chosen from every 15 houses to assume the responsibility of carrying out concrete tasks. Such representatives together formed Area Committees. They had to conduct regular meetings with members of the 15 houses and be a link for communication between them and between this group and the rest of the community. This mechanism is used even today to keep every person in the community informed, ensuring that the communication chain is maintained. The women chosen to be members of Area Committees had to acquire various skills and play specific roles. They were required to learn to involve everyone and also to facilitate collective decision-making. They received support and feedback on their work from SPARC and members of the community. These women representatives, because of their communication skills, became trainers in other communities.

To collect basic information necessary for planning their alternative settlement, each cluster had to do a simple exercise of counting the exact number of families that lived there. Since they had never been involved in such a task before, the exercise was important for undertaking the gathering of statistical information about themselves and using it with confidence in discussions to support their arguments. Besides, SPARC's experience had showed that an enumeration can be used as a powerful tool for mobilizing people. For these reasons, it was decided that Area Committee members would perform this task for their individual groups of 15 houses (although information about each cluster existed in the census of pavement dwellers conducted earlier by SPARC).

This exercise was a watershed in the training program. An anomaly surfaced: the number of structures (huts) did not match the number of families living in the cluster—because of renting out of part of the huts, huts being used for income-earning activities, vested interests attempting to claim more space, stronger families trying to outdo weaker ones, and so on. There was tension that had to be resolved. Enumeration was conducted in each cluster several times until the findings satisfied a majority and a consensus was reached. The whole process contributed significantly to group building.

For women, the enumeration exercise was the first major concrete task that they did collectively. This gave them a sense of accomplishment and boosted their confidence. They got insights into the community dynamics and began to understand processes by which Area Committee members could be coopted by outsiders or community members. The process made them aware of the need to set norms carefully for space allocation so that the needs of every community member could be fulfilled. They developed a team spirit which formed a basis for a collective leadership in place of traditional leaders.

The next step in the training was to design the dwelling and settlement. While women dreamt of the kind of houses they would want to live in, they were realistic about their means and resources and needs of the community. They analyzed the existing allocation of space for various functions in their dwellings. This helped to identify family space against collective/ community space. The importance of sharing space and amenities was discussed. On the basis of this analysis, requirements of individual dwellings were worked out. They were discussed with professionals. Women defended their choices/decisions.[17] Architects/engineers explained the importance of natural light and proper ventilation and space management. They discussed the importance of developing a prototype. The presence of SPARC at these meetings ensured that the professionals were informed and sympathetic, that they were neither overbearing nor romantic about people's participation, and that there was frank dialogue. After a series of meetings, designs of dwellings and settlement evolved.

The training program included a discussion of existing public housing schemes for the poor. Officials from the housing authority were invited to make presentations before groups of women. Visits to public housing projects by a core group of women were arranged in Bombay and other cities. Pamphlets giving information about various housing schemes were obtained and translated by SPARC staff members into appropriate languages. Women compared their dwelling and settlement designs with those in official schemes and assessed public housing designs for suitability for their own needs. During visits to housing projects, they asked their residents those questions that they had asked themselves when they planned their dwellings. They explained their design choices to these residents. In this process, a critique of public housing projects emerged.

The whole exercise involved:

1. An analysis of their own life styles and their means and resources to arrive at a relevant dwelling/settlement design.
2. Articulating their design choices to professionals and defending their decisions.
3. Developing prototypes with the help of professionals.
4. Collecting information on public housing schemes and assessing them for suitability.

Subsequently, full-scale dwelling models were built by women (using timber, cloth, and paper in the first training program; in subsequent programs, other materials such as brick and concrete were also used). An exhibition was organized which was visited by slum dwellers, professionals, and government officials. Women showed and discussed the dwelling models with the visitors who had diverse interests in the exhibition. To slum dwellers, it demonstrated ways of upgrading their houses and settlements; to government officials and professionals, it was not only a clear expression of people's ability to plan shelter meticulously but also broke stereotyped images of the poor as incapable of working out suitable alternatives.

Starting from an analysis of their existing situation to working out a concrete structure for shelter took a period of nearly 18 months. Having conceptualized dwelling and settlement designs, the next phase in the training program was to discuss the "hardware" of housing (i.e., the three major components of building materials, finance, and land).

1. Building materials: Women visited building material depots to determine which of them were appropriate for their use and inquired about prices. They also learnt actual construction, estimating cost of construction, delivery systems, and later supervising construction work.
2. Finance: Pavement dwellers are fully aware that alternative shelter would not be given free of cost. They started putting aside small amounts of money regularly in a bank

for paying for shelter. In addition, they made inquiries about loan facilities for housing from established credit sources.

Each household has an account in a bank in the name of the woman. Community leaders assist each family to open a bank against the target set on the basis of estimates of dwelling cost. Women who once regarded entering a bank intimidating and operating bank accounts formidable now do this work with ease and confidence. Regular saving of money has inculcated discipline among the people and awareness regarding planning for the future—both values alien to those leading a hand-to-mouth existence.

Discussion with housing finance institutions have now been initiated and are going on. Considerable amounts put aside as housing savings so far by pavement dwellers as a group show the level of preparedness of the people to participate in housing projects. This is contrary to a normally held view by government authorities that pavement dwellers are neither willing to pay toward housing nor capable of saving money regularly.

3. Land: In the case of pavement dwellers, acquiring land is the most difficult proposition. They have had to start with a struggle for recognition of their legitimacy. Even this has been achieved only marginally. Establishing a right to land to live on is a distant goal. Negotiating with government authorities for land has been initiated but constitutes a drawn-out and painful process.[18]

Urban land is a highly valuable resource. To tilt its allocation in favor of the urban poor (i.e., those who are incapable of competing in the land or housing market) is a major political battle.[19]

The complexity of and enormous difficulties in the task of obtaining secure shelter have not so far deterred pavement dwellers from refining their training program or assisting other groups of urban poor in developing their shelter alternatives. It is continuing evidence of solidarity among marginalized groups that pavement dwellers have assisted those groups of slum dwellers who have been allotted land to design and construct their homes, although their own quest for land remains unfulfilled. Because the struggle for shelter is a part of the larger struggle for social change, every small step forward in either the specific shelter situation or in the context of urban poverty and deprivation is also a step forward in the other.

Illustrating the Outcome of Popular Education

In conclusion, this section illustrates various elements described in the paper. There are:

1. The challenge of ensuring women's participation in the process of change and, specifically, in the shelter situation.

2. Strategies of popular education which not only create the means for people to participate in formulating these strategies but in reproducing them in a manner which ensures women's central participation and community control over the adaptation and reproduction of these processes.

Most existing shelter training material for women exhibits a top-down approach.[20] It embodies an approach which refers to the "condition" of women and not to their "position." Such an approach has severe limitations for improving the status of women. In the shelter training program devised by SPARC, the focus is on empowering women. It has, firstly, created a positive self-image of women and, secondly, has created mechanisms to sustain it. This has transformed their perception of themselves from individuals who are not worthy of associating with the better-off and professionals and who are incapable of making any contribution to individuals who can act as catalysts in the process of change. Their increased self-esteem has changed their role within their families and the community. Thirdly, by locating the process of reproduction of this training within women's collectives, it has ensured that women's participation is sustained in all decision-making both in their communities and in federations of which these communities are members. For example:

A. This empowerment process acknowledges women's need to integrate their own empowerment with the fulfillment of needs of their families and communities. This has always remained a challenge to educators working with poor women. In SPARC's approach, women's self-esteem is enhanced by taking up issues in those priority areas which have helped resolve crises faced by such communities. For example:

   1. Obtaining ration cards which have entitled the families to buy food grains, cooking oil, and fuel at subsidized rates.

   2. Dealing with harassment by the police—changing humiliating treatment by officials to due respect for women's opinions.

   3. Transforming the feeling of intimidation by and a lack of access to institutions like banks into a situation where bank staff welcome poor women to open bank accounts and invite women's collectives to advise them on loan applications by members of their communities.

   4. Dealing with municipal officials at the local wrd level—transforming the fear and the feeling of helplessness caused by repeated demolitions into ensuring accountability from public servants.

Table 1: Mahila Milan Housing Unit Bank Saving Analysis

	A/C Holders	Amount in Bank of Baroda Rs. Started 1986	Amount in HDFC Rs. Started 1991
APNA	99	71,542	6,450
Water Street	85	75,249	16,100
Tank Pakadi	23	7,101	500
Dimdimkar Road	53	49,516	11,800
Peer Khan	33	36,575	9,560
Sophia Zubair	41	8,158	41,860
Shanti Nagar	41	12,118	57,560
Jula Maidan	45	27,519	18,690
Dockyard Road	19	1,570	38,150
P.D. Mellow Road	117	12,864	47,500
TOTAL	556	302,212	248,170

Total Amount: Rs. 503,382

Analysis as of March 3, 1992

Table 2: Mahila Milan—HDFC* Deposits

Date	Amount Rs.
9.15.1990	5,150
4.03.1991	200
4.05.1991	200
4.10.1991	160
5.23.1991	150
7.03.1991	12,990
7.31.1991	110
8.21.1991	8,920
9.09.1991	30
10.16.1991	13,640
10.23.1991	560
11.06.1991	12,320
11.14.1991	14,700
11.27.1991	12,410
TOTAL	92,540

*HDFC: Housing Development Finance Corporation—a private financing agency.

Account Holders: 534

Women's judicious decision-making has established their credibility among not only their community

Table 3: Dharavi Mahila Milan Savings and Loan

Area (Society Name)	No. of A/C Holders	Savings Rs.	No. of Loans Disbursed	Amount Disbursed Rs.	Amount Repaid Rs.
Ashirwad Society	17	468			
Bharatiyar Society	169	5,022	3	700	
Chambra Bazar	169	26,791	15	27,672	1,430
Maharashtra Seva	30	1,839			
Rohidas Society	26	2,442			
Ro Vilas		56			
Sakinabai Chawl	30	980			
Tagore Society		453			
Vijay Nagar	5	106			
Virasavarkar Society	24	363			

Analysis as of March 31, 1992.[22]

members but also larger federations and public authorities. This has created an effective spiral in which women's capacity to undertake tasks related to community well-being is supported by the community. This, in turn, creates the space for collective introspection into women's strategic interests.

B. The empowerment approach devised by SPARC uses shelter as a focus because this is regarded as the most pressing and critical problem by pavement dwellers with whom SPARC has chosen to begin its work. However, resolution of the question of shelter is only a means to achieving the alternative vision that women have built collectively. Devising a strategy for action is a complex process, for it must be harnessed both to immediate problems and to long-term goals. In the case of pavement dwellers, their efforts to gain access to secure shelter address their immediate predicament. At the same time, these efforts lay the foundation for the fulfillment of an alternative vision.
This approach acknowledges that, having explored possible alternatives, isolated efforts at achieving them cannot bring much success. Mobilization of increasing numbers of communities is essential. Creating educational strategies to give impetus to larger and larger numbers of people to take action contributes to this end.

A number of federations of slum and pavement dwellers now have educational tools to assist communities.

1. To undertake enumerations—a process by which they create a database required for designing strategies and negotiating with the state.[21]

2. To design mechanisms of savings and credit to fulfill community members' needs for tiding over family crises, needs for loans for small businesses, and saving for shelter (see Tables 1, 2, and 3).

3. To design dwellings, construct houses, and manage basic amenities.

4. To link communities doing any of the above with those who aspire to take action through horizontal exchanges between them.

While the scope of the work that SPARC, MM, and NSDF have embarked on together has expanded, it has so far primarily involved internal reorganization of poor and deprived groups. The challenge of securing adequate shelter has now moved to a larger arena, for it is a struggle for a greater share of resources. This is related to the political economy of urban development. The struggle for secure shelter is even harder in the present context of globalization and liberalization of the Indian economy and proposed privatization of various services, for access to even basic necessities of decent living for the poor cannot be achieved without the intervention by the state in their favor.

Notes

1 Member federations are the Pavement Dwellers Federations, the Railway Slum Dwellers Federation, Dharavi Vikas Samiti, Dharavi Vyavasay Ekta Samiti, the Federation of the Airport Authority Land Dwellers. Taken together, these federations have a membership of nearly 315,000 families.

2 The following review draws extensively on an overview presented by Shirley Walters, in "Her Words on His Lips: Gender and Popular Education in South Africa," *ASPBAE Courier,* No. 52, 1991.

3 Sen, Gita, and Caren Crown: *Development, Crises and Alternative Visions.* Third World Women's Perspective Monthly Review Press, 1987.

4 Moser, Caroline: "Gender Planning in the Third World: Meeting Practical and Strategic Gender Needs," *World Development,* 1989.

5 This "tool" for analysis has been developed by Kate Young and is cited in Walters, *op. cit.*

6 Walters, *op. cit.*

7 The differentiation identified by Maxine Molyneux, referred to in Walters, *op. cit.*

8 Developed by Kate Young, referred to in Walters, *op. cit.*

9 Walters, *op. cit.*

10 Walters, *op. cit.*

11 It is estimated that 35,000 families lived on pavements.

12 See Kate Young, referred to in Walters, *op. cit.*

13 SPARC: *We, the Invisible,* Bombay, 1985.

14 The demolition of pavement dwellings in Bombay was expected to begin any time after 31st October (the end of the monsoon) that year. In a judgment rendered by the Supreme Court, the Bombay Municipal Corporation (BMC) was directed not to remove dwellings on pavements during the monsoon in order to save the residents hardships caused by being made homeless in the rain. In 1981, after the BMC attempted to evict payment dwellers after demolishing their huts, a writ petition was filed in the Supreme Court challenging this action. The Supreme Court in its judgment given in 1985 ruled that the BMC was empowered by the Bombay Municipal Corporation Act to remove encroachments, including huts from pavements.

15 What is undertaken under this training program is, no doubt, an exercise in community organization/mobilization. We call it "training" because it is a process which, once developed, can be used by other marginalized and poor groups in their struggle to achieve their goals. It is essentially a systematization of knowledge and information and designing of strategies to develop requisite skills.

16 By negotiations, we mean a debate between people holding different points of view to arrive at a consensus/agreement. Deprived groups generally do not have any experience of negotiating with authorities who allocate resources. The poor are regarded as beneficiaries for whom decisions are made. The training process provides opportunities for them to build skills to negotiate.

17 For instance, women opted for shared toilets—one toilet to be shared by four families. This was contrary to the professionals' view that each dwelling should have its independent toilet facility. Women argued that placing a toilet in the confined space of their small dwellings is not hygienic. Further, community toilets would be constructed by the authorities at their cost while internal toilets would increase considerably the dwelling cost to be borne by the occupier. Further, shared toilets would serve as a deterrent to higher-income groups buying out the poor households and dispossessing them of the dwelling.

18 Even today, no public housing scheme mentions pavement dwellers. However, the Planning Commission, Government of India, has allocated Rs. 750,000/ in 1988 for each of the four metropolitan cities in India toward setting up rehabilitation projects for pavement dwellers. This money to this day remains unutilized in Bombay because the local authority still refuses to acknowledge the presence of slum dwellers in the city, let alone allocate land for rehabilitating them.

19 Bapat, Meera, "Allocation of Urban Space: Rhetoric and Reality—Evidence from Recent Jurisprudence," Economic and Political Weekly, Vol. XXV, No. 28, 14 July 1990.

20 For example, Moser, Caroline and Sylvia Chant: *The Role of Women in the Execution of Low-Income Housing Projects Training Module,* DPU Gender and Planning Working Paper No. 6. Development Planning Unit, London, 1985.

21 See SPARC: *Beyond the Beaten Track: Resettlement Initiatives of People Who Live Along the Railway Tracks in Bombay,* 1988. Nearly 18,000 families (97,000 people) who live along railway tracks in Bombay were enumerated in conjunction with government officials. An enumeration of pavement dwellers in Madras in the state of Tamil Nadu in south India was conducted in 1989–90 to design a rehabilitation scheme for pavement dwellers.

22 Tables compiled by Meera Bapat and Sheela Patel, SPARC, Society for Promotion of Area Resource Centers, Post Box No. 9389, Bhulabhai Desai Road, Bombay 400 026, INDIA

Chapter 24
Women's Participation in the Production of Shelter

Aliye Pekin Celik

Aliye P. Celik has been working with the United Nations Centre for Human Settlements (Habitat) for the past ten years. Dr. Celik received her Bachelor of Architecture and Master of Architecture from the Middle East Technical University and Princeton University. She has a Ph.D. from Istanbul Technical University. In the UNCHS (Habitat) headquarters in Nairobi, she worked in the Research and Development Division, concentrating on building materials, construction technologies in developing countries, energy in human settlements, and women and shelter. As the focal point for women at UNCHS from 1984 to 1987, she was instrumental in the preparation of the initial work done in the area of women and shelter. She is currently in the New York office of UNCHS (Habitat).

Women represent 50% of the world's adult population and one-third of the official labor force. They perform nearly two-thirds of all working hours and receive only one-tenth of the world's income and own less than 1% of the world's property. Women's participation in formulating policies, plans, and programs related to the construction sector, as well as women's participation in decision making and managing construction programs and projects, are far from being at a satisfactory level. The construction sector is one of the areas where women's involvement is marginal. Most of the countries that had statistics on the number of women in the construction industry indicated that women's involvement in this field is below 10%. The involvement of more women in the activities of the construction sector would improve output, as well as empower women with more choices and effectiveness in mainstream development activities, creating income-generating activities.

The construction sector makes significant contributions to the socio-economic development process in developing countries, employing a large proportion of a country's labor force and helping in the improvement or acquisition of skills. The sector also stimulates other sectors through economic multiplier effects. Therefore, women's exclusion from the sector is detrimental both to the sector and to women. Women's involvement in the construction sector would increase the available skilled and semi-skilled labor force and would also result in their involvement in the construction sector activities at every stage of construction (e.g., making policy decisions, planning, design implementation, and maintenance of buildings). Women's entrepreneurial roles would contribute to the small-scale industries in the construction sector.

However, women are ill-equipped for participating in the planning, decision-making and building of human settlements, not only because they lack training and education in the sector activities themselves, but also because they do not have the kind of basic education and training that would be necessary to acquire shelter. Women in developing countries usually have two sets of handicaps in participating in the planning, decision making, and building of human settlements. They lack basic knowledge, such as literacy and mathematics, necessary for access to information about housing markets, eligibility for loans, and opportunities in community participation. Second, women lack the education and training to have an active role in the design, planning, management, operation, and construction of human settlements. The solutions are to provide basic education to women and facilitate their participation in training programs in the construction sector and to create incentives for women to be involved in the planning, design, and management of human settlements.

Women's access to employment, income, and services is directly affected by their involvement in the planning and execution of national policies, as well as women's management and participation in local government, housing, and real estate. Even in developed countries with relatively strong institutional frameworks to ensure women's advancement, women's participation in sectoral decisionmaking has been weak. Although today there is a stronger trend for women's participation in the construction sector than ever before, the weakest area is still in decision making and political decisions. Women's professional representation is low in housing cooperation and grassroots organizations. Even if women are in a clear majority as cooperative members and on committees, they tend to be underrepresented in executive positions.

Usually, there is a strong grassroots participation of women, thinning out at managerial and bureaucratic levels, in improvement of housing. The number of women entering the human settlements sector is traditionally low. Even though there is an increase in many countries, however, women continue to confront difficulties and are pushed into low-paid, low-prestige jobs. There is a tendency to steer women away from building design or decision making positions into interiors, public relations, programming, planning, public sector, and even teaching, whereas positions related to decision-making still remain with men. Men appear to hold absolute domination over administrative and managerial positions and are reluctant to entrust women with power or to promote them.

Women's Role in the Informal Construction Sector

As women are usually unable to gain high-level formal sector employment, they turn to the informal sector. The informal construction and real estate sector forms an important part of human settlements activity in most developing countries. Small-scale contractors, craftsmen, apprentices, unskilled laborers, building materials producers, building materials suppliers, real estate agents, and landlords contribute to the human settlements sector considerably. This is especially true in developing countries where about 60–70% of the urban population live as squatters and 30–50% of housing

stock is in squatters' settlements. One can see that the informal construction sector is as important and strong as the formal one. So one can see the tremendous potential that exists for women in the construction sector. The informal sector is a basis for developing an indigenous construction industry in these countries. There is an enormous potential for expanding production and opening up entrepreneurial roles for women. In some countries, such as Ghana, women play an important role as entrepreneurs, contractors, and owners of plants. Women can invest their savings in these areas, if the informal sector is supported and if such supportive action is directed equally to women and men by:

— Strengthening organizational and managerial capabilities of informal enterprises and promoting relevant skills among women;
— Providing legislative support for the strengthening or establishment of financial institutions, such as credit agencies, cooperatives and building societies, where women can participate on an equal footing with men;
— Providing credit facilities and promoting saving schemes giving equal access to women and men;
— Providing non-financial assistance through training and communications directed to both women and men;
— Promoting self-help programs which aim at facilitating women's participation at all levels; and
— Awarding subcontracts to informal-sector contractors, craftspersons, and others, and using informal-sector products, when appropriate, in government-sponsored projects.

Strengthening the informal sector would help women to get access to income-generating activities within the sector and enhance women's access to formal and informal sector jobs in other non-traditional fields. In many countries, women take an active part in construction and, in some, they help in the preparation of mud bricks and other construction materials. Though it is rare for women to get into income-generating activities, many of them are now helping to produce building materials. In Mexico, a factory assisted by the Inter-American Foundation drew two-thirds of its workforce from women. Projects in Jamaica and Brazil have trained women in metalwork and welding, to produce furnishings and equipment such as show stalls and shelving. A woman in Honduras owns and operates a floor-tile factory. Women have also been involved in the production of building blocks in several countries. In Mombasa, Kenya, women have, on their own initiative, set up a cooperative to make concrete blocks.

The entrepreneurial capacity of women involved in construction is sometimes expressed through women's groups. For instance, Ogago Usafi Women's Group in Kisii, Kenya, is a rural building group that formed in 1984 to initiate income-generating activities by growing maize and beans on rented land and by contracting out labor. Later, the group decided to start a brick-making business and, after trial and error, sent one member for training who then taught others. After 20 months, the group had made and sold about 25,000 bricks. The members have also learned how to build houses for themselves, using a team of about 20 women who volunteer their time. They have found that a house can be nearly completed in a day, if detailed preparation has been done. In their first 20 months, they constructed 66 houses. With the initiative of the Council for Human Ecology, Kenya, a women's cooperative was established to make sun-dried, cement-stabilized bricks. To this end, the Kenya Ministry of Culture and Social Services trained 60 women who started their production by using locally made equipment. The Kabiro women's group in Nairobi is having problems in their block-producing unit due to insufficient land; however, Dandorra women's group is running a profitable building-block production unit.

In Zimbabwe, the rural brick-making industry is dominated by women. This was a result of the post-independence, school-building program which required labor to be mobilized to meet the target for schools in Zimbabwe. Since women were required for the construction of buildings and were the traditional clay workers, it was obvious that they should be employed in the production of bricks. They have since continued developing this industry. Other examples of women in the production of building materials are to be found in Malawi and Mozambique. In Malawi, women have been given the opportunity to learn how to produce fiber-concrete tiles, and some women who have been involved in this scheme have expressed interest in setting up their own businesses, though this has not yet happened. In Mozambique, a series of carpentry and ceramics cooperatives, six in total, involve a large number of women in the making of clay tiles and bricks. In small-scale production units, women and even children play an important role in the production line. There is also a great potential for women to play an entrepreneurial role in building materials, owing to the low investment needed in small-scale production. The exclusion of women from the many skilled occupations in the construction sector not only discriminates against women but also is against the interests of the industry itself. There are examples of women taking positive

action to secure appropriate training and skilled positions within the construction industry. These demonstrate the potential for women in the industry throughout the world.

Women's Role in the Formal Construction Sector

Constraints that hinder women's participation in the formal labor force of the construction sector are, to a large extent, similar to those they face in other mainstream sectors. Limited access to training and education is one of the main constraints to women's involvement in the construction sector, and labor regulations are often used as an excuse for excluding women, although, in reality, women are well used to heavy manual labor, and women in developing countries often carry out hard, unskilled labor for low pay. Certainly, this is no argument against their equal participation in light, technically skilled, and well-paid artisan jobs in the sector.

In Jamaica, a training project was established to equip women to participate in the construction industry. A small-scale training and employment project, focusing on the construction industry, was designed to meet identified needs of the industry and specific job openings. At the beginning of the project, 10 women were trained, and there were commitments from contractors to place them on sites on a trial basis on completion of their training. Every woman who pursued these openings was hired. The group was then extended to 34 women from different communities, with national and international support. At the end of the course, more than 90% of the women trained had been placed in such jobs as plumbing, masonry, carpentry, electrical installation, painting, and steelwork erection. By achieving these skills, women increased their earnings, and the construction industry benefited from the skills generated. Employers were happy with the women's performance and reported reduced violence and pilferage on site and increased productivity, indicating the positive influence of women on the building sites.

The Women in Construction Advisory Group (WICAG) in the U.K. works in consultation with employers, trades unions, policymakers, and training bodies to increase jobs and training opportunities for women in craft and technical jobs. WICAG was set up in 1984 by groups working on women's employment issues, tradeswomen, women trades trainers, and trades union officials. The group felt that an independent project was required, first to examine the underrepresentation of women in craft

and technical jobs, and secondly to work with mainstream industries to bring about changes that
tradeswomen themselves have largely initiated.
WICAG provides information, resources, and advice to
employers, training agencies, education authorities,
community groups, career services, trade unions, and
women.

WICAG is contacting schools to encourage girls to take
up relevant scientific and technical subjects and to learn
manual skills. Local building colleges and employers
who take trainees from these colleges are contacted so
that "positive action" may be offered to young women to
"unlock the doors." A number of women-only training
centers, providing courses in electricity, plumbing,
plastering, bricklaying, carpentry, joinery, painting, and
decorating have been evidence of the considerable
numbers of women from all different groups who want
to learn these trades. WICAG works with employers in
the construction industry to convince them that women
can do the jobs in the industry, to discuss with them
issues of particular concern with respect to hiring
women, to explain the many indirect ways in which
existing recruitment practice discriminates on the basis
of gender and race, and to suggest "positive action" that
would increase the number of female applicants. As a
result, employers are now advising WICAG of vacancies, and some changes in recruitment practices have
already taken place.

The Non-traditional Employment for Women (NEW)
group was set up in 1979 to help poor women find
economic self-sufficiency through work in construction
and other blue collar trades. NEW trains 300 women
each year in blue-collar trades such as construction,
building maintenance, and air-conditioning. Trainees
have become sheet-metal workers, carpenters, plumbers,
ironworkers, electricians, painters, and lathe-operators,
and they work with railways, public utilities, housing
authorities, and private contractors. In NEW's twelve-
week, pre-apprenticeship course, women study mathematics, shopwork, tool usage, drawing interpretation,
and physical fitness, and they are instructed in civil
rights and legal matters so as to prepare them for any
challenges they might meet on the job. There is also a
program for high-school girls to educate them about the
range of career opportunities open to them. A special
literacy and self-sufficiency program concentrates on
low-income and single mothers. NEW maintains a
computerized job bank to help graduates find positions
on construction projects. The construction industry is
particularly prejudiced against women, and many
graduates suffer on-the-job harassment and discrimina-

tion. Nevertheless, NEW has been able to find a job for
every woman who has graduated.

A training program for Caribbean women in non-
traditional skills was launched to provide an orientation
for women in plumbing, refrigeration, and electrical
installation that would allow them to assess whether
they wanted to pursue long-term training in those areas.
Eighteen young women between the ages of 18 and 25
participated: 14 from Grenada and 4 from Dominica
and Saint Vincent. After the assessment, a special two-
year accelerated program was planned for the Grenada
participants, most of whom did not have the initial
academic qualifications to enter the regular program at
the Grenada Technical and Vocational Institute (GTVI).
They did, however, have the potential to complete the
entire technical training, and graduates will receive the
normal GTVI diploma. Programs for women in non-
traditional fields are being started in other Caribbean
countries and are benefiting from direct contact with the
Grenada program. In Dominica, participants are being
helped to undertake apprenticeship programs that will
qualify them to enter the technical college if they wish.

Increasing Women's Participation in the Construction Sector

There are also many successful projects helping women
to get access to housing. Technical cooperation projects
undertaken by UNCHS (Habitat) often contain components assisting women, training components involving
women, and women as active participants and often
counterparts. An example is the low-income housing
project in Zimbabwe which consists of two pilot projects
in KweKwe and Gutu. These pilot projects are being
jointly implemented by the communities and the local
authorities in the two respective urban and rural areas,
together with the Ministry of Construction and National
Housing of Zimbabwe, with technical assistance from
the United Nations Development Programme and
UNCHS (Habitat) and capital cost funding from the
United States Agency for International Development
and the Beverly Building Society. One of the immediate
objectives of these projects is to test and monitor new
methods of organization in aided, self-help cooperative
and communal efforts, including building teams which
enable the beneficiaries to be involved closely in the
achievement of their own housing solutions. Women in
these projects gained experience in community participation, learned how to set up and manage credit facilities, participated in the design and construction of their
homes, and availed themselves of employment opportunities in and around the project areas. The value of

women's initiative was shown further in their setting up of a women-headed housing cooperative. Further, women built the houses more speedily than men, who found time to build only when off duty and on weekends (women household heads often took advantage of the building teams to construct their homes).

Women, either as household heads or as part of a family, formed significant target groups. In these pilot projects, housing allocation criteria were designed to consider heads of household regardless of sex. In these projects, 36% (Gutu) and 20% (KweKwe) are women household heads (separated, divorced, deserted, widowed, and single). All are either wage earners or self-employed and support their families with very meager earnings. The pilot projects clearly demonstrate that, with appropriate training and information programs, women heads of household and female spouses can contribute significantly toward successful housing project implementation and management. After the selection and verification of the project's beneficiaries, one-day weekend workshops on the housing process were organized both in KweKwe and Gutu for groups of 50 families each (these workshops were used to highlight such topics as community participation, house designs, construction methods, building materials stores, administrative structures, and financial arrangements). In most cases, the majority of workshop participants were women who not only took an active part in the workshop but also demonstrated their concern for adequate shelter for their families. They voiced doubts and raised questions of interest to them (e.g., concerning loan repayment through a building society). Some of the women showed community leadership qualities and later became prime movers in aided, self-help, and cooperative modes of construction.

Women also played a significant role in the planning, design, and construction of homes. After being allocated plots, they were helped to choose their house plans from among the alternatives available or to design plans of their own. They proposed changes and amendments to suit the circumstances of their families. The project's beneficiaries were provided with a choice of the method of construction either through aided self-help, housing cooperatives, or building brigades. The majority of women heads of household chose the aided, self-help method. Thirteen of them, together with one male household head, formed the first housing cooperative in Gutu, the Masimba Evanhu Housing Cooperative. It has a woman chairperson who took the leadership role to mobilize the group. Most of the members are self-employed vegetable sellers in the nearby market ,and

one of them is a 70-year-old widow who now has her first house in Gutu. As of January, 1985, they had completed eight houses, with others at various stages of construction. The actual work is done by labor which they hire and supervise, each contributing Z$10 each month to the cooperative.

Regardless of the mode of construction, project beneficiaries were given loans in the form of building materials from a central stores building on the site. Since the stores operated seven days a week, the women heads of household and spouses played a major role in the procurement and delivery of materials to their plots. It was a common sight to see women with their babies carried on their backs transporting materials in wheelbarrows, in the tractor/trailers provided by the project, or by hand. Women also took on responsibility in supervising and managing the construction of their houses. When men were employed elsewhere, the women would do the work themselves. During weekends, construction became a family responsibility, with men, women and children living and eating in a temporary shelter while their homes were being built.

Not only were women involved directly and indirectly in the day-to-day construction, management, and maintenance of their houses, they were also employed in various income-generating activities both within and outside the settlements. Women who were actively involved in the construction of houses (mixing concrete and laying the blocks, for instance) acquired new skills from the project. They in turn were hired by other aided, self-help builders and thus supplemented their incomes. The project also offered on-the-job training for two women who did their final field assignments as potential social workers there. Among the project staff are a female development officer and a woman architect. This has been a satisfactory example of the involvement of women in UNCHS (Habitat) technical cooperation projects, many of which deal in part with the integration of women in human settlements development, taking into account their needs and upgrading and making use of their skills. The project showed women participating at different stages in the provision of shelter in different capacities without any additional cost to the project, proving that involvement of women in human settlements development can be an organizational issue rather than a financial one.

In Zimbabwe, the women could choose among different types of construction possibilities (aided self-help, building brigades, etc.). In some cases, only possibilities of aided self-help are considered for women, as in

Panama. The Women's Self-Help Construction Project (WSHOP) of Panama had the goal of constructing 100 houses in San Miguelito, a neighborhood adjacent to Panama City. The project was to be built entirely by women living in slums who had no experience in construction. Fifty houses were completed in 1982. Women had low incomes, low education levels, and high unemployment rates. Forty-five percent of women were heads of households. Short-term training courses for masonry, plumbing, and carpentry were organized. The project supervision and the materials for construction of the houses were provided. Among those households in the project, 45% were headed by women, 35% by men, and 20% by women and men jointly. In households headed by women, 41% of women were not working, 33% were community workers, and the rest were involved in several jobs. The women could cope with the construction work with the help of other members of the family; usually the older children help in domestic activities. The project contributed to the construction skills in the community, although none of the women used their skills again. Living conditions improved, as did commitment to a better neighborhood. However, it is questionable whether such a project should have been carried out only by women versus providing complete equality with men, with emphasis on women's problems. Time was spent on acquiring construction skills that were not used again. Providing training in construction skills would be more useful if that led to continuous income. The training prepared the women to expand their houses and take care of the units, to organize a construction cooperative, and to work as independent contractors on small construction jobs. Only those women who specialized in plumbing and carpentry were interested in applying their skills to generate income in cooperatives or as independent contractors. Women trained in masonry found construction work tiring.

In the traditional societies of Africa, women play a very important role in constructing buildings, e.g., in Dagombas, Mambrusis, and Konkombas in Ghana. Women begin building after celebrating the usual ritual on the chosen site by weeding and sweeping the ground and watering it. After the men complete the walls and roof construction, women plaster in and outside of the buildings, lay and beat the floor, and apply decorative finishes to the walls in the form of incised patterns. In Ghana, women have developed high artistic skills in decorating finished walls. These examples show that women are very successful in the construction sector. The problem is that usually they are not allowed to be involved in jobs requiring any skills. But when they are involved in jobs requiring skills, they have a very high performance.

Women's access to the construction sector can be achieved through the promotion of women's cooperatives and providing means of finance to women in human settlements activities. Making a special effort to incorporate women is the key issue for women's access to housing and their involvement in the construction sector. Access to credit is important and usually difficult for women to obtain, whether they live in rural or urban areas. Self-help programs through cooperatives and similar thrift institutions are worth supporting by the public sector, but usually are not adequate to meet the demand. Private lending institutions, public information campaigns, and guaranteed loans could be needed. Facilitating access to credit involves adding flexibility to the criteria used to make decisions about credit, and removing some of the arbitrary legal/institutional discriminatory barriers to approving credits to women who head households. Innovative approaches to keeping the cost of credit affordable, thus increasing the probability of cost recovery for the creditor and decreasing the chance of default for the person receiving the loan, are needed.

Cooperative banks geared to women's needs can be one solution for solving women's housing problems, providing institutional infrastructure to commercial banks. They participate in serving the self-employed, providing custody of the cash women receive as loans, aiding in promoting individual and cooperative purchasing, processing and marketing, managing women's savings and the repayment of loans, conducting training programs in the banking habit, and providing social security to members in housing.

Collaboration is needed among researchers, women's organizations, and NGOs in a plan of action concerning women and shelter construction, including: campaigns for changes in social attitudes and public policy, development of technical courses in building for women, promotion of self-help, low-income housing schemes that include infrastructural support, and recognition of the need for full participation of women. Programs should focus on women's interest in entering non-traditional fields and should initiate training programs, keeping in mind lessons learned from others' experiences.

1. The market should be assessed for the need or local demand for certain skills and potential job opportunities.

2. Adequate time should be allowed for pre-planning and preparation to clarify objectives and assess available human and material resources.

3. Thorough screening of participants, taking into account their level of education and paying attention to upgrading female trainees' competence in mathematics and basic science skills to ensure that they are not at a disadvantage compared to their male counterparts.

4. Begin with an orientation program for potential trainees to help them understand what will be expected of them during the training program.

5. Sensitize tutors to the situation/needs and learning styles of women trainees, as well as the interrelatedness of the various skills being taught.

6. In addition to basic theory, include appropriate tools for "hands-on" experience, as well as a personal development component to foster self-confidence and group cohesion and to cope with attitudes that trainees are likely to face in society.

7. Pay particular attention to the needs of trainees who have children, so that their participation is not constrained by their domestic responsibilities.

8. Ensure that the program design includes exposure to role models of local tradeswomen, as well as audio-visual presentations by women working in different fields in the region.

9. Contact governmental and private agencies to get their commitment for apprenticeship and job opportunities for trainees.

10. Document the training experience, particularly the factors that promote or inhibit women's participation, and disseminate to authorities and other groups interested in promoting such programs.

Governments should take measures to incorporate women in general adult education programs; specific classes for women's groups in locations accessible to them with child-care facilities, as needed, would be appropriate. NGOs and community groups should pressure authorities to look at the needs of poor women, promote cooperatives or building groups based on existing communities, and promote building materials, products, and industries based on local natural resources.

International Seminars on Women and Shelter

Since the World Conference on Women in 1985, the United Nations Center for Human Settlements (Habitat), which has always placed housing policies and programs in the context of national development plans, has been actively engaged in the promotion of women both as beneficiaries and as agents of change in the area of

human settlements. One of the Center's first follow-up activities after the World Conference was an international seminar on women and shelter, organized jointly by the Center for Social Development and Humanitarian Affairs/Division for the Advancement of Women and the United Nations Center for Human Settlements (Habitat). That Seminar, held in December, 1985, in Vienna, brought together representatives of governmental and non-governmental organizations for women from many countries of the world.

The purpose of the Seminar was to familiarize women's organizations with key issues of settlements management. It was felt that, through familiarization with mainstream development issues, women's organizations could formulate proposals related to them for inclusion in a national agenda for action. At the end of the Seminar, the participants had an increased appreciation of the broad scope of settlements, but felt that, to achieve the greatest impact, it was not enough for women's organizations alone to be made aware of the issues; policy-makers in the settlements sector also had to be familiar with women's perspectives on housing and residential environments. It was stressed that only through joint collaborative efforts could realistic and practical national plans of action evolve. The Commission on Human Settlements, at its ninth session in 1986, recommended regional or subregional seminars to exchange experiences on pilot projects and to define and evaluate the role of women and the organizations that represent them. As a result, work intensified to promote the role of women in the management of settlements. In addition to the resources of the United Nations Center for Human Settlements (Habitat), funding required for regional seminars was received from the Governments of The Netherlands and of Norway. The following regional and subregional seminars were organized by the Center and the respective host countries in 1988 and 1989:

1. Asia and the Pacific: 24–29 February 1988 in Indonesia;
2. French-speaking African countries: 28 March–1 April 1988 in Tunisia;
3. Caribbean countries: 6–10 June 1988 in Saint Vincent and the Grenadines;
4. English-speaking African countries: 31 October–4 November 1988 in Zambia; and
5. Latin American countries: 27–31 March 1989 in Argentina.

The participants, who were drawn from governmental and non-governmental organizations as well as from donor agencies, were all involved in human settlements activities, particularly those concerning women. The objectives of the seminars were:

1. To provide policy and procedural guidance to high-level policymakers in such ministries as housing, public works, and industry on the incorporation of women's concerns in their programs;

2. To provide technical information to representatives of governmental and non-governmental organizations on means of ensuring the effective participation of women in human settlements development and management, with particular emphasis on community participation;

3. To facilitate the identification of special problems concerning the participation of women in settlements development and management;

4. To enhance communication and cooperation between institutions dealing with issues concerning women and those dealing with mainstream sectoral development issues;

5. To create a readiness in institutions to support policies, programs, and projects to mobilize the participation of women in the development and upgrading of settlements;

6. To discuss the effectiveness of different communication and information technologies in promoting gender awareness in the formulation, implementation, and evaluation of policies, programs, and projects; and

7. To develop national advocacy strategies for the continuous promotion of the involvement of women in the development and management of settlements.

The following key issues were deliberated upon at each regional seminar:

1. The role of women in the formulation and implementation of housing policies;
2. Women and land;
3. The participation of women in housing finance;
4. The participation of women in the construction sector;
5. The participation of women in shelter projects;
6. Women, water and sanitation;
7. Community participation as a means of enhancing the role of women in the development and management of settlements; and
8. Communications and information as instruments to enhance the participation of women in the development and management of settlements.

The Interregional Seminar to Promote the Full Participation of Women in all phases of the Global Strategy for Shelter to the Year 2000 was convened to give further impetus to the process begun by the earlier series of seminars. The participants (governmental and non-

governmental), observers, resource personnel, and donors were drawn from each of the five earlier seminars. The Seminar built on regional experiences to develop a plan of action for the continuation of the process which the United Nations Center for Human Settlements (Habitat) had initiated, intended to achieve the following long-term development objectives:

1. To involve women at all levels of the planning and implementation of human settlements policies and programs; and

2. To improve the residential/work environment of women, especially urban and rural low-income women, their families, and communities.

Conclusion and Recommendations

The women in the human settlements development program are now taking a new form with the support of Danida, Global Training Program for Community Participation in Improving Human Settlements, and Strengthening Community Participation in the Development and Operation of Facilities and Services. Both these programs actively support the mainstreaming of women and gender issues. Therefore, emphasis has been given to women's participation and a gender-aware attitude in their activities. The joint FINNIDA/UNCHS project for the planning, implementation, monitoring and evaluation of the national shelter strategy in Uganda is also aware of the need to support the empowerment of women and has specifically asked a consultant to pinpoint women's particular interests and needs so as to include them in the elaboration of the strategy.

UNCHS (Habitat) has a program in the pipeline, entitled Training and Capacity-Building for Women's Groups in Shelter and Shelter-Related Services. A collective effort with UNIFEM, it will be in Indonesia and in Sri Lanka. UNCHS (Habitat) activities and outputs planned for 1992 include:

1. A poster on women, human settlements, and sustainable habitats for International Women's Day on 8 March 1992;
2. A flyer, "Why focus on women?"
3. A video on gender-aware, community-oriented, and environmentally sound approaches to human settlements development;
4. An *ad hoc* Expert Group Meeting on progress achieved to date on women's full participation in the Global Strategy for Shelter (in Africa);
5. A workshop on women and sustainable habitats (in Latin America); and

6. A workshop on regional policy and consultation and gender awareness (in Asia).

We can summarize the approach by saying that women should participate in decision making and in management of construction programs. Training must take account of women's special needs to facilitate their full participation in building work. Women should be encouraged to be involved in income-generating activities in the informal construction sector either as entrepreneurs, contractors, or building materials producers. Appropriate technologies that would promote the fullest and most economic development of local resources of material and labor within overall development objectives should be used, incorporating women in their application and serving women. Building standards should be based on minimum health and safety requirements with particular reference to needs of women and children; standard designs and construction manuals should be elaborated, keeping in view the requirements of women.

References

Celik, Aliye Pekin, Women and Human Settlements, 20–21 September 1992, International Symposium on "Women, the Working Environment and Sustainable Development in the Urban Communities," City University of New York, New York.

Celik, Aliye Pekin, Women and Construction Technology, 9–20 December 1985, Women and Shelter U.N. Advisory Service Seminar, UNCSHA, UNCHS, Vienna.

Case Study of Women Blockmakers in Kenya, 1988, United Nations Centre for Human Settlements, Nairobi.

Low-Income Housing Pilot Projects, Zimbabwe, 1986, UNCHS (Habitat) Technical Cooperation Monograph, Nairobi.

Schreckenbach, M. Abankwa, J., 1982, *Construction Technology for a Tropical Developing Country,* GTZ.

Towards a Strategy for the Full Participation of Women in All Phases of the U.N. Global Shelter Strategy to the Year 2000, 1990, UNCHS (Habitat), Nairobi, pages 14–16.

Women in Human Settlements Development and Management, United Nations Centre for Human Settlements (Habitat), Tilden Communications Ltd., pages 51–57.

Women and Shelter, 1985, JUNIC/NGO Program on Women, Vienna, pages 1–19.

Chapter 25
Community Planning in Developing Nations: Land Use Planning, User Participation, and Appropriate Technologies

Ann H. May and David K. May

Ann H. May is an assistant professor of Landscape Architecture in the Department of Architecture and Landscape Architecture at North Dakota State University. She has a Master of Landscape Architecture from the University of Michigan, Ann Arbor. She joined the United States Peace Corps in 1988 and was assigned to Jamaica, West Indies, where she worked with a multiplicity of groups as a design professional. She has eight years of professional work experience as a landscape architect in a number of offices throughout the country.

David K. May is an assistant professor of Landscape Architecture in the Department of Architecture and Landscape Architecture at North Dakota State University. He has a Master of Landscape Architecture from the University of Massachusetts, Amherst, with an emphasis on land use planning. He joined the United States Peace Corps in 1988 and was assigned to Jamaica, West Indies, where he worked with a variety of groups providing design and planning expertise. In addition to his Master of Landscape Architecture, he has a Bachelor of Science in Psychology with an emphasis in environmental psychology.

Often, there is a basic misunderstanding of what the real housing needs are, as perceived by the designer and, therefore basic assumptions fail to provide adequately for the individual's wants and desires. When dealing with the needs of those who live in the Third World, there is frequently an arrogance associated with the "helper" towards the "helpee." A corollary to this is an attitude that says, "I know what is best for you," often exhibited by designers as well. Many times, the techniques proposed by aid givers are not within the economic means of those they are intended to protect or help. This reflects a lack of understanding on the part of the "helper," resulting not only in the use of unsuitable materials but also relying on inappropriate technologies.

We will use the community of Highlite View, a squatters' settlement in the hills above Kingston, Jamaica, to explore the issues of user involvement in housing design, appropriate technologies and materials, and community planning. Many of its residents are single mothers faced with raising a family and receiving very little outside help. An interesting phenomenon took place here, one in which the women assumed the role of community leaders in a male-dominated society, and have become the driving force behind the decision-making process. The situation at Highlite View emphasizes the need for First World countries, when offering assistance, to develop appropriate building technologies that are sympathetic to the vernacular architecture of the area. In this case, a mother and her children needed to be able to assist in the construction of the dwelling and to undertake the periodic maintenance with minimal assistance from others. Our involvement in this project has provided us with a rare insight into this predicament.

Designer Biases

When discussing the issue of adequate housing, it is imperative to understand the needs of those who will be the eventual residents, whether in this country or a Third World nation. Many contemporary designers come from a middle- to upper middle-class background. As a result, their aspirations, perceived needs, and desires are often much different from those of a single mother who is trying to provide for her children. Added to this socioeconomic disparity is the fact that, historically, most designers have been white and male, resulting in yet another barrier to understanding the needs of those for whom they are designing, the ultimate user. The designer bias problem experienced in Jamaica, discussed later in this paper, was not due solely to cultural differences between countries. Within the United States, nowhere is this difference in backgrounds and

208   Shelter, Women, and Development

designer bias better exemplified than in the design of inner-city housing and parks. The public housing projects which had to be demolished at Pruitt-Igo are a well-known example of a complete lack of understanding on the part of the designers of the needs and living situation of those for whom they are supposedly designing living spaces.

A further example of this chasm between the designer's beliefs and those of the true client, the resident, is best portrayed by the history of an urban park designed by a group of white, upper middle-class suburbanites for an inner-city neighborhood. Given the success of the exploratory playgrounds found in their suburban communities during the late 70s, the designers decided, without input from the "real client," that this type of park would be the most appropriate solution. Sadly, the inner-city residents perceived the final product as a reflection of their own plight. Many of the elements used to construct the playground were recycled materials, i.e., tires, barrels, large timbers, etc., which the community equated with junk. These same types of elements were already prevalent in their neighborhood, (i.e., abandoned automobiles, remnants of buildings, etc.). In the end, someone burned the playground to the ground. These two examples serve to stress the necessity of the designer fully to understand the needs and desires of the TRUE clients, the final user, not some domineering public agency.

Global Housing Issues

A critical problem facing many nations today is that of meeting the need for new housing. It has been estimated that the demand for additional housing, worldwide, would necessitate the construction of 53,000 new houses per day to bridge the gap between supply and demand (Hamdi, 1991, p. 4). This situation has far-reaching implications for many countries, given the fact that to provide conventional, formal sector housing on this scale would consume 25–50% of the gross national product of most countries in the world today. To meet this continuing demand, new methods for providing affordable, adequate housing need to be developed. An integral part of this process entails defining not only the needs of the population but determining minimum building standards for the different regions of the world experiencing increased growth.

The Case of Jamaica

To explore these issues, we will relate the situations we encountered while serving in Jamaica in the U.S. Peace Corps. Both physically and culturally, Jamaica is a very different place from that which is portrayed in the American tourist brochures. This is a society in which there is a huge disparity between the many poor and the few very wealthy. Beyond the well-known beaches, in the mountainous countryside, many people live in wood and zinc shacks and children carry their shoes to school so they don't ruin their only pair. It is a culture in which many families are headed by a single mother, women who must provide for all the needs of their family.

Jamaica is an island located in the Caribbean basin with a land mass of approximately 4,244 square miles, an area slightly smaller that the state of Connecticut. This is a country with a diverse population of 2.2 million people whose ethnic backgrounds include European, Middle Eastern, Chinese, and East Indian, but of whom the majority come from African ancestry. This diverse background is best expressed in the national motto "Out of many, one people." As in this country, there is a disproportionate number of blacks who occupy the lower socioeconomic classes, and a well-defined class system aligned with or seemingly based on ethnicity. Many single mothers in Jamaica are from an African heritage.

The physical character of the island consists primarily of a mountainous terrain, half of which lies at or above 1,000 ft. above sea level. There are more than 100 hundred rivers and streams flowing from the mountains, carving their way through the plains and finally into the ocean. As a result of serious deforestation across the island, the fisheries just off the coast have been seriously damaged due to the increased sediment transported by the rivers. The Jamaican Agricultural Ministry estimates that throughout the island areas that have been cleared, either for agriculture or settlements, lose approximately five tons of top soil/acre/hour/inch of rain (May, 1988). Evidence of this claim can be found whenever it rains in the "rivers of mud" that flow from the mountainsides.

One of Jamaica's most hospitable natural characteristics is its climate, a climate very forgiving to the homeless and those with substandard housing. Temperatures range from the 80s to the 90s throughout the year. The rainy seasons (of which there are two, May-June and September-October) are the most destructive times of the year for land that is cleared. As discussed previously, erosion is a very serious problem facing this nation, resulting in very complex planning issues which will be discussed shortly. Furthermore, due to the rainy season, there is a greater need for satisfactory housing because of the dampness which causes increased illnesses.

In the sixteenth century, when Europeans discovered the island, they found a peaceful and healthy native population, that of the Arawak Indians, who numbered over 100,000 people. In less than a century, the new inhabitants from Europe managed to decimate the Arawak nation completely. This genocide was the result of both the introduction of disease and the hunting of the Arawaks for sport. During the next 400 years, the Europeans took the most productive and flatter lands for the development of plantations to grow sugar cane, bananas, and coconut. The attitudes of these "absentee landlords," who never had any intention of settling on the island permanently, set a precedent that would shape future attitudes toward the island's natural resources. In addition, since the European land barons confiscated all of the most productive lands, the other inhabitants of the island, mostly slaves from Africa, and indentured labor from India and China, were left with the marginal areas that should never have been cleared or developed for subsistence farming. When slavery was abolished in the year 1834, many of the emancipated slaves moved into the mountain areas and set up small farms. The vast majority of present-day Jamaicans are descendants of slaves who worked for the British land owners.

Current Land Use Concerns

This historic pattern of land ownership has led to the current situation in which a very small number of people own over three-fourths of the most productive lands in the country, again, leaving only the marginal areas for the majority of the population on which to eke out an existence. The land ownership patterns are the result of the deeding of properties before Jamaica obtained its independence from Britain in 1962. Less than one hundred years ago, Jamaica was still an island paradise, with dense forests covering the mountainsides. In recent years, large areas of mountainside have become barren slopes due to deforestation and the ensuing erosion. Concern has been raised that Jamaica could follow the same disastrous path that Haiti has taken, the result of which is that there are now large areas of desert unable to support plant life. Haiti's experience is the direct result of deforestation—"in order to survive people have cut down 91% of the island's trees" (Callwood, 1988). The resulting erosion depleted the topsoil over much of the island so that large areas can no longer support plant life.

Socioeconomic Conditions

As of 1988, the average Jamaican family, many headed by a single mother, consisted of 4-5 people. Sadly, there is a current trend where the father of the children will leave the family to fend for itself, creating a poverty class of young, single mothers or grandmothers with small children. Often, a grandmother will raise the grandchildren while the mother is away at work, either on another part of the island or in another country. This has resulted in a situation not dissimilar to conditions we find in many large cities in this country today. These women often find themselves living in substandard and unsafe housing. This socioeconomic group is often not represented in the political arena nor does it participate in funded programs sponsored by countries such as the U.S., Canada, or Great Britain.

Currently, there is a great deal of pressure on both public and private land by the disenfranchised, those who can neither afford to own or rent a dwelling place, where whole communities of people have been drawn together by the common thread of homelessness. Frequently, these people will erect a shack on government or unattended private land, and if they live there for seven or more years, it is very difficult to evict them legally. In 1989, the ruling government was at odds with itself about how to react to squatters using public property, and turned a blind eye to the situation. Usually, the people inhabiting these settlements are the working poor, those holding jobs in places like Kingston or one of the resort communities but unable to afford the high rent demanded by the landlords in these areas. In addition, the ownership of land is highly prized and a sign of status; therefore, Jamaicans will go to great pains to procure a site for a dwelling. The pressures on squatters' land are great. Besides using the land for their housing, many families must raise some type of crop to supplement their income. It has been found that it takes approximately one-quarter acre of land to sustain one family (May, 1988). But this agricultural use also contributes to the erosion problems facing the island today.

Minimum Building Standards

In Jamaica, as is happening in many Third World countries, there is a dramatic move from the rural areas to the urban centers. As a result, there is increasing pressure on existing housing, creating a need for new development. In many communities around the world, the use of a "quick fix," deliberate construction of substandard housing, is really only creating a future slum, defeating the basic purpose of housing. Minimum standards must be adhered to at all costs to avoid or these future slums (Payne,1977, p. 65). Building codes and design restrictions in many Third World countries are rarely geared toward the needs and available resources of either the builder or the eventual inhabitant. They generally tend to emulate those standards found in more affluent countries (Payne, 1977, p. 201). For example, the "requirements in a New Delhi low-income housing competition stipulated separate bathrooms and W.C.'s, something that is not even required in official housing in Great Britain" (Payne, 1977, p. 202). This typifies the lack of understanding on the part of the designer of the needs of the eventual user.

A number of case studies in Third World communities have explored the notion of soliciting advice from the residents in the slum areas during the early phases of urban housing programs and have come to the same conclusion that including the poor in the decision-making process greatly increases the potential for success. Geoffrey Payne, in his study of the Rouse Avenue settlement in New Delhi, India, found that the vast majority of the residents interviewed to be quite capable of developing or planning their living environment. This finding supplants the notion that the "designer knows best" and reinforces the concept of self-help or user involvement in the determination of one's own destiny.

New Concerns

Day Care

Problems are beginning to appear in Third World countries similar to those that developed nations have been grappling with for years. For example, with the disintegration of the extended family, there is a greater need for some type of day-care system in many developing nations today. Third World countries are just now trying to deal with this issue, which, sadly, the U.S. has yet to resolve: the need for an equitable national day-care program that provides for the needs of all families, not just the upper middle class.

Security

Security in one's home, as well as in the public spaces, has become an increasingly more urgent issue in many cities worldwide. Many Third World countries are now facing rising crime rates and increased drug use that is

changing the social fabric and character of these societies. In the U.S., when middle-class neighborhoods begin to deteriorate, the residents either move further out into the suburbs or fortify their homes with security systems. This is a luxury that few residents in developing nations can afford. What is the appropriate response by the designer to these phenomena? Many Jamaicans live with the fear that their unsecured homes are easy prey for thieves. It is not uncommon for robbers to cut through the walls of a stick frame structure with a saw to gain access. As a result, the housing type of choice is a concrete-block structure with iron bar grates covering all windows and doors.

Appropriate Technology

Many developing countries face the problem of inappropriate technology; that is, when countries such as the U.S. offer assistance, it is often in a form which the host country is unable to use. Furthermore, as Payne notes:

> Recent developments in this field [housing] now make it unnecessary (and undesirable) to continue applying capital intensive, inappropriate, and expensive techniques in the field of housing construction. Such technologies are not only beyond the resources of most developing countries but frequently represent a source of environmental pollution and a high degree of energy waste. (Payne, 1977, p. 205)

As a result, these projects are doomed to failure even before they are implemented.

The following case studies epitomize this notion that designers and aid organizations are often misguided in their assumptions concerning their client. The first was a program sponsored by both the U.S. and Canadian governments to help residents in the Caribbean Basin make their homes more hurricane-proof. The program was entitled "GO STRAPLESS TODAY, TOPLESS TOMORROW" and the solution, according to the building consultants who studied the problem, was to install galvanized metal straps tying the roof joists to the top plate. The problem with this strategy was that the recommended piece of hardware (wood connectors) such as joist hangers or hurricane anchors (twist straps) cost $.89 to $1.50 in this country, an acceptable cost in any building construction. However, in Jamaica the same hardware would result in great financial hardship to the average home owner, given the cost of living and the average rate of pay.

Attempts to find other more appropriate solutions included the use of tin snips to cut the straps from any available metal, e.g., sheets of zinc-plated metal used for roofing. Here again, the dilemma was ready access to the required tools. A pair of tin snips necessary to cut the heavier metals would cost up to $100 Jamaican, totally out of the question for the average family. Eventually, it was found that a can, such as for vegetables, could be torn open and used as a pseudo hurricane strap, a technique more in line with the economy and technology of the country. This solution is an example of the approach Ortega *et al.* suggested, that of "exploiting whatever resources are at hand and applying basic ingenuity to exploiting their potential" (Payne, 1977, p. 205). Ortega's notion should be the basis for problem solving in most, if not all, design or planning situations, since it implies that the most appropriate solutions should employ the proper technologies and techniques for any given circumstance.

After Hurricane Gilbert: Aid with Conditions

As previously discussed, designer bias is an insidious threat to the design process, often resulting in failure of a project. This need to exert control often accompanies offers of aid as well. Historically, those giving aid to Jamaica have imposed conditions that disregarded the needs and desires of the people. Theirs is a history of having been coerced into embracing First World ideas regarding their way of life, from the crops they should grow to building types they should use to the method by which they should run their schools.

Hurricane Gilbert swept over the island on the morning of September 12, 1988. This was the strongest hurricane ever recorded in the Northern Hemisphere. It caused a catastrophe of monumental proportions, resulting in severe damage throughout the island, washing out many of the roads and destroying large numbers of buildings. There was an outpouring of international aid, but much of it came with conditions attached. For instance, a Canadian philanthropist hired an architect to design replacement housing for the people devastated by the storm. This designer, who was trained and lived in a very different climate, culture, and socioeconomic situation, was expected to develop the most appropriate housing type for a foreign situation. A prevailing attitude among the "helpers" or aid-givers was that "any housing was better than none"; "I will help them," an attitude that does not recognize the needs, desires, or rights of the recipient. Based on the architect's design, the philanthropist arranged for donated building materials to be sent to Jamaica. He then offered to help rebuild the community, but the design decided upon was a stick frame structure clad with fir siding (over stock and

seconds) donated by a wood products firm. The problem? As mentioned earlier, security is a major concern and this type of building is easily broken into by cutting through the wood siding with a simple hand saw. Furthermore, the preferred building type (concrete block) is able to sustain the impact of a hurricane with less damage, making it more suitable for the climate. The residents expressed their concern to the philanthropist, concerns that were echoed by volunteers who had been working on the island for sometime. The philanthropist became incensed at the notion that his design was inappropriate for these conditions, proclaimed that he would not change his plans, and then took his aid elsewhere.

A Squatter's Community in Jamaica

We will use the experiences of Highlite View, a squatters' community outside Kingston, Jamaica, as a vehicle to explore the issues associated with housing and planning. Many people living in Jamaica are so poor that not only is owning land or a house out of the question, but they cannot even afford to rent a home. As a result, there is a growing trend toward squatter settlements. As mentioned earlier, if an individual has lived on a piece of land for more than seven years, it is very difficult ever to evict him or her from either private or public property. Many of these communities have a disproportionate number of single mothers, resulting in a new set of needs associated with this type of development. These developments need to deal with many of the same issues that are confronting communities throughout this country, such as affordable, safe day-care and secure housing. Something atypical is happening here; the women are taking control of the planning and decision-making process, a role traditionally reserved for the male leaders of the community. A small core of women, assisted by a British community development person, is taking responsibility for making the decisions that affect their community. They confronted a number of potentials and problems. A cornerstone of the community was to be a community center that would include:

Day-Care Facility

Many of the single mothers must commute to various areas in Kingston and often have no one with whom to leave their children. As a result, there was a great need for a community day-care center where several of the mothers who do not work in the city could take care of the children who live in the community.

Concrete Block Production

An area needed to be set aside for the production of concrete blocks used to construct new housing in the community. As mentioned earlier, the most secure homes are made of block, and since many of these women commute to work, their homes were easy prey for thieves. In addition, the blocks' price made their purchase from local manufacturers out of the question.

As an aside, we would like to point out that the traditional building technique employed in these types of settlements was wattle. This technique involves the use of poles or sticks interwoven with slender vines or branches. Stones are then worked into the weave. Finally, multiple layers of concrete are applied to create an exterior surface. The stones worked into the wall provided additional security from both intruders and the elements. Sadly, this type of structure is no longer prevalent due to the stigma associated with it, since it was widely used by the poor and the fact that only a few of the older men left in the country still know how to do it.

Biogas (Methane Gas) Production Facility

There was an interest in developing a biogas facility with a 4,000 gallon tank for storage. It was to be constructed of a wire mold frame and then rendered with a thin wall of cement and used to produce biogas (methane gas), derived from manure, to provide a ready fuel supply for cooking. It was believed that the proceeds from the gas could be used to supplement their incomes.

Community Tree Nursery

Several of the community leaders wanted to develop a tree nursery to grow fruit-producing trees to be planted throughout the immediate area to supplement their diets. This involvement in the planning process is an important departure from historical attitudes which fostered a dependency on aid from other countries, not only money, but also advice and decisions. A prevailing attitude has developed in Jamaica over the years that stresses the need for aid in order to help oneself, emphasizing participation, not dependency. These women believed that they could and should take a responsible role in planning their futures. This is an uphill battle in a male-dominated society where women are not typically allowed access to the resources necessary to complete such projects.

This male dominance prevails throughout all levels of the society. For example, after Hurricane Gilbert, many homes were destroyed in a mountain community northeast of Kingston. One project involved the rebuilding of houses for the elderly and infirm with funds from foreign aid organizations. In one instance, an elderly woman in her 80's, known as Auntie, lived in a zinc structure in very poor condition. She was practically bed-ridden and had a number of health problems, including a severe case of diabetes resulting in very poor vision. Her home, for all intents and purposes, was destroyed during the hurricane. When locals tried to build a new block house for Auntie, her son, who lived in Kingston, flatly refused. Furthermore, he had no intention of improving her living condition, claiming other commitments necessitated his attention. He was simply too busy to help and did not want anyone else to help her either. The reason for this was rooted in male pride and by the prevailing traditional attitudes "that it was up to the men of the society to make this kind of decision and take care the women." It must be noted that the offer of help came not from outsiders but rather, from locals of the community who wanted to help. Unknown to him, only the funding was to come from outside sources. This is another example of an injustice against women by society. The root of the problem in this case was not designer attitudes but an underlying collective male ego exerting control over the destiny of women.

Planning Problems at Highlite View

Soil erosion was another serious problem facing this community. The prevailing mentality in this society is "cleared land is good land" and that included the area around one's house. The problem is that cleared land has nothing to hold the soil in place and, as mentioned previously, this creates a serious erosion problem. The immediate hazard to Highlite View was that of mud slides, which threatened many of the homes already built on the steep slope of this squatters' community. Erosion due to slope clearing had already washed out the major road and a number of trails in Highlite View.

The people had previously tried employing their own method of erosion control called tire bonding, which entailed building retention walls made of old tires (abundant throughout the island) to hold back the encroaching slope. The tires were fastened together with old steel cable and then filled with rocks and soil and planted with deep-rooted trees, such as ackee and soursop. Tire bonding stops erosion temporarily at the original trouble spot but typically can worsen the problem in adjacent areas, causing even greater threats to the inhabitants. The only real cure to this problem was to reforest the slopes above and around the houses. Sadly, there was not much support for this plan of action.

Carrying Capacity

Good management for the squatter communities is essential but hard to enforce due to a shortfall in the supply of land given the demand. Studies have shown that this problem is only getting worse worldwide (Hamdi, 1991, p. 3), despite all the innovations and investment with regard to providing housing for the poor. Determining and enforcing density limits in a squatters' community are very difficult for several reasons. First, none of the home owners typically own their lot, so they cannot tell others looking for a place to live that their community is "full." Secondly, there are usually no zoning regulations governing these areas, no government enforcement, and, as a result, no control over how many people can settle in the area. At Highlite View, despite early squatters, siting buildings with adequate setbacks between houses, as densities increased, houses were put in between the existing homes. This led to increased erosion, due to runoff from roofs, and more extensive trail systems that threatened the community as a whole.

So what is the point of discussing Highlite View? The traditional strategies associated with improving the living standards of those in need, whether in this country or in a developing nation, need to be drastically altered. The women at Highlite View needed outside assistance but did not need someone to come in and take control of their destinies. They required a "consultant," someone who would provide expertise in a problem area and would recommend the best course of action. The critical issue here is that the decision-making power remains in the hands of the community.

Conclusions

We believe that a common agreement should exist amongst all rational design professionals concerning the value of "user involvement" in the design and planning process. Sadly, when budgets are tight and scheduling is a problem, this is one of the first elements to be cut. And what a travesty. How can we develop the most appropriate solution to a problem without understanding all the issues? We find a similar mentality with the aid organizations; the experts know best and asking the

recipients what they want and need is of little value. Another problem occurs with the economies of scale. It is much easier in most scenarios to get a very large grant for development, hundreds of thousands to millions of dollars, than to obtain funding for small communities to improve their living standards. This mentality serves only to emphasize the lack of respect for those who have little political power, whether it is a single mother in a developing nation or in this country. Designers and planners need to take a leading role in defending the right to participate by those who are affected by these decisions.

References

Callwood, June. "Millionaire Whirls Around the Caribbean Like a Benevolent Hurricane," *The Globe and Mail:* Ontario, October 26, 1988.

Hamdi, Nabeel. *Housing Without Houses: Participation, Flexibility, Enablement,* Van New York: Nostrand Reinhold, 1991.

May, Ann. Discussion with Department of Agriculture Official, Main Office, Kingston, Jamaica, 1988.

Payne, Geoffrey, K. *Urban Housing in the Third World,* Boston: Routledge and Kegan Paul, 1977.

Theme 5
Shelter and Income Opportunities

Photo: *Hemalata C. Dandekar*

As Kusow states in the first paper in this theme,

> Historically, traditional family or kin systems have provided
> some social security for poor women, thereby reducing their
> need for cash income. However, current structural
> economic and social changes, such as the fragmentation of
> land, technological changes, and migration, have increased
> the necessity for these women to earn incomes. The
> changes resulting have also pushed women into the
> secondary job market which is characterized by low-skill,
> low-paying jobs. Moreover, cultural restrictions on some
> Third World women have excluded them from participation
> in the public domain.

The forces Kusow describes have been particularly
strong in Third World countries during the last five
decades of planned develpment. Therefore, an increasing number of Third World women have sought to earn
income in the informal sector, often from work that can
take place in the family home. The success of women in
such income generating activities often depends upon
their access to proper shelter and its ownership. This
observation surfaces directly or indirectly from the four
papers in this theme which look at the relationship of
shelter and income for women in the Third World. The
first paper, by Kusow, provides an overview of the
perceptual and structural factors that limit women's
access to shelter, and therefore to opportunities to earn
an income. The perceptual and cultural factors that
exclude women from attaining housing are underscored
by Miraftab. Salat presents a fine-grain case study of
Malaysian women skillfully organizing their dwellings
and larger social and physical environment to support
their income-generating activities. Concluding this
theme, Mahajan looks at home-based economic activities of women in rural and urban India and highlights
the importance of this work in the national economy.
She calls for a more gender responsive physical planning of urban areas to facilitate and support this work
rather than hinder it, as is presently the case. The first
two papers of Theme 6, which are based on case studies
in urban India, voice a similar need for planning and
regulation of services and infrastructure at the project
level.

Chapter 26
The Role of Shelter in Generating Income Opportunities for Poor Women in the Third World

Abdi M. Kusow

Abdi M. Kusow received his Bachelor of Arts in Sociology from Michigan State University in 1990 and a Master of Urban Planning from the University of Michigan in 1992. His areas of interest, as they relate to Africa and the Third World, are in urban and regional development, housing and community development, agricultural development, urban and rural migration, food insecurities and shortages in Africa, and the role of farmer empowerment. He plans to focus research on the constant food and hunger crisis in the Horn of Africa, particularly among the poor peasants and farmers of southern Somalia.

This discussion of poor women's income opportunities seeks to identify some of the salient factors that hinder women from obtaining shelter and proper employment. Particular consideration is given to the ways in which the current economic structure of the world, industrialization, technological changes, the fragmentation of land ownership, and migration have affected women's social and economic status. This discussion is further intended to examine the conditions of home-based women workers in the urban and rural areas of India, and the potential of shelter in providing economic opportunities for these women (Mahajan). Selat examines the role of self-employed women and their significant contribution to the family income and the importance of shelter in the status of women in a small locality in Malaysia. Thus, the aim of this discussion is to show the importance of residential space and the centrality of shelter in providing long-term income for poor women in the Third World. Finally, policy implications for the future are examined, showing how women's organizations can influence such policies in the future.

Background

Women constitute more than half of the membership of societies. They are also great consumers or users of the housing objects. In most Third World countries, they are important participants in the actual production of shelter (Sheriff, 1991: 76). Yet, historically, women's economic contributions to the family income and the role of shelter in generating this income were largely overlooked. In Bangladesh, wives and children of small and marginal landowners work for wages to meet family needs. The same situation is apparent among the urban poor. Male heads of households often earn less than 50% of the total household income and secondary earners, such as women and children, contribute the remainder of the income. Moreover, one-third of all households in the Third World are headed by women and in some cases the percentage is closer to one-half (Charlton, 1984: 48). Despite this fact, a very small number of women in the Third World gain access to proper employment and legal ownership to shelter and land. This partially explains why a majority of female heads of households are among the poorest in the Third World (1984: 48).

Historically, traditional family and/or kin systems have provided social security for some low-income women in Third World countries, thereby reducing their need for cash income. However, current structural economic and social changes, such as the fragmentation of land, technological changes, and migration have increased the necessity for these women to earn income. These changes have pushed women into the secondary job market which is characterized by non-skilled, low-paying jobs. Moreover, cultural restrictions on some Third World women exclude them from participation in the public domain. Therefore, an increasing number of Third World women have sought income from work such as making pastries, frying fish, or braiding hair. For the most part, the production of these services and activities took place in the family home (Tripp, 1989: 604). Ownership and access to shelter thus become very important in women's livelihoods and their access to income-generating activities. In Muslim countries, the need for such shelter is even more apparent. The differentiation between male and female space represented by purdah mandates a division of labor that limits women's spheres of activities within the boundaries of the home (Charlton, 1984).

The Current Economic Structure

Since the introduction of industrialization and the capitalist mode of production, many Third World countries have been unable to offer job security to most of their population, resulting in a severe surplus of unemployed labor. Much of this surplus population, including the displaced, landless wage workers, and the marginally self-employed, joined the informal sector to survive. The urban informal sector helps reduce labor costs for the large corporations by decreasing the relative size of the formal labor force, thereby providing abundant casual labor. Under this capitalist social condition, a large proportion of women who have been displaced from or never entered the formal economic sector before constitute a reserve labor force whose surplus labor power is absorbed into the domestic domain of the social economy (Harrison, 1991: 179). Thus, this displacement process has affected women more drastically then men.

There is a sexual division of labor within the informal economic sector. In Nairobi, Kenya, women are restricted to producing and marketing household consumer goods such as foodstuffs, cooking utensils, and clothing mainly used in the home. Similar circumstances also exist in Oceanview, Jamaica. For example, close to 33% of the working women in the informal sector are involved in some sort of domestic service (1991: 180). This feminization of employment in the informal sector has increased the number of low-income females who participate in survival and subsistence

activities. The situation of women is not any better in the public sector. Most women are overwhelmingly concentrated in the teaching and nursing professions, areas that can be perceived as basically extensions of domestic duties. In Zimbabwe, between 1980 and 1983, the number of women employed in the public sector increased from 30 to 44% (Kazembe, 1988: 397). These figures indicate an increase in the female public sector labor force participation, but, as in Jamaica, the greatest increase occurred in the fields of health and education.

Women in most Third World countries have also been excluded from participation in the political sphere. Like the public sector, women's participation in the political field is also confined to areas considered an extension of traditional female roles. The largest number of women leaders are concentrated in the revival churches and school associations, areas not generally considered or designated as political (Harrison, 1991: 198). Thus, women's overall lack of access to political positions impedes their ability to help other less fortunate women gain access to shelter and property ownership.

The Impact of Development and Technological Changes on Women

A large part of the negative impacts of development and industrialization, particularly on women in the rural areas, may be due to the changes they create in the family structure. In agrarian societies of the Third World, the family has been the unit of production. Both women and children have traditionally participated in the production process. Once a society moves from these traditional roles of production and becomes more urbanized, the traditional division of labor ceases to exist. Another important consequence of these altered family roles is that the family itself becomes smaller and less stable (Charlton, 1984: 33). This is not to say that social and economic changes are inherently disadvantageous to women, but when women are unable to find employment in the absence of traditional family support systems, they can be reduced to poverty.

Agricultural modernization, such as the introduction of high-yielding seeds and cash crops, can be both beneficial and harmful to women. On the one hand, the introduction of rice as a cash crop in the Cameroon has increased women's workloads and increased their income at the same time. However, the net increase in women's incomes was only 25% of the increase of men's. On the other hand, the development of high-yielding crops, such as maize in Zaire, proved disadvantageous to women. As in many African and Asian countries, women and men farm different plots and have different responsibilities. For example, women are in charge of the home gardens which provide the much-needed food for the family, but men grow maize and other cash crops. These new crop varieties increased production and demanded more labor, which was provided by women. But, because maize was planted in the men's fields, men kept the profit (Buvinic and Yudelman, 1989: 26).

Another important issue is the appropriateness and access of available technology for women. The failure on the part of national governments to involve women in the decision making about new technologies has meant that appropriate technologies to facilitate the agricultural tasks of women have been neglected. In most Asian, African, and Latin American countries, the greatest impact of technology has been on cash crops, such as cotton, coffee, and tea, whose cultivation is predominantly a male activity. The dis-couragement of significant attempts to upgrade the female-controlled poultry sector by men in Kenya, while introducing new technologies for cash crops earning men a high income, is a good example of the lack of support for the development of female-controlled resources. The effects of the Green Revolution are similar. The people with the largest land holdings have generally been the most benefited, taking advantage of high-yield crops. This process has aggravated the income inequalities between men and women and increased the workload of women. In Africa,

> Women do 70–80% of the planting, seeding, weeding and harvesting and 100% of the processing of cassava, a root crop critical in times of food scarcity. Compared to wheat and rice crops that men control, limited money has been devoted to research on cassava and for extension services. Cassava is easy to plant but demands time to harvest. Processing is very labor intensive. The natural cyanide in the tuber must be washed out, and approximately 18 five-hour days are required to process one ton of cassava into gari, a paste that can be eaten. Research has concentrated on producing bigger tubers or high-yielding varieties, ignoring the development of processing techniques that would increase both the productivity of women farmers and the demand for, and the price of the crops (Buvinic and Yudelman, 1989: 30).

Access to technology is closed to women both in rural and urban areas. One of the reasons for the inability of women to obtain access to technology is their lack of information and awareness. The people who supply information such as extension agents are all men and are not willing to provide this information to women. More importantly, land and shelter ownership to be used as collateral for equipments exchange are not available to women. Therefore, shelter and property ownership should be seen as the basic pre-condition for a woman's access to credit and autonomous income.

Access to Land and Property Ownership

Systems of land inheritance vary from one society to another. In some cases, as in the Sudan, land is owned by the government; the people are allowed to share the land collectively. The amount and the availability of land depend on the individual's capacity to use it. In a few other societies, as in much of Malaysia, most of the ancestral clan land is transmitted through the mother and men gain access to land through their wives or mothers (Stivens, 1985). Nevertheless, under the customary laws of most societies in the Third World, women have no land-use rights in their individual capacity. Land is inherited by the male only who is, at the same time, the head of the family. Upon the death of the husband, the wife does not inherit her husband's land. The fields are reassigned to her male in-laws (Kazembe, 1988: 385).

In the past, these customary arrangements, prevalent in many Third World countries, have been less problematic than they are today. The family, as a whole, has been the unit of production and land was shared collectively, or in most cases, land was not scarce. Any community member could clear land and it belonged to him or her. Upon the death of a husband, the wife used the land inherited by her male offspring. If she had no children, upon the death of her husband she could move back and use the land of her father or her other male relatives in her natal area. On the eve of industrial modernization and the arrival of the colonial rulers, land tenure systems were introduced to many of the Third World countries, whereby land was surveyed and individual titles were given mostly to men (Oboler, 1985: 334). When land was not automatically appropriated to men, they still ended up controlling the land, due to their access to cash income. In some areas of Tanzania, men and women inherited equal portions of land, but land that was acquired through purchase was all owned by men because more men had enough money to buy land than women. For widowed or divorced women, the effects of land tenure and monetization was even more severe. Furthermore, only men holding ownership to land meant that credit was available only to them (Oboler, 1985: 316).

Women-Centered Projects

Despite efforts by local governments and international development agencies to improve the overall economic, shelter, and health conditions of women in the world, particularly Third World countries, most women continue to be poor and lack access to employment and proper shelter. Even though a substantial number of women today are better educated and are more active economically and professionally than they were few decades ago, women continue to be disadvantaged in every aspect. Social and economic structures in most countries still relegate women to second-class citizenship (Buvinic and Yudelman, 1989: 8).

In the past, international development agencies and local governments alike favored women-centered income-generating projects. Three major types of projects have been designed for poor women in the past two decades: (1) the micro enterprise designed to provide credit and technical assistance to women artisans and vendors, (2) income-generating projects designed to offer skill training and other services to women, and (3) vocational education training. The income-generating and vocational-training projects have both failed to achieve their goals due to a lack of technical experts and financial resources. The micro enterprise projects for women vendors and artisans have been relatively successful in providing women with credit and other necessary resources. The Working Women's Forum in Madras, India, has been relatively successful in helping poor women. The organization has enabled over 10,000 women to receive short-term loans for small businesses. Another important example of a relatively successful micro enterprise project is the Women's Construction Collective, established in Kingston, Jamaica, in 1983 to train and place unemployed women in the construction field. In its first two-and-a-half years, this organization trained 34 women and placed over 90% of them in plumbing, masonry, and carpentry. It has also initiated a revolving fund to assist working women in purchasing tools (Buvinic and Yudelman, 1989: 40).

Thus, the point here is not to suggest that income-generating projects are inherently bad for poor women's economic well-being in the Third World. Rather, they do not address the root causes of the lack of decent income for women. In addition to such projects, women's access to shelter should be given priority. Once women gain access to proper shelter and property ownership, they can freely engage in home-based economic activities and thus secure credit for improving their businesses.

The Role of Shelter

Women are generally the primary users of shelter both as a resting and reproduction space and as an income-generating entity. As Farida Sheriff points out,

.... housing is more than just an architectural, physical object which provides a roof over one's head. It is a concept most adequately defined and explained when situated within the societal dominant regime of accumulation and mode of regulation.... [H]ousing acquires a double character: On the one hand, it is an essential spatial object which satisfies a basic social need for shelter, rest and reproduction. In relation to the very poor women heads of households, it often provides a spatial base for their income-generating activities" (Sheriff, 1991: 78).

Using this definition, shelter becomes a central entity in determining the economic well- being and the survival of women in general and Third World poor women heads of households in particular. Thus, to appreciate the role of shelter in providing income opportunities for poor women in the Third World, one needs to look at the nature of their work. As mentioned, an overwhelming majority of women in Third World cities are concentrated in the urban informal employment sector. In India, 43% of self-employed women work in their homes. This is also true in other countries of the Third World, where a majority of women engage in petty commodity production, such as cooking small snacks to sell in the streets. This indicates that the nature of women's work is different from wage work because the site of their production is the home (Mahajan). Thus, because the nature of women's work is related to their home, the provision of shelter becomes a very important commodity.

Another important feature of property ownership and shelter is its basic requirement of land and accumulation of wealth. By land, I mean the ownership of an appreciating asset which can be exchanged for other valuable material, in this case credit. Ownership of shelter then indicates the simultaneous ownership of land and, without access to land rights, women are unable to gain access to credit, for land is generally used as a collateral (Sheriff, 1991, Moser, 1987). The location of shelter is another important factor in the economic condition of Third World women. For example, zoning laws which separate income activities from the residential sphere hinder women from engaging in income-generating activities in the home or around the neighborhood (Mahajan, Moser, 1987). For example, in Delhi, India, 700, 000 squatters were relocated to new settlements on the outskirts of the city between 1975 and 1977. As a result of this relocation and lack of efficient transportation, many women could not combine domestic and income-generating activities. Thus, the rate of female employment among the relocated fell five times more than that of men in the same area (Moser, 1987: 20). The concept of women's access to shelter should therefore be understood in the context of land, capital, and power. Ownership and access to land determine the capital base of the individual in relation to the overall society and thus his or her negotiating power in acquiring credit and access to loans and modern technology.

Future Policy Implications

Implications for future policy should be analyzed, first, by dividing women's short- and long-term needs in their integration in the overall development process. This can be done by creating a distinction between the condition and the situation of women. Following this line of analysis, Kate Young provides this distinction and writes: "By condition, I mean the material state in which women find themselves: their poverty, their lack of education and training, their access work burdens, their lack of access to modern technology, improved tools, work related skills, etc." By position is meant women's social and economic standing relative to men (Young, 1988: 1–2). In the past, both researchers and international agencies have concentrated on assessing women's conditions. However, this emphasis, as Kate Young further indicates, has had its share of negative consequences. First, it emphasizes women's day-to-day practical needs, thus focusing on ameliorative measures. Second, it makes it very difficult for the structural problems concerning women's issues to be raised (Young, 1988). A negative impact of income-generating projects on women's conditions is their tendency to create too many small projects in trying to solve every single women's problem in isolation from the rest (Pareja, 1988).

To overcome this dilemma, national government and other related agencies should not try to address every single women-related problem, but should limit themselves to those that have the greatest impact on a number of other aspects of social and economic life. This is an issue of prioritizing needs. Once the most fundamental are met, a base for other actions will have been created (Pareja, 1988: 57). Thus it is very important to examine

the relation of cause and effect between certain structural and social variables and how they relate to women's status. In the Third World, for example, access to shelter and land rights is one of the most important, if not the most important, variable in determining women's overall employment and social status; many women in the Third World are single mothers with children, most are employed in the informal sector with a majority of them working in their homes. Thus, shelter becomes not only the physical housing and the roof needed by all women to survive and feel secure, but also an income-generating entity. Therefore dealing with the shelter needs of women can prove more beneficial than other quick-fix solutions.

In the long run, however, structural factors that impede women's position in relation to men must be addressed. First, the current economic structure that pushed women into the lower paying, less influential secondary and tertiary markets should be reorganized so that women can play more important roles in the formal market economy. Second, training programs for women should not be confined to skills that are extensions of women's traditional roles. Rather, such training should be diversified to include skills that have been seen as traditionally male occupations. Third, access to higher education must be provided to women, especially in the sciences, politics, and engineering without discrimination by sex. Fourth, women should be given access to decision-making positions. For example, in most countries in the Third World, a large number of women work in the field of education as teachers, but few women occupy decision-making positions in their respective ministries of education.

The Role of Women's Organizations

Despite relative advances in the health, education, and the number of women who joined the labor force over the past twenty years, governments worldwide have not been successful in implementing policies that increase substantially women's share in the paid labor market. The International Labor Organization reports that the percentage of women in the labor force has decreased from 35% in 1975 to 34.6% in 1985. The ILO's medium-term plan for the years between 1990 and 1995 identifies women as the most likely group to be disadvantaged by the negative impacts of restructuring and technological change (Lycklama a Nijeholt, 1991). To integrate women into the development process, both international agencies and national governments have, in the past, concentrated on setting up income-generating projects that were hardly part of the initial planning process. The purpose of these projects was mainly to increase the share of women's employment opportunities. Such projects have based their objectives on the assumption that women require only an additional income to supplement their overall family income. Most of these projects are thus based on occupations that are traditionally extensions of female roles. Women-targeted projects also suffer from a number of market-related problems. On the one hand, they have to compete with more sophisticated, lower-priced industrial products. On the other hand, the smaller sizes of such projects makes it difficult to employ more than a few women at a time. Another less apparent problem is the dependency of such projects on outside funding sources. Once a funding agent completes his funding obligations, these projects often die (Pareja, 1988: 57).

Thus, it is in this spirit that women's organizations ought to assume an aggressive role in meeting the income and shelter needs of women, especially those of women-headed households in the Third World. Policies relating to women's income-generating projects should consider the nature of women's work and its relationship to ownership and access to land rights and shelter. Women's organizations can play an important role in identifying and addressing women's needs, and bring their views to the attention of the state and other related agencies. However, the objectives of women's organizations should not be confined to exposing women's needs to the outside world. Rather, these organizations should mobilize to present a united front against the male-dominated governments of the Third World. This does not necessarily mean that women should not form alliances with other groups, including men. As Julius Nyerere, the past president of Tanzania pointed out, "The history of the world shows that the oppressed can get allies—and need to get allies—from the dominant groups as they wage their struggle for equality, human dignity and progress. But no one and no other group can be liberated by others. The struggle for women's development has to be conducted by women, not in opposition to men, but as a part of the social development of the whole people" (Lycklama a Nijeholt, 1991: 157).

Nevertheless, before women's organizations can start to articulate and implement meaningful income-generating projects for women, several problems inherent in today's women's organizations should be resolved. First are the problems related to class, ethnic, and racial differences within women's organizations. Even though all women may support the demand for better health for women and children, wealthier women may withdraw

their support if they feel their privileges are threatened by such demands. Some organizations have overcome such problems to some extent. The Self Employed Women's Association of Ahmedabad (SEWA), India, The Women's Working Forum in India, and the Sistern Theatre Collective in Jamaica all represent an interesting form of cooperation whereby middle-class women share their leadership and other resources with working-class women (Lycklama a Nijeholt, 1991: 156). Thus, even though forging alliances is very difficult, women's organizations should strive towards achieving that goal, or at least maintaining and reinforcing such alliances.

Finally, by documenting the relationship between shelter and income opportunities for women, all the papers in this section contribute to ongoing research on the condition and the situation of women and the potential of shelter in providing economic well-being to the (largely women) heads of households in the Third World. On the one hand, Selat examines how the earnings of self-employed women in a small locality in Malaysia are decisive to the family income and enable them to enjoy a better lifestyle than other ordinary working-class families. He thus traces the experiences and the contributions of several self-employed women, either through long-distance trade or through working in their homes. Selat concludes that, in Malay households, despite the cultural expectation that the man will be the breadwinner, women take up tasks that contribute to the family income. Thus their contribution should be recognized and their income activities should be facilitated.

On the other hand, Mahajan explores the condition of home-based women workers and the potential of shelter in facilitating such activities. She further examines the role of Mahatma Gandhi's economic thought in relation to home-based workers and how that affected women's organizations in India today. A key argument of Mahajan's paper is related to the influence of Western town planning concepts of zoning on the settlement patterns and the development of Indian cities and towns. Mahajan indicates that women in such centers have been removed from productive roles as production activities have been separated from the domestic spheres. Thus, this process created what Mahajan refers to as "housewifization, isolation, and dependence." Mahajan calls for alternative rural and urban planning strategies based on the practical needs of women.

Finally, my contribution to this debate examines the role of shelter in enhancing women's income opportunities. I emphasize the importance of prioritizing needs and selecting those which, once met, can serve as a basis to meet others. My conclusion calls for stronger and more cohesive women's organizations, for they are the most important actors in enhancing women's overall economic well-being in the Third World.

References

Buvinic, Mayra, and Sally W. Yudelman. 1989. "Women, Poverty and Progress in the Third World." *Deadline Series. Foreign Policy Association.* No. 289.

Charlton, Sue Ellen M. *Women in Third World Development.* 1984. Boulder and London: Westview Press.

Clark, H. Mari. 1986. "Women-headed Households and Poverty: Insights from Kenya," in: B. Gelpi et al., *Women and Poverty.* Chicago: University of Chicago Press.

Harrison, Faye. V. 1991. "Women in Jamaica's Urban Informal Economy: Insights from a Kingston Slum," in: C. Mohanty and A. Russo (eds), *Third World Women and the Politics of Feminism.* Bloomington: Indiana University Press.

Kazembe, L. Joyce. 1988. *The Women Issue. Zimbabwe: The Political Economy of Transition: 1980–1986,* Codesira, Dakar.

Lycklama a Nijeholt, Geertje. 1991. "Policies and Strategies: A Reflection." In: Geertji Lycklama a Nijeholt (ed.), *Towards Women's Strategies in the 1990s: Challenging Government and State.* The Hague: Institute of Social Studies.

Moser, Caroline. 1987. "Women, Human Settlement, and Housing: A Conceptual Framework for Analysis and Policy-making," in: C. Moser and L. Peake (eds.), *Women, Human Settlements, and Housing.* London: Tavistock Publications.

Oboler, Regina Smith. 1985. *Women, Power, and Economic Change: The Nandi of Kenya.* Palo Alto: Stanford University Press.

Pareja, Francisco. 1988. "Problems that Concern Women and their Incorporation in Development: The Case of Ecuador," in: K. Young (ed.), *Women and Economic Development: Local, Regional and National Planning Strategies.* Berg/Unesco.

Ramzi, A. Sonia. 1988. "Women and Development Planning: The Case Of Egypt." in: K. Young (ed.), *Women and Economic Development: Local, Regional and National Planning Strategies.* Berg/Unesco.

Sheriff, Farida. 1991. *Shelter and Beyond: The State, Gendered Residential Space and Survival in Tanzania,* in: Lycklama a Nijeholt, Geertje (ed.), *Towards Women's Strategies in the 1990s: Challenging Government and State,* The Hague: Institute of Social Studies.

Stivens, Maila. 1985. *The Fate of Women's Land Rights: Gender, Matriliny, and Capitalism in Rembau, Negeri Sembilan, Malaysia.* In Haleh Ashraf (ed.), Women, Work, and Ideology in the Third World. London and New York: Tavistock Publications.

Tripp, Mari Aili. 1989. "Women and the Changing Urban Household Economy in Tanzania," *The Journal of Modern African Studies,* 27(4): 601-23.

Young, Kate. 1988. *Women and Economic Development: Local, Regional, and National Planning Strategies.* Oxford, New York, Berg, Paris: UNESCO.

Chapter 27

Shelter as Sustenance: Exclusionary Mechanisms Limiting Women's Access to Housing

Faranak Miraftab

Faranak Miraftab is currently a Ph.D. candidate in the Department of Architecture at the University of California, Berkeley. Her dissertation research examines the spatial and social impacts of women's home-based production in urban areas of developing countries. She has a Master of Architecture from the Norwegian Institute of Technology, Trondheim, Norway. Her undergraduate architectural studies were at Tehran University in Iran. Her work in the U.S., Norway, Latin America, and Iran has helped her develop a social understanding of the built environment.

This paper discusses the role of shelter for the sustenance of women in cities of the developing world and the ways in which women's access to shelter is limited in these societies. This problem is particularly important since processes of economic change and urbanization that bring women to cities in the developing world often strip them of forms of social support and force them to seek shelter in a commodified environment in which they lack adequate monetary resources and/or legal or social rights.

Shelter is an essential resource for sustenance of both men and women, but it plays different roles in and fulfills distinct aspects of their lives. In this paper, the relation of women and housing in developing countries is discussed with two different concerns. One is the particularities of the role played by shelter in women's lives. The other is the particularities of women's limitations in acquiring adequate shelter. The multiple roles of shelter for women; as a nexus of social bonding and integration into urban life; as a place for reproduction and raising a family; and as a place of production and economic activities are addressed. Emphasis is placed on the increasing economic importance of shelter for women in the context of global economic restructuring and the new international and sexual division of labor. The focus will be on Mexico, where national and multinational firms are increasingly integrating their production into residential neighborhoods by subcontracting work to women.

Also addressed are the cultural and perceptual limitations women face in obtaining adequate shelter. Just as women's subordination in society is often complex and systematic, so too is their exclusion from social amenities such as housing. Long-term efforts are needed to remove obstacles women face in obtaining housing at a multitude of social, economic, and cultural levels. While structural factors inherent in a patriarchal-capitalist system push women into low-paying jobs and make market-rate housing unaffordable to them, low-income housing programs also fail to consider women's specific needs and thus exclude them as program beneficiaries. Furthermore, women's access to shelter is also often limited by cultural norms and/or discriminatory rules that prohibit women's independent living in cities without male authority. Women's own perceptions also often play a limiting role. Where women do not value their own work at home, perceptual factors may hinder their access to adequate shelter.

Shelter as a Sustenance Resource

During the primary migratory experience of women, shelter plays an important role in their social integration into urban areas. Women migrants settle close to people from the same rural point of origin, and it is through their neighbors that new migrants learn about city life. Residential neighborhoods are the nexus for creating a new urban identity. For migrant newcomers, neighborhoods become the springboards to urban life (Blondet, 1990).

This is especially true for rural women in Latin America, often the pioneers of urban migration in their families. In Latin America, migration flow has consisted largely of young women who moved to cities in search of jobs (Crummett, 1987; Momsen and Townsend, 1987; Brydon and Chant, 1989).[1] Latin American migrant women do not follow male members of their families.[2] They move alone, either to break free from familial and rural restrictions, or to assist with overall family income (Blondet, 1990). In either case, urban neighborhoods are central to women's initial adjustment and integration into city life and the establishment of their new identity.[3] The social role of the neighborhood is also very important in the establishment of networks of support for women's daily domestic work. In the absence of economic resources, low-income women are excluded from using institutional support systems for child care and family assistance. These women often have no choice but to rely on neighbors for such help.

Reproduction and Daily Domestic Tasks

Home and neighborhood play important roles in the lives of women who, based on a gender division of work, are traditionally responsible for making a home and raising children. Women spend more time around the house and its conditions are of greater concern to them than to men (Moser, 1989; Schmink, 1985; Chant, in Moser and Peake, 1987). An empirical study by Chant in Queretaro, Mexico, confirms the notion that the improvement of home conditions is a high priority for women. Her comparative study revealed that within the same income group women heads-of-households had invested more of the household's income on improvement of housing conditions than men heads-of-households. Furthermore, in male-headed households, housing improvements were less common among nuclear families than among extended families, where the authority of a male head-of-household was often reduced by the existence of older family members, a

condition also possibly increasing the degree of decision-making authority for women (Chant, in Moser and Peake, eds., 1987).

The role of the home for women is even more important in Moslem societies that practice the seclusion of women. In societies which confine women to their walled homes, courtyards within houses may be the only daily outdoor experience of women in *purdah*. In these cases, insensitivity of designers to the role of the home for women and the differential spatial needs of men and women can cause severe psychological effects on women. A survey of two newly developed low-income housing projects in Tunis[4] revealed that the design of small courtyards increased psychological depression, neuroses, and suicide among women residents.

The domestic tasks and responsibilities of women make the structures of the neighborhood important to them as well. The existence of neighborhood services such as water pipes, laundry rooms, sewage systems, street pavements, and garbage pick-up are important to women's daily lives. The quality and location of such services affect women's lives directly by determining how difficult and time-consuming their domestic responsibilities will be (Schmink, 1985).

Production and Income-Generating Tasks

Women of the developing world have always produced goods at home for use by their families and themselves, and for exchange. To manage their poverty, women often must combine child-rearing with income-generating activities. For this reason, the home has traditionally been a place of work for women. In Moslem societies, performance of productive tasks at home is further motivated by the conditions of women's seclusion.

For Third World women, there is no valid dichotomy between the home as a private sphere of non-paid household services and the workplace as a public sphere of paid economic activity. Such conceptualizations of private and public do not respond to the daily realities of low-income women in developing countries. For Third World women, the home bridges between the two spheres, as both a place for raising a family and for generating income (Tiano, 1984; Blondet, 1990).[5]

Although the types of production and economic activity performed at home were once limited to traditional female occupations such as the production of garments and weaving, recent global economic transformations have radically expanded the types of production women perform at home. Today, with the overall increase of informal economies in developing countries, women's productive activities also include the assembly of manufactured goods such as electronic devices. The home has gained the interest of international manufacturing firms, and international capital is increasingly integrating manufacturing into the homes and neighborhoods. International firms have realized that production can be treated as an extension of women's daily domestic tasks, and may thus be accomplished at less cost than through formal labor in a factory.

The Home as a Place of Industry

New levels of flexibility in production and transportation have allowed the fragmentation and globalization of production so that different phases in the manufacture of goods can take place in different places around the world. Investment by core industrial countries in the countries of the periphery is no longer necessarily based on the availability of raw material; it is now often based on the competitive capacity of different countries to manufacture goods for export.[6] Therefore, the position of the national economies of the countries of the periphery within a global context is altered and defined by their export capacity (Portes, Castells, Benton, 1989).

With the new international division of labor, the availability of cheap labor has become an important factor for international capital in decisions to locate export-processing plants.[7] In this context, the employment of women,[8] whose labor in patriarchal systems comes more cheaply than men's, has become central in exploitative relationships between the center and the periphery (Mies, 1982, 1986; Mies *et al.,* 1988; Tiano, 1990).[9] In the context of new developments in the relations of the core and the periphery, feminization of labor clearly demonstrates the close linkages between the international and sexual divisions of labor (Fernandez-Kelly, 1983; Lawson and Klak, 1990; Mies, 1986; Ward, 1990). It shows how the interactive mechanisms of patriarchy and capitalism make the foundations of a system that, as an integrative whole, perpetuates the relations of dominance between genders, social classes, and nation states (Fernandez-Kelly, 1983; Nash and Safa, 1985; Leacock and Safa, 1986; Roldan and Beneria, 1987; Mies, 1986).

The reflection of this global trend began to appear in Mexican economy during the late 1960s and the early 1970s with the move of the multinational export-processing manufacturing plants to the Mexican side of the U.S.- Mexico border.[10] The *maquiladoras* border

industry increased their profit by targeting young single women workers whose labor, under a patriarchal system, came more cheaply than men's (Fernandez-Kelly, 1983; Tiano, 1990).[11]

International capital has paid attention to the potentials of women's work at home, and manufacturing firms are increasingly targeting married women at home for piece work.[12] Married women at home who, under a patriarchal system are responsible for child-rearing and homemaking activities, are less mobile and thus their labor can be gained at even less cost than that of single and young women. In Mexico, women home-workers on average accept jobs for less than one-third of the minimum wage—and this often fails to include the unpaid labor of their children (in Portes et al., and Beneria, 1987; Gonzales de la Rocha, 1986). By employing women at home, national and international capital saves on production costs in three ways: first, it saves directly on labor cost by employing married women with minimal job mobility; second, it saves on work-space cost, with production to take place in workers' homes; and third, by using informal channels of production, it saves on the cost of benefits, taxation, and regulatory expenses (Portes, Castells and Benton, 1989; Lawson and Klak, 1990).

The fact that women subsidize industry in this way is justified by the false patriarchal assumption that their production is a side activity to their daily domestic chores. Women's production at home becomes an extension of their homemaking activities, which is not seen as "productive work," and is thus valued less (Ward, 1990). While compartmentalization of women's time between their domestic tasks and their income-earning tasks is rarely possible, the real hourly wage of women's work at home is even lower than that assumed by their informal contracts. Today, a combination of patriarchal and capitalist relations is behind the increasing move of production into the homes. The role of shelter for sustenance of Third World women is coming to be defined at the intersection of women's underprivileged position within existing social relations of gender and their country's peripheral position within the global economy (Lawson and Klak, 1990).

Exclusionary Mechanisms Limiting Women's Access to Shelter

Economic Factors

Lack of economic power in the housing market is one of the most important factors that excludes a large portion of urban women in developing countries from access to adequate shelter. The structure of labor markets based on the sexual division of labor systematically pushes women into low-paying jobs. Women's low income further limits their access to institutional assistance for child-rearing, reducing their job mobility. This vicious circle perpetuates women's underprivileged position in the job market, and concentrates women in unstable and low-earning activities such as domestic service, street vending, and informal-sector activities.[13] Economic limitations to acquiring adequate shelter are especially important for women heading their own households.[14] Where employment opportunities of women are confined to low-paying jobs, female-headed households suffer from relatively greater poverty than male-headed households (Merrick and Schmink, in Buvenic et al., 1983; Charlton, 1984).[15]

Considering that the changing composition of households is increasingly putting the burden of acquiring shelter on women's shoulders—at the same time that economic realities make housing prices unaffordable to them—it is crucial that national and international shelter programs target women as specific beneficiaries. However, critiques of interventions in the area of informal housing—and their appraisal of site-and-services projects, one of the most widespread forms of housing intervention in Developing Countries during the past two decades—have highlighted the gender insensitivity of these projects. By overlooking the multiple roles shelter plays in the lives of women, such programs have not only failed to reach women, but they have also often harmed women by increasing their travel time to work or causing them to lose their jobs (Moser and Peake, 1987; Moser, 1988; Schmink, 1985; Van Vliet, 1988; Carlson and Bhagat, 1984).

A major feature of these shelter programs is the patriarchal assumption that homemaking is the only role of women. This often leads to the conceptualization of home as a mere place of reproduction and domestic activity. This view ignores the multiple responsibilities of women (as producers as well as reproducers and homemakers) and the fact that women's economic activity inside and outside the home accounts for a large portion of any household's income.[16]

The invisibility of women's economic role within the home (a result of considering their home-based production merely as an extension of their domestic tasks) not only directly contributes to women's economic disadvantage through lower wages, but it excludes women from obtaining credit support and assistance from shelter programs (Moser, 1988).[17] Once the economic role of women is overlooked and it is assumed that only men are income providers in the family, housing loans may be granted based only on the income of the male member of the family. Title to the housing may also thus be granted only to the male member, and the location of project sites may often be decided based only on proximity to male-type occupations such as industrial sites. Since women's occupations are mostly in the informal sector and in central-city areas, the location of housing projects away from city centers harms women more than men.[18] Furthermore, a disregard for women's work at home is often reflected in zoning laws that regulate project sites for residential use only, and thus harm women's economic conditions.[19]

The inadequacies of shelter programs in reaching low-income women exemplifies the interconnection of relationships within a patriarchal system. This often limits women's access to adequate shelter directly through economic disadvantage, but also indirectly through their exclusion from assisted, low-income shelter programs. The complexity of the exclusionary mechanisms at work will be further understood by exploring the cultural and perceptual dimensions of this exclusion in the following section.

Cultural Factors

Cultural factors are those shared values in a society which determine social norms and the range of acceptable behaviors. In this respect, the patriarchal stigma of women living alone or without male authority often limits women's access to adequate shelter. According to cultural codes that define women's independent living as "sexual or social looseness" (Mernissi, 1975), women are often prohibited from changing their living arrangements from the home of the patriarch, even if this arrangement does not respond to their spatial or psychological needs. Cultural norms can also make shelter economically unaffordable for women where they have to pay higher prices for the same unit than men. At times, women have to gain the accord of their landlords and compensate for their "deviance" from social norms.

For example, in most countries of North Africa and West and South Asia, protection of women by men is highly valued as a representation of female modesty and male honor.[20] Cultural norms in these societies function beyond the economic access of women to housing. In societies where Islamic laws are observed, in fact, women may have legal rights for ownership, and they may own property. However, their legal and economic access to property might be limited based on non-institutionalized social rules. Even a single woman who lawfully owns her home may thus feel prohibited to live independently. This is an appropriate example to show the importance of differentiating between women's *access to* and *control of* resources. This distinction is emphasized by Overholdt and others (1985) involved with development projects to improve women's conditions.[21] The increased access of women to resources, whether this is accomplished economically or legally, does not necessarily result in benefits for women if it is not accompanied by control over the resources.

Cultural factors are a powerful exclusionary mechanism that may not be directly reflected in laws and regulations, but which nevertheless indirectly affect women's access to adequate shelter. This may take the form of an external force imposed on individual women based on norms of "acceptable" female living arrangements, or an internal force that is self-imposed. Where women internalize social values of male protection and female modesty, they often limit their own options for shelter.

Perceptual Factors

Exclusion of women's access to housing cannot be explained only in relation to exogenous factors socially imposed on women. Women's limited access to adequate shelter is also embedded in interpersonal factors. Both exogenous and endogenous factors play roles in the systematic limitation of women in social amenities. Limitations in adequate housing must be examined at both structural and individual levels. Structure and agency are in a reciprocal relationship. Women as individuals affect the structures of dominance among genders both by changing it or reinforcing the patriarchal relations of gender.[22] However, individuals are also affected by the structure by internalizing patriarchal social relations and values. This reciprocal mechanism pertains as well with regard to shelter, as women often do not value or acknowledge their own spatial needs.

In "Gender and Cooperative Conflicts,"[23] Sen presents an excellent analysis of the deep-seated notion of legitimacy of needs for women. He argues that women's perceptions of the value of their work define their sense of entitlement, and thus the sense of the legitimacy of their needs. He argues that perceptions of men and women of their contribution to household welfare affect how they define their sense of entitlement, and how they bargain for the distribution of welfare in the household. In this relation, Sen

argues that different perceptions among men and women can become a matter of survival, as women sometimes exclude themselves from an equal share of family resources such as food and medical care.[24]

In this context, the role of perceptual factors for women in defining the legitimacy of their spatial needs is significant. Women's perception of the value of their contribution to family well-being through their "productive" and "reproductive" activities plays an important role in what they can claim as their need, and how they can bargain for their share of family resources. When work is legitimized only by its monetary value, women's activities at home are not perceived as "work" and their contribution to the family well-being is not acknowledged. Thus, women, themselves, are often not convinced of the legitimacy of their own spatial needs. This condition is similar in some respects to that of women who work for pay at home. Beneria and Roldan (1987), in their study of women home-workers in Mexico City, point out that, although these women contribute to the monetary resources of the family, they often perceive their work to be secondary to that of their husbands, and thus less valuable than that of men.

The low allocation of value (in space and time) to women's activities also limits the managing role women can play in neighborhoods when it comes to issues of hygiene and urban services. While the same role played by men is perceived as being an organizational and managerial activity deserving time and space, for women it is assumed to be merely an extension of daily domestic activities. Moser (1988) points to "convenient myths" about women having more free time around the neighborhood. Women may have internalized these myths, and may perceive their work around the neighborhood of little value, and thus not the basis for a legitimate claim to time or space.

Conclusions

Just as women's subordination in society is a systematic and complex phenomenon, so too is their exclusion from social amenities such as housing. Factors that contribute to women's limited access to housing are manifold and account in both the realms of production and consumption. While economic limitations often create a need for low- income shelter for women, often the gender insensitivities of housing programs exclude women from access to benefits. On the other hand, cultural and perceptual factors often limit women in the consumption and/or use of the housing they are able to obtain. To guarantee women's access to resources, long-term efforts are needed to remove obstacles at both structural and individual levels. This will involve addressing a range of economic, cultural, and perceptual factors that contribute to the asymmetrical access of men and women to shelter.

Therefore, besides efforts that address the improvement of women's economic condition to increase their access to shelter, consciousness raising is necessary to increase women's control of the use of resources such as housing. This will involve increased gender awareness at both institutional and individual levels. At the institutional level it will involve promoting gender awareness in design and implementation of shelter-development programs. This will enhance awareness of the significance of shelter to women and of the limited access women have to housing. At the individual level it will involve the inclusion of educational components in shelter programs to increase women's sense of the value of their work and their contribution to the well-being of the household. Change in women's perceptions of the value of their activities at home and in the neighborhood may contribute to an improvement in women's living conditions by legitimizing their spatial needs. In the long term, changes in individuals' value systems will enhance a process of cultural change that alters broad social values.

Any attempt to improve conditions of shelter for women must address both the economic and ideologic bases of women's exclusion from adequate shelter. Such an effort needs to go beyond provision of physical shelter, and contribute to a process of change in gender relations.

Notes

[1] Between 1965 and 1975, in Latin American cities, there were 109 women for every 100 men (Brydon and Chant, 1989).

[2] Boserup (1970) explains that a higher rate of female migration to cities of Latin America is a result of local systems of agriculture and a colonial past reliant on haciendas and tenant farming systems. In this region, farming relies heavily on the operation of animal draughts by men, and thus female members of the household are more likely to leave the rural areas. She further explains that where farming most heavily relies on female work, as in paddy cultivation as in parts of Southeast Asia, or in slash-and-burn cultivations as in Sub-Saharan Africa, responsibilities of women have restricted their move from the rural areas and encouraged male migration. The exception to this general pattern is in Arab countries where, despite male farming systems, migration is predominantly of males.

[3] Blondet (1990) examines processes of establishing social identity for women migrants in low-income settlements of Lima, Peru. She emphasizes the role of building a home and neighborhood, particularly in the primary phase of women's urban living. She argues that the establishment of a new identity is more influenced by their migration experience than by their rural origins.

[4] These were Mellassine, a squatter upgrading project, and Ibn Khaldun, a planned community financed jointly by the Tunisian government and USAID.

[5] Tiano further argues that "the degree of separation between the two spheres could thus be viewed as a variable, and factors such as social class which might increase or decrease the separation could be specified empirically" (1990:22).

[6] Between 1963 and 1985 the share of the Third World in producing the world's manufactured goods increased from 4.3% to 12.4% (Tiano, 1990:195).

[7] The advantage of cheap women's labor in assembly lines has been one of the major factors in reducing production costs for export-oriented manufacturing goods in the countries of Southeast Asia. While hourly wages in the U.S. and Japan were $6.96 and $5.97 respectively, in Indonesia and Malaysia wages were as low as $0.45 and $0.42 (Lin, 1985, cited in Momsen and Townsend, 1987).

[8] Lourdes Arizpa and Josefina Aranda (1981) call the process by which women have become an attractive labor force a "comparative advantage of disadvantages." The underprivileged position of women in the labor market and the availability of their cheap labor based on the "advantage" of social subordination offers them wider employment opportunities (in *Signs*, 1981, 7: 453–473). No doubt, this argument will raise the question of whether, at an average 15-hour working day for women in maquiladoras (Fernandez-Kelly, 1983), we could still call this an advantage or a further exploitation.

[9] "Women aged 16–24 make 80–90% of the export-processing labor force in Mexico, Southeast Asia, and other export platform nations" (Tiano, 1990).

[10] This process was supported by the Mexican government through the Border Industrialization Program (BIP) which was initially motivated by the 1964 cancellation of a pact between the U.S. and Mexico for immigrant workers, after which the U.S. expelled 200,000 Mexican immigrant workers. Most of the expelled population settled in the border towns of Mexico. As a result, the rate of unemployment among men in these towns reached 50%. Soon, however, the international firms that were encouraged to invest in export-oriented industry in these border towns found it was cheaper to employ women than men. Although the plan did not meet its initial objective of reducing male unemployment, it nevertheless improved the economic conditions of border towns and their inhabitants by providing gainful employment for female members of households (Tiano in Ward, ed., 1990).

[11] Feminization of labor in Mexico is reflected in the increase of the female labor force between 1930 and 1974 from 4.5% to 19.1% (Nash and Safa, 1986).

[12] Beneria and Roldan (1987), in their study in Mexico City, found that some multinational manufacturing companies were contracting out 70% of their production. They also found that 85% of the women involved in home-based industrial work were directly or indirectly subcontracting for multinationals.

[13] For example, in Latin America in the early 1960s, 67.2% of women were employed in the service sector (Nash and Safa, 1985). Domestic services alone have absorbed about 40% of the working women in Latin American cities (Youseff, 1976), while in Ile-Ife, Nigeria 94%

and Chonburi, Thailand, 80% of the street vendors are women (Tinker, 1987).

[14] The increase in female-headed households is an international trend that has been most dramatic in developing countries and among low-income groups (Aguiar, in Nash and Safa, 1976). It is estimated that, on average, one-third of the households in developing countries are headed by women (Buvenic, 1983; Tinker, 1976). This number varies across the developing countries and is greater among low-income groups. In urban areas of Latin America, due to unstable unions between couples and high migration rates, female-headed households make up half of all households (Momsen and Townsend , 1987; Tinker, *et al.* 1976). In refugee camps of Central America, this number is as high as 90% (Moser and Peake, 1987). In a squatter settlement near Nairobi, a study shows that about 50–80% of women were independent heads-of-households (Nelson, 1979 cited in Momsen and Townsend, 1987). In general, the increase in the number of female-headed households is a global trend that is partially due to labor mobility (Brydon and Chant, 1989). Buvenic and Youssef (1987) cite migration, mechanization of agriculture, urbanization, and marginalization of low-income workers as reasons for the increased number of female-headed households in the developing countries (cited in Buvenic, *et al.,* 1983). In Africa, this trend has been encouraged by colonial policies that moved young men to cities to work on plantations. Women who were left behind in villages married older men. This increase in age difference, motivated by the colonial employment policies, eventually led to an increased number of female-headed households in both rural and urban areas of Africa (Boserup, 1970; Wilkinson in Momsen and Townsend, 1987).

[15] Machado in her study of female-headed households in Brazil found that of all the female-headed households, 20% had no income; this number for male-headed households was only 1.3% (Machado in Moser, 1987). For those female-headed households that had an income, 43% earned only half the minimum wage (UNCHS, 1987). Machado also found 80% of daughters in female-headed households missed school in order to assist their working mothers with domestic responsibilities (Machado Neto quoted in Schmink, 1982).

[16] I use the terms "producer" and "reproducer" based on the definition presented by Brydon and Chant, 1989. They define production as "direct generation of income," and reproduction as "unwaged activities contributing to the maintenance and welfare of household members" (1989: 188).

[17] In Jamaica, where almost 40% of households are female headed, 75% of working women were not eligible for housing loans at private financing institutions because of their low official income (Schmink, 1985). In Solando Sites-and-Services Project, Quito, Ecuador, 30% of all benefit applicants were female-headed households. From that number, 46% did not qualify for the program, because their income levels did not meet the eligibility criteria (Moser, 1987).

[18] An example of a site-and-service project in Dakshinpuri Settlement, Delhi, India, is illustrative of such. In this project, which involved the relocation of 60,000 inhabitants of a settlement to a site closer to industrial areas, 27% of the women involved in informal-sector jobs mostly close to the central city lost their jobs, while only 5% of men lost theirs (cited in Moser and Peake, 1987).

[19] An example of this is Dandora Site-and-Service Project in Nairobi, Kenya, where zoning restrictions caused more than half the local women to discontinue their small enterprises operated from the home (Nimpuno-Parente, 1985; cited in Moser and Peake, 1987).

[20] For an excellent anthropological work on concepts of female modesty and male honor among Moslem societies, see the work of Lila Abu-Lughod (1986), *Veiled Sentiments, Honor and Poetry in a Bedouin Society,* University of California Press. This study explores the importance of these cultural codes as mechanisms of social control.

[21] Also see Beneria and Roldan, 1987. In their study of women home-workers in Mexico they found that though women had increased access to monetary resources but often they did not have the control of their income, they emphasized the role of consciousness raising, along with material resources for increasing control of women of their resources.

[22] Sen in Irene Tinker (ed.), 1990, refers to this duality in roles of women for structural change by making a distinction between viewing women as "patients" or as "agents." While women's perception of their contributions and claims is influenced by socially constructed values, women also act as agents of change who affect the society's structure and culture.

[23] In Tinker, Irene (ed.), 1990.

[24] Sen also makes a serious linkage between women's perceptions of their value and contributions and their life expectancy and rates of mortality. He demonstrates that, in developing societies where women have a higher rate of outside home activity (Sub-Saharan Africa, East and Southeast Asia), women's life expectancy is higher. "Since mortality and survival are not independent of neglect and care," he argues, this reflects the importance of perceptual factors in acknowledging women's contribution as "productive" and valuable.

References

Antrobus, Peggy 1987. "Feminist Issues in Development," in *World Education Inc. Report,* Fall.

Beck, Lois, and Keddie, Nikki (eds.), 1978. *Women in the Muslim World,* Cambridge, Harvard University Press.

Beneria, Lourdes, and Roldan, M. 1987. *The Cross Roads of Class and Gender: Industrial Homework, Subcontracting, and Household Dynamics in Mexico City,* Chicago: University of Chicago Press.

Beneria, Lourdes, and Sen, Gita, 1981. "Accumulation, Reproduction, and Women's Role in Economic Development: Boserup Revisited," *Signs,* 7 (21):279–298.

Blondet, Cecilia, 1990. "Establishing an Identity: Women Settlers in a Poor Lima Neighborhood," in Elizabeth Jelin, ed., *Women and Social Change in Latin America,* London, Zed Press.

Boserup, Ester, 1970. *Women's Role in Economic Development,* London: George Allan and Unwin Ltd.

Brydon, L., and Chant, S., 1989. *Women in the Third World, Gender Issues in Rural and Urban Areas,* Hants, England: Edward Elgar Publishing Ltd.

Buvenic, M. et al. (eds.), 1983. *Women and Poverty in the Third World,* Baltimore: The John Hopkins University Press.

Charlton, Sue Ellen M., 1984. *Women in the Third World Development,* Boulder, Colorado: Westview Press.

Carlson, E., and Bhagat, 1984. *Housing and Economic Development: A Women's Perspective,* New York, Report of a Symposium, Conference of Non-Governmental Organizations in Consultative Status with UN/ECOSCC (C.O.N.G.O.)

Chant, Sylvia, 1976. "Family Formation and Female Roles in Queretaro, Mexico," *Bulletin of Latin American Research,* No. 4, pp. 17–32.

Crummett, M., 1987. "Rural Women and Migration In Latin America" in: Deer, C.D., and Leon, M. (eds.), *Feminist Perspectives in Latin American Agricultural Development,* Boulder, Colorado: Westview Press.

Fernandez-Kelly, Maria Patricia, 1983. *For We Are Sold, I and My People: Women and Industry in Mexico's Frontier,* Albany: SUNY Press.

Gonzales de la Rocha, Mercedes, 1986. *Los Resources de la Pobreza, familias de Bajo Ingresos de Guadalajara,* Guadalajara: El Colegio de Jalisco.

Hansen, Karen Tranbergh, 1987. "Urban Women and Work in Africa," *Trans Africa Forum,* 4 (3).

Jaquette, Jane, 1982. "Women and Modernization Theory" *World Politics,* 34/2.

Kendiyoti, Deniz, 1988. "Bargaining with Patriarchy" *Gender and Society,* 2 (3).

Lago, Maria Soledad, 1987. "Rural Women and the Neo-Liberal Model in Chile" in Deere, C.D., and Leon, M., (eds.), *Rural Women and State Policy,* Boulder: Westview Press.

Lawson, Victoria, and Klak, Thomas, 1990. "Conceptual Linkages in the Study of Production and Reproduction in Latin America," *Economic Geography,* 66.

Leacock, Eleanor, and Helen Safa (eds.), 1986. *Women's Work: Development and the Division of Labor by Gender,* South Hadley, Mass.: Bergin and Garvey.

Mernissi, Fatima, 1976. "The Moslem World" in: Tinker, I., and Bramsen, M.B., (eds.), *Women and the World Development,* New York: Prager.

_____, 1975. *Beyond the Veil,* Cambridge: Schewkman Publishing Company.

Mies, Maria, and Bennholdt-Thomsen, Veronika, and Von Werlhof, Claudia, 1988. *Women the Last Colony,* New Delhi: Kali Women Press.

Mies, Maria, 1986. *Patriarchy and Accumulation on a World Scale: Women in the International Division of Labor,* London: Zed Books.

_____, 1982. *The Lace Makers of Narsapur, Indian Housewives Produce for the World Market,* London: Zed Press.

Molineux, Maxine, 1981. "Women in Socialist Societies" in Young, K., Wolkowitz, C., and McCullagh, R., (eds.), *Of Marriage and the Market: Women's Subordination in International Perspectives,* London: CES Books.

Momsen, J. and Townsend, J., 1987. *Geography of Gender in the Third World,* Albany: SUNY Press.

Moser, Caroline and Peake, Linda (eds.), 1987. *Women, Human Settlements, and Housing,* New York: Tavistock Publications.

Moser, Caroline, 1982. "A Home of One's Own: Squatter Housing Strategies in Guayaquil, Ecuador," in: Gilbert, A., Hardy, J., and Ramirez, R. (eds.), *Urbanization in Contemporary Latin America,* New York: John Wiley.

_____, 1988. "Housing Policy and Women : Towards a Gender Aware Approach," *DPU Gender and Planning Working Paper,* No.7, London Development Planning Unit, Bartlett School of Architecture and Planning, University College.

_____, 1989. "Community Participation in Urban Projects," *Progress in Planning,* Diamond, D., *et al.* (eds.), 32, part 2, Oxford: Oxford University Press.

Nader, Laura, 1989. "Orientalism, Occidentalism and the Control of Women," *Cultural Dynamics,* 2(3).

Nash, June, and Safa, Helen, (eds.), 1976. *Sex and Class in Latin America,* New York: Prager.

_____, (eds.), 1985. *Women and Change in Latin America,* South Hadley, Mass.: Bergin and Garvey.

Overholt, Catherine, *et al.* (eds.) 1985. *Gender Roles in Development Projects,* West Hartford: Kumarian Press, Inc.

Portes, Alejandro, Castells, Manuel, and Benton, Lauren, 1989. *Informal Economy,* Baltimore: The John Hopkins Univ. Press.

Schmink, Marianne, 1985. "The Working Group Approach to Women and Urban Services", *Ekistics 310,* Jan./February issue, pp. 76–83.

Sen, Gita, and Grown, Caren, 1987. "Development Alternatives with Women for a New Era," in Gita Sen, and Caren Grown, *Development, Crisis, and Alternative Visions: Third World Women's Perspectives,* New York: Monthly Review Press.

Smith, Joan, Wallerstein, Immanuel, and Evers, Hans-Dieter 1984. *Households and The World-Economy,* Beverly Hills: Sage Publications.

Tiano, Susan, 1984. "The Public-Private Dichotomy: Theoretical Perspectives on Women in Development" in *Social Science Journal,* 21(4).

Tinker, Irene, et al., 1976. *Women and the World Development,* New York: Prager.

Tinker, Irene, 1987. "The Case for Legalizing Street Foods," *Ceres,* 20 (5).

Tinker, Irene (ed.), 1990. *Persistent Inequalities: Women and World Development,* New York: Oxford University Press.

UNCHS, 1987. "The Involvement of Women in Grassroots efforts and Low Income Shelter Projects" in: *Women and Human Settlements Development,* Nairobi, UNCHS.

Van Vliet, Willem, (ed.), 1988. *Women, Housing and Community,* Vermont, Avebury: Gower Publishing Company.

Ward, Kathryn (ed.), 1990. *Women Workers and Global Restructuring,* Ithaca: Cornell University, IRL Press.

Ward, Peter, and Chant, Sylvia, 1987. "Community Leadership and Self-help Housing," *Progress in Planning,* 27, part 2. Pergamon Journals Ltd.

Youssef, Nadia, 1972. "Differential Labor Force Participation of Women in Latin American and Middle Eastern Countries: The Influence of Family Characteristics," *Social Forces,* 51:135–53.

Chapter 28

My Home Is My World: Women, Shelter, and Work in a Malaysian Town

Norazit Selat

Norazit Mohd Selat has a Ph.D. in Anthropology from Monash University, Melbourne, Australia, and is currently associate professor in the Department of Malay Studies at the University of Malaya in Kuala Lumpur. He was a Fulbright Fellow at the College of Architecture and Urban Planning at the University of Michigan.

This paper focuses on two basic issues facing the laboring class of a locality[1] situated in the town of Muar, Johor, Malaysia. The first is related to the problem of finding a home, which, however small or shabby, working people can call their own. (And if they rent it, the rent should be minimal so that they can save money to buy or build their own house later on.) The second issue is related to the role of women, especially with regard to the Malay saying "my home is my world" (*rumah itu dunia ku*). The home should not only provide basic shelter, it should also be comfortable to live in and beautiful so as to be the envy of the neighborhood. Comfort is measured not only in space but also in amenities the homeowner possesses.

The Locality and Its People

The locality, here fictitiously named Lorong Sembilang, is situated about 1 km away from the center of the town Muar. Muar is approximately 180 km south of Kuala Lumpur, the capital of Malaysia, and 160 km north of Singapore.

It has been said that "[modern] urbanization is essentially the product of capitalist development and expansion" (Roberts, 1978:11). The town of Muar is no exception. Structurally, it was the outcome of British capitalism as well as the positive will of the then ruler, Sultan Abu Bakar. Muar was born as the rest of the state of Johor became embroiled in the production of pepper and gambier (Selat, 1987; Trocki, 1979). The town of Muar was planned to grow from a few shophouses that had sprung up in the context of developing capitalistic production into a modern Malaysian town. Like all Malaysian towns, Muar too reflects plural characteristics. While the Chinese and Indians form the majority in the town center, the Malays settled in ethnically defined communities and localities on the outskirts of the town. Lorong Sembilang, although not one of the Malay pioneering communities, is one such settlement. It is the product of the urbanization process, which sees the growth of a large population of landless people, and Lorong Sembilang itself came into being as the need for housing became greater. The locality houses a majority of Malay wage earners of the laboring class.

Lorong Sembilang has been built up on reclaimed swamp land. In a sense, it is a "coastal" Malay locality; the sea at high tide is only half a kilometer away, and the area between the settlement and the sea is covered with thick mangrove swamps. The sea is not visible from any point in the settlement and is accessible only by way of the two drainage canals, Parit Betuk and Parit Lokan. The settlement consists of sixty-four houses, of which sixty are occupied. One of the four unoccupied houses is used as an occasional lodging house for the Indonesian migrant workers who use the locality as their embarkation point. Ethnic composition of the locality is made up of 1 Indian family, 2 Chinese families, and 57 Malay families. The total population is 227 people, consisting of 70 men, 62 women, and 96 children. Of the 57 Malay families, 5 are renting their houses.

The people of the locality trace their origin to three different areas: Indonesia, Terengganu, and Muar, especially from the Malay community close by. Of the people from Indonesia, only one is a recent migrant. The local people of Muar who moved into the settlement also include those who worked in the town as laborers but upon retirement had nowhere else to go. With the money they received from their Employee Provident Fund, some constructed modest houses for themselves and their families. The rest of the settlers consist of the married children of the residents and others who have moved in from the neighboring areas.

As land available for housing close to the road or canals that service the locality is now scarce, the children of the residents have to build their own homes farther in the swamp land. People wanting to settle in Lorong Sembilang must either be sponsored by a resident or be relatives of one. The applicant does not need the support of the whole community, but it is essential that the applicant's immediate neighbors approve. This is important because it can then be ensured that the land is not earmarked by the neighbors for their immediate kin. The settlement keeps expanding as immediate neighbors of each family build their own houses. There is no physical limit to the development of the locality as yet, for the land is still plentiful for those who are willing to put in a lot of labor to reclaim the swamp land. Those who do so also have to bear with the inconvenience of not having basic amenities like electricity and water.

There are three types of houses built in the locality: (a) the traditional wooden stilt house, (b) the traditional stilt house with a ground level kitchen, and (c) the house built on the ground level but on a raised foundation. Because of the marshy character of the land, clay and rubble are brought from the outside (from demolished buildings) and are pounded into the ground before laying the foundation. A house usually consists of the bedroom, a separate living room, and a kitchen. Houses with two or more bedrooms are rare.

These people are squatters[2] and, as is common with squat-ter housing, the houses are built close together and most do not have a clear boundary demarcating claims, although at the initial stage they may have an imaginary one. Each individual plot is often drawn by convention and usage. Complaints about intrusion are sometimes made but they usually come to nothing; the dwellings, by then, have been raised. As squatters, they have no legal avenues to redress the problem, nor can they bring the issue up with the headman, as the locality does not have one.

More often than not, the houses form into clusters belonging to a single kinship group, often an extended family. Why and where the housing comes into being can be best understood from an actual example. The Celak family built five houses on a plot approximately 100 meters long and 30 meters wide. There is still a vacant lot between the fourth lot and the fifth house for another house. The house nearer to the road is the main house built by Celak when he first settled in the area and is now occupied and owned by his second daughter. The parents gave her the house at the time when she was a tenant in sufferance elsewhere. Celak then built another house behind the original home. The front of the new house is only 2 meters from the kitchen of the original home.

Later Celak decided that, as his eldest daughter did not own a house in the area, he should build one for her to inherit, even though she does not live in Muar. Celak constructed the house on a site immediately beside the kitchen of the original house. The land space is approximately 10 meters which is just enough to construct a two-bedroom house complete with a kitchen, lounge, and attached bathroom and toilet. There is even a small verandah in the front of the house. Celak managed to fit in the house by building it along the wall of the original kitchen. As it shares a common wall, one of the bedrooms is always dark. The dwelling was built by Celak with the help of his sons and sons-in-law. The bulk of the money for the construction was provided by the eldest daughter's husband. When the house was completed, the son-in-law told Celak that "since he was not coming back yet," Celak could rent the place and use the income as his "cigarette money" (duit rokok). Celak spends the rent in the town on his morning coffee. Celak charges M$80 a month rent for the house while the tenant pays his own electricity bill.[3] The water rate is shared as there is only one meter for the five households sharing the water. The water charges are about $10M a month for each house.

The fourth house is an extension of Celak's present house. The extension was built when his second son (Tarmimi) married. He had been working then as a laborer/carpenter with the Town Council for only six months and had no savings. His wedding was financed by the family. After the marriage, the young couple stayed with Tarmimi's parents, his younger brother, and his niece. Tarmimi since became an enterprising young man with responsibilities and built himself a separate house with its own lounge room and entrance annexed to the main house. His part of the house can also be entered through a door from the lounge room of the main house. At the back of this house there is another small house. This is constructed on stilts. Celak built the house for his third daughter who works and resides in Johor Baru with her family. Her husband has property and a house nine kilometers away from Johor Baru, and it is unlikely that she too will return to Muar. Celak cannot rent the house as it has no electricity, so it was turned into a hostel for the itinerant Indonesian immigrants waiting for boats to take them back to Sumatra. Celak charges M$2 per night for each individual.

Squatting: The Urban Poor's Solution to Shelter

Land, both in the town and its hinterland, has become an expensive commodity and many of the people cannot afford to own it. As a result, the urbanization process has also included the growth of squatter settlements for the urban poor. The birth of Lorong Sembilang is a result of such a process. The characteristics of Lorong Sembilang are clearly reflected in Roberts' observation on the squatter settlement in general: "in most cases, squatter settlements appear in the outskirts of the city and in government-owned land that has relatively little infrastructure for commercial or industry purposes. Striking but common examples are location of land used for rubbish dumps, on swampy ground, or over lagoons" (1982: 375).

Squatting in Lorong Sembilang has evolved from its early beginning to what it is now a response to the urban residents' need to provide their own shelters (cf. Roberts, 1982: 376; Drakakis-Smith, 1981: 63). The excessive cost of housing in relation to their low income means that most of the urban dwellers cannot afford legally to own their houses. In urban Malaysia, the cheapest house is around M$40,000. In most areas, the housing developers are reluctant to build low-cost houses. They would rather construct double-story terrace houses and maximize their profits. Loans from

the banks are also difficult to secure as the banks need collateral.

Lorong Sembilang, however, is somewhat different from the squatter settlements found in larger towns such Johor Baru or Kuala Lumpur. There, the squatter settlements are overcrowded and housing space is difficult to find (Kassim, 1983; Suratman, 1979). As living spaces reach the saturation point in a locality, new settlements are established. The poor and the indigent are willy-nilly colonizing the cities and towns, for it is in these centers that the fruits of capitalistic development are most concentrated.

The growth of the squatter settlements in the larger town is, in the main, a result of a continuous rural-urban immigration, for the larger towns offer better opportunities (McGee, 1972). On the other hand, Lorong Sembilang's growth is still slow and is still taking place. As yet, the locality has no serious problem of housing space. Unlike the squatter settlement in Kuala Lumpur and other towns, Lorong Sembilang has managed to avoid being labeled as a squatter area (*rumah setinggan*) and having its houses referred to as illegal houses (*rumah haram*).[4] The absence of labeling indicates that the authorities in Muar do not as yet view squatting as a threat. More than that, the people of Lorong Sembilang had the protection of UMNO (United Malay National Organization), the main component of the National Coalition Government.[5] In this sense, the settlement exists as part of a system of state-party patronage. UMNO, and hence the government, need the residents politically to offset the numbers of Chinese who support the opposition party. The state parliamentary seat of Muar is held by the MCA (Malaysian Chinese Association), so the Malay vote is crucial. As the Chinese vote is split between the MCA and the opposition DAP (Democratic Action Party), the Malay vote tips the balance to the MCA, the ally of UMNO.

Most of the homes in Lorong Sembilang are built by the owners themselves. While in the field, I was able to observe the construction of two houses. The first house was built with the help of some relatives. The owner of the house, after buying all the necessary materials, sought the help of his father and four brothers. They took two months to complete the house. The work done is not refined or *halus*. From a distance, it can be seen that the house tilts slightly, but, as the owner said, it is his own. He rewarded his brothers with cigarettes and money, totalling only one-tenth of the market value of their labor. The other house was constructed using the neighbors' labor. The owner requested the help of a few neighbors two or three days prior to the raising of the house's structure and, because the dwelling was a small one, it did not take long before the structure was raised and the floor and roof laid. The nailing of the wall was completed later in the day. The owner, in appreciation of the help of his neighbors, served them rice and chicken curry. During the work, he also served them coffee, biscuits, and cigarettes.

The cost of materials for building a house is high, so a few persons constructed parts of their houses with pilfered materials, especially the timber and planks from the nearby construction sites. I was informed that one man in particular had constructed his house, barring the nails, from materials that he had pilfered and accumulated over a period of time. From time to time, those who have the means will renovate or extend their houses. One in particular built a porch with cement bought cheaply from a man who stole it from his workplace. There are others who have built extensions to their houses using discarded materials or materials they have brought home from their workplace.

The Women of Lorong Sembilang and Work

The women of the locality make significant social and economic contributions to the household economy. Most of the women's work is household labor and therefore not statistically recorded. It remains hidden and unappreciated by most economic and anthropological research, and yet women make positive contributions to the household and the community in creating use values. Furthermore, when they toil as wage earners, petty commodity producers, or self-employed business-women, their earnings are decisive to the family income and enable the family to enjoy a lifestyle better than that enjoyed by ordinary working-class families.

However, before I discuss this further, it is pertinent to discuss first the status of women in the Malay society. The Malay residential and economic unit is the house-hold (Djamour, 1965: 53; Swift, 1963: 277). It is defined by Djamour "as a group of people who live in the same house and engage in a large number of common activities as well as sharing a common budget" (1965: 53). More frequently, the household consists of a married couple living together with their unmarried children. Heads of the household, the majority of whom are men, are usually the chief money earners (Djamour, 1965: 53; Swift, 1965: 37 and ch. 5; Manderson, 1983: 5). Marriage is what gives sanctity to the Malay household and it is emphasized in the performing of the

family's objective requirements. A wife's primary task is to carry out domestic duties, cook, run the household, and care for the children. The husband is considered the primary provider of the family (Swift, 1963: 277; Roose, 1963: 290). Thus, there is a clear distinction between men and women in the division of labor.

However, the division of labor is not rigid and, when necessary, husbands will undertake work normally carried out by wives (Swift, 1963: 278). For example, a Malay man seldom washes clothes, but he will do so if his wife falls sick and he cannot find any female relatives to help him. The dominant position of the husband in a Malay household prompted Swift to write the following: "There is no question that in the Malay's image of their society the husband is regarded as the dominant partner in a marriage. Not only do they maintain that this should be so, but also seem to believe that it is so" (1963: 278).

This image of the husband as the dominant figure is, in reality, only partly true, for a woman also has authority over matters pertaining to the family. She does not hesitate to express her opinion particularly if the issue discussed concerns her as, for example, in the building of a new house or the choosing of a son- or a daughter-in-law (Swift, 1963: 279). Swift also notes that he has seen instances of women exerting their influence in economic matters (1963: 279). Thus, he concludes that, although the Malay husband is regarded as the dominant partner, it must be realized that the Malay family, and the relations between husband and wife, are much more egalitarian than they appear at first sight and than the people say they are (1963: 279). In short, there is a disjunction between ideology and the realities of day-to-day life and its attendant decision making.

It is also generally agreed that the household, as a basic unit of production and consumption, comes under the authority of the women. The women manage domestic finances as well as budget the various needs of the household and its members (Firth, 1966: 27; Manderson, 1975: 95). They usually receive the necessary cash earned by their husbands and assume responsibility for spending and saving (Manderson, 1983: 6). Research on the rural economy also demonstrates that women contribute significantly to the household economy (Firth, 1966: 30; Barnard, 1983; Ng, 1984). Apart from being involved in housework such as cooking, sweeping, and washing, women's labor is crucial in the production of rice as well as in the fishing industry.

It can be clearly seen that women are engaged in every aspect of the economic production of the household, whether in the production of use values or in commodity production. Unlike their rural counterparts, people in the urban centers have to earn their living away from the family estate. Living in a monetized economy, they obviously depend on money to live. One important feature of the urban economy is that in the towns foods such as rice, tapioca, edible ferns, bananas, bamboo shoots, and coconuts which, in the countryside, are grown or gathered, have to be bought. For the most part, urban women's work is also limited to wage employment as factory workers or domestic help. Only a few have been privileged enough to set up their own small businesses.

The majority of women in Lorong Sembilang (68%, N=42) do not work at any form of outside work. Only ten of the active adult females in the locality are wage earners. Of these, four are in full-time employment as factory workers while the other six work part-time as washerwomen. Among the women wage earners, there is a correlation between age and the type of work a person does. The factory workers are young, unmarried girls in their late teens or early twenties, while the washerwomen are married with children and are above forty years old. All the teenage females who work in the factory left school at sixteen when they failed their Lower Certificate Of Education exam (at form three). These girls did so badly that they themselves decided to seek wage work rather than resit the examination. This paper will not focus and discuss the work of the wage earners, especially the factory workers, as the issue has been discussed in great length and detail by a number of social scientists doing research in Malaysia (see Ariffin, 1980; Ong, 1983; O'Brien 1981; Lim, 1983; Lin, 1985; Yun, 1984; Karim, 1985). Instead, this paper will focus on the work of the self-employed women in the locality.

The Self-Employed Women of Lorong Sembilang

Only seven of the women in the locality are self-employed. Six of them run petty businesses, four of whom sell mainly clothing materials bought in Singapore, while the other two sell items such as *batik* cloth, *songket* (cloth made of gold thread) and brassware from Terengganu. One other woman is a seamstress. To understand the nature and mode of operation of these women, we need to look at a few case studies. One of the women involved in buying clothes from Singapore is Gayah who, apart from being a self-employed business-woman, is also a mother and a housewife. Although Singapore is 160 km away, it holds a great attraction for the people of Muar because of its duty-free goods. There are many others like Gayah and they go on an organized bus trip to Singapore at least once a month. The chartered bus trips cost M$17 each time. So far, all travel has been on Fridays as this is the most suitable time for Gayah. The school is closed and her daughters are therefore able to cook for the family and do the rest of the domestic chores.

In Singapore, the bulk of Gayah's shopping consists of dress materials for women, which she resells. Occasionally, she buys domestic electrical appliances such as blenders and toasters or other household items such as plastic flowers, Pyrex plates, dried longan (fruit), aluminum tea pots, and bath towels. She buys these items only when she has special orders from her clients. The electric blender is in great demand among her clients because it makes the task of grinding spices easier. Gayah can buy only one such item on each trip because the blender is a taxable item, and it is cumbersome and bulky, she smuggles it through the custom checkpoint at Johor Baru.

Gayah has evolved her own method of escaping duties on the goods that she buys in Singapore. She and the rest of the passengers leave the bus just before it reaches the checkpoint enclave. The bus is then driven to the other end onto Malaysian territory and waits for the passengers there. The passengers sort out their own belongings and declare them to the officers. Generally, Gayah avoids the check by walking across the checkpoint laden with the shopping bags containing part of her haul while the custom officers are busy with the other passengers. Even if the custom officers detect her, they can only yell at her as they cannot leave their posts. As there are so many people around, Gayah soon loses herself among the crowd.

When the security is tighter and there are more custom officers on duty, Gayah employs other methods to protect her goods. She stuffs the clothing material into her handbag or into the teapots that she has bought. At times she places the material right at the bottom of her shopping bags, leaving one or two pieces of material on the top to escape prying. She also makes sure that the cloth pieces are distributed among all her shopping bags and are not stacked in just one bag. She hopes to make it tiresome for the customs officer to place his hands right into each of the bags and check all the contents. The materials placed on the top are meant to make the officers believe that she has just "bought a few but they are for my own use." Gayah always removes the packaging bearing brand names prior to the customs check up. By removing the boxes and wrappings, she visibly reduces the bulk of the goods, as well as their actual volume and weight, thereby making it innocuous.

Gayah's mother, Limah, is active in the small business domain too, but she is not a regular visitor to Singapore. She goes shopping only when she visits her two daughters and their families who live in Johor Baru, for a few days once every two to three months. On these occasions, she goes to the Woodland shopping center, the nearest shopping center after the causeway in Singapore, at least twice to do her shopping. She then leaves the bulk of her clothing materials at a relative's house, who lives close to the shopping center, carrying only a few items across herself. Again, because of the small quantity she is not taxed at all. When Limah gets back to her daughter's house in Johor Baru, she asks her granddaughter (daughter's daughter), who works in one of the electronic factories in Singapore, to take the materials across the causeway, one or two pieces a day as she returns from work. Given that the material that her granddaughter brings across is small in quantity, she also is not taxed. Thus, bit by bit, all Limah's materials are taken through the checkpoint and it will be time for her to return to Muar.

Mode of Business

The customers of these small businesswomen are located not only in the district of Muar, but also in the district of Batu Pahat. Gayah's customers, for example, are also located in Melaka and even as far away as Kuala Lumpur. In Muar itself, Gayah developed a network of customers who themselves expand the network further by word of mouth. Pahl refers to these sets of relationships as "gossip networks" (Pahl, 1981: 149). Thus, when Gayah delivers an order to a customer, other women in the neighborhood who happen to be around may also have a look. If they are interested, they too can place an order with Gayah. In turn, they might introduce their friends or relatives to Gayah as well.

In Batu Pahat, and in Kuala Lumpur, Gayah's younger sister and youngest brother assist her in the sale of the clothing material. In Melaka, she has a distant female relative to act as her agent. Gayah's younger brother also sells materials belonging to the mother, Limah. But the brother finds it easier to sell Gayah's material rather than his mother's because his mother's taste in designs is old (*tua*). What Limah considers to be beautiful is

seen as old-fashioned by customers in Kuala Lumpur, many of whom are fashion- and status-conscious women at the son's workplace. These customers prefer Gayah's materials because they are not only modish but also are not available in Kuala Lumpur. Gayah pays her brother and sister, plus her distant relative in Melaka, either in cash or kind, for acting as her sales agents. While the relative in Melaka is paid at a fixed rate of 10% for her efforts, Gayah pays her brother a token sum. The sister prefers her payment to be in kind; sometimes she receives materials in payment, but once she asked Gayah to find her a blender or an electric rice cooker. Instead Gayah soon bought her sister a rice cooker because she felt that the labor expended has reached the monetary value of the rice cooker.

Gayah's relationship with her brother and sister is not solely based on money. In fact, the relationship is founded on the notion of reciprocity and need. Knowing that her sister is relatively poor (her husband is employed as a carpenter and is only seasonally employed), Gayah often buys her sister's children clothes or fruit on her Singapore trips. The sister too gives Gayah some of the produce from her garden every time Gayah visits her. While in Kuala Lumpur, Gayah sleeps at her brother's house. Gayah depends on her siblings' continuation of her business for, apart from selling, they also collect the money owed by the customers and Gayah needs the cash flow.

Gayah and the rest of the businesswomen sell their products on credit. The people in and around Muar repay a standard installment of M$5 a month, so it takes a person six months to pay a debt of M$30. Gayah keeps all the details of the debts in a little black book which she carries around when the repayments are collected. Gayah's "agents" also sell her products on the same terms. The only difference is that, because her customers in Kuala Lumpur, for example, have regular employment, they pay off their debts at M$10 a month. She also encourages them to pay cash by telling her brother to charge up to M$5 less than the credit price. Thus, if Gayah buys a piece of material for M$22, she'll sell it for M$40 on credit and M$35 if the customer pays cash. Gayah charges more for credit payments because of the inconvenience of having to collect the debts, having to wait for cash and also because this method of payment entailed a few risks. Many of them have deferred payments or reneged on payments.

In her line of work, Gayah faces intense competition from other businesswomen, not only from within the locality but also from elsewhere. To maintain an advantage over her rivals, Gayah sometimes goes to the extent of creating her own market, forming a demand for items that will give her a good return. Once Gayah found that there was a woman in Muar who was good at sewing floral embroidery with her sewing machine and whose prices were reasonable. So Gayah bought plain-colored materials from Singapore to make tablecloths or bed sheets and pillow cases and got the woman to embroider them. They cost Gayah M$50 to produce and she sold them at around M$70. I saw another example of Gayah's ingenuity when I first moved into my rented house. As decoration, I hung various kinds of bamboo hats on the wall. Gayah saw them, liked the idea, and promptly went and bought some hats. But she went one better. On one of her trips to Singapore, she bought a variety of silk cloth flowers and wove them through the hats. She set a new trend and soon she had orders for them from neighbors and visitors to her house.

Gayah also sells goods that she casually buys on her local business trips. She once bought some brooms made from the spines of the coconut leaves and sells them at a profit of 20 cents each. She also sells grated coconut from her house. She originally bought the electric coconut grater for her daughter's wedding, but because she can get coconut cheaply from one of her customers, she decided to sell grated coconut as well. She has a profit of 15 cents on each coconut. Thus, Gayah's business is not limited to selling high-priced products. She sells anything as long as the product has an exchange value. According to her, 20 cents would buy her a small packet of salt or a bunch of herbs, which she uses to flavor the fish dishes.

Most of the time, Gayah is also able to make some money by selling the products of her own household labor. A few of the Indonesians who move regularly in and out of Lorong Sembilang eat their meals at her house; consequently, they pay Gayah a small sum for the meals she cooks and also pay her for the afternoon teas and snacks. Gayah does not see this as an extra chore for she has to cook for the whole family any-way—she simply prepares an extra quantity of food.

Gayah is not the only one among her relatives who engages in this form of business. Her mother as well as her sister-in-law do not miss an opportunity either. They have their own Indonesian customers, charging them M$3.50 for a packed meal (*nasi bungkus*), which consists of a generous portion of rice, fish curry, *sambal* (chilly condiment), vegetables, and plenty of gravy. On a good day, these women may make around M$30 to

M$50. This source of money is seasonal in nature. Nevertheless, when the Indonesians are around Gayah never fails to sell them some of her materials as well as items such as bath towels and embroidered pillow cases. Gayah sells *kretek* (Indonesian clove cigarettes) which she buys from the newly arrived Indonesians who desperately need Malaysian currency for their onward fares. The *kretek* are resold through her networks in Melaka and Kuala Lumpur. In Kuala Lumpur, for example, the kretek are sold through her brother-in-law (sister's husband). The brother-in-law takes whatever money Gayah gives to him as his *duit kopi* and *duit minyak* (coffee and petrol money). The reference to "the expenses for coffee and petrol" is a hint to Gayah that the money to be given should be an adequate reward. Yet this is not a source of strife because her brother-in-law is never placed in the position of having to demand compensation or reward as Gayah gives freely of her own accord. Here again, the elements of kinship and give-and-take interweave.

One of the women in the community works at home as a seamstress to earn extra income for the family. The work is seasonal, the bulk of her orders coming just before *Hari Raya* [6] and the beginning of the school year. She specializes in women's dresses and charges M$10 for the *baju kurung* (loose blouse) and M$12 for *baju kebaya* (tight fitting sarung and blouse). She does all her sewing inbetween her household tasks, so it takes her between two and three days to sew a Malay dress. The *baju kurung* takes slightly longer as the collar of the dress has to be embroidered with herring-bone stitching. In these intricate relationships among customers, relatives, and the trader, gift exchanges, kinship, and commerce are combined with feminine identity to create and sustain the small business structure.

Self-Employment and the Appropriation of Nature

The women in Lorong Sembilang also depend on the swamp, not only for their own food but also for extra income. The mangrove swamp is a source of various types of shellfish and edible snails. The shellfish collected are *lokan,* which are semi-circular in shape and can reach the size of the palm of a young child, and *sepetang,* which are tubular in shape and are around five to seven centimeters long. A good snail is about the size of a thumb. The work of collecting is laborious. If the shells gathered are for sale, then (because of the number to be picked) the work will take a lot longer than if the women gather them for food. The mode of collection and the time required varies according to the type of shellfish.

The food items are gathered by women in groups. *Lokan* are collected during dry weather when they can be easily located and when walking on the dry mud is a lot easier. The *lokan* are found close to the surface, but only a trained eye can detect the slightly open shells which enable the creature to breathe in air. Sometimes all that is visible is a small crack about two or three centimeters long on the surface of the mud. In a good dry season, the women may gather the *lokan* in areas far away from Lorong Sembilang. When this happens, they place the bags, as they fill, at well-marked locations and walk home. Later, their husbands will bring these bags back to them on their motorcycles or bicycles. Thus there is much cooperation and interdependence between the men and the women.

Sepetang (the other kind of shellfish) are collected when the swamp is still wet. The *sepetang* have to be dug out from the ground with a sharp stick or a *parang* (machete). Not only is the task more laborious than the collecting of *lokan,* but the *sepetang* are also more difficult to find. The gathering of *sepetang* is not popular with the women even though they fetch a better price in the market. Snails or *siput* are easier to collect, but they are best gathered during high tide. At low tide, the snails scatter over the ground to forage and are thus difficult to detect, whereas at high tide they climb the trunks of the mangrove trees to escape the rising water. They can be gathered easily from the trees. A person can collect a bucketful within an hour or so.

The shells and snails the women gather are sold to both Malay and Chinese dealers in the market. The *lokan* fetch M$2.80 per 100; the *sepetang,* because they are difficult to gather and popular with the Chinese, are worth M$6.00 a kilogram. The snails are the cheapest at M$0.80 a kilogram. For a few hours work, the women can earn between M$5.00 to M$10.00 a day. The women keep some of the *lokan* and *snails* for their own family, although the snails have to be kept in a covered basin for a few days for them to "spit out" the mud in their bodies. Otherwise the consumer is likely to suffer a bad stomach ache.

Conclusion

As stated earlier, the Malay culture expects the husband to be the breadwinner of the family but the situation in reality is different. In Muar, the earnings of husbands in many families are barely enough to meet the families' basic needs. The husbands take on supplementary work to earn enough money not only to provide more and better food for the family but, in a few cases, to buy luxuries such as television sets, armchairs, and hi-fi sets. The women work as wives, mothers, and housekeepers but also take up tasks that will bring in cash to increase the family income. There are women in the community, usually with small children, who cannot participate in any form of money-earning activity. Such women are invariably poor. I would also like to note here that four of the women in the community have little choice but to work. Three of them are widows while the other's husband is crippled. All four women work for themselves (and in one case for the husband as well), but as their children are already grown up, their needs are limited. Two of the women work as small business-women while the others are washerwomen.

The rest of the women in the locality who work do it for various reasons. Some work so as to be able to afford clothes for themselves and the children. The money they earn is also used to buy jewelry which the husband cannot afford. One woman wants to save her earnings so that she can make her pilgrimage to Mecca. But all the women, whether working or not and for whatever reason, avoid being overly dependent on their husbands. As one of them said, she does not have to put up with her husband's growls or questions every time she asks him for money.

Gayah works so that she can afford to buy goods which, apart from being useful, also bring her prestige. With the money earned so far, she has managed to install a new asbestos ceiling in the house, replacing the plastic sheetings made from sugar bags sewn together, install a ceiling fan, buy a gas stove complete with oven, paint the house, buy a coconut grater, and install a sink in the kitchen. Gayah is able to lead a life style characteristic of white-collar workers. She is the first person in the community to own a color television set and a hi-fi set. With her earnings, Gayah has also bought her four daughters gold bangles, necklaces, and earrings. She has a savings of about M$1,000 in the bank too. Gayah's contribution to the family income is much appreciated by her husband, who believes that he is a very lucky person to have Gayah as his wife. Apart from being a good wife, mother, and good to kin, Gayah's efforts enable the family to enjoy a good life style.

Thus, urban women, because of greater opportunities not only in self-employment but also in selling their labor, even if only as domestic help, have a degree of independence. They can afford to buy personal items such as jewelry and household goods such as rice cookers and blenders.

Notes

[1] I use the term locality and not community because Lorong Sembilang not only does not have a proper territory, it also does not have a headman, a prayer house, or a community center which are normally associated with a community. The initial field research in the locality was undertaken over two extended periods. The first was between June and December, 1983 and the second between February and September, 1984. Thereafter, regular visits were made to the locality because the landlord and his family, whose house I rented during my stay there, had adopted me. Each visit normally lasts for three to seven days and during each visit I inquired about and made observations of the progress of the locality and its people. The last visit was in 1990 during the Malaysian election. A colleague from the University of Malaya stood as the ruling party's candidate and I went to Muar to help campaign for him. Lorong Sembilang is part of his constituency.

[2] I use the term squatter to mean: "illegal or unlawful occupation of land, whether alienated or unalienated by individuals or groups of individuals" (Kassim, 1983:60).

[3] I stayed in this house during my stay in the locality.

[4] Rumah haram literally means illegal house. It is also known as rumah kilat or lightning house, referring to the speed with which these houses are built. Normally, it is built overnight. Now it is commonly known as rumah setinggan or squatter house.

[5] Malaysia is governed by the Barisan Nasional or National Coalition party consisting of the various ethnic-based parties, such as the United Malay Organization Party (UMNO), the Malaysian Chinese Association (MCA), the Malaysian Indian Congress (MIC), Parti Bansa Dayak Sarawak (PBDS), etc. UMNO is the main component party and the constitution states that the Prime Minister must come from this party.

[6] Hari Raya is celebrated by the Malays, who are Muslims, immediately after the fasting month of Ramadan.

References

Ackerman, S.E., 1980, *Cultural Process in Malaysian Industrialization: A Study of Malay Women Factory Workers,* Ann Arbor, Michigan: University Microfilms International.

Ali, A.H., 1983, "Degradation of Rural Factory Workers: A Study of Their Instrumental Orientation Towards Work," *Ilmu Masyarakat,* Oct.–Dec.

Ariffin, Jamilah, 1980, "Industrial Development in Peninsular Malaysia and Rural-Urban Migration of Women-Workers: Impact and Implications," *Jurnal Ekonomi Malaysia,* 1,1.

Barnard, R., 1979, "The Modernization of Agriculture in a Kedah Village 1967–1978," *Review of Indonesia and Malayan Affairs,* 13.

Barnard, R., 1983, "Housewives and Farmers: Malay Women in the Muda Irrigation Scheme," in L. Manderson (ed.), *Women's Work, Women's Roles,* Canberra: Development Studies Center Monograph 32, Australian National University.

Bell, C., 1974. "The Use of Gossip and Event Analysis in the Study of Suburban Communities," in C. Bell and H. Newby (eds.), *The Sociology of Community: A Selection of Readings,* London: Frank Cass & Co.

Bell, C. and Newby, H., 1971, *Community Studies: An Introduction to the Sociology of the Local Community,* London: George Allen & Unwin.

Djamour, J., 1965, *Malay Kinship and Marriage in Singapore,* London: The Athlone Press.

Drakakis-Smith, D.W., 1979, "The Role of the Private Sector in Housing the Urban Poor in West Malaysia," in M. Rudner & J.C. Jackson (eds.), *Issues in Malaysian Development,* South East Asian Publications, Series 3, Hong Kong: Heineman Asia.

Drakakis-Smith, D.W., 1981, *Urbanization, Housing, and the Development Process,* London: Croom-Helm.

Evers, Hans-Dieter, 1979, "On the Evolution of Urban Society in Malaysia," Second Colloquim, *Change in Malaysia,* James Cook University, 11:43.

Firth, Rosemary, 1966, *Housekeeping Among Malay Peasants,* London: The Athlone Press.

Karim, Wazir Jahan, 1985, "Electronic Woman," *Inside Asia,* Nov–Dec.

Kassim, Azizah,1983, "The Genesis of Squatting in West Malaysia: With Special Reference to the Malays in the Federal Territory," *Malaysia in History,* Vol. 6, No.4.

Lim, Y.C., 1983, "Capitalism, Imperialism, and Patriarchy: The Dilemma of Third-World Workers in Multinational Factories," in: J. Nash and M.P. Fernandez-Kelly (eds.), *Women, Men, and the International Division of Labor,* Albany: State University of New York.

Lin, V., 1985, "Women Workers in the Semiconductor Industry in Singapore and Malaysia: A Political Economy of Health Perspective." Paper presented to the Center of Southeast Asian Studies, Melbourne: Monash University, Nov. 21, 1985.

McGee, T.G., 1963, "The Cultural Role of Cities: A Case Study of Kuala Lumpur," *Journal of Tropical Geography.*

McGee, T.G., 1972, "Rural-Urban Migration in a Plural Society: A Case Study of Malays in West Malaysia," in D.J. Dwyer (ed.), *The City as a Center of Change in Asia,* Hong Kong: Hong Kong University Press.

Manderson, L., 1975, "Women and Work: Continuities of the Past and Present," *Kabar Seberang,* No. 5–6.

Manderson, L. (ed.), 1983, *Women's Work and Women's Roles: Economics and Everyday Life in Indonesia, Malaysia, and Singapore,* Canberra: Development Studies Center Monograph No. 32, The Australian National University.

Ng, Cecilia, 1984, "Production and Reproduction in a Padi-Farming Community in Kirau, Perak," *Ilmu Masyarakat,* 5.

O'Brien, L.N., 1981, "Women and Development: New Directions," Paper presented to the Australian Anthropology Society 1981 Conference, Canberra: Australian National University.

O'Brien, L.N., 1983, "Four Paces Behind: Women's Work in Peninsular Malaysia" in L. Manderson (ed.), *Women's Work, Women"s Roles,* Development Studies Center Monograph 32, Canberra: The Australian National University.

Ong, Aihwa, 1983, "Global Industries and Malay Peasants," in J. Nash and M.P. Fernandez-Kelly (eds.), *Women, Men, and the International Division of Labor,* Albany: SUNY Press.

Pahl, R.E., 1981, "Employment, Work, and the Domestic Division of Labor," in: M. Harloe and E. Lebas, *City, Class, and Capital,* London: Edward Arnold.

Roberts, B., 1978, *Cities of Peasants. The Political Economy of Urbanization in the Third-World,* Beverly Hills: Sage Publications.

Roberts, B., 1982, "Cities in Developing Societies" in H. Alavi and T. Shanin (eds.), *Sociology of Developing Societies,* London: McMillan Press.

Roose, H., 1963, "Changes in the Position of Malay Women," in B. Ward (ed.), *Women in the New Asia,* Paris: UNESCO.

Selat, Norazit, 1985, *Kapitalisme Tahap Pertama di Negeri Melayu Tidak Bersekutu: Johor 1840–1844,* Siri Laporan 5, Projek Penyelidikan Johor, Universiti Malaya, Kuala Lumpur.

Selat, Norazit, 1986, *The People of the Swamp: Work and Money in a Malaysian Town.* Unpublished Ph.D. dissertation, Melbourne: Monash University.
Selat, Norazit, 1987, "The Emergence of Commodity Production in a Malay District: Muar, Johor," *Journal of Contemporary Asia.*

Strange, J., 1981, *Rural Malay Women in Tradition and Transition,* New York: Praeger.

Swift, M.G., 1963, "Men and Women in Malay Society," in B. Ward (ed), *Women in the New Asia,* Paris: UNESCO.

Swift, M.G., 1965, *Malay Peasant Society in Jelebu,* London: The Athlone Press.

Suratman, Yusuf, 1979, *Kemiskinan di Kalangan Orang Melayu di Bandar - Satu Kajian Setinggan di Bandar Johor Baru,* Kuala Lumpur: unpublished M.A. thesis, Department of Anthropology and Sociology, University of Malaya.

Trocki, C.A., 1979, *Prince of Pirates,* Singapore: Singapore University Press.

Wazir, J.K., 1985, "Electronic Woman," *Inside Asia,* Nov–Dec.

Yun, Hing Ai, 1984, *Orientasi Kerja: Satu Kajian Kes Pekerja-Pekerja Kilang di Semenanjung Malaysia,* Siri Laporan 2, Projek Penyelidikan Masyarakat Negeri Johor, Kuala Lumpur: Universiti Malaya.

Yun, Hing Ai, 1985, "The Development and Transformation of Wage Labour in West Malaysia," *Journal of Contemporary Asia,* 15, 2.

Chapter 29
Shelter and Income Opportunities for Women in India

Sulakshana Mahajan

Sulakshana Mahajan is a senior architect with Gherzi Eastern Limited in Bombay. She received her Bachelor of Architecture from the University of Bombay in 1972 and a Post-Graduate Diploma in Product Design from the Indian Institute of Technology in Powai in 1974. She has sixteen years of work experience as an architect planner, with four years of teaching at Sir J.J. College of Architecture. She has also participated in women's organizations and is presently connected with projects for creating destitute women's shelters, creches, and employment for women in Bombay.

In India, most working people, male and female, are "self-employed." The self-employed include all those people who have to earn their living without a regular or salaried job. There are basically three categories of self-employed women:

1. The small-scale hawkers, vendors;
2. Home-based producers; and
3. Laborers selling their services.

This essay explores various issues related to home-based producers and studies the conditions of home-based women workers in the urban and rural context.

The invisibility of home-based women workers is of great concern to the women's movement in India. Mahatma Gandhi had recognized the special role of home-based workers in general and women in particular. In fact, it was the central issue of his economic thought. Today, many organizations are working for the betterment of these women workers and their efforts are also important for this study. The potential of shelter in providing economic opportunities to women is quite high in India. It is important for architects and planners to address the needs of the home-based women workers, creatively supporting them in their designs for housing, neighborhoods, townships, and city development plans.

Family, Occupations, Shelters and Settlement Patterns

Human economic activities (i.e., production of goods and services) have a great bearing on settlement patterns. In India, the majority (70%) of the population is engaged in agricultural production. This divides India into two basic settlement units: rural and urban. These two categories have very few things in common. Hence it is necessary to treat them separately here.

Rural Production and Settlements

People in rural India are basically engaged in agriculture. This is both land-intensive and labor-intensive. Mechanization and automation are not widespread. A large work force is necessary. In the absence of irrigation, most of the agricultural work is seasonal. The dependence upon monsoon rains dominates the working pattern of the people. At harvest time, the demand for labor is very great. This provides continuous work for three to four months of the year. But after the main crop has been harvested, there is little work on the farms. Processing of agricultural produce is then shifted to the residential sphere and women have a greater role in this. Dairy and animal husbandry are the other two main occupations of the rural population. In such a situation, women as laborers have to contribute to production. Division of work based on the sex of worker exists but is not clear-cut. Both men and women work together on farms and residences. Hence rural "domestic space" in India has a very different meaning from what is generally understood by the term "house" or "home." In typical farmers' houses, there are no specific areas for sleeping, living, children's play, dining etc. The built-up space and surrounding open land, semi-covered areas, and courtyards are used in multidimensional ways.

Regional differences in space planning as they have evolved over centuries, construction materials, and methods are well maintained. The built form is largely governed by the environment and the nature of human activities. The whole process of designing, planning, and construction is determined by the family members. The regeneration, maintenance, and addition to the rural house takes place outside the planning process of state or governing authorities, architects, engineers or planners, the so-called specialists. The houses in rural India are designed as:

— Shelters for family members
— Shelters for animals
— Areas where agriculture produce is processed
— Store for agriculture produce and grains
— Space for caste-based production of goods; e.g., weaving, shoe making, pottery, carpentry, etc.
— Space for storage of raw materials and finished goods

All the necessary services are related to domestic spheres. Families are large and children, old people, and the disabled are cared for in the residence itself. Functions such as marriages also take place in the residences. Many of the large houses have special rooms for childbirth. Necessary medical experts and help are brought to the houses. Many trading families have storage, go-downs, and workplaces in their houses. Houses also act as retail outlets for small goods and daily necessities and food items. The Brahmin caste (priest) families have a close relation with the village temples or schools where knowledge is being imparted.

Such examples are numerous. One can very well imagine that such houses provide very close spatial relations for all human activities. And these are very common even today in rural areas. In such a situation,

there cannot be a very sharp division of labor based on sex. Men and women necessarily have to participate in all human activities together. The houses in rural areas are not branded as "women's sphere." And as compared to their urban counterparts, the role of women in practice is not secondary. This does not mean that women have "equal" social status in society. The religions do not allow such views. However, the "economic" role of women is well recognized in reality. When men and women work in fields as casual laborers, they are given a share of the produce, not always cash. While cash can be easily appropriated by men and spent, the share in grain remains for the use of family members. Education and training in trade or production of goods also take place in the domestic sphere. Girls and boys from one caste learn the same trade and processes from childhood on. And when girls get married, they generally carry on the same work , since the marriages generally take place within the same caste.

Even today, villages composed of such households are more or less self-sufficient but only at the subsistence agricultural level. The lands of villages, before the British rule, were distributed to the families according to their needs as well as the status and number of family members. Production of other goods was entrusted to particular castes and families. This production of goods was undertaken for the entire village population and craftsmen were paid for their services in kind. The production of particular goods was the responsibility as well as the right of the families. One caste was not allowed to indulge in the trade of another caste.

The village settlement pattern is based on castes. Families within one caste are grouped together. Upper castes command the "prime" locations of villages, near temples or water sources. Occupations which create pollution are located on the outer peripheries. There is not much vehicular traffic. Hence roads and lanes are narrow and houses are closely packed. The village population always remains limited. This is generally decided by the sustainable level of production. When population pressure is felt, the surplus laborers have to move out. In the past, when such pressure was felt, new lands were brought under cultivation and new settlements, based on old village patterns, were created. The kings and rulers had the responsibility of creating and facilitating such new settlements. Today, the population pressure on land is so great that the surplus population migrates to the urban centers in search of work and sustenance.

Urban India

In the past, before the British Raj, there were few towns. These settlements varied little from village settlement patterns, except that these were centers along trading routes and comparatively richer than villages. The population in these towns was composed of various castes and there were more traders and artisans settled in towns. However, caste- based settlements were the norm. Towns were planned by the town planning experts and natural phenomena like sunpath, wind direction, water sources, etc., were well considered. Various castes were located according to hierarchy and type of goods produced (many of the historical towns still maintain their spatial divisions). The roads and lanes were named by the caste names: Brahmin Lane (Priest Caste), Chamar Ali (Cobbler Street), Tambat Galli (Coppersmith Street), Gavli Gally (Dairymen's Street), etc. Life in these towns varied little from that in villages, except that women had less access to production and agriculture as compared to women in villages. The trading towns were also attractions for bandits, thieves, and frequent outside interference by and the rivalries of kings. Hence, there was greater need and tendency to "protect" women. Areas having a high frequency of attacks like the Rajasthan, Northern, and North Western regions of India restricted women more than did the South.

Present Indian towns and cities are the products of colonial rule as well as post-independence industrialization policies. Settlement patterns in urban India are more or less governed by "market" processes. These towns have few links with traditional settlement patterns. Most people in urban areas have no link with agricultural production. The growth of the towns is influenced by Western town planning concepts of zoning. Women in such centers have been thrown out of traditional economic spheres as the production activities and services have been removed from the domestic spheres. Industry, business, services, hospitals, schools, etc., have taken over the "traditional" family functions. And there has emerged a clear-cut "domestic" sphere exclusively used as residence. Women's activities, to a large extent, are limited by this "domestic" sphere. Traditional, informal participation of women in the production of goods and services has received a setback. The growing affluence of industrial workers in the formal and organized sector is affecting women's roles. Activities of the "domestic" sphere have a secondary position in the "market" economy, and most of the women in the middle and upper layer of society have been subjected to the "housewifization" process.

However, due to very limited growth of the formal and organized sector of production after independence and limited job opportunities, most urban residents have no choice but to look for self-employment. And there are larger numbers of self-employed women than men even in urban areas. Large numbers of women have to work in their homes for their livelihood. Large-scale migration from villages to urban areas has created difficult conditions in urban centers. Traditional crafts and skills have little place in urban economy. They have great difficulty in getting a livelihood, shelter, services, etc., in urban areas. Modern town planning, land-use patterns, and zoning do not recognize the need for such large numbers of migrants to cities. Ghettos and slums seem to be the only places for the migrating population.

Self-Employment In India

A large number of the people in India are self-employed. The self-employed category in the labor force accounts for about 57.3%. The growth of the organized sector in Indian economy has been rather slow. The organized work force accounts for only a tenth of the total employment. The percentage of women in the self-employed sector of the economy is higher than that of the men. Sixty percent of the 98,400,000 female workers (59,100,000) are self-employed. In rural areas, the percentage of self-employed women is larger than that in the urban areas. Of self-employed women, 43% work in their homes and are engaged in various occupations. The total lack of salaried jobs in rural areas forces women to seek a means of self employment. The seasonal agriculture work also limits their opportunities to find permanent employment outside their homes.

Self-employment, by and large, constitutes the dominant sector of employment in our economy. This sector is characterized by "easy entry" and "less waiting time," where the choice of activity is mainly guided by the association of other members of the family in a particular activity, or their "previous experience," or their acquaintances. Most of the activities involve no or little capital. The capital requirement is met almost entirely through family and informal sources. This sector, by and large, generates its own capital. This sector is also characterized by almost unrestricted working hours.

Home-Based Women Workers

Home-based workers, a majority of whom are women, can be divided into two broad categories. The prominent category is that of the piece-rated home workers, working for some other employer or small artisans. The second is own-account small entrepreneurs or small artisans. The problems and hardships faced by these two groups, though both are home-based, are different. The piece-rated home workers are "exploited" by outsiders like contractors and are paid very low wages. The workers in this category need better wage protection and implementation of labor laws. Own-account workers need better facilities and arrangements for raw materials, marketing, credit, storage, workplace, and better prices, and protection from harassment by public authorities. These women face forcible eviction from their workplaces or confiscation of their goods by municipal authorities and police, as their activities are often viewed as illegal.

The self-employed section of the population is the poorest in the society. Their need for work is for sheer survival. Men and women have to undertake any kind of work. And the availability of a large, unorganized work force reduces their wages further. In a sense, there are no idle and unemployed workers. The poverty of these people forces them to live on a "day-to-day" basis and survival without a job, even for a few days, is difficult.

Profile of Economic Activities

The type of economic activities women undertake in their homes varies according to their rural and urban status. More than 50% of the women in rural areas are engaged in dairy, poultry, and animal husbandry, followed by weaving and spinning and tailoring. A significantly low percentage of women are engaged in manufacturing of other goods. Tailoring is the only manufacturing activity which women undertake in rural areas. In urban areas, 26% of the women are engaged in dairy and animal husbandry. Tailoring is the activity in which 40% of urban women are engaged, followed by spinning and weaving (15.25%). Many women prefer part-time activities. This is because responsibility for the household and the family are the primary concerns of women.

The households in rural areas have many tasks to be performed for the betterment and functioning of the family. Besides cooking, cleaning, and other household services, many women have to spend time in fetching water, collecting firewood, collecting fodder for animals, and making cowdung cakes for use as fuel. The lack of basic amenities in rural areas has an adverse effect on the economic potential of women. Next to agriculture (which includes animal husbandry), manu-facturing constitutes the single biggest source of

employment. The proportion of women engaged in this sector has shown the tendency of growth in last two decades. But within this sector, a large number of women are engaged in the traditional sector. Food, beverages, tobacco, textiles, wood and wooden products, and ceramics account for 86% of female workers engaged in the manufacturing sector.

Compared to the rural areas, the opportunities of generating income from self-employment in urban areas are more and varied. A large number of educated urban women undertake economic activities in their spare time, especially in the service sector of the economy. Job opportunities in this sector have shown the tendency of growth in the last two decades. Many professional women, such as doctors, lawyers, architects, engineers, accountants, and teachers, like to operate from their residences. Many financial institutions have provided employment for women, viz., Indian Postal departments, Life Insurance Corporation, Unit Trust of India. After completing their household duties, women are gainfully engaged in their spare time and these activities provide them with independent incomes. Many women also operate trading and retailing business from their homes. Modern technological developments also have a potential of generating income from the residential premises, e.g., computers and electronics are two areas to which women from urban centers are attracted.

There are large numbers and types of activities that women undertake in their homes that generate an independent income. In fact , Indian women have found many indigenous ways of generating their own incomes. In many of the poorer families, women's work provides for a subsistence-level livelihood for the whole family without which the families would not survive. It is not the lack of work that women can undertake in their homes which is of more concern: it is the lack of recognition of the fact on the part of society in general, which many times discourages women and affects them adversely.

Adaptation of Shelters

It is observed that construction of houses takes place outside the field of physical planners and architects. But the general pattern of development has thrust many changes on the villages. Governmental policy decisions are affecting the settlement patterns. Developmental activities pertaining to irrigation projects, power projects, and large public and private sector investments in chemical, fertilizer, and nuclear industries, in petro-chemical complexes, and in transport and communications all have an impact on rural areas for the better as well as for the worse. Changes in land-use patterns, agricultural production, cultivation methods and marketing facilities have affected the total population. Traditional social and economic institutions are undergoing rapid changes. People get dislocated in such development processes. A large, landless work-force is generated and thrown out of villages where land has become an exchange commodity. Large-scale migration is accelerated. Traditional, stable life patterns are shaken, and mobility is on the increase. Urbanization on a large scale is expected to grow still further. Large population growth is also a cause of concern.

Migration on a large scale has caused unprecedented urbanization. Most of the poor migrating from rural areas in search of opportunities are not welcome in the cities. The strain on urban land is such that poor people are forced to live in already crowded slums. They lack modern technical skills, and education. However, on their arrival in urban areas, most people acquire small skills. Old, large-family relations and regional ties make their survival in cities possible to start with. Hard work, self-help, and opportunities of work and education allow the migrants not only to survive in urban centers but to do much better economically than they could have dreamed of in villages. These people, men, women, and children, are engaged in many useful activities without which Indian cities could not function. This self-exploitation of unorganized masses, their work, and real value added to the economy are never properly understood by authorities, economic planners, and urban planners. There is a tendency to look at these hard-working people as burdens, while in actuality they are assets to the economy.

The slums, in reality, are busy economic units like houses in rural areas. The "spaces" in slums are used in multidimensional ways, especially by women. Very small rooms with poor light and ventilation and lack of other facilities such as water and sanitation are used as shelters for a number of people in the family. After the men depart from home for their jobs or economic activities, women use the homes as "space" for generating incomes of their own. Cities like Bombay have very crowded localities. But women manage to put the spaces to productive purposes. The activities are independently carried out by women alone or other family members also participate in such activities. "Dharavi," the largest slum in Bombay, is also a thriving business and manufacturing locality. Leather work, wood work, small industrial goods assembly, and

manufacturing also take place. Handicraft, basket weaving, rag picking, food processing, packaging, tailoring etc., which do not need large areas, are undertaken by women as economic activities. Some of the cities and towns have become special production centers, where a large number of women are engaged in the activities at their homes. "Bidi rolling" (making a kind of indigenous cigarette) is one such activity in the town of Nipani in the tobacco-growing region. Handloom weaving in Bhivandi and other towns, papad (a snack) making, and food processing, are some of the common activities undertaken at homes. Women also operate from homes as vendors and do some small retail business. In fact, every family in the slum area and all the members, including the children, participate in a number of activities which generate income (it may be very small, but is very useful) which allows them to survive in the cities. And even when few opportunities are provided, many manage to do even better than just subsistence level.

Many industries, large and small, take advantage of the situation. Many jobs, otherwise undertaken in factory premises, are handed to women to do in their homes on a piece-rate basis. This way, the cost of providing space, and the need for facilities such as water, sanitation, electricity, and minimum wage or other benefits which would have been necessary by the law, can be circumvented. This reduces the costs for the industries, and their profit margin increases. The slums and domestic spaces near the industries thus help the industries, on the one hand, and provide economic opportunities to poor women on the other. This mutual relationship is also very important in a business district like crowded office areas of south Bombay. Providing very cheap food is a great thriving business for many families. Semi-cooked food is prepared in the domestic areas or in slums and is sold on the streets for the benefit of a large number of white-collar workers at very low prices. Quality and hygiene are at stake, and the streets become eating places during lunch time. This is an example of the failure of physical planners to understand the relation of the informal sector and the business district and to provide facilities for both. It is also an example of the failure of following the Western zoning norms without proper adaptation to local needs and local conditions.

This large, unorganized, largely home-based sector of workers has another kind of impact on the organized workers' movements and struggles. Whenever large-scale industrial unrest and disputes take place in organized sectors of the economy, the unorganized sector of the economy absorbs the shock. On the one hand, it allows the struggle of organized workers to last longer than would have been possible without it. On the other hand, it takes over the production of goods thus affected by strikes and closures in the factories, and reduces the ability of the working class to force the management to settle. Thus, there is not much loss of production, and the availability of goods to the society is not necessarily affected. This was witnessed in the strike of textile workers in Bombay.

The strike in Bombay Textile Industry in 1984 involved about 200,000 workers. The strike continued for two years. The Textile Industry owners were least interested in finding a solution for the simple reason that the industry had become unprofitable. Modernization was opposed by workers. And the industry was not able to compete in the market. The industry had become a burden to them. However, the strike continued. But this did not affect the supply of textile goods in the market. The production was shifted to a nearby town, Bhivandi, where the powerloom and handloom sector increased its capacity and the goods were branded and sold by the textile mills. The families of the striking workers in such conditions had to survive and had to find solutions to the economic needs. Many workers were supported by the women who started their own economic activities, in an unorganized way. Subsequently, these unorganized women were supported and got organized to promote their own activities. It was the beginning of organizations for home-based workers in Bombay.

Home-Based Women Workers and Their Organizations

Home-based women workers are one of three groups of self-employed women workers. The three groups are:

1. Small-scale vendors, small traders, hawkers selling goods such as vegetables, fruits, fish, eggs, and other staple foods, household goods, garments, and other similar products.
2. Home-based producers such as weavers, potters, bidi workers, milk producers, garment stitchers, and processors of agricultural products, and handicraft producers.
3. Laborers selling their services or their labor, including agricultural laborers, construction workers, contract laborers, hand cart pullers, head loaders, washerwomen, cooks, cleaners, and other providers of services.

The home-based, self-employed women workers are literally invisible to society; they work within their homes and do not appear in the census or other official statistics. These are the workers whose organization is very difficult. The home-based workers, because of their isolation from general workers and even from their own group, remain unnoticed and, hence, are exploited in many ways. They have no employer, yet they have to obtain raw materials and deal with the consumers in the market, financiers, and middlemen in case they are not able to sell their goods directly. The self-employed lose income when:

— They buy raw materials and inputs
— They hire tools and equipments
— They need cash for working capital; and
— They sell their produce in wholesale or retail markets

The self-employed generate income when they:

1. Buy inputs in bulk
2. Provide tools on hire purchase
3. Obtain capital; and
4. Organize marketing of their produce

It is clear from this that the home-based women workers have a greater need of organization if they have to generate proper income from their activities. It was Mahatma Gandhi who first recognized the importance of the promotion of home-based workers in general and women in particular. His strategies for economic self-reliance had roots in the traditional Indian methods of home-based production.

K V I C (Khadi and Village Industries Commission)

This is a large and important organization of home-based workers in India. Established in 1956 to carry out the work of rural reconstruction through development of the economic activities, KVIC activities have proved important to poor women, as one of its objectives is to provide employment for women at their doorsteps. The major activities of KVIC are in spinning, weaving, leather industry, soap making, rice pounding, bee keeping, oil milling, woolen and silk textiles, as well as food processing. Recently, KVIC has also entered the field of electronics in a big way. In the state of Kerala, KVIC gives training to women and then provides work at home. Work such as assembling electronic circuit boards is provided. KVIC has a very large marketing network and large showrooms in the large cities and towns in India.

S E W A (Self-Employed Women's Association), Ahmedabad

Inspired by the Gandhian philosophy and expanding on the basic idea, this independent organization has been actively involved with a large number of self-employed women and home-based women workers since 1972. The women felt that, as a workers' association, SEWA should establish itself as a trade union. This was a novel idea because the self-employed have no real history of organizing. The first struggle SEWA undertook was to obtain official recognition as a trade union. The Labor Department refused to register SEWA because it felt that, since there was no recognized employer, the workers would have no one to struggle against. SEWA argued that the union was not necessarily against an employer but for the unity of workers.

A similar problem was faced by Illa Bhatt of SEWA at the International Forum in 1974, when she was told that she was ahead of her time by ILO in Geneva. Talking about her experience, she says, "In 1981, I was ridiculed when I talked of recognizing piece-rate, home-based workers as 'workers' and providing them with legal protection and social security. I was ridiculed at the national and international forum. In 1988, the ICFTU (International Confederation of Free Trade Unions, Brussels) World Labor Congress at Melbourne passed [SEWA's] resolution to bring home-based workers within the fold of the labor movement."

The success of SEWA is in its approach of combining three movements: the labor movement, the co-operative movement, and the women's movement. SEWA was born in the labor movement with the idea that the self-employed, like salaried workers, have the right to fair wages, decent working conditions, and protective labor laws. They deserve recognition as a legitimate group of workers with status, dignity, and the right to organize bodies to publicly represent their interests. Most importantly, most workers in India are self-employed and, if unions are to be truly responsive to labor in the Indian context, then they must organize them. This requires going beyond the western model of the trade unions as practiced in the advanced countries where labor is mainly composed of wage earners working for large-scale manufacturers or enterprises.

In addition, SEWA feels that the co-operative movement is very important for the self-employed. Not only is it important for the self-employed to struggle for their rights, but they also need to develop an alternative economic system. The co-operative movement points the way to such a system in which the workers themselves would control their own means of production, an alternative system without employer and employees, but in which all own what they produce. SEWA accepts the co-operative principles and sees itself as attempting to reach the goal of social change and economic relations.

The women's movement in India began with the social and religious reforms movement in the late nineteenth century. Under Mahatma Gandhi, women actively participated in the freedom struggle and became active in their own liberation. In the 1970's, the women's movement took a new radical turn, with women participating actively in social movements and demanding capabilities and opportunities in all spheres of life. The women's movement pointed out that women constitute 50% of the world's population and do two-thirds of all the work in the economy. For this work, women are paid only 10% of all wages, salaries, and remunerations. At most, 1% of this income is owned by women. All this is because women's work is not recognized as work and, hence, is not paid for or is paid for at a very low rate. SEWA has been part of the growing women's movement. It is felt that the bulk of women in India are poor, self-employed, and mainly rural. For the movement to be successful, it must reach out to these women and make their issues— economic, social, and political—the issues of the movement.

Annapoorna Mahila Mandal (AMM), Bombay

The textile workers' strike in Bombay was mentioned earlier. The women of the striking workers had no option but to support their families. Some were already engaged in providing food to the migrant workers. Most new migrants to Bombay leave their families behind in the rural areas. The women engaged in supplementing their family incomes now had a greater need for more income to support their families. The need for better organization was realized through the Annapoorna Mahila Mandal. (Annapoorna is the Goddess of Food.) The AMM today has a large membership (50,000) and a consolidated base in the working-class area of Bombay. The organization arranges for the soft loans that are required by women to start their own catering business and gives support to women on many issues. The members of the organization are also motivated to participate in many social programs such as literacy, adult education, family planning, cleanliness, and other women's issues such as dowry and family counseling.

This well-knit organization has successfully evolved market support for the food products.

Mahila Grih Udyog (Lijjat Papad)

This co-operative is exclusively for home-based women workers. The main activity of this organization, i.e., production of papad, is undertaken by many women in their homes. The rolling of papad is based on the easily available skills of the women. The prepared dough, with all its ingredients, is provided to the women after a very short training in achieving uniformity of the product. The women roll the papads in their homes and deliver the product in semi-dried condition to the collection centers. Hundreds of women members of this co-operative from a large number of towns are engaged and generate incomes regularly. The organization has a large domestic market and has been successful in exporting the products to many countries and popularizing the product through modern marketing techniques. The organization is also diversifying in many other products and is establishing a large network of packaging centers. It has been a very popular organization among women and, at the same time, a very successful commercial venture.

Home-Based Women Workers and Related Issues

Invisibility

Recognizing the category of home-based workers poses a great problem. Most of the issues related to the well-being of the home-based women workers remain unnoticed due to their general invisibility.

Health Hazards

Many of the home-based women workers suffer from multiple health hazards. Not all are necessarily related to their economic activities. However, the living conditions of poor women are so bad that all the activities become inter-related. Most of the women have little idea of health hazards and, even if they do, they have very little control of their environment. There are no safety regulations or health services. Crowded residences in the cities lack sanitation and water supply. Many handicraft workers suffer from bad eyesight caused by lack of proper lighting conditions and lack of electricity. In the case of the Bidi (a kind of cigarette) workers, who roll tobacco in leaves by hand, poor ventilation and fine tobacco dust cause tuberculosis

and cancer. Continuous back-breaking work, unlimited working hours, and awkward postures with general malnutrition cause many ailments. Most family members, including young children, are adversely affected by the working conditions.

Poverty

Illiteracy, lack of education and training in skills, as well as many social drawbacks such as the caste system, untouchability, and traditional social practices adversely affect women's work, health, and status. Women are doubly exploited. They are exploited by the traditional joint family system of patriarchy and the modern economic system. Barring a very few professional and educated women, most of the home-based workers lack the ability to interact with the outside world effectively. Hence, they do not become independent in spite of their economic activities and incomes of their own. Their isolation in the home is not so total in the Indian context. On the other hand, women in India have very little or no privacy.

Effects of Technology

With the introduction of modern technology in production processes, traditional skills and production are challenged. However, a number of crafts and skills are still preserved through family traditions. The artisans are economically exploited by the market system. However, artists also benefit from the modern communication system and market expansion if they are able to organize themselves. Many of the performing arts are not only preserved but have received a great boost through modern media.

Lack of a modern communication network interlinking large numbers of villages is a major cause of isolation of the rural communities. There is an additional cause for concern. The introduction of modern technology in only a few fields such as electronics and computers without corresponding changes in other fields can aggravate the situation. Introduction of appropriate technology in most of the fields can, on the other hand, help society in general and women in particular. "Operation Flood" is an example of the successful combination of the innovative use of modern technology and old forms of production organization. The scheme promotes production of milk by giving support to individual producers, many of them women, and central collection, processing, and distribution of milk and milk products to the urban population. This approach provides remunerative prices to the individuals for their product. This approach also has the advantage of distribution of wealth to a large population.

Conclusions

In India, a large number of women generate income from various activities undertaken in their homes. Home-based women are the most exploited section of the self-employed workers category and form the poorest strata of society. The organization of these women is an important task. Various issues related to home-based workers need greater attention from planners. It is essential to give special attention to the needs of this section of the economy so as to strengthen its position in society.

Residential settlements devoid of any income opportunities reduce women to the "housewifization" process, isolation, and dependence. Separation of all the economic activities of production and services from the domestic sphere necessarily limit income opportunities for women. This also leads to spatial determinism and wasteful travel and energy consumption which are the results of present zoning plans.

Division of work based on sex and division of space in commercial and industrial zones and non-economic residential zones are closely related. This relationship, at present, is governed by market forces. Alternative urban and rural planning strategies based on the needs of the people and women in particular have to be developed, if they are to be effective. Architects and physical planners have the responsibility to create a better environment for the future. Hence, they must seek active participation of women in the planning processes.

Home-based economic activities of women are important to society. Creating better opportunities through physical planning is the responsibility of the architects. Such opportunities need not be only for women but can also be extended to include men. This approach can help in overcoming the present division of work based on sex and can provide equal status to men, women, and their works.

References

Baily, Ann M., and Tosep R. Llobera. 1981. *The Asiatic Mode of Production—Science and Politics.* London: Routlege and Kegan Paul.

Bensman, Joseph, and Arthur Vidich (eds.) *Metropolitan Communities.* New York: New York Times Company.

Bhatt, Ela. 1989. *Grind of Work.* Ahmedabad: SEWA, pp. 136.

Bhave, H.A.. 1990. *Kautiliya Arthashastra.* Pune: Varda Books.

Bourne, S. Larry (ed.). 1971. *Internal Structure of City, Readings on Space and Environment.* New York: Oxford University Press.

Cheruniliam, Francis, and Odeyar D. Heggade. 1987. *Housing in India.* Bombay: Himalaya Publishing House.

Gadkari, Jayant. 1981. *Prachin Bharatiya Samajrachanetil Shudranche Sthan.* Bombay: D.D. Kosambi Partishthan.

Government of Maharashtra. 1981. *Report of the High Power Steering Group for Slums and Dilapidated Houses.*

Kosambi, D.D. 1974. *Ancient Indian History and Culture.* Bombay: Popular Publishers.

National Commission on Urbanization. 1987. *Interim Report.* New Delhi: Government of India, Ministry of Urban Development.

Pandey, Divya, and Mira Savara (eds.). 1990. *Between the Farm and Thali, Women and Food Processing.* Research Centre for Women's Studies, Bombay: S.N.D.T. Women's University, pp. 195.

Pandit, Nalini. 1984. *Gandhi.* Bombay: Granthali.

Sane, Geeta. 1986. *Bharatiya Stree Jeevan.* (Marathi) Bombay: Mauj Printing Beaurau.

Sanjanwala, Jyotsna (ed.). 1991. *Women's Perspective on Environment. Research Centre for Women's Studies.* Bombay: S.N.D.T. Women's University.

Schumacher, E.F. 1990. *Small is Beautiful.* India: Rupa and Company.

SEWA in 1988. Ahmedabad: Mahila Sewa Trust 1988.

SEWA in 1990. Ahmedabad: Mahila Sewa Trust 1991.

SHRAMASHAKTI, Report of National Commission on Self-Employed Women and Women in the Informal Sector. New Delhi: Publications Division, Government of India.

Tabb, William K., and Larry Sawers (eds.). 1984. *Marxism and the Metropolis.* New York: Oxford University Press.

Theme 6
Women and Shelter-Related Services and Infrastructure

The social services and the physical infrastructure that women need in their homes and in their immediate neighborhood are related to culture, ethnicity, and race as well as shaped by the responsibilities women have for sustaining the family. Rapid technological and economic changes throughout the world have resulted in many women working outside the home, by choice or necessity. This has affected their needs for services inside and outside the home. Their ability to meet the responsibilities for domestic life has been limited by concerns for personal safety, inadequate transportation, long travel distances between the home and workplace, and by the lack of convenient services such as shopping, health care, and child care. The papers in this theme reveal a need to bring about reforms in housing and neighborhood design so as to allow women to meet their responsibilities to work and family. The first two papers articulate the needs, perceptions, and priorities of lower-income women coping with the pressures of looking after their families and earning a living in the Indian metropolitan cities of Bombay and Madras (Dandekar, Adarkar). El Safty describes the importance of easy access to appropriate health care for Egyptian women. Feldman and Stall document the efforts of resident activists in public housing in Chicago to attain control over their physical and social environment.

Photo: *Hemalata C. Dandekar*

Chapter 30
Women's Views of Shelter-Related Services and Infrastructure in Charkop, Bombay, and Mogappair, Madras

Hemalata C. Dandekar

Hemalata C. Dandekar is Professor of Urban Planning at the University of Michigan and chairs the International Planning and Development concentration in Urban Planning. She has a Bachelor of Architecture from the University of Bombay, a Master of Architecture from the University of Michigan, and a Ph.D. in Urban Planning from UCLA. She is a licensed architect who has practiced in India, Tokyo, and on the east (Boston) and west (Los Angeles) coasts of the U.S.A. Her dissertation research provided the initial material for a book titled Men to Bombay, Women at Home: Urban Influence on Village Life in Deccan Maharashtra, India, 1942–82. *She has been a consultant to the Urban Projects Department of the World Bank on projects related to physical infrastructure and shelter planning in Calcutta and for UNESCO's Human Settlements Division in the training of officials implementing shelter and settlement projects.*

That women in housing settlements of low- and moderate-income families need infrastructure of two kinds, tangible, physical structures and less tangible social and institutional ones, is well substantiated in the literature on shelter, women, and development.[1] Both kinds of infrastructure are addressed in this book in a variety of contexts.[2] This illustrates the multifaceted nature of shelter-related infrastructure that is needed if women are to benefit in both pragmatic and strategic ways from their new homes.[3]

In the established traditions of architecture and physical planning, rarely are infrastructure needs determined specifically from a woman's perspective. Such consideration as has been given to such needs has generally centered on technical aspects of appropriate design at the micro scale of individual housing unit, and, at the macro (neighborhood) scale, on the provision of supportive amenities such as shopping centers, clinics, and schools. Sometimes, particularly in formerly British colonies in the Third World, such as India, these design standards have been based on British Town and Country Planning formulae. In more enlightened efforts, some adaptations are introduced to meet women's particular needs within a specific culture. International agencies such as UNCHS and the World Bank have attempted to look at differential impact by gender of technical and design choices in infrastructure.[4]

A house, no matter how badly needed, has only limited potential to help a woman achieve long-term empowerment. A range of efforts has emerged to change the larger social and institutional environment in which women live and seek access to housing. These efforts have included working for the passage of legislation to allow women to own housing in countries where they do not now have such rights; facilitating social organizations that empower women to collectively determine what activities and investments are appropriate for their neighborhood; and using women's involvement in housing creation to shift the socially acceptable relationships between men and women in that culture. Words such as participation, empowerment, enablement, self awareness, confidence, and rights weave through the descriptions and discussions of such efforts.

A typology of what has been observed to be women-supportive infrastructure could prove to be quite useful in the formulation of the kind of housing policy sensitive to women's needs called for in this book. But developing this typology, important as it might be from a policy perspective, would be beyond the objectives of this paper. What is intended here is much more limited. This paper will extract from a larger examination of two low-income housing projects in India some women's views of what works for them in the services and amenities they are provided, and the needs they have for additional, more supportive infrastructure.

Rationale and Need for This Research

The observations presented in this paper and the photographs by the author throughout this book were obtained in a pilot study initiated by this author between 1989 to 1991 in two low-income housing projects: Charkop 1, located in Kandivali, Bombay, and Mogappair East, in Mogappair, Madras. These projects have been developed with funds from the World Bank and the Housing and Development Corporation (HUDCO) of the Government of India. The intent of the research project, titled *Women's Access to Shelter for the Poor: The Case of Bombay and Madras* [5] was to identify, in two quite different metropolitan cities in India, those physical and organizational characteristics which have implications for women's abilities to gain access to units of shelter and which can make for a good or bad fit with women's needs. Large-scale publicly financed housing projects such as Charkop and Mogappair, include investments by international agencies, and are being replicated in various regions of the country. There are thus opportunities to make judicious changes in the material and the institutional design, improving the ways they meet the needs of their women occupants.

At the time this research was initiated there appeared to be a great deal of confidence that the right issues in housing were being addressed in appropriately rational and scientific ways. But the specific needs of women were not receiving particular attention.[6] Traditionally acceptable, economic issues such as housing preference, shelter finance, infrastructure standards, and land policy were investigated. But the spatial and concrete in shelter projects, affecting the quality of life and of the environment, were not, and these issues have immediate impact on women and children, the population that spends most of its time in these settlements. Other approaches to shelter projects which can have great implications for the extent that women are able play a role in shelter creation, were also neglected: e.g., options for incremental investment strategies, for participation, self-help, and appropriate technology in shelter design and construction. A collection of essays on spontaneous shelter, which had included some of these topics germane to women's access to shelter, had

not directly addressed the issue of women's specific roles in, and needs for, shelter.[7]

In South Asia in particular, little systematic has been work initiated to better understand the role of women, women's organizations, women's special needs, and the access of women to the benefits of programs providing housing and infrastructure. In India, there has been considerable experimentation with public sector investments in shelter. Most low-income Indian women have been assumed to be in traditional families and their housing needs have been thought to be subsumed in the larger effort to meet the needs for shelter of the poor. Perhaps the need of poor women for shelter and infra-structure has traditionally not been given separate attention in India because the proportion of women documented as heads of their households is not large. But evidence suggests that modernization and develop-ment are undermining some of the traditional marital nets that sustained women in patriarchal societies like the Indian, and that this phenomenon is occurring across class lines.

The feminist literature makes clear that opportunities for autonomy and economic independence are enabling women to resist the oppressive or physically aggressive behavior of men, such as wife beating, that they had traditionally accepted. Various chapters in this book have alluded to the fact that, for women, ownership of one's shelter can be critical in attaining autonomy and economic independence. The norm in India is for the man of the household to be the sole title holder of the family house. That women do not usually hold title to their homes inhibits them from assertive actions on their own behalf. It is useful to look at a country like India, to examine the access of women to shelter to which they hold title, as there has been an active feminist movement in the major cities which could bring about change. The Indian constitution has provided the underpinnings of legislation that would assist these groups to act through the judicial system. Feminist scholars working on Indian women's development are pointing out that access to, and ownership of, housing in urban and in rural areas is crucial, across class, in empowering women by enhancing their personal security and enabling them to gain a foothold in the modern economy of the city.[8] They are highlighting the importance of women's unique and special needs for housing.[9]

The authors work in Charkop 1 and Mogappair East helped reveal some of these needs by looking at the situation from the vantage point of women who had obtained an opportunity to build a new house. The overall results of this research are to be reported elsewhere. This paper presents some of the insights that this investigation has yielded about technical and institutional infrastructure needed by women occupying shelters in these sites and services projects.[10]

Mogappair and Charkop Case Studies

The sites and service approach to creating shelter options for the poor, as reflected in Charkop 1 and Mogappair East, represents an important shift in national housing policy related to low-income populations. Faced with, and rendered helpless by, the growing housing and physical infrastructure needs of the burgeoning populations of large and medium-sized cities of the Third World, governments and international aid institutions have moved away from their earlier negative attitudes about the illegally constructed shelters of the poor and have experimented with strategies to harness and guide this activity constructively. The sites and service approach represents an effort to tap the creative potential of poor people's ability to house themselves. As this approach has unfolded over the last two decades, it has attempted to address the needs of the poor for housing and infrastructure through a variety of programs providing different combinations of house sites and services. The particular design and execution of the various phases of the Charkop and Mogappair sites and services projects in themselves illustrate the ongoing evolution and adaptation that have characterized this approach to shelter creation in the Indian context. The common denominator in these projects has been the provision of quite modestly sized plots of land. Here various combinations of services and infrastructure are provided. The poor obtain title to the property and build themselves housing.

The two projects, Mogappair East (which at the time of the field survey was in the process of construction: see Figure 1), and Charkop 1 (which was in the construction and design stage: see Figure 2) were jointly funded by the World Bank and HUDCO. The implementing agencies were Tamil Nadu Housing Board, Mogappair Division, and Maharashtra Housing and Area Development Authority (MAHADA), respectively. Oversight and planning supervision over the two projects were provided by Madras Metropolitan Development Authority (MMDA) and Bombay Metropolitan Regional Development Authority (BMRDA). Information on, and an understanding of, the various parameters of these projects were obtained from the following four types of sources:

MOGAPPAIR

Fig. 1: Overall plot plan for Mogappair East, Madras. Area where data was collected for this project is indicated in heavy outline.

1. Interviews of officials in the above-mentioned agencies at various levels of the administrative pyramid, from Vice Presidents and Chief Executive Officers to site engineers, planners, designers, administrators, and community development officers. These provided an overview of official attitudes and positions vis a vis women plot holders.

2. Documents and data which were generously and freely made available by the officials in these agencies. These provided good technical and quantitative information on allotments of plots, financing, background of women who were plot holders, and design and construction norms.

3. On-site observations, documentation, and analysis of the physical construction process and the site-level management systems. In Bombay these included conversations with local contractors involved in housing construction. Site surveys were executed to establish the extent of building completion and occupancy status as well as turnover in ownership of properties which were in women's names. Given the emphasis in this research on

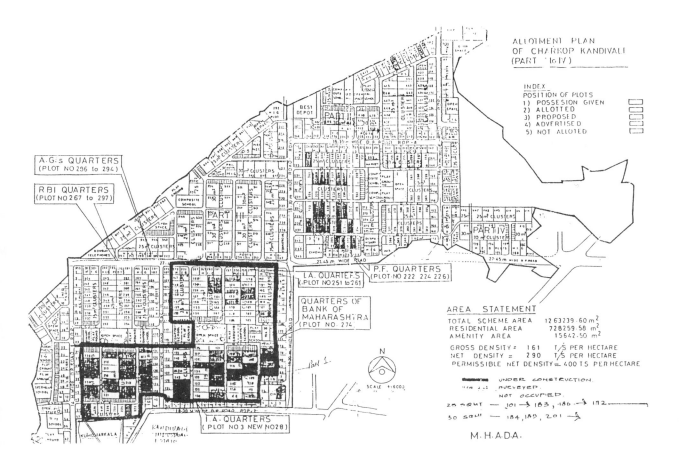

Fig. 2: Overall plot plan for Phases 1 through 4 of the Charkop sites and services scheme in Kandivali, Bombay. Area in Phase 1 where data for this project was collected is indicated in heavy outline.

poor women, the areas which were selected for observation contained only those plots which were designated for low-income groups, which the World Bank terms Economically Weaker Sections (EWS) and which it classifies into subcategories by level of income.

4. Open-ended interviews with, and photo documentation of, women title holders of the newly created housing. This latter source has been the most heavily drawn upon in this paper.

Charkop 1 and Mogappair East represented, at the time of field work, in their design and execution, the more recent experimentation in, and thinking about, the sites and service approach. The two projects differed in the process by which housing was expected to be constructed. In Mogappair East, some 6 miles from downtown Madras, allotments were made in 1983/84. Individual plot holders were required to construct their individual housing. Besides water, sewer, and electrical hookups and service roads, several permutations of core units were made available on two basic plot sizes.

Layout of plots within sectors followed the more conventional pattern established in sites and service projects (see Figure 3 and background site plan on cover). To consolidate their claim to the property, owners were required to start construction and build at least to plinth height within two years from time of allotment. Cooperation with adjoining neighbors in the construction of common walls was required. By 1990 it was clear that some allottees were not building on the site; others were constructing only the minimum structures to meet the MMDA requirements to retain ownership. The slow rate of construction and occupancy was a disappointment to the authorities. The state's investment in infrastructure was buried under the ground. The new housing, to result from the investments by the private sector in the form of individual owners, was not forthcoming.

In Bombay allotments were made two to three years later in 1985/86. House sites were laid out into residential clusters of 46 plots around a central courtyard (see

Detail of Sector

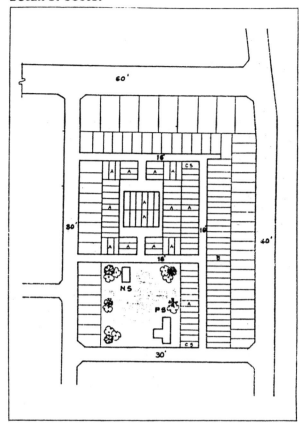

Fig. 3: Detailed layout of one typical residential sector in Mogappair East showing arrangement of individual plots, levels of service roads, and open space.

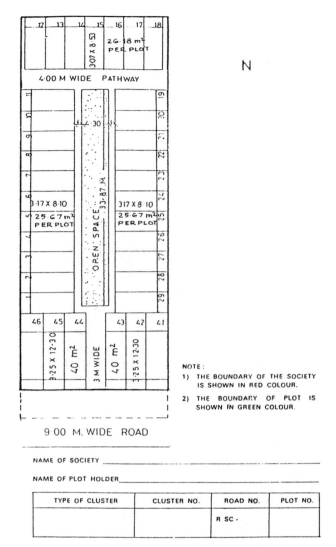

NOTE :
1) THE BOUNDARY OF THE SOCIETY IS SHOWN IN RED COLOUR.

2) THE BOUNDARY OF PLOT IS SHOWN IN GREEN COLOUR.

9·00 M. WIDE ROAD

NAME OF SOCIETY _____

NAME OF PLOT HOLDER_____

TYPE OF CLUSTER	CLUSTER NO.	ROAD NO.	PLOT NO.
		R SC -	

Fig. 4: Typical layout of one housing cluster in Charkop 1, showing arrangement of 46 individual plots in a housing cooperative, of open space, and of pathways.

Figure 4). Each cluster was provided with a connection point for Bombay municipal water, sewer, and electrical services. The distinguishing feature for the Charkop 1 project was that construction of the housing within each 46 plot cluster was done cooperatively through housing societies whose formation was facilitated and mandated by MHADA. Consolidation into group housing made the proposed construction sufficiently large to be attractive for bidding by small local contractors. The objective was to reduce the time required for housing construction and occupancy, compared to more conventional projects in which decisions to build were left to individual allottees.

The neglect of gender as a category of analysis in shelter creation and assessment, described in the introduction to this book, manifested itself in a variety of ways in the Mogappair East and Charkop 1 projects. For example, very good financial and background data on plot allottees did not specify the gender of the allottee, precluding an overall analysis by gender. We expended considerable effort in manually scanning allottee lists for female names to establish a reliable list of women allottees on each site. Ultimately in Mogappair East we determined that 522 of a total of 3,129 plots (17%) belong to women allottees. In Charkop 1 out of 5,804 plots, 411 belonged to women (7%). That the percentage was higher in Madras, the socially more conservative city, was interesting: one might have anticipated the opposite, given that women in Bombay are such a visible part of the work force. Local community development workers in Madras attributed this to the fact that sites and service schemes have been introduced to a greater extent in Madras than in Bombay and have been implemented and in place for a longer time. The value of the properties has been better established and families make multiple applications in the name of all eligible family members when the lottery for plots in a site and service project is announced and applications are solicited.

To determine whether institutional barriers were operative in women's access to these properties, we looked in some detail at the gate-keeping aspect of the plot allotment process in Bombay. Recipients of these serviced plots, from the pool of applicants who generally far outnumber the plots available, are generally selected though some form of lottery. Although, as mentioned above, we did not have a data base of applicants by gender and therefore could not assess statistical representation of applicants by gender to see if the pool of female applicants itself was small, we found nothing in the process of selection by lottery that seemed to be particularly biased against women applicants. We did examine how availability of plots was advertised, the systems through which application forms were obtained, and the income criteria that were applied. Contrary to our expectations, income criteria too did not appear particularly to discriminate against those women allottees who were establishing an ability to pay through informal sector work. Our trail of documents revealed how applications by women, initially rejected because they were employed in informal sector, self-employed work and could not produce the required affidavits of earnings and employment stipulated in the application forms, were accepted after an established process of appeal was followed. Administrators appeared to be willing to accept other ways of establishing an ability to pay beyond statements by formal sector employers.[11]

When we questioned women allottees about the application and selection process in both projects, by and large they appeared to have experienced it as an orderly and fair one. Some had received assistance in obtaining and filling out forms from male relatives but others had navigated the complexities of the process on their own. It is to be noted, however, that women eligible for plots in sites and service projects such as these have more resources (finances, education, family connections and wage work), than, for instance, the pavement dwellers that Bapat and Patel speak about in their chapter. Our interviews revealed that these individuals moved to these projects from the chawls, tenement structures, and settled squatter communities that Adarkar writes about in her chapter.

In comparing the status of construction of plots owned by women in the two projects, we found that, despite the up to three years' time difference in date of allotment of plots (Mogappair East having been allotted in 83/84 and Charkop 1 in 85/86), 49% of the women owned plots in Mogappair; 47% of those in Bombay had been completely built; and another 9% in both projects were almost complete. Thus the Charkop 1 approach of mandating construction of houses through housing cooperatives appeared to be working: the gestation period for constructing a house appears to have been reduced. Because geography and size and growth of the metropolis, the pressures on, and therefore price of, land for housing is much higher in Bombay, which partially explains the relative speed in construction. However, this appears to have a cost for some women. When we questioned the women owners in both projects about how satisfied they were with the housing they had obtained, we found that the Mogappair house owners seemed, by and large, to be quite satisfied with their houses. They had been able to build them incrementally, as and when they could afford it, and to design their units and allocate space to meet their individual life styles. In Charkop 1, the level of satisfaction seemed to vary between various clusters. In some, women expressed a great deal of frustration and anger at being discounted in, left out of, or not understanding the technical decisions made in their housing cooperative. The decisions involved the level of per unit cost that they would commit to as a group in their contract with the builder, about the types of materials and finishes that would be provided, about the specifics of the design of their units, particularly the bathroom and sanitary fixtures that were selected and the layouts of kitchens and toilet blocks. As one woman, who was widowed, had a small son to support, and was earning a living as a domestic servant, as a sweeper in a health clinic, and in petty trade in coconuts or other seasonal products, expressed it:

> I don't mind working very hard to earn and pay the price for a good house. I don't care if I have to do three full-time jobs to earn the money. I am not afraid of hard work. What I am sad about is that I am paying a lot and I did not get the house I wanted. I can see where my money is just wasted and that hurts me. Everyone who lives around me has more money than I do and they just made these decisions for all of us in this society. They don't listen to a woman like me.

Several factors were at play in this and other women's expressions of disenchantment with the decision making in their housing cooperatives. Initially they were intimidated by the technical process, did not always understand the plans and drawings presented by project officials and later the private contractors, and hesitated to volunteer for leadership positions on the cooperative committee. One woman confessed that she had not understood, even after the drawings were explained to her, that hers would be a row house that had common walls with her neighbors. As their adverse experiences increased, women in some of the clusters took over decision-making positions in some of the cooperatives. It appeared clear that some training and assistance on technical matters in the earlier stages of project evolution might have saved them considerable pain and expense and allowed them to participate in a more constructive and efficient way earlier in the process. The Charkop 1 approach is a particularized one, but even in the more prevalent situation of owners building on their own, as in Mogappair East, construction components are needed that promote self-help. Technical skills need to be taught and approaches to shelter formulation need to be found to encourage participation of poor women in the design and implementation of projects. That would help more women to attain the houses they want and can afford.

Such participation and input by women communicating with the technical designers of these projects would have resulted in a better physical solution, for instance in the layout of the wet core in each housing unit. In our interviews with women in both Mogappair and Charkop 1 the location of the water closet, the bathroom, the location of entry doors to these facilities, and the placement of the kitchen sink and drain were of great concern to women. At issue were whether the designs and layouts were seen as convenient and provided the required sense of privacy and propriety by the women who would use the housing and do much of the domestic work, and what configurations the technical planners, the architects, civil and sanitary engineers, and planners deemed to be most efficient and economic to construct. In Mogappair we found that most allottees had demolished or greatly altered the configuration of the wet core that was provided on their plot. Because the supply of piped water was rather unreliable in Mogappair, many families had dug private, individual wells in the location of their bathrooms to ensure some supply of water for the family. Of our interviewees, 93% had made this investment in a private well and 61% had relocated their bathroom.

In Charkop 1, in the units developed by each cooperative society, we found several permutations on the original, approved layout of the wet core. Figure 5 is the typical plan of the 25-square-meter plot that is pre-approved for construction by the Bombay Municipal Corporation.[12] Figure 6 presents our sketches of the

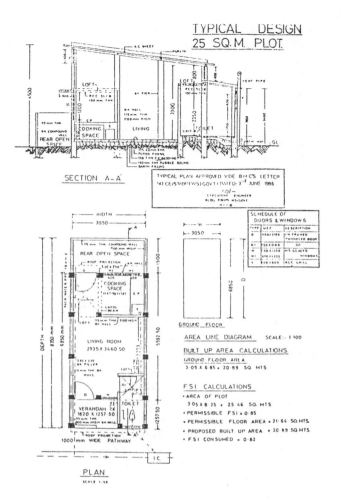

Fig. 5: Typical approved plan for 25 square meter plot in Charkop 1.

various reconfigurations of the layout we found in our survey work. Clearly preferred by women were options that divided the water closet from the bathing/washing area as in alternative 1, relocated the entry door to the sanitary core to provide more privacy as in alternative 2, moved the washing and bath area to the outside porch as in alternative 3, and finally the most expensive but also most desired alternative, 4, relocating the washing areas and bathroom to the outside, rear courtyard. The last option was the most expensive because, in the approved plan and the first three alternatives, one main drainage pipe could be installed down the middle of the central courtyard of the housing cluster. The drained washing spaces on the rear in alternative 4 would require two other piping runs along the exterior walls of the cluster. For efficiency and lower costs, adjacent housing societies could cooperate in sharing these secondary waste pipes. But the construction and administrative

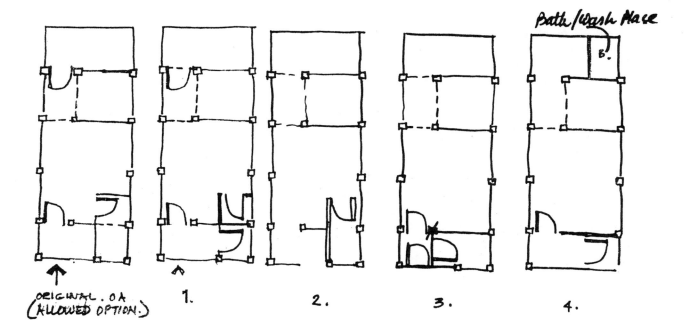

Fig. 6: Four alternative reconfigurations of the approved plan noted during our field work in Charkop 1.

logistics became much more complex. But this option substantially improved the usability of the house for many of the women The project designers and planners in MMDA had heard this before and were trying to respond in future projects. But this still left several thousand housing units under construction or about to be constructed with a plan that was less desirable from the vantage point of the women occupants. This illustrates how the design of public housing projects is first driven by technical rationality, what works for the women who will spend the most time in these facilities, is often left out. We should be able to develop processes that allow inclusion of women's views in the early design stages.

To obtain more information on what a plot represented to a woman allottee, we completed systematic, open-ended questionnaires and in-depth interviews with 28 women in Mogappair and 16 in Charkop 1. From these we assessed various characteristics of the respondents including the level of autonomy they were exercising with respect to decisions about, and responsibility for, their house; their interest in establishing income-generation activities in the project; and whether they now had fewer or more amenities and infrastructure available to them relative to the homes they had left. We found that 25% of the informants in Mogappair were

acting in a highly autonomous fashion and another 45% in a moderately autonomous way while in Bombay, as we expected, 50% were highly autonomous and another 25% were moderately so. We looked at factors such as investment of assets in the house construction, participation in the design and construction phase, and whether the woman was solely or partially responsible for the maintenance of the household. It appeared that, in both projects, and contrary to the popular perception of housing administrators in India, the majority of women we questioned were very active in obtaining and sustaining their housing and households.

It has been recognized in the literature on women and shelter that the stress of resettlement to the peripheries of major cities to occupy new sites and serviced plots such as those in Mogappair and Charkop is expected to be greatest on poor women. This is because they have children and housekeeping responsibilities to fulfill as well as money to earn. Resettlement usually results in longer commuting time for those women who have middle-class, wage-work occupations. In our interviews women in such jobs voiced their frustration with the level of bus service and the paucity of travel options to get to work and the amount of time needed every day for commuting. For those women engaged in domestic work, usually in service to households in their old neighborhoods, resettlement generally results in loss of such jobs and other income-augmenting home occupations possible when one is located in older, more developed, settlements. Resettlement in the new housing locations needs to take these circumstances into account. Poor and middle-income women might, for instance, require the creation of facilities that support income-generation activity.

In this regard we found in our interviews that women in both projects were most articulate about wanting to start, or needing support for, existing income-generation activities. They cited the need for employment possibilities in the vicinity of the project area. They expressed the need for child care that they could depend upon. They described the crèches they had started that they needed more space for. They took pride in showing or telling us about the various petty trade activities they were involved in that enabled them to earn some income. One animated and strong woman in Mogappair (see cover photograph) who runs a small hotel in her housing unit which enjoys a corner location (caption photo for Theme 6 is of the kitchen of her hotel) told us:

> I have always worked hard and earned a living for my family. I have been on my own from a very young age. My husband left me with several children to support and I have worked hard to raise them. I have the ability and the will to turn this place into "a first class hotel" if only someone would give me a substantial loan to do so. And I mean substantial. When they have programs of loans for women to start some work to earn more they never talk about access to some REAL money. What am I going to be able to do with just a couple of thousand rupees here and there? I need much more. And they won't let me use this house as collateral for a loan because it isn't paid up yet. Give us some real help and we can show what we can turn that into.

Conclusion

In my work on these particular projects and in my ongoing work with a group of rural women from a village in Maharashtra, India, I have found strong, motivated, women clear and evocative in their claims for a chance to make good on their own.[13] The ability to attain shelter in their own names and to utilize this precious resource so that they can stand on their own feet is a common need that I have heard articulated by women from all classes of Indian society. The feminist movement in India has taken the position that it is necessary to provide special access to housing and entitlement to house ownership for single women, be they unmarried, divorced, abandoned, or widowed as, in a patriarchal

society such as the Indian, they are a most vulnerable sub-population. One feminist demand is that a certain percentage of plots in new public housing projects be earmarked for single women. Our work indicates that there is a need to seriously consider this type of action. Certainly quite appropriate follow up questions about shaping such policy will arise. What happens if and when remarriage occurs? What protections and rights do women have vis-a-vis fathers, sons and brothers that would enable them to maintain ownership and control over this shelter? In our interviews we noted how obtaining title to plots had strengthened the hands of the women owners and at the same time made them vulnerable to pressures from their male relatives and their relative's spouses. It had forced others to take these women's claims to home and shelter more seriously. This fact in itself may be sufficient reason to press ahead on implementing policy for expanding women's access to shelter and for providing the supportive infrastructure that will enable women to hold on to their homes in their own right.

As this book demonstrates, the issues regarding women, shelter, and development are highly complex, widely divergent, and very grave. The planet's burgeoning population, particularly in those countries whose resources are already overly stressed, suggests the urgency with which these issues need to be confronted. But there are some grounds for cautious optimism. The very fact that the issues are not out in the open is among them. The strength, resiliency, and resourcefulness of many of the women described herein should also be included. Academics, journalists, intellectuals, lawyers, governmental officials, entrepreneurs, planners, architects, designers - need to all look, and listen, and learn, and then act together.

Notes

[1] A forthcoming review article, Hemalata C. Dandekar, "Women and Housing," in Rita S. Gallin, ed., *The Women and International Development Annual,* Volume 4, Westview Press, 1984, delineates the literature on shelter, women, and development in some detail and discusses its implications for research and policy. For a representative example of the positions of international agencies see, United Nations Centre for Human Settlements (UNCHS), *Women in Human Settlements Development and Management,* Nairobi, Kenya, 1989 which reflects the UNCHS approach to thinking about gender and physical infrastructure. See also, Mine Sabuncuoglu, *Communications, Development and Women's Participation in Human Settlements Management,* United Nations Centre for Human Settlements (UNCHS), Nairobi, Kenya, 1988.

[2] See, for example, Bapat and Patel's call for social support networks and for political mobilization, Celik's call for technical and managerial knowhow, Neela Dabir's call for counseling, Bhatt's articulation of the

importance of common open spaces adjacent to shelter that are capable of flexible use, and Larsson, Oruwari, and Scarneccia's illustrations of the need for legislation that will enable women to obtain control over the housing asset.

3 Bapat and Patel discuss this issue at some length in their chapter. See also Aliyar and Shetty's discussion of Maxine Molyneux's delineation of gender interests and needs.

4 See, for instance, the United Nations Centre for Human Settlements (UNCHS) publications, *The Role of Women in Execution of Low-Income Housing Projects Training Module,* Nairobi, Kenya, 1986, and *Building-Related Income Generation For Women: Lessons – From Experience*, Nairobi, Kenya, 1990. Frannie Humplick's presentation at the conference titled "Women and Infrastructure Services," based on the application of an analytic model to a project in Istanbul to investigate empirically the issue of gender differentiated choice in infrastructure technology, illustrated the World Bank's approach to this topic.

5 Field work for this project was supported by a senior research fellowship grant from the American Institute of Indian Studies and supplemented by travel funds from the University of Michigan's Office of the Vice President for Research.

6 See, for example, Dandekar, review of Lloyd Rodwin, ed., *Shelter, Settlement and Development,* Allen and Unwin, Boston: 1987, *Economic Development and Cultural Change,* 1989 and *Journal of the American Planning Association,* Winter 1989, pp. 111–113. See also, review of G. Shabbir Cheema, *Urban Shelter and Services: Public Policies and Management Approaches,* Praeger: 1987, *Journal of the American Planning Association,* Winter 1989, pp. 111–113.

7 See Dandekar, review of Carl V. Patton, ed., *Spontaneous Shelter International Perspectives and Prospects,* Temple University Press: 1988, *Journal of the American Planning Association,* Winter 1989, pp. 111–113.

8 In our in-depth interviews of women plot holders in the Charkop 1 and Mogappair East, we did in fact find several instances where ownership of their houses was providing a great deal of security to women who were vulnerable because they were single, divorced, aged, and economically dependent.

9 In this context, groups such as SPARC, headquartered in Bombay, whose work has been documented in this book by Bapat and Patel and received recognition internationally, Pennurimai Yakkam located in Madras, and the National Campaign for Housing Rights have been significant.

10 An article describing the overall findings of this project and documenting various aspects of women's access to the sites and services plots in Charkop and Mogappair is in progress.

11 Many officials in the various agencies were generous with their help, for which I am grateful. Of particular note were the overviews provided by Mr. V.K. Phatak, Chief Planner, BMRDA, permissions to obtain data and documents provided by Mr. Sunder Burra, Director World Banks Projects, MAHADA, the computer data manipulation provided by Dilip Muglikar, MHADA, Mr. A Lakshmanan, Chief Urban Planner, MMDA, and Ms. Lilian Premkumar, Community Development Officer, MMDA.

12 In Bombay help in data gathering was provided by Ms. Leena Kharkar. My familiarity with Bombay and ability to speak Merathi, the local language, allowed me to complete much of the field work and survey myself. Ms. Lilian Prem Kumar provided very able assistance in data collection, and in-depth interviewing in Mogappair East. She served as a translator and guide during my site visits and provided an extremely dedicated voice on behalf of the women in Mogappair. Her in-depth background knowledge of the project, the rigor of her approach to the material, and carefully collected and documented data did much to enhance the quality of this research.

13 The exceptions to this observation are the individuals who have been allocated plots and are part of a forced resettlement in which the government is trying to free up public lands in more desirable parts of the city where these individuals had acquired squatters rights. These resettled allottees, some of whom we did interview in Mogappair, are often least able to bear the costs of construction and maintenance of their new homes as they tend to be some of the less literate and poorer segments of the population.

14 This is a service provided by the more recent sites and service projects and represents a considerable savings in time for the builder, time that would have normally been spent in the generally acknowledged to be frustrating process of obtaining a building permit.

15 The book on rural women, a follow-up to my *Men to Bombay, Women at Home,* (1986), (working title *Where Shall I Go? What Shall I Do? Rural Indian Women Face Development*, CSSEA Publication, the University of Michigan) will be available in late 1993.

Chapter 31
Shelter-Related Infrastructural Needs of Women in Low-Income Settlements of Bombay

Neera Adarkar[1]

Neera Adarkar received her Bachelor of Architecture, University of Bombay and diploma in Industrial Design from the Indian Institute of Technology in Bombay. She has been active in the feminist movement in Bombay since 1980 and she is a member of Stree Uvach, a feminist publication group, and a member of the Women and Shelter group. She was active in the National Campaign for Housing Rights (NCHR) during its initial stages and helped in organizing a special workshop on Women and Shelter under NCHR in Madras in 1987. She helped in organizing "Expression," a women's cultural festival in 1990.

The issue of shelter-related amenities is linked to the urban problems and the political ideology of the state. The existing power and social relations in class, patriarchy, and culture affect the shaping of built environment, and women are adversely affected by these factors. Patriarchy is its most expressive in the institution of family to which the concepts of shelter and infrastructure are closely linked. Women's contribution as reproducers is not valued and as producers is not recognized, resulting in the invisibility of their needs in policy.

The growing feminist awareness of the planning of environment has led to many hypothetical solutions. This paper examines several within the reality of the sociocultural context of low-income settlements of Bombay. The aims of the study are: (a) to analyze how the amenities provided by the state in the settlements fulfill the needs of women; (b) to identify the chores for which immediate relief is required and culturally acceptable; and (c) to explore the women's response to proposed new amenities to improve the quality of their lives and provide necessary infrastructure for a non-sexual division of labor.

Long-term structural changes are needed in the society to improve the status of women, including a reformulation of housing policy addressing gender issues. Certain practical measures are suggested in the present context. However, a holistic gender-aware approach would require joint efforts of professionals, and feminist activists, and other progressives.

Conceptual Framework

The need for shelter-related infrastructure cannot be seen in isolation. It is closely linked to the urban problems of housing, which in turn are closely linked to the political ideology of the policy makers. The present deteriorating housing situation is proof of this fact and therefore needs to be critically examined.

The development model adopted by India is of a mixed economy but in reality negates all socialist measures, clearly leaning toward capitalist policies. This is most apparent in a city like Bombay. As a result of maximum industrialization, it has expanded into one of India's fastest growing urban centers, with maximum capital accumulation and the most unequal distribution of land. The problem is further aggravated by the continuing arrival of migrants from rural areas, because of lopsided economic development benefiting only urban areas. The land is concentrated in the hands of few agencies. With their manipulative power, prices have risen phenomenally, compelling the working class, especially unorganized labor, to occupy any available vacant lands and form slum colonies. The upper classes of the society make use of this cheap labor, but neither they nor the government wish to improve the quality of their lives by providing better housing or infrastructure. During the pre-independence and early independence period, the state authorities did provide formal housing for the working class population, but soon this became inadequate. The present government policy is to dispense with government-built formal housing, and instead finance housing through the newly formed housing banks, encouraging them to buy from the private builders at market rates. Needless to say, the low-income population will never have access to formal housing. "The nexus that exists between the rich in the city, the higher echelons of bureaucracy and the politicians belies any possibility of a people oriented rational housing policy (Jha: 1986, p. 146)."

Women are the worst affected, suffering the property relations of class and the property and social relations of a patriarchal culture. Women's access to housing is mediated through their relationships to males—father, husband, or son. Patriarchy is its most expressive in the institution of family, to which the concept of housing is closely linked. There exists a strict hierarchical order in the family: the husband or the father-in-law is at the top of the ladder and the women are at the bottom, and labor is strictly divided based on sex. Family also conveys a set of values attached to this division of labor. A home becomes a strong medium to keep women dependent, and they suffer the deprivation and oppression to retain shelter. Women's reproductive role (biological and social) is not valued economically and culturally; their productive roles as wage earner are not recognized; and therefore the needs of amenities like crèches are not taken seriously.

With the World Bank investing a large amount of money in the low-income housing projects, in the last five years the issue of housing is on the political agenda of the Indian government, as in other Third World countries. To study gender awareness in planning the infrastructural amenities, we decided to approach women in the housing settlements with the following aims:

1. To identify women's needs in the low- and middle-income housing settlements of Bombay for the physical infrastructural social amenities.

2. To see how the existing amenities help women in their daily lives, and to pinpoint inadequacies.
3. To examine the existing planning standards stipulated by the state housing policy.
4. To explore the response of the women to a new set of proposed amenities that would help to improve the quality of their present lives and change their social status.

Existing Planning Standards for Provision of Infrastructure

Development Plan of Bombay

The Bombay Municipal Corporation stipulates the standard for all the development activities of Bombay by devising Development Plan and Development Control Rules, including the planning standards for the infrastructure, i.e., the ratio of minimum plot area for an amenity to a certain number of population. The amenities include playgrounds, primary and secondary schools, health and medical facilities, markets, libraries, fire stations, parking, lots, cinema theaters, burial and cremation grounds, road depots, and welfare centers, including a gymnasium facility. The welfare center is the only amenity in the existing settlements which could be, and which is very occasionally, used for women's activities. The allotted area for a welfare center, of 15,000 sq. ft. per ward (a ward may constitute about 500,000 to 2 million people) is ridiculously low. Owners of the land reserved for public amenities are allowed to use 50% of the buildable area for commercial purposes, provided they use the remaining 50% for the amenities.

The proposed new low-income housing is through World Bank funded "site and services" projects implemented by the state authority of MHADA (Maharashtra Housing and Area Development Board) (Murphy: 1990).

Provision of Infrastructure in the Existing Slum Settlement

The existing "authorized" low-income housing stock in Bombay is the slum settlements and "Chawl" settlements. Provision of infrastructure in the existing authorized slums is under two authorities, the Slum Improvement Board of BMC and the MHADA Slum Improvement Board. They concentrate mainly on physical amenities like common toilet blocks, water taps, electricity, etc. The World-Bank-aided "Slum Upgrading Program" also provides similar services. But electrical services in interior lanes are provided only if they are wide enough for a maintenance vehicle to pass through. Needless to say, the settlements don't always meet this condition.

Provision in the New Housing Schemes Funded by the World Bank

In the new housing under the "Site and Service" scheme, the World Bank package includes provision of an individually constructed toilet block and a demarcated plinth on which the owner builds as per his/her needs. In addition, the package includes roads, water supply, and amenities like markets and schools. Plots for welfare centers (30,000 sq. ft. for a population of 35,000) are earmarked. Although the norm for welfare centers is better than the provision in the Development Plan of BMC, the welfare centers' chance of getting built is remote because, as per the authority, the residents have to undertake the responsibility of building them.

Provision of Social Services by the State Welfare Department

The Bombay City Social Education Committee, funded by the government, started in 1939 by opening adult education classes in low-income settlements. Unfortunately, even at present, the emphasis is only on adult education; 1,000 classes are run in Bombay. Although the committee claims to have activities for women, they are limited to two kindergarten classes, two child nutrition centers, and eleven "motherhood development centers" in the entire city of Bombay. This organization's plans for the future do not indicate any quantitative or qualitative modification of the existing policy.

The Study

Selection of Settlements

Three types of settlements were selected on the basis of physical development, available infrastructure, and socio-economic status of the residents, namely (1) Slums, (2) "Chawls," and (3) Blocks. Only women belonging to low- and middle-income groups were selected as subjects for the study, with an emphasis on the low-income category, as they form the majority of the women's population in the city. The city of Bombay is a linear development with the business and commercial center concentrated on the southern tip. The city was divided into three zones, south, central, and north. Each type of settlement was selected from every zone so as to allow maximum representation. A total of 17

settlements was selected. Specific characteristics of each type of settlement selected are given below.

Slums

Important characteristics of a slum settlement are unplanned growth without any initial infrastructure, extreme high density, low-rise development with only narrow lanes dividing the rows of tenements, and no common open spaces within. Electricity, common sanitary block, and water supply are subsequently provided wherever possible by the Slum Improvement Board. The slum settlements have a mixed culture as the residents are mostly migrants from all over India.

"Chawls"

"Chawls" belong to the formal housing stock provided by the Bombay Development Directorate of the state between 1945 and 1965, built at subsidized prices for working classes. This is a planned layout of the ground plus three-story buildings, with a playground and community welfare center. The two-room (kitchen and outer room) tenements, about 8 to 10 per floor, are accessible by a common corridor in the front. A similar corridor on the rear provides access to the common toilet block on each floor. The population is mainly of early migrants from the rural areas of Maharashtra, economically better off than people living in the slums.

Block of Flats

Small independent flats of not more than 500 sq. ft., accommodated in a cluster of 4–5-storied buildings, form a housing colony. There are four flats on each floor. The income strata are low- to middle-income, and resident are of varied cultural backgrounds.

Populations staying on pavements, which are below the poverty line, and upper classes staying in big apartments were excluded from the study.

Selection of Women from the Settlements

On an average, three women in the age group of 25 to 50, selected with a preference for earning women, from each type of settlement were interviewed with the help of a structured questionnaire. A total of 66 women from all the three types of settlements were interviewed: 28 women from slums, 18 from chawls, and 20 from flats.

Earning women constitute 91% (N=60) of the total sample. Two remaining 9% (N=6) are non-earning, full-time housewives.

Findings

The findings are presented in two parts. The first part includes information about the existing physical and social infrastructural amenities provided in the settlements visited, and the second part includes information obtained from individual women.

Table 1: Existing Physical and Infrastructural Amenities in the Settlements

No. of Settlements Surveyed	No. of Slum	No. of Chawls	No. of Block Flats
	7	4	6
Physical Infrastructural Amenities:			
Toilets:			
1. Common toilet blocks	6	common toilets/floor	individual toilets
2. Distance to the toilet from residence	6 min.	1 min.	–
3. Average waiting period	20 min.	12 min.	–
4. No toilet facility	1	–	–
Water Source:			
1. Common	6	–	–
2. Individual	–	4	6
3. No water source	1	–	–
Electricity	6	4	6
Drainage	open	covered	covered
Internal Roads	4'–0" narrow lanes	4	6
Garbage Disposal	–0–	4	6
Social Infrastructural Amenities:			
1. Welfare center	–0–	4	–0–
2. Mahila Mandal (informal groups of women)	6	3	3
3. Kindergarten classes	5	4	5
4. Adult education classes	4	2	1
5. Distance to public dispensary	30 min.	30 min.	Private

Existing Physical Infrastructure

As Table 1, giving physical and infrastructural amenities in the selected settlements, indicates, infrastructure varies with the category of the settlement. However, one can make a general observation that all the amenities provided are inadequate.

Sanitation

In slum settlements particularly toilets are inadequate and inconvenient for women. Lack of enough privacy, insecurity at night, long waiting periods and unhygienic conditions due to bad maintenance are common problems. In chawls the problems are less because the common toilets are on each floor of the building. However, problems of privacy, inadequacy, and bad maintenance remain.

One of the slums located in the richest downtown commercial area has no toilet block. Women suffer the most due to the lack of toilets, e.g., they avoid meals during the day to save themselves from the embarrassing and insecure situation of having to use secluded places at night. The norm of the Slum Improvement Board is to provide one W.C. (water closet) per 25 to 50 people. This is inadequate as seen from the average waiting time; and there is no provision of water inside the toilet in all the settlements. Three slums out of seven had no lights in the toilets, and two slums had no lights in the access to the toilet. The women's toilet blocks were observed to be dirtier because the children accompany their mothers, and, due to the dark, unsafe conditions of the W.C. units, prefer to use the outer steps or the corridors between the W.C. units.

Water Supply

In the slums the norm for common water taps is one standpost for 150 to 200 people, which is inadequate. The tap is on average five minutes away, and women have to wait in queues at odd hours for their turn to fetch heavy buckets to their tenements. Few households have spent collectively for a private connection. Most of the tenements have a small enclosure for bathing in a small corner of the back room or outside, if space permits. The stored water has to be enough for washing the clothes and utensils, for cooking, and for drinking. It is stored in drums mostly outside the tenements in the narrow access lanes which are 4 to 5 ft. wide.

Existing Social Infrastructure

No space is earmarked for any social amenities except welfare centers provided in government-built "chawls." Social amenities in slums and "chawls" are limited to adult education classes and kindergarten classes either provided by the welfare department of the government or as a part of N.G.O. community development activities. The kindergarten classes are mostly run privately on a commercial basis.

Welfare Centers

The "Chawls" built by the Bombay Development Directorate have a community hall and a playground in each cluster. The community hall is almost totally appropriated by men for sports from which women are excluded. However, in one of the centers a few sewing machines were kept on the mezzanine floor by the welfare department for use by women. Women seem to be too inhibited to use the welfare centers for their "Mahila Mandal" activities, because the men have been the dominant users of the community hall as well as the outside playground.

Mahila Mandals

Mahila Mandals are informal groups of women who get together in the community. This is a culturally accepted structure mainly for middle-class women who come together to plan some entertainment and/or charitable activities. However, this structure is now common in "chawls" and to some extent in slums. Unfortunately, the activities are limited to celebrations of religious festivals only. For lack of common meeting places, women meet in one of the tenements or on terraces.

Local Residents' Committee

Each settlement has some local committees composed of the active and enthusiastic residents, all men, who undertake various activities at the settlement level. However, the most common and popular activities are celebrations of religious festivals. The committee also does minimum liaison work with the state authorities for basic infrastructure, such as lights and water. Not a single local committee in all the settlements surveyed had a woman member on it, and we found no desire to take up issues related to women.

Dispensaries

Public dispensaries are at a walking distance of half an hour, on the average. On the other hand, private doctors are available near all the settlements. People spend a large sum per month for their services.

Interviews with the Women of the Settlement

To identify women's needs in the roles of producer and reproducer, we need to learn their perception of the status and value attached to the domestic chores both in the Indian cultural context and in the context of their double role. The interviews therefore included questions about sharing the domestic burden by other family members, especially the husbands; the hobbies and other interests of the women which could be pursued were their burden reduced; and their mobility within and outside the city. We also tried to learn the subjects' perceptions of their needs for services such as counseling/crisis centers for women, and child care facilities in the settlements. The findings are presented separately according to the types of settlements, i.e., slums, "chawls," and block of flats, to compare the needs and aspirations of women from the three socioeconomic levels.

Income-Earning Activities of Women

Figure 1 indicates the distribution of women respondents' earnings in home-based and outside home activities. It is seen that middle-class women who live in the blocks of flats are engaged in outside employment because of their higher education and class backgrounds, whereas in low-income settlements such as slums and chawls women are engaged both in home-based earning and outside employment.

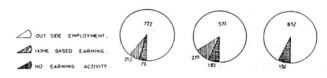

Fig. 1.

Table 2. Average Daily Working Hours Per Settlements

Earning Activity	Slum	Chawl	Block of Flats
Home-based	5.0	5.0	–
Outside earning			
Small production units	8.0	8.0	–
Service sector	7.0	6.0	7.0
Self-employed	5.0	8.0	–
Commuting time	0.5	2.0	2.0–2.5

Home-Based Earning

Women in home-based work are exploited to a greater extent than women in outside employment because the women do not form part of the organized sector. The Bombay Municipal Corporation's zoning regulations affect women's self-employed earning activities at home. In one of the "site and service" projects aided by the World Bank, women have started home-based informal shops through windows of their outer rooms, facing the access lanes to sell small grocery items, catering to the daily needs of the residents. In the residential zone, this kind of commercial activity is illegal, and these informal "shops" are liable to legal action.

A home-based worker spends, on the average, 5 hours at work, in addition to the time spent in obtaining the unfinished material and returning the finished product. The household chores and the income-generating activities always overlap, which allows no rest. Most of these activities involve a risk of pollution from the raw materials, in addition to the mess in a small room of 10' x 8' which the woman has to clean up every time this activity overlaps with other chores when other family members are present. The work is done in isolation even if women in adjoining tenements are engaged in the same work.

Outside Earning

Slum residents work mainly as contract laborers such as domestic servants and sweepers, and as job workers in the unorganized sector. In "chawls" the majority are workers employed in small-scale production units. The women in flats are employed mostly in white-collar administrative jobs as clerks, receptionists, accountants, etc. Table 2 shows the working hours in different earning activities.

Middle-class women in flats have to commute by local trains to South Bombay's commercial area, whereas slum residents seek work within walking distance to save on transportation costs.

Perception of Household Chores

Household work is considered a natural primary activity for women, and it is assumed that women enjoy performing domestic chores. In reality, the domestic responsibilities which are solely the women's restrict them irrespective of their class, in pursuing either an earning activity or any other work of their own interest. The average time spent on household tasks was 6.5 hours per day. Women spent an average of 4.5 hours on these tasks. They thus contributed 70% of the labor for household chores.

To find out how women assess their chores, the value they attach to each, and the physical labor required for each, they were given a list of common domestic chores like cooking, preparation for cooking, sweeping, cleaning utensils, washing clothes, fetching water from the common water source, child care, serving meals, buying vegetables, and buying necessities like grains and fuel (kerosene) from government subsidized ration shops and private grocery shops. They were asked to categorize these as enjoyable chores, strenuous chores, and chores which give them some status. Sixty-one women from a total number of 66, said very vehemently that all the chores are very strenuous and questions of pleasure do not arise. The five exceptions were women who stay in flats (see Figure 2). When pressed on this matter, some of the women identified a few chores which gave them some pleasure in spite of the fatigue. The positive values assigned to some tasks vary with the status of the settlements; more women living in flats claimed to get pleasure from activities such as cooking, child care, and shopping (Figure 2).

The affordability and variety of foods and the status attached to exclusiveness of personal cooking seem to be the main reasons for middle-class women's higher values assigned to cooking. For slum and "chawl" women, shopping is mainly standing in long queues in front of government-subsidized ration shops for daily necessities and fuel almost every alternate day, and therefore it is not enjoyable. Home-based income

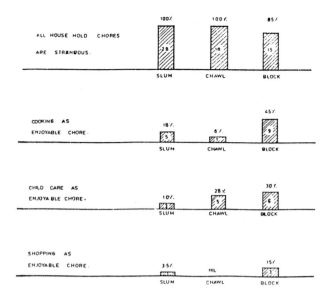

Fig. 2.

Fig. 3.

generating activity is the only domestic activity conferring status, as reported by all the women who undertake home-based earning work.

Sharing of Work by Husband and Other Family Members

The relationships between husbands and wives in sharing the domestic work were examined by finding out whether the wives ask their husbands to help them. Of the respondents, 81% (54) women (in slums, chawls, and blocks) replied that they never ask for help. The reasons varied by class. Slum and chawl women expressed hopelessness and anticipated negative replies to such requests. They responded with, "I know he is not going to help so why ask?" Women in the flats said, "I can manage on my own, so why ask him?" Maximum help in the family is provided by the daughters, mothers in-law, and very occasionally sons, in extended households of single women. Figure 3 shows the help extended by other family members.

It was amusing to find out that the chores in which the husbands help are very similar. The chores are restricted to "clean," fast, and outside jobs, namely, shopping, getting the children ready for school, and occasionally fetching water during the wife's illness. In the most tiring and time-consuming jobs, cooking, cleaning, and washing, the husbands do not extend help. However, four women said they do receive their husbands' help in all the chores. The women were asked to identify the chores which other family members can possibly undertake. Fetching water, buying rations from ration shops, and looking after school-going children are prominently identified.

Collective Organization of Services

The concept of socialization of domestic chores was unheard of by all the women who were interviewed. This was expected, and therefore the questions under this head were framed carefully. Certain consumer items and services, like buying ready pickles and getting ready flour from flour mills, were part of household chores a few decades ago, but are well accepted as commercial services today, even in the low-income households. By citing these examples, further response was sought to the proposal of similar organized help for cooked "chapatis" (bread), cooked vegetables, and collective services for washing clothes by a set of washing machines in the community. Basic affordability of these services was assured. In some of the earlier informal discussions with middle-class women, such a proposal was turned down as unrealistic and ridiculous. However, in the present study, the uninhibited responses came as a pleasant surprise. The proposal was not discarded as unrealistic but was probed into with curiosity. The degree of acceptance of the unfamiliar concept of organized help is shown in Figure 4. On the whole, it was observed that cooked chapatis and cheap laundry would be welcome. Chapati-making is a laborious process involving rolling and roasting of flattened dough on the kerosene stove, which increases chances of the sari catching fire in the small multipurpose room.

Women who get regular help from the family members are not so much in favor of outside service. The charts show that women from all the categories are eager to be relieved from the chore of washing clothes. It is interesting to see that in one of the poorest slums surveyed, where women work mostly as domestic maids, they cannot comprehend paying for the very services they sell, like washing clothes, whereas they do cherish the dream of getting ready-made meals. On the

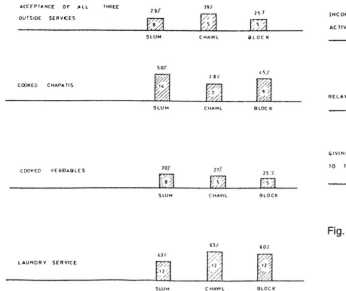

Fig. 4.

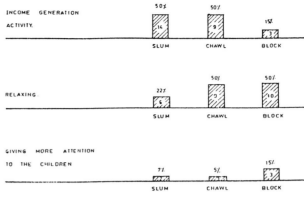

Fig. 5.

other hand, middle-class women are less interested in cooked items than in laundry services. This may reflect the difference in the attitudes of the two classes towards the status attached to different chores.

Activities Which Women Would Like to Undertake If They Got Relief from Domestic Chores and Hobbies They Would Pursue

Through the interviews the women were asked to identify their hobbies encouraging them to carve out at least some part of their time exclusively for their own interests. Yet the answers show how difficult it is for these women to allow themselves to think about their own satisfaction. As can be seen in Figure 5, for 50% of the slum and chawl women, the priority is income generation in the saved time rather than any leisure activities. The concept of hobbies is alien to nearly 50% of the women in slums. They laugh it off as an unthinkable luxury at the first instance. Women in blocks could specify a few hobbies, and almost all the women said they had pursued some hobby before they got married. Tailoring and knitting are culturally accepted hobbies, encouraged by parents in all classes: they restrict the girls to their homes and make them self-sufficient in stitching their own clothes. These may also be potential income-generating activities in their married life,

especially in an emergency situation, e.g., the husband's death or desertion.

Mobility

Women get inhibited due to lack of mobility. Many factors in patriarchal society restrict the mobility of women, domestic responsibilities among them. The degradation of life in slums adds to the insecure atmosphere. In the study, the mobility of the women was judged from their use of time in the holidays, out station travel in vacation, mobility in the settlement, and within the city of Bombay. Mobility within the settlement is found to be negligible compared to that of the men, as shown in Table 3.

Mobility of women is found to depend mainly on the place of work and commuting. Women from low-income settlements choose to work close to their homes, thus minimizing their mobility. Inflation has curtailed pleasurable activities of traveling or sightseeing within the city; 85% of the women in the slums and 55% of those in chawls are not even aware of the activities in the main downtown commercial and administration area. Faulty town planning, totally segregating commercial and residential areas, added by the real estate pressures, segregate the middle- and low-income population from the main town. "Women are the most affected population, who become extremely inhibited and scared to venture beyond their immediate environment" (Matrix: 1984). However, in this respect it should be noted that the original unplanned character of Bombay has been advantageous to a majority of women in that commuting for work is necessary. Women who work are therefore forced to and become competent in navigating the city.

Table 3: Sightseeing Mobility of Women

Destination	Slum %	Chawl %	Block %
Sightseeing in the vicinity of settlement	64	85	100
Beach	53	95	100
Main railway stations	64	88	100

A very good system of public transport in Bombay also helps women to be mobile.

Awareness of Services Such as Crèches and Women's Counseling Centers

Whether the women are aware of services like crèches or counseling/crisis centers, and whether they perceive the necessity of having these services in their settlement or in the vicinity is indicated in Figure 6. Many women in slums who had not heard of crèches earlier felt that, if such services were to exist, in part, their children would not have missed their schooling by having to look after the siblings while the parents went out to earn money. Awareness of women's counseling centers and the need felt for this service is also indicated in Figure 6. It was found that the awareness for this service is seen only if such organizations are working in women's own settlements.

Conclusions

The study establishes that there is an apathy toward inclusion of women's needs in the process of planning housing and its infrastructure. The study sought to identify and analyze the needs of women in the two categories of low income and one category of middle income, as indicated by where they lived, namely slums, chawls, and block of flats. It led to the emergence of new insight and also confirmed the hypotheses, e.g., it has shown that the needs of women in the three different socio-economic categories vary in degree but not in kind. The variation is attributable mainly to the degree of internalization of patriarchal values and upholding of many myths, especially about the status and value attached to domestic chores.

Women's perspectives of domestic chores are changing due to their increased awareness of the importance of their roles as producers. Analysis of the double burden of earning and household responsibilities confirms that

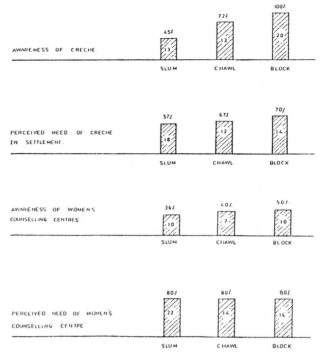

Fig. 6.

immediate measures are needed to socialize some of the most strenuous chores for which women would be willing to accept outside help. Most women no longer consider cooking as a status-giving activity, contrary to what has been assumed in the Indian cultural context.

The socialization of chores as with the "British Restaurant" of post-war England (Matrix: 1984, p. 108) and the "Common Kitchens" of the socialist countries like the Soviet Union, would, within the Indian social framework, run into factors related to caste, religion, and regionality. These might play a restrictive role in socialization of domestic chores, especially cooking. Caste pollution and caste and regional identity may adversely affect eating meals cooked by women of other castes. Thus one would have to start with a limited scale to make this a workable concept. Instead of all the daily items of meals, only a few basic items could be prepared and managed at the community level. This should be encouraged and financed by the state welfare department.

The local residents' committee would play an important role here. It was observed that in all 17 settlements not a single local committee had a woman member. This fact contradicts Caroline Moser's analysis of the triple role of women in Third World countries, woman as a producer, a reproducer, and a community manager (Moser and Peake: 1987, p. 13). In the Indian urban context, the leadership capabilities of the women at the community level are revealed, unfortunately, only during crisis situations like religious riots or police repression during compulsory eviction. The degradations of life in the low-income settlements due to the corrupt political climate affects the lives of the poor to a great extent. They are divided on caste and religion lines for political gains, and the local residents' committees are used by the nexus of politicians and criminals in the power game. In such a situation women are further marginalized.

With this background, it seems practical that the existing structure of Mahila Mandals (informal groups of women in the settlement) should be imbued with feminist consciousness. Women should be mobilized around tangible demands such as crèches, community space for collective domestic work, etc. The examples of SPARC and of Maitrei, a feminist women's organization, are worth noting. Maitrei's, through the Mahila Mandal, stimulate social awareness among the women by taking up issues such as domestic violence, health, sexuality, etc. Such "consciousness-raising" would help to link the concept of socialization of work with the sexual division of labor. The study shows that the women have begun to realize the unjust division of work between men and women, even on the domestic front. Equal sharing of household responsibilities by the husband is a part of the long-term process, but simultaneous efforts are needed to empower women to make demands on both fronts.

Changes in the State Housing Regulation

The present political and economic policies of the Indian government are heavily inclined toward a private market economy. All welfare expenses are being heavily cut and women are going to be the worst sufferers. In this situation, on the one hand, demands based on the state provision for housing and infrastructure will have to be made with renewed efforts in collaboration with all other progressive movements. On the other hand, demands will have to be made for changing norms in favor of women, in the building regulations, and within the private sector development.

Some of the changes which could be implemented in the state policy are:

— Inclusion in the development plans of BMC and World Bank-funded projects of MHADA, the amenities of

welfare/community centers especially for women, e.g., crèches and shelter homes/crisis centers for women. The state should also ensure the construction of these amenities rather than leaving it to the private owners as in the present provision.

— Zoning regulations need to be reformulated to allow women to undertake home-based small-scale commercial activities. The critique of zoning regulations of Third World countries by Caroline Moser applies accurately to the Indian situation. Zoning regulations which separate residential and business activities may prohibit the development of small-scale self-employed income-earning activities at home, e.g., women selling products from their front door (Moser and Peake: 1987, p. 21).

— Slum Improvement Board and World Bank-funded Slum Upgrading Program for existing settlements should incorporate the suggested social amenities in their package of services, in addition to the quantitative changes needed, e.g., addition of low-cost open-air toilets for children will go a long way to keep the women's toilet block less dirty.

In conclusion it appears that to change the situation documented in this paper two areas need to be addressed.

— Policy makers should be aware that the definition of shelter cannot be complete without the provision of physical and social amenities for women.

— The infrastructural needs of women have to be identified in the feminist perspective and in the cultural context, giving equal weight to their double roles of production and reproduction. Solutions should be geared toward long-term objectives ("strategic"), empowering women to live free of exploitative power relations within the society, not token welfaristic measures of quantitative modifications as in the existing provision. Even short-term measures ("practical") should be aimed toward structural changes in the social status of the women. The participation of men in domestic and child care would have to be enhanced by consciousness-raising of the women of the settlements through existing social services like adult education classes and Mahila Mandals.

To make such demands of the state authorities and to mobilize the women of the community, forums of progressive architects and feminist groups would have to collaborate and work at multiple levels, at the level of research, at the level of lobbying, and at the level of activism. All shelter-related struggles therefore go hand in hand with women's movements: the struggle for subsistence production, the struggle of the unorganized sector, and the struggle for a balanced and healthy ecology.

Note

[1] This study was assisted by Sandhya Naik, Nandadeep Society, Goregaon, Bombay, India.

References

Jha, S. S., *Structure of Urban Poverty.* Bombay: Popular Prakashan, 1986.

Karkal, Malini, "Can Family Planning Solve Population Problems," Stree Uvach Publication, 1989.

Lawyers Collective, "Special Issue on Housing," 1987.

Lind Jenness, ed., *Feminism and Socialism,* New York: Pathfinder Press, 1976.

Matrix Book Group, *Making Space,* London: Pluto Press Limited, 1984.

Moser, Caroline, and Peake, Linda, eds., *Women, Human Settlements and Housing,* London: Javistock Publication, 1987.

Murphy, Denis, "A Decent Place to Live: Urban Poor in Asia," Asian Coalition for Housing Rights, 1990.

Royal Institute of Technology Department of Architecture, Stockholm, *Shelter for the Urban Poor—A Case Study of Bombay,* 1987.

Singh Andrea Menefee, *Women in Cities: An Invisible Factor in Urban Planning in India,* Population Council, 1980.

SPARC – Society for Promotion of Area Resource Centres, "We, the invisible—a census of pavement dwellers" (1985).

Chapter 32
Women and Shelter-Related Services and Infrastructure: The Case of a Vulnerable Group

Madiha El Safty

Madiha El Safty studied at the American University in Cairo and received a Bachelor of Architecture in 1972 and a Master of Architecture in Sociology-Anthropology in 1976 . She received a Ph.D. in Sociology in 1980 from Ain Shams University, Egypt. She has been involved in research in different areas of sociology in Egypt, with a special emphasis on health, sanitation, education, and housing. She has been teaching at the American University in Cairo since 1977 and has lectured in a number of Egyptian academic institutions, including the Military Academy. She is currently a member of an advisory body on health matters, which is directly responsible to the president.

As a sociologist who has long been involved in field research in Egyptian society, I have written this paper as the outcome of my own experience, most of it being first-hand information from the field. It is based on a number of studies that I have supervised, in addition to published articles in both the Arabic and English languages. Additional information has been included from the Ministry of Health, the Central Agency of Public Mobilization and Statistics, and the study titled *Structural Adjustments in Health Sector to Protect the Vulnerable Groups*. Badran: 1989. The data presented here is somewhat dated, but more recent information is not available.

Women: Citizens with Equal Rights

For the Egyptian woman, the year 1954 marks a significant landmark, because it was then that an official declaration of women's rights was made for the first time. The Egyptian constitution explicitly recognized the status of women as members of society and as such granted them legal rights equal to those that men had always enjoyed. Women came to be legally entitled to education, job opportunities, and all other civil rights which had previously been restricted to the males as their exclusive privileges, if not on the formal, official level, then definitely on the level of actual practice. This declaration of equal rights for women represents a milestone in the Egyptian woman's long struggle for emancipation, which had been thwarted by the strong hold of Egyptian and Islamic tradition. Since then, both educational and job opportunities have opened to women. They have likewise been participating actively in political life in voting, running for office, and being elected. Their salaries are equal to those of men. They do not complain of any form of discrimination at work.

The fact remains, however, that the cultural base of a historically male-dominated society creates a discrepancy between the legal formal situation and the actual informal one. The prevailing norms in society lead, in many cases, to an unequal situation between the sexes, which can be detected clearly on the socio-cultural level where the dynamics controlled by tradition operate. The reflection of such a condition can be seen in many aspects of life. Educational and job opportunities are examples. The area of health is another major illustration of the underprivileged position of women. It is the sad truth that the health conditions of the Egyptian population, like those in most developing countries, are very poor. Morbidity and mortality rates are high; life expectancy is very low; and above all, the infant mortality rate, though significantly reduced in the last decade, remains very high. Such health problems exist in spite of the intensive and extensive measures taken to deal with them. The position of women as a disadvantaged group in the area of health cannot therefore be understood out of context. It is part and parcel of the broader problem of a poor health status for the population at large, as has already been mentioned.

Why the Bypass?

In an attempt to face that situation, the Egyptian government, since the Alma-Alta declaration, has been developing plans to extend health services to all segments of the population. It has undertaken the task of providing health coverage in the context of a broad and comprehensive program initially started in the mid-fifties with the purpose of extending different services to the underprivileged strata of the population. In line with this policy, the Ministry of Health has been taking measures to increase the number of health facilities throughout the different parts of the country, especially those concerned with maternal and child health. It should be remembered that governmental health centers in Egypt are meant to offer their services free. However, in spite of the many efforts exerted in this respect, the Egyptian Ministry of Health has not succeeded in eradicating many of the existing health problems. Neither has it been able to cover all the population nor improve the health standards. The effectiveness and efficiency of the present health care system are thus open to question.

Studies have shown that some health facilities are underutilized, which raises the question of accessibility. To which segment(s) of the population is the governmental health system meant to cater? If health services are presumed to be available to the population, what intervening variables account for underutilization of these services and continuing poor health standards, specifically, what are the existing conditions among the various communities of intended beneficiaries of health services that might account for bypassing the government health care delivery system? The question is simply: Why the bypass?

To answer this question, a set of complex factors must be understood in the context of the socio cultural milieu. Environmental and urban conditions, socio-economic and demographic characteristics of the population, problems of cost involved in the provision of health care, and the available equipment in the health facilities are but some of the relevant factors that might help explain the pattern of utilization of the health centers.

The issue is therefore a multifaceted one, and necessitates a multidimensional perspective.[1]

Any approach to the phenomenon of bypassing the formal health system has therefore to seek an explanation in the cultural base and it is through probing into this cultural base that a major variable of the underutilization of the health services can be highlighted. In the first place, prevailing Egyptian values, beliefs, and norms support the traditional healing system against the formal health services. As is often the case in developing societies, the traditional healing system exists in Egypt side by side with the formal health system. One explanation why the former tends to be more effective in the lives of the people than the latter can be sought in the approach of the traditional healers to their patients. Traditional healers are the midwives (untrained in medical care in most cases), health barbers, and herbalists. A major difference between folk medicine, represented by these traditional healers, and the so-called "scientific modern medicine," represented by physicians, is the perception of causation in illness. In the former, causation is rooted in the interpersonal world of tradition, magic, and the supernatural, whereas in the latter, it is rooted in the non-personal, observable, and predictable natural phenomena of nature. The traditional healer, therefore, interacts with the client through the channel of a shared belief system which is strongly rooted in their culture, and shapes the way of thinking of both healer and clients, which is not the situation with the "modern scientific" interpretation of the causal factors in illness.[2] One interesting paradox that can be noted in the relationship between "modern" and folk medicine is apparent in the utilization of the formal health system for children. In one study in a traditional neighborhood outside Cairo,[3] mothers reported that when their children are ill, they first resort to folk medicine, particularly to elderly women of the household or neighborhood, who offer prescriptions for every ailment. Only after all methods of traditional treatment are exhausted do the mothers finally resort to the health center, and then the child has already become seriously ill.

Mothers do, however, utilize the maternity and child care centers for vaccinating their children. In fact, vaccination ranks as the number one reason for utilization. Of the mothers surveyed, 53% indicated that they visit the centers only for this service. The paradox lies in the fact that mothers tend to seek traditional treatment for their infants under conditions considered "normal," yet resort to the formal system for vaccinations. The paradox can be understood, however, in the light of the

Table 1: Maternal Mortality for Every 100,000 Live Births

Year	Maternal Mortality Rate	Year	Maternal Mortality Rate
1951	16,000	1980	9,310
1955	11,000	1980	7,690
1970	11,000	1982	7,660
1965	9,000	1983	7,490
1970	11,000	1984	5,690
1975	7,360	1985	5,000
1976	8,090	1986	6,500
1977	8,040	1987	6,500
1978	8,220	1988	7,800
1979	7,790		

Source: Ministry of Health Statistics: 1989

Table 2: Causes of Female Mortality

Postpartum hemorrhage	22.8%
Ruptured uterus	12.9%
Antepartum hemorrhage	12.2%
Eclampsia	16.2%
Caesarian section	9.3%

Source: Ministry of Health, "Causes of Maternal Mortality," 1984–87.

motivating factor that leads the mothers to vaccinate the infants. Parents who do not vaccinate their children are fined by the government. It is not so much the acceptance of the "modern" health system, that motivates the rate of utilization, but rather the fear of a penalty. This should not be interpreted as acceptance but as coercion.

Women—The Vulnerable Group

In this drama of underutilized health services in Egyptian society, women are at a greater disadvantage. They represent a broad segment of what can be considered the vulnerable groups. Vulnerability here is defined with reference to the definition adopted by the World Health Organization as including "underprivileged social groups" in society. The Egyptian women can fit into this category very well, since the culture obviously supports male domination and tends to enhance it. It actually extends to all aspects of life. Even as infants, females are at a disadvantage. Studies have shown that the incidence of infant mortality is higher among females. Especially in the traditional subcultures of Egypt, a female infant is of very low value and may be neglected, and her rights denied, even in health care.

Significant in this situation is the high mortality rate among females of reproductive age. Women in this age group represent the most vulnerable of the vulnerable group. They are highly exposed to the incidence of death as a result of pregnancy and childbirth complica-

tions. The significance of the problem is clear from the proportion of females at the age of fertility: 21% of the total population.[4] The fact remains, however, that the rate has been decreasing over the years. Table 1 reveals the direction of change for the maternal mortality rate in Egyptian Society.

It must be noted that the table shows some fluctuations in the maternal mortality rate, but there is a downward trend starting in the seventies when there was an expansion in state health services. However, the increase in the mid-eighties is the result of a growing concern and enforcement on the part of the government for the registration of vital statistics. Here can be seen another cultural fact: accurate registration, not only of mortality cases, but also of births is highly doubtful. Again females are highly disadvantaged in this respect.

The seriousness of maternal mortality and its related aspects can be further highlighted by the following table which shows the female mortality rate as the result of different causes. Table 2 is based on a field study conducted in Egypt in an attempt to investigate prevalent causes of maternal mortality.

In studies done by the Ministry of Health in Egypt it was found that one out of eight women died of postpartum complications, the incidence being highest among the poor, illiterate women who delivered at home and who lived far from the available health services.[5] Another study showed that the incidence of mortality among women under 20 reached 2–5 per thousand and among those above 35, was 3 per thousand.[6] Both studies were conducted by the Ministry of Health. Relevant to these results is the traditional culture in which women are expected to marry at an early age; both family and societal pressures are strong. In addition, a woman's fertility is a major part of her identity as a female and guarantees her security in marriage. Consequently, females marry early and start having babies as soon as possible. They continue to reproduce until a late age. A barren woman or one who loses her fertility culturally represents very good grounds for divorce. In a society where most women are economically dependent on their husbands, divorce is a tragedy and a threat of insecurity. Such an attitude toward women's fertility is one important variable in the prevailing high birth rate and is one major constraint in family planning programs.

Relevant Variables

The above situation, serious as it appears, is a reflection of the inadequacy and also inefficiency of the health system, especially in the area of maternal care. One major reason here can be seen in the discrepancy between village and city in this respect. The unavailability of sufficient maternal care in the countryside is in large part responsible for the high female mortality rate. The results in a demographic survey of the Egyptian population have revealed that the overall percentage of women who receive maternal care does not exceed 14%. The village women receiving this care represent only 5% of the total, while those in the urban centers that seek such a service are 34% at best.[7] Moreover, as has already been mentioned, utilization of the health facility is largely determined by the individual's concept of illness. Therefore, neither pregnancy nor childbirth, including prenatal and postnatal care, is defined as requiring the services of the health facility. Such conditions are perceived as normal events and taken care of in the context of the traditional system. The midwife thus appears as an important figure in the community. Not only is her credibility high in the indigenous culture, but what is more is her affiliation with this culture as a member and equal in a network of close relationships.

A childbirth which may be initially complicated because of medical reasons during pregnancy or one that might develop complications during delivery cannot be handled by the midwife in most cases, and the condition may be far beyond her limited skills and knowledge. Consequently, it is common in such situations that the mother is transferred to a health facility after such complications arise. It may happen that because of the delay in transfer or deterioration of the condition, the arrival at the facility is too late and death occurs, whether of mother or infant. Such an outcome is in many cases attributed to the health facility's failure to handle the patient, and is responsible for the negative perception of the formal health system. The women therefore bypass the factors/problems preceding the transferal to the health facility and associate the death/ complications with its provided service. Such a negative

Table 3: Incidence of Anemia Among Mothers

Status	Percent	No. of Cases Investigated
Not pregnant	17.0	402
Breast feeding	25.0	823
Pregnant	22.1	253
TOTAL	22.4	1478

Source: "The Egyptian Child," Central Agency for Mobilization and Statistics (CAPMAS) and Unicef, June 1988.

image on the part of the potential beneficiaries of the health system, common as it is, is one important variable in its under utilization.

In some traditional subcultures in Egypt, a husband may deny his wife health care if it is provided by a man. A female provider is sought, which may well explain the importance of the traditional midwife among a large segment of the population. The formal health system has realized this cultural fact and has consequently been utilizing the services of female medical doctors in large numbers. In general, there is a growing demand in society for female physicians, especially as gynecologists-obstetricians, in particular with the growing movement of Islamic revival. The result is that home deliveries are frequent. A demographic survey in 1988 revealed that 77% of the deliveries that took place between 1984 and 1988 were at home, only one-third by a doctor or nurse; the rest were handled by the traditional midwives. The percentage of home deliveries is definitely higher in rural than in urban areas, reaching as high as 89% in the former and 59% in the latter.[8]

Nutrition also stands out as a major variable affecting the high maternal mortality rate, related, of course, to economic conditions. A significantly high proportion of the population is living under the poverty line. Moreover, women in a traditionally male-dominated society are underprivileged in matters of nutrition. The following table shows the incidence of anemia among mothers as revealed by a study on children.

These data were consistent with an earlier study by the Nutrition Institute in 1981, which revealed that 22.2% of urban families and 33% of rural families distribute food unequally among their members, with women and children receiving the least shares.[9] In 1987, the World Health Organization and the Egyptian Ministry of Health studying maternal mortality, found out that protein calories were very low in women's nutrition. In both situations the rural women ranked even lower than urban women.[10]

The role of environmental conditions cannot be underestimated in the prevailing health problems. Sanitation is poor, especially in villages. Water and sewage problems persist in spite of increasing concern, simply because of the inability of the supply market to meet the growing demand. Intensive water and sanitation projects are launched both through government and foreign funds, but cannot meet the increasing needs in this respect. The 1986 census showed that only 73.8% of households had running water, 55.9% of which were rural and 92.4%, urban. Only 87% of urban households had electricity. According to the World Health Organization in 1987 only 80% of urban households had sewage disposal; but in 1990 the percentage reached 100% in the cities and 65% in the villages.

A Final Word

In the multitude of factors that affect women's health, education is a significant variable, as it is in the inferior status of women in general. Education, or rather the absence of education, is the underlying factor behind the high maternal mortality rate and the high incidence of disease among women, among other health problems. Education can likewise be seen as both cause and effect of women's underprivileged status. A lack of awareness of their rights not only on the level of the family but on that of society at large is the result of a lack of educational opportunities. At the same time their inferior position in the culture leads to a denial of many of their rights, education being only one among them. In a traditionally male-dominated culture with limited resources, preference usually goes to educating the male rather than the female child. In 1991 the overall female illiteracy rate was 62.5%; in the rural areas, 77%. The dropout rate from school among females is likewise high, especially when girls reach puberty.

The demographic survey mentioned above showed that education plays a role in reducing the proportion of home deliveries among illiterate women. The percentage of home deliveries was as high as 87%, while among those with a high school degree, it was 43%. Moreover, response to family planning programs has been higher among women with more education. For this reason, any approach to improve women's status has

to start with extending educational opportunities to cover all the female population.

Opportunities to work are another relevant variable in women's pursuit of equality. But a large segment of Egyptian women are exploited. Because of their dual role in society, women are currently undergoing a role conflict which has not helped in their vulnerability. As is true elsewhere, working women without education find it very difficult to escape their disadvantages.

The state has tried to make education available to all the female population. And health services are being upgraded, in both quantity and quality. In addition, the Egyptian Ministry of Health, following the 1978 Alma-Ata declaration, has attempted to incorporate the traditional health system into the formal one by initiating a training program for the traditional midwives. This program is to teach health awareness and upgrade the midwife techniques of prenatal/postnatal care for their practice, while maintaining the midwives' role within the cultural milieu as accepted providers of medical care. This policy, as undertaken by the Ministry of Health, is a step toward promoting primary health care in Egypt. It remains to be seen how far these measures can affect women's lives to eradicate, or at least reduce, vulnerability.

Notes

1 El Safty, "Planning for Primary Health Care: Socio Economic Factors Influencing Utilization of Health Services in Egypt," in: *Women Health and Development, The Cairo Papers for the Social Sciences.* Cynthia Nelson, ed., vol. 1, Monograph 1, 2nd edition, Sept. 1983, pp. 111–114.

2 Ibid., p. 115.

3 El Safty, "The Attitudes of Traditional Mothers towards the Treatment of Diarrheal Diseases," unpublished paper for the National Program for Combating Diarrheal Diseases in Cairo, p. 9, May, 1983.

4 Egyptian Ministry of Health Statistics: 1990.

5 Ministry of Health, "Causes of Maternal Mortality," 1983–85, p. 11.

6 Ministry of Health, "Causes of Maternal Mortality," 1981–83, p. 3.

7 Ministry of Health, Demographic Survey, 1989, p. 23.

8 National Population Council Demographic Survey, 1988, p. 35.

9 Nutrition Institute, *Report on Food Consumption and Patterns in Egypt,* 1981, p. 11.

10 A. Badran, *Structural Adjustments in Health Sector to Protect the Vulnerable Groups UNICEF,* 1989.

Chapter 33
The Politics of Space Appropriation: A Case Study of Women's Struggles for Homeplace in Chicago Public Housing: An Abstract[1]

Roberta M. Feldman and Susan J. Stall

Roberta M. Feldman is an architectural educator, researcher, and activist who advocates for and supports socially responsible design. Dr. Feldman's work focuses on housing and community planning and design, with an emphasis on underhoused Americans. Presently, she is engaging in participatory research with community women activists in Chicago Public Housing. An associate professor and Director of Graduate Studies at the School of Architecture, University of Illinois at Chicago, Dr. Feldman also is Editor of the Journal of Architectural and Planning Research, *an international, multidisciplinary resource for professionals and scholars.*

Susan Stall is a teacher, activist, and sociologist. As a housing activist Dr. Stall coordinated two conference projects: "Women and Safe Shelter: Creating and Recreating Community" in 1986, and "Women and Public Housing: Hidden Strength, Unclaimed Power" in 1987. As a community consultant, she has worked with residents in public housing, including representatives from Wentworth Gardens, to form the citywide advocacy organization, Chicago Authority Residents Taking Action (CHARTA). Dr. Stall's research focuses on women and community-building in both rural and urban settings. Dr. Stall is an assistant professor in the Department of Sociology, Northeastern Illinois University. In addition, she coordinates the Student Internship Program and is a core faculty member in the Women's Studies Department at NEIU.

Appropriation of place is conceived of as a fundamental process of "becoming-at-home." It is a concept that has been used to describe how people create, choose, take possession of, personalize, modify, enhance, and care for, or simply intentionally and routinely use the residential environment to make it their own.

The focus of current inquiry has been on the universality of the individual experience of appropriation of place. This chapter seeks to extend this inquiry and situate the inquiry within its socio-political context. This concept will be examined in the context of the power relationships that frame people's transactions with the residential environment. In particular, we will examine how racism, sexism, and classism intersect to mediate people's relative power to appropriate place and its outcomes.

In the United States public housing is the residence of many of this nation's poor. It houses primarily low-income, minority, female-headed households—one consequence of the feminization of poverty. This housing environment is beset by high crime rates, poor maintenance and services, and physical deterioration. For policy makers and the public alike, the role that women in public housing have played in their struggles to save their homeplaces, as well as the struggles of other low-income women of color, all too often remain invisible. Information from an ongoing case study of the history of women residents' activism in one Chicago public housing development, Wentworth Gardens, offers an alternative portrayal of women's struggles to save their homeplace. Our participatory research findings demonstrate how women resident activists, despite actual limited power over the places they live, persist in a continual struggle to appropriate places within their housing development in order to improve their own and their neighbors' lives. These appropriated places include the on-site field house and the laundromat. In the process of taking possession of, modifying, and utilizing these spaces, residents cultivate confidence, skills, and collective resources for greater social and political power.

The activism of women at Wentworth Gardens illustrates the importance of considering the homeplaces in which, and over which, the everyday power struggles to maintain households and communities are manifest. To take control of the physical settings of their housing development, Wentworth women have had to defy conventional conceptions of their capabilities and institutional regulations of their rights to control these settings. Their ongoing struggle for the appropriation of homeplace has not only provided a site for resistance, but has itself come to be resistance. Finally, these local struggles suggest that homeplace is an accessible and central site for groups of limited resources to engage in social change.

Note

[1] Forthcoming in *Women and the Environment,* in the *Human Behavior & Environment* Series, Irwin Altman & Arza Churchman, Eds., Volume 13.

Theme 7
Non-traditional Living Arrangements: Beyond the Nuclear Family

There has been a mismatch between the diversity of family structures that exist in the world and the nuclear family norm assumed by policy makers. Usually women are worse off for not being recognized as heads of families (de facto or de jure) in the planning and design processes. The papers in this theme raise our awareness of the diversity of households that women find themselves in around the world and the needs that result out of their particular situations. The papers address the following four areas: Who are the non-traditional households? What are their shelter needs and problems? Why are these not being met?, and What are the strategies to address these needs in the context of personal, community, and national development? Pothukuchi provides a typology that encompasses the range and diversity of non-nuclear households and suggests directions for shaping more responsive policy and design. Scarnecchia presents a historical case study of women from Harare, Zimbabwe. He illustrates the discrimination against women outside nuclear families that has prevailed since colonial times within the policy guiding the allocation of legally sanctioned housing. Varley, very appropriately, cautions against an exclusive emphasis on the needs of women in non-nuclear households. She presents, drawing on her work in urban Mexico on how shelter is shared in traditional families, the very real needs of women in traditional families. Thompson observes how care facilities substitute for shelter for women in some countries of Central Europe. Finally, du Plessis provides a case example of a process by which single teenage mothers in Ontario, Canada, have embarked on a process for improving their access to quality affordable housing. This process and the efforts described in Theme 8 are responsive to the intangible needs for independence, control, community, security, and opportunities for growth, which are important, given the disadvantaged status of women in general and particularly of women in non-traditional family settings.

Photo: *Hemalata C. Dandekar*

Chapter 34
Non-traditional Living Arrangements: Beyond the Nuclear Family

Kameshwari Pothukuchi

Kameshwari Pothukuchi received a Bachelor of Architecture from the University of Bombay. She has worked in Bombay and Bangalore, India, as an architect. She obtained a joint Master in Architecture and Urban Planning degree from the University of Michigan in 1990. She is a doctoral student in the Urban and Regional Planning Program at the University of Michigan, studying for a Ph.D. in Urban, Technological, and Environmental Planning. Her interests include participatory community planning, empowerment of women through access to shelter and employment, and international development planning.

Sociologists and anthropologists have reported on the wide diversity around the world of household structures, and of their internal and external functions.[1] There has been a good deal of discussion on the historical development of households, and of the demographic changes they have undergone over the years due to various forces of urbanization, modernization, and technological change, as well as cultural change. There is evidence of this from all around the world. Writers[2] have cautioned against the tendency of referring to *the* household, as if it were possible to impart universal significance to the term. It is clear that there is enormous variety in kinship and residential arrangements and that it is important to place these in their historical and social contexts when addressing issues of shelter for women.

This paper addresses issues of shelter conditions, strategies, and policies related to non-nuclear households.[3] Perspectives from the developed as well as the underdeveloped world are presented. It is, of course, difficult to cover any single aspect of this topic in depth, given the breadth of the phenomenon of non-nuclear households and the diversity of their antecedent conditions. Nevertheless, the paper seeks to provide a broad framework for the other papers on this theme. The purpose of the paper is to emphasize the following points, which will be clarified and illustrated in the following sections of this paper, as well as in other papers on the theme:

1. Shelter and urban policies related to shelter often presume a norm of a male-headed nuclear household with stereotypic notions of gender roles. Sometimes they actually help create it.[4] This is true for the developed[5] as well as the developing world.[6] Hence not only is the concept of nuclear household reinforced as universal and ideal, but the non-nuclear households that do exist in increasingly large numbers are rendered invisible. Their conditions, needs, and problems are not recognized and incorporated into policies.

2. There is great diversity *within* the category of non-nuclear households around the world. Family life-cycle changes, extension or division of households due to migration, separation, divorce, death, granny fostering, etc., can singly or in combination lead to the emergence of non-nuclear households. Household structures and functions are dynamic and flexible, and these households represent adaptive ways of coping with economic, psychological, and social insecurity (even physical abuse).[7] To blame these households for the poverty and insecurity they face is to put the cart before the horse.

3. Of the non-nuclear arrangements, the needs of women-headed households are especially critical for various

reasons, and have to be incorporated into policy, planning, and design of shelter.

4. By understanding the situation of women in non-nuclear households, we may gain a better theoretical as well as practical understanding of the shelter and related needs of women in general.[8] There is evidence that women do not always gain when "the household" is the unit of analysis in shelter and development policies as this hides internal dynamics of power distribution and resource allocation.

5. Non-nuclear household strategies for shelter and related services can occur at many levels and can come from many sources. These may be micro-level household or community strategies, institutional, or public-policy oriented. At all levels, however, an integrated and holistic approach to shelter issues for women is urgently needed. Women also need to organize themselves around shelter issues for non-nuclear households, and take leadership roles at political and institutional levels.[9]

Household: Conceptualization and Definition

The concept of "household"[10] is not everywhere congruent with the concept of "family" as a kinship arrangement of people related to each other by blood, by marriage, or by fictive relationships. This distinction is discussed elsewhere.[11] The term "household" also escapes universal definition given the degrees of flexibility of these arrangements in different regional and cultural contexts. There is some debate about whether and how useful the concept is in the first place.[12] This paper assumes that it is indeed relevant. Households are defined variously, and sometimes in combination as *co-residence* and as a *unit of shared production and consumption.*[13] The United Nations[14] defines household as the "arrangements made by persons individually or in groups, for providing themselves with food or other essentials for living." It may be a one or multi-person household. The persons in the group may pool their incomes and have a common budget to a greater or lesser extent; they may be related or unrelated or a combination of both.

"[H]ouseholds may usually occupy the whole, part or more than one housing unit, but also may be found living in camps, boarding houses or hotels or as administrative personnel in institutions, or they may be homeless. Households consisting of extended families that make common provisions for food or for potentially separate households with vacation or second homes may occupy more than one housing unit." The conceptualization distinguishes two concepts: "housekeeping," which is sharing resources to provide household members with food or other essentials, or the

domestic unit, and "housing unit," which is occupying all or part of a dwelling unit, or co-residence.

It is also important to place households in the social, political, and historical contexts of their specific region or culture.[15] How households relate to each other and how they function as units that are complementary or in conflict with the larger society are also critical issues as these have implications for the role of women within and outside households,[16] and therefore, for their shelter. An understanding of households is critical as they constitute arenas wherein gender roles are defined, presumed, or idealized. Households constitute separation between the public and private spheres, however ill-defined these may be, or however ephemeral the separation. The structure and functions of households are also defined by class, and there is usually status attached to certain types of households, and this has implications for women within and without these households. For instance, in cultures where women derive their status in relation to men, women-headed households would automatically have very low status.

Non-Nuclear Households: Some Examples, Conditions, Needs, and Problems

Following are some examples of non-nuclear households in First and Third World settings, along with some explanations for their prevalence and how they affect women in particular. This is by no means an exhaustive listing, and must be seen as partial evidence of the diversity of households worldwide. Non-nuclear households may have a male head or may be headed by women—*de facto* or *de jure*. These arrangements constitute opportunities for women in the flexibility they afford them, as well as constraints arising out of the "invisibility" of these non-nuclear households. The assumptions of sex-role specialization that are attached, however inaccurately, to *nuclear* households clearly do not apply to women-headed households. This makes a study of women-headed households especially important and interesting. However, as Varley cautions in her paper, care should be taken when addressing women-headed households, so as not to render women in other household forms invisible.[17] Hence, shelter issues need to be seen in a context of women's participation in subsistence, wage earning, and production, their participation in reproductive activities, and their needs for security and community as well as for personal development, health and education, transportation, child care, etc.

Example 1: Women-Headed Households

Female-headed households are increasing in numbers in the First as well as the Third World. In the U.S. alone, roughly one-third of all households are headed by women.[18] In 1988, there were 3,600,000 women-headed families living below the poverty level, up from 2 million in 1970. Of these, about 1,700,000 belonged to minority racial and ethnic groups. A majority of the poor is in these households.[19]

Women-headed households tend to suffer from a number of disadvantages vis-à-vis their shelter and related needs. Marans and Colten (1985),[20] in a study involving 1,007 tenants of rental housing, have reported that 37 percent of these households are headed by women, with minority groups over-represented. They tend to be concentrated in inner-city locations.[21] These households usually have trouble finding suitable and secure housing, and move more frequently than others.[22] The majority of children (55 percent) is in these households. This suggests a great and growing need for inexpensive child care in the near future. Ahrentzen reports, based on longitudinal data comparing female-headed with jointly headed households, that women heading households also pay a higher proportion (more than 35 percent) of their incomes for housing, and settle for less desirable housing. They are also less likely to own homes than their male counterparts or working couples.[23][24] Women in these households are also more vulnerable to sexual harassment by landlords and managers.[25] Sometimes women-headed households come about through the woman's voluntary decision to leave an abusive marital situation.[26]

In the Third World too, there is evidence that the numbers and proportions of women-headed (*de jure* or *de facto*) households are increasing.[27] Tinker (1975)[28] suggests that one of the reasons is the breakdown of customary protection afforded divorced women. In some cases, modern laws and customs have created female-headed households in African countries. Laws have been adopted to make monogamy the only form of marriage, taking away legal protection afforded by customary law for women who are second wives. In Uttar Pradesh, a largely conservative northern state in India, Ranjana Kumari[29] found in a study of 814 households that 12.5 percent of these were headed by women, a figure about one-third higher than the official census figure of 9.5 percent. Migration of men to urban areas for employment, widowhood, divorce, or physical incapability on the part of the male are cited as the main causes of this occurrence in India and other parts of

Asia. These reports also show that the absence of the male does not substantially alter traditional norms concerning women's place or the division of labor, or in any way increase their authority or control.[30] This has also been found to be the case for the 85,000 wives left behind (according to 1975 data) by Basotho mine workers working in South Africa.[31]

It appears that this is an urban phenomenon in the Third World too. For instance, even in a traditional culture such as Morocco's, as many as 21 percent of urban households are headed by women. In Latin America, the incidence is especially high: 20 to 25 percent in Venezuelan cities, one-third in Honduran towns, around 50 percent in Managua, Nicaragua. In Africa, the situation is not much different. In Mathare Valley, Nairobi, for example, over 50 percent of households are headed by women. The reasons for the existence of non-nuclear households are manifold and vary in each region and culture. Female migration seems to be one of the major contributors to the urban phenomenon. Latin American women who migrate to work in domestic service and unskilled informal and service sectors far outnumber men in rural-urban migration. Cultural factors also play a big role: men subscribing to the ideology of *machismo* father many children and desert them to escape financial obligations. Widespread existence of polygamy is a factor in Africa, with individual wives living with their own children outside of the conjugal residence.[32]

The constraints that women face in some Third World contexts are somewhat different, although in many cases, the difference is just a matter of degree from the First World situation. Women's status, and legitimacy, and therefore entitlement to different basic needs such as shelter and food is often tied to their relationship to the men in their households and to their own position within it. Further, while formal social participation is mostly proscribed for women, the burdens of fetching fuel wood and water, subsistence food production, food processing, etc., still remain.

Women in patriarchal societies of the Middle East and Asia and to some degree in Latin America tend to be restricted to their neighborhoods, fulfilling such socially determined functions as child care and household maintenance. Women also face restrictions regarding ownership of land and property. There are hence debilitating consequences for women heading households who do not have a source of subsistence, or who have to be employed outside the home as in urban contexts. Hence entering in non-nuclear arrangements with kin or other women is a strategy aimed at dealing with poverty and potential destitution.

In a rapidly industrializing context where gender roles tend to be polarized, women are the most disadvantaged as they are forced to seek employment outside the home with little relief from burdens of household work and child care. Furthermore, they are also discriminated against, unequipped in skills and literacy to qualify them for employment in more modern sectors. And finally, there is discrimination in the labor market itself, with unequal access and unequal pay for women.[33] Women tend to be seen as a reserve labor force, with incomes considered merely to supplement the household income. This has negative effects on women heading households, especially those that start out poor.

Women's access to various types of development schemes is also inhibited by gender-blind planning. When housing policies assume the nuclear, male-headed family as norm, women are denied access simply on account of their sex. Brydon and Chant (1989)[34] give as an example a Brazilian low-income housing program which granted serviced land plots for self-building, in a sites-and-services scheme. In one of the projects in Vila Velha in southeast Brazil, it was explicitly stated that applicants had to be the *father* of at least two children.

Shelter needs of women and their households cannot be seen in isolation from the prevailing ideology, and especially the confluence of patriarchy and industrial capitalism. Hence a more holistic approach to shelter is also needed, where opportunities for income generation, provision of child care and health services, education, and the development of skills are included as integral to the shelter package. Another aspect is that since it is at the community, grass-roots level that discrimination occurs and is experienced, solutions too need to work at this level.

Example 2: Extended Households

Extended households, almost everywhere, constitute opportunities and constraints for women somewhat distinct from those for women-headed households. Extended households, as they occur in Latin America, Africa, or Asia, are households with vertical or lateral arrangements of kin. A non-traditional extended household may be formed when women choose to live with their relatives, or when they take on additional members, consanguinal or fictive, male or female, to function as a domestic or a residential unit. As Chant and Ward[35] point out from a study of Latin American

contexts, both, the extended and the female-headed systems arise as a positive response to combat poverty, to accommodate changes in the life-cycle, to share domestic labor, and to minimize social and psychological insecurity arising out of the ideology of *machismo*.[36] Their data show that women in non-nuclear arrangements fare better than their counterparts in nuclear households.

Morris[37] has also studied households in Mexico City located within four separate housing clusters in impoverished areas, and suggests that such patterns of domestic organization are geared to solve basic and related problems of child care and home maintenance. The household demonstrates ambiguity of membership and flexibility of structure for residence, economic cooperation, and reproduction.

However, extended households do not give as much cause for optimism in some other contexts. In London, lack of adequate affordable housing has led to "doubling-up" in extended family units. This has been reported to be very unsatisfactory.[38] Ann Varley, in her research in Mexico City, has found that not only do daughters of tenants of the housing project lose out due to preferences for sons and their families, but also that the internal family dynamics of the extended households between the mother-in-law and the daughter-in-law need to be looked at more carefully when addressing issues of shelter for women in these extended households.[39] This tension between in-laws may get very oppressive for the daughter-in-law in situations where the son is absent, due to migration.[40]

Younger couples in nuclear households, in many cases, not only have more physical and economic independence due to greater access to cash income, but women also have a greater potential for influencing decisions in the household. However, the nuclear family represents a double-edged sword especially for low-income women, as we have seen, in the isolation of housework, lack of help with child care, etc.

Example 3: Polygamous Households

This is a form that is permitted and practiced in Africa and Islamic countries. The benefits and disadvantages of the situation for women are especially difficult to analyze, especially in a shelter context. Policies influenced by Western, middle-class perspectives of the normative family have made the situation very uncomfortable for women in traditional contexts. There is some ambivalence about whether women consider the polygynous arrangement to be beneficial. On the one hand, there are reports that the polygynous arrangement permits a man relationships with many women, preventing the formation of strong conjugal bonds with individual women, and that married women see their co-wives as rivals thus preventing the development of any genuine female solidarity.[41] On the other hand, there are studies showing that women favor polygamy, as it allows sharing the burden of household work and cooking, allowing one to go off into trade while the other stays at home to carry out household chores.[42]

Shelter projects based on policies that are blind to household composition hurt women as a group. One such project was the creation of Lake Volta in Ghana in the early 1960's.[43] Resettlement of areas to be flooded was undertaken with no thought for local social organization and practices. The new houses constructed by the government took no account of prevailing polygynous family structures. Thus there were no separate sleeping rooms for individual wives, nor were there separate kitchens or store areas.

The above were just three examples of non-nuclear households, with a discussion of the problems they encounter from gender-blind policies that have underlying assumptions that do not appreciate flexibility of household structures. There are other forms of non-traditional households not addressed here. For instance, in developing countries, the needs of single women, who migrate to cities to work in the growing export-processing zones, are met in working-women's hostels. While hostels satisfy some needs, they are also insensitive to others.[44] Other groups of non-nuclear households are women living singly or with other people in apartments. It may be difficult to call them "women-*headed*," if they have an egalitarian system of living, which brings into question what, exactly, constitutes headship.[45] The above examples need to be seen as a sampler of the existing wide variety of household types that get shortchanged by gender-blind policies and policies that presume the nuclear, male-headed household as the basic unit of society.

Implications for Shelter Policy: Planning, Theory, Research, and Design

The great diversity of household types and in particular the increasing prevalence among them of women-headed households calls for shelter policy that appreciates such diversity. Greater choice of residential alternatives, affordability, and increased access to shelter and related services of those previously denied by virtue of restrictive definitions of the households are critical to this requirement. Shelter policies aimed at addressing the needs of non-nuclear households also need to appreciate their current strategies, so that these may be facilitated with a lesser commitment of resources and tap the creativity that already exists. All over the world, human settlement policies vis-à-vis women tend to be looked at in the framework of women's roles in reproduction.[46] Policies and plans need to incorporate an integrated approach to shelter and infrastructure as well as to the community-management roles and needs of women in non-nuclear households, particularly of women-headed households. Shelter policies need to be based on a theoretical understanding of how existing policies ignore or render invisible existing non-nuclear households or force the formation of nuclear households; and of the conditions that would increase access of women to shelter and opportunities for their development.

1. The general condition and shelter and related needs of non-nuclear households, especially those headed by women, need to be recognized as of great importance.[47] The importance of understanding these in the local cultural contexts, as well as of the allocation and control of resources within the household are underscored. In First as well as Third World contexts, these have implications for plot and house design, tenure, recruitment of residents to self-help settlements, and for the process of dwelling construction itself.[48] They also bear on urban land-use planning, the structure of credit and lending policies, and provision of social and physical infrastructure. Consideration of female-headed households needs to be guaranteed in national and local habitat policies.[49] Women heading families should have the same priority of access to self-help shelter projects as do male heads of families, and greater priority than men without family obligations. Collaborative and cooperative arrangements within and among non-nuclear households need to be supported and encouraged.

2. Social and physical infrastructural needs are especially critical in the context of women-headed and other non-nuclear households. Child care in close proximity, available and affordable, transportation that is based on an understanding of the time-budgets of women in these households, opportunities for skills and job-training, shopping, water, health care facilities, etc., all need to be an integral part of shelter policy.[50] An understanding of the networks that these non-nuclear households form within the community to satisfy shelter needs, as well as of the local context, is also crucial to physical interventions. Living quarters for single women living away from their families, such as working-women's hostels, need special attention in Third World contexts.

3. Land-use and zoning policies need to be informed by the need to incorporate income-generating and production activities for women in non-nuclear households.[51] Strategies and designs to allow residents to keep small stock or poultry and cultivate gardens or otherwise engage in occupations that may need some space around and outside the house are some examples. In the First World, these should also allow for greater mixed use and higher densities than a single-family housing layout may offer.

4. Women in non-nuclear households should also be provided with easy access to credit, as well as information regarding other institutional arrangements to obtain shelter. There is evidence that some sources of credit work have worked better for women than others.[52] These should be expanded and replicated. The myth that women are bad credit risks has been debunked in the literature,[53] but this understanding has not yet permeated lending policies. Barriers to access or availability to credit need to be identified; in many cases women are unprepared or unwilling to deal with bureaucratic credit processes and sometimes they are ignorant of their availability. Traditional sources of credit such as rotating funds that have historically provided resources for women need to be encouraged and supported.

5. The participation of all women, and those in female-headed households especially, in the design, implementation, and management of projects needs to be encouraged. For this to be effective, it is necessary to know the work they are already doing, their time availability, and physical and cultural barriers to participation. Higher levels of gender consciousness do not always result in high participation: projects need to be geared specifically to their needs. Requests for voluntary labor may not be reasonable under many circumstances. Efforts need to be made to develop self-sufficiency in implementation and management and the development of local skills. In many cultures, women project personnel and decision-makers are necessary to mobilize participation of local women. Mechanisms and contexts to facilitate participation need to be designed.[54] Women also need to organize to participate effectively in advocating for their own needs.[55] An explicit understanding that the needs of women cannot be met in the family that is represented by men only also needs to permeate shelter policy and planning.[56] The representation of women in greater numbers in planning and policy decisions has the potential also to bring women's concerns to the fore.

6. Legal access to land and property needs to be effected or implemented more vigorously; in many countries around the world, legal aspects of women's access to land, property rights, and credit are linked closely to customary constraints on women's roles and relationships with men.[57] Women heading households are usually unable to secure collateral, given the restrictions on their ownership of property. Financing institutions need to recognize non-formal and flexible sources of income for women in non-nuclear households.[58]

7. Women also need to be taught building skills, making credit and materials easily available. Self-help situations all too often presume the availability of skilled labor and capital. In many rural contexts around the world, women have traditionally been engaged in the construction of shelter; this is not a very novel idea. Unrealistically high building standards constitute barriers to shelter. The use of small-scale technology that facilitates construction by women as well as giving them opportunities for income generation needs to be considered.[59] The introduction of technology to lighten the burden of women's tasks in these households and to increase their efficiency in all aspects of production should also be part of shelter policy.[60]

8. Models that have successfully mobilized awareness of these issues, or have provided shelter to non-nuclear households from the First[61] as well as the Third World[62] should be studied for some general principles and lessons. These strategies have taken various forms, e.g., organizing women around issues of shelter, and cooperative arrangements that combine economic activities as well as child care. It is also important that evaluations have criteria for success that are meaningful to women and important for their development, rather than simple cost-benefit types of analyses. Planning also needs to shift emphasis from physical and administrative considerations, which constitute barriers to non-nuclear households, to human considerations. Design is a powerful tool to raise and advance ideas; to build a body of research about the kind of housing that is facilitative of diversity in household type; and to provide visions by involving experts as well as the people affected.

9. A new paradigm of the home, the community, and the city needs to be developed to describe accurately and support rather than restrict the physical, social, and economic activities of a multiplicity of households.[63] Research is also needed on the internal dynamics and development of the households, and the conditions in which they provide the most benefits or constraints for women. How households interact with each other, and within the larger economy and society, are other areas of needed research.

Notes

[1] Harris, Olivia, 1981, "Households as natural units," in: Kate Young, Carol Wolkowitz, and Roslyn McCullagh (eds.), *Of Marriage and the Market,* London: CSE, pp. 48–67; Hutter, Mark, 1981, *The Changing Family: Comparative Perspectives,* New York: John Wiley; Lenoro-Otero, Luis (ed.), 1977, *Beyond the Nuclear Family Model. Cross-cultural Perspectives,* London: Sage.

[2] For instance, see Harris, 1981, *op. cit.*

[3] The term "non-nuclear" is used here to signify essentially "non-normative" households. This is important because of the ambiguity of the title of this paper. Whether a household is "traditional," or "non-traditional" is not as important as the issue of match/mismatch between diversity of households as they exist, and the norm as assumed by policy. In an international context, what may be

traditional, such as the extended or the polygamous family, may actually be non-normative in that context, because of the existence of policies based on norms alien to the traditional culture.

4 For a good example, see Scarnecchia, Timothy, 1992, "Housing and gender ideologies in rural and urban Zimbabwe: Life histories and the nuclear family," in this publication.

5 For examples of planning circumscribed by assumption of family and women's role of mother and wife as sacrosanct in twentieth century London, see Roberts, Marilyn, 1990, *Living in a Man-Made World.* London: Routledge. Frank discusses how ideas about gender and family help determine the physical design and location of dwellings, places of work, and other designed environments. These settings then support the ideas of gender and family that generated them. [Frank, Karen A., 1988, "The social construction of the physical environment: The case of gender," in: Willem van Vliet (ed.), *Women, Housing and Community,* Brookfield, VT: Avebury.]. For a description of the conditions of women heading households, and an analysis of the phenomena that have led to their concentration in central cities, see Stimson, Catherine, Elsa Dixler, Martha Nelson, and Kathryn Yatrakis (eds.), 1981, *Women in the American City,* Chicago: University of Chicago Press.

6 For a general discussion of the invisibility of women and the discrimination they face as a result of policies that ignore women's productive activities and the relation of these to their homes, and the additional burdens these policies constitute for women, see Rogers, Barbara, 1980, *The Domestication of Women,* New York: St. Martin's; Moser, Caroline, and Linda Peake (eds.), 1987, *Women, Human Settlements and Housing,* London: Tavistock; Daswani, Mona, Oct., 1987, "Shelter and women—a perspective," I*ndian Journal of Social Work, 48*(3):273–285; and Chant, Sylvia, and Peter Ward, Feb., 1987, "Family structure and low-income housing policy," *Third World Planning Review, 9*(11):5–19; also provide insights from different regional and cultural contexts.

7 *Ibid.*

8 This is elaborated in a following paper on this theme. See Du Plessis, Valerie, 1992, "Young mothers and affordable housing: Information and organization for change," this publication.

9 For an interesting case study see Du Plessis, *ibid.*

10 The term *household* is used as a compact version of *living arrangement,* as in the title of the panel, and is useful given the mass of theory associated with the concept.

11 For a very simple description and explanation of these terms, see Brydon, Lynne, and Sylvia Chant, 1989, *Women in the Third World,* New Brunswick, NJ: Rutgers University Press. See also United Nations, 1987, *Demographic Yearbook.* Special topic: Household and Family Statistics. 39th issue. New York: United Nations.

12 For instance, see Brydon and Chant, *op. cit.*, pp. 9–10.

13 *Ibid.*, pp. 47–68, 134–60.

14 United Nations, 1987, *op. cit.*, p.4.

15 Harris (1981), *op. cit.*

16 See Brydon and Chant, 1989, *op. cit.*

17 Varley, Ann, 1992, "The house of two." The provision of rent free accommodation for young adults in urban Mexico," this publication.

18 Franck, Karen A., and Sherry Ahrentzen (eds.), 1989, *New Households, New Housing.* New York: Van Nostrand. Caplow, Theodore, Howard M. Bahr, John Modell, and Bruce A. Chadwick, 1991, *Recent Social Trends in the United States 1960–1990,* Montreal: McGill-Queen's University Press, pp. 82–89.

19 *Ibid.*

20 Marans, Robert, and Mary Ellen Colten, 1985, "U. S. rental housing policies affecting families with children: hard times for youth," in: Willem. van Vliet, Elizabeth Huttman, and Sylvia Fava (eds.), *Housing Needs and Policy Approaches: Trends in Thirteen Countries,* Durham, N.C.: Duke University Press.

21 Stimson *et al.,* 1981, *op. cit.*

22 Klowdawsky, Fran, Aron Spector, and D. Rose, 1985, *Single Parent Families and Canadian Housing Policies: How Mothers Lose,* Ottawa: Canada mortgage and housing corporation.

23 Ahrentzen, Sherry, 1985, "Residential fit and mobility among low-income, female-headed households in the United States," in: W. van Vliet *et al., op. cit.*

24 Harris, Richard, Fall, 1985, "Women and homeownership: A research note," *Women and Environments.* Harris reports that female single parents (61 percent) are less likely to own their own homes than their male counterparts (44 percent). Male single parents earn more and tend to be older. When income is controlled, the gender difference disappears, except for the bottom quartile. This implies, he suggests, that income is the overwhelming factor and that others (for example, discrimination) are not significant except in the bottom income quartile.

25 Fuentes, Annette and Madelyn Miller, 1988, "Unreasonable access: Sexual harassment comes home," in W. van Vliet, *op. cit.*, pp. 153–160.

26 Shelter issues for women in crisis, and those who may have suffered physical or mental abuse are addressed in theme three in this book.

27 For instance see, Brydon and Chant, 1989, *op. cit.*, pp. 54–56, 145–151.

28 Tinker, Irene, and Michele Bo Bramsen (eds.), 1975, *Women and World Development,* Washington, D.C.: Overseas Development Council, pp. 32–33.

29 Kumari, Ranjana, 1989, *Women-Headed Households in Rural India.* London: Sangam, p. 42.

30 UNESCO, 1984, *Women in the Villages, Men in the Towns* (Yogesh Atal, ed.), Paris: UNESCO. Around one-third of all households worldwide are made up of women-headed households. (Moser, Caroline, and Sylvia Chant, 1985, *The Participation of Women in Low-Income Housing Projects,* Gender and Planning working paper no. 5, London: Development Planning Unit, University College.

31 Gordon, Elizabeth, 1981, "An analysis of the impact of labor migration on the lives of women in Lesotho," in: Nelson, Nici (ed.), *African Women in the Development Process*, London: Frank Cass.

[32] Brydon and Chant, 1989, *op. cit.*, pp. 146–48.

[33] This is a very brief and general statement of underdevelopment faced by women in developing countries around the world. For a more specific understanding of development theories and their special significance for women, cf. Rogers, 1980, *op. cit.*; Tinker and Bramsen, 1975, *op cit.*; Afshar, Haleh (ed.), 1985, *Women, Work and Ideology in the Third World,* London, Tavistock; and Anker, Richard, and Catherine Heine (eds.), 1986, *Sex Inequalities in Urban Employment in the Third World*, Basingstoke: Macmillan.

[34] Brydon and Chant 1989, *op. cit.*, p. 216.

[35] Chant and Ward 1987, *op. cit.*

[36] Blumberg (Rae Lesser, 1975," Fairy tales and facts: economy, family, fertility and the female," in: Tinker and Bramsen, 1975, *op cit.* also debunks the myth of the "disorganized female-centered family pattern" as a cause of poverty, and states that it is rather the poverty and the economic prospects of women in a patriarchal society that combine to produce the female-headed family. She observes an adaptive pattern of sharing, and a network of give-and-take among close kin, especially on the female side, and suggests that female-headed families emerge under certain marginal economic conditions when women as well as men have independent access to subsistence. Cf. Brown, Susan E., 1972, *Lower Economic Sector Female Mating Patterns in the Dominican Republic: A Comparative Analysis*, Ph.D. dissertation, Ann Arbor: University of Michigan. She suggests that women following traditional middle-class ideals of the single mate pattern seem to be better off in traditional, material measures (land, wealth, etc.), whereas women in non-traditional, multiple partner pattern tend to do better in various indices of well being (number of surviving children, shelter conditions, food quality, etc.).

[37] Morris, Lydia, 1981, "Women in poverty: domestic organization among the poor of Mexico city," *Anthropological Quarterly, 54* (3):117–24.

[38] Ash, Joan, 1985, "The effects of household formation on housing needs in Britain," in van Vliet, *et al., op. cit.*

[39] Varley, 1992, *op. cit.*

[40] Cf. Gulati, Leela, 1986, "Male migration from Kerala—some effects on women," *Manushi., 7* (1). She studied women in Kerala whose husbands were away in the Gulf for extended periods of time. While these women have taken on a more active role in the management of family affairs and are less dependent, she also found that women between 15 and 25 showed alarming rates of mental disturbance. Incompatibility with in-laws was the cited as the main cause; UNESCO, 1987, *op. cit.*, reports similar findings.

[41] Brydon and Chant, 1989, *op. cit.*, p. 26.

[42] Tinker, 1975 (in Tinker and Bramsen, 1975, *op. cit.*) reports on a survey conducted in the Ivory Coast in the sixties that showed that 85 percent of the women were in favor of polygamy (p. 32). Ocloo, Esther, 1974, *The Ghanaian Market Woman*, paper prepared for the 14th World Conference on the Society for International Development, Abidjan, Ivory Coast) reports similar findings, with women in polygamous marriages enjoying a sense of economic and psychological independence from their husbands, which makes their "liberation" more real than that of literate professional women in nuclear households.

[43] Brydon and Chant, 1989, *op. cit.*, p. 104.

[44] A study by the YWCA (1975, *A Place to Live: a Study on Housing for Women.* Bombay: Allied Publishers) surveyed hostel residents and identified the following factors as important: choice in room type, affordability, some degree of organization and supervision, safety and security, fear of isolation, decent neighborhood, and the special needs of older women. However, the hostel situation can be unpleasant, as indicated in a letter to the editor in a women's magazine in India. Hostel residents' belongings were forcibly thrown on the road by the landlady, after residents began taking sole responsibility of managing hostel affairs following conflicts with the management. (Bhatt, Sharada, 1986. Letter to the editor, *Manushi., 6*(4). Mehra and Kaul [1986, "Last priority: Women in the IARA," *Manushi* 6(5)] too recount how women students of the prestigious Indian Agricultural Research Institute were shortchanged by policies that assumed that their shelter needs were being met in their families. The students, who did not have hostel accommodations, were afraid to protest for fear that their scholarships would be withdrawn as punishment. This was also the case when married students always got preference above single women students. See also Foo (Gillian Hwei-Chuan, 1987, "Work and Marriage: Attitudes of Women Factory Workers in Malaysia," University of Michigan: unpublished dissertation for a good description of hostel conditions for women working in electronics industries in Malaysia.

[45] For a discussion of the definition of "head," see United Nations, 1987, *op. cit.*; as well as Ranjana Kumari, 1989, *op. cit.*

[46] Moser and Peake, 1987, *op. cit.*

[47] Moser and Peake, 1987, *op. cit.*; Moser, Caroline O. N., 1989, *Community Participation in Urban Projects in the Third World*, New York: Pergamon; Smith, Diana L., "Nairobi 1985: Women and habitat," *Women and Environments.* 8(1). Ranjana, Kumari, 1989, *op. cit.*; Wekerle, Gerda, 1981, "Women in the urban environment," in: Stimpson *et al., op. cit.*; Cf. Schlyter, Ann, 1989; *Women Householders and Housing Strategies: The Case of George, Zambia.* She focuses on how women-householders manage their housing situation in a neighborhood where an upgrading project was executed in the 1970's.

[48] Chant and Ward, 1987, *op. cit.*

[49] Smith, 1986, *op. cit.*; Ranjana Kumari, 1989, *op. cit.*

[50] Smith, 1986, *op. cit.*

[51] Markussen, Ann R., 1981, "City spatial structure, women's household work and national urban policy," in: Stimpson *et al., op. cit.*

[52] Berger, Marguerite, 1989, "Giving women credit: The strengths and limitations of credit as a tool for alleviating poverty," *World Development,* 17(7):1017–32. She suggests that intermediary programs, parallel programs, and poverty-focused development bank approaches have been more effective than bank schemes in improving women's access to credit.

[53] Wekerle, 1981, *op. cit.*

[54] Cf. Farge, Brenda D., 1986, "Women's leadership in Cooperatives: Some questions," *Women and Environments*, Fall 1985. She observed, in a fascinating study by the Cooperative Housing Federation of Toronto, that women constitute a majority of adults in Toronto co-ops. However, while 59 percent of committee members and 60 percent of all committee chairs are women, 38 percent of presidents, 52 percent of treasurers and 72 percent of secretaries are women. Women thus

tend to be underrepresented in executive positions, except for the traditionally female position of secretary. Farge suggests insightfully that perhaps the question is not so much "why are women not involved?" as it is "is this a forum which reflects the manner in which women typically express themselves?" There may be some lessons here for planners seeking participation.

[55] Du Plessis, 1992, this publication; Bapat, 1992, this publication.

[56] Moser and Peake, 1987, *op. cit.*

[57] Cf. Hosken, Fran, 1988, "Women and property," in W. van Vliet, *op. cit.* She discusses the importance of property rights and access to land and other sources of capital. Cf. also *Women and Habitat,* 1985.

[58] Ranjana Kumari, 1989, *op. cit.*

[59] Childers, Erskin, 1975, "The development approach to liberation: Suggestions for planning," in: Tinker and Bramsen, *op. cit.*

[60] Boulding, Elis, 1975, "Women, bread and babies: Directing aid for fifth world farmers," International Women's Year Studies on Women, paper no. 4., Boulder, Colorado: University of Colorado, Institute for Behavioral Sciences, Program for Research on General Social and Economic Dynamics.

[61] Many strategies at different levels have worked for providing shelter for non-traditional households, several in this publication itself. Cf. France, Ivy, 1985, "Hubertusvereniging: A transition point for single parents," *Women and Environments,* Winter, 1985; Soper, Mary, 1980, "Housing for single parent families: A women's design," in: Wekerle, Gerda R., Rebecca Peterson, and David Morley (eds.), *New Space for Women,* Boulder, CO: Westview; Klodawsky, Fran, and Aron Spector, 1985, "Mother-led families and the built environment in Canada," *Women and Environments,* Spring, 1985.

[62] Moser and Peake, 1987, *op. cit.*; Andreas, Carol, 1989, "People's kitchens and radical organizing in Lima, Peru," *Monthly Review* *41*(6):12–21; Bapat, 1992, this publication.

[63] For an example, see Leavitt, Jacqueline, 1985, "A new American house," *Women and Environments, 7*(1).

[64] Hayden, Dolores, 1981, "What would a non-sexist city be like?" in: Stimpson *et al., op. cit.*

Chapter 35

Access to Housing in Urban and Rural Zimbabwe: Historical Observations on the Nuclear Family[1]

Tim Scarnecchia

Tim Scarnecchia is currently completing his dissertation in Modern African History at the University of Michigan. His thesis, "The Politics of Space and Gender in Salisbury, Rhodesia, 1940–1956," examines the formations of specific uses of urban space, and the resultant contests over such spaces. He received a Fulbright-Hays Dissertation Fellowship for this work. He has lectured on American Economic History for the Department of Economic History, at the University of Zimbabwe.

The Geographical Setting and Current Scope of the Problem

Harare is the capital city of Zimbabwe, and since the 1950s, when it was called Salisbury, the capital of Rhodesia, has been the largest city in the country—the center of industry and government. The population has never ceased growing, experiencing a higher level of population growth during the Liberation war (1965–1980), as many people migrated for security reasons. After Independence in 1980, the population has continued to grow with an increase in the number of women and children coming to stay in the city. About 64% of the country's population lives in the three largest urban areas of the country (Vakil, 1991). Most of this African population live in what are called "high-density areas," located for the most part on the periphery of one side of the city. Harare itself is an extremely spread-out urban area, the product of ninety years of suburban growth, and poor use-planning of urban "open spaces." The other side of Harare is the low-density suburbs, a euphemism for the previous all-white suburbs from the pre-Independence period. This area, often with minimum one-acre stands, security walls, and night-security guards, takes up the majority of urban residential land area. It is also where Harare has achieved the dubious honor as the city with the greatest density of swimming pools in the world (Vakil, 1991).

In contrast to the rich side of town, the population in the high-density areas are confronted with a growing population density due primarily to the increased reliance on the lodger system both for revenue, and, for many, the only available housing alternative. Harare does not have extensive squatter settlements in the peri-urban areas and those that have been built are subject to harassment, eventual forced removal and relocation either to farm land or to the high-density areas.[2] Because of the continued "vigilance" against squatter areas, the lodger system and overcrowding of existing housing in the high-density areas hide the true proportions of inadequate provision of housing for the majority of the urban population. Of Harare's population in 1982, at the time of the last census, an estimated 15% are made up of women-headed households, of which more are self-identified as such in the middle- and higher-income groups than in the poorer population.[3] This low percentage reflects the historical prevalence and preference for "single" male labor in the urban economy, as well as the inability of census data to enumerate the higher number of poor women who do not fit neatly into nuclear family categories. In Zimbabwe, unlike in South Africa, even domestic service jobs remain dominated by men. The current estimates of population are that 70% of Zimbabwe's women live in the rural areas; approximately 30% of peasant families operate on a "split-family survival strategy," and 40% of all farming is done principally by women. (Herald, 1992; Potts and Mutambirwa, 1990).

Unintended consequences of the Government's pre-Independence promises, and the post-Independence view of "housing as a social right," led to the further entrenchment of the existing prevalence of male dominance in access to urban housing. The policy to make all municipality-owned housing in the high-density areas open to home ownership by the sitting tenants offered an immediate solution to demands for access to home ownership. This solution, however, also removed the great majority of the existing housing stock from municipal control, therefore limiting the state's ability to provide accommodation to women (Schlyter, 1989, p.192). Even the existing single-sex hostels were transformed into family housing at Independence, which placed further emphasis on the recognition of the nuclear family to obtain access to these one-room "flats."

Beyond the existing stock at the time of Independence, newly constructed residential housing has been far less than promised and anticipated. The new housing that has been legally built has been primarily of the self-help core housing type, which necessitates individual capital. For this reason, such new housing has been predomi-nantly built and occupied by male workers who have access to capital through their employers, informal employment, or extended family. Such access is not officially or legally restricted to men. As Ann Schlyter's recent study has shown, women are able to succeed in these new areas of residential development, but their numbers are relatively few (Schlyter, 1989, p.195). For poorer women with children the main form of accommodation in the urban areas remains lodging—often in small one-room shacks built on the stands of existing houses in the high-density area. Rents range from approximately $40 to $100 dollars per month, which is often one-half or more of the tenants' monthly income. Recent demolition of "illegal" lodger structures in Epworth reportedly included one area consisting of over 400 one-room shacks, dubbed the "Epworth Sheraton," which was occupied almost exclusively by women tenants all paying rent to one landlord.[4] Al-though racial and sex discrimination in housing has been officially removed since Independence, numerous problems and limitations remain, reflected in class and gender differences in access to housing.

The next section will examine the historical precedents specific to housing policies, which have been partially responsible for the continued emphasis on married housing and the nuclear family unit.

Accommodation for the Urban African Population: The Colonial City and the African Worker

From its origins in 1890, colonial Harare's population was always more African than European, but the settlers chose to deny Black Africans permanent resident status in the city. The dominant idea was that while Africans could come into the city as workers, they should never become residents. This attitude was challenged by the reality of a growing European demand for African domestics, and from a growing industrial and service economy entirely reliant on African laborers for unskilled and some skilled labor.

After World War II, job opportunities for African men increased and the African population more than doubled in the first five-year period. Lack of accommodation for single male workers as well as married workers caused the state to attempt legislation to force industrial employers to provide resources for housing their workers. In an attempt to avoid "slum" conditions, the state and municipality took responsibility for building and supervising such housing. While providing access to housing, the colonial state went to great lengths to control urban residential space. African occupancy was limited to municipal or government-built townships, and then only for male workers who could prove employ-ment, and to African women who could prove marriage and/or employment. At the same time, the state at-tempted further to regulate the lives of African men and women living in the city. Pass laws were more strictly enforced, and marriage was promoted among the African working classes by subsidizing rents for married housing with the rents paid by employers to house single men living in hostels. Frequent raids in the Township were carried out by the municipal police to evict women without proof of marriage (Mnyanda, 1954).

The early expressions of the frustrations caused by such measures were voiced through the Reformed Industrial and Commercial Worker's Union, which owed a large part of its existence to township and housing issues. The example given by Julius Mpazeni, of the African Waiters Association, at an August, 1949, meeting of the Union, points to the untenable living situations reached by this stage:

[he] told the meeting of an African who was arrested for trespassing on European property in town. At the Court this African was told that he had no right on that property and he must go to the Location. The African went to the Location and was given a house to share with three others. The wife of this African came along, and she lived with him in a spare room. The Location Police then raided and found the married woman in the spare room, she was not registered and was arrested for vagrancy, even though she was living with her husband.[5]

Such harassments, and the recounting of them, along with frustrations caused by the increasingly high cost of living in the city, were key grievances used by nationalists in the urban areas to organize workers' opposition to white rule.

Stability and Labor Efficiency

In the period of rapid industrial expansion following World War II, particularly that of tobacco processing in Harare, women's labor also became sought after. The most influential lobbyist of European industrial and reform groups, the National Joint Council, organized the Government in 1951 to investigate the further expansion of employment opportunities for women. The Joint Council's observations on the role of women in the urban economy reflect the more general tendencies to view Africans first as production inputs:

It appears that the majority of African women living in the locations or Townships, unlike those living in the Reserves, have little with which to occupy themselves and from this aspect alone it appears that employment of some kind would be beneficial.... There are objections to the employment in industry of married women with home responsibilities. It would be an advantage if married women in the Locations could be trained in some profitable home craft which they could use in their homes and would bring in some money.... Employers on the whole appear to think that repetitive work done by women and girls compares very favorably with that of the African male and that they could be employed in great numbers and in a greater variety of jobs.[6]

The investigation that followed revealed, among other things, that the majority of employers hiring women in the early 1950s preferred to hire the wives of workers already working in town, as such women already had secured accommodation in the married section. This meant the employer did not have to worry about finding accommodation, while at the same time limiting options for women who were not married and seeking employment (NNLB, 1952). Such hiring practices placed

further emphasis on the nuclear family model for African working-class housing.

African Elite Demands for Married Housing

An unintended consequence of previous European attempts to "rationalize" urban and peri-urban space along racial lines was to confine Africans from diverse backgrounds and classes within the same limited space and style of housing (Vambe, 1976; Mnyanda, 1954). A cross-section of educated clerks, government workers, teachers, etc.—the elite of the male African population—were forced during the period after 1945 to share accommodations with newly arrived male migrants coming to work in Harare's burgeoning unskilled labor market. These educated single men were indignant about having to live "cheek by jowl," with the uneducated, and demanded better housing away from the existing African Townships. Married elites were demanding as well that their wives and children should not have to be exposed to the moral degradation of the Township, and therefore a new African elite neighborhood should be created. J. Z. Savanhu reported that some in the African middle class argued they "would help to produce racial harmony. Unfortunately, it was general among Europeans to regard Africans as belonging to one class." He described the African middle class as "frustrated and hemmed in by government laws and municipal by-laws." Savanhu recommended creating "a separate area contiguous to the present location," where middle-class Africans could buy land and set an example for the other Africans. He stressed this was not

segregation from one's people, but the middle class African has a better sense of hygiene, cleanliness and culture. For these extra amenities they are prepared to pay.... The middle class did not wish complete separation from their own people. They wished to combine the best of their own traditions and customs with the best of Western Culture and civilization (Savanhu, 1953).

African elites used the productivist arguments of greater stability and performance to further their demands for better accommodation in the urban areas, and specifically for security of tenure in the urban areas. Such demands from the African elite eventually coalesced with the state's goal to provide a more stable African residential area based on married family life, as opposed to the existing location which was dominated by male-only single-sex hostels. The new African suburbs were built in the mid-1950s, with the largest being New Highfield.

The 1950s, therefore, saw an official emphasis on "properly married" nuclear families in the African residential areas. This ideal community materialized, to a large extent, as women and men settled down to a lifestyle which afforded them unprecedented opportunities to create the model home and model nuclear family. But beneath this idyllic image of suburban bliss—often enough showcased by the colonial government to the outside world—remained hidden a myriad of familial and social relations which betrayed European and African notions of the nuclear family.

Mapoto Wives: The Antithesis of Respectability

Both the colonial authorities and the African elites shared an antipathy to a living arrangement that was seen to threaten the moral fiber and the stability and productivity of the African male worker: *mapoto* wives (literally wives with pots)—an informal relationship in which single women traded domestic work and sex for access to housing and/or income. Women who entered such relationships were different from prostitutes, although in commentary by African men and women little distinction is made between mapoto and prostitution. Views expressed in the African press in the mid-1940s express the victimization attributed to women who lived outside of the narrow range of acceptable marriage relationships:

> I would like to air my disgust at the woman who lives as a mapoto wife. To me, she is wicked, and such people are responsible for the lack of development in our country. The single young man in the city is losing direction because of such women. If he gets paid at the end of the month, the wicked woman takes the money and does not leave him enough to buy clothes, thus rendering him a strolling beggar.[7]

Women's views were seldom expressed through the media, but when they were, men responded overwhelmingly negatively, as above. One letter from a single woman living in the African Location in 1944 asked "What shall we do?" as their white employers did not provide accommodation for single women, and in the location "there are standing regulations that forbid home-ownership for women."[8]

The actual prohibition against single women living in the African location went back to the "Natives Registration Act of 1936." The Act was passed to "safeguard native society, especially in regard to its women kind," through attempts at greater interventions by the state to control relationships between men and women. The Secretary for "Native Affairs" in 1937 outlined the purpose of this control to the municipal officials:

> In regard to the difficult question of Native sexual life, there can be no doubt that we must aim at the elimination of immorality. Regarding the women, sometimes loosely termed "concubines" [mapoto wives], who have formed alliances with men, but have not married, gradual pressure should be brought by the Location Superintendents to the end that the parties shall either marry by civilized rites, or see that their union is in accord with native custom, and register it. The Location Superintendent should not issue passes to women who indulge in a succession of merely temporary unions.[9]

For the state, the letter goes on, the ideal is that the worker with permanent employment should marry. For the temporary worker, however, "it is not thought that sexual intercourse is a necessity for young bachelors ... if facilities are provided for games and recreation."[10] Obviously, such sentiments were not shared by the young bachelors, as interviews with men who lived in hostels and women who lived with relatives reveal elaborate and numerous ways for men and women to have had relationships. Besides prostitution and male homosexual relationships inside the hostels, the mapoto arrangement was the most prevalent.

Interviews with women who were single and living in town prior to the 1950s reveal that becoming a mapoto wife was a common alternative for women, especially for those who had been divorced or abandoned. There was a respectable form of mapoto relationship, in which the man, if he was "morally decent," would first go to the woman's rural area and visit her parents, even if he was unable to afford lobolo.[11] Many such relations developed between mapoto wives and men from outside Zimbabwe. The men were unwilling to enter into a "proper marriage" in Zimbabwe, having left a wife in their home country.

Accommodation, however, was difficult for mapoto wives and their husbands. They could not participate in the married accommodation scheme easily, although many were able either to bribe or to trick the municipality's allocation officials. For the most part they would live with married relatives, outside the city in the peri-urban areas, or on nearby commercial farms. Relations were often strained for mapoto wives living with married couples, as the mapoto husband was looked down upon by the other man, and the mapoto wife was seen as a constant danger because she might seduce the properly married husband.[12] The availability of mapoto wives on nearby commercial farms was encouraged by the European farm owners who had a difficult time attracting farm labor, competing as they were with better paying industrial work in the city. One man, originally from Malawi, told how he left a job with the municipality after 20 years (1940s–1950s) to go live and work on the nearby Beatrice Farm because of mapoto wives. He explained the relationship between hostel men and mapoto wives:

> To visit women, we would go to the cottages, go where the lady stayed, we could visit the lady, but she wasn't allowed to visit us. I used to go to Old Bricks [section of the Location] for women. I used to have mapoto wives. Mapoto wasn't a girlfriend. They would stay with the babies. Men would say the children were not theirs; the parents, anyway, would not let the men take the babies as they hadn't paid *lobolo*. I so many children that way. Back then, Men with no wives were known as soldiers. I himself never lived in a cottage but went from the Hostel to Beatrice Farm. On Beatrice Farm I was able to build my own hut, that was when I got a mapoto wife. In the Hostels, women were not allowed; if you had an affair, you had to do the things outside.[13]

Such stories make it clear that the municipality was to some extent able to limit women without proper marriage certificates from occupying legal housing in town, and through harassment made illegal occupation of housing difficult. At the same time, some women were able to manipulate the municipal authorities and gain access to married housing, as were men with unregistered marriages.[14] For those mapoto wives unable to gain access to legal housing, or to have relatives to live with, the alternative was to live illegally in the house with her husband (and usually other men) and to run when the police came searching for marriage certificates.[15]

Women who lived through this period in the Townships often give an alternative interpretation why the Municipality forbade single women from occupying housing. They do not talk about the "moral degradation" which was often cited by colonial and African elites. Rather, in many cases, it came down to the difficulties caused by men who fought with, and over, mapoto wives. As an example, one woman told the following story:

> A woman named Sekisei, a mapoto wife, didn't come one night to visit her man, because she was proposing to another man. The next day her man showed up, asked for some

water, and when she turned her back to get it for him, he took out a knife and stabbed her many times in the back and in the front. She died. Before the police arrived the neighbors beat the man up badly.[16]

Not all the stories are about murder, but the violence perpetrated against mapoto wives is constantly referred to by both men and women when asked about how mapoto wives were treated. Compared with wives married with the consent of the wife's parents, and with lobolo paid, the mapoto wife was often treated worse. In a sense, their mobility was also a liability, as men often abused them physically for reasons of jealousy or spite.[17]

The treatment and experiences of mapoto wives contrast greatly with those of the model wife responsible for "a normal and happy family life." Living as a mapoto wife was a necessity for many women unable to fit into the life-cycle strategies of the majority of urban and rural women in Zimbabwe who became "proper wives." It is clear that colonial labor policies, and housing policies manipulated to serve labor efficiency, helped to foster the growth and maintenance of the mapoto system. Such policies were also responsible, in large part, for the precarious and difficult existence many such women faced living in the city. This situation is indicative of most African urban areas. The literature on women in some larger areas may be useful to researchers and planners (e.g., Hansen-Transbert, 1984; Bozzoli and Nkotsoe, 1991).

The mapoto wives represent a minority of women in the urban areas, but they show clearly the precarious position many women were in, given the choices made concerning housing policy in the past. There are certainly other choices for married and single women than the mapoto arrangement, but the scope of this paper limits adequate discussion of such options. I have presented the previous historical sketch in the interest of emphasizing to what extent past policies have worked against equal access to shelter for women in the urban areas. These inequalities continue, contributing in many ways, among predominantly poor women to a bevy of social and health problems for women and their children.

Life Outside the Nuclear Family Today

The lack of a coherent housing policy directed at single women, or more specifically women outside of the nuclear family, continues a legacy of dependence and violence against certain groups of women and their children. Perhaps the most desperate result of a lack of policy, and the subsequent reliance on the predatory private market of the lodger system, with its makeshift one-room wooden houses, has been the alarming rise in "baby dumping" in the urban areas such as Harare. A case can be made connecting this crisis, in which mothers abandon or kill newborn babies, to the lack of shelter alternatives for women. Many young women, living with relatives or parents in an existing urban household, become pregnant by young men of another urban household. Traditionally, the father is responsible to provide shelter for his child and the mother. When the father is unwilling or unable to meet his responsibilities, the young woman is sometimes forced out of her relatives' house. In such a case, a child may be too much of a responsibility, and such babies end up abandoned or killed.[18] This example is a dramatic indication of the dilemmas facing Zimbabwe policy makers, which need to be addressed as part of a concerted effort to move away from housing based primarily on the male wage earner and nuclear family.

The majority of single women are not driven to these desperate measures, and like a number of women in the grandmother's generation, they fend for themselves and their children in a difficult and sometimes hostile environment. Due to the short supply of housing, however, even those with supportive families and boyfriends often live similarly to the *mapoto* wives of fifty years ago. The primary difference is the reliance on a private landlord system that makes it possible for young couples to cohabit, but certainly not in conditions they would choose were a choice available. Another similarity to earlier times is the continued reliance among many young men on prostitutes. Young women prostitutes are able to afford the high lodger fees charged in the existing residential areas. These women service men, often "regulars," who are young men living with their families in the same or another residential area. Just like those of the 1940s, these men are often waiting to be able to afford marrying a "proper wife," while, in the meantime, they contribute no small portion of their current income to prostitutes or girlfriends.

The problems of urban housing in Zimbabwe, as in many African countries, continue to be linked to the rural areas, where some of the same contemptuous attitudes against single women continue. The urban areas in Zimbabwe are in no way severed from the rural areas, and therefore such attitudes continue to be important when planning future policies.

Rural Attitudes toward Single Women

In the rural areas, as in the city, the predominant preference expressed among the older generation of interviewees has been toward a nuclear family norm. The same is true of the younger generation, but for them, there is also the understanding that economic and housing pressures make it difficult for everyone to realize that ideal. In the rural villages where I carried out research, older men tend to express hostility toward single women in town, referring to them as prostitutes. The presence of "loose women" is another reason to justify keeping their wives in Chikwaka.[19] This view is usually expressed by men, who, on the other hand, are likely to express privately that they had affairs with such women when they were younger.

Women in Chikwaka tended to express their preference for staying in Chikwaka for economic advantages, rather than joining their husbands in town. Women in the urban survey often expressed their choices as something their husbands had decided, and therefore what they must do. In Chikwaka, the tendency was to stress the savings life in the rural areas provided for the family: no rents, self-sufficiency in certain foods, such as maize, eggs, and milk; lower school fees for the children, etc. Most of the women have spent time in Harare, often during the war for security reasons, but still argue the rural area is a better place for their families to live.[20] The views expressed about their husbands working in town were generally evasive, no doubt because I knew some of their husbands from town, and they wouldn't readily confide in me.

For single women, living in Chikwaka meant (and still means) living by another set of rules that restrict access to housing and land for women. First and foremost, as in the colonial city, women are denied access to land on their own. The two cases when a woman may be allowed land are those of widows or divorcees, but these decisions are left up to the male headman, who uses the arbitrary criterion of the woman's age. The reasoning behind this selection process remains one of "social peace." If a woman is "young," she would pose a threat to married couples as she "might seduce their husbands." For this reason, only women seen as mature enough to support their families were allocated stands on their own. According to some of the oldest members of the community, women rarely got access to stands unless they were living there before their husbands died or left them. This helps, in turn, to explain the added pressures forcing urban divorced and abandoned women to stay in the urban areas.

Most of the wives of men originally from Chikwaka were brought into the village from a nearby village. They were then usually expected to live with the husband's parents for a few years, until the husband was able to establish a separate home nearby. One women recounted how she and her husband lived in a converted granary at the husband's parents' house for the first two years after getting married, until they could afford to build their own home. Throughout the marriages the husbands would return to their homes on weekends and during annual leaves. In many ways the married couples in Chikwaka and the Highfield sample shared similar life-cycle experiences. The majority in both cases benefited from the organization of housing based primarily on the nuclear family as the most privileged group.

For those women in Chikwaka who were unable to live within the options of marriage, housing in the rural areas could present difficulties, depending primarily on the stage in the women's life-cycles. The most common difficulty is for women who choose to leave for the city before marrying in the rural areas, or for those girls who become pregnant and are chased from their homes by their fathers. In the old days, many such women would become *mapoto* wives in town. Today, the connotations from the viewpoint of much of Zimbabwean society seem to be similar to the ones applied to *mapoto* wives, even if the name is no longer current. The views expressed by older respondents in Chikwaka still hold such women and girls in contempt. Older women explained how they would, during their youth, ostracize their peers who had left for the city unmarried. They were labeled prostitutes, and very often had difficulty returning to Chikwaka, even if they returned with husbands willing to pay lobolo. Later, as women in Chikwaka married, they continued to feel contempt for such women, as they now were seen as potential seducers of their husbands working in town. In this way, the pervasive image of all unmarried women in town as prostitutes is still shared by many of both the men and women in Chikwaka villages.

The young woman who was divorced or abandoned by her husband who has already paid her lobolo was considered part of the husband's parents' family and allowed to remain living with them at their homestead.[21] Evidence collected about the children of the men and women in the urban surveys revealed that in most cases

a divorced daughter lived in the same house with her parents. This was not the case with divorced sons, and reveals a crucial aspect of current housing options for women in Harare. It is along these lines that these rural and urban examples are also evidence of what Pauline Peters has described as:

"... certain points of vulnerability in development cycles when, given particular political economic conditions, a developmental phase of disadvantage or failure can feed into an exacerbating spiral and thence longer-term, inter-generational reproduction of disadvantage" (Peters, 1983, p. 117).

Such reproduction of disadvantage is indicative, in the Zimbabwean urban and rural evidence, of historical and present difficulties women outside of "nuclear family" units face in access to accommodation.

Conclusion

The preceding discussion has attempted to present the factors which have historically created the emphasis on the nuclear family as the fundamental category for the perception and allocation of legally sanctioned housing in both urban and rural Zimbabwe. The discussion has remained at a general level, with all the inherent problems of over-generalization and simplification of diverse human activity and strategies. The structural constraints, however, concerning access to housing for women are great. For this reason, generalizations are warranted and valid even as such evidence distorts the ability of individual women to overcome these con-straints to achieve their goals. Clearly there are a number of women who have managed on their own to provide themselves and their children with urban and rural housing (Schlyter, 1989). It is, however, an achievement made difficult by prevailing attitudes in society, and by prevailing discrimination within the overall direction of state housing policies.

It has been pointed out by Ann Schlyter that gender-neutral housing regulations are not sufficient to over-come the past discrimination against women. She calls for "positive discrimination" to allow women better access in the future to housing. Another element must be incorporated into this critique. It is the need to understand how current class biases influence the future goals for housing policies in Harare. The current emphasis within government housing programs is toward what is now called "medium-density" housing as a solution to the severe shortage of middle-income housing. It is possible to see such housing as primarily for young married couples, the children of the elite of the previous generation, who are currently forced to live with their parents either in the low-density wealthier suburbs, or in houses in high-density areas owned by their parents. The need for such housing is real enough. But the transformation of policy at a time when the housing backlog for low-income housing continues to increase reveals a choice in priorities not very different from that made in the 1950s. The colonial state, as well, in its allocation policies attempted to appease the most vocal and politically important sections of the urban African population when it opted to invest in homes to foster "a normal and happy family life." Interestingly, both the colonial government and the current government turned to foreign aid to finance such plans: the Colonial Development Corporation in the 1950s, in the interest of colonial labor efficiency and political stability, and today, USAID, in the interest of "Third World" economic and social development. In both cases, however, these interests have overlooked fundamental needs of women who are not to be found in a nuclear family unit.[22]

The formation of middle and elite classes was fostered, in part, by past state policies of family housing. Attitudes towards housing and rural ties are today conditioned by such class views. The elites of the 1950s are now much in command of economic and political resources, having obtained the middle-class lifestyle they demanded. For these classes, housing continues to be a political issue, this time for their children. The elites as well are less likely to see their rural homes as a necessity beyond that of status for the family. For the poorer classes, however, of whom women are in the majority, such emphasis on housing for the nuclear family has been, and continues to be, a major and difficult hurdle to overcome as individuals and extended families struggle for urban and/or rural survival.

Notes

[1] This paper is based on primary research and observations made during 16 months' research in and around Harare, Zimbabwe, 1991–1992. Special thanks for help in preparing this paper to Rita Aggarwal.

[2] This process was recently carried out days before the arrival of Queen Elizabeth for the Commonwealth Heads of Government Conference in August 1991. For an account of squatters' strategies and organization see Bourdillon, 1991.

[3] Such estimates are highly suspect, as the last census in 1982 did not count women living within households designated as having a "male head" other than their husbands. (Schlyter, 1989, p. 28).

[4] The name is a play on the most luxurious hotel in the City Center built by the Chinese after Independence. *The Herald*, Zimbabwe, June 1991.

[5] "RICU Meeting," 14 August 1949, Reported by Detective R. Robinson, Criminal Investigation Division, National Archives of Zimbabwe (NAZ) S517.

[6] Joint National Council, Race Relations Committee, "African Women and Industry," Sept. 18, 1951, NAZ S2788/19.

[7] Letter to Editor from Edwards Sillew Zaranyika, Mangwende Reserve, Mrewa (June 21, 1944), *African Weekly* p. 5. (Translated from the Shona by Simba Handiseni.)

[8] "Homeless Women," Letter to Editor from Sarah Shoniwa, *African Weekly*, June 7, 1944.

[9] C. Bulluck, Secretary for Native Affairs, to Town Clerks, 1937, NAZ S482/535/39.

[10] *Ibid.*

[11] Interview at Machipisa Market Highfield, October 19, 1991.

[12] *Ibid.*

[13] Interview, Highfield, Sept. 24, 1991.

[14] Interview at Machipisa Market Highfield, October 19, Survey #9, Highfield, December 4, 1991, Miss Scott, Sept. 10, 1991.

[15] Survey #38.

[16] Interview, Highfield, Sept. 10, 1991.

[17] The "true" wife of a mapoto wife's man was also a potential and real physical threat to the woman. There are numerous references to men beating mapoto wives in the surveys and interviews. Surveys were carried out by a team of Research Assistants: Joseph Seda, Aaron Jonasi, Peter Mayavo, and Nhamho Samasuwo. See also Jeater (1990) for the complex issue of women's limited freedoms in the urban areas compared to the rural areas, and the new forms of oppression developed to meet such freedoms.

[18] The connection between "baby dumping" and economic hardship is clearly seen when one compares the dramatic increase in such cases in the past two years, a period of economic hardship for the poor in urban Zimbabwe.

[19] The rural interviews were carried out during a number of visits by the author in a 12-month period. The area is Chikwaka, a section of Goromonzi District some 50 kilometers east of Harare. Interviews were collected in Ndamba and Mapfumo villages, five kilometers from the main tar road between Harare, Muhrewa, Mutoko, and the Mozambican border. These areas are the most populated rural sections of Zimbabwe, and historically the source of the majority of Harare's population.

20 Interviews in Ndamba Village, January 30, 1992: Mapfumo Village, February 1 and 5, 1992. The following materials were collected in these 10 interviews.

[20] Interviews in Ndamba Village, January 30, 1992: Mapfumo Village, February 1 and 5, 1992. The following materials were collected in these 10 interviews.

[21] Susan Jacobs' (1989, p. 166) research argues that wage labor allowed young men to be free from familial obligations derived from parents paying lobolo for his wife. This led to less responsibility for the family to look after daughter-in-laws, and for more "arbitrary behavior" and "incidence of divorce without just cause" on the part of men.

[22] In the decade 1980–1990, USAID provided $51,000,000 earmarked for housing to Zimbabwe, which was 12.2% of total aid to Zimbabwe (U.S. Embassy, 1990). Another $50,000,000 has recently been approved.

References

Bourdillon, M.F.C., 1991, *Poor, Harassed, But Very Much Alive,* Harare: Mambo Press.

Bozzoli, Belinda, and Mmantho Nkotsoe, 1991. *Women of Phokeng: Consciousness, Life Strategy and Migrancy in South Africa, 1900–1983,* Portsmouth, NH: Heinemann.

Hansen-Transberg, Karen, April, 1984. "Negotiating Sex and Gender in Urban Zambia," *Journal of Southern African Studies,* 10(2):219–238.

Jacobs, Susan. 1989. "Zimbabwe: State, Class, and Gendered Models of Land Resettlement," in: Jane L. Parpart and Kathleen A. Staudt (eds.), *Women and the State in Africa,* Boulder: Lynne Rienner, pp. 161–184.

Jeater, Diana, 1990, "Marriage, Perversion and Power: the construction of Moral Discourse in Southern Rhodesia" Oxford: Oxford University. D.Phil. dissertation.

Mynanda, B. J., 1954, *In Search of Truth: a Commentary on Certain Aspects of Southern Rhodesia's Native Policy.* Bombay: Hind Kitabs.

National Native Labour Board (NNLB), 1952. *Investigation into the Conditions of Employment for African Women in the Major Cities ... 1952. Evidence,* Godlonton Collection, University of Zimbabwe Library.

Peters, Pauline, October, 1983, "Gender, Development Cycles and Historical Process: a Critique of Recent Research on Women in Botswana," *Journal of Southern African Studies,* 10:(1):99–122.

Potts, Deborah, and Chris Mutambirwa, December, 1990, "Rural-Urban Linkages in Contemporary Harare: Why Migrants Need Their Land." *Journal of Southern African Studies,* 16(4):677–698.

Savanhu, J. Z. October, 1953, "Development of an African Middle Class," *National Affairs: Official Organ of the Rhodesia National Affairs Association,* 4(10):4.

Schlyter, Ann, 1989, *Women Householders and Housing Strategies: The Case of Harare Zimbabwe,* Stockholm: National Swedish Institute for Building Research.

U.S. Embassy (Zimbabwe), 1990, "United States and Zimbabwe: Celebrating a Decade of Cooperation," Harare.

Vambe, Lawrence, 1976, *From Rhodesia to Zimbabwe,* London: Heinemann.

Vakil, Anna, 1991, "Community-Based Housing Organizations in African Cities: Case Studies from Zimbabwe." Paper presented at the Center for Afroamerican and African Studies (University of Michigan) Colloquium Series.

Chapter 36
Gender, Household Structure, and Accommodation for Young Adults in Urban Mexico

Ann Varley

Ann Varley has worked on urban housing in Mexico for over ten years. She directed a major research project on renting, funded by the British Overseas Development Admin-istration and codirected by Alan Gilbert. This led to the publication, in early 1991, of Landlord and Tenant Housing for the Poor in Urban Mexico *(Routledge).* Her other main area of interest is in land tenure regularization as an upgrading strategy or political response to self-help housing. She is currently developing a research interest in migrant women from developing countries living in Britain. Dr. Varley is based at the Department of Geography, University College London.

In research on gender and housing the usual definitions of "traditional" and "non-traditional" households have been reversed: "female-headed" rather than nuclear households dominate the literature. There is a danger of rendering women in "traditional" nuclear households, once again, invisible. It is important not to r*estrict* discussion of gender and housing to the problems facing single mothers or women living alone.

This paper approaches "non-traditional" housing arrangements in urban Mexico in a different way. "Sharing" occurs when two or more households occupy the same plot of land: one household owns the plot, allowing the other/s to live there rent-free. Sharing mostly involves the adult sons or daughters of the plot owners, and may be regarded as a variation on the extended household structure. Sons are more likely to be allowed to bring their wives to their parents' home, whereas daughters are more likely to leave. Women living with their in-laws lack security of tenure and there is often conflict between wives and members of their husbands' family of origin, particularly their mothers-in-law. The anthropological literature has identified male-dominated authority structures as the source of conflict between women in extended households. Sharing reduces the potential for conflict by giving the younger household greater autonomy. Furthermore, concern for their daughters' welfare leads many parents to offer accommodation to married daughters as well as to sons. Single mothers, however, are more likely to live as part of their parents' household than to share. In this respect, the nuclear household norm is reinforced, since sharing seems to be a privilege accorded only to those who are married.

Traditional and Non-Traditional Households in Research on Gender and Housing

Women's housing needs do not seem to attract much attention. They do not figure prominently in the housing literature, as can be seen, for example, from the contents of journals such as *Habitat International* or *Housing Studies.*[1] Similarly, housing has received little attention in the gender studies literature. There are relatively few books on the subject. Notable exceptions, in recent years, include Sophie Watson's (1988) book on Britain and Australia, *Accommodating Inequality: Gender and Housing,* and the collections on *Women, Housing and Community* and *Women, Human Settlements and Housing*, edited by Willem Van Vliet (1988b) and Caroline Moser and Linda Peake (1987), respectively.[2] In comparison with other subjects, there are few entries on housing in Janet Townsend's and Sarah Radcliffe's

(1988) bibliographies on women in developing countries, and the authors surveyed tend to take "squatter settlements" as a context for their study rather than focusing on housing *per se*.[3]

How can we explain this? In part, it may result from unwillingness to accept the relevance of gender: "most authorities responsible for development planning have only very reluctantly recognized gender as an important planning issue" (Moser, 1991: 84). In their introduction to Lloyd Rodwin's edited collection on *Shelter, Settlement and Development*, published to mark the International Year of Shelter for the Homeless in 1987, Rodwin and Bishwapriya Sanyal call for special attention to be paid to the shelter needs of women and especially of female-headed households. But there is no chapter on this subject. The United Nations/IYSH leadership decided that it "should be dealt with in other ways" (cited in Varley, 1989: 116).[4]

But what of feminist scholars? Could their apparent reluctance to work on housing stem from the fear that they will be criticized for suggesting that "a woman's place is in the home"? Such fears would not be groundless. In his foreword to *Women, Housing and Community*, Willem Van Vliet deprecates "the limited scope of feminist critiques that have juxtaposed the private home and the public community as a dichotomy of female and male spheres" (Van Vliet, 1988a: ix). This criticism is misdirected: feminist writers have played a central role in exposing the ideological nature of the supposed dichotomy between public/male and private/female spheres, work and home, production and reproduction (Hayden, 1981; McDowell, 1983; Harris, 1984; Watson, 1988; Jelin, 1991a). Nevertheless, given "the empirical foundation to this dualism" (Harris, 1984: 151), it is all too easy to reinforce the notion of home and work as separate female and male spheres rather than recognizing their interdependence (McDowell, 1992). Rather than trying to "reconceptualise the links between home and work" (*ibid.*: 19) it may (deceptively) seem safer simply to steer clear of the domestic sphere. As Janet Momsen (1989: 119) has written, "recent work on women in Third World countries has, in most cases, concentrated on moving the research focus from women's reproductive roles to their productive contributions," emphasizing paid employment outside the home.

Unconscious anxiety about upholding an unacceptable ideology may also explain why research on gender and housing in developing countries has largely portrayed women outside the confines of the nuclear household. The literature emphasizes, first, "female-headed households," and, second, women as "community managers" mobilizing around housing construction or the introduction of services to their settlement.[5] Most chapters in the Moser and Peake collection, for example, focus on female-headed households, and a series of parallel projects on women householders in Africa has led to several publications (Larsson, 1988, 1989; Schlyter, 1988, 1989). The theme has also been taken up in a Latin American context (Falú and Curutchet, 1991).[6] Regarding women as community managers, all but two of the case studies in *Women, Human Settlements and Housing* are concerned with housing/upgrading projects, and Moser's chapter on Ecuador documents women's struggle for services. An emphasis on specific housing projects is also apparent in the other studies cited (see also Volbeda, 1989).

There is a clear rationale for work on female-headed households. First, as they tend to be more common in cities, continuing migration and urbanization increases their numbers (Brydon and Chant, 1989). Second, female-headed households are likely to be among the poorest members of society, although this is by no means universally or inevitably the case (Townsend and Momsen, 1987). Third they have been neglected by planners (Buvinic *et al.*, 1978; Moser, 1991). In particular, they have been marginalised by the way in which "housing policy and provision ... assumes, and is structured around, the patriarchal family form" (Watson, 1988: 21). Thus, an emphasis on female-headed households is intended to redress a general imbalance, and specifically to expose discrimination against women (see Machado, 1987; Nimpuno-Parente, 1987).

However, the emphasis on female-headed households may have some rather unfortunate consequences. There is a danger of exaggerating the quantitative importance of female-headed households, surely not a good way to convince the planning community of their importance. And there is a danger of rendering many women (the majority?) once again "invisible."

It has become almost commonplace to argue that "one third of the world's households are now headed by women" and that "in urban areas, especially in Latin America and parts of Africa, the figure exceeds 50 percent" (Moser, 1987: 14; see also Chant and Ward, 1987; Smith, 1988; Muller and Plantenga, 1990; Sayne, 1991; Wilson, 1991).[7] Given the difficulties of working with National Census data on household structure (Youssef and Hetler, 1983), information on household structure is often based on small-scale surveys of particular locations. Taking Mexico as a case study,

Table 1: Percentage of Female-Headed Households in Mexican Cities, 1981–91

	Single women/ mothers only*	All female heads**	N		Single women/ mothers only*	All female heads**	N
VARIOUS 1980S+				**PUEBLA 1986**			
Low-income settlements	7	12	9,464	Young self-help settlement (owners) C	2	5	100
				Older self-help settlement (owners) D	6	14	76
MEXICO CITY 1981–82				Older self-help settlement (tenants)	11	15	80
Young self-help settlement (owners) A	16	16	25	Inner city rental area (tenants)	9	12	115
Older self-help settlement (owners)	0	4	25				
Young self-help settlement (owners) B	16	16	25	**PUERTO VALLARTA 1986**			
Older self-help settlement (owners)	0	4	25	Young self-help settlement (owners)	13	17	23
				Older self-help settlement (65% owners)	9	20	69
MEXICO CITY 1991							
Older self-help settlement (owners) B	8	15	78	**LEON 1986**			
Older self-help settlement (owners) A	6	11	72	Young self-help settlement (96% owners)	4	9	23
				Older self-help settlement (72% owners)	6	11	54
GUADALAJARA 1985–86							
Young self-help settlement (owners)	5	12	102	**QUERETARO 1982–83**			
Older self-help settlement (owners)	9	13	64	Young self-help settlement (owners)	9	14	92
Older self-help settlement (tenants)	10	16	96	Young self-help settlement (owners)	8	10	52
Inner city rental area (tenants)	15	19	120	Young self-help settlement (owners)	10	15	100
PUEBLA 1991				**OAXACA 1990**			
Young self-help settlement (owners) C	0	5	55	Older self-help settlement (66% owners)	18	42	50
Older self-help settlement (owners) D	12	33	33				

Sources

Various, 1980s: Selby *et al.,* 1990 (plus own calculations)

Mexico City, 1981–82: Varley, 1985

Mexico City and Puebla 1991: Questionnaire survey, summer 1991 (author)

Guadalajara and Puebla 1985–86: Gilbert and Varley, 1991

Puerto Vallarta, León, Querétaro: Chant, 1991b

Oaxaca, 1990: Willis, 1992

Notes

\+   Mexico City, Mexicali, Mérida, San Luis Potosí, Querétaro, Tampico, Villahermosa, Mazatlán, Reynosa, Oaxaca.

Definition of female-headed households: see note 5. Percentages for different cities are not strictly comparable. Chant (1991b: 235) excluded male-headed one-parent households, single-person households, households shared by adolescent siblings, and households with sharers. The Mexico City, Guadalajara and Puebla data include such households, where found. All figures based on random sample questionnaire surveys.

*   Excludes extended households headed by women.

**   Includes extended households headed by women.

"Young" self-help settlements are those in which most of the households interviewed had arrived within the last 15 years. In Guadalajara, Puebla, León, Pto. Vallarta, and (with one exception) Querétaro, these areas were 2–7 years old; in Mexico City and the third Querétaro settlement, they were 10–12 years old.

"Older" self-help settlements are those over 15 years old. In León, Pto. Vallarta, Querétaro and Mexico City, these areas were about 20 years old, whereas the one in Oaxaca was about 30 years old, the one in Guadalajara about 35 years old, and the Puebla one, about 40 years old (1985–86).

A, B, C, D – letters identify the same settlement surveyed in different years.

Table 2: Percentage of Female-Headed Households in Various Latin American Cities 1968–1990

Country and town/city	Type of area	Percentage of house-holds with female head	Year	Source
Brazil, Belo Horizonte	Various, all income groups	17	1983 1983	Merrick and Schmink
Brazil*	Various	18	1984	Goldani 1990
Brazil, Sao Bernardo do Campo	Housing project	13	1980s	Volbeda 1989
Brazil, Córdoba	Housing project	16+	1988–90	Falú and Curutchet 1991
Colombia, Pereira	Various self-help areas	20	1987	Gough, 1992
Costa Rica, various	Low-income	14–15	1989	Chant 1991a
Ecuador, Manta	Low-income	13	1970s	Middleton 1991
Honduras, various	Various	33	1970s	Cited in Chant 1991b
Mexico, Oaxaca	Self-help area	18	1968–72	Higgins 1974
Mexico, Oaxaca	Low-income	22	1977	Hackenberg, Murphy and Selby 1984
Mexico, Mexico	Various	17	1969–70	García, Muñoz and de Oliveira 1982
Nicaragua	Various	48	1975	Vance 1987
Venezuela	Various	20–25	Various	Cited in Chant various1991b

Notes

* Figure from 1984 National Household Survey, which includes some rural areas but is more representative of the urban areas (Goldani, 1990: 536).

+ See note 9. It should be remembered that some housing projects may discriminate against female-headed households (Machado, 1987).

\# One-half of the Nicaraguan population lives in Managua.

Table 1 presents the results from various micro-surveys and one larger study of Mexican cities in the last decade. In only two cases does the figure for women-headed households reach one-third of all households.[8] The findings for tenants are particularly significant. Female-headed households face particular difficulties in building their own home. They may therefore be underrepresented in self-help settlements, but not in rental accommodation (Gilbert and Varley, 1991; Chant and Ward, 1987; Volbeda, 1989). If, therefore, fewer than 20 per- cent of tenant households are headed by women, it is unlikely that female-headed households constitute 50 percent of urban households.

Earlier Mexican work and other Latin American studies also suggest that the proportion of female-headed households is lower than has been proposed. Figures below 20 percent are often reported (see Table 2 and note 7).[9]

The significance of female-headed households is, as I have indicated, not merely a question of statistics. But a legitimate concern for the housing needs of single women should not lead us to neglect the housing problems facing women who live with male partners. Otherwise, there is a danger that many women will once more be rendered "invisible"—this time, ironically, by feminist scholars. Discussion of the housing strategies of female- and male-headed households, for example, easily slips into a comparison of "women" and "men," as if there were no women in the (so-called) male-headed households.

It is tempting to see the gender and housing literature's emphasis on single women as an example of the irony identified by Anne-Marie Goetz:

> the liberal feminist language of *integration* has been based upon a *separating* out from the context of development of the category "women" as a self-contained identity…. The effect has been to ignore the importance of relations between men and women ... with the result that women, seen as separate rather than central, have been added into the process of development *at the margin* (Goetz, 1991: 140; my emphasis).

If the archetypal gender-and-housing study concerns female-headed households in a housing project, the danger of marginalization is increased by the change of emphasis in World Bank thinking, with ramifications for national housing policies. Individual projects such as sites-and-service schemes are no longer in favor.[10] Instead, city-level attempts to unblock housing markets characterize the new emphasis on shelter delivery/urban management systems or *programs* rather than *projects* (Rakodi, 1991; Burgess, 1992; Fiori and Ramirez, 1992).[11] This change should be acknowledged in research on gender and housing. A land tenure legalization program, for example, is likely to influence far more women's lives, for better or for worse, than all the sites-and-services projects in the country. We need to understand the housing problems facing low-income women from both "traditional" and "non-traditional" households, and not only those headed by women. The next section tries to put this principle into practice.

The Provision of Accommodation for Young Adults in Urban Mexico

The housing problems of Mexico City, with a population of some 20 million people, and Puebla, Mexico's fourth largest city, with over 1 million inhabitants, are well

documented.[12] The economic crisis of the 1980s aggravated a situation in which two-thirds of the population was already denied access to ownership via the conventional private or public housing markets (Ward, 1990; CIDAC, 1991). Extensive areas of self-built housing had grown up since the 1940s, but the pressures on incomes, land prices, and building material costs in the 1980s created further difficulties for people seeking to house themselves in such areas. Mexico City and Puebla already had an unusually high proportion of tenants and the recession of the 1980s seems likely to have increased the number of families unable to gain access to ownership (Gilbert and Varley, 1989, 1991; Coulomb, 1988).

One response to such difficulties is to share accommodation with kin. As here defined, "sharing" refers to two or more separate households occupying the same plot: one household owns the plot, and the other/s live there rent-free as a result of kinship or friendship links with the owners.[13]

Table 3 provides basic information on sharing in four self-help settlements of different ages and degrees of consolidation: two in Mexico City, and two in Puebla.[14] Overall, one in three owners currently shares a plot with at least one other household (excluding tenants). Most sharers are the sons or daughters of the owners. They are "married" and around 30 years of age, with an average of two children (see also Gilbert and Varley, 1991; Coulomb, 1990; Gilbert and Ward, 1985).[15]

Table 3 also reveals that plot owners tend to let their sons share more often than their daughters. About two-fifths of sharers are women.

If, instead of living as separate households, the members of these families all lived together, they would form extended households. As the literature on extended households is highly relevant to the following discussion, Table 4 provides some information on extended households in the case-study settlements to complement Table 3. The finding which I wish to underline concerns the proportion of those still living with their parents who are women. Overall, women with a husband or child are as likely to form part of their parents' extended household as their male counterparts; but if single parents are excluded, the proportion falls to less than two-fifths, the same as for sharers.

These findings suggest that providing accommodation for young adults in this way is characteristic of what

Table 3: Basic Information on Sharing in Case-Study Settlements

	MEXICO CITY		PUEBLA		
	Loma de la Palma	San José	El Salvador	Veinte de Nov.	ALL
Percentage of owners who share their plot with other household(s)	37	38	7	27	29
Mean no. of sharer households*	1.6	1.6	1.0	1.8	1.6
N	78	72	55	33	238
Of sharers:					
Percentage who are daughters/sons of owners	85	77	75	100	84
N	47	44	4	16	111
For sharers who are daughters/sons of owners:					
Median age (years)	29	29	26	33	29
Percentage who are women	33	44	67	38	39
Percentage with spouse + child/ren	95	85	100	94	91
Percentage with spouse but no children	5	12	0	6	8
Percentage with children but no spouse	0	3	0	0	1
Mean no. of children	2.3	2.1	1.7	2.3	2.2
N	40	34	3	16	93

Source: Questionnaire survey, summer 1991.

Notes

In El Salvador, there are as yet few sons/daughters of plot owners forming their own families; hence the very small number of sharers.

"Sharer": within the sharing household, the person with the closest blood relationship (or friendship) with the owners of the plot.

* Only for plots with at least one sharer household.

anthropologists have described as the patrilocal "stem" or "grand" family (Selby *et al.*, 1990: 101; Lomnitz and Perez-Lizaur, 1991: 124).[16] These multi-generation households are formed when, rather than moving to a new house on marriage, sons bring their wives to live with their parents. Later, older siblings and their families may move to independent accommodation. Such households have been found in "peasant communities in state societies" (Lamphere, 1974: 104), including Latin America, China and India (Croll, 1978; Sharma, 1978; Wolf, M., 1974; Wolf, A.P., 1984). They have often been mentioned in studies of rural Mexico (Foster, 1967; Chiñas, 1973; Whitecotton, 1977; Gross, 1978; Ingham, 1986; Stephen, 1991).[17]

Some authors have argued that patrilocality is no longer significant in urban Mexico. Selby *et al.* (1990: 101) argue that the tendency to live with the man's parents "has disappeared from urban households," and Lomnitz and Perez-Lizaur (1991: 126) find that "instances of patrilocality are not substantially greater than those of matrilocality." However, in the case study on which this statement is based, Lomnitz (1977: 119) argued that "patrilocality is predominant in the shantytown," although it declined over time as married children moved away from their parents' home. Thirty-five percent of households was classified as patrilocal at the time of study, compared with 25 percent which was

Table 4: Young Adults Living as Part of Their Parents' Extended Household in Case-Study Settlements

| | MEXICO CITY | | PUEBLA | | |
	Loma de la Palma	San José	El Salvador	Veinte de Nov.	ALL
Percentage of owners with an extended household including daughters/sons with spouse/child	9	18	15	151	4
Mean no. of daughters/sons with spouse/child in these households*	1.1	1.2	1.1	1.0	1.1
N	78	72	55	33	238
For daughters/sons with spouse/child living in their parent's household:					
Median age (years)	21	24	27	24	24
Percentage who are women:					
Overall	25	67	33	60	49
Excluding single parents	14	50	25	60	36
Percentage with spouse + child/ren	38	47	67	80	54
Percentage with spouse but no children	50	7	22	20	22
Percentage with child/ren but no spouse	13	47	11	0	24
Mean no. of children	1.0	1.3	1.9	1.6	1.4
N	8	15	9	5	37

Source: Questionnaire survey, summer 1991.

Notes

The table refers to extended households including one or more daughters/sons with spouse/child.

* Only for households extended in this way.

matrilocal (giving a ratio almost identical to the one noted above) (*ibid.*: 120).[18]

In this study, information was sought about the housing status of *all* living children of the people interviewed. If there is a tendency to patrilocality, those living with their in-laws should display the opposite pattern from the one described above: more women than men should live with their in-laws. Table 5 shows that this is indeed the case. Again, the patrilocal bias is not dramatic, but it is noticeable: whereas the ratio of men to women is about 3:2 for those living with their parents, the ratio is reversed for those housed by in-laws.[19]

Further evidence comes from people's accounts of how they decide which of their children should share their

plot. In one house in La Palma, one son was sharing with his parents. Another son, who now owned his own home, also used to share; but their two married sisters were both tenants and had not shared with their parents since marriage. The explanation for this was that "*se las llevaron*": the daughters' husbands had taken them to live elsewhere. This phrase was echoed by other people interviewed. It is a husband's responsibility to house his wife, particularly when, as this phrase hints, the couple eloped. (The custom by which a young man "steals" his girlfriend from her parents, sometimes with the explicit support of his own relatives, has been widely documented in rural areas [Foster, 1967; Chiñas, 1973; Whitecotton, 1977] and is also, apparently, common in the cities.) Other people interviewed were quite clear that sharing is a privilege granted to *sons*. Parents may

Table 5: Young Adults Relying on Their In-Laws for Accommodation

	MEXICO CITY		PUEBLA		
	Loma de la Palma	San José	El Salvador	Veinte de Nov.	ALL
Percentage of those sharing with their in-laws who are women:	50	89	100	0	68
N	10	9	2	1	22
Percentage of those living with their in-laws' extended households who are women:	71	57	60	–	63
N	7	7	5	0	19

Source: Questionnaire survey, summer 1991.

Notes

The table includes the daughters/sons of interviewees who share with their in-laws or live as members of their in-laws' extended household.

In all, 379 sons/daughters of interviewees who were over 15 and had a spouse/child were recorded. Of them, 171 (45 percent) of them shared/ lived with their own parents/their in-laws, and women constituted 47 percent of this latter group.

build additional accommodation in anticipation of their sons getting married, or a man may build a room on his parents' plot to set up a home with his girlfriend.

The Implications of Sharing and Extended Households for Women's Housing Options

The effect of the patterns observed is to increase women's dependence on others in their efforts to accommodate themselves and their children. Tenure has been identified as a key concern in women's access to housing: "For women, tenure rights are a strategic gender need which ensures protection for themselves and their children" (Moser, 1991: 93). The problem of tenure becomes particularly acute for a woman whose right to her home depends on her relationship with a man who does not himself have any right to the house, and whose family may view her with hostility (see below).[20] If the relationship breaks down, she will probably have to leave, as the owners are likely to support their son, and continued co-residence is likely to be distasteful to all concerned.

The difficulties facing women-headed households wishing to build their own home have already been noted. On separation from her husband, a woman who has been living with her in-laws would seem to have few options but to return to her own parents' home, or to move into rental accommodation. Regular rent payments pose particular problems for families with only one earner, when the children are still young (Volbeda, 1989).

On the other hand, women who live with their husband's family may find themselves upwardly mobile in the housing market. The full implications for their subsequent housing histories cannot be addressed here, but there is evidence to suggest that sharing can help people become owners (Gilbert and Varley, 1991). It enables them to save money that would otherwise have gone on the rent, until they have enough for the deposit needed for their own plot.[21] Later, they can dedicate a larger share of their income to purchasing building materials than tenants would be able to do.

The Problems of Living with In-Laws

Shared accommodation entails living in close daily proximity with one's in-laws. To date, studies of the extended household in urban Mexico have tended to argue that it has positive implications for women, because of the opportunities for cooperation which it allows. But this is only half the story: there is also considerable potential for conflict.

Larissa Lomnitz (1977) sought to counter the derogatory aspects of some writings on urban marginality by analyzing the mutual support networks enabling people to cope with extreme poverty. In her book, she wrote:

> one will find no stress on the more sensational aspects of poverty: the filth, the promiscuity, the arguments and fights between people who must live together in a tiny space (Lomnitz, 1977: 31).

The social resources mobilized by people in their efforts to survive included networks of reciprocal exchange and institutions such as *compadrazgo* (*ibid.*: 3). Although networks could be based on friendship as well as kinship, "kinship is the most common social foundation for reciprocity networks" (*ibid.*: 156), and extended or "joint" household structures played a key role in these networks.

Sylvia Chant (1984, 1985, 1991b) also emphasizes cooperation in extended households. Women in extended households can "share and/or delegate gender-assigned duties" (Chant, 1991b: 156) more than women in nuclear households. They therefore face fewer restrictions on their ability to enter the labor market (see also García *et al.*, 1982; González de la Rocha, 1988; Selby *et al.*, 1990). Decisions on household budgeting become more democratic, housework is shared, "the full-time mother-wife role tends to become redundant" and women seem to have "far greater personal liberty" (Chant, 1985: 22). In short, extended households "reduce some of the excesses of patriarchy" (*ibid.*: 26).

Chant (1991: 144-53) examines different types of extension to the household in support of her arguments, particularly those involving the inclusion of women's sisters or mothers. The focus of this paper is narrower, since it is restricted to the incorporation of sons- or daughters-in law; this is, however, the most common pattern in household extension and sharing. The literature on patrilocal extended households suggests that this type of extension is likely to lead to conflict between female relatives rather than cooperation:

> The authority structure of the patrilocal, patrilineal extended family, where father has authority over son and husband over wife, brings about conflict rather than cooperation between women in these groups (Lamphere, 1974: 105).

Since authority is in men's hands, women have to manipulate their relationships with men—their husbands, and later their adult sons—to gain influence.

Mothers- and daughters-in law therefore have conflicting interests. The stem family "introduces in the role of daughter-in-law a woman whose only hope of personal autonomy is division of her husband's natal family" (Wolf, A., 1984: 281). The consequences of this for daughters-in-law have been documented, for rural China, by Elisabeth Croll (1978) and Margery Wolf (1974), and for rural India by Ursula Sharma (1978), although they stress that daughters-in-law are not without resources (including women friends) in dealing with their mothers-in-law. The emphasis women place on strong relationships with their sons and the consequent strains between mother- and daughter-in law are summarized by Croll (1978: 50):

> It was by forming and nurturing ties with her son which were personal and exclusive that women cultivated a source of power in a social structure dominated by men. Any potential threat to this relationship by the daughter- in-law was felt deeply. Trapped all their lives, women, with the authority of being the mother-in-law, appeared to compensate for their own former suffering and impotence as outsiders by repeating the very same process of domination.

This type of conflict has also been reported in rural Mexico (Stephen, 1991: 40-62; Chiñas, 1973: 59; Ingham, 1986: 64).[22] Although the context of modern urban Mexico is a very different one, tension between in-laws is still a significant problem, for which gender relations are ultimately responsible.

The fundamental emotional significance of sharing was highlighted by one woman who answered my question why her married children (all daughters) didn't live with her by saying "all my children hurt me a great deal." She was referring, not to a family quarrel, but to the pain of childbirth. In a cultural context in which girls are seen as inherently less "valuable" than boys (Díaz-Guerrero, 1990: 35; Stephen, 1991: 49), a certain resentment of daughters, a feeling that they should stand on their own two feet just as their mothers had to do, can sometimes be detected, and probably helps to explain the gender bias in sharing. One woman who thought neither sons nor daughters should live with their parents *particularly* disapproved of married daughters bringing their husbands home, because they would expect their mothers to cook for them.

Women's attitude to their sons is different, reflecting the privileged nature of the mother-son relationship in Mexico (Díaz-Guerrero, 1990; Leñero Otero, 1987). In Puebla, a woman who blamed Mexican mothers for their men's *machismo* said that when a son marries, his mother will use all kinds of emotional blackmail to get him to bring his wife to live with them, including pretending to be ill, and fainting. In this context, it seems almost inevitable that mothers will dislike their daughters-in-law. One woman (whose own children were all still single) summarized the problems of sharing in these terms:

> supposing your son comes home drunk one night, and you go out to tell him off about it. Then, his wife comes out and starts having a go at you for scolding her husband: she tells you to lay off and mind your own business.

To avoid such problems, she thought it better that children should find their own place to live: "I love you a lot, but you have to go.... As another woman put it: "I don't like having the daughters-in-law around. They [her sons] had better not bring the wife here to my house."

The misery that these problems can cause, for the older woman as well as the younger one, had become apparent during my earlier work in Puebla. An old woman spontaneously approached me in the street one day, and started to tell me about the wickedness of her daughter-in-law; another was locked out of her house by her daughter-in-law; and one 86-year-old woman without children of her own preferred to live alone in a *vecindad* rather than living with her godson and his wife, because the two women didn't get on.[23]

For a woman sharing with her in-laws, the problem may be not only her husband's mother but also his sisters. It is common for some single daughters still to be living with their parents. If, for example, a child is hurt in a fall, her mother may be blamed and made to face the opprobrium of being a "bad mother" by her sisters-in-law as well as their mother: they react as though it is *their* child that has been hurt. Moreover, it may not be easy for women who are sharing to develop friendship networks to help them counteract such pressures, insofar as such networks depend on friends having access to each other's homes. Friends of whom the owner disapproves are unlikely to be welcome on the plot, and grounds for disapproval could readily be found by a hostile mother-in-law. Shopping or other work performed away from the home may provide some opportunity for women to resist such restrictions; but spending too much time "in the street" (which has strong sexual implications) can give a prying relative the chance to tell tales to a woman's husband.[24]

The House of Two: Responses to the Problems of Dependence and Conflict

The kinds of problem outlined above are widely recognized by people in low-income settlements in urban Mexico. What, then, can they do about them?

In the first place, sharing may be seen as a way of trying to reduce the potential for conflict associated with the extended household. Work in rural Mexico has shown the importance of having separate cooking facilities "as a focus of identity" (Whitecotton, 1977: 254); the so-called extended household is actually composed of two or more nuclear households, undermining the notion that the extended household is the basic unit of domestic organization (Gross, 1978). The importance of having separate accommodation and facilities also emerged in the case-study settlements in Mexico City and Puebla. Tables 3-5 show that sharing is more common than living as part of the parental household. The reason for this was explained by one woman in Puebla. Her mother, she said, had taught her that "*casados*" ("married") meant "*casa [de] dos*" ("house of two"). In other words, married children must be given some independence. Although they might have little option but to live with their parents for a while, every effort should be made to provide somewhere for them to be together, in private. Even if the room was so small that they could push the door shut from the bed, the important thing was that they should have a door to shut behind them.

Thus, sharing can be seen as an attempt to avoid some of the problems associated with the patrilocal extended household.

Second, conflict between women is not a structural necessity. Instead of vying for their son's/husband's affections, women *can* cooperate with each other to resist the exercise of patriarchal authority. As Chiñas (1973: 59) notes in her study of the Isthmus Zapotecs:

> A surprising number of wives do adjust remarkably well to living with their mothers-in-law ... and sometimes very strong bonds of affection form between them over the years. Frequently mothers-in-law side with the wife against their own son, especially when his behavior is obviously at the root of the trouble.

Nash (1969: 2/9) also talks of relationships between mother-in-law and daughter-in-law which are "characterized by mutual cooperation." At the least, a conscious intention *not* to interfere was apparent on the part of many of the women I interviewed. Several women stressed that it was up to their sons and daughters-in-law to choose where they wanted to live, even if their personal preference would be to have all their children close at hand. One widow with five married sons and daughters living elsewhere said she would happily evict her three tenants to make room for them, but accepted with philosophical resignation that "daughters-in-law don't want to live with you...." Once married, as another woman put it, sons "will live wherever their wives like—because they *don't* always like [to live with their in-laws]." Thus, many parents respect their children's need for autonomy, whatever their own feelings in the matter.

Third, the fact that almost two-fifths of sharers are women indicates that parents also recognize their daughters' needs. In particular, they are concerned about the consequences of their daughters' marriages breaking down. One man, who expressed the idea that sharing is for sons, not daughters, more clearly than anyone else, nevertheless stated that, in addition to the accommodation he was building for his two (as yet unmarried) sons, he was also trying to make room for his daughters as well. He would like to be able to help them if their marriages didn't work out well and they were left with nowhere to live. The daughter of this man's neighbors had just left her parents' plot. According to her mother, she wanted one of her married sisters to take her place, because "her in-laws are being right so-and-sos with her." And in Puebla, one woman, aged 22, was sharing with her parents. After getting married, she had spent a short time with her in-laws, but after problems with her mother-in-law she and her husband had moved to her parents' plot.

Conclusion

I have argued that, in research on gender and housing in developing countries, the notion of "traditional" and "non-traditional" households has almost been reversed: women-headed households have held a prominent place in such studies. While there was clearly a need for research on the housing needs of women as single parents or single-person households, there is a danger of rendering women in nuclear households, once again, invisible. Therefore, it is important not to *restrict* discussion of gender and housing to the needs of female-headed households.

Forms of domestic organization involving patrilocal extended households or the sharing of accommodation may have negative consequences for women. These include women's dependence on their husbands' relatives for a roof over their heads, and the potential for conflict between wives and members of their husband's family of origin. As Lamphere (1974: 112) concludes: "women quarrel with or dominate other women when it is in their interest to do so; they share and exchange with other women when it suits their own goals." When women see their interests as involving the manipulation of their relationship with their sons or husbands, rather than solidarity with other women in resisting male authority, then conflict rather than cooperation is likely to result. It is not, however, an *inevitable* outcome.

Thus, to understand the implications of sharing as a housing strategy, we must take gender relations into account. Moreover, it is also important to remember that the home is *not* a separate sphere: state regulations permeate and circumscribe the supposedly private sphere. The next step in the exploration of sharing as a housing strategy should perhaps be to ask how the state intervenes in the interaction among gender relations, household structure and the housing process.

Finally, to return briefly to the question of "traditional" and "non-traditional" households: while married daughters as well as married sons were recorded sharing with their parents, single mothers were, in all but one case, counted as part of their parents' extended house-hold. It seems that it would be regarded as inappropriate for them to *share* their parents' plot as a separate, independent household. Sharing therefore reinforces the patriarchal norm of the nuclear family, insofar as it is a privilege accorded only to those who are "married." If, moreover, women without a partner are more likely to rent or to depend on their parents for accommodation, whilst sharing leads to home ownership, then the patriarchal norm is also reinforced by material rewards for those who ascribe to it. In this sense, sharing is a highly "traditional" housing strategy.

Notes

[1] A study evaluating research on low-income housing found that only 13 of 126 studies reviewed provided any information on the particular problems faced by women (Van Vliet, 1988: x).

[2] A number of specific issues have received more attention. Housing design has been addressed, in a British context, by the Matrix Collective (1984) and Marion Roberts (1991); for the U.S.A., see Hayden (1981). Homelessness is a growth area in the literature as well as on the streets. It is examined, for Britain, by Watson and Austerberry (1986), Miller (1990) and Dibblin (1991); for the United States, see Stoner (1988) and Golden (1992).

3 Housing is mentioned, but not analyzed in any depth, in several recent studies of gender and the environment (Rodda, 1991; Dankelman and Davidson, 1988; Sontheimer, 1991; Levy, 1992).

4 An IYSH seminar on "Women and Shelter" was held in Harare in December 1987 (Schlyter, 1989).

5 Despite the unsatisfactory implications, this paper follows the convention in the literature of describing households in which there is no resident male spouse as female-headed households. The term "community managers" is used by Caroline Moser (1987, 1991).

6 The United States and United Kingdom literature also emphasizes single women and women as single parents (Watson and Austerberry, 1986; Wekerle, 1988; Mulroy, 1988; Sprague, 1991; Golden, 1992).

7 The source of these figures is often given as Buvinic *et al.*, 1978; but in two-thirds of the Latin American countries analyzed in that study, women are described as *de jure* heads of between 10 and 20 per cent of all households. The only figures over 30 per cent are for Chile (32 per cent) and Panama (40 per cent) (Buvinic *et al.*, 1978: 87–88; figures mostly for the 1970s).

8 The temporary absence of men working illegally in the USA could account for under-reporting of *de facto* women-headed households; but in surveys in ten Mexican cities, Selby *et al.* (1990: 201) found that only 11 percent of households had members working overseas.

9 The traditional concept of the household (usually defined as a residential unit sharing food and at least some budgetary resources) has been criticized as too static and too concerned with boundaries. Methodologically, it is argued that questionnaire surveys elicit responses falsely depicting a "normal" conjugal family (Fonseca, 1991). Such problems have led some authors to uncover *de facto* or "hidden" women-headed households, doubling the overall proportion reported (Falú and Curutchet, 1991), or to emphasize the importance of mother-child units in situations where "the overwhelming majority of households are normally nuclear" (Fonseca, 1991: 135). Unless the criteria used for defining *de facto* female-headed households are clear and consistently applied (following, perhaps, the categories proposed by Youssef and Hetler, 1983), there is a danger of playing *cherchez la femme* in some of these approaches.

10 They were, in any case, never of great importance compared with the vast areas of "spontaneous" housing in Latin America.

11 The shift to a broader institutional level of intervention is unlikely to decrease discrimination against women unless specific safeguards are introduced. Brion and Tinker (1980) and Watson (1988) have shown how women in Britain and Australia are marginalized by housing allocation and finance systems, although Munro and Smith (1989) argue that particular patriarchal outcomes cannot be assumed, because of the intervention of labor market variables.

12 For Mexico City, see, for example, COPEVI, 1977; Connolly, 1982; Gilbert and Ward, 1985; Michel *et al.*, 1988; Schteingart, 1989; Ward, 1986, 1990. For Puebla, see Mele, 1984; Universidad Autónoma de Puebla DIAU-ICUAP, 1986; Jones, 1991; Gilbert and Varley, 1991.

13 Most sharers make some contribution to the costs of services consumed. Although the literature often fails to distinguish between extended households and sharing (see below), the question *"cocinan juntos o aparte?"* ("do you cook together or separately?") clearly makes sense to people, and generally elicits a direct, clear response to questions seeking to establish the number of households present.

14 Fieldwork in 1991 included participant observation in a young self-help settlement on the eastern periphery of Puebla and a questionnaire survey in areas already studied in 1981–82 (Mexico City) or 1985–86 (Puebla). *Loma de la Palma* developed in the 1970s on a hill in the north of Mexico City. Legalized in 1976, it received water and drainage in the 1980s and was being paved by the residents in summer 1991. *San José de los Leones* is a regularized and consolidated settlement in the west of Mexico City; it dates from the late 1960s. *El Salvador* is a ten-year old illegal settlement on the eastern periphery of Puebla. The streets are unpaved and many plots still unoccupied. *Veinte de Noviembre,* founded in the late 1940s as an illegal subdivision of private lands in north-west Puebla, now has a complex mixture of owner occupation, renting and sharing.

15 Although the words "married," "wife" and "husband" are used, no distinction is made between couples who are legally married and those living together in a consensual union.

16 Arthur Wolf (1984: 281) defines a "grand" family as having a minimum of *three* nuclear units – two married siblings and their parents. He defines a stem family as having only two nuclear units. If sharing is to be described as a variation on this theme, it is clear that there are both stem families and grand families involved.

17 In an interesting exception to the rule, Nash (1969) found that in Amatenango del Valle, Chiapas, where recently married couples used to live with the bride's parents, they were now equally likely to live with either set of parents.

18 The figures for "initial residence" were 46 percent and 29 percent. The implication is that nuclear households were in the minority: "the extended family prevails in the great majority of households" (Lomnitz, 1977: 100). This finding is contrary to most studies of Mexican urban households, although it is difficult to draw comparisons between Lomnitz's household classification scheme and those used by other authors. Many of the households she classifies as extended are more easily enumerated as nuclear sub-groups (*ibid.*: 102). Sharers as defined in this study are found in Lomnitz's "single-roof" and "single-plot" extended household categories rather than what she classifies as "jointed households."

19 More daughters and sons are recorded as living with their parents than with their in-laws; this calls for comment. It may reflect under-reporting; but there is another explanation. Whereas almost all owners in the case-study settlements have enough space to accommodate another family, this is not necessarily true of their children's in-laws, who will come from a variety of housing types. Some, for example, will be tenants, who are more likely to lack the space to accommodate any other relatives (Gilbert and Varley, 1991).

20 The additional problems facing a woman whose husband has children from a previous marriage was discussed by one woman in Mexico City. Her sister's step-children had become extremely hostile at the time of legalization, arguing that she had no right to the house and threatening to throw her out. For this reason, the woman interviewed said that she and her husband, both of whom had children from previous relationships, would *not* consider letting them share.

21 Gilbert and Varley (1991: 112) suggest that the deposit, rather than the regular monthly payments on a plot of land, is one of the key elements dividing persistent tenants from prospective owners.

22 Interestingly, Croll (1983: 83) notes that tension between mother- and daughter-in-law was the most common cause of divorce in 1980s Beijing.

[23] Interestingly, in her study of a village in Chiapas, where married children can live with either set of parents, Nash (1969) found apparently more harmonious relations between in-laws.

[24] As Selby *et al.* (1990: 91) write "Living alone is almost unthinkable in urban Mexico," particularly for a woman in her eighties.

[25] The phrase "subir y bajar" ("to go up and down") is used in two contexts: to-ing and fro-ing (as in visits to a government office in search of documentation, for example) and sleeping around. Women may be expected to take a child with them on "legitimate" outings.

References

Brion, M,. and Tinker, A., (1980), *Women in Housing: Access and Influence*, London: Housing Centre Trust.

Brydon, L., and S. Chant, (1989), *Women in the Third World: Gender Issues in Rural and Urban Areas*, Aldershot: Edward Elgar.

Burgess, R. (1992), "Helping some to help themselves: Third World housing policies and development strategies," in K. Mathéy (ed.), *Beyond Self-Help Housing*, London: Mansell, 75–91.

Buvinic, M., and Youssef, N.H., with Van Elm, B. (1978) *Women-headed households: The Ignored Factor in Development Planning*, Washington D.C.: International Center for Research on Women.

Chant, S. (1984), "Household labour and self-help housing in Querétaro, Mexico," *Boletín de Estudios Latinoamericanos y del Caribe, 37*, 45–68.

Chant, S. (1985), "Family formation and female roles in Querétaro, Mexico," *Bulletin of Latin American Research, 4*, 17–32.

Chant, S. (1991a) "Gender, households and seasonal migration in Guanacaste, Costa Rica," *European Review of Latin American and Caribbean Studies, 50*, 51–85.

Chant, S. (1991b), *Women and Survival in Mexico Cities: Perspectives on Gender, Labour Markets and Low-Income Households*, Manchester: Manchester University Press.

Chant, S. and Ward, P. (1987), "Family structure and low-income housing policy," *Third World Planning Review, 9*, 5–19.

Chiñas, B.L. (1973), *The Isthmus Zapotecs: Women's Roles in Cultural Context*, New York: Holt, Rinehart and Winston.

CIDAC (Centro de Investigación para el Desarrollo) (1991), *Vivienda y Estabilidad Política: Alternativas para el Futuro*, México D.F.: Editorial Diana.

Connolly, P. (1982), "Uncontrolled settlements and self-build: what kind of solution? The Mexico City case," in P.M. Ward (ed.), *Self-Help Housing: A Critique*, London: Mansell, 141–74.

COPEVI (Centro Operacional de Vivienda y Poblamiento) (1977), *Investigación sobre Vivienda II: La producción de vivienda en la Zona Metropolitana de la Ciudad de México*, México D.F.: COPEVI.

Coulomb, R. (1988), "Vivienda en renta y dinámica habitacional en la Ciudad de México," in M.A. Michel, A. Azuela, P. Connolly, R. Coulomb, G. Garza, A. Iracheta, M. Maydon, and M. Schteingart (1988), *Procesos Habitacionales en la Ciudad de México*, México D.F.: Universidad Autónoma Metropolitana- Iztapalapa y Secretaría de Desarrollo Urbano e Ecología, 141–82.

Coulomb, R. (1990), "Inquilinato y vivienda compartida en América Latina: Inquilinato en cinco colonias populares de la ciudad de México," México D.F.: Centro de Estudios de la Vivienda, mimeo.

Croll, E. (1978), "Rural China: segregation to solidarity," in P. Caplan and J.M. Bujra (eds) *Women United, Women Divided: Cross-Cultural Perspectives on Female Solidarity*, London: Tavistock, 46–76.

Croll, E. (1983), *Chinese Women Since Mao*, London: Third World Books.

Dankelman, I., and Davidson, J. (1988), *Women and Environment in the Third World: Alliance for the Future*, London: Earthscan.

Díaz-Guerrero, R. (1990), *Psicología del mexicano*, 5th ed., México D.F.: Editorial Trillas.

Dibblin, J. (1991), *Wherever I Lay My Hat: Young Women and Homelessnes*, London: Shelter.

Falú, A., and Curutchet, M. (1991), "Rehousing the urban poor: looking at women first," *Environment and Urbanization, 3*, 2, 23–38.

Fiori, J., and Ramírez, R. (1992), "Notes on the self-help housing critique: towards a conceptual framework for the analysis of self-help housing policies in developing countries," in K. Mathéy (ed.), *Beyond Self-Help Housing*, London: Mansell, 23–31.

Fonseca, C. (1991), "Spouses, siblings and sex-linked bonding: a look at kinship organization in a Brazilian slum," in E. Jelín (ed.), *Family, Household and Gender Relations in Latin America*, London: Kegan Paul International, 133–60.

Foster, G.M. (1967), *Tzintzuntzan: Mexican Peasants in a Changing World*, Boston: Little, Brown and Company.

García, B., Muñoz, H., and de Oliveira, O. (1982), *Hogares y Trabajadores en la Ciudad de México*, México D.F.: El Colegio de México.

Gilbert, A.G., and Varley, A. (1989), "From renting to self-help ownership? Residential tenure in urban Mexico since 1940," in A.G. Gilbert (ed.), *Housing and Land in Urban Mexico*, San Diego: University of California, San Diego, Center for US-Mexican Studies, 13–37.

Gilbert, A.G., and Varley, A. (1991), *Landlord and Tenant: Housing the Poor in Urban Mexico*, London: Routledge.

Gilbert, A.G., and Ward, P.M. (1985), *Housing, the State and the Poor: Policy and Practice in Three Latin American Cities*, Cambridge: Cambridge University Press.

Goetz, A.M., (1991) "Feminism and the claim to know: contradictions in feminist approaches to women in development," in R. Grant and K. Newland (eds.), *Gender and International Relations*, Buckingham: Open University Press, 133–57.

Goldani, A.M. (1990), "Changing Brazilian families and the consequent need for public policy," *International Social Science Journal, 42*, 523–37.

Golden, S. (1992), *The Women Outside: Meanings and Myths of Homelessness*, Berkeley: University of California Press.

González de la Rocha, M. (1988), "Economic crisis, domestic reorganisation and women's work in Guadalajara, Mexico," *Bulletin of Latin American Research, 7*, 207–23.

Gough, K. (1992), *From bamboo to bricks: self-help housing and the building materials industry in urban Colombia*, unpublished Ph.D. thesis, University College London.

Gross, J.J. (1978), "Marriage and 'family' among the Maya," in A.F. Marks and R.E. Römer (eds.), *Family and Kinship in Middle America and the Caribbean*, Leiden: University of the Netherlands Antilles and Royal Institute of Linguistics and Anthropology.

Hackenberg, R., Murphy, A.D., and Selby, H.A. (1984), "The urban household in dependent development," in R.McC. Netting, R.R. Wilk, and E.J. Arnould (eds.), *Households: Comparative and Historical Studies of the Domestic Group*, Berkeley: University of California Press, 187–216.

Harris, O. (1984), "Households as natural units," in K. Young, C. Wolkowitz, and R. McCullagh (eds.), *Of Marriage and the Market: Women's Subordination Internationally and its Lessons*, 2nd ed., London: Routledge and Kegan Paul, 136–55.

Hayden, D. (1981), *The Grand Domestic Revolution: A History of Feminist Designs for American Homes, Neighborhoods, and Cities*, Cambridge: M.I.T. Press.

Higgins, M.J. (1974), *Somos Gente Humilde: Etnografía de una Colonia Urbana Pobre de Oaxaca*, Mexico City: Instituto Nacional Indigenista.

Ingham, J.M. (1986), *Mary, Michael and Lucifer: Folk Catholicism in Central Mexico*, Austin: University of Texas Press.

Jelín, E. (1991a), "Family and household: outside world and private life," in E. Jelín (ed.), *Family, Household and Gender Relations in Latin America*, London: Kegan Paul International, 12–39.

Jelín E. (1991b) (ed.), *Family, Household and Gender Relations in Latin America*, London: Kegan Paul International, 12–39.

Jones, G.A. (1991), *The impact of government intervention upon land prices in Latin American cities: the case of Puebla, Mexico*, unpublished Ph.D. thesis, University of Cambridge.

Lamphere, L. (1974), "Strategies, cooperation, and conflict among women in domestic groups," in: M.Z. Rosaldo and L. Lamphere (eds.) W*oman, Culture, and Society*, Stanford: Stanford University Press, 97–112.

Larsson, A. (1988), "The housing situation of urban female-headed households in Botswana," *Habitat International, 12*, 3, 17–27.

Larsson, A. (1989), *Women Householders and Housing Strategies: The Case of Gaborone, Botswana*, Gävle, Sweden: National Swedish Institute for Building Research.

Leñero Otero, L. (1987), "Valores familiares y dramaturgia social," in: A. Hernández Medina and L. Narro Rodríguez (eds.), *Cómo somos los mexicanos*, México D.F.: Centro de Estudios Educativos (CEE), 253–99.

Levy, C. (1992), "Gender and the environment: the challenge of cross-cutting issues in development policy and planning," *Environment and Urbanization, 4*, 1, 134–49.

Lomnitz, L.A. (1977), *Networks and Marginality: Life in a Mexican Shantytown*, New York: Academic Press.

Lomnitz, L.A., and Pérez-Lizaur, M. (1991), "Dynastic growth and survival strategies: the solidarity of Mexican grand-families," in: E. Jelín (ed.), *Family, Household and Gender Relations in Latin America*, London: Kegan Paul International, 123–32.

Machado, L.M.V. (1987), "The problems for woman-headed households in a low-income housing programme in Brazil," in C.O.N. Moser and L. Peake (eds.), *Women, Human Settlements and Housing*, London: Tavistock, 55–69.

McDowell, L. (1983), "Towards an understanding of the gender division of urban space," *Environment and Planning D: Society and Space, 10*, 59–72.

McDowell, L. (1992), "Space, place and difference: a review of ten years of feminist geography," mimeo.

Mele, P. (1984), *Los Procesos de Producción del Espacio Urbano en la Ciudad de Puebla*, Puebla: Instituto de Ciencias, Universidad Autónoma de Puebla.

Merrick, T.W., and Schmink, M. (1983), "Households headed by women and urban poverty in Brazil," in: M. Buvinic, M.A. Lycette, and W.P. McGreevey (eds.), *Women and Poverty in the Third World*, Baltimore: John Hopkins University Press, 244–71.

Michel, M.A., Azuela, A., Connolly, P., Coulomb, R., Garza, G., Iracheta, A., Maydon, M., and Schteingart, M. (1988), *Procesos Habitacionales en la Ciudad de México*, México D.F.: Universidad Autónoma Metropolitana-Iztapalapa and Secretaría de Desarrollo Urbano e Ecología.

Middleton, D.R. (1991), "Development, household clusters, and work-wealth in Manta," *City and Society*, 137–54.

Miller, M. (1990), *Bed and Breakfast: Women and Homelessness Today*, London: Women's Press.

Momsen, J. (1989), Review of C.O.N. Moser and L. Peake (eds.) (1987), *Women, Human Settlements and Housing*, London: Tavistock, *Transactions, Institute of British Geographers*, N.S., *14*, 119–20.

Moser, C.O.N. (1987), "Women, human settlements, and housing: a conceptual framework for analysis and policy-making," in C.O.N. Moser and L. Peake (eds.), *Women, Human Settlements and Housing*, London: Tavistock, 12–32.

Moser, C.O.N. (1991) "Gender planning in the Third World: meeting practical and strategic needs," in R. Grant and K. Newland (eds.), *Gender and International Relations*, Buckingham: Open University Press, 83–121.

Moser, C.O.N., and Peake, L. (eds.) (1987), *Women, Human Settlements and Housing*, London: Tavistock.

Muller, M.S., and Plantenga, D. (1990), *Women and Habitat: Urban management, empowerment and women's strategies*, Amsterdam: Royal Tropical Institute.

Mulroy, E.A. (1988), *Women as Single Parents: Confronting the Institutional Barriers in the Courts, the Workplace and the Housing Market*, Dover, Mass.: Auburn House.

Munro, M., and Smith, S.J. (1989), "Gender and housing: broadening the debate," *Housing Studies, 4*, 3–17.

Nash, J.C. (1969), *Social Relations in Amatenango del Valle: An Activity Analysis*, Cuernavaca: Centro Intercultural de Documentación (CIDOC).

Nimpuno-Parente, P., (1987), "The struggle for shelter: women in a site and service project in Nairobi, Kenya," in C.O.N. Moser and L. Peake (eds.), *Women, Human Settlements and Housing*, London: Tavistock, 70–87.

Radcliffe, S.A., with Townsend, J. (1988), *Gender in the Third World: A Geographical Bibliography of Recent Work*, Brighton: Institute of Development Studies.

Rakodi, C. (1991), "Cities and people: towards a gender-aware urban planning process?," *Public Administration and Development, 11*, 541–59.

Rodda, A. (1991), *Women and the Environment*, London: Zed Books.

Rodwin, L. (ed.) (1987), *Shelter, Settlement and Development*, Boston: Allen and Unwin.

Sayne, P.L. (1991), "Food for thought: making women visible," *Environment and Urbanization, 3*, 2, 46–56.

Schlyter, A. (1988), *Women Householders and Housing Strategies: The Case of George, Zambia*, Gävle, Sweden: National Swedish Institute for Building Research.

Schlyter, A. (1989), *Women Householders and Housing Strategies: The Case of Harare, Zimbabwe*, Gävle, Sweden: National Swedish Institute for Building Research.

Schteingart, M. (1989), *Los Productores del Espacio Habitable: Estado, Empresa y Soicedad en la Ciudad de México*, México D.F.: El Colegio de México.

Selby, H.A., Murphy, A.D., and Lorenzen, S.A., with Cabrera, I., Castañeda, A., and Ruiz Love, I. (1990), *The Mexican Urban Household: Organizing for Self- Defense*, Austin: University of Texas Press.

Sharma, U. (1978), "Segregation and its consequences in India: rural women in Himachal Pradesh," in P. Caplan and J.M. Bujra (eds.), *Women United, Women Divided: Cross-Cultural Perspectives on Female Solidarity*, London: Tavistock, 259–82.

Smith, D.L. (1988), "Women and habitat: Nairobi 1985," in: W. Van Vliet (ed.), *Women, Housing and Community*, Aldershot: Avebury, 185–89.

Sontheimer, S. (ed.) (1991), *Women and the Environment: A Readerr—Crisis and Development in the Third World*, London: Earthscan.

Sprague, J.F. (1991), *More than Housing: Lifeboats for Women and Children*, Boston: Butterworth Architecture.

Stephen, L. (1991), *Zapotec Women*, Austin: University of Texas Press.

Stoner, M.R. (1988), "The plight of homeless women," in: W. Van Vliet (ed.), *Women, Housing and Community*, Aldershot: Avebury, 135–51.

Townsend, J.G. (1988), *Women in Developing Countries: A Select Annotated Bibliography for Development Organisations*, Brighton: Institute of Development Studies.

Townsend, J.G., and Momsen, J.H. (1987), "Towards a geography of gender in developing market economies," in: J.H. Momsen and J.G. Townsend (eds.), *Geography of Gender in the Third World*, 27–81.

Universidad Autónoma de Puebla, Departamento de Investigaciones Arquitectónicas y Urbanísticas del Instituto de Ciencias (DIAU-ICUAP) (1986), *Memoria de la Primera Mesa de Trabajo sobre Investigaciones Universitarias de Urbanismo*, Puebla: Universidad Autónoma de Puebla.

Vance, I. (1987), "More than bricks and mortar: women"s participation in self-help housing in Managua, Nicaragua," in: C.O.N. Moser and L. Peake (eds.), *Women, Human Settlements and Housing*, London: Tavistock, 139–65.

Van Vliet, W. (1988a), "Communities and built environments supporting women's changing roles," in: W. Van Vliet (ed.), *Women, Housing and Community*, Aldershot: Avebury, 1–5.

Van Vliet, W. (ed.) (1988b), *Women, Housing and Community*, Aldershot: Avebury.

Varley, A. (1985), *Ya somos dueños: ejido land development and regularisation in Mexico City*, unpublished Ph.D. thesis, University College London.

Varley, A. (1989), Review of L. Rodwin (ed.) (1987), *Shelter, Settlement and Development, Transactions, Institute of British Geographers*, N.S., *14*, 115–17.

Volbeda, S. (1989), "Housing and survival strategies of women in metropolitan slum areas in Brazil," *Habitat International, 13*, 3, 157–71.

Ward, P.M. (1986), *Welfare Politics in Mexico: Papering Over the Cracks*, London: Allen and Unwin.

Ward, P.M. (1990), *Mexico City: The Production and Reproduction of an Urban Environment*, London: Belhaven.

Watson, S. (1988), *Accommodating Inequality: Gender and Housing*, Sydney: Allen and Unwin.

Watson, S., with Austerberry, H. (1986), *Housing and Homelessness: A Feminist Perspective*, London: Routledge and Kegan Paul.

Wekerle, G.R. (1988), "From refuge to service center: Neighborhoods that support women," in W. Van Vliet (ed.), *Women, Housing and Community*, Aldershot: Avebury, 7–22.

Whitecotton, J.W. (1977), *The Zapotecs: Princes, Priests and Peasants*, Norman: University of Oklahoma Press.

Willis, K. (1992), "Women's work and social network use in Oaxaca City, Mexico," paper submitted for publication to the *Bulletin of Latin American Research* (mimeo).

Wilson, E. (1991), *The Sphinx in the City: Urban Life, the Control of Disorder, and Women*, London: Virago.

Wolf, A.P. (1984), "Family life and the life cycle in rural China," in R.McC. Netting, R.R. Wilk, and E.J. Arnould (eds.), *Households: Comparative and Historical Studies of the Domestic Group*, Berkeley: University of California Press, 279–98.

Wolf, M. (1974), "Chinese women: old skills in a new context," in M.Z. Rosaldo and L. Lamphere (eds.), *Woman, Culture, and Society*, Stanford: Stanford University Press, 157–72.

Youssef, N.H. and Hetler, C.B. (1983) "Establishing the economic condition of woman-headed households in the Third World: a new approach," in M. Buvinic, M.A. Lycette, and W.P. McGreevey (eds.), *Women and Poverty in the Third World*, Baltimore: John Hopkins University Press, 216–43.

Chapter 37

The Care Facility in Central Europe as a Form of Shelter: Implications for Women

Carolyn Thompson

Carolyn Thompson *is an assistant professor in the College of Architecture and Design, Kansas State University. In 1990, she was sent with three other faculty members of the college on a fact-finding tour of Central Europe to explore opportunities for exchange, professional development, and research. This paper offers some of the observations from that tour. She has a Bachelor of Arts in the History of Art from Mount Holyoke College and a Master of Architecture from Columbia University, with twelve years of professional practice in architecture and interiors.*

In November of 1990 four faculty members of the College of Architecture and Design of Kansas State University (KSU) were sent by the College to Central Europe to explore opportunities for exchange, professional development, and research. As a member of that group, among my personal interests were facilities which offer care: relatively short-term in the form of the hospital, or long-term in institutions such as orphanages or nursing homes. As the only female member of the group, I made a point of observing the status of women in the society at large, and the degree to which policy and cultural attitudes affecting them also influenced the care facility.

The classic Soviet conception of its citizens is best depicted in Social Realist art, where human forms are idealized, as in ancient classical sculpture. In this depiction of humankind, there is little place for the concept of uniqueness or diversity, which has led Western cultures to the notion that "special" populations deserve special attention, so they may participate fully in the life of the community. Many of the social developments of the last three decades in the West have dealt with the fact that economic distinctions, which Soviet regimes initially purported to remove, are not the only limitations which may hinder equality. Viewing social realist images of the family, one does not perceive, for example, the ethnic differences to which Central Europeans have clung for decades; nor does one see the traditional family roles which women are obligated to fulfill despite full-time employment; nor is it evident that many citizens of formerly Soviet regimes are physically and/or mentally disabled. The *denial* of these phenomena is painfully evident to an observer from the West, where these issues have been addressed continuously for a generation. The inattention which they have received in these formerly Soviet countries suggests that in Central Europe, as in the West, ethnics, women, and the disabled may share a common cause.

The previous Soviet regimes in the region were committed to the provision of care, for as long as possible, to anyone requiring it. In the limited exposure to these facilities which our 1990 tour provided, it seemed that there was more reliance upon the care facility than is conventional by current Western standards. Stays are longer, and confinement to such a facility seems to be the physician's solution of choice more frequently than in the West. The average stay in a Polish hospital, for example, is 28 days (Niemiatowski, 1990); such a lengthy stay could thus accord the facility the status of *shelter.* The care facility is of special concern to women, who are frequent recipients of health care services due to their reproductive capability, and because they or their children may be born with disabilities, which in these societies could confine them to an institution for the duration of their lives.

The inclusion of this paper in this conference is based on the premise that (1) the care facility in Central Europe is a form of shelter; (2) women are strongly affected by the facility and policies surrounding its delivery of services, and (3) those policies do *not* facilitate women's personal control over their bodies or their lives.

In the view of current Western concepts of care, the heavy reliance upon the care facility may be seen to contribute to a dependency that Americans, at least, would view as inconsistent with the change in economic structure that we presume to be taking place. This perception, however, may be based not on a Western vs. Eastern economic dichotomy, but rather on a European vs. American cultural one. In a 1988 article in the *Journal of Aging and Human Development* (Gelfand, 1988, 57–65), the author compares the character of German social services to those of the United States. German services, like those in Central Europe, are almost always performed by professionals, and supported by government funds, available on an *unlimited* basis. The idea of a time limit, such as one finds in the U.S., on government-supported health care to those who need it is not paramount in Germany, as it is not in countries of Central Europe.

An article describing Czech psychiatric care in the *International Social Science Journal* (Vencovsky, 1973, 547–554) mentioned no programs that were *not* the creation of the government, and none that was operated without the supervision of a psychiatrist. By contrast, women's self-help and support groups in the U.S. and chemical dependency groups, such as A.A., adamantly reject professional help. Even many federally sponsored programs in the U.S. are simply grass-roots initiatives, such as meals-on-wheels, which have eventually received funding, due to the demands of aggressive interest groups. Both illustrate a strong cultural bias toward voluntarism and community control, rather than the more traditional European assumption that the professional's decisions, whether those of physicians or planners, are always best (Gelfand, 1988, 60). To the American mind, influenced by social movements of recent years, especially feminism, this policy suggests a type of patriarchal control, however protective and benevolent, that remains basically inattentive to specific human needs.

In a recent talk to the Forum on Environmental Issues in Central Europe at KSU, Lech Klosiewicz, a Polish architect specializing in housing, demonstrated that plans for housing and population growth were conceived on a nationwide basis by planners, and implemented from above, with little consideration for micro-level issues such as the occupants' desires, or even their health. The physical organization of a certain housing estate, which Dr. Klosiewicz presented, followed a Beaux-arts formal prototype which is balanced and artful as a two-dimensional plan drawing. However, the plan in application, downwind from a factory, could not have more effectively drawn the factory's atmospheric pollutants into its inner court area, thus seriously affecting the health and comfort of the residents. This housing estate thus symbolized the frequent contextual inappropriateness of housing and health care policies on a larger scale.

Decisions concerning the location of health care facilities in Central Europe seemed also to be the product of a plan for the health care infrastructure imposed from above. This observation is confirmed by the article on Czech psychiatric care previously mentioned, in which the nation's definitive Medical Act of 1966 is described in the following terms: "(Its principles) constitute *directives for establishing the network of hospitals and health centers* .... Medical care is a fundamental duty of the State, and it must have a *scientific basis*" (Vencovsky, 1973, 548). Similarly, the network of hospitals and health centers is "scientifically" planned, which seems to mean without any interaction with user groups. Thus the Central European attitude toward care, so much a product of Soviet policy and culture, has implications which were evident in the organization of the public environment, and in the location and internal arrangement of care facilities themselves. Examples presented will follow the chronology of the tour, beginning in Poland.

1. The KSU group had the privilege of a review, provided by the Director of Design and Construction of Hospitals in Poland, of drawings and photographs of many major hospitals constructed in the nation since 1970 (Niemiatowski, 1990). This was the first evidence we encountered that many facilities were dedicated to only certain specialized functions, such as oncology, and none other, and that these facilities were limited in number, and located according to a master plan. As a consequence, patients had to travel far from home and family to receive treatment for the more serious illnesses. The holistic support that could be offered by a more general facility, and a sense of community context during treatment, were in these cases evidently not available.

The decentralized care facility, with its emphasis upon the patient remaining in the home and in her/his community—such as the community hospital, the out-patient clinic, the half-way house—seemed relatively rare in this overview of Polish hospitals. If a diagnostic test must be performed, the patient must use public transit to access a large hospital, where diagnostic and out-patient services are located near the entrance, as opposed to freestanding facilities throughout the community. Before we become complacent about the superiority of American care, we should recall that our data are drawn from our experience with the private sector. The scenario just described is not limited to Central Europe, however: it is well-known to any poor person in any large American city, who needs to use the services of the city hospital.

Reports by Dr. Charles Bascom and others of Romanian health care are similar: here antibiotic treatment is given largely by injection, not taken orally. Thus one travels to the hospital to receive several injections, which must be dispensed over six-hour intervals (Dr. Charles Bascom, KSU Student Health Services, 1991). This method of treatment, one would imagine, reinforces the dependency of the recipient upon the services of the institution; antibiotics taken orally obviously permit a patient greater control over her/his care.

2. At the Institute for Industrial Design in Warsaw, an atelier of designers of textiles and garments was composed exclusively of women. The group presented "a line" of garments for bedridden patients; the garments were designed to facilitate care-giving—the turning and moving service provided by an aide or nurse—rather than to improve the mobility of the patient. Again, the status and control of the caregiver is reinforced through design: the patient is characterized in this transaction as essentially passive.

3. The tour of Central Europe by the team from the College of Architecture and Design included many discussions with faculties of academic disciplines similar to our own—in the Department of Interiors at the Technical University of Brno, Czechoslovakia, the faculty presented a student's thesis project, which offered a view of the social context of Czech long-term care facilities. The project involved the renovation of one of the two extended care facilities for the handicapped in the entire nation. Placement in the facility obviously required separation from family and community. Physically and mentally disabled were confined to the same institution, with no recognition of their disparate needs. While the students' proposal stressed improved mobility of patients within rooms and through corridors, there was no evident intent to use the configuration of the facility to nurture independence or reintegration into society—this was evidently a setting in which patients were cared for virtually indefinitely. The absence of handicapped accessibility in the public environment at large seemed to play a major part in the retention of

persons, even those with a relatively minor disability, in these facilities.

4. Romania was not on our itinerary, but a discussion of Central European care facilities, especially with a focus upon the status of women, is not complete without reference to this country. Western journalism has recently documented the orphanages and Ceausescu's pronatalist policies, instituted in 1966, designed to increase the nation's labor force. Under the plan, each family was obliged to produce five children, contraceptive devices were impossible to obtain, and legal abortions were so limited that self-induced procedures became the norm. According to an article which used data collected in 1976, police were placed in hospitals to enforce the ruling during the first two years, causing the birthrate to increase dramatically. However, clandestine abortion procedures became so common that the birthrate eventually returned to its pre-1966 level (Moskoff, 1980, 602). This remained true until the end of the regime in 1990: thus Ceausescu's desire to increase the labor force was never realized (Kruh, August 19, 1990, 22A). One result of this policy was large numbers of normal as well as physically and mentally deficient children—often the products of unsuccessful abortion attempts—whose families could not provide for them. Their numbers included children with disabilities as minor as cleft palates and club feet, which can be corrected with current orthopedic surgical techniques. The state's solution was to create institutions to house these children. The Ceausescu regime ultimately did not have the resources to continue to maintain the facilities nor to provide adequate care—thus most of these children, even those with any initial degree of ability, languished into physical and mental deficiency.

The conditions described above received the most notable press attention in the U.S. through a feature story on *20/20* in 1990. Another example of popular although excellent coverage was a series of articles by Nancy Kruh, journalist with the Dallas *Morning News*; Kruh was sent to Romania to investigate not only the poorly maintained facilities and their residents, but the policies and social context responsible for this phenomenon. Her conclusions support the view that Ceausescu's policies imposed their greatest burden on women. To review some of her data: punishments for women convicted of having abortions consisted of fines of as much as two years' salary, or five years imprisonment.

Over the 23 years of Ceausescu's rule, some 15,000 women died of abortion complications; this estimate is considered conservative. The orphan population is now estimated at 100,000; this means that 1 in 60 Romanian children is housed in one of the 500 state-run facilities. Since conditions of life were so severe, many women would risk death rather than have another child. After the ban was lifted in 1990, deaths resulting from abortions were immediately reduced by 80%; the rate will probably be seen to decline further by the replacement of dilation and curettage by the safer technique of aspiration (Kruh, 1990).

Dr. Charles Bascom of the Student Health Service of Kansas State University has labored in the orphanages and hospitals of Romania each summer to improve facilities and to provide care as a physician. Bascom brought plumbing supplies from the U.S. to install additional showers in one orphanage; previously one shower head served 200 children (Bascom, 1992). Walter Bacon of the faculty of political science of the University of Nebraska in Omaha, and of the Midlands Aid for Romania organization, reports the current condition of these facilities since Kruh's articles and the *20/20* feature of 1990: many, but not all of the 500, have been upgraded to model institutions, at least for the time being, through assistance provided by voluntary groups such as World Vision (Bacon, 1992).

Romania's large orphan population and its conditions apparently resulted from women's inability to choose contraception, let alone abortion, but contraceptive methods, mostly supplied by relief organizations, are now more available Education in the use of the devices and the creation of a more positive attitude toward them are now being supported by the state. Still, the majority of women of child-bearing age suffer from side-effects of illegal abortions, obtained before the lifting of the ban; these complications seriously affect the methods required in the prescription of contraceptives for them (Kruh, August 24, 1990, 3C).

The earlier article, using 1976 data, asks why Ceausescu did not consider other means of increasing the labor force, employed by Romania's neighbors Czechoslovakia and Hungary, such as raising the retirement age, or positive methods of increasing the birthrate, such as substantial financial incentives for the birth of additional children, and 2 to 2 1/2 years paid maternity leave. The amount of leave permitted in 1976 in Romania was only 112 days (Minskoff, 1980, 612–613). Why, indeed, is the question: perhaps the control of human beings, particularly females, is for some individuals wielding power a far more compelling priority than the achievement of any stated objectives.

The above examples offer evidence of the rootedness of care facilities in the total approach to planning that characterized previous Central European regimes. They also suggest that the resulting concept of care itself, and the environment in which it is offered, should be re-examined in the light of policies which foster personal independence, regardless of the degree of disability. The development of living skills and the creation of sources of support and accessibility in the environment could render the services of the care facility as a provider of long-term shelter unnecessary.

References

Bacon, W., April, 1992. *Big Eight Forum on the Environment in Central Europe*, Kansas State University.

Bascom, Charles, M.D., 1992. Kansas State University Student Health Services and World Vision. Interview.

Gelfand, D.E., 1988. "Directions and Tendencies in Aging Services: A German-American Comparison." *International Journal of Aging and Human Development, 27* (1), 57–69.

Klosiewicz, L., April, 1992. *Big Eight Forum on the Environment in Central Europe*, Kansas State University.

Kruh, N., August, 1990. "Bitter Legacy: Romania Faces Tragic Effects of Ceausescu's Social Policies." The Dallas *Morning News*, August 19, 1990: 1A, 22A, 1F. August 20, 1990: 1C, 10C. August 21, 1990: 1C, 10C. August 22, 1990: 1C, 7C. August 23, 1990: 1C, 3C. August 24, 1990: 1C, 3C.

Moskoff, W., April, 1980. "Pronatalist Policies in Romania." *Journal of Economic Development and Cultural Change, 28* (3): 597–614.

Niemiatowski, Z., 1990, Director, Biuro Studiow I Projektow Sluzby Zdrowia. Warsaw, Poland. Interview.

Vencovsky, E., 1973. "Some Aspects of Psychiatric Care in Czechoslovakia." *International Social Science Journal, 25* (4): 547–54.

Chapter 38
Young Mothers and Affordable Housing: Information and Organization for Change

Valerie L. du Plessis

Valerie L. du Plessis *is a master's student in International Rural Development Planning at the University School of Rural Planning and Development, University of Guelph in Canada. Her thesis is entitled "Young Mothers and Affordable Housing: Information and Organization for Change." She is the Assistant Coordinator for the University of Guelph Women and Development Subcommittee, Chair of the Graduate Student Gender Relations Committee, and a member of the university's Advisory Committee on Sexual Harassment. She has a Bachelor of Arts and highest honors in Geography and Religion from Carleton University, Ottawa, Canada.*

"Accessing Information for Young Mothers" (AIYM) is a group of young mothers living in the Region of Halton, Ontario, Canada, who want to improve their access to quality, affordable housing. Since its formation in 1989, AIYM has provided young mothers in the Region with personal and practical support. Under the age of 25, mostly single, and living on limited incomes, members have educated one another about ways to find affordable rental housing, helped each other fill out application forms for subsidized housing, and accompanied each other to agency appointments. To increase awareness of community services, members have developed a "Helpful Resources List" that includes phone numbers for parent-child centers, government and non-profit children and family services, credit counseling, emergency food, employment services, housing services, legal aid, and social assistance. To improve their understanding of regional housing issues and realities, members interviewed representatives of the Halton Region Housing Authority in February, 1990, and surveyed 40 young mothers in local shopping centers in June, 1990. AIYM has shared the information gained through these initiatives at presentations to young mothers' groups and service providers.

Currently, the group is completing an initiative called the "Low Income Solvation Project" that links the issues of young mothers' housing and health. Through this initiative, Halton young mothers are learning about the relationship between the cost and quality of their housing and health, and discussing ways to improve their situations by working together. This Project combines four processes: documenting and analyzing young mothers' housing situations, organizing on a regional basis, working with service providers, and initiating collaborative community planning to address young mothers' needs. This paper is an integration of ideas raised in the context of the young mothers' initiative with issues discussed in the literature on women and housing.

In the first part of this paper, context, content, and process of AIYM's Project are explained. Highlighted is the fact that the young mothers' initiative represents a very innovative and promising strategy for addressing non-traditional household needs. The important connections that AIYM's Project makes between housing conditions, gender issues, personal, community, and regional development are stressed. In the second part, the contributions of AIYM's work to international discourse on women and housing in three areas: theory, project design, and research are discussed. It is important to emphasize that AIYM's Project is still in progress. Consequently, this discussion is preliminary rather than comprehensive or complete.

Part I: AIYM's "Low Income Solvation Project"

We are going to gather real information about the housing needs of young mothers in Halton and build an organization of young mothers concerned about affordable housing. This organization will be a group that can meet formally with service providers and community members to solve affordable housing problems for young mothers and examine other health/support needs as identified by the mothers (AIYM, 1990b:3).

Regional Context

With a population of over 300,000, the Region of Halton covers an area of 960 square kilometers in the Greater Toronto Area of southern Ontario, Canada. Within the Region, there are four area municipalities: the towns of Milton and Halton Hills in the north, and the cities of Burlington and Oakville in the south.

In aggregate terms the Region is wealthy. According to the 1986 Canada Census, the median household income in Halton was almost 25% higher than the corresponding Provincial median. Social service providers and low-income residents find that this aggregate wealth "... leads to an assumption [by local politicians] that Halton doesn't need services" (AIYM, 1992:1). In reality, however, the Region's wealth is not distributed evenly. For example, although the number of women and men reporting income in 1986 was relatively close, the median male income was just over 60% higher than the median female income. Among female income earners, almost 70% earned less than CDN $20,000[1], as compared to 35% of male income earners. Also, 16% of families were living in poverty[2] (Statistics Canada, 1986). In 1986, 9% of families in the Region were led by single parents. This represents a 72% growth in the number of lone-parent families since 1976. Approximately 80% of these families were headed by females (Statistics Canada, 1986). According to Halton District Health Council, 60% of the 302 unmarried mothers who gave birth in 1989 were between the ages of 13 and 24 (AIYM, 1992:1).

The Region's housing stock is dominated by ownership units and low-density housing designed for traditional families. In 1986 almost three-fourths of all units were owned and almost two-thirds were single-family detached houses (The Starr Group, 1991a). Costs in both the rental and ownership markets are high. How-

ever, while vacancy rates are healthy in the ownership market (4% in 1988), they are nonexistent in the rental market (0% in 1988) (Halton Regional Information Systems Committee, as quoted by The Starr Group, 1991a). Despite high costs and a low rental vacancy rate, there has been almost no development of private low-cost housing in recent years (Kendrick, 1987; The Starr Group, 1991b). Furthermore, local politicians have not shown leadership in addressing the lack of low-cost housing. Instead, they have actively supported upscale residential development designed for high-income families (McFadden, 1990).

Project Origin and Rationale

The roots of AIYM's "Low Income Solvation Project" are in young mothers' experiences of the affordable housing crisis in the Region of Halton. For example, of the 40 Halton young mothers AIYM surveyed in June 1990, 80% were paying over 50% of their income on rent; 36% were paying more than 70% of their income on rent (AIYM, 1992:1). Constantly faced with difficulties obtaining quality, affordable housing and discouraged by a lack of political commitment to the issue, AIYM members developed the Project because they wanted "... to take some action to improve [their] situation and that of others like [them]" (AIYM, 1990a).

Their Project is based on the rationale that housing is an important issue for young mothers, that it is central to their lives, and that there are significant links between young mothers' housing situations and their health. In its Project Proposal, AIYM explains

... that without quality, affordable housing the health of young mothers and their families is at risk. The cost of housing, characteristics of the home environment and housing location can impact on both physical and emotional health. For some young mothers, the cost of housing absorbs more than 70% of monthly income, leaving few funds for other basic needs including food. Other young mothers are living in homes in need of major repair, with inadequate heating, ventilation or poor insulation. Also, some young mothers are living in homes that are located near polluting industries, in isolated areas or areas with high crime rates ... these factors can ... [also impact] on self-esteem, if a young mother is embarrassed about her living situation or if she feels that she is not adequately providing for her family (AIYM, 1991:1).

Project Approach and Participants

While the origin and rationale of AIYM's "Low Income Solvation Project" are grounded in young mothers' housing problems, the group's collaborative Project approach builds on and supports the young mothers' ability to find creative solutions. The "Low Income Solvation Project" is a young mothers' initiative. A core group of AIYM members initiated and designed the Project, facilitating the participation of larger numbers of young mothers in Project implementation. At the same time, part of AIYM's strategy was to involve a broad base of community members to increase awareness of, and to get assistance with, their work. More specifically, the group invited and established collaborative relationships with local service providers, planners, and policy-makers; housing and community development activists and consultants; as well as planning and social work students. To varying degrees, a total of over 150 young mothers, 15 local decision-makers, 2 activists and consultants, and 4 university students have participated in the Project.

In meeting and working together, young mothers from across the Region have recognized and supported each other as organizers, surveyors, advisors, leaders, friends, and resource people. They have developed each other's research, networking, communication, and presentation skills. Furthermore, by facilitating work with a broad base of community members, AIYM has created a unique opportunity for mutual learning and sharing of ideas, knowledge, and experience across sectors, as well as between professional and academic fields.

Project Funding and Budget

Funding for the Project was provided by the Ontario Ministry of Health through its Health Promotion Grants Program. More specifically, AIYM was awarded a one-time-only grant of CDN $10,000. Since AIYM is not an incorporated body, it required a Project sponsor. The Halton Social Planning Council accepted this role, which included receiving and administering the funds on AIYM's behalf. The consultants have supported AIYM in its relationship with the Project's sponsor by assisting with bookkeeping and negotiations. In addition, the university students have helped AIYM complete monthly progress reports required as part of the funding agreement.

The most important budget items were transportation, day care and honoraria for young mothers. AIYM allocated over 80% of the Project budget to these three expenses, which enabled and supported young mothers' participation. All the young mothers involved in key

Project positions have limited incomes. By covering the costs of transportation and day care, the Project did not tax their personal and family resources. Moreover, by providing honoraria for time spent organizing and surveying, the Project contributed to the young mothers' incomes. Whenever possible, AIYM hired young mothers to provide Project-related day care as a way of maximizing income opportunities. By providing these supports, AIYM respected young mothers' practical interests. By meeting these needs, the group enhanced the opportunity for young mothers to work together to address their common strategic interests.

Project Design and Implementation

The goal of the Project is to work with young mothers in the Region of Halton to generate information necessary for young mothers to better understand their housing situations and health related risks, as well as to start to change their situations in ways that improve their health status. This includes increasing young mothers' skills and confidence to find solutions by working together (AIYM, 1991:3).

To meet this goal, AIYM planned, and is currently implementing, four interrelated activities:

1. a region-wide survey of young mothers,
2. presentations to young mothers' groups,
3. meetings with local service providers, and
4. a public workshop to begin identifying strategies for change.

Together these activities combine participatory education, group building, and action aimed at improving young mothers' situations. More specifically, the survey is contributing to a new definition and analysis of the Region's affordable housing problem grounded in young mothers' experiences. At the same time, it is increasing young mothers' awareness and understanding of their situations and needs, as well as their opportunities for action. Through presentations to groups, young mothers are organizing and networking, sharing their knowledge, discussing issues of importance, and building skills, self-confidence, and self-esteem. By working with local service providers and publicly presenting Project results, young mothers are adding their voices to regional politics. They are introducing AIYM as an organization of young mothers able to work on its own, and in cooperation with other community groups, to identify and address specific housing and related health interests and needs. Moreover, they are initiating a long-term community planning process aimed at resolving the problems identified. Implementation of each Project activity is explained and discussed below:

Young Mothers' Survey

The central activity in AIYM's "Low Income Solvation Project" is a Region-wide survey of young mothers designed to document young mothers' housing situations and the impacts of housing costs and conditions on personal and family health. More than ten young mothers helped to develop, pretest, and finalize survey questions. Two questionnaires were prepared: a long version with 96 questions for distribution in group situations, and a short version with 16 questions for individuals.

The survey begins with an affirming message and question concerning young mothers' accomplishments, both of which recognize and emphasize the importance of young mothers' efforts. In addition to questions concerning personal information (marital status, age, number of children, income), physical housing conditions (utilities, repair and maintenance, relationship with landlord, etc.), security and location (personal safety, location, etc.), the long survey addresses interpersonal dynamics within the home environment, including mother/child relationships, issues of abuse, sources of stress, and assistance from co-residents in the areas of meal preparation, dishes, transportation, emotional and financial support. While identifying young mothers' housing and health problems, the survey also records young mothers' ideas and strategies for improving their situations. On the one hand, the survey documents young mothers' knowledge and use of community support services, such as the women's shelter, food banks, legal aid, parent child centers, rent review, and life skills groups. On the other hand, it addresses young mothers' interest in working to together to access better, more affordable housing, and day care.

Ten young mothers were trained as Project Assistants to distribute the survey in their local areas. Also, two young mothers provided baby-sitting services. Surveys were distributed at a local shopping mall, among friends, and during presentations to young mothers' groups (the second Project activity). Each strategy involved direct dialogue and interaction between the surveyors and respondents and provided the opportunity for survey respondents to learn about AIYM and the Project. In total, AIYM surveyed 141 Halton young mothers, completing 62 long and 79 short surveys. Currently, the group is working on data analysis.

Presentations to Young Mothers' Groups

Presentations to young mothers' groups form the second Project activity. To date, (May, 1992) AIYM has completed eleven presentations: two at social events organized by local community groups, three during prenatal and postnatal classes offered by Halton Adolescent Support Services, and six to Teen Education and Motherhood (TEAM) classes, a high school program run by the Halton Board of Education.

In addition to their function as an important survey strategy, these presentations have supported group building. At every presentation, AIYM's coordinator and one of the Project Assistants or a university student have introduced AIYM and the "Low Income Solvation Project" and responded to questions. They have distributed AIYM's "Helpful Resources List" and invited each participant to complete a survey. At the end of every session, the presenters have explained the opportunities for further involvement in AIYM's work and facilitated a discussion about the survey process by asking general, open-ended questions, such as: "What did you think of the survey?" "What issues are most important?" "What is housing like in your area?"

These discussion sessions have been important occasions for open dialogue and learning. Examples of issues raised by presentation participants include child custody issues, sexual abuse, use of drugs and alcohol, the cost of day care, and the importance of free day care provided by Halton's Teen Education and Motherhood (TEAM) Program. One young mother talked about the double prejudice she faced in her community, first because she was a young mother, and second because her child was a different race from her own. Another young mother felt very strongly that housing for young mothers (subsidized housing) was built "way out in the middle of nowhere," on the edge of the city, because "the public considers young mothers to be a bad influence" and wants to keep them out of sight. Other housing issues discussed included tenants' legal rights and the poor condition of housing accessible to young mothers. At every presentation, young mothers emphasized that there was a lack of quality, affordable housing in their area.

Meetings with Service Providers

The third activity is to build an interactive relationship with Halton service providers by inviting them to participate in the Project as resource people, and keeping them informed about Project progress and results. At the start of the Project, AIYM established a Public Advisory Committee, including local service providers, planners and policy-makers from the Board of Education, Adolescent Support Services, Social Planning Council, Children's Aid Society, Children's Services, Parent-Child Centers, District Health Council, and Regional Health Department. The committee has met four times to provide advice regarding survey content, give feedback on Project progress, and support AIYM in solving problems of survey distribution and analysis. Also, the young mothers have contacted individual members on an informal basis at various times during the Project to get input on particular Project tasks.

In addition to their encouragement and suggestions, Public Advisory Committee members have made a number of other contributions to the "Low Income Solvation Project," such as providing Regional statistics, contacts for local groups and services, office space, and access to computers for data input and analysis. Also, a number of the members are helping to organize the public workshop.

Public Workshop

This event was planned for the end of May, 1992. AIYM invited all the young mothers who have been involved in the Project, including Project Assistants, baby-sitters and survey respondents, as well as local service providers, planners and policy makers, local politicians and the public to participate. AIYM hoped to engage everyone who attended in small group discussions about the results and to involve everyone in making recommendations about future action.

AIYM's Coordinator understands this public workshop to be the first stage in a longer-term community planning and action process. Groups were to leave the presentation with the survey results and ideas that they could discuss further over the summer. In September, a second meeting was to be planned in which the groups could come together, share their individual plans for action, and work together to develop a community plan of action. In this way, while representing the final event in the "Low Income Solvation Project," the May meeting was to launch a new and important Regional planning process.

Significance of the Young Mothers' Strategy

Young mothers living in unaffordable housing are typically the objects rather than the initiators, organizers, and owners of housing research. For young mothers in

the Region of Halton, AIYM's "Low Income Solvation Project" is the exception to this rule. Consequently, its significance stems from both content and process. To begin with, the "Low Income Solvation Project" is expanding young mothers' understanding of their housing situations and available services. To the extent that knowledge is power, AIYM is creating a unique source of power for young mothers in the Region, a quantitative and qualitative data base about their housing and health realities. One of the Project's products will be the first Regional analysis of young mother's housing situation. This analysis will provide a new perspective on housing needs, one that reflects the young mothers' housing experiences.

By combining knowledge creation with organizational development, AIYM is increasing young mothers' skills and confidence to take action to improve their situations. In particular, the Project is enhancing young mothers' research, networking, communication, and presentation abilities. At the same time, it is contributing to young mothers' experience as community organizers and planners. AIYM has strengthened the significance of its work for local service providers by involving these decision-makers in Project implementation. This initiative has been a unique opportunity for mutual learning and sharing of ideas, knowledge, and experience among a broad spectrum of people: young mothers, university students, consultants, local service providers, and decision-makers. Moreover, it has introduced an important model for community collaboration and increased the possibility that young mothers and service providers will be able to work together to address young mothers' housing and related health needs in the future.

Part II: Contributions to Women and Housing Discourse

> Women's mobilization for improved habitat and human settlements symbolizes new directions for the development process (Carlson and Bhagat, 1985:1).

My objective here is to initiate dialogue between AIYM's Project and international literature on women and housing. What can the international community learn from the young mothers' housing initiative? What new directions in theory, Project design, and research are these young mothers pointing to? It is important to recognize the limitations of this dialogue. To begin with, it is at best introductory. As already explained, AIYM's Project is still in progress. Some of the most interesting parts, including the young mothers' analysis of the survey data and the public workshop, are not yet complete. Furthermore, it is only a brief dialogue based on selective references to the literature.

Theory: Women's Housing and Human Settlement Needs

Within the international literature, women's housing and human settlement needs are conceptualized as specific, diverse, and changing. Two main arguments are presented in support of the idea that women have gender-specific housing and human settlement needs. The first states that, because women generally control fewer resources than men, they have different experiences, interests, and needs within human settlement systems. For example, with lower incomes than their male counterparts, women have greater problems in rental and ownership housing markets. This is particularly true for women in the Region of Halton. As noted earlier, there is a 60% wage income difference between the median female and male income earner. All the women participating in AIYM's initiative live on limited incomes. Affordability is one of their key housing concerns.

The second argument states that women's specific housing and human settlement needs arise from their gender-specific roles and responsibilities (Moser, 1987). Most often referred to are women's roles as mothers, income earners, or farmers, and community organizers. The majority of the women participating in AIYM's initiative have the triple role and accompanying responsibilities of single mothers, income earners, and active community participants. In addition, most of the young mothers are high school students. This fourth role, which is not focused on in the literature, is critical to their personal development, relationships with peers, and their futures. The significance of being students is evident in the survey questionnaire. For example, the question related to housing location addresses proximity not only to jobs and support services, but also to schools (see Table 1).

The theme of diversity relates to the fact that "women" is not a unitary category. For example, single parents and married women, elderly and young women, as well as women of different cultures and ethnic groups do not all share the same needs. Similarly, women's needs vary with context, between countries as well as rural and urban areas (Wekerle, 1990; Sorock et al., 1984). During survey pretesting, AIYM learned that "young mothers" is not a unitary category either. For example, respondents who were expecting their first child voiced special concerns. They emphasized that pregnancy is a traumatic experience for single teenagers. In need of extra personal support and assistance preparing for their first child, they are often rejected by their family and peers. Asked to leave their parents' home, they enter the housing market for the first time. Their needs for timely, supportive, affordable housing are different from those of a young mother who has experience finding rental accommodation and who is not in the midst of a crisis.

In addition to being gender-specific and diverse, women's housing needs are changing. Since women's lives are dynamic, their needs change over time. For example, the same woman, as a youth, adult, and elderly individual, will have different housing needs. Similarly, a women who is divorced has different housing needs from those when she was married. For young mothers, housing needs can change frequently and quickly, as job status or location changes, as relationships with boyfriends or common-law husbands are formed or ended, and as their children's needs change. One implication seems to be that young mothers move frequently. Therefore, AIYM's work enhances the conceptualization of women's housing needs as specific, diverse, and changing. While providing a young mother's perspective on the issues in general, it makes visible young mothers' student responsibilities in particular.

Project Design: Enabling Women's Participation

> Whatever the objectives of participation, ultimately it is a question of who is participating and the accessibility of a project to a target population, that determines the extent to which real participation occurs (Moser, 1987:15).

Most of the international literature on women's participation in housing focuses on construction or upgrading projects. The Halton young mothers' housing initiative provides a unique example of a community planning and research project. Initiated by young mothers for young mothers, AIYM's Project is very sensitive to issues of accessibility. As discussed earlier, over 80% of the budget was allocated to transportation, day care, and honoraria. Clearly, the Project values young mothers' participation and respects their need for these very practical supports. Transportation, day care, and honoraria received high priority because the organizers were young mothers whose own participation required these supports.

Research: A Process Agenda

At the end of the International Year of Shelter for the Homeless, seventy women representing thirteen countries and two liberation movements met in Zimbabwe for the Harare Seminar on Women and Shelter. The first and most important priority identified by consensus and unanimity at this African regional meeting was women's need for information to understand and change their shelter situation. The Seminar focused attention on the inadequacies of information on women and shelter, specifically the lack of data disaggregated by gender and researchers' assumptions about households that seldom take into account women's perspectives. Seminar participants agreed that the key to producing new data relevant and useful to women at the local level is to focus on the process of data collection. More specifically, they emphasized the need for women to set research priorities, define data categories, and assess the results of shelter research and development (Smith, 1990).

AIYM's "Low Income Solvation Project" is a housing research initiative designed and implemented by Halton young mothers with the goal of understanding and changing their housing situations. Young mothers living in unaffordable housing set the research priorities and implemented a survey process. Currently, they are analyzing the results. While representing an important example of the Harare research model, AIYM's Project contributes a new dimension. In addition to being participatory, AIYM's work is collaborative, involving a broad base of community representatives. By involving local decision-makers as advisors and resource people, AIYM has gained community support for its work and increased the possibility that young mothers and service providers will be able to work together to solve the needs identified.

Conclusions

AIYM's "Low Income Solvation Project" is an important example of women in non-traditional households organizing for improved housing and human settlements. The Project represents the first step in a long-term collaborative community planning and action process to address young mothers' needs. As a strategy for change, it combines participatory education, group building, and public involvement. The content of AIYM's work links the young mothers' housing and health issues while the process enhances personal, community, and regional development.

AIYM's work to date contributes an understanding of housing and human settlements needs from a young mothers' perspective. Young mothers' needs relate to their low incomes, multiple responsibilities, and to their differing life experiences. As teenagers and young adults, the needs of community acceptance, personal support, and opportunities for growth are also crucial. With respect to Project design, the young mothers' sensitivity and commitment to Project accessibility indicates the significance of combining the roles of participant and organizer. Also, AIYM's work adds an important community dimension to the participatory research model.

Notes

[1] To convert Canadian currency to the US$ equivalent, reduce the Canadian amount by 15%. In this case the equivalent figure is US $17,000.

[2] The definition of poverty used here was an annual income of less than CDN $25,000 for a family of four.

References

AIYM. 1990a. Cover Letter to the Ontario Ministry of Health, Health Promotion Grant Program Application. September 28, 1990. Accessing Information for Young Mothers. Region of Halton, Ontario.

AIYM. 1990b. The Low Income Solvation Project Proposal. November 20, 1990. Prepared for the Ontario Ministry of Health, Health Promotion Grants Program. Accessing Information for Young Mothers. Region of Halton, Ontario.

AIYM. 1991. Final Revisions to the Low Income Solvation Project Proposal. March 20, 1991.

Correspondence with the Ontario Ministry of Health, Health Promotion Branch. Accessing Information for Young Mothers. Region of Halton, Ontario.

AIYM. 1992. Opportunity Planning Project Proposal. April 16, 1992. Prepared for the Ontario Ministry of Social Services Opportunity Planning Pilot Projects. Accessing Information for Young Mothers. Region of Halton, Ontario.

Carlson, Eric and Susheila Bhagat (eds.). 1985. *Housing and Economic Development: A Women's Perspective.* Report of a Symposium organized by the Working Group on Housing and Shelter of the Committee on Development. Conference of NGO's in Consultative Status with UN/ECOSOC. Non-governmental Liaison Service. United Nations. New York.

Kendrick, Robert. 1987. *Affordable Housing in Burlington.* Halton Social Planning Council. Region of Halton, Ontario.

McFadden, Jeff. 1990. "Who can afford to buy house in Burlington?," *The Burlington Post.* January 17. Burlington, Ontario.

Moser, Caroline. 1987. "Women, human settlements, and housing: a conceptual framework for analysis and policy-making," in Moser, Caroline and Linda Peake (eds.). 1987. *Women, Human Settlement and Housing.* New York: Monthly Review Press.

Smith, Diana Lee. 1990. "Women and Shelter in Africa." Lecture given on January 29. University of Toronto. Toronto, Ontario.

Sorock, Margery, *et al.* 1984. "Women and Shelter," Occasional Paper Series. Washington: Office of Housing and Urban Programs, Agency for International Development.

The Starr Group. 1991a. *The Region of Halton Municipal Housing Statement: Demand and Supply.* Preliminary Draft for Discussion. February. Region of Halton, Ontario.

The Starr Group. 1991b. *The Region of Halton Municipal Housing Statement: Creating and Sustaining Balanced Residential Communities—Recommended Policies and Strategies.* Preliminary Draft for Discussion. May. Region of Halton, Ontario.

Statistics Canada. Census 1986. Ottawa, Canada.

Wekerle, Gerda. 1990. "Women and Housing: A Research Agenda." *Canadian Women Studies.* 11(2), 66–67.

Theme 8
Design and the Creation of Shelter for Women

Photo: Hemalata C. Dandekar

Professor Donna Salzer, who was the faculty moderator for this theme and brought to it needed energy and vision, died suddenly in October 1992. This theme is dedicated to Donna.

Historically, cultural and religious perspectives on the status and position of women have produced distinct typological, functional, and even stylistic solutions in the domestic architecture of various civilizations. In western societies, despite the growing literature on women's issues, women's perspectives and needs have tended to be excluded from the core of architectural theory and practice. Yet recent social and economic changes have resulted in urgent problems that call for immediate architectural solutions. These may, and perhaps should, require a fundamental rethinking of the power relationships that exist within the family, particularly those that are based on gender. The above observations are elaborated in the papers in this theme through examples from South Asia and the United States. Mangana provides an overview of the papers and a context for this discourse. Chowdhury delineates the limits of the public domain that rural, Muslim women in northwest Bangladesh are privy to and the ways in which this shapes the articulation of their private space within the house. Bhatt illustrates, through a case study of a low-income settlement from South India, the importance to women of the particular configuration of public or common space. The need of female-headed, single-parent families for housing that will provide protection, security, safety, and a homelike appearance is addressed by Sprague, who offers an approach to designing appropriate solutions. Follenweider, drawing on the revisioning by women writers of myth and archetype in literature, calls for a reconceptualization of house design to answer women's need for sacred space. Silverman and Taylor echo this theme. In poetic form they call for a redefinition of shelter.

Chapter 39
Design and the Creation of Shelter for Women: An Overview

Vassiliki Mangana

Vassiliki Mangana *is a candidate in the Ph.D. program in Architecture at the University of Michigan. She received her Diploma in Architecture from Aristotle University in Thessaloniki, Greece, and her Master of Architecture from the University of California, Los Angeles. Her area of study is history and her research topic centers on the History of Urbanism with Thessaloniki, Greece, as a thematic case study.*

As the considerable body of work produced in theoretical writings on women's issues has shown since the nineteenth century, various cultural, political, and economic aspects of contemporary societies reflect assumptions that have often failed to consider the nature of women's needs. Architectural theory and design, produced primarily by male theorists and practitioners, have traditionally accepted such assumptions and reproduced them especially in the morphology, typology, and spatial arrangement of domestic architecture. However, as the papers on the theme *Design and the Creation of Shelter for Women* indicate, due to recent social developments and a new theoretical orientation of scholars from various fields (architecture, urban planning, anthropology, sociology, etc.), women's issues are beginning to appear in architectural research programs.

The influence of theories focusing on women's issues on both urban and housing design is not new. Since the nineteenth century, various branches of feminist discourse have approached the question of women's position and role in society from different points of view. "Socialist feminists," for instance, "saw the dominance of men over women and class politics as acting together in the oppression of women, whereas radical feminists argued that male dominance formed the motor force behind women's subordination from which all men, of whatever class, benefited."[1] Women from minority groups, on the other hand, have advanced such issues as cultural conventions and religious requirements[2] as the primary sources in which the oppression of women originate. This approach could be viewed as introducing a distinction between the problems that constitute the main concerns of women in the First and the Third Worlds. Sexuality has been another issue which has determined yet a different approach to the women's movement. Some lesbian women "see a society which values heterosexual relations to the exclusion of all others as being intensely problematic ..." while others "see themselves as placed more firmly within a socialist tradition which places an emphasis on class."[3]

The above approaches to women's issues, to which many more can be added, constitute theoretical positions that seek not only to explicate the problems of women in contemporary societies but also to question conventional cultural practices and norms, the effects of modern economy and politics and even the traditional arrangement of family life. They could, therefore, be viewed as having an at least implicit effect on the physical, architectural form of housing. However, there have also been other feminist movements, based on the technological advancements and economic developments of the late nineteenth and early twentieth century, which succeeded in revolutionizing domestic environments. Such is, for instance, the case of the material feminists. As described by Hayden, the material feminists "demanded economic remuneration for women's unpaid household labor. They proposed a complete transformation of the spatial design and material culture of American homes, neighborhoods, and cities. While other feminists campaigned for political and social change with philosophical and moral arguments, the material feminists concentrated on economic and spatial issues as the basis of material life."[4]

As a general comment, then, it could be said that much of feminist discourse has focused on theoretical and pragmatic proposals that could transform gender assumptions, social conditions, cultural norms, and stereotypical images of women, and could subsequently change the form of urban spaces and houses to serve the particular needs of specific groups of women. The papers on the theme *Design and the Creation of Shelter for Women*, however, are characterized by a different orientation: rather than proposing new approaches to architectural design as a means to satisfy women's material/pragmatic needs, they argue for an architecture that reflects the special qualities of women's inner world and consequently represents their true being. As Professor Donna Salzer argued, in her summary of the design theme, the papers of this panel "ask that we look at alternative ways of inhabiting, ... that we consider how women occupy space differently than the much generalized and standardized western dwellings might imply."[5]

The first two papers on the Design theme focus on case studies from the developing countries and examine "how women ... occupy housing—the way in which forms are created specifically in response to women's way of using and inhabiting spaces."[6] Reporting on an organically grown settlement (slum) in Bangalore, India, Neema Bhatt in her paper "The Socio-Economic Impact of Open Spaces on Women in a Spontaneous Settlement" examines the role of open and semi-closed spaces attached to the main housing unit and their beneficial effect on the psychological and economic well-being of women.[7] In another paper entitled "Segregation of Women in Islamic Societies and Its Effects on Rural Housing Design: Bangladesh," Tasneem Chowdhury deals with the elaborate system of spatial separation that has developed in a rural community as a reflection of the

cultural and religious (Islamic) requirements of gender segregation. Those requirements, Chowdhury argues, have produced a distinct, secondary network of communication for the exclusive use of women, in addition to a variety of typological and morphological characteristics in the design of housing. Along with the strict principles of women's segregation, however, economic considerations constitute a significant issue: while the poverty that the local population faces has become a source for creative solutions, it also constitutes a considerable restriction often preventing women from following the rules determined by their religion and culture.

The first group of papers clearly notes the need for future research to focus on the analysis of the specific socio-economic and cultural contexts in the developing countries and to examine their implications on the design of housing and its main consumers: the female population. Yet a second group of papers primarily dealing with recent social developments introduces actual and urgent problems that have begun to emerge in the United States and require immediate solutions. The increasing percentages of single women heading households,[8] and the issue of homelessness of women often resulting from purely economic reasons but also from domestic violence, alcohol, and drug abuse, are some of the problems that describe an actual social crisis for which theoretical inquiry and architectural explorations should provide answers.

As Joan Forrester Sprague notes in her paper "Women and Shelter-Related Services and Infrastructure," a variety of housing types has already begun to develop in response to the above needs. Those types which Sprague calls "lifeboat" housing can be categorized as emergency, transitional, and permanent housing and have taken various architectural forms. In her description of a wide variety of such institutional shelters throughout the United States, Sprague notes that an essentially communitarian aspect characterizes everyday life in lifeboat housing. Beyond the conventional four zones of use (personal, household, community, neighborhood), she argues, lifeboats incorporate two additional ones: "one between household and community and another between community and neighborhood."[9]

Institutional housing that is often created by particular communities constitutes a solution that can considerably assist women in crisis and even, as Sprague mentions, transform and save their lives.[10] Yet the architectural expression and the aesthetic value of such shelter, resulting from unimaginative designs and the strict adherence to existing building codes and standards remain unresolved problems. This is the issue on which the three final presentations on the Design theme focus.

In her presentation "Redefining Standards: Toward a Positive Ambivalence," Kim Tanzer dealt with a project for a shelter for battered women. Through a comparative analysis of the project as conceived and implemented, she discusses two types of changes that the initial design underwent during the stage of its execution: (1) the transformation of unconventional heights to standardized ones, and (2) the removal of its protective layers (built in shelves and cabinets, tongue and groove interior siding, porches, built in benches[11]). While questioning the validity of existing architectural norms and standards for the design of transitional housing for women in her analysis, Tanzer also argues "for an architecture which could accommodate intimacy, protection, security, and home-like qualities."[12]

Another paper dealing with the issue of aesthetics and architectural expression in transitional housing is that of Mary Follenweider. In "Language, Sacred and Transitional Housing," approaching her topic from a theoretical point of view, Follenweider argues for a feminist aesthetic that should be tactile, physical, erotic, spiritual, mediative, mystical. A new architectural language expressive of such qualities and endowed with the elements of the sacred, she argues, is conceivable and could become particularly important for the design of transitional housing because "it [could] provide the means by which new kinds of lives may facilitate new kinds of structures as a real force of change ... [and could] also connect individuals to the greater universal myth of human existence."[13]

The final paper of the Design theme, "Shelter: a Place of the Telling, A Chimerical Cookbook," by Tamy Silverman and Chris Taylor, seeks to extend and generalize the discourse on housing for women by focusing on the question of shelter as such. The objective of transforming conventional conceptions of shelter by including heterogeneous, subjective, unthematized views and experiences constitutes a central theme in this work. "Through this paper" Taylor and Silverman write, " we hope to define shelter in terms which extend beyond the limits of accommodation and begin to deal with issues of place involving the individual and the personal within society."[14] The cookbook as a conventional form able to contain dissimilar elements and chimera as the female myth being able to accommodate and transform the real and the phantastic become the metaphors through which women are brought into the center of a reconsidered notion of shelter.

A common objective that seems to characterize at least the second group of papers is the need for the architecture of transitional and single-female-parent family housing to be expressive of such homelike qualities as intimacy, protection, security, safety. These qualities that seem to serve the special needs of women could also be related to the notion of dwelling as it is discussed by Martin Heidegger. "The fundamental character of dwelling," Heidegger argues, "is ... [the] sparing and preserving."[15] "Real sparing," he continues, " is something *positive* and takes place when we leave something beforehand in its own nature, when we return it specifically to its being, when we 'free' it in the real sense of the word into a preserve of space."[16]

Building for oppressed women, then, should produce spaces that allow them to dwell and subsequently provide the preconditions that will lead to the emergence of their true being. This abstract requirement, however, should not be viewed as limiting the architectural project. The sociologist Georg Simmel has noted that "insofar as the woman lies beyond both of these tendencies—which are actually eccentric, that of sensual desire and transcendent form—she might even be described as the authentic 'human being', as the being which is situated in the human in the most unqualified sense."[17] The creation of an architecture expressive of such qualities as safety, protection, stability, and homeliness that the authors in this panel advocate, not only will contribute to accomplishing a significant social mission, but will also provide the means by which the true nature of women's being and, through it, the true nature of the being of human kind in general can emerge.

Notes

[1] Marion Roberts, *Living in a Man-Made World , Gender Assumptions in Modern Housing Design*, London: Routledge, 1991, p. 2

[2] See M. Roberts, *Living*, p. 2

[3] M. Roberts, *Living*, p. 3

[4] Dolores Hayden, *The Grand Domestic Revolution: A History of Feminist Designs for American Homes, Neighborhoods, and Cities*, Cambridge, MA: MIT Press, 1982, p. 1

[5] Donna Salzer, Theme Summaries and Future Directions, International Conference: *Shelter, Women and Development, First and Third World Perspectives*, The College of Architecture and Urban Planning, The University of Michigan, May 9, 1992.

[6] D. Salzer, Theme Summaries and Future Directions.

[7] Bhatt also notes that in a few cases the income generating activities that open spaces allowed contributed to the physical degradation of women.

[8] As J. Sprague notes "conservative census figures show that roughly a quarter of all households with children in the United States are headed by women. Joan Forrester Sprague, *More than Housing, Lifeboats for Women and Children*, Boston: Butterworth Architecture, 1991. 7

[9] Joan Forrester Sprague, "Women and Shelter-Related Services and Infrastructures," abstract.

[10] J. F. Sprague, "Women …," abstract.

[11] Kim Tanzer, "Redefining Standards: Toward a Positive Ambivalence," presentation, May 7, 1992, International Conference: Shelter Women and Development: First and Third World Perspectives.

[12] D. Salzer, Theme Summaries and Future Directions, presentation, May 9, 1992, International Conference: Shelter Women and Development: First and Third World Perspectives.

[13] Mary Follenweider, "Language, Sacred and Transitional Housing," abstract.

[14] Chris Taylor, Tamy Silverman, "Shelter: A Place of the Telling, A Chimerical Cookbook," 2

[15] Martin Heidegger, "Building Dwelling Thinking" in *Poetry Language Thought,* New York: Harper and Row, 1971, 149.

[16] M. Heidegger. "Building …," 149.

[17] Georg Simmel, *Georg Simmel on Women, Sexuality and Love*, New Haven: Yale University Press, 1984, 111–2.

Chapter 40
Segregation of Women in Islamic Cultures and Its Reflection in Housing: A Study of Spaces for Women in a Bangladesh Village

Tasneem Chowdhury

Tasneem Chowdhury, *an architect from Bangladesh, presently resides in Canada. Graduating at the top of her class in 1979 from the Bangladesh University of Engineering and Technology, she worked for eleven years as an architect and graphic designer in the Middle East, designing everything from residences to office buildings to mosques. Immigrating to Canada in 1990, she attended the Minimum Cost Housing Program at the School of Architecture, McGill University, Montreal, and received a Master of Architecture in 1992. She is a research assistant at the Center for Urban and Community Studies at the University of Toronto.*

In Islamic societies, religion plays a significant role in shaping the home and the environment. An important feature of the Islamic culture is the segregation of women from males other than next of kin. This influences the female pattern of activity and movement, both in the home and in public areas. The organization of space in the Muslim home reflects this particular pattern. Consequently, there is a general separation of male and female domains in the domestic architecture of almost all Islamic societies. This duality of space in turn reinforces the seclusion and segregation of women. This paper attempts to examine this socio-physical phenomenon in a particular setting—a community in north-west Bangladesh, where the author carried out a study in October, 1991.[1] Some of the findings from this study are presented in this paper.

Bangladesh, a country of more than 100,000,000 Muslims, is one of the least urbanized nations in the world, with ninety percent of its population living in rural areas. Poverty, the blight of this region, also plays an important part in shaping both societal standards and the living environment. This paper examines the spatial response to gender segregation norms in rural housing, taking into consideration the very serious issues of poverty and lack of resources prevailing in rural areas.

The system of segregation, seclusion, and veiling of women is known as *purdah* in Bangladesh, as elsewhere in South Asia. *Purdah*, which literally means curtain, refers to the physical segregation of living space, as well as the covering of body and face. In broader terms it also refers to the modest and deferential behavior of women and the restrictions on their movements. Societal and religious norms of segregation have far-reaching effects in every rural woman's life. These norms determine a woman's role and status in society, her life cycle changes, her activities, and her access to different institutions. All these, in turn, are realized by rules about the organization of living space. The study was approached by focusing on the living patterns of rural women. Women's activities, occupations, and mobility were addressed as these directly affect women's use of space, both in private and in public areas.

The Village

The field study was undertaken in two adjacent villages, Bajitpur and Shadashivpur (Fig. 1), in the district of Chapai Nawabganj near the Indian border. This region is mainly dependent on agriculture. Mango, sugarcane,

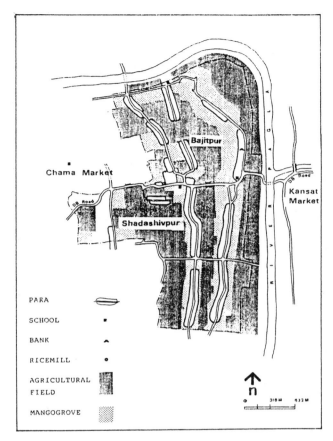

Fig. 1: Map of Bajitpur and Shadashivpur.

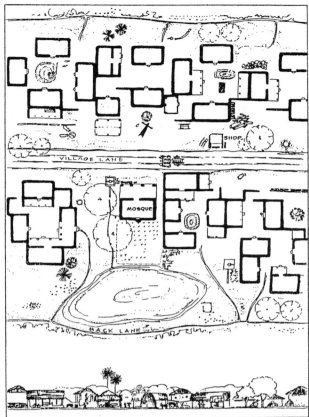

Fig. 2: A Village Lane and Part of a Neighborhood.

and paddy are the main crops. Jute, pulses, mustard vegetables, etc. are also important cash crops. Three socio-economic groups were studied—the landless laborers, who make up sixty percent of the villagers, the farmers (including both surplus and subsistence farmers), and the landlords.

The two villages are divided by a main circulation spine (D.B. Road) connecting two markets. The main public institutions—the schools, the bank and the ricemill are located on the main road and on its main subsidiary, the road along the edge of Bajitpur, parallel to the river. The individual settlements or neighborhoods are arranged on two sides of the village roads which branch off from the main road. These neighborhoods are known as *para*s and are generally named after an occupational group or a former neighborhood chief. Narrow footpaths join the *para*s at the back of the homesteads.

A definite hierarchy of spaces was found in the circulation pattern. How much or how little women will use

these circulation spaces depends on their position in this hierarchy. Women usually do not use the main road, especially on market days when the traffic increases. Women often take longer routes to visit other neighborhoods, rather than walk through a busy main road. The secondary roads, which are the village lanes, have homesteads organized in a linear pattern on both sides of the village lanes (Fig. 2). Men walk along these roads and congregate to stand and talk. Mosques and small neighborhood shops on the roadside also encourage social gatherings. Children play all day long in safe surroundings. Women are almost totally missing from the street life. Their appearance there is conditional to necessity and to modest behavior. Sometimes women are visible in the entrances of their homesteads, looking out at the road. Their role in the street life is as discreet spectators, never as participants.

The third category of roads is the network of backlanes and footpaths at the back of the homesteads. These lanes, which are often nothing more than narrow dirt paths created by walking feet, meander through mango

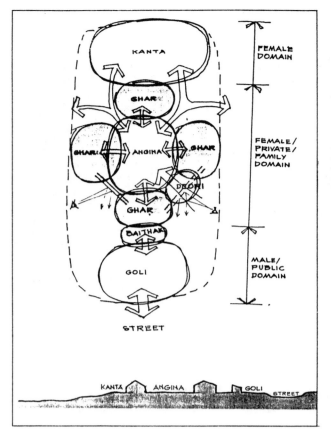

Fig. 3: Sequence of Spaces in the Home.

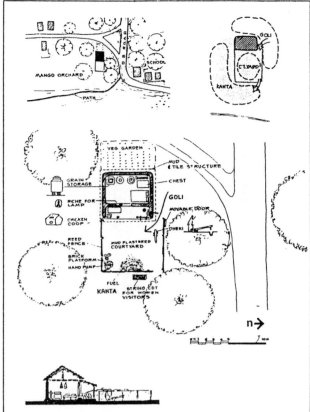

Fig. 4: Homestead of a Landless Nuclear Household.

groves and crop-fields and link the different *para*s. These lanes are freely used by women to get about, but men also use them to get to their fields or as shortcuts.

Generally public spaces are conceived as "male spaces." Women do not visit public institutions such as the mosque or the bank. They avoid open fields and public roads. Societal norms prevent women from working in agricultural fields or mango orchards, which are acknowledged "male" preserves. The open market has connotations of being an indecent place for women to be in. Women usually do not visit the marketplace or neighborhood shops, where men congregate not only for trading purposes, but also to socialize. Although women are not totally excluded from public spaces, their use of such spaces is conditional to necessity and discretion. Women cannot and do not use public space in the casual and relaxed manner permitted to men. When a women ventures out of her home, veiling the body and face with her sari and discreet behavior are the norms. While bicycles are the common mode of

transport for rural men, women travel in covered oxcarts or boats, or curtained rickshaws.

The Dwelling

In the Islamic world, the most common dwelling form is the inward-looking courtyard house. Closed to the outer world, it opens toward a central court, thus fulfilling the need
for privacy, as well as for adequate light and ventilation. Islamic norms for seclusion of women have given rise to several architectural devices and elements which are more or less common in the domestic architecture of all Islamic countries. These include:

— organization and orientation of the elements of the house
— secluded and private open space
— small exterior openings
— entrance with screen wall for visual privacy
— multiple entrances to segregate paths of men and women

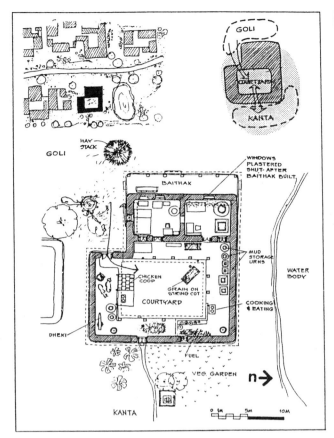

Fig. 5: Homestead of a Farmer.

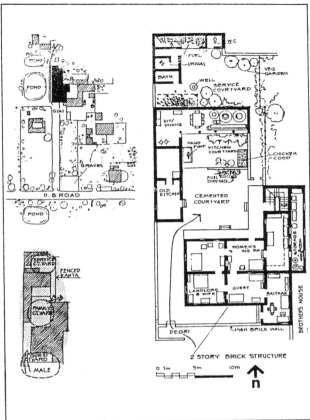

Fig. 6: Homestead of a Landlord.

The traditional Bangladeshi homestead employs all these devices. It is usually an aggregation of loosely spaced free-standing units grouped around a central courtyard. In this region, however, the more compact layout with adjoining rooms is also noticeable. The size and number of huts and the size of the courtyard is a good indicator of the economic condition of the family. Each house is unique and changes with the needs of the family and reflects the pattern of its growth and modifications.

The spaces in an individual homestead are laid out in a distinct hierarchical sequence (Fig. 3). The total plot is not built on. There is a fairly large transition space on the street side of the plot. This is a semi-private space known as the *goli*.[2] At the back of the house is an open space with vegetation known as the *kanta*. The living area is made up of several huts (*ghar*) grouped around and facing a square or rectangular courtyard. This courtyard, known as the *angina*, is the heart of the

homestead where most activities take place. The courtyard is entered on the street-side by the *deori*, the indirect entrance which acts as a visual barrier. There are one or more huts around the courtyard, which are used only for storage and for sleeping. Most huts have attached semi-open covered spaces known as *baranda*, which act as transitions between the open courtyard and the enclosed hut.

The dwellings of different socio-economic groups (see examples in Figs. 4, 5, and 6) from the survey were examined and compared to understand the interaction between status and the dwelling form. Although the three main groups—the landlords, the farmers, and the landless laborers—share basic norms of *purdah* and a basic concept in dwelling design, each adapted the different spaces of the traditional dwelling form to their own particular lifestyle. The concept of male and female domains at the front and the back of the homestead, respectively, is present in the homesteads of all

Fig. 7: A *Baithak.*

Fig. 8: A Courtyard.

income groups. There are some differences, however, in how these domains are achieved and how visual privacy is maintained.

In farmers' homes, the spacious *goli* in front of the homestead is used mostly for feeding livestock, threshing produce, and keeping the haystack and farming implements. Men usually gather here in the evenings to converse. Male landless laborers use their considerably smaller *goli* for socializing or manufacturing articles for home consumption or sale. The landlords usually did not rear cattle (except perhaps a milk-cow) and used the *goli* mainly for socializing. Several landlords built walls around their *goli*s and planted elaborate flowering gardens in this space. The *goli* is considered to be "male" space, although women too use it to some extent for work that often spills over from the courtyard, for example, drying grain or making mud storage bins. They, however, do not linger there for extended periods of time, and it is obvious that they do not feel at home in this space, although it is part of their homestead. In many of the homesteads, there is a long shaded porch facing the *goli* for receiving male guests. This is known as the *baithak* (Fig. 7). In poor households, the *baithak* is often absent. Sometimes a male guest is important enough to be brought into the courtyard. Some women reported that, in such cases, they hid in their kitchens or rooms till the visit was over.

The homestead is usually entered through a corner of the courtyard between two huts. This entrance—the *deori*—is generally indirect with specially built walls for visual privacy. In affluent households the courtyard has boundary walls with entrance doors that can be locked. Often in poor households, the entrance is not visually obstructed by staggered walls. Nevertheless, there is always an attempt to create visual barriers, either by

hanging a jute-mat or old quilt in the doorway or by a movable door made with leaves in a reed-frame. The gaps between the individual huts are fenced, at least on the street side. Among the poor, where adherence to *purdah* is less stringent due to practical needs, the fences are lower and more transparent, and sometimes even non-existent. As the families move up the social ladder, the boundaries of the house become more defined and solid, the walls become higher, with entrances that can be locked and barred. Apart from the need for privacy, this also reflects the need to safeguard wealth.

The courtyard of the house is the focus and spiritual center of the home. This is the space where women spend most of their time, the space for the majority of their activities. The courtyard supports all the activities of work and leisure. Processing paddy, manufacturing household items, rearing children in a safe environment, cooking, and socializing all take place in this central place (Fig. 8). There are built-in mud stoves in the courtyard for open-air cooking during fair weather, which is most of the year. Landlords' courtyards are usually divided into spaces with separate functions: a cemented portion for general household work; a small vegetable and flower garden; and another cemented space for work connected to the kitchen. The courtyards of the other two groups are more multifunctional. Women visit neighboring courtyards almost every day. Neighboring courtyards are usually inter-connected so that women can visit each other without having to go out on the road. Women, known or unknown, never need permission to enter a courtyard. It is quite acceptable for women to use courtyards to get from one place to another. Men other than family members, however, will never enter a courtyard unless invited. For a male, entering a courtyard without permission is an act of symbolic violation.

Fig. 9: The Backyard or *Kanta*.

Fig. 10: The Women's Pond.

The *baranda* is the transitional space between the open courtyard and the enclosed space of the hut. These semi-open porches are usually attached to a *ghar* and face the courtyard, but they may also be attached to the courtyard wall. The *baranda* is a shaded space used as an extension of the courtyard to support outdoor activities during hot or rainy weather. It also protects assets such as storage urns, animal coops, and cooking implements.

The individual huts known as *ghar* are usually single- or two-room multifunctional structures used mainly for sleeping and storage. They are also used for other household activities during inclement weather. In the typical village home, usually one nuclear family shares one room until the son grows up and marries. Then another hut is built for him. Homesteads of the landless are usually organized loosely with separate one-room structures surrounding the courtyard. Farmers' houses tend to be more compact with adjoining rooms and walled corners for additional living and storage space. With increasing wealth, more semi-covered space is needed to shelter animals, household implements, and storage urns. This need has given rise to the walled courtyard with long wide *baranda*s attached to the wall. The mud huts often have no windows and only one doorway as a source of light. If there are windows present, they are very small, usually only a horizontal slit or round narrow holes. The reason given for absence of windows or for their small size is visual privacy and, more importantly, a safeguard against evil spirits entering the room. Bigger windows are screened by shutters or tiles from passers-by.

The *kanta* is the backyard of the homestead, which usually contains the vegetable patches, bamboo groves, and family hand pump where women wash their utensils and clothes (Fig. 9). It was found that private hand pumps, even when shared by several families, were located in the backyard, while public hand pumps provided by the government were invariably placed on the roadside. Women who used public hand pumps usually carried the water to the backyard to wash and clean. The *kanta* in the landlords' houses are enclosed with walls, creating an additional service courtyard for latrines, bathing spaces, and fuel storage. In the other two groups, the *kanta* remains unfenced, although the vegetation in the back of the house provides privacy for the women while they work or bathe. The *kanta* is considered primarily women's space.

Most homes are built with family labor unless the family is wealthy enough to be able to afford hired help. The building of a new home involves separate established roles for men and women. Women dig and prepare the mud, while men build the walls and the roof. The plastering and repair of the walls and the floor is also considered women's work.

Mobility in the Public Realm

Women also bathe at a special spot in the riverbank, commonly referred to as the "women's pier." There is also a women's pond (Fig. 10) near Kanapara in Shadashivpur, where women from as far as one kilometer away come for their daily bath and to wash clothes. These spaces are considered to be essentially women's spaces and men usually avoid them.

For natural functions the usual practice is to use the fields or bushes. None of the landless houses surveyed had latrines in their homesteads. Of the twenty-one farmers' houses surveyed, five had latrines in their

Fig. 11: Grameen Bank Meeting.

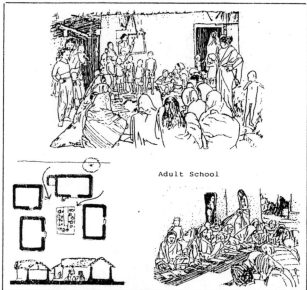

Fig. 12: Adult School for Women.

backyards, indicating the changing sanitation practices with increase in wealth (and stricter adherence to *purdah* for women). All the landlords' dwellings had well-built latrines. The absence of enclosed latrines is the source of complaint for many of the women. Several women reported waiting until dark or going before daybreak, in order not to be seen. A sanitary slab is not expensive, only about two dollars, but men do not see a latrine as a priority and women, although the main consumers of domestic space, do not have much say in the decision-making process. The few homesteads that have sanitary toilets are of the pit-latrine type, usually placed in the *kanta* at a safe distance from the house (up to twenty meters).

The production of rice, an important crop, also has a definite division of roles. Women spend considerable time in productive work in the agricultural sector. Women work daily in processing and storing the farm produce. Men grow paddy, but women are responsible for paddy processing, storage, and seed germination, in

short, all the activities that can take place within the home. For poor women, processing paddy for richer families is one of the few income-generating opportunities available to them. An electric ricemill set up a few years ago, although viewed by the villagers as a symbol of development for the village, was actually detrimental to the income-earning capacity of the women, as getting rice husked at the mill was cheaper for the affluent families. Thus opportunities for work, which are normally limited, decreased even more.

Women are excluded from daily and weekly markets, both as vendors and buyers, but they are not totally excluded from commercial activities. Door-to-door vending is very common. Most women do not observe *purdah* in front of male vendors, as they are mostly considered village "brothers." Wholesalers also visit the homesteads to buy eggs, vegetables, or chicken from the women.

There is an agricultural bank in the village, but no woman has ever visited the bank. Grameen Bank, a mobile bank which gives income-generating loans mainly to poor landless women, has started operations in one of the *para*s. Grameen Bank recognizes the limited mobility of rural women and sets up a weekly office in one of the courtyards/*baranda*s of their members' homesteads (Fig. 11). Because of cultural constraints regarding the mobility and use of the public domain,

Fig. 13: Sari Vendor in a Courtyard.

women tend to cluster in a limited range of occupations based within the home. Processing paddy, sewing embroidered quilts or clothes, manufacturing household utensils, working as domestic help, or raising livestock, fowl, or vegetables are some ways that women can generate an income. However, the constraint of working at home and having to depend on male intermediaries makes them vulnerable to exploitation.

There is an adult education program run by an NGO active in this region. Classes for women are held in a courtyard in a farmer's house (Fig. 12), while the men's school is held in the *goli* of another homestead. There are about twenty-five women in the class. The course that they follow is known as "functional education" and lasts for six months. This school is fairly successful, with no dropouts to date and a waiting list for the next course. All the women, however, were from the same part of the neighborhood. Distance from home seems to be a determining factor in attendance at school.

Women in this area have little access to health care. The usual practice is for husbands to describe the symptoms of their wives' illness to the male doctor in Kansat or to the two homeopaths in Bajitpur and bring medicine for their wives. Unless it is absolutely necessary, women are not taken to the doctor. Women's lack of mobility and the long distance that has to be covered to reach government health facilities in Kansat means that women are mostly left out of modern health services. Thus they are compelled to rely on indigenous health care practices which are easily accessible and which operate within the given social constraints imposed on them. There are several village practitioners, known as *kobiraj*, who dispense traditional herbal medicine.

The study confirmed that access to public, political, and economic institutions, insofar as they are situated in the

public domain, is difficult and often impossible for rural women. However, the courtyard house in Bangladesh supports private as well as public functions like marketing, banking, and school, although exclusively for women. When vendors come into the courtyard, several women from the neighboring homesteads congregate to create a small market in the courtyard (Fig. 13). The success of the adult education program for women is due to a great extent to its location in one of the neighborhood courtyards. It facilitates the attendance of women with limited mobility and also assures that women feel comfortable in familiar surroundings. Rural women tend to be intimidated by alien environments.

Conclusions

Although architecturally the rural house facilitates the segregation and confinement of women, it provides an environment that is not claustrophobic or confining. The design and arrangement of the courtyard house mitigate the effects of confinement in several ways. The courtyards are fairly large with a feeling of openness. One courtyard flows into another, heightening the sense of space and movement. Three kinds of spaces— enclosed, semi-open, and open—satisfy the separate spatial needs for different activities. Access to neighboring courtyards assures frequent visits from other women; total isolation is not the norm. Most of the families studied were nuclear, often sharing a homestead with separate cooking arrangements. The spatial arrangements of their shared living quarters and common courtyards assured many of the support systems of the traditional extended family, such as combined child rearing, household help during illnesses, companionship, and emotional support, especially for the women.

The creation of domains and the physical boundaries within the homestead are instrumental in achieving a segregated existence for women, but these boundaries are not the crucial factor in the separation of men and women. Societal standards and religious injunctions are far more effective in maintaining the separate world of women. The field study revealed that, rather than a strict physical separation of domains with the exclusion of either sex, behavior and space use determined the limits of the domains. The separating physical boundaries exist, but are made flexible by time zoning, use/ avoidance, and behavioral norms. Age, status, and financial standing also determine the rigidity of the spatial barriers between domains. For example, the physical boundaries of the homestead define the limits of living space more for younger women than for older. For newlyweds or new mothers, these boundaries are absolute and impossible to disregard. But generally, for other women, the physical boundaries are flexible and vary according to time, period, and occasion. However, the kinship boundaries of the family and the physical limits of the homestead and the immediate neighborhood very much define the world of the average woman.

The special needs and problems of women in the provision of shelter has long been a neglected field, especially in developing countries. Any development work or upgrading of settlements in gender-segregated societies must take into account the value system and needs of women. This is not to say that the status quo—that is, the segregation of women—should be upheld; rather, physical interventions should be sensitive to the prevailing norms of society, which are changing, although very slowly. Reports from elsewhere in Bangladesh suggest that more and more women are coming out of seclusion and entering work places which are traditionally considered "male" spaces, such as construction and road maintenance sites. Any rural development must recognize the transition in societal norms and must attempt to incorporate the essence of the change in planned interventions in the built environment.

Notes

[1] The field study was funded by the Humanities and Social Sciences Research Grants Subcommittee of McGill University, Montreal, Canada.

[2] All spatial terms used are in the local dialect.

Chapter 41
The Socio-Economic Impact of Open Spaces on Women in a Spontaneous Settlement

Neema Bhatt

Neema Bhatt received her Bachelor of Architecture from Bangalore University, India, in 1989. She worked at HUDCO as a student-trainee for a period of twelve weeks and has been associated with HUDCO since then. She has worked at the architectural planning and research laboratory (APRL) at the University of Michigan. Her current professional interests are in urban planning and landscape architecture, particularly in the context of the Third World.

The impact of pockets of open spaces, resulting from organic growth in an economically weak, low-income group (LIG) settlement, on the female inhabitants was studied. On the one hand, the open spaces provided a venue for women to carry out small businesses, a forum for their participation in social exchanges, and a miniature playground for their small children. On the other hand, increased usage of open spaces led to their physical degradation, resulting in unhygienic surroundings. The role of open spaces in the everyday life of women in degraded settlements is thus complex.

The data reported here are from one of the five degraded settlements surveyed in Bangalore, an Indian city which has the highest growth rate in Asia. The settlement consisted of 272 families spread over 3.35 acres and was uniquely divided into two distinct cultural groups. A typical dwelling consisted of a multifunctional space separated from the wet core areas (kitchen and bath) in front by a short wall. A prominent feature was a veranda which formed the link between the interior and the exterior. This provided the platform for the socio-economic activities. The veranda was the women's locus for gossip, light-hearted banter, and some arguments. It provided passive recreation for the women while they kept a watchful eye on their young children who played in the open spaces. Side by side, many women, aged between 10 and 45, worked on the veranda doing unskilled jobs for the small-scale industries that employed them. The women "earned" a better status for themselves in the male-dominated home. In an LIG settlement, household income supersedes all other factors for survival. Open spaces are thus useful and should be an integral part of the socio-economic and physical set-up. Housing authorities and cooperative societies should incorporate at least a mandatory 51% open area in their rehabilitation schemes. Small-scale industries can make use of the vast amount of unskilled labor for mutual benefit.

The global phenomenon of accelerated urbanization has been increasingly evident during the past fifty years. The most striking characteristic of this phenomenon is the upsurge of urban growth in the developing world. In just four decades, the urban population in developing countries registered a five-fold increase; the population figure of large metropolises recorded an eight-fold increase. Urbanologists note that the rapid population growth of developing world cities has no parallel economic growth and does not accurately indicate industrial development or social progress. Further, very sizable proportions of population of the major cities in the developing world consist of low-income group (LIG) settlements. Bangalore, a city in south India, which has registered the fastest growth rate among Asian metropolises, exemplifies this trend. Case studies in cities like Bangalore explain a common scenario in a majority of Third World metropolises. Because of their financial dependence on men, women in LIG settlements are susceptible to extra hardships in life. To alleviate additional hardships, these women have to find ways to help themselves. Any available option they find, although very limited in scope, is thus of interest.

Formation of a Bangalore Slum

While a final definition of the term "slum" needs extensive study, based on a general survey of five low-income-group settlements, an interim definition for a typical Bangalore slum is as follows: A slum is an LIG urban settlement in unsanitary condition, generally overcrowded, characterized by make-shift dwellings or those in a state of deterioration, either totally unserviced or with facilities far below the minimal acceptable standards of the city, tending to make the area hazardous to the physical and social well-being of its inhabitants. A common characteristic of a Bangalore slum is its proximity to industries and/or the mass transportation network. It is often found in open areas with a nearby water body.

The People

The settlement in the slum studied started in 1944 when families from the neighboring state of Tamilnadu settled in the then outskirts of Bangalore. After India gained her independence in 1947, many industries were started in this area, and that was a major contribution to this particular slum's growth. In 1983, about 120 families from Gulbarga, a district in the northern part of Karnataka state, joined the slum for economic reasons. When this study was conducted in the summer of 1989, the population of the slum had reached a total of 1,496 in an area of 3.35 acres.

Ethnic Composition

From an ethnic point of view, the slum can be divided into two categories: people who originated from Tamilnadu, 150 miles southeast of Bangalore, and those from Gulbarga, 500 miles north. These two groups of people speak different languages, and also differ in their cultural and social behavior. They do not mix with each other on any account.

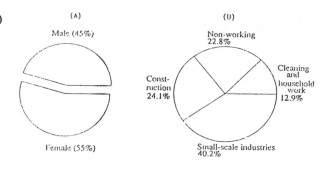

Fig. 1: Gender Distribution and Women's Work in Settlement.

Religion

Differing religious preferences of the two groups from Tamilnadu and Gulbarga led to the designation of several makeshift structures as shrines, where they conduct regular cultural events to worship their favorite deities. The Moslems have a mosque within two miles and the Christians worship in the local church about a half mile from their settlement.

Economic Activity

In this settlement many of the men are construction workers in the ever-expanding city of Bangalore. Given the nature of the construction industry they can find only seasonal employment. Another category, albeit a small one, consists of industrial laborers who have regular jobs and are economically secure. Many of the laborers send money back to their villages. A still smaller group of people belongs to the lower middle class (monthly income greater than Rs. 1,250) who continue to live in slums for various reasons. Some own a piece of land or a house; and the cost of living is lower in the slums. This group consists of elementary school teachers, clerks, and petty businessmen. A sprinkling of such people is found in most slums. These people are instrumental in changing certain areas from the slum to the non-slum category.

The survey indicates that women constituted 55% of the slum population. Figure 1 shows the work distribution of these women. The average income of a family per month is about Rs. 1,250. Unemployment is very high.

Open Spaces in a Slum

A typical housing unit consists of a multifunctional space separated from wet core areas in the front by a

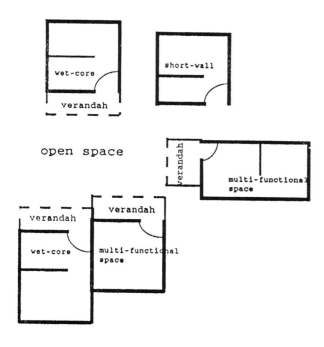

open space

Fig. 2: Typical Cluster of Housing Units and Open Space.

short wall. The walls are made of semi-permanent materials such as unbaked, undried mud, hay, or straw, with a thatch roof on top. These walls do not reach the minimum height according to the acceptable standard for a residential house and do not span large lengths, and hence are built thinner in section than the acceptable standard. These units have very little or no ventilation. The wet core areas are grouped in front because they do not have a drain system and the refuse has to be put out to the front. The housing units have grown organically within the settlement with no organized orientation or pattern, and open spaces have been created spontaneously. The dwelling units look inward at the pockets of open spaces thus created. The outermost part of the dwelling unit, the veranda (analogous to a porch), is the first physical and spatial link to the outside. The veranda may or may not have a shelter on top, but is mostly open on the sides, the front, and the back, forming the first wall of the house (Fig. 2).

Most open spaces have at least three units surrounding them, but some may have up to five units. There is hardly any ground cover in these open spaces in the form of plants, but one can occasionally find small plants, of Tulasi, a sacred plant for Hindus. The ground immediately in front of the housing unit is coated with cow dung paste. The open spaces are well ventilated compared to the interior of the dwellings, with plenty of

light and sunshine. The air is tunneled through the gaps in between the houses. If the orientation is against the local wind direction, the air inside the open spaces is stale, but the ventilation is still better than inside the housing unit where the smoke from the mud-baked ovens is suffocating. The open spaces form a physical means to drain the refuse from the kitchen and bath areas toward any kind of natural slope in the land formation. Indeed the open spaces are a visual delight in a way after one reaches the expanse of spaces traveling through a narrow corridor. The surrounding walls have brightly painted colors with vernacular patterns which can instill a festive mood in anybody responsive to subtleties in artistic expression.

Open spaces as defined above are more common and abundant within the earlier group of huts where the settlement grew gradually. Open spaces are nonexistent within the group dwellings of people from Gulbarga where settlements took place very quickly. The socio-economic impact of open spaces in the former case can therefore be sharply contrasted with the later.

Socio-economic and Physical Aspects of Open Spaces

In the absence of electricity, the waking hours of a household were mostly limited from dawn to dusk, i.e., from about 6 a.m. to 6:30 p.m. The settlers believed in rising and retiring early. Not surprisingly, an average woman spends two to three hours outside on the veranda. Considering the amount of activity that had to be fitted in her limited time schedule, this was of particular significance. When two or more women gathered outside their houses on their respective veranda the scene was set for gossip, light banter, and sometimes volatile arguments. This interaction provided passive recreation, an essential ingredient in their strife-torn world. Young children enjoyed playing with marbles and wooden toys outside their homes. Young children found diversion from closed space and their mothers kept a watchful eye on them in the open spaces.

An important aspect of the study concentrated on the economic activity of the "outdoor" women. Even though passive recreation was an integral part of their lives, many women were busy with the jobs they got from the local light industries which employed the women as unskilled labor—an ideal condition wherein jobs came to women's doorsteps, literally! Such jobs included basket weaving, agarbathi (incense sticks) making, and casting construction elements in molds. All these activities took place in the proximity of open spaces in the veranda.

Income is the most important factor for survival in a society. The contribution of women almost doubled the monthly income of their families. The consequences of income generation by women resulted in the following:

1. In a male-dominated society, an earned income provided these women a say in family matters.
2. Women were now financially independent and bought new clothes for themselves during a festival.
3. If their husbands deserted them, which was not uncommon, these women had their earnings to fall back on.
4. Instances of child labor were low in families with working women. More children were sent to nearby schools for education.

Overall, since the work was not physically intensive, and did not involve traveling to distant places but staying in their verandas, there was a congenial relationship between these women's working and family lives. Most of the women interviewed (85%) felt that the quality of their lives improved since they started earning money. A small percentage (11%) of working women thought that their lives had gotten worse due to increased health problems and their husbands' unchanged attitudes. It is interesting to note that women from the early settlement group were more approachable during data collection and seemed to be more active in work than the women from Gulbarga.

The advantages of these spontaneously created open spaces were many. However, there were a few disadvantages too. Misuse of the space occurred in a number of ways. Since there was no site planning of any type, a low point in an open space could act as a tiny water spot to collect refuse from the wet core areas from surrounding dwellings, thereby becoming a breeding ground for mosquito larvae and bacteria. When the water shortage was acute, the contaminated water was being reused by the people, increasing the risks of health hazard. Children between the ages of 2 and 4 used the space to defecate and increased the levels of pollution. All these factors leading to degradation of open spaces did not foster any beneficial activity. Therefore, slum dwellers needed to exercise some level of health consciousness.

Municipal Service and Public Utilities

In 1984, the local slum development board intervened to provide some basic amenities with the financial backing from the Housing and Urban Development Corporation (HUDCO). As a result, five borewells were dug at different locations within the settlements, roads were designated and a public toilet was built. Availability of

drinking water improved the condition of women to some extent since they could concentrate on their family and work. However, one of the borewells dried out by 1989 and another had stopped working due to a mechanical failure. Only three borewells were in operation at the time of the study reported here. Long lines were noted in the morning between 8 a.m. and 10 a.m. and evenings between 4 p.m. and 6 p.m. Summer months brought in more demand for water but less availability.

The roads were demarcated with no design logic. The main road was 30 feet wide while all the other roads were 20 feet wide. In a settlement where most of the people walk and a few own bicycles, the money spent on those roads could have been invested for some other improvement. There was no management of public toilets either. The group psychology perhaps had a big role in this. People used the toilets irresponsibly. As a result, open spaces served as spots for defecation.

Conclusion

Urbanologists now use the approach of slum rehabilitation and slum resettlements instead of slum clearance. Most of the rehabilitation schemes in the Third World end up as monotonous rows of (semi-permanent building materials used for construction with poor technology) houses with no interesting street scapes. But this survey indicates that a site-specific response is necessary to cater to the activities of women and their level of sensitivity to change. Clusters of dwelling units around open spaces are conducive to women's psychological, economic, and physical well-being. This was found to be true in all five slums that were surveyed in general and in the specific slum that was studied in detail. This is an emphatic recommendation for open spaces to be a part of resettlement schemes and to be a part of the layout of every single unit. Most rehabilitation schemes executed in the past fifteen years have less than 5% of the area devoted to open spaces. It is argued that providing such a facility reduces the number of dwelling units provided. A possible solution is to vertically stack units within the range of local building laws. This can provide the advantage of open spaces without sacrificing the number of dwelling units. A low-cost paving and planting system would go a long way toward improving the aesthetics of the environment by reducing the impulse to spoil the surroundings.

Roads within the settlements were used for the transportation of pedestrians and two-wheelers. A maximum of 25 feet and a minimum of 15 feet for the main and the arterial roads within the settlements can meet any such transportation needs. In this study, the wider roads seemed unnecessary, an investment which could have been channeled to other basic facilities for women and children.

Economic Rehabilitation

This case indicated that, given proper conditions, a women's potential to provide unskilled labor in an economically weak LIG settlement is tremendous. A slum rehabilitation scheme can be located near heavy or light industries which need vast amounts of unskilled labor. Incentives can be given to women to make use of this economic opportunity. Essentially this means that the industries have to take the initiatives and approach the women in settlements like these for their mutual benefit.

Education and Health

Cleanliness is not unfamiliar to women in an economically weak LIG settlement. For all the filth outside their home, the interior of their homes is surprisingly clean. This means that they just lack the belief that the quality of space just outside their dwellings is their concern. They are unaware of the health risks of not maintaining a clean surrounding. Children become the main target of disease. As a result, infant mortality is high due to illnesses such as diarrhea, malaria, cholera, and tuberculosis. Most children can be seen plagued with chronic cold symptoms. Since the main reason for pollution of the open spaces is dumping refuse from their wet core areas or defecating, a special place can be designated and designed to wash vessels and wash clothes. The women are eager to maintain their public facilities like water sources and public toilets. This would ensure a better quality of open space linked to their dwellings so that they can reap the benefits of what the space has to offer. A small initiative on the part of administration to educate the women about basic hygiene and to teach them organizational skills could go a long way to help the women use the open spaces where they live for much greater benefits.

References

Cook, E. (1988), "Women helping women: Humanism at work in Bombay slums," *Humanist*, 48: 22–25.

Freeman, A. (1987), "Vernacular village of low-income houses at sea ranch," *Architecture*, 76: 64–67.

Hashmi, S.H. (1975), *The slums of Karachi: A Case Study*, Lahore, Pakistan: Aziz Publishers.

Marcussen, L. (1990), *Third World Housing in Social and Spatial Development: The Case of Jakarta*, Brookfield, Vt.: Aldershot.

Mookherjee, D., (1982) "A profile of slums in a third world city," *Ekistics*, 49: 476–480.

Qadir, S.R. (1975), *Bastees of Dacca: A Study of Squatter Settlements*, Dacca, Bangladesh: Local Government Institute.

Thorbek, S. (1988), "Women and urbanization," *Acta Sociologica*, 31: 283–301.

Chapter 42
Lifeboats, More than Housing

Joan Forrester Sprague

Joan Forrester Sprague *has lectured at many universities and conferences in the United States and abroad in the Netherlands, the People's Republic of China, and the former Soviet Union. Her grassroots technical assistance publications have been used nationally and she has contributed chapters in several edited works. Her book,* More Than Housing: Lifeboats for Women and Children, *received a 1991 Citation of Excellence from the International Book Awards of the AIA. With an architecture degree from Cornell and a Master of Education in Organization Development from Harvard, she is a registered architect in Massachusetts and with NCARB. She cofounded a number of feminist initiatives, which include the Open Design Office, the Women's School of Planning and Architecture (WSPA), the Women's Development Corporation in Providence, Rhode Island, in 1978, and the Women's Institute of Housing and Economic Development in Boston in 1981, where she was president and executive director until 1988.*

We know that households of single mothers and children will determine the future of the planet and that more and more women and children worldwide are in need of housing and stable lives. We have seen that many kinds of sponsors in the U.S. have developed new models of housing that include sharing and services and that many more are needed. These models are at the leading edge of redefinitions of home. What is yet to be discovered is how living in these diverse models affects personal experience. This is the area of the writer's current work, using the six zones of use to chart personal experience in housing for single mothers and children and for a wider mixed population. Others are asked to contribute and participate in this work to enlarge its usefulness.

From the writer's perspective, poor women and children, out of their critical and particular needs, are beginning to change the face of housing from the idea of the isolated "castle of man," sheltering dependent and/or abused women and children, to home spaces that include sharing and support. The writer suggests future expansion of these concepts through feminist leadership in development, which can change the face of architecture from monuments-as-usual to more conserving and pluralistic building characteristics and approaches.

The combination of decrease in affordable housing for the poor with the rise of single-mother households as a primary poverty population in the U.S. has brought new issues to public attention. A crisis was necessary before the problem of housing for single mothers, long hidden within the problem of affordable housing, became acknowledged, or has almost become acknowledged. Demographics affirm the need to take a new look at changes in family life and housing. The percentage of American households composed of married couples was about 75 percent in 1960; by 1991 it was only 48.9 percent and only half of the married couples represented by that figure had minor children living at home (U.S. Census Report quoted in *USA Today,* 1992).

The Census in '89 documented a 19 percent decrease in affordable housing for the poor between '78 and '85, a trend that continues (U.S. Census, 1989). This is only one among a number of trends that impact on housing for women and children. Single mothers now head roughly a quarter of all households with minor children in the U.S. From 1970 to 1988, the number of single-mother households more than doubled. In 1988, over 8,000,000 single women were rearing 13,500,000 children. Although divorce rates have stabilized, births to unmarried women have risen: the percentage of single mothers who were never married increased from

4.2 percent in 1960 to 32.4 percent in 1989. Some of these are middle- and upper-class women who have careers and made a choice to have children before their time clock ran out (Sprague, 1991). But there are over 8,000,000 poor white and over 4,000,000 poor black children in this country, and more than half of these 12,000,000 poor children are reared in single-mother households (Edelman, 1987). Close to half of all single mothers, 44.6 percent, are poor. An additional 14.8 percent are near poor. Yet over two-thirds of single mothers are employed (Pearce, 1990). Without others to turn to, crisis often forces these mothers and children into homelessness. When asked, most homeless women cited their social worker or their children as their only supportive relationship (Bassuk *et al.,* 1986). Single mothers and children are estimated as 40 percent of the homeless population. They often have been cited as the fastest growing subgroup of the homeless. Surveys in cities showed 90 percent of all homeless families were headed by women. In 1987 there were 11,000 children in New York City's emergency shelter system, more than the total number of single homeless adults in the city (Dumpson, 1987).

This crisis has had an effect on policy. With the Stewart B. McKinney Act of 1987, HUD's focus for the homeless became innovation: linking services with housing. This new federal approach reinforces the perceptions and actions of a very diverse group of development sponsors: grassroots women's organizations, century-old nonprofit institutions, religious groups, colleges, corporations, and concerned individuals. Together these sponsors have created a new housing type that I call lifeboats, because they rescue and transform the lives of women and children (Sprague, 1991). This support allows single mothers to work toward economic self-sufficiency. This can make a great difference to all Americans. A South African proverb seems apropos: "When the women move, the nation moves."

Lifeboat Housing Types

My examples of lifeboat housing include emergency, transitional, and permanent housing. These definitions are most meaningful in understanding how projects are financed and what the sources of their development and operating funds are.

Emergency

This type of housing serves to mitigate the crisis of homelessness using federal and state shelter funds for those who cannot afford to pay any rent. This is the

money that has been used to pay welfare hotels in cities like New York. It has been more than the cost of building or buying housing. But until very recently, for special instances, narrow bureaucratic definitions have restricted the use of these emergency funds.

Transitional Housing

For some this is a temporary solution until permanent housing is found. For others, it is a transition to the objective of self-sufficiency: education, a job, a career. It is funded through combinations of private and public (including McKinney) funds. Residents pay a percentage of their incomes for rent.

Permanent Housing

This may be achieved through a rental or an ownership program. If it is designed to encourage a community of support and includes services, the homeless cycle can be broken. The housing concept and design helps single mothers to achieve stability in their lives. Combinations of funding make permanent housing possible; state or federal rent subsidies enable it.

In actuality, the three categories are blurred. Some programs take emergency residents and call themselves transitional. Some transitional housing has a residency period that lasts two or more years, a more permanent period than a household may have ever experienced. Some transitional housing is planned to evolve into permanent cooperative home ownership. I therefore have used these categories to show the diversity of characteristics in the choices of how space is allocated in unique settings and circumstances.

In a futurist book I read recently, *Creative Work,* seven laws of ecology were described. The first six were familiar to me: everything is connected to everything else; there is no such thing as a free lunch; nature knows best; everything must go somewhere; continuous growth leads to disasters; competing species cannot exist indefinitely. It was the seventh that was of special interest, called the law of the retarding lead. "Adaptive changes come not from the species dominant in their niche but from species and individuals existing on the fringe and forced to be more resourceful." (Harman & Hormann, 1990) I was fascinated to find a concept so applicable to my experience in analyzing housing derived from the needs of single mothers and their children, who clearly exist on the fringe of our society and who have inspired a resourceful approach to housing.

Zones of Lifeboat Housing

Through studying these lifeboat models I found an expansion from four common zones to six zones of use in what I call "lifeboat" housing. In addition to the four basic familiar zones: the personal zone, the household zone, the community zone (for all those who live in the same development or building), and the neighborhood zone (which is the larger setting), two new zones have been introduced: a zone between household and community and another zone between the community and the neighborhood. Each of these zones has more or less importance depending on each person's life and capacity to be self-sufficient, economically and personally. Their relative dominance depends on the design of the development, which reflects the values and attitude of the sponsors, and on the characteristics of the neighborhood in which the housing is set.

The fixed personal zone is the center of a private world. It has decorations with personal meanings that we have placed there as reflections of ourselves in addition to our bed and storage for clothing and other possessions. Particularly in emergency housing, single mothers may share this zone with their child or children, similar to the way coupled adults share the personal zone.

The personal zone exists within the household zone, generally a cluster of rooms only used by those in a single household, or by people who are sharing to form new kinds of extended households. The household zone is also used temporarily by invited guests. In a typical housing unit, we are accustomed to a household zone that includes the bedrooms, bathrooms, a kitchen and dining area, living room, storage, and circulation space. Bedrooms are typically the personal places within the household zone. The bathroom in use is commonly serially claimed as a personal zone by self-sufficient adults. Typical dwelling units in the household zone are designed for nuclear families. But single parents in this kind of unit can experience isolation in a world of children unless there is easy access to other adults offering a community of support. There is also a parent need for respite from children. In a thesis video by Wendy Garber, "Housing Ideals and Disappointments: Alternative Housing Options for Single Parent Families," a single parent says she cared less about having a large living room than having a large bedroom, a private space for retreat. For children without siblings, the typical household unit can also mean isolation from other children.

Most of us need little, if any, intervention from others within the personal or household zone. But for children, the elderly, and others in times of illness and recovery, care-taking by others providing food or assistance with shopping, cleaning, or personal support may be necessary. This kind of help is ordinarily provided by others in the household. But for single adults and especially for single parents, others in the community or neighborhood can offer needed assistance when household connections are lacking. Friends living nearby can help with food, shopping, or informal child care. Without this kind of support, single mothers experience the kind of crises which, compounded, cause homelessness.

A developed zone between household and community contributes to the support network that is important to lifeboat housing. It encourages adults' and children's friendships, informal child care, and an extended family experience. This zone can include laundry units shared by several households, or kitchens, or a place to watch television, or a table for sharing meals, or a place for children to play. This zone is a subpart of a community zone that is divided and dispersed in close proximity to private household places.

Households are also linked in the larger community zone, which exists in most multi-family housing that has common building entries and mailrooms, elevators and staircases, lobbies, hallways, and sometimes laundries, yards, and roof-decks. Depending on design and individual preference, all these can be places to make social connections.

The community zone is largely undeveloped in traditional single family houses, where it is typically only the street or a shared back alley that gives access to a series of houses. A dead-end street is more of a community zone than a through street which is used by strangers in transit. Adjacent outdoor household zones may be unfenced and joined to create a visual community zone. But this is not a place that a group can choose to use without the participation or permission of the householder.

For affluent homeowners the community zone can be a jointly owned recreational area, a dock, a clubhouse, or a golf course. Condominium and cooperative homeowners, members of a land trust, or a co-housing development may have community, social, or workshop rooms or land in common. In housing for single mothers, most of whom are poor, a community zone connecting residents requires a critical number to support on-site services such as child care and social services. A critical number is also necessary in co-housing for guest, hobby, and exercise rooms, large entertaining spaces, or group cooking and dining space. Small-group privacy is an asset in a community zone, particularly if it includes functions that create a zone between the community and the neighborhood.

In the zone between community and neighborhood, lifeboat housing often offers space in a child-care center to children living in the neighborhood. It may offer social services or invitations for meals as part of a neighborhood eating club, or extend use of laundry, workshop, exercise, gardening, or play space to others in the neighborhood. This offering to a neighborhood can make the difference between welcome for a lifeboat project or its being shut out when NIMBY (Not In My Backyard) is a neighborhood issue. The zone between community and neighborhood is a social bridge creating a neighborhood center. It can foster connections between generations and is designed as protected place, safe from strangers, vandalism, and crime.

Communities, households, and single people without communities, and strangers, who may be benign or threatening, all meet in the neighborhood. Group connection and awareness in the social bridge between community and neighborhood can expand safety by sponsoring crime-watches and marches to take back the streets.

The six zones and their characteristics differ in the examples I researched for my book, *More Than Housing: Lifeboats for Women and Children*. The differences are the result of the development sponsor's values and choices. For some, small-scale development is a priority in creating an intimate domestic approach. For some, large-scale development responds to the magnitude of need. The difference between small and large and the characteristics of residents influence the way zones are planned.

Particularly for more than 50 households, and where men, women, and children are housed, private apartments are typical and the zone between household and community may be minimal or nonexistent. When communities include women and children only, functions that are typically private to a household, such as a kitchen, dining, or living room, may be shared, creating an active zone between household and community.

Accent on the zone between community and neighborhood is inversely affected by scale. A larger number of residents makes a development more prominent in the neighborhood and makes the incorporation of services and spaces that can be shared with the neighborhood more economically feasible. But there are also small sites that invite neighborhood residents, particularly children, into their community spaces. Examples from around the U.S. include a progression of household space sizes in former houses, apartment buildings, hospitals, and schools that have been renovated for use as lifeboat housing. Some of the examples are newly constructed, some planned and/or built using modular prefabricated systems of concrete or wood. The spatial organization often separates service spaces from residential areas. In others, spaces for counseling and informal living are used interchangeably.

Conclusions

This statement from a single mother in a Red Cross emergency-transitional shelter in New York is compelling and persuasive:

> We want to achieve something in our lives, you know. We have children. We don't have no men taking care of us. We're doing this on our own. We need somebody to push us and this place has. We don't want to be on welfare the rest of our lives, we don't. But we can't afford condominiums and co-ops.... We want someone to be behind us, [to say] "hey, you can make it. I trust you. I believe in you. Believe in us, you know, 'cause we can do it.... Just because we are homeless doesn't mean we don't have a future. We have a future. (Sprague, 1991)

We know these families are a large part of the future of the world. If they are helped to have decent lives, they can contribute to better futures for all of us on this planet. What else do we know? We know that more and more women and children worldwide are in need of housing and stable lives. We know that many kinds of sponsors have developed new models of housing that include sharing and services. We know many more are needed.

The new lifeboat models described here are the leading edge of redefinitions of home. But what I don't know and what I am working on now is the discovery of how living in these diverse models affects personal experience. Are experiences tied to differences in physical space or personal backgrounds? How do differences in the experiences of those in lifeboat designs compare with experiences of those who have more stable lives and who live in conventional housing? I am pleased to be able to investigate these "Consequences of Design Choices" in a study I have recently begun, supported by an National Endowment for the Arts Fellowship. I am working with the diagram of concentric zones of use to ask residents of lifeboat housing and others concerned with home to map the locations of experiences such as: friendship, conflict, safety, learning, success, trust, rejection, difficulty, help, celebration, and other new, good, or bad experiences.

I have some information from the first site visit I made where residents mapped the experiences I have listed. I discovered from three women in a domestic violence shelter that the location of their friendships in the personal and household zone and the location of their conflicts in the outside neighborhood, where their abusers were located, were both also the locations of their learning. I discovered that their limited household space in a single room encouraged them to join others in community spaces to form friendships and learn to trust, experiences from which they had been isolated living with their abuser. The close space fit is an antidote to isolation. I also discovered in discussion with a service manager of transitional housing that conflict within the expanded housing setting was embraced as an opportunity to teach and learn conflict resolution. For those to whom conflict has been associated with abuse, becoming adept and aware of how to negotiate conflict is particularly important.

I am using the same diagram with a study group in Boston. We are members of IONS, the Institute of Noetic Sciences, an organization founded by astronaut Edgar Mitchell to become a vehicle for exploring human consciousness. This work is part of a larger study I am doing called Finding Home, exploring social, psychic, and physical qualities. The zones I have identified for a diverse population of women, men, and couples living in more conventional settings include the personal, household, community, neighborhood, town or city, region, the nation, the planet, and the universe. The greatest variations and dilemmas have emerged in the community zone, which, for some, does not exist or which may be located at work.

I have tried to show that poor women and children, out of their critical and particular needs, are beginning to change the face of housing from the idea of the isolated "castle of man," sheltering dependent and/or abused women and children to home spaces that include sharing and support. More women and children need this opportunity. How can this happen? The projects I have shown were created as if by magic. But the magic was and is the result of the vision and commitment of groups deciding to take action. There is latent magic at this conference. The magic rests in creating a goal. Money supports the magic, but need not be there at the outset. All development, private and nonprofit, uses OPM (Other People's Money). Greedy private developers working with savings and loan institutions around the U.S. used all our money for their commercial ventures. We are paying for it now and will be paying for it for years out of our taxes.

For innovative ventures, how and where to access money becomes clearer as the details of the goal emerge. There is no one way to do it, but money can always be found to deal with crisis. Crisis money can fatten the *status quo* coffers but it can also create a wider base of self-sufficiency for our world. The clarity of the goal, which is helped by having a site and/or architectural drawings, makes access to money easier. That may be the most important lesson we can adopt from our capitalist patriarchal traditions of development. We are only at the beginnings of feminist leadership in development that can change the face of architecture from monuments-as-usual to more conserving and pluralistic building characteristics and approaches. Patriarchal control and assumptions are still embedded in policy, education, and the leadership of form-making, zoning, housing regulations, business, economics, banking, real estate, and development.

Can more advocates for women chip away at the edges of outmoded traditions by becoming developers? Can these new developers bring a new morality to a planet choking on pollution, much of it caused in the U.S. by commuting from suburbs designed to isolate women and children? What can we do with all the unaffordable and deteriorating single family houses that are vulnerable to or which have already faced foreclosure? The big question is: Can an army of new nontraditional developers, an army of Eves, recreate the garden we have lost through centuries of patriarchal domination of building and land development?

References

Bassuk, Ellen, Lenore Rubin, and Alison Lauriat, "Characteristics of Sheltered Homeless Families." *American Journal of Public Health*, 76 (September 1986):1097–1101.

Dumpson, James R. *A Shelter is Not a Home: Report of the Manhattan Borough President's Task Force on Housing Homeless Families.* New York: Office of the President of the Borough of Manhattan, 1987.

Edelman, Marion Wright. *Families in Peril: An Agenda for Social Change.* Cambridge: Harvard University Press, 1987.

Harmon, Willis and John Hormann. *Creative Work.* Indianapolis: Knowledge Systems, 1990.

Pearce, Diana. *The More Things Change: A Status Report on Displaced Homemakers and Single Parents in the 1980s.* Washington, D.C.: National Displaced Homemakers Network, 1990.

Sprague, Joan Forrester. *More Than Housing: Lifeboats for Women and Children.* Boston: Butterworth Architecture, 1991.

U.S. Bureau of the Census and Department of Housing and Urban Development. *American Housing Survey for the United States in 1987.* Washington, D.C.: U.S. Department of Commerce, Bureau of the Census, 1989.

Chapter 43
Language, Sacred Places, and Transitional Housing

Mary J. Follenweider

Mary J. Follenweider earned her degree in mathematics and science from DePaul University and a Master of Architecture from the University of Colorado at Denver. She works for Robert E. Herndon and Associates Architects as a project manager and head of computer services. For a number of years, she had her own part-time business as an interior design consultant. She is an associate member of AIA, a member of ACSA, a board member of the Denver professional organization, Women in Architecture, and is on the Colorado Artists' Registry. She has given several talks about women's spaces as imagined through women's writings, both fictional and nonfictional.

Concepts of sacred place are rooted deep within the cultural myths of a society. The revisioning of myth and of archetypal patterning done by women writers, grounded in "her" experience of the sacred, provides a new language for the creation of women's sacred places. The creation of a physical sacred space to inhabit can not only empower women through its design, but also transform architectural language to a language which speaks with a truly human voice. By incorporating elements of women's sacred place with the physical needs of transitional housing, the process may not only transform the residents, but also ultimately transform the language of the built environment. In this paper it is the context of white, middle class women in the United States, which is primarily considered.

Language—A System for Change

Language is a sign system which attempts to assimilate how a culture understands itself in relationship to the universal mystery of life. To explore this relationship, language provides the vehicle by which the culture acquires meaning through defining reality into a usable medium. By interpreting and organizing the world which individuals experience through their senses, words not only become symbolic expressions of thoughts and ideas, but also provide an order for formulating these thoughts and ideas. Thus words image the world, and this imagery provides structure to everyday existence. Since language is a human convention, it is influenced by cultural values, which filter the extent of the reality which can be ordered and the extent to which language can express this reality (Miller, 1976, 137). When this expression is inadequate language changes or new languages emerge.

Is this the origin of a "women's" language? Possibly, although to separate a distinct sign system is not easy; it requires that the "word" be judged in its real world context, and this revolves around a complex combination of judgments (Lakoff, 1975, 59). Nothing can ever be entirely isolated from its environment, and to operate in a vacuum is self-deception. However, because of entrapping social norms, gender roles which challenge women's authenticity and tension between "her" power and "her" powerlessness, women withdraw from hostile environments, seeking personal modes of self-exploration (Pratt, 1981, 67). Virginia Woolf was thinking of books whose writers withdrew from the patriarchal culture into self space to generate new modes of being, new language, books which were female in their vision, in their narrative structure, and in their language (Fryer, 1986, 44).

Ostriker in her book, *Stealing the Language* (1986, 211), states that "it is a vigorous and varied invasion of the sanctuaries of the existing language where women write strongly as women." It is her belief that women writing "subvert and transform" life and literature by revisionist use of gender imagery. Adrienne Rich defines revision as: "the act of looking back, of seeing with fresh eyes, of extending an old text from a new critical direction" (Fryer, 1986, 235–236). This new experience through revision gives old words new meanings. The emerging of a women's language through revisioning allows for the opportunity of change and transformation of social and cultural structures.

Archetypal Patterning

All language originates from basic archetypal concepts of the sacred. Archetypal imagery derives from the reoccurrences of patterning in life experiences. This repetitiveness transcends everyday existence, but is intimately woven into the fabric of the culture. Jung saw these images as being derived from the unconscious. Archetypal images mark a visible transition from the unconscious through the consciousness of the human condition. For women there exists a commodity of experience which images itself through repeated patterning woven throughout stories, rituals, images, and symbols (Pratt, 1981, 3).

Helen Campbell wrote: "Cleaning can never pass from women's hands ... for to keep the world clean, this is the one great task for women" (Torre, 1977, 18). Homekeeping is an archetypal pattern going back even to paleolithic times when women have been credited with inventing containers. In the late nineteenth and early twentieth century, as women increasingly went outside the home, causing a then-perceived social imbalance, the model home became the rigid structure imposed as a means of establishing and maintaining order and control (Fryer, 1986, 28). Mary Pattison defends this structure with the statement, "Better homes will give a better government, and better politics better homes" (Torre, 1977, 18). This patterning continued into the 1960's with Martha-Ann Kirk's song, "Washer Woman God":

> Washer woman God, we know you in the water,
> Washer woman God, splashing, laughing free,
> If you didn't clean the mess where would we be,
> Washer woman God,

But by the 1980's the archetypal patterning of keeping house and cleaning seemingly has lost some of its sacredness.

> We had simply ceased to consider the room a parlor. Who would think of dusting or sweeping the cobwebs down in a room used for the storage of cans and newspapers, things utterly without value ... (Marilynne Robinson, 1980, 180).

Cleaning and housekeeping are still women's domain, but through revisioning it is being desanctified. Women need to discover patterning that are common among themselves and/or to create new images and stories which could lead to change in the language system, (Lauter, 1984, 208). Through a change in the language it is possible to affect the language system of architecture and the built form.

Myths

Myths change, are rejected, or new myths are created, when the existing ones can no longer adequately express the experience of the individual. They are the way that the culture attempts to understand itself in relationship to the universal whole. This understanding results in a better knowledge of self. Although culture cannot be totally assessed through direct perception or recognition, it does become an integral part of how individual lives are structured (Lauter, 1984, 209, 1–2). Myth reaches into preconscious experience and into symbolic order, emerging in that which is expressed through language, ritual, and symbols (Ecker, 1986, 19–20).

Myth forms a common ground of women's experience, strains of resonating inner journeys. Women's exploration of myths is a necessary part of remembering, because, by claiming the words, "her" reality is affirmed. The chief vocation then is to become conscious of the acts of myth making that do occur, and to establish a viable relationship with those myths relevant to every woman's experience. This ongoing process collectively reclaims and remembers both new and ancient intuitions, rituals, symbols, and patterning (Lauter, 1984, 213, 4). The connection among women is acknowledged by the recognition that the faces in mythology are really our own.

> Whenever a poet employs a figure or a story previously accepted and defined by culture, the poet is using myth, and the potential is always present that the use will be revisionist; that is, the figure or tale will be appropriated for altered ends, the old vessel filled with new wine, initially

satisfying the thirst of the individual poet, but ultimately making cultural change possible (Ostriker, 1986, 212–213).

This is myth-making. The revisioning used by women writers in myth-making provides symbolic meaning and importance beyond itself, accessing the realm of the subconscious where memories and dreams are engendered, where the interior reality is an intuitive mapping of the true self (Pratt, 1981, 178).

The "home" myth can represent a trap, a tomb. Much has been written about this myth's seemingly finer qualities, but still the entrapment imagery remains sharp and strong. Marilyn French calls it the fantasy it is and writes:

> Jack, Jack pumpkin eater
> Had a wife and couldn't keep her.
> Put her in a pumpkin shell
> And there he kept her very well.
> After the ball, after the finery,
> Cinderella's coach turns into a pumpkin shell.
> Yes that was what that was all about" (1980, 188).

Still the myth lives on: women's trap is her salvation, her identity, her reason for existence.

The myth of "room" has also been a continuing myth within women's writings and offers images of inner space denied externally. As the myth of home exists for the convenience of others, the imagery of room denotes a personal space, singular and sacred for women. Coexisting with the myth of the entrapment, women have placed the "room" in otherness. Ellen S. Richards (in her article "The Cost of Shelter," written in 1916) stated: "The comfort in living is far more in the brain than in the back." The imagery of real space continues to exist in the mind. Rika Lesser writes: "I try to keep my house within my head" (Torre, 1977, 186). Marilyn French (1980, 77) puts it quite adamantly when she writes: "It takes room, the room to choose, the room to entertain possibilities." Women have not had the room. It has been controlled and ordered by others. French (1980, 50) also alludes to the idea that men have many "compartments" for their women, sports, work, etc. and in each space they act differently, while women have only one room and act the same whatever they do. Mary Daly revisions the imagery, "as she creates her self, she creates new space, semantics, cognitive, symbolic, psychic, physical spaces. She moves into these spaces and finds room to breathe, to breathe forth further spaces" (Daly, 1990, 340). The imagery changes from room to rooms, new spaces, physical spaces as women's new experience of self-revising myth.

Sacred Place

Elizabeth Dodson Gray (1988) in her book, *Sacred Dimensions of Women's Experience,* defines sacred space as a "magic ring, a ring of sanctification … consecrated by the dailyness of incredible nurturing care." The definition is boundary restricted and centers on mothering, reinforcing once again women's spiritual confinement to the domestic imagery. Annis Pratt defines sacred space as "the sanctuaries and rooms into which women withdraw from society … fantastic but in a positive sense (Pratt, 1981, 165). They are projections of an ideal world." The power is to create new ways of being for women in new worlds. By creating new worlds for new beings, a new definition of sacred place is created. This space is dynamic; it affords movement. There is a real sense of fluid motion, energy, excitement, and empowerment. There is freedom. The imagery of the mystical force, "magic circle" is alien to an image of the empowering spiral, which allows movement by its form but also is managed by its own internal integrity. It allows movement simultaneously inward and outward by self-propulsion. Everyone has watched a slinky go down the stairs and marveled at its seemingly innate ability to be self-propelled, self-directed, flexible, expansible and contractible, controlled, and ordered all at the same time. It seems to have a life and power of its own. This reimaging of sacred space as a dynamic spiral transforms boundaries from solid enclosures of space, to movements which occupy space.

The spiral image of sacred place applies easily to physical space. It acknowledges the order and the discipline of an interior domain, entrusting the responsibility for self-protection, self-assertion, self-expansion, and self-actualization to the woman, while maintaining control and order. Mary Daly uses a similar imagery when she refers to women as "Spinning Voyagers," creating centers within movement. The spiral imagines a vast space while remaining intimately connected. Rooted in revisioned myth, the revisioning of the spatial imagery of sacred spaces grant the possibility for transformation. Only through entering a space that is psychically innovative is it possible to fundamentally affect one's nature and outwardly affect the environment (Fryer, 1986, 310).

As the rhythm became faster and more complex, the normally docile women threw off their wraps and danced with movements that were unrestrained and frankly erotic.... Their pent-up emotions, so repressed in everyday life, were released in the uninhibited motion. Tensions drained in a catharsis of freedom...(Auel, 1980, 93).

This imagery originates in a new myth of the sacred. Even though Jean Auel writes of ancient times, her language is of today, and she writes of sacred places. To be truly free is to create dynamic spaces in which women are free to dance, to spin, to imagine, to journey. Women's spiraling sacred places are places which are tactile, physical, "frankly" erotic, spiritual, mediative, and mystical (Fryer, 1986, 301).

Physical, Erotic, Spiritual, Mediative, Mystical

Space is experienced by engaging the senses. If woman's unique experience impacts her sensory approach, then her aesthetics, i.e., relationship to matter and material, her perception, her means of processing tactile and temporal rhythms can express itself in a distinctive form.

The question then is: Is there a feminist aesthetic? This may be true as an aesthetic awareness, or modes of sensory perceptions, and not necessarily as a theory of art, although Bovenschen in "Is There A Feminist Aesthetic?" seemingly takes a revisionist approach when she writes that feminine artistic production takes place by means of a complicated process involving conquering and reclaiming, appropriating and formulating, as well as forgetting and subverting. This can be found both in artistic tradition as well as breaking with it (Ecker, 1986, 47–49). Virginia Woolf (1929, 87) writes:

> The rooms differ so completely, they are calm or thunderous, open on to the sea, or on the contrary, give on to a prison yard; are hung with washing, or alive with opals and silks; are hard as horse hair, or soft as feathers—one has only to go into any room in any street for the whole of that extremely complex force of femininity to fly in one's face.

The complexity of women's spirit may need to be unraveled before a feminine aesthetic will truly be defined.

Simone de Beauvoir severely doubted that the female body could provide a new vision of the world (Ecker, 1986, 33). Van Vliet in *Women, Housing, Community* (1988, 3) states that "it is hard to conceive of a theoretical frame work from which to derive such uniquely feminist guidelines," guidelines which could offer a

solution to real life issues. Revisionist theory offers that a feminist aesthetic is possible; however, it may be far too early to assess its ability to impact real issues, although based upon the above discussion transformation is possible. Ultimately, the definition must be a truly human one, not theory in abstraction or isolation, because a narrow definition would create its own bondage, become culturally invisible and lack forms to visualize the meaning (Tregebow, 1987, 136–137).

Physical

Women have been confined, restricted to the space of one's body, and not even allowed to acknowledge that. Spaciousness has always been a luxury for women. Spaciousness implies freedom to move, great spaces in which to lodge "her" universe (Fryer, 1986, 49–50). The image of vessel has long been an archetypal form of the feminine, and the power over the mysteries of life has been preserved in this symbol. It orders boundaries and its enclosures. As an archetypal form it defines "dwelling," as the sacred domain of women, both controlling her and ordering her as she orders and controls, eliminating any possibility of freedom (Neumann, 1963, 282). This has been done even to the point, as discussed earlier, as a means of control of social problems by ordering domestic space, without regard to the damage inflicted upon woman's spirit. The outcome has been disastrous. Under male-oriented repetitive space frame, places in which women dwell have been defined by language created by men, designed by men and built by men without female input or alternative choices of organization and design. Women have always transformed these empty dens with bric-a-brac and surface expressions of domestic tranquillity. The vessel imagery as an archetypal symbol of the feminine should provide empowerment and transformation for women, but for great spans of time it has imprisoned her spirit and kept her in her wrongful place.

Jung built in stone a mythic structure in order to learn to inhabit a world of words and symbols to which he belonged by right. The stone and permanence of his tradition (Fryer, 1986, 339) validated his existence. Women have the same right to claim through shape and structure, a spaciousness in which to actualize their uniqueness not confined to a domestic reality. This need for a reawakening of sensitivity of physical space, an actualization of sacred place, should be of primary importance for women (Ecker, 1986, 128).

Erotic

Through the exploration of myth residing within women's collective experience of their unconscious, their dreams, their psyche, women have become aware of "self," body and spirit, and realize that the two are one. There is no hierarchical division, as in Jung and Erich Neumann's versions of the female Being, into Sky Goddess and Earth Mother. Female writers do have the tendency to reunite the flesh and the spirit into an integrated whole. The result is a revolt against defining the universe into sacred and profane space, redeeming and uniting that which has been excluded and rejected. Reclaiming self and annihilating the edge, relocating directly in the center, creates a new definition of sacred (Ostriker, 1986, 219, 195–197).

Placing spirituality within the body is the undeniable acknowledgment of the erotic, and the embracing of the feminine sexuality is an integral part of sacred. Women's sexuality provides a sacred joy which when embraced creates movement, new space, a new sense of authenticity of "her" universe (Ostriker, 1986, 220). Images and form replace words, locating meaning in the incomplete pieces of memory (Fryer, 1986, 320). Fryer in talking about Willa Cather states:

> concentration on her inner vision, she pares down language so that words exist as objects, physical things implying spiritual connectedness, as she searches for a form simple and pure enough to express her desire, to contain it exactly. (Fryer, 1986, 291)

The power of language is in its ability to connect the body and the spirit.

Spiritual, Mediative, Mystical

Spirituality is at the center. In many cultures the tower, the pole, the pillar has symbolized the center of sacred place connecting the upper and lower cosmos. Because of the unified self, women place themselves at the center. We are the center. There is no pillar or tower. There is no separation, no hierarchy, all is one. By finding the center of one's boundless desire, and to give form to it, is a creation of sacred space (Fryer, 1986, 338, 293). Sacred place becomes the physical form originated in myths both personal and collective by which women affirm their unique identity.

Space

Space is by no means a neutral entity. It is a formidable task to impact such a cultural mediator, but there has always been the belief that environments, particularly domestic environments, bring about social change (Torre, 1977, 127). In periods of social stability, space is shaped by culturally accepted values, and reinforces these values. However, during periods of transition, when the difficult task of value changing is going on, such as today, when economic and political systems and their ideological supports do not conform to values and needs of specific segments of society, when the myth changes, physical forms are seen as inadequate and inappropriate. In order to make significant changes to physical space, social values need to change and to be integrated into the socio-political fabric (Birch, 1985, 251).

Charlotte Perkins Gilman in *Herland* states that the patriarchal modes of competition upon which our socio-economic system is based must change because it is antithetical to the female experience (Fryer, 1986, 41). Virginia Woolf in *A Room of One's Own* believes that financial independence and a room of one's own is the solution to women's plight, but in order for the socio-economic system to change, the physical environment must also change. Then women can enjoy economic freedom (Fryer, 1986, 38). A woman's needs are linked to "her" role in society and to the decision making processes linked to that role, which directly impact those spaces which she occupies. The chances that women can significantly alter the landscape are slim, because of how the present socio-political system and design profession are aligned (Mazey, 1983, 66).

Feminist critics have been analyzing women's writings for over ten years and although much has been written and critiqued about women's changing role in social and economic terms, the physical environment seems to be taken for granted or generally overlooked (Van Vliet, 1988, 1–3). Most women architects, like women writers, are outside the mainstream practice and the present socio-political structures (Werkerle, 1980, 214). Architectural schools and the professional community are still male domains, and women are seldom in positions of power. The power to birth a physical form is a "God" mythology which will not be easily rewritten.

Adele Chatfield-Taylor in "You Can't Make a Silk Purse Out of Suburbia," writes: "Architecture is, next to men, the most oppressive force in our society, obsolete architecture is one of the things that is holding us back" (Torre, 1977, 167–168). Architecture does lag behind in developing a viable feminist critique. It has yet to come to grips with the fact that little or no input by women has gone into architectural forms, while these same forms impact women's lives (Tregebow, 1987, 129–131).

Birnkey and Weisman (1975) state: "If women's needs are to be environmentally supported, then each woman must become her own architect, that is, she must become aware of the ability to exercise environmental judgment and make decisions about the nature of spaces in which she lives and works." There has been a reluctance among women designers to use existing architectural forms because of the patriarchal message of dominance and power which they envision, even to the point of creating anti-architecture–no architecture. Women have not wanted to identify themselves with any built form because of its inherent imagery (Torre, 1977, 161, 132). Women's spaces have been a language of control and submission. However, as difficult as it is to confront this stronghold on symbology, it is necessary for women not to back down from the challenge of transforming the language and the message, and begin the task of form-making. Revisioning forms creates new expressions of spatial imagery which can support and nurture those spaces which women inhabit on a daily basis.

Women and Architecture

What is important is that what has been imposed upon women through the oppressive value system of the present socio-political system not be further perpetuated in women's aesthetics (Ecker, 1986, 16). Going where women have created spaces for themselves, or going where women have temporarily made space for themselves and their activities presents the opportunity for form-making (Ecker, 1986, 132). Transitional housing is an initial phase in the evolution/revolution of women's spaces. The woman in crisis has felt threatened and insecure both inside and outside the home to the point that the situation has become intolerable (Refuerzo, 1990, 34). The psycho-social loss is exacerbated by a corresponding loss of control over the immediate spatial environment and one's life. Crisis intervention does provide a limited time of safe haven, but because of the highly traumatized situation in which such women find themselves the woman, in most cases, may not be capable of reconnecting with "her" space as an essential component of the healing process. As

women have been denied space for a long time, reclamation becomes important for all women, but particularly for those who suffer displacement due to inhabiting "unsafe" spaces.

Transitional housing harkens back to women's cooperative housing of the late nineteenth and early twentieth century. Each of these experiments in living was unique, but all were based on the principle of equality and acceptance (Mazey, 1983, 62). Transitional housing can provide the means by which new lives through revisioning and concepts of sacred places can facilitate new kinds of structures as a real force for change. It can connect individuals to the greater universal myth of human existence, allowing women to feel the essential connection to the greater whole and begin the much needed process of healing. This type of housing can also be the beginning of the transformation of women's built environments, transforming the individual, and ultimately transforming the society and the language of the built form.

Women always remain individuals and their sacred places remain uniquely their own. Residents of transitional housing need to be in control of their environments. Boundaries need to be fluid but under direct control of the woman. Women's concern for safety and security are in direct proportion to how much uncertainty has been alleviated. In talking about their newly installed transitional housing, the director of the Boulder County Safehouse, a crisis intervention center for battered women in Boulder, Colorado, stated that the need for control goes as far as to include control over natural light, hot water, heat, and room temperature. Refuzero's (1990, 46, 49) study of four shelters in Los Angeles and two in New Orleans reiterates this need to control one's immediate environment as a means of coping with the lack of control in one's life. According to the study, the job of the shelter is to buffer out unwanted visual elements and noise, creating a calm, non-chaotic setting while allowing surveillance of site and quality views of the surrounding environments. The spiral imagery of sacred place promotes the layering of spaces from public to private, which remain flexible and expandable, subject to the needs of the residents. Through design, transitional housing can address broader issues such as economic opportunities, and can be organized to blend the physical needs of shelter, the economic advantages of sharing, and the social aspects of community service (Birch, 1985, 44–45).

However, the most important element that transitional housing can provide is sacred space, a sacred place for each woman, independent of any living space, but a space specifically catering to the woman's spirit. The idea of the French "boudoir" may have come the closest to this concept. In a 1987 interview in the Boulder Daily Camera newspaper, Lizzie Borden, the film-maker of the movie, *Working Girls,* a documentary about "madam" houses stated: "There was a kind of a drawing room atmosphere. It's so much of a woman's space...." It should be remembered that the patriarchal society has done an exceptional job of defining its reality by creating sacred places as an outward manifestation of its mythological roots. These sacred places have translated into hierarchical structures, such as churches and as skyscrapers, separate from everyday existence, but visual and ideological perpetuators of the mythology. Woman's sacred reality is a necessary and integral part of her life. It is not hierarchical and separate, but it is distinct and it is essential that it be acknowledged as a real part of her environment.

This requires there be an actual physical space from which woman's daily life radiates outward into the everyday world. The imagery of the spiral reorients the dwelling from a box polarity to one of radiating spokes, layers, or nodes. Mary Daly (1990, 396–397) uses the imagery of a spider's web as a spiral net diverging from a central point where the spider sits as the symbol of the center of the world. Judith Thuman writes: "My life alone within that room has evolved a precise shape, a formality like that of a web" (Torre, 1977, 188). The power is that the architectural form would change, be revisioned, and the language right along with it, because women could choose freely from a range of potentially available "neutral" architectural forms with their capacities for new narrative and symbolic expression based upon a new vision of sacred place (Tregebow, 1987, 142). The imagery of radiating spokes is an adaptable imagery to possess and to translate, to form-make, to revision form. It is "room which breathes forth more rooms" (Daly, 1990, 340). Women would have a sense of their own space as a tangible reality, validating and empowering outward from the center of their being. The difference is that it is a dynamic revision based upon women's own unique interpretation of their mythological experience. The rootedness in the revisioned myth manifested in women's sacred space would allow for success where it has not existed. It would be powerful because of this grounding. This reorientation could be so empowering that, a truly human transformation could result from which a new language of community would emerge.

References

Auel, Jean M. *The Clan of the Cave Bear.* New York: Bantam Books, 1980.

Birkley, Noel Phyllis, and Leslie Kanes Weisman, "A Woman-Built Environment: Constructive Fantasies Quest," A Feminist Quarterly," 1975.

Birch, Eugenie Ladner., ed. *The Unsheltered Woman: Women and Housing in The Eighty's.* New Jersey, Center for Urban Policy Research, Rutger's University, 1985.

Daly, Mary. *Gyn/Ecology: The Metaethics of Radical Feminism.* Boston: Beacon Press, 1990.

Ecker, Gisela., ed. *Feminist Aesthetics.* Boston: Beacon Press, 1986.

French, Marilyn. *The Bleeding Heart.* New York: Summit Books, 1980.

Fryer, Judith. *Felicitous Space: The Imaginative Structure of Edith Wharton and Willa Cather.* Chapel Hill, North Carolina: The University of North Carolina Press, 1986.

Gray, Elizabeth Dodson., ed. *Sacred Dimensions of Women's Experience.* Wellesley, Massachusetts: Roundtable Press, 1988.

Lakoff, Robin. *Language and Women's Place.* New York: Harper & Row, 1975.

Lauter, Estella. *Women as Mythmakers: Poetry and Visual Art by Twentieth Century Women.* Bloomington, Indiana: Indiana University Press, 1984.

Mazey, Mary Ellen, and David Lee. *Her Space, Her Place: A Geography of Women.* State College, Pennsylvania: Resource Publications in Geography, Commercial Printing, Inc., 1983.

Miller, Casey, and Kate Swift. *Words and Women.* New York: Anchor Press/ Doubleday, 1976.

Neumann, Erich. *The Great Mother.* Princeton, New Jersey: Princeton University Press, 1963.

Ostriker, Alicia Suskin. *Stealing The Language: The Emergence of Women's Poetry in American.* Boston: Beacon Press, 1986.

Pratt, Annis., and Barbara White, Andrea Loewenstein, Mary Wyer. *Archetypal Patterns in Women's Fiction.* Bloomington, Indiana. Indiana University Press, 1981.

Refuerzo, Ben J., and Stephen Verderber. "Dimension of Person Environment: Relationships in Shelter for Victims of Domestic Violence." *The Journal of Architectural and Planning Research*, vol. 7, no. 1 (Spring, 1990).

Robinson, Marilynne. *Housekeeping.* New York: Farrar Straus Giroux, 1980.

Torre, Susan, ed. *Women in American Architecture: A Historical and Contemporary Perspective.* New York: Whitney Library of Design, 1977.

Tregebow, Rhea., ed. *Work in Progress: Building Feminist Culture.* Toronto, Canada: The Women's Press, 1987.

Van Vliet, Willen, ed. *Women, Housing and Community.* Aldershot, England: Avebury, 1988.

Wekerle, Greda R., and Rebecca Patterson, David Morley. *New Space for Women.* Boulder, Colorado: Westview Press, 1980.

Woolf, Virginia. *A Room of One's Own.* New York: Harcourt Brace Jovanovich, 1929.

Chapter 44

Shelter: A Place of the Telling
a chimerical cookbook

Tami Silverman and Chris Taylor

Tami Silverman attended the Art Institute of Pittsburgh and Kent State University for Art/Photography from 1978 to 1982. In 1982, she became a retailer and traveler for six years. In 1988, she received a Bachelor of Arts in Sociology from the University of South Florida and later began work as a freelance photo assistant in New York City. In 1990, she did graduate work in photography and literary criticism at the University of Florida.

Chris Taylor studied architecture at the University of Florida from 1983 to 1987. In 1987 he attended the Cambridge Graduate School of Design where he focused on the model as a design tool. He received a Master of Architecture from Harvard University in 1990.

Shelter is thought of as an enclosed space, a refuge of safety, hidden. Institutional shelter is defined in the moment of re-domestication. "Not conforming to the dearly held ideals of hard work, property ownership and family membership" (Lesley Harman, When a Hostel Becomes a Home, p.21), vagrants are perceived as a threat to society and must be controlled. Forced back into the fold, they return to the invisible state of submission. The language of the institution becomes unacceptable in its intransigence. There is a need to invent a language that is neither shameful nor pejorative, a language that includes and places. This becomes the language of the telling, a language which merges desire and action. The language of the institution separates desire from action especially when those desires do not coincide with the agenda of the institution.

We are re-defining shelter of the displaced other, of the woman without her home. The hope is that she may create a place for herself, beyond the interminable structure of the institution. We need to reinvent the strategies to make ourselves, to realize our own stories. Throughout time, his-story has been considered fact, documentable truth, denying interpretation. Her-story has been seen as fiction, hysteria, old wives tales, stories for children. The woman has remained invisible, without a visible place to speak, without a place to tell her-story. Because she can not tell, given neither the opportunity nor the vehicle. She keeps. "Women hold the repositories of life and death, or of time in them, women know that both the material and the measure of living is time." (Kathy Acker, In Memoriam To Identity, p.156)

Silence will not protect us from our fears. We must challenge our fears beginning the search of woman as miner, woman as time-keeper (with her own time and rhythm). Woman as story-teller, visible and no longer shamed by her-story or visibility. The ritual of mining empowers her to collect/access the fragments of her memory/time. In the moment of the telling, the woman begins to weave the found/mined fragments visibly, creating for herself a place and an identity, unrestricted. Shelter is defined in the moment of telling. Shelter strives to release her from the dependency on the institution by imparting the tools for mining her own identity. Digging through and under white male doctrine and history, shelter becomes a place for the telling, a place for the under-mining. Digging deep into her own truth/time/memories she invents her own language, weaves her own identity, tells her own story.

Entering into a dialogue of questions, rather than a monologue of polemics, we explore the definition of shelter. Not only for women, but for all people who fall-out of the putative culture, people who do not fit neatly into the graveclothes of hegemony. This is a collaboration relying on serendipity revealed through action, an associative dialogue rather than a categorical examination. We are encouraging people to step away from their houses and onto the streets, to challenge themselves and reflect upon the definition of shelter. "If identity is a house, then what is safety?" (Kathy Acker, In Memoriam To Identity, p.119)

Through this paper we hope to define shelter in terms which extend beyond the limits of accommodation and begin to deal with issues of place involving the individual and the personal within society. The traditional (institutional) notion of shelter (an enclosed space of protection, a refuge of safety, a place of hiding) with its objective of correction, is not capable of extending beyond accommodation and addressing questions of fundamental concern to our social/urban existence. To attempt the re-domestication of those who have fallen out of the putative culture merely reifies the position and the legitimacy of that culture. Laying claim to the fact that the women/people in question must adapt to the unbending norms of that culture. Adaption is required to survive within a structure dominated by the language of mathematical reason, the facts of logic and proof, a structure built up to preserve the power of the status quo.

There is a need to explore a model for making shelter that is based on transformation, rather than adaption. A model which openly instills invention and dialogue, asserting the position of the personal as valid. A model which questions the relation between personal and public by challenging the objective with the subjective. A mode of operation that is driven more by association than by logical progression.

The cookbook is borrowed here as an organizing vehicle, an active model to contain (house-hold) the work of the under-miner. The cookbook is an analogy. A practical handbook. It serves as a vehicle to focus and empower the prevailing kitchen table talk. It presents a strategy for the formation of a collective voice, an opportunity to generatively weave personal, public, and political forms of knowledge.

Packed with heterogeneous components, the cookbook contains ingredients which can be used to compose a discourse (dialogue) on transformative shelter. A working model of collection and distribution. The cookbook is a conductive demonstration, merging action

and reflection in a theory (critical) which is both visible and accessible.

The cookbook is a deliberate attempt to provide a frame of research which engages both the symbolic and the analytical modes of inquiry.[1] It does not lend isolated, objective, answers. Instead it orients a specific direction. It establishes momentum.

Academic men and women engaged in the production of feminist theory must be responsible for setting up ways to disseminate feminist thought that not only transcend the boundaries of the university setting, but that of the printed page as well. It is also our responsibility to promote and encourage the development of feminist theory by folks who are not academics. As long as the university remains "the" central site for the development of feminist scholarship, it will be necessary for us to examine the ways in which our work can and is undermined.[2]

There is a need to undermine the language of mathematical reason with a mythos, a variable order, a personal voice, which embraces chimera as a valid and intersubjective mode of operation.[3]

chimera 1 a : a she-monster in Greek mythology represented as vomiting flames and usually as having a lion's head, goat's body, and dragon's or serpent's tail b : a similar imaginary monster : a grotesque animal form in painting or sculpture compounded from parts of different real or imaginary animals c : a horrible or frightening manifestation d : an often fantastic combination of incongruous parts, esp. a fabrication 2 : an illusion or fabrication of the mind or fancy 3 : an individual, organ, or part consisting of tissues of diverse genetic constitution occurring esp. in plants and most frequently at a graft union[4]

Notice the connection between SHE-monster and fantastical schemes, improbable notions and incongruous parts (non-conforming action). Is the monster a she because fantastical schemes and unrestrained imagination are her characteristics, or is it because when she has visible dreams and unrestrained imagination, does she, by virtue of this, transform into a monster?

"chimera ... are much more permanent reference points than fixed mile markers—in the manner, for example, of the right and the left, which also change as one turns.... When one considers that thought is constant mobility, in the end it may only be chimera that are usable references, pole stars."[5]

Shelter, a place to mine for clues, gaps, pole stars. Shelter is created with Chimera in mind.

Chimera is becoming.

She is the process of transformation. Her transformation is not only internal, but also visi ble. She pursues the links, the connections by under-mining all she can access.

Culture, Society, History, Language

Chimera is becoming a model because she is thought to have "unattainable" goals and "unrealizable" dreams. She is chimerical because she has an intention to affirm and weave herself into an active subjective position within culture.

Because she wants to work within a context that will not accept her, except as a dupe of itself, she under-mines and dis-mantles the deceptions of language that have been forged upon her.

> The fundamental axiom of the sciences since 1800, as well as of the humanities, has been 'invariance,' which rejects, or at least is unable to cope with the richness and ambiguity of symbolic thought.[6] The rhetoric of scientific proof has debased the validity of personal story and myth. As an independent entity, the power of logical and mathematical reason is a force which has affected our entire culture. The language of objective reason has been appropriated to support a patriarchal system of oppression and exploitation. As a language of control, it dictates the conventions of production for a truly "modern" knowledge, that is, a universal knowledge, information devoid of the personal, subjective, or symbolic. Information relegated to the realm of verifiable facts. The voice of the personal has been systematically displaced from the language of our culture.

Digging deep into her mine she re-collects memories, pieces of her-story. Chimera is the tool of the under-miner. Subverting the material that has traditionally appropriated her,[7] she weaves it into a context that includes, affirms, and encourages her participation. Chimera re-means what she dis-covers to allow her own voice to e-merge from the mine. The under-miner adopts a subjective position.

> Throughout time, his-story has been considered fact, documentable truth, denying interpretation. Her-story has been seen as fiction, hysteria, old wives tales. The woman has remained invisible, without a visible place to speak, without a place to tell her-story. Because she can not tell, because she is given neither the opportunity nor the vehicle. She keeps. "Women hold the repositories of life and death, or of time in them, women know that both the material and the measure of living is time."[8]

Reconstructing, she begins the ritual of telling. Gathering her voice. It becomes her mission to affirm her own self, dis-covering the subjective, weaving a dialogue that merges the personal within a visible, public context.

> "To write in public with others carries a quite different meaning: the construction of another space for the manifestation of the plural word, the place of confluence of different voices, currents, traditions."[9] Made visible, the collective voice of renga[10] is not monolithic. Neither authoritarian nor objective it is a voice of broken units, individual threads conjoining to weave a fabric of personal dialogue. Not a product of generalization, "renga is, before everything, a mode of practice."[11] An active model of confluence and transference. Reading and writing the collective voice.

Chimera is not anarchistic. Chimera is the under-miner. She uncovers the tools which assist in dis-mantling the facts that have been inscribed upon her by the dominant patriarchal structure. Under-mining is not merely an exercise in demolition. She develops a place of resistance.

> "... we have to create ...
> 'communities of resistance' — so that there are places where we can recover, and return to ourselves more fully.[12]

The material is re-worked in a way that re-asserts it into a public context, a way which includes memories, stories, as they begin to unwind and disclose themselves.

> Renga provides a model for the re-assertion of the personal within the public. Renga is an act of collaboration, a series of incongruences, split or broken verse. Operating with simple rules of tangency (association), renga creates an opportunity for chance to appear within the construction of a collective voice.

Affirming her place within, she gains empowerment and accountability in becoming part of the collective.

> *Dialogue is transformative.*

In telling she transforms.

> "True dialogue cannot exist unless the dialoguers engage in critical thinking—thinking which discerns an indivisible solidarity between the world and men and admits of no dichotomy between them—thinking which perceives reality as process, as transformation, rather than as a static entity—thinking which does not separate itself from action,

but constantly immerses itself in temporality without fear of the risks involved."[13]

The circulation of personal stories within a social/public context is critical. History as the preservation of old facts and hard exclusive evidence has atrophied into cultural rigormortis.[14] The permutable nature of reality is denied, left out, displaced, hidden.

Chimerical shelter is metamorphosis, not carapace.[15]

Shelter is a place of be-coming visible. Indoctrination. Suggesting that myth become an active agent of transformation. A way to gather material for re-invention and re-imagination. Chimerical shelter is a visible and resumptive process, not a refuge or an ephemeral glance at safety.

If identity is a house, what is safety?[16]

The distinction between house as object, and home as subject is crucial. When the house becomes an object of identity, describing a position within society, the values and needs of home as subject are buried, hidden, displaced, left without a visible place to speak.

Chimerical shelter provides a place to strip oneself of the identity of house. An identity that has been in-scribed onto us by the dogma of the dominant social structure. Required to wear the dog obediently and faithfully, we are cloaked in graveclothes. When we bark too loud or begin to shed in the process of be-coming visible, we are ushered into the house and retro-fitted for another suit. The same constricting, homog-enous suit.

Control always works through the imagination by making it invisible and domesticating it.[17] Women are especially (deliberately) alienated in the market place society. Made to stay, behave, be invisible, obey the norms, buy the right deodorant, be good and obedient consumers. When visible fallout occurs they are shuffled into a shelter for re-adaption, or re-integration as it is commonly referred to. Questions that challenge culture are never raised in the process of re-domestication.

Chimera recognizes the need for women to emerge from the carapace of culture. To work within, embrace, what has traditionally been used to subordinate them (femi-nism, fantasy, incoherence, emotion, ambiguity, subjectivity, and the ability to cook). To begin to strip the graveclothes and dig into the mine. Not mine as for

me, but mine as my connection to it/you/us. My place in the collective voice of difference. Mine as in we. We mine within the existing material in search of e-merging our-selves into our-culture. To collect and tell our stories.

We are searching to uncover the material that makes us, to collect the fragments of our time and being, to affirm our existence as something other than a market share, to weave our stories (personal) into culture which has abandoned the need for mythos, for a subjective body of knowledge that is passed on between people. Clues of survival. Sense-making (sense not in terms of facts, but in terms of existence. sense of place and being).

Storytelling

the story depends on everyone of us to come into being. It needs us all, needs our remembering, understanding and creating what we have heard together to keep on coming into being ... they call it the tool of primitive man, the simplest vehicle of truth. When history started separating itself from story, it started indulging in accumulation and facts.[18]

Rituals are tools to access memory.
Not made by history, but through informal participation, rituals define personal memory.
The story to be told.

Stories include and circulate. Nomadic wanders. Restless. Transmutable. Stories invoke the teller to re-invent their lives through collection and distribution.

History claims its ground in facts. Denying the transfer of personal engagement. Essentially removing itself from anything but the epitaph on its tombstone, which reads,

here lies history
frozen
will spoil if opened
please don't touch.

The story, her-story embodies exchange, a dialogue that is permutable, that can be passed on.

for the vision of a story that has no end, no middle, no beginning, no start, no stop, the vision of a madwoman ...[19]

Chimera tells her story. Inter-weaving the past and present, en-visioning and re-working the language of the future.

... incorporating into a language of the future, which means that one must learn to argue with unexplained terms and to use sentences for which no clear rules of usage are as yet available. Just as a child who starts using words without yet understanding them, who adds more and more uncomprehended linguistic fragments to his playful activity, discovers the sense-making principle only after he has been active in this way for a long time ... in the very same way the inventor of a new world view must be able to talk nonsense until the amount of nonsense created by him and his friends is big enough to give sense to all its parts.[20]

Through telling Chimera re-leases and re-kindles. Taking up the work of Time. She cooks. Telling invokes transformation. Affirming in its state of alterability. Taking an active role in the re-making of the self and the world.

Alchemy takes place in the same spiritual category: the alchemist takes up and perfects the work of Nature, while at the same time working to 'make' [her]self.[21]

Chimera undermines language to un-cover the things which oppress and objectify her. Digging in the gaps, she cooks up her itinerary of meaning, she e-merges as her own being.

... thus if the dead, if those who are to come, need an abode, what refuge could be more agreeable ... than this imaginary space? this enforces the connection that they wish to make, an abode for those yet to come ... which would be domicilitated neither in outer space nor entirely in inner consciousness ... but rather an imaginary space from which we can hear one another.[22]

Searching to join the personal (chimerical) within a visible public context she dwells in the gaps she has un-covered. She begins to speak and listen at the same time. Breaking down the dichotomy of speaking and listening in oppositional terms. Communication links cooperating subjects.

No longer can the work of shelter (the voice of women, personal) be contained. It spills out into the street. Kitchen table talk begins to mobilize as we share recipes. Making the cookbook. Chimera e-merges from the kitchen. Pushing the kitchen table out onto the street.

Chimera is becoming.

Notes

1   Gregory Ulmer, "The Euretics of Alice's Valise," *Journal of Architectural Education* (November, 1991)

Ulmer's study of euretics contains clues for the construction of this new frame of research. *Euretics is a cognitive practice coming into formation as an alternative to (not opposed to, but supplementing) hermeneutics and critique. The term, related to 'Eureka! I found it!,' is synonymous with thinking as discovery rather than as interpretation.* (Ulmer, 1991, p. 4)

2   bell hooks, *Talking Back: thinking feminist, thinking black* (South End Press, 1989), p. 36.

3   Alberto Perez-Gomez, *Architecture and the Crisis of Modern Science* (MIT Press, 1983)

For many architects, myth and poetry are generally considered synonymous with dreams and lunacy, while reality is deemed equivalent to prosaic scientific theories. In other words, mathematical logic has been substituted for metaphor as a model of thought. Art can be beautiful, of course, but only seldom is it understood as a profound form of knowledge, as a genuine intersubjective interpretation of reality. And architecture, particularly, must never partake of the alleged escapism of the other fine arts; it has to be, before anything else, a paradigm of efficient and economical construction. (Perez-Gomez, 1983, p. 6)

4   *Webster's Third New International Dictionary* (Merriam-Webster Inc., 1986), p. 389.

5   Jean DuBuffet, *Asphyxiating Culture* (Four Walls Eight Windows, 1988), p. 70

6   Alberto Perez-Gomez, *Architecture and the Crisis of Modern Science* p. 6.

7   Peter Sloterdijk, *A critique of Cynical Reason* (University of Minnesota Press, 1987)

What Diogenes demonstrates to his fellow citizens through his life-style would be designated now to the level of an animal. Because of this, the Athenians deropatorily call him "dog," for Diogenes had reduced his requirements to the living standards of a domestic pet. In doing so, he had freed himself from civilizations chain of needs. He thus also turned the Athenians' nickname around against them and accepted the insult as the name of his philosophy. (Sloterdijk, 1987, p. 165) As Diogenes embraced nd identified his title of dog, we work through ours as miners, working beneath the surface of our institutional existence, under-mining ourselves in order to embrace and identify ourselves.

8   Kathy Acker, *In Memoriam To Identity* (Grove Weidenfeld, 1990), p. 156.

9   Octavio Paz, *Renga: A Chain of Poems* (George Braziller, 1971), p. 27.

10   Hiroaki Sato, *One Hundred Frogs: From Renga to Haiku to English* (Weatherhill, 1983)

Renga is a collaborative form which evolved in Japan between the Heian period (794-1192) and the Moromachi, in the fourteenth and fifteenth centuries. *A renga consists of two to a hundred alternating parts of 5-7-5 and 7-7 syllables, usually written by two or more persons, with the linking made in such a way that any two consecutive parts must make an intelligible whole, but three may not. ... AB, BC, CD, but not ABC, BCDE, DEF, and so on ... It is collaborative poetry with 'disjunctive linking.'* (Sato, 1983, p. 3–18)

11   Octavio Paz, *Renga: A Chain of Poems*, p. 18.

12   bell hooks, *interview in Angry Women* (Re/Search #13, 1991), p.85

13   Paulo Freire, *Pedagogy of the Oppressed* (Continuum, 1984), p. 81.

14   Alberto Perez-Gomez, *Architecture and the Crisis of Modern Science* (MIT Press, 1983).

In the history of modern architecture this predicament is clearly visible. The provable themes of mathematical reason and universal truth continue to direct the making of architecture and the values of a culture which consumes it. The quest for universal knowledge, for an architecture of truths (to be applied anytime, anywhere), continues to plague the evolution of architectural theory and practice. [The] *functionalization of architectural theory implies its transformation into a set of operational rules, into a tool of an exclusively technological character. Its the main concern becomes how to build in an efficient and economical manner, while avoiding questions related to why one builds and whether it is justified in an existential context.* (Perez-Gomez, 1983, p. 4)

15   **carapace 1 a :** a bony or chitinous case or shield covering the back or part of the back of an animal **2 a :** a hard surficial crust **b :** any hard protective covering (Webster's Third New International, Dictionary 1989, p. 335)

16   Kathy Acker, *In Memoriam To Identity* (Grove Weidenfeld, 1990)

17   Ibid., p. 141.

18   Trinh T. Minh-ha, *Woman, Native, Other: Writing Postcoloniality and Feminism* (Indiana University Press, 1989)

19   Ibid., p. 123.

20   Paul Feyerabend, *Against Method* (NLB, 1975), p. 256–257.

21   Mircea Eliade, *The Forge and The Crucible: The Origins and Structures of Alchemy* (Harper & Row, 1971)

22   *Avitail Ronell, The Telephone Book: Technology, Schizophrenia, Electric Speech* (University of Nebraska Press, 1989)

Theme 9
Shelter Options for Elderly Women

As women grow older, shelter which is appropriate to their changing needs is often difficult to locate and secure. Just when issues such as housing affordability, home maintenance, and personal mobility become most challenging, women tend to find themselves alone in their struggle to meet these challenges. In developing countries, where elderly women have traditionally remained part of an extended family unit, some face uncertainties as this unit begins to dissolve in the wake of industrialized development. In light of these challenges, consideration of shelter options for elderly women must necessarily be linked to the provision of those services critical to the health and well-being of older women. The papers in this theme evaluate the shelter options for elderly women across countries and cultures. Yen and Keigher provide an overview to the papers and delineate areas for further research. The housing situation of elderly women in the United States is described in the next paper (Keigher). The constraints and opportunity to attain the right kind of housing in the context of current design standards, construction costs, zoning regulations, and cultural norms are delineated. The effort at a local level to provide elderly people with information on housing options such as retirement centers, home share, ecogenic housing, and accessory apartments is described by Hastings and Yen. Pastalan and Schwarz elaborate the ecogenic housing option. The topic of older women in Third World countries is addressed in the next two papers. Sethi highlights the need to look at elderly women in India and elderly women who have immigrated to North America, both of whom are finding their traditional support systems altered or completely erased. Stucki illustrates the way in which ownership of housing allows elderly Ashanti women of Ghana to obtain a stable and secure old age. The papers in this theme serve to underscore the notion that the various options for facilitating the housing of elderly women in a society need to be evaluated not only in terms of affordability, access to services, maintenance requirements, and safety, but also in terms of cultural fit. By bringing together academics, activists, and elderly women, appropriate policy can be formulated to enhance the shelter choices available to women as they grow older.

Photo: Hemalata C. Dandekar

Chapter 45
Shelter Options for Elderly Women:
An Overview

Maria M. Yen and Sharon M. Keigher

Maria M. Yen *is a doctoral student in City and Regional Planning at the University of California, Berkeley. She received a Bachelor of Arts in Chinese and Political Science and a Master of Urban Planning from the University of Michigan, Ann Arbor.*

Sharon M. Keigher, *Ph.D., A.C.S.W., is associate professor of Social Welfare at the University of Wisconsin-Milwaukee. She previously taught at the University of Michigan and received her degree from the School of Social Service Administration, University of Chicago, in 1985.*

The multiple discourses on gendered approaches to shelter and development naturally converge at a common reality: all women, if fortunate, will grow old. Age exacerbates the crises they face, accentuates the difficulties of linking shelter to income-earning opportunities, emphasizes the supportive infrastructure. At a time when women should be able to review their struggles for personal and societal development with a sense of satisfaction, they are forced to keep up the fight for decent, enabling shelter, and often to fight alone. It is the struggle of our mothers and grandmothers, and eventually of us all, which the authors of the following papers consider.

The sequence of these pieces reflects the systematic approach the "Shelter Options for Elderly Women" panel took during the conference. Speakers moved from examining broad themes which cut across cultures to suggesting specific shelter alternatives for older women. Each panelist brought into sharper focus the challenges facing elderly women and the options available to them.

Sharon M. Keigher comprehensively outlines the difficulties older women have in finding decent shelter in the United States of America. Her paper, "In Search of the Golden Girls: Why Is Affordable, Adaptable and Assisted Housing for Older Women So Hard to Find?" reveals the reality of aging in America—as women grow old they are more likely than men to live alone, and the housing they can afford will likely be unsuited to their needs. The U.S. shelter environment fails older women in three key respects—lack of affordability of housing for a significant proportion of older women, lack of housing adaptability as women's needs change, and lack of in-home assistance options.

In "Crossing Oceans: A Cross-Cultural Look at Elderly Immigrant Women in the United States and Elderly Women in India," Rama Sethi focuses on the needs of foreign-born elderly women in America and their counterparts in industrially developing India. Rapid modernization, driving both rural-urban and international migration, can rend the fabric of the extended family. Older women may find themselves in unfamiliar situations—some are left behind in Indian villages as sons and daughters seek employment in the city, while some immigrant women find themselves stranded in the auto-dependent environment of U.S. suburbia. Rama Sethi urges shelter practitioners to conduct research on the needs of older immigrant women, drawing upon experiences of other nations as models.

Crossing continents to Africa, Barbara R. Stucki adds the voices of Ghanaian matriarchs to our increasing awareness of the links among housing, development, and well-being. Her paper, "Housing and the Creation of Security in Old Age by Rural Women of Ghana: A Development Perspective" examines the side effects of modernization on rural housing shortages. The author, who has first-hand field research experiences in Ghana, describes how housing shortages may benefit the elderly in general by reinforcing their traditional role of providing shelter for their families. However, elderly women may have fewer opportunities to secure the necessary resources to build a family compound. Housing as a determinant of women's old-age security should be incorporated in the design and implementation of housing policy—a lesson applicable throughout cultural settings.

The final two papers describe ongoing efforts to provide enabling shelter for older women. The experience of an advocacy organization is described in "Housing Needs of Elderly Women: The Washtenaw County Experience," by Carolyn Hastings and Maria M. Yen. The Housing Bureau for Seniors of Washtenaw County, Michigan, assists older women especially in their search for appropriate shelter. In the paper, the authors describe an array of housing options available to older women, from relatively independent to relatively assisted living environments. They highlight the powerful attachment many older women feel toward their family homes and describe a HomeShare program which attempts to make aging in place a viable alternative.

Leon A. Pastalan and Benyamin Schwarz likewise explore the importance of home to psychological and physical well-being in "The Meaning of Home and Ecogenic Housing: A New Concept for Elderly Women." Faulting institutional settings as being antithetical to a home-like environment, the authors present the Ecogenic, shared housing option as a design alternative which enhances autonomy while easing loneliness. Affordable, adaptable, and assisted—the three shelter criteria established in Sharon Keigher's paper—are found in this innovative design concept.

Several themes emerge repeatedly in addressing the unique housing issues of older women, regardless of whether it is a First or Third World view. First, women have distinctive needs that can be met by appropriate housing design and resources. It follows that older women's best housing would be somehow connected to the ideal housing they had as younger and mid-life women. However, we must acknowledge that housing needs change over the life course. How, then, can we get housing that is appropriately adapted? Or perhaps even better, how can we assure that our housing will adapt as we age?

Second, as women have relationships with each other they seem also to have very real relationships with their environment. Themes that come up repeatedly in discussion of housing that are meaningful for older women are familiarity, preferences, and attachment to place, and the ability to control these or have mastery over decisions about the space in which we live. Security is a critical notion as is the idea that we are socialized into the housing patterns we experience. What we seek in or expect of housing can be fractured by the need to relocate or by significant dislocations.

Third, proactively establishing or building the kind of housing we might perceive as ideal, or even just adequate, costs money. It requires expertise which relatively few women have: architectural and design skills, financial management knowledge, legal knowledge of real estate, etc. Such skills are absolutely vital, however, for any communal action or organized efforts to develop new housing options in communities.

Thus, several areas of research were suggested by our discussion. Research in these areas might facilitate and heighten further development of housing options for older women.

First, we need better to understand how women relate to their immediate environment and the power of that and other relationships in their lives. We need to understand how relationships with other people, vital social support, are sustained and facilitated by space and place. A critical dimension of this would include where relationships take place in the household itself, and also in the immediate neighborhood and the larger community. How important are qualitative factors such as familiarity, predictability, security, and choice in the preferences older women express when faced with adapting their homes or relocating?

Second, what are the effects of social class and especially poverty on density and relocational choices? Co-residence and proximity to others are often viewed as disadvantages or necessities for lower class or poor persons, yet they provide built-in advantages in access to care and reciprocal support. Home ownership and the locational choices that accompany it can evolve into the isolation and lack of security women fear in old age.

We must better understand how women's preferences interact with their resources, and how both function as constraints as well as present opportunities.

A related issue might be to explore how notions of private property have shaped these expectations. What does "ownership" really mean for women? Does it have to mean "private property" (mine) or is there also a sense of legitimacy in the idea of shared ownership, of living in "our" home, of sharing communal space with others?

Third, how do women use their physical space and what are considered to be the real resources needed? Is there a kind of minimum and maximum limit in the accouterments that a home should have, say in a given community, to make it appropriate and also acceptable to women?

Finally, we must recognize that, as women, we need to understand the ways older women wish to live for self-interested reasons. A basic dimension we can and should keep in focus is how we wish to develop housing options for ourselves. How options are developed now for women will very much shape what is available to us as women in thirty to fifty years from now. While on one level this makes shelter development a most self-interested investment, what could be more legitimate? We all certainly have a vital stake in where we will live.

Taken together, these papers serve to clearly define the need for enabling shelter for older women and to propose ways to meet this need. Whether calling for detailed research, better informed policy, or more sympathetic design solutions, each author shares the conviction that older women, in searching for a place to call home, should not have to fight alone.

Chapter 46

In Search of "The Golden Girls": Why Is Affordable, Adaptable, and Assisted Housing for Older Women So Hard to Find?

Sharon M. Keigher

Sharon M. Keigher, Ph.D., A.C.S.W., is associate professor of Social Welfare at the University of Wisconsin-Milwaukee. She previously taught at the University of Michigan and received her degree from the School of Social Service Administration, University of Chicago, in 1985. Her policy analyses of home-care services from a feminist perspective include coauthorship of Wages for Caring: Compensating Family Care of the Elderly *(Praeger Press, 1992). Her study,* Housing Risks and Homelessness among the Urban Elderly *(Haworth Press, 1991) examines the needs of elders in Chicago who experienced housing-related emergencies. The paper in this volume reflects research conducted for the National Older Women's League in 1991 and was supported by the Gerontological Society of America's Technical Assistance Program.*

Housing is a serious problem for many older American women. The problem varies among different populations and communities, as do the policy options and potential solutions. This paper presents an overview of the housing problems confronting mid-life and older women. Originally developed for the Older Women's League, it is intended to assist women and their advocates in assessing housing issues confronting individuals and their communities. To identify key issues facing women, it draws from the growing literature on housing and older people, the smaller literature on the housing needs of women, and policy discussions with national housing advocates, researchers, and older women concerned about housing.

Housing problems are experienced differently by older American women of different ages, racial and ethnic backgrounds, and marital and socioeconomic statuses. For some, housing is not perceived as a problem at all; for others, it is only a subtle concern that health and expenses could be a problem at some future time. For some, however, where and how one will live as needs change at different life stages has profound implications. The very heterogeneity of older women's incomes, resources, cultural expectations, preferences, and opportunities assures that different groups will have differing needs. Differing regions, communities, and neighborhoods offer uneven levels of housing adequacy and in-home assistance. Many American homes and neighborhoods are not well suited to the aging society of the 1990s and the next century. Escalating housing prices, utility costs and property taxes, dislocation, home maintenance problems, isolation, and lack of options increasingly threaten the security of many mid-life and older women. Unfortunately, for a growing proportion of women, both old and young, housing difficulties pose increasingly serious dilemmas.[1]

Housing as a Women's Issue: Domesticity, Caring, and the Powerful Meaning of Home

In the most basic of ways, women's homes shape their view of the world as well as their lives, opportunities for self-determination, and control over personal and public presentation of self. Where one lives, with whom, and how well are intrinsically tied to the self-image most women have of themselves. "One's home is a symbol of one's self and one's achievements" (Streib, 1988, p. 6).

In much the same way, today's housing stock reflects powerful societal patterns set by financial institutions, the design and home building industries, community planners, and public policy decisions made decades ago.

Because little consideration was given to women's needs when most suburban communities were originally built, many homes lack access to public transportation, and proximity to neighbors, employment, shopping, recreation, and health care. For younger women these communities lack access to child care, vocational training, job opportunities, and even schools. As such communities have aged, they have become isolating and even threatening to their frail elderly residents.

The post-war period was one of unprecedented focus on the nuclear family and of mass migrations from city neighborhoods into the suburbs. Throughout the twentieth century, but especially in the period immediately following World War II, the nuclear family, already housed separately from the extended family, became smaller and more scattered around the country. Concomitantly, the uses to which homes were put have evolved (Hayden, 1984; Wright, 1988). Today, women are less "tied down" at home, spending less time there, working more time on the job, and spending more money on fast food, cleaning services, transportation, and work-related expenses.

Many of today's older women moved into their present homes when they married, had babies, and watched the children grow—important work which occupied substantial portions of their adult lives. With roles centered on domestic life and "reproductive tasks," many women naturally developed strong attachments to their homes over the years. Along with one's neighborhood and friendships, the home, established at a critical formative stage in life, took on significant meaning. Women were accustomed to being house-bound, walking or sharing the family car, cooking all the meals, sewing, gardening, canning and freezing, and doing laundry and cleaning without the aid of dishwashers, disposable diapers, microwave ovens, or maids.

These experiences have implications for the lifestyles women anticipate and the options they normally consider as they age. Whether married or widowed, today's retired women still have habits they developed in those early years. They are the age group most likely to own their homes (three-quarters are homeowners), buy groceries, and eat their meals at home (Exeter, 1991, p. 6). But "the little woman" does not retire from housework; she still cooks, cleans, shops, and "keeps house." For persons who remain there, the family home has "become too large," as the grown children have moved away (although increasing numbers of grown children are returning to live there at least for a time). Home still has vital meaning and importance to the whole family, and many women remain attached to it even when it becomes unaffordable, isolating, or even dangerous. Its familiarity is comforting and unchangeable in a way nothing else can be.

Researchers have noted that although people adapt at different life stages, homes do not (Lawton, 1982; Carp, 1975). Indeed, American housing stock today is remarkably inflexible. Only 27% of households still fit the nuclear family stereotype of a married couple with children under 18. Only 22% of married couple householders contain a male breadwinner and a female homemaker, down from 61% in 1960 (Riche, 1991, p. 44). Yet, neither community nor housing designs have altered appreciably to accommodate this changing family or our society's increasing age. Patrick Hare, a noted expert on home adaptation, points out that most Americans live in "Peter Pan housing," designed for people "who will never grow old." Housing is located in largely suburban tracts with yards and maintenance requirements, stairs, snow, and excess space that needs to be heated, cleaned, secured, and paid for. Older women's "role" in the home after "retirement" continues to be much what it was in earlier years, although the uses to which the home is put are gradually reduced in scope. For many at advanced ages, maintaining and securing the home grows increasingly difficult, even as the attachment to it often increases.

Going It Alone

A new study by the American Association of Retired Persons (AARP, 1991) finds that a major shift occurred within the older population between 1980 and 1987. The percentage of older persons in rural areas decreased while the percentage in non-metropolitan areas increased: the "graying of suburbia." While many suburban homes do not meet the needs of families having unprecedented rates of mobility, divorce, family disruptions, remarriage, and two "breadwinners," neither do they meet the needs created by increasing longevity. By 1989, nearly one-fourth of housing units were occupied by only one person; 7 million of those 22.8 million units, nearly one-third, are occupied by women aged 65 and over.

The living arrangements of men and women differ remarkably as they age, not surprising given the likelihood that women will eventually be living alone (see Figures 1a and 1b). Since women outlive men by an average of 7 years, there are many more women in each aging cohort. While the proportions of men and women living with a spouse are quite similar in their

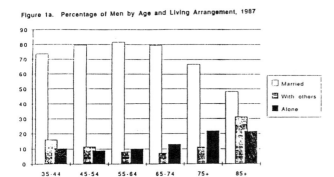

Figure 1a. Percentage of Men by Age and Living Arrangement, 1987

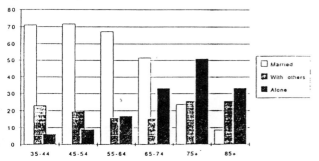

Figure 1b. Percentage of Women by Age and Living Arrangement, 1987

Source: Current Population Survey, March 1988, US Census

Figs. 1A and 1B: Living Arrangements of Men and Women.

early 40s, they differ dramatically by their 70s and 80s. After widowhood and divorce, men remarry at a significantly higher rate than women. With the average age of widowhood estimated to be 55.1 (Norton and Miller, 1990) and the average age about 68 (Schoen *et al.*, 1985), women are left alone with roughly one-fourth to one-third of their lives to go.

As a result, half of all women over age 75 live alone, as do less than 22% of men. This disparity is even greater after age 85 when only 8.5% of women are living with a spouse (see Table 1 below). Meanwhile, half of the men aged 85 and older still have a wife, and typically receive care from her as well (Longino, 1988). After age 85, over 25% of women are living in a home for the aged compared with 15% of the men. The longer women live, the more their housing choices become restricted. To reassert control over their own housing choice, women need to see it as the women's issue it really is.

As can be seen from Table 1, in 1987 women comprised over 58% of the 29,000,000 persons aged 65 and over. They were 70% of persons 85 and over, the population most likely to be frail, poor, and isolated. Of the 8.8 million elders who don't have spouses, slightly over 7,000,000 (79%) are women, or 3.94 women per each man without a spouse (AHS, 1987). While similar proportions of women, 61%, and men, 66%, now own their homes, there are many more women living alone.

Table 1: Living Arrangements by Gender and Age

	Total		Married		With Others		Alone	
	Men Number	Women Number	Men %	Women %	Men %	Women %	Men %	Women %
35–44	17,077	17,606	73.6	71.0	16.1	23.0	10.4	6.0
45–54	11,520	12,275	79.5	71.6	11.6	19.5	9.0	8.9
55–64	10,186	11,456	81.6	67.3	8.2	15.8	10.2	16.9
65–74	7,736	9,736	79.5	51.2	7.3	15.4	13.1	33.2
75+	4,101	6,955	66.8	23.6	11.3	25.5	21.9	50.9
85+*	676	1,521	48.2	8.5	31.2**	58.2**	21.6	33.3
All 65+	16,691	11,836	8,889	6,627	1,028	2,507	1,811	4,655

Sources: U.S. Census, 1988.

Notes: **Longino (1988) based on 1980 Census.*

              **Includes 15.1% of men and 25.4% of women in homes for the aged and nursing homes.

Shelter, Women, and Development   379

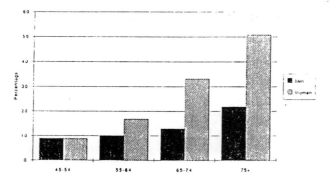

Source: Current Population Survey, March 1988, US Census

Fig. 2: Percentage of Older Persons Living Alone by Age, 1987.

Twenty-four percent of all renters who live alone are elderly women, while only 6% are elderly men (AHS, 1985).

The 1980 census indicates that 7 in 10 of the 6,500,000 elders aged 65 and older who live alone are women, as are 7 in 10 of the 3,500,000 elders who live with others. However, only 4 in 10 of the 15,500,000 married elders are women. In contrast, among people aged 75 and older, women are still 7 in 10 of the 2,500,000 who live alone, and 6.8 in 10 of the 1,400,000 who live with others. They are 3.7 in 10 of the 4,900,000 who are married. By age 85, however, dramatic changes occur in living arrangements. Longino (1988) found that of 1,500,000 elders aged 85 and over, less than 1 in 10 (8.5%) women had a living spouse, 2.4 in 10 were living with others, and 3.3 in 10 were living alone. Fully 2.5 in 10 had relocated to a home for the aged or to a nursing home.

In addition to their prevalence among single-person households, elderly women have lower incomes and a greater rate of poverty than any other age group living alone. As can be seen in Figures 3a, 3b, 3c, the only age/gender cohort in any living arrangement who experience more poverty than older women living alone are women under 45 living with children. (That group faces discrimination as well as other costs because of their children.)

Among elders who do not live with spouses, about three times as many women as men also live with others, both relatives and non-relatives. Women who do this are much more likely to provide valued assistance to those co-residers, as well as to depend upon them for income and assistance. This is particularly true of African-American women, over 18% of whom live with others

Figure 3a. Married Couples (N=3,371)

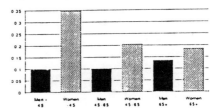

Figure 3b. Householders Living with Others (N=4,193)

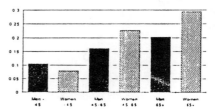

Figure 3c. Householders Living Alone (N=4,211)

Source: Current Population Survey, March 1988, US Census

Figs. 3A, 3B, 3C: Poverty Households by Type, Gender, and Age, 1987 (in Thousands).

(as do only 7.7% of white women). Elderly white women are more likely to be living with a spouse (45%) than African American women (28.8%), while about 35% of both groups live alone (AHS, 1987, Table 7–9, p. 320).

Following widowhood or divorce, but also disability of a husband or self, women are likely to find their home no longer appropriate for their needs, that repairs and maintenance are too difficult or expensive, that the home is too large, and/or that their reduced household income does not meet the costs of increasing mortgages, utilities, and taxes. If the home's location requires maintaining and driving a car or taking public transportation, and if neither is available, women are severely isolated. At this point many women feel forced to sell the home. (It is frequently sold also if a divorce occurs.) Life can become a process of coercion and disabling dislocation.

Women who have never experienced the "American Dream" of home ownership find themselves with other difficulties at widowhood, divorce, or retirement, since women of all ages tend to pay a greater share of their incomes for housing costs. They experience more "shelter poverty," paying more than 30% of household income for housing and utility costs. Families that were unable to accumulate a down payment or overcome racial segregation or redlining patterns, women who were single parents, and single women who have been discriminated against by mortgage lending practices and low wages, encounter increasing difficulties in housing markets where costs escalated dramatically in the 1980s, especially in urban areas on the East and West Coasts. Poorly paid or disabled women, displaced homemakers, and women who have experienced prejudice that prevented a choice of housing options over time are at the mercy of the housing rental market. Many search in vain for affordable rental housing that meets their modest expectations. Thirty percent of women living alone have incomes below the poverty level and fully half have annual incomes only $2,800 ($233 per month) above the poverty level. Thus frail older women who are widowed, divorced, or single are especially vulnerable to being forced to leave their homes because they cannot afford to stay, or because they cannot afford the support services they need to remain there independently. Even among women above the median income, options are limited. A 1990 survey by AARP found that only 5% of the elderly are living in specially age-segregated planned senior housing; 27% are living in "naturally occurring retirement communities" in neighborhoods with a preponderance of older people; 43% had lived in their present home for over 20 years.

All women, but especially older women, have strong feelings about their homes. Whether one lives alone or with others, home is a refuge, a comfort, as a character in Robert Frost's poem "The Death of the Hired Man" said, "a place where, when you have to go there, they have to take you in." It provides privacy, familiarity, and comfort, especially as activities become restricted by reduced mobility and frailty. At best it is a place where one is surrounded by supportive people; ultimately, a place to die in peace and dignity. Access to shopping, medical care, nutrition, personal care, and social life is vital, and could be improved in most places with better community planning, program design, and use of technology. The home should facilitate independence and safety, even when women can no longer reach, or see, or walk, or remember well. Home's familiar surroundings should aid, not impede, one's remaining a part of life as long as possible in the way

one wants. But such housing is difficult for many to find.

Three Critical Needs

Research on housing policy and design suggests that the housing problems of older women cluster around three central issues: affordability, adaptations, and assistance needs. Each issue affects age cohorts, racial and ethnic groups, socioeconomic groups, and urban and rural women somewhat differently. Affordability has to do with the actual housing available to a person, given limited social and financial resources. Adaptability pertains to the willingness and ability one has to change one's home or situation, given the financial but also emotional investment one has in it. Assistance refers to the range and severity of physical and social help needed from either family, friends or paid helpers to remain at home. Without provisions for all three, many women eventually settle for less than they need.

Affordability

Persons with low and moderate incomes have difficulty paying for housing in every community which relies entirely on the private market to provide it. In the U.S. only about 5,000,000 of the 92,000,000 units of housing receive any governmental assistance (Congressional Budget Office, 1988, p. xi). The federal government has never treated housing assistance as an entitlement, and so many needy individuals have been unable to obtain it. The assisted units available at the end of fiscal year 1985 were enough to house only 25% of poor persons eligible for it (Dolbeare and Stone, 1991). A significant proportion of elders, and especially elderly women, need such assistance, as their housing expenses require an excessive proportion of their incomes.

Between 1975 and 1988, real rent levels increased by 17% while real incomes of renter households actually fell by 4%. Higher interest rates and operating costs, gentrification, and abandonment all contributed in varying degrees to a shortage of rental units affordable to low- and moderate-income households. By 1988, more than two-thirds of all poor renters spent more than half of their incomes for housing (Turner and Reed, 1990, p. 2). And hardship continues to grow.

For example, while there were 16,000,000 elderly households in 1980, there will be 23,000,000 by 2000, resulting in a demand for at least 7,000,000 more units of housing. Federal housing efforts fell far short of keeping up with this growth during the 1980s. In 1984

Table 2. Elderly Women Living Alone ("one person householders"), selected measures, 1987 AHS

	Numbers (000s)	Who Rent	Are Poor	In Substandard Housing	With <$5K*	With <$10K	Median Income**
All	7,024	37.8%	29.4%	6.96%	22.8%	64.5	$8,260
Black	603	49.9	62.5	24.87	55.06	88.5	$4,521
Hispanic	173	58.9	50.3	16.2	43.9	84.9	$5,742

Source: American Housing Survey, 1987, Table 7–9, pp. 320–323.

Notes: *The median housing cost burden for all households with incomes under $5,000 was 48%; while for black and hispanic women heads of household, it was more than 70%.*

**The 1987 poverty threshold for single elderly persons was $5,447.*

there were 1,100,000 elderly renter households with incomes below the poverty level. Only 444,000 of them, not quite 40%, lived in subsidized housing. The remainder paid well over 30% of their incomes for housing and many lived in substandard units. The National Low Income Housing Coalition estimates that at a minimum the 700,000 elderly renters and 1,500,000 elderly homeowners with incomes below the poverty level need financial assistance of various kinds (Senate Special Committee on Aging, 1990, p. 317).

Affordability, then, by far the most critical housing problem facing aging America, is one we could solve by "throwing some money at it." A national pledge "to house all Americans" was made in 1937 with the establishment of the first public housing, but it has never been honored. Instead, housing has remained a private speculative market good rather than a public good. Provision, whether through private means or public subsidies, has benefited the basically entrepreneurial housing industry which often produces homes and apartments poorly located or adapted to women's life long needs. Lack of affordability means that housing options (both social and financial) are severely restricted for the bulk of mid-life and older women, and these restrictions are growing worse as we enter the twenty-first century.

Home ownership alone does not help. The tax and equity benefits of home ownership are generally received by wealthy men, not women. By the time a house deed is in the woman's name, after widowhood or divorce, her household income has dropped by more than half. And renters have been particularly hard hit in recent years, as rents remained high, even as unemployment grew and wages generally fell. The poorest of elderly women and those who live alone are at greater risk, as are those who rent. The median income in 1985 for the 2,700,000 elderly single female renters was $6,446; and 40.2% of them had incomes below the poverty level (Dolbeare and Stone, 1991). Of the 11,600,000 renter households with annual incomes under $10,000, 61% were maintained by women and more than 5,000,000 spent at least half their incomes on housing in 1985. Over 2,000,000 spent 70% or more.

A recent study comparing the 1980 and 1987 American Housing Surveys notes that the number of older renters with incomes below $5,000 has increased by 33% (AARP, 1991). Renters over age 75, who have the lowest median income among renters of all ages, experienced a decline in median incomes from $7,513 to $7,200. Two-thirds of this group paid more than 30% of their incomes for housing. Fully 85% of this poorest group of renters are elderly women.

The women in the poorest set of renters present an even grimmer picture. The 1985 Annual Housing Survey reported that elderly women are 43% of all single renters with incomes under $5,000 per year and on average they pay some 70% of their income monthly on housing costs. Elderly women are 44% of all single renters with incomes under $10,000 per year, and their housing cost burden is 45%. Over one-fourth of all elderly single renters have incomes above $10,000. As can be seen from Table 2, on average, African-American and

Hispanic women living alone bear the highest housing cost burden.

Home Ownership Offers Little Security to Many Older Women

Home ownership—having "a piece of the dream" — has long been the basic standard of American prosperity. By this standard America is in the midst of a major housing crisis affecting not only women and lower-income socioeconomic groups, but the majority of middle class, middle aged, and older Americans. An estimated one in three Americans—and 70% of Californians of all ages—cannot afford to buy a home (Porcino, 1991, p. xvi). As with annual income, however, older Americans today appear to have done better in recent years than younger people. Having lived through severe housing shortages immediately after World War II and then assisted by the availability of VA and FHA mortgage insurance and low interest rates in the 1950s and 1960s, they bought single-family detached homes in suburbia. Indeed, over 60% of the present housing stock in America was built during this post-war building boom.

Today, the elderly are more likely to be homeowners than any other age cohort. Three-fourths of them own 14.8 million units. They represent one-fourth of all American homeowners (AHS, 1987), an increase from one-fifth of all homeowners (only 8,400,000) in 1970. But given the difficult times, especially during the 1980s, home ownership among the elderly grew at a time when the prospect of home ownership was becoming increasingly remote for younger American families (M. Stone, 1990). Home ownership increased from 72.1% of the elderly in 1980 to 74.9% by 1987, while it declined from 63.9% to 60.9% among householders under age 65 during this same time (AHS, 1987).

But does this likelihood of home ownership make elderly women better off? Not necessarily. Ownership presents particular problems for women when it involves older homes, maintenance problems, poverty, and family obligations. Although there have been significant improvements in quality of housing in recent years, the housing of older homeowners has the highest rates of severe inadequacies, especially housing owned by minorities. Partly because 30% of older homeowners occupy housing built over fifty years ago (AHS, 1987), 7% of older women living alone are in substandard housing. Twenty-five percent of Black women and 16% of Hispanic women are in substandard housing. Housing of the elderly is nine years older on average

than that of other homeowners and its value is less. Of all elder occupied housing, one-fourth is valued at less than $40,000, and the median home is valued at $62,000. Some 489,000 women living alone are in substandard housing, as are another 356,000 couples, and 191,000 women who are living with others (AHS, 1987, p. 320).

The nature of deficiencies vary. For example, 23% of elderly homeowners had leaking roofs, but only 17.9% replaced a roof in the past two years and only 9.2% had storm doors and windows installed. Such housing can be unsafe and energy-inefficient; but the cost and complexity of rehabbing and upgrading it is prohibitive for many, and many women find dealing with such unfamiliar problems a major difficulty.

Typically homes are purchased by families making the largest purchase in their lifetimes. Couples buy and hang on to their homes until retirement, often intending to die there. Fully 90% of elderly couples are homeowners, as are only 60% of elders who live alone. Eighty-three percent of elderly homeowners own the home free and clear of mortgage payments. The equity in the home is a legacy, a resource, and a source of great financial as well as emotional security, so if elders can just keep up with the property taxes, utility costs, and maintenance, they are substantially better off than retirees with similar incomes who rent. Elderly couples who own their homes have median incomes of $18,400 while those who rent have median incomes of $12,650 (M. Stone, 1990).

In contrast, elderly women homeowners living alone have median incomes of $8,260 (only a $6 increase in 1987 over 1985) (AHS, 1987). One-fourth of all single homeowners have incomes of under $5,000 and despite having paid off their mortgages, the average cost burden in taxes and utilities for them is still 57% of their income. Elderly women are the homeowner group living alone most likely to be poor. Of the 4,100,000 elderly single females who own their homes, 63% had incomes under $10,000 in 1985. More than 86% of all elderly owner-householders living below poverty are women. So, while even extremely poor elderly women are homeowners, they have real problems with the home's adequacy and usefulness, and often have serious problems just keeping it.

Twenty-three percent of elderly female homeowners live with others, usually caring for family members, but sometimes taking in relatives or boarders. In 1987 there

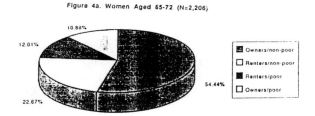

Figure 4a. Women Aged 65-72 (N=2,206)

10.88%

12.01%

54.44%

22.67%

- Owners/non-poor
- Renters/non-poor
- Renters/poor
- Owners/poor

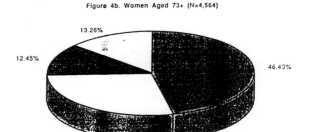

Figure 4b. Women Aged 73+ (N=4,564)

13.26%

12.45%

46.43%

27.87%

Source: 1987 American Housing Survey, US Census

Figs. 4A and 4B: Tenure of Elderly Women Living Alone by Poverty, Status, and Age, 1987 (in Thousands).

were 4,366,000 elderly women living alone while another 1,327,000 lived with others, a total of 5,693,000 elderly women who own their homes (AHS, 1987). These homes comprise a vital, sometimes inadequate, and often underutilized resource in times of shortage of affordable housing for families and individuals.

Many women make a transition to rental housing as they get older, usually as they lose their spouses. As can be seen from Figures 4a and 4b, there are over twice as many women living alone over 72 as there are between ages 65 and 72. Of women between ages 65 and 72, 65.3% are homeowners, of whom 10.9% are poor; 34.7% are renters, including 12% who are poor. In women over 72, however, a significant shift occurs. Fewer women, 59.7%, own their homes but the proportion of these homeowners in poverty grows to 13.3%. The number of renters grows while the proportion in poverty remains virtually the same. It appears that some women sell their homes and rent, maintaining a decent standard of living, whereas women who do not or cannot sell face increasing risks of poverty and other inevitable difficulties. Home ownership presents multiple problems to widows who are poor as they get older.

Because the elderly are so likely to be homeowners, older women face quite different housing problems than older men and younger people. Often the older woman

is saddled with financial as well as emotional burdens, crippling isolation, and lack of information as she considers whether and how to remain in her home. For some, afflicted with medical problems, immobility, or cognitive incapacity, the "American Dream" can turn into a nightmare.

Inaccessibility to Home Buying Markets

Some population groups have historically encountered significant barriers to home ownership. Among the 25% of the elderly who rent their homes, most have never owned a home because of low wages throughout their earning years and difficulty accumulating a down payment and qualifying for a mortgage. Renters have significantly lower discretionary incomes than homeowners among both the young and old. They include a disproportionate share of racial minorities whose income deficits have been compounded historically by segregation and discriminatory lending patterns.

While the rate of home ownership among whites is now 74.9%, among African Americans elders it is 62.0%, and among Hispanic elders it is 56.3%. Women predominate among the groups of older persons who experience difficulty in buying property. While gradually the proportion of women entering old age as homeowners is increasing, the proportion is still 61% compared to 66% for men.

Erosion of Affordable Rental Housing

Women are more likely to be renters because we are more likely to lose spouses, be poor, and live longer. While only 9% of older couples rent, fully 38% of elderly women living alone rent. Nearly 80% of the 2,900,000 elderly householders who rent have incomes below $10,000 (AHS, 1985). Their median income is $6,446, lower than any other category of householder. Women compose 82% of all poor elderly non-family renter households. Ninety percent of all poor elderly non-family renter householders in publicly owned or subsidized housing are women. Nevertheless, 46% of poor elderly female non-family renters are in *un*subsidized, private-sector units.

These women struggle to find and keep the very housing that has been disappearing from the market throughout the 1980s because of changing urban dynamics, high interest rates and operating costs, and the tax code revisions of 1986. Dolbeare (1984, pp. 20–21) notes how much this reality has changed. In 1970 there were 5,700,000 householders with incomes below $3,000 and

8,200,000 units available for rents of less than $75 per month (30% of these renters' incomes). By 1980 there were 3,300,000 householders with incomes below this level, but only 2,400,000 units they could afford, and the situation eroded dramatically after that. By 1985, there were only 2,100,000 rentable units costing less than $125 per month, but 5,400,000 renters who could afford no more than this—nearly four times as many poor renter households as there were affordable units (Dolbeare and Stone, 1991, p. 112).

This increase in demand created a precipitous rise in homelessness as well as in rents. It has put mid-life and older women on fixed and modest incomes at serious peril competing with other poor households. The "housing crisis," which has pressured especially urban dwellers on the East and West Coasts, has affected all persons on fixed and low incomes in sometimes frightening ways. It has severely eroded the stock of available rental housing in most central city areas (through condo conversions, gentrification, razing of downtown housing to build high-rise office space, and speculation). Changes in tax laws in the late 1980s left little incentive for investors to continue to write off rental property that could be converted and put to more lucrative uses. Further, erosion of the federal government's commitment to subsidized housing decreased the options available to low-income householders. This economic hardship has thrust excessive burdens on the young as poverty rates among families with children, many of whom are headed by single women, have risen. These mothers face lifelong hardships in the rental market and diminished prospects of ever accumulating equity in a home for their futures.

The paramount housing problem, then, is not a shortage of housing units so much as a severe and growing shortage of units that low-income households can afford to rent, much less to buy, in neighborhoods which sustain a decent quality of life. In terms of rental subsidies, the elderly are somewhat better off now than are younger families. Of 4,954,000 units of housing rented by the elderly in 1987, 30% were receiving subsidies of some type (AHS, 1987). These included 789,000 units owned by Public Housing Authorities, 373,000 receiving other federal subsidies, 89,000 receiving state or local subsidies, and 235,000 receiving other subsidies; 3,467,000 units rented by the elderly received no subsidy, although 268,000 of them were rent-controlled.

Renting is a more serious disadvantage than a mortgage burden, because renters have no accumulation of equity

against which to cushion other hardships and most elderly homeowners no longer pay a mortgage anyway. Because increasing "housing cost burdens" and "shelter poverty" affect a growing share of all women, increased numbers of today's mid-life women will enter old age without even the security and equity of a modest home to cushion social and financial hardships in their later years.

Minority Women and Geographic Variations

Special problems are encountered by older black , Hispanic, and immigrant women who are more likely to have experienced poverty and housing discrimination throughout their lives. Minority women are much less likely to live alone, and their co-residence has many benefits, mostly economic and social. Elderly minority women often provide much more in the way of financial resources and social care to their families than they receive, but their contributions tend to be highly valued.

When they live alone, however, black women tend to encounter very serious economic difficulties. Women who have outlived their children, whose children have moved, or who are the last survivors in their families, and who have inherited an old family home, are often burdened with cares difficult to manage alone. Half of elderly black women who live alone own their dwelling, despite the fact that 63% live below poverty. Their median income is only $4,521, $926 below the poverty level. As was shown in Table 1, elderly minority women living alone clearly suffer the most hardship of any age and gender group. The 1987 American Housing Survey found that half of the 301,000 black elderly women who live alone in the U.S. lived in the South, and 88% lived in urban areas. Virtually none was in homes or apartments newly constructed in the last four years, and only 1.6% were living in mobile homes (AHS, 1987, p. 320).

Hispanic women are slightly better off in income, but even less likely to own their homes. Their median income, $5,742, is $295 above the poverty level, but only 41% of them own their dwellings. Forty-three percent of the 102,000 elderly Hispanic women who lived alone lived in the South, 26% in the Northeast and 26% in the West; again, 86% lived in urban areas; 4.6% lived in newly built structures, and 4.6% lived in mobile homes.

Despite these marginal circumstances when minority women live alone, federal policy penalizes living with others. SSI recipients (the poorest among elderly

Table 3: Number of Units of Public Housing for the Elderly (in 1,000s)

Year	Total	Occupied	Under Construction
1960	18.9	1.1	4.1
1970	249.4	143.4	65.7
1980	358.3	317.7	11.5
1985	373.5	361.1	2.1
1986	373.0	363.9	3.0
1987	378.6	374.2	1.3
1988	382.5	374.7	1.4

Source: U.S. Senate Special Committee on Aging, 1990.

women) have their SSI and Food Stamps benefits reduced by one-third if they live with their families or in shared households of non-relatives (U.S. House of Representatives, 1991, p. 736). This deters cohabitation when the economies of scale and benefits of social living should be encouraged and supported rather than made even more difficult. Of the nation's 4,600,000 SSI recipients, including about 2,000,000 aged recipients, only about 6% live in the household of another. Yet to each of them this penalty represents a loss of some $1,628 annually; removing it would increase their incomes by some 50%. Removing it for all SSI recipients would cost the government about a half billion dollars per year, money that would add directly to the pockets of the poorest among the disabled and elderly, of whom some 85% are women (U.S. Social Security Administration, 1990, Table 9.E5).

Older women with strong ethnic family ties are the ones most likely to choose to live with others. The substantial immigration of non-English speaking elders during the 1980s, especially from Southeast Asia and Central America, has meant an increase in women who have traditionally lived with their adult children. Such persons are highly dependent upon their family members who work hard, earn little, and often live in overcrowded conditions. The increase in this chosen family configuration highlights the unfairness as well as poor targeting of the SSI and Food Stamp penalties. If anything, the experiences of minority families provides evidence of the benefits of co-residence and insights for successful intergenerational living and home sharing programs.

In addition, 30% of elders live in rural areas. Many are minority women with special cultural circumstances which tend to be overlooked entirely. Rural housing has twice the incidence of structural defects. Rural elders have lower incomes, tend to be isolated, and live in much older housing valued at half that of urban areas (U.S. House of Representatives, 1988, p. 7). Some rural dwellers are reluctant to seek government assistance for housing problems (Streib, 1988, p. 8). Again, cohabitation is often the only alternative to institutionalization, but receives little if any government assistance.

The Government's Response

Since 1947 the federal government has operated various programs of mortgage guarantees and capital and rent subsidization to encourage construction of housing for the elderly. Construction of public housing for the elderly, begun in the late 1950s, has been very popular, but implementation takes many years from the time funds are appropriated until new construction is completed and units can be occupied.

Programs designed to create more decent and affordable housing stock, such as public housing, are called "supply side" approaches to housing policy. Government funds have been used to support construction and operating costs of local public housing authorities, and the federal government has directly supported private and non-profit builders through the Section 236 program, Section 202, and Section 8 mortgage interest guarantee programs.

Throughout the 1980s, however, the number of poor households added to the federal rental assistance rolls plummeted each year. New commitments fell from more than 375,000 in 1977 to fewer than 108,000 in 1988, slowing the growth in the total pool of available aid (Congressional Budget Office, 1988, p. xiv). New budget authority for housing assistance was reduced by over 80% from 1970 levels. Table 3 shows how public housing stock, which grew slowly at first, was dramatically cut in the 1980s. The number of units under construction virtually stopped after 1980.

In addition to the erosion of new federally subsidized construction, nearly 1,000,000 of the nation's 4,000,000 low-income housing units are threatened by prepayment and expiration of subsidized mortgages. Fully half of the present stock of federally subsidized housing is threatened over the next two decades by terminations, prepayments, and buyouts of federally assisted mortgages (Dolbeare and Stone, 1991, p. 16). Most of these losses will occur between 1991 and 1996, but the attrition had begun in the 1980s. Subsidized housing will be lost by:

1. Owners' decisions to opt out of low-income housing and convert their units to other uses;
2. Default or foreclosure because rising costs have out-stripped the subsidies provided; and
3. Expiration of subsidy contracts to for-profit owners who had agreed to keep rents low, but only for a specified period of time. Furthermore, many older subsidized housing developments have not been adequately main-tained and need major repairs and renovation because the operating subsidies have not provided enough to cover full costs. (Dolbeare and Stone, 1991, p. 116)

The prospect for the future is grim. Substantial federal funding commitments will be required just to avoid losing ground over the next 15 years. Yet, unless the trend of rising costs and lower real renter incomes is reversed, even if the existing subsidized stock is preserved, we will fall farther and farther behind because the need for additional subsidized housing will grow ... (Dolbeare and Stone, 1991, p. 117)

In addition, management and maintenance problems now threaten most public housing. This has contributed to the growth of homelessness, waiting lists, deteriora-tion of many existing housing facilities, the threat of displacement, and other housing scandals. A 1989 University of Illinois study of the Section 202 program documented eleven older persons for each available unit in urban areas, and 28.5 applicants per unit in new facilities.

Massive cuts have been made in the popular 202 program, which serves only six elderly units per every 1,000 elderly in the country. The Senate Select Com-mittee on Aging report of February, 1990, observed:

Indeed, the housing needs of several million elderly—housing that is affordable, safe, accessible, and suitable in terms of neighborhood amenities and services—have gone unaddressed. Program cuts have come not only at a time of current high demand, but also at a time when demand is expected to increase. The enormous projected growth of the elderly population suggests the prospect of rapidly increasing shelter and service needs that the Nation has just begun to recognize (p. 301).

A more recent housing policy approach, favored by the Reagan administration, provides "demand side" subsi-dies to meet the gap between the renter's available income and the actual rent. These include Section 8

vouchers and certificates. The low-income renter is expected to pay 30% of available income for rent and utilities. The adoption of certificates and vouchers has substantially changed the way we account for housing assistance now. The government puts out far less money "up front" to provide about the same number of units, while beneficiaries (who are often frail or dis-abled) compete for places on the private market.

In view of the erosion of our nation's low-rent housing stock, as well as our federal government's commitment to housing the poor, it is paradoxical that government grants the largest housing subsidies to the rich in the form of tax expenditures. Tax expenditures are the total cost to the Treasury of the various housing-related tax deductions and other tax-reducing provisions of the IRS Code, in this case tax deductions taken by homeowners affluent enough to itemize deductions on their income tax returns (Dolbeare and Stone, p. 118). The major housing-related tax expenditures are homeowner deductions for property taxes and mortgage interest. These are of no benefit to the 83% of elderly homeowners whose mortgages are paid off.

While federal housing payments in the form of direct assistance declined from $26.9 billion in 1981 to $10.5 billion in 1988, tax expenditures increased from $33.3 billion in 1981 to $53.7 billion in 1988. Thus govern-ment now pays the equivalent of $81 of every $100 in federal housing assistance in the form of tax expendi-tures to homeowners who itemize deductions. Wealthy homeowners (and virtually no households headed by women) receiving tax subsidies in the form of mortgage interest and property tax deductions in 1989 received more than 4 times the amount currently spent by government for low-income housing assistance. Con-gressional analysts estimate that 57% of mortgage interest deduction dollars and 62% of real estate tax deduction dollars benefited taxpayers who had adjusted gross incomes above $40,000 (U.S. Congress, 1985). However, only 6% of households headed by women have incomes above $40,000 and elderly women, whose mortgages are paid off and whose incomes are too low to benefit from itemizing deductions, benefit from none of this (Dolbeare and Stone, p. 120).

While the need for direct assistance to shelter-poor homeowners, who are mostly women, has been recog-nized for a long time, it has yet to be taken seriously by Congress. In 1971, the White House Conference on Aging called for 120,000 units of specially designed housing for seniors per year (Report of the White House Mini-Conference on Older Women, p. 45). If these had been built, we would now have some 2,300,000 units more than the 132,000 units that were actually built between 1971 and 1991. Instead, as Table 3 shows, less and less is constructed. Ironically, these affordability problems should be our easiest ones to solve. It is easy to identify what could be done at the federal level, but a lack of political will is even easier to discern.

Policy Solutions

If the government supported housing creatively and powerfully, women would truly benefit. The government has several possible ways to do so. First, housing benefits could be provided as entitlements, available automatically to householders with incomes below a certain level, say 50% of the median. Current housing voucher and certificate programs could be expanded to reach all who are currently eligible, rather than the lucky 25% who find their way to the top of the waiting list now. Second, the federal government could adequately support local governments and non-profit operators to assure the retention of the current stock of subsidized housing. Third, the supply of affordable housing could be expanded through its direct operation and government support of non-profit development. Such housing could be far more creatively designed, recognizing and supporting women's special needs throughout the life cycle in the community.

In the late 1990s the first new housing legislation in over a decade, the National Affordable Housing Act (NAHA), was finally passed. More symbolic than substantial at this time, NAHA spells out avenues through which solutions to the crisis in affordable housing may be found, if sufficient annual appropriations to housing can be secured. Among its provisions, this law mandates that local city and county planning bodies develop coordinated five-year Comprehensive Housing Affordability Strategies (CHAS) before the Department of Housing and Urban Development (HUD) provides assistance to state or local governments. These will replace the Community Development Block Grant (CDBG) funded Housing Assistance Plan, and the Comprehensive Homeless Assistance Plan (CHAP) formerly required for receipt of McKinney Act funds, and must also address local public housing resources. Citizen participation is required and local plans must be publicly reviewed annually. The strategy must address local housing needs, including the nature and extent of homelessness, characteristics of the local housing market, the effects of local tax policies, land use controls and growth limits, the strengths and gaps of the local housing delivery system, how additional public and private resources will be leveraged, how public housing, CDBG, and McKinney Act funds will be used, how coordination will occur with other state and local entities, and more.

The keys to influencing priorities will be to identify the local authorities preparing the plan, to obtain the public documents pertaining to it, to attend the public hearings, and to pin down local officials about the real priorities in the plan. HUD will review complaints if such citizen input is ignored. Advocates pressing any agenda may get special consideration, so here is an opportunity to highlight and address the needs of older women. Women's advocacy organizations can demand an "Impact on Women" discussion in the CHAS, forcing attention to the lifelong housing needs of women who are poor, disabled, and in need of assistance.

Beyond this, low-income home owners and those living in substandard housing, of whom women are the most vulnerable, need special attention. As the 1980 White House Mini Conference on Older Women noted:

> As long as the incomes of older women remain on a poverty level, housing assistance will be a survival need. Ingenuity and creative use of public dollars can result in some solutions. But many women cannot wait until there is a turnabout in national priorities, so ... we will have to create some viable alternatives for ourselves (p. 47).

On this note, we will turn to alternatives that might be considered.

Adaptability

Older people in general are reluctant to relocate, and show remarkable inclination to be satisfied with their present housing (Carp, 1975), because the home investment they have is both financial and emotional. One's willingness to make changes or to move is highly dependent on one's perception of options available for doing so. This attachment to place and home raises issues of housing design, and financing, as well as community planning, and the willingness of neighborhoods to let homes and common space be used in more helpful ways. A recent survey of the American Association of Retired Persons (AARP, 1990) found that 76% of older people prefer to live (or stay) in intergenerational neighborhoods; half would consider living in shared housing. Seventy percent currently live in single-family detached homes, 30% in other types, mainly low-rise buildings (7%), mobile homes (7%), and 10% in retirement communities or senior buildings ("congregate housing"). Women over 80 are most likely to live in this latter arrangement.

Planning Ahead and Relocating

Assessing Alternatives. Considerations when thinking about housing needs should include age, health, anticipated longevity, cost and resources, social or communal living opportunities, access to services, and appropriateness of the physical structure and community conveniences. AARP offers several helpful workbooks and resource guides for persons considering making a move or modifying a home. One AARP survey found that while a small percentage of older persons move across state lines, most remain close to or in the same house. Fifty-one percent had lived in the same community for over 30 years, 15% had lived there 21 to 30 years, and 15% had lived there 11 to 20 years. Eighty percent had remained there for 11 years or more and 46% had remained in the same house for at least 20 years. Only 5% lived in institutions at any given time (Streib, 1988, p. 3).

While making any move is difficult for most people, women especially seem to feel that moving means giving up a part of the self. Many feel that altering the home environment is also difficult. All women have limits, and the need for privacy and private space can be paramount. Some who have tried home sharing note, "I can't have someone else in my refrigerator." Others have found that "I can't share a home with other women" or "I don't want to live around children. I get too nervous." Others say that "I don't want to live with a lot of old people."

Yet the likelihood of living alone, as well as the risks involved in being alone, both increase with age. Living with or near others whom women enjoy and on whom they can rely has distinct advantages, including financial, mental, health, and social support. Having such support around requires personal planning, since most of today's single-family detached or suburban housing does not provide for this "naturally."

Women who have always lived alone and been independent may be more accustomed to "taking charge" and planning ahead, but they are not necessarily better adapted to the give-and-take of shared housing or communal living arrangements. Fortunately, a wide range of options incorporate privacy, as well as opportunity for social interaction, depending on people's preferences and resources. Women observe that future financial cost and access to social supports are the most critical factors to consider. To many, staying in a familiar environment is particularly important and beneficial. Depending on one's age and anticipated needs, options certainly exist but they must be discovered and sometimes invented.

Relocating: The Options. Traditional retirement housing and retirement communities include a wide range of costs and features. Less costly rental options include simply remaining in or relocating to friendly and supportive neighborhoods composed of a large number of older residents. Such neighborhoods, known as "naturally occurring retirement communities" (NORCs) are highly desirable when located near services, good transportation, and free or low-cost activities. Especially popular settings are near universities, in resort communities, and in dense urban neighborhoods of small apartment buildings and small homes. Other traditional options are congregate living facilities (both subsidized by HUD and non-subsidized), some offering meal services and activities, although long waiting lists characterize government-subsidized buildings (202 and Section 8). Other arrangements include cooperatives offering market, limited, or fixed-equity arrangements, and mobile or manufactured housing. While generally services are not available in these settings, they do offer access to social support and amenities important to many older people. Informal assistance is available when neighbors are familiar and share mutual interests and obligations. Indeed, depending on the pre-planning that accompanies this choice, an extraordinary amount of mutual aid can be facilitated.

A second level of security is offered by condominium ownership and by specific retirement communities. Private congregate housing complexes have sprouted in all kinds of places, many of which are barely noticed as "senior buildings." The unfortunate feature of some is their obscure location, necessitating special transportation and effort. The easy give-and-take with the larger community is sometimes lost.

More upscale versions of "buy in" arrangements include what are often self-contained adult retirement or leisure communities. Continuing Care Retirement Communities (CCRCs) require an "endowment" or down payment, and life care communities do not. In 1988 endowments ranged from medians of $30,000 to $90,000, depending upon the unit size. Usually part of this is refundable. Both have provisions for nursing care on site, whatever level of care is required, and offer the security of a permanent place to live. The difference is in the additional fees for service of the life care communities, including the current top of the line favorite, Assisted Living. Both provide an independent apartment, with housekeeping and personal care services, as well as medical care as necessary, usually for an additional fee. Median monthly fees range from $695 to $938 depending on size (U.S. Senate Select Committee on Aging, p. 325). Generally people make a move to such communities only when they anticipate a need for care, and obviously, when they have the income and assets to afford it. About 1% of the elderly live in some 700–800 CCRCs nationwide.

Living with one's children remains the choice of many women. It was recently found that 15% of young men between the ages of 20 and 40 were living with their parents, usually their mothers, while only about 8% of young women the same ages live with parents (Gross, June 16, 1991, p. 1). Cohabitation offers financial benefits for both generations and an exchange of services can be beneficial for both older women (who receive help around the house, security, and maintenance) and young men (who often have meals, laundry, and/or cleaning provided). While the young men appear to be benefiting from a very good deal, this arrangement evidently fits their needs and those of their mothers better than do similar arrangements for young women.

Alternative Communities. Households of non-related adults grew by 140% during the 1970s, while family households grew by only 11.5%. There were 3,500,000 non-relative households in 1980, and since then the numbers of elders living with others has doubled (AHS, 1987). Communal households, co-housing, and large intentional communities are examples of newer residential forms that are emerging. Intergenerational communities shared by a number of households, households shared by from 5 to 30 individuals, and small shared houses owned by a resident or a cooperative group are examples of alternative living than can improve the quality of life for women in the future (Porcino, 1991).

Communities of persons with specific ideological commitments exist, as do networks of like-minded persons with households in several communities. Networks of lesbian retirement communities can be found, but most do not advertise widely and must be sought out. Other communities are guided by devotion to meditation, religious beliefs, or commitment to holistic lifestyles, service, or spiritual or utopian philosophies. Some are only a place to live while others offer a whole range of work, activities, and philosophy. As a type, these arrangements are self-planned communal settings, as opposed to commercial enterprises, a

characteristic especially important to persons on limited incomes. Local organizations all over the country are discovering creative housing alternatives as an exciting idea in self-help and empowerment. Their most difficult challenges involve packaging the expertise, financial planning and resources to make such projects affordable to women who need them most.

Should the project include only older people or be intergenerational? Only women or singles or married couples? Low incomes or mixed incomes? There is need for expert advice from local zoning authorities, public funding sources, builders, architects, banks, and mortgage companies. According to the U.S. Senate Select Committee on Aging (p. 327), shared housing for seniors like this can also be an important low-cost means of revitalizing neighborhoods; abandoned buildings can sometimes be made suitable with little renovation or contributions of "sweat equity." Some of the most interesting and exciting new housing designed specifically to address women's needs has been transitional housing. This has integrated women with children and older people and provided day care and social services in planned and largely self-managed communities (Saegert and Leavitt, 1984; Sprague, 1992).

Adapting An Owner-Occupied Home

For many women, sharing their own home is a way to create immediate financial and social support. While "aging in place" is the ideal, it is honored more in the breach than reality, since even by doing nothing one can stay put. The U.S. Senate Select Committee on Aging notes that 670,000 elders now share housing with non-relatives, a 35% jump over a decade ago (p. 327). The National Shared Housing Resource Center established by Maggie Kuhn in Philadelphia lists over 1,000 Home Matching programs around the country and works to develop more.

An impediment to shared housing includes the reduced SSI and food stamp payments to participants living with others, as mentioned above. In addition to accepting the idea of having someone else around, home sharing often requires adapting the home's physical structure itself.

Accessory Apartments and Echo Housing

Accessory apartments are another form of shared housing. When privacy is highly valued and resources are available, construction of a separate unit with a separate entrance, kitchen or bathroom can provide significant benefits. Such apartments have traditionally been shared with family members, but today students, parents with young children, or other singles, including elders, fit just as nicely. Proponents of accessory apartments note that America could create a substantial amount of low-income housing by making it easier to build accessory apartments. If only 10% of older women who live alone in their homes were to share that space, nearly half a million units of affordable housing could be created, a substantial amount to a nation experiencing a critical shortage of affordable housing. Women who are "over housed" can offer a substantial resource to individuals or families having difficulties finding adequate housing arrangements. Services such as errands, shopping, and home or car maintenance can be traded for reduced rents. On the other hand, the daily presence of an older woman can be of great benefit to a renter, providing surveillance, financial assistance, child care, cooking or shared meals. Of particular benefit would be the provision of affordable space to mothers with young children, a low-income group as disadvantaged in today's tight housing market as are older women who live alone.

Unfortunately, only about 40% of the single-family hous-ing stock in the country is now zoned to permit accessory apartments (U.S. Senate Select Committee on Aging, p. 327). Once zoning is changed in a community, there are typically a number of applications to legalize existing accessory apartments, but few new ones are built because homeowners face many difficulties with local government zoning and building regulations, as well as with contractors, banks, and tenants. The process can be intimidating, and reliable advice can be difficult to find. Partnerships are needed between local real estate agents and remodelers to market accessory apartments and to assist in understanding this often complex process (U.S. Senate Select Committee on Aging, p. 327). Here again local non-profit organizations are needed to take the lead in linking these two necessary services, remodelers and real estate agents. Older owners would benefit because "getting started" is always the most formidable part of this process and easier access to "know how" would facilitate it.

A similar innovation is the "granny flat" or "ECHO" (elder cottage housing opportunity) housing, movable units placed on property to accommodate elderly parents near their families while maintaining the independence of both parties. Again, this has been tried in a variety of creative ways, sometimes with governments even loaning out movable units. Unfortunately, rigid zoning laws, lack of public information, and concern about property values can be barriers, but increasingly it

appears that civic leaders, public officials, and organizations are expressing interest in these ideas.

Home Equity Conversions. Home equity conversions allow a homeowner to withdraw some of the equity in a home to cover remodeling, specific expenses or a living allowance, while keeping the right to occupy the home for a set period of time or for life. Types of conversions include reverse equity mortgages, sales plans, and deferred payment plans allowing the homeowner to use the equity for home improvements, tax deferrals or other purposes. Usually conversions are worked out with a bank, a development corporation which wants the property, or with an intended heir. Government support is needed to encourage private lenders to get more involved in this kind of financing, however, if it is to yield greater benefits to homeowners, especially ones who need assistance the most. Thus far, only limited benefits are available to a limited set of homeowners. Unfortunately, the asset value of homes owned by most older women is not great enough to attract much investment interest.

Regulatory and Financial Expertise Needed

More support from governments at all levels is needed to develop the innovations proposed above. These are complex and politically loaded proposals. Some communities make adaptations and construction of accessory apartments quite difficult through community regulations, mandatory standards, and imposed costs, fees, zoning, and complex financing requirements. A pilot program of the FNMA (Fannie Mae) includes loans to finance accessory apartments (as part of a single-family residence), ECHO cottages, one-to-one home shares, and sale lease backs (sale to investors), allowing each to gain from the sale while the elder's right to stay is protected. This provisions are still very limited, however.

An increasing number of non-profit technical assistance and lending groups are established to disseminate knowledge of how shared equity housing projects can be established. These include the Institute for Community Economics of Springfield, Massachusetts, which works to establish Community Land Trusts, the Enterprise Foundation, which is building a loan fund, and the Local Initiatives Support Corporation (LISC).

Commercial and manufacturing businesses and home builders are increasingly recognizing that it is in their interest to consult older women as they create new homes and developments. National organizations are sponsoring demonstrations such as "The Hartford House" and the National Association of Homebuilders "Adaptable Home." Safer products (such as stoves with timers and non-flame burners, bathtub seats, and grab bars), adaptive devices for kitchen and bathroom, and better designs for aesthetics and comfort are available, but still are not marketed widely. Until such features are built into the infrastructure of every new and remodeled home, the threat will remain that our homes will not accommodate us as we age in place.

Women will have to demand the attention of builders, architects, financiers, and planners to make known what should be included, when it is necessary, and how it could work better. Older women are continually aggravated, and unnecessarily handicapped, by lack of closet and storage space, placement of shelves that are too high, and sockets that are too low. Hazards in the home can be identified and fixed, particularly ones that create the danger of fires, falls, and accidents. People building new homes must install structures that can be adapted as the owners age. Women's organizations can also facilitate the difficult packaging of financial resources and hiring of contractors that is required to complete home adaptations and could be especially helpful in identifying ways to facilitate the work of contractors and older people together.

Finally, developers should ask older women for such input. Those who will spend most of their time in these new and remodeled homes know best if they are places that will remain comfortable and functional and really facilitate independence.

Availability of Assistance

Under most circumstances, if a frail elder is to live comfortably, a range of personal needs (social as well as physical) must be met in one's home, basically with personal assistance from either family, friends, or paid helpers. Although increasing disability may require increasing levels of assistance, by no means does this make a nursing home placement inevitable. Stone and Murtaugh (1990) estimate that between 411,000 and 4,100,000 non-institutionalized disabled elders (1.5% to 15.5%) require assistance with activities of daily living to remain in their own homes. Their needs range from assistance with housecleaning, cooking, and shopping to grooming, eating, dressing, and toileting. However, having even one of these needs chronically unattended and troublesome can make living alone risky if not downright impossible.

Women have the greatest stake in obtaining services to facilitate their "aging in place," because they are more likely to be placed in nursing homes if these needs are not met. Women are 75% of nursing home residents, and increasing proportions of women are institutionalized as they grow older. In a recent projection, Kemper and Murtaugh (1991) estimate that of all the persons who turn 65 in 1990, 43% will end up in a nursing home for some time before they die. One in three women and one in seven men who reach 65 in 1990 will spend at least one year in a nursing home, and more of the women (25%) will have a total lifetime nursing-home use of 5 years or more, compared with 13% of the men. Clearly, nursing home policy is a women's issue.

Given these odds, the determination of many women to stay out of a nursing home at all costs is admirable, but the obstacles are formidable. To do so with dignity requires planning. For most, this ultimately means receiving care in the home that is personalized, sensitive, and affordable. Most frail elders receive such care informally from family members and sometimes friends and neighbors. Unfortunately, formal services do not always supplement, facilitate, and truly relieve family and friends because many programs explicitly disallow the substitution of formal services for assistance already provided informally. Some women in every community languish in isolation and discomfort unattended by anyone; too often, pride, fear, and lack of information, as well as limited resources, prevent them from even asking for services.

It is surely worth considering what alternative caring communities can do to meet the needs of frail and dying members. Experiments in many places with "care credit" schemes are attempting to learn how services can be expanded through formal reciprocal mechanisms, to make fairness and contribution the basis for entitlement to care in the future. To avoid burdening or "burning out" caring helpers too strenuously, it is often necessary for many helpers to be involved. Ideally the care receiver is able to manage such care, provide direction, and take charge. Many examples of such persons exist, but obviously better provisions, including guardianship and protective services, will be required for some elderly women. As our whole society "ages in place," consideration and rearrangement of gender role expectations are needed, and especially how men of all ages can provide more care. More public discussion of issues heretofore left only to families and individuals could do even more to expand community-wide effort. Ultimately more care will also require more public monies so that mid-life women, who inevitably bear a disproportionate burden of this work, are not unsupported.

In addition, there are inevitable social and cognitive reasons for nursing home admissions. Women enter nursing homes largely because social support services are lost, not available, or have been exhausted. Institutionalization, as measured by length of stay in a skilled nursing facility or a hospital, is found to have a strong relationship with living alone (Wan and Weissert, 1981; Townsend, 1965). Except for post-hospital stays, admission of women over 65 is rarely only for health reasons. No wonder states have taken the initiative in recent years to divert and deter such admissions, to develop group homes and adult foster care, and alternative living settings in which home health and personal care can be provided more economically and efficiently.

Whether such alternatives meet the physical, social, and emotional needs of frail and elderly women or their family caregivers, especially those 85 or older who require "institutional" care now, remains to be seen. States' initiatives in this regard, just as in their determinations of guardianship, bear very close scrutiny because of the extreme dependency and vulnerability of elders who are at their mercy. The cost-saving motivations of state Medicaid programs for reforming long-term care are, unfortunately, sometimes more powerful than their concern for quality assurance.

Federal Initiatives

The latest federal government long-term care initiative has been to recognize that "supportive services" that will allow people to return home after hospitalization are needed in subsidized congregate housing. The National Affordable Housing Act appropriates $10,400,000 in FY 1992 for HUD to initiate some pilot supportive service programs in Section 8 housing for 1,500 seniors. It also allocates $26,100,000 for HUD and FNMA to provide services to persons in HUD 202 and Section 8 congregate housing, including coordination of Older Americans Act services (Dolbeare, 1991, pp. 20–23). These initiatives are long overdue, but pitiably small.

The problem with proposals to enhance "supportive services" in congregate housing is the source from which such "extra" resources are to come in today's fixed budget environment. The federal funding for the Older Americans Act nationwide has eroded relative to the growth in the population needing services. Strains on state Medicaid and Social Service Block Grant monies have yet to recover from the devastating cuts

they suffered in the early 1980s. Although most states are now funding much more, the focus of service has become increasingly "medicalized" and services have become means tested. Further, the effects of the recession of 1990–91 continue to whipsaw most states. Reeling from revenue shortfalls of all kinds, they are still reducing home care, personal care, respite, day care, and home health services. This means eligibility limits are more restrictive, cost controls limit the number of visits or services allowed, co-payments and deductibles are required, and outreach is trimmed. Obviously, in this environment, the service that could make it possible for many women and their caregivers to remain decently and comfortably at home will be denied. In such a zero-sum game, with continual cutbacks instead of new federal monies from a progressive tax base, new supportive services in congregate care, or anywhere else, can only come at the expense of persons already being served. Unfortunately, cutbacks in Older Americans Act services (rationing), and state Medicaid programs throughout the 1980s have so eroded the base of services for everyone that without new monies, coordination and case management is rather superfluous. Meeting the needs of the growing elderly population at home in the next decade becomes an increasingly elusive ideal.

Unfortunately, residential care or nursing home placement, even when it is inevitable, is sometimes a source of terror and dislocation for many women. The legacy of the Poor House still haunts today's institutions. Many resemble an acute care setting more than home-like and normal living. A recent proposal by Rosalie and Robert Kane (1991) observes that the austere environment in nursing homes has been created by regulations and structures developed for medical care settings. We could alter this environment by separating the government reimbursement through Medicare and Medicaid for housing and medical care. This reform would assume first that one lives in a home, and secondly, that medical and nursing care are provided there. This presumes that residents move "into the home" with their own beds, chairs, and other furnishings for daily living that provide security, and that they continue to use them there.

The Kanes' proposal highlights the rigidity in our present institutions and formal home care services, that invariably favors medical, routinized, and production-oriented regimens over the social, individualized, and personalized care and support that most human beings prefer. Inevitably, reforms of our institutional long-term care system will require that policy makers address the deficiencies of our housing system for poor people. The lower-cost alternative to nursing homes is obviously affordable, adapted, assisted, and socially supportive housing. Older women know better than anyone the profound lack of vision and commitment our nation has shown to that basic alternative.

Conclusions and Recommendations

So, what can women's housing advocates do about problems of such gravity? And what can governments do more vigorously and effectively?

A first task would be to understand better how women are coping now with housing hardships, in the short term and over time. Research is needed to identify key hardships for older women. Much more should be known about the housing preferences of mid-life and older women, and their possible options. Annual national panel surveys of older women, controlled for income and marital status, monitoring residential transitions might be one way to enhance such knowledge. The experiences of older women in the current tight housing market would be especially informative. Such baseline data will be increasingly important in the future. Women's experiences documented on a longitudinal basis, along with data on their changing housing preferences, would yield new knowledge.

It would also be informative to explore with women's organizations members' interests in planning their own future living arrangements and the adaptations they are currently making to their own environments. Such investigation could anticipate the kind of security the next generation of older women can truly expect. Documented in a longitudinal fashion, middle-aged women's plans, preferences, and choices could be particularly useful to researchers interested in housing choices and normal aging.

Research is also needed to assess which types of assistance work best in the home, how such arrangements might be created for low-income women, and what arrangements work best in settings usually composed largely if not entirely of women. The increasingly gender-segregated experience of old age needs to be addressed very directly by gerontological research. Models of communities composed in different ways could test, or at least track, the advantages of various age, household composition, income and lifestyle combinations. Reciprocal models (barter economies or "care credit schemes"), whereby services are exchanged for reduced rent, need to be tested, as do various adaptive arrangements as researchers learn to

integrate personality types with housing design, and long range community planning. Such data will be valuable to consumer markets as well as to policy makers.

The social aspects of shared living are just as important as the community and structural design of physical space. The increasingly gender segregated experience of old age will be an integral, and one hopes, vital part of that experience for us all.

Note

[1] Research for this paper was supported by the Gerontological Society of America Technical Assistance Program and the Older Women's League in summer, 1992.

References

AARP (1984). *Housing Options for Older Americans.* Washington, D.C.: American Association of Retired Persons.

AARP (1990). *Understanding Senior Housing for the 1990s.* Washington, D.C.: American Association of Retired Persons.

AARP (1991). *Comparisons of the 1980 and 1987 Annual Housing Survey.* Washington, DC: American Association of Retired Persons.

AHS: see U.S. Department of Commerce, *American Housing Survey.*

Bierbrier, Doreen (1986). *Living with Tenants: How to happily share your house with renters for profit and security.* McGraw Hill.

Carp, F.M. (1975). Ego-defense or cognitive inconsistency effects on environmental evaluation. *Journal of Gerontology, 30:* 707–711.

Congress of the United States (1988, December). *Current Housing Problems and Possible Federal Responses.* Congressional Budget Office.

Dolbeare, C. (1984). The Housing Needs of the Elderly, *Social Thought* (winter): 16–27.

Dolbeare, C., and Stone, A. (1991). Women and affordable housing, pp. 94–131 in *American Woman, 1990–91.* Women's Research and Education Institute. New York: W.W. Norton.

Dolbeare, C. (1991). *Section by Section Summary of the National Affordable Housing Act of 1990.* Washington, DC: Low Income Housing Information Service and National Coalition of the Homeless.

Exeter, T. (1991, January). Finding food markets, *American Demographics,* p. 6.

Gross, J. (1991). More young single men clinging to apron strings, *New York Times*, Sunday, June 16, p. 1.

Hare, Patrick, and Ostler, Jolene (1987). *Creating an Accessory Apartment.* New York: McGraw-Hill.

Hayden, Dolores (1984). *Rebuilding the American Dream: the Future of Housing, Work and Family Life.* New York: W.W. Norton & Co.

Kane, R, and Kane, R. Funding for housing and nursing care should be separated. *New York Times*, Aug. 18, 1991, Op Ed page.

Kemper, P. and Murtaugh, C. M. (1991). Lifetime use of nursing home care. *The New England Journal of Medicine, 324* (9): 595–600.

Lawton, M.P. (1982). Competence, environmental press, and the adaptation of older people. In *Aging and the Environment: Theoretical Approaches*, edited by M.P. Lawton, P.G. Windley, and T.O. Byerts. New York: Springer Publishing.

Longino, Charles F. (1988). A population profile of very old men and women in the United States. *The Sociological Quarterly, 29* (4): 559–564.

McCammet, Kathryn, and Durret, Charles. *Co-housing: A Contemporary Approach to Housing Ourselves.* Berkeley, CA: Ten Speed Press.

National Corporation for Housing Partnerships (1988). *Preventing the Disappearance of Low-Income Housing.* Washington, D.C.: Report of the National Low Income Housing Preservation Commission.

Norton, A.J. , and Miller, L.F. (1990, December). Remarriage among women in the U.S.: 1985. Washington, D.C.: National Institute of Child Health and Human Development.

Porcino, Jane (1991). *Living Longer, Living Better.* Continuum Press.

Riche, M. F. (1991, March). The future of the family, *American Demographics*, pp. 44–46.

Ryzbdy, W. (1986). *Home: A Short History of an Idea.* Penguin Books.

Saegert, S., and Leavitt, J. (1984, summer). Women and abandoned buildings: a feminist approach to housing, *Social Policy, 15*: 32–39.

Schoen, R., *et al.* (1985, February). Marriage and divorce in 20th century American cohorts, *Demography*, 22 (1).

Sprague, J.F. (1991). *More than Housing: Lifeboats for Women and Children.* Boston: Butterworth Architecture.

Stone, M. (1990, Dec.) *Housing Affordability and the Elderly: Definitions, Dimensions, Policies.* Boston: U of Mass., Gerontology Institute.

Stone, R., and Murtaugh, C.M. (1990, May). The elderly population with chronic functional disability: Implications for home care eligibility, *The Gerontologist, 30* (4): 491–496.

Streib, Gordon (1988). Where will the old live? Paper presented at the Society for the Study of Social Problems, Atlanta, August 21–23.

Townsend, P. (1965). On the likelihood of admission to an institution. In Shanas, E., and G.F. Streib (eds.), *Social Structure and the Family: Generational Relations.* Englewood Cliffs, NJ: Prentice Hall.

Turner, A.A., and Reed, V.M. (1990). *Housing America: Learning from the Past, Planning for the Future.* Washington, D.C.: Urban Institute.

U.S. Department of Commerce, Bureau of the Census. *American Housing Survey, 1985.* Washington, D.C.: U.S. Government Printing Office.

U.S. Department of Commerce, Bureau of the Census. *American Housing Survey, 1987.* Washington, D.C.: U.S. Government Printing Office.

U.S. Department of Commerce, Bureau of the Census (1990). *U.S. Statistical Abstract.* Washington, D.C.: U.S. Government Printing Office.

U.S. Senate Select Committee on Aging (1990). *Developments in Aging, Vol. 1.* Washington, D.C.: U.S. Government Printing Office.

U.S. Social Security Administration, *Annual Statistical Bulletin, 1990.* Washington, DC: U.S. Government Printing Office.

U.S. Statistical Abstract: see U.S. Department of Commerce.

U.S. House of Representatives Committee on Ways and Means. (1991). *Overview of Entitlement Programs, Green Book.* Washington, D.C.: U.S. Government Printing Office.

U.S. House of Representatives Select Committee on Aging (1988, November). *Section 202 Housing Budget Crisis, a Report by the Chairman.* Washington, D.C.: U.S. Government Printing Office.

White House Mini Conference on Older Women (1980). *Growing Numbers, Growing Force.* Report of the White House Mini-Conference on Older Women, Des Moine, IA. Older Women's League Educational Fund, Oakland, and Western Gerontological Society, San Francisco.

Wan, T.H., and Weissert, W.G. (1981). Social support networks, marital status, and institutionalization. *Research on Aging, 3* (2): 240–256.

Wright, Gwendolyn. (1988) *Building the Dream: A Social History of Housing in America.* Cambridge: MIT Press.

Chapter 47
Housing Needs of Elderly Women: The Washtenaw County Experience

Carolyn Hastings and Maria M. Yen

Carolyn Hastings has served as the executive director of the Housing Bureau for Seniors since its inception in May 1983. Before that she was employed at a small local organization that assisted senior citizens to live independently in their own homes. She has also worked with families of emotionally impaired children, psychiatric patients, and the American Red Cross assisting families of servicemen and women. She has a Master of Social Work from the University of Michigan with a specialty in agency administration and received her Bachelor of Social Work in 1966 from the University of Wisconsin.

Maria M. Yen is a doctoral student in City and Regional Planning at the University of California, Berkeley. She received a Bachelor of Arts in Chinese and Political Science and a Master of Urban Planning from the University of Michigan, Ann Arbor. She lived in the South Indian city of Visakhapatnam during the 1989–1990 academic year, interviewing recent migrants from rural areas to urban squatter settlements. She is interested in grassroots, collaborative planning projects which tap the energies and wisdom of community residents.

The Housing Bureau for Seniors is an organization which serves the older residents of Washtenaw County in Southeastern Michigan. Staff members are concerned with the shelter needs of all the county's senior citizens (defined as age 60 and above). Of the elderly in Washtenaw County, 59% are women, and they represent a significant proportion of the organization's client base. In addition, when an adult child of an elderly person comes in for advice on housing options for Mom or Dad, that child is typically a daughter. Thus, daughters and mothers are often seen in the corridors of the Housing Bureau for Seniors' offices—concerned women searching for ways they or their loved ones may live their later years in enabling shelter which enhances their comfort and dignity.

The elderly of Washtenaw County, some 30,000 out of a total population of over 280,000, live throughout its rural and urban areas. The county has one large city, one small city, and seven towns and villages. Yet 33% of the county's elderly live in the rural areas, presenting challenges for service organizations such as the Housing Bureau for Seniors. The isolation of these senior citizens living in the rural areas is compounded by the fact that 23% of them are classified according to Housing and Urban Development (HUD) standards as having a low or very low income.

The Housing Bureau for Seniors is determined to serve the entire county's older adults by providing them with information on a range of living choices. The organization, established in 1983, runs three primary programs which recognize the need for appropriate and affordable housing for Washtenaw County's senior citizens. The programs are: (1) information and counseling on the range of housing choices; (2) the HomeShare Match-Up Program; and (3) the Property Tax Foreclosure Prevention Program.

In this paper we first introduce the type of information sought by the older women who come to the Housing Bureau for Seniors: the shelter options available to them as they age. These choices are arranged on a continuum from very independent to more assisted living environments. After listing these choices, along with an evaluation of each, we focus on two ways the Housing Bureau for Seniors helps support women in their own homes: the HomeShare Match-Up and the Property Tax Foreclosure Prevention Programs.

Housing Options: A Continuum

Depending on a woman's financial resources, health, and mobility, desire for socialization, and overall preferences, she may choose from a variety of shelter options. At the Housing Bureau for Seniors, these choices are arrayed along a continuum ranging from the more independent shelter environment to the highly supportive or assisted environment. In this section we describe each option and identify some advantages and disadvantages of each. After this, we evaluate some of the options according to standards important to elderly women. The shelter choices are ordered starting with the most independent situation (remaining in one's own home) down to the most assisted situation (relocating to a retirement center).

Own Home

For older women especially, the family home is their territory—the place where they raised their families and over which they have had a measure of control. While the aging process may make the home less of a friendly environment, even a dangerous one, women are quite understandably reluctant to leave their houses for new, untried alternatives. In this paper, we define "own home" largely as a single-family dwelling which has served as a home for a woman and her family. We acknowledge the fact that one can make a home in any type of housing—apartments, cooperatives, etc. For the sake of clarity and to reflect the living situations of many older women in the Washtenaw County area, this section on older women's own homes focuses on single-family houses. The attachment to one's own home, along with the fact that this option provides the most independence, compels many older women to try their hardest to remain in their familiar environments.

Thus, the first advantage of remaining in the family home is that of familiarity. An older woman is used not only to the home's interior, but also to its exterior yard spaces. The neighborhood itself is also familiar (although older people may witness changes in their neighborhoods as the years pass). A woman's own home is designed in a way she prefers, a way she is used to. Being in control and familiar with one's personal surroundings may convey a sense of power for an elderly woman—a sense she may lack as she tackles other challenges of aging. Another advantage is that one's own home provides more privacy and peace and quiet than other, less independent options. Many elderly women cherish these qualities in their living environments.

However, remaining in one's own home has disadvantages as well. The housing stock in Washtenaw County, and indeed in much of America, is simply not designed for older adults' changing needs. Older women who come to the Housing Bureau for Seniors report there are parts of their homes which they rarely see. One inaccessible part is the basement, an area which often contains the washer and drier. Yet the trip down to the basement can be perilous for an older adult, and she may make that trip with a constant fear of falling down the stairs. Then she faces the possibility of not being found for days after the accident. The design of the typical single-family house is not well adapted to or adaptable for an aging population, and the results may be dangerous.

Maintenance of the family home can also pose difficulties. As people age, so do their houses, which causes never-ending upkeep problems for older adults. It is not always easy to find someone to handle various maintenance problems, and older adults may have trouble paying for the ever-increasing prices of decent maintenance. Sometimes an elderly person may not realize that a part of the house needs maintaining, especially if it is the attic or the basement where she may not go often.

Thus, while there are powerful reasons for an older woman to try to stay in her own home for as long as she can, there are some very compelling disadvantages to this choice. Many women who come to the Housing Bureau for Seniors are in search of other options, such as the ones listed below.

HomeShare

If an elderly woman decides on the HomeShare option, typically she owns her home and wishes to remain there, but needs assistance to overcome the types of disadvantages listed above. Under a HomeShare program, an older adult is able to stay in her home because another person, often a young woman, is located, matched with a senior, and moves into the home. The new resident may help with the maintenance of the home, will provide some rent, often helps to run errands, and provides companionship for the older adult.

We discuss this option more thoroughly in the section on supporting women in their own homes. Briefly, an advantage of the HomeShare option is that it enables an older adult to remain at home while conquering, at least in part, some of the difficulties of that choice. Another advantage is that it provides another source of income, a critical consideration for older women. There are also disadvantages, the most notable being a lack of privacy. Another disadvantage is the very real chance of personality conflicts. Shared spaces such as the kitchen, a place over which older women may have a particular feeling of control, may be potential conflict zones.

Accessory Apartments

An accessory apartment is a second, completely private living unit created out of the extra space in a single-family home (Linda Hubbard, 1984, 23). They are sometimes known as "mother-in-law apartments." This is increasingly becoming a popular option in the Washtenaw County area. An advantage of converting part of a house into an accessory apartment is that the tenant can be a helper and friend who is *close* to you but not *with* you. This diminishes the opportunities for personality conflicts. Another advantage is that the accessory apartment provides extra income for an older woman.

However, a major disadvantage in the Washtenaw County area is that zoning rules often restrict and deny the building of accessory apartments in certain neighborhoods. Just as our homes do not accommodate the changing needs of an aging population, neither do our local ordinances. Another disadvantage many older people do not consider before going ahead with this option is that it forces one to become a landlord, a job which is often full-time and not easy. An elderly person then has the responsibility for maintenance, not just in her part of the house, but also in the accessory apartment. She may even have to evict a tenant, a situation faced by some older people who come to the Housing Bureau for Seniors for advice.

Mobile Homes

Manufactured homes which are clustered into communities are popular options in the Southeast and Southwest of the United States of America, but not common in Washtenaw County. A significant advantage of a mobile home is its general affordability. A mobile home often includes furniture in its cost and may include the lot and certain services if the home is located in a mobile home park. Today's mobile homes are subject to strict quality standards, making this option quite cost-efficient (Hubbard, 1984, 6). Another advantage of moving into a mobile home community is that it provides ample opportunities for socialization. Many mobile home parks have organized activities for their residents.

A disadvantage of owning a mobile home is that it can be difficult to resell. Another dilemma, at least in Washtenaw County, is that many mobile home communities are located outside city limits, thereby making city services such as mass transit inaccessible.

Condominiums

Down the continuum from the more independent options and bordering on the more assisted options are condominiums. For an elderly woman who wants or is forced by the aging process to leave the frustrations of home ownership behind, yet who is not ready to relinquish much independence, a condominium is a natural consideration. A condominium "... refers to housing in an apartment building or detached or semi-detached town houses in which individuals hold title to their living unit but share ownership of the 'common elements' with other owners in the development (Hubbard, 1984, 8)." Common elements include walls, parking areas, grounds, recreation areas, walkways, and utility buildings. Thus, a clear advantage of condominium dwelling is the ease of maintenance of the living environment. Shoveling snow and cutting grass are no longer burdens nor are utility problems. Another advantage is that a condominium can be a good investment for a senior citizen since its equity is likely to grow. A disadvantage is the expense—this is often not a viable option for an older woman with a low income. A condominium dweller must make monthly payments and may be paying for services she does not use, such as the club house.

Subsidized Apartments

Providing all the advantages of apartment dwellings (i.e., the landlord is responsible for maintenance) at a reduced rate, subsidized apartments are much sought after by senior citizens. The greatest advantage of this more assisted (in the financial sense) option is that the rent is related to one's income. An elderly woman needs to pay only 30% of her income for rent, with the remaining 70% free for her other needs.

Yet there are disadvantages as well. Subsidized apartment units tend to be very small, lacking the space an elderly woman may need to host friends or grandchildren or store important possessions from home. The greatest problem is the long waiting list which seniors face when they apply for these units. There are simply not enough units in Washtenaw County to meet the growing demand, making a waiting period of two years the norm. A woman on the brink of senior citizenship would be wise to apply early for a unit, before her need is critical.

Ecogenic and Other Types of Shared Housing

A more assisted option than the ones described above is an arrangement in which three or more unrelated people live together in a house, usually having private sleeping quarters while sharing the other spaces. An innovative design solution is the Ecogenic House described in more detail elsewhere in these proceedings (Pastalan and Schwarz).

Retirement Centers

This option actually includes a range of possibilities from communities in which a senior citizen can purchase or rent a dwelling specifically designed for older people to institutions which provide full, around-the-clock care for the aging. Next to a hospital, retirement centers are the most assisted or supportive environments for an elderly woman. The advantages are many: security, opportunities for socialization, less worry over chores and maintenance. There are cases when an elderly couple comes to the Housing Bureau for Seniors, and it is the wife who prefers this option. Retirement for a husband means less work and more time to enjoy hobbies and friends. However, a woman who works inside the home never retires, and while her husband enjoys his newly found freedom, she continues to cook, clean, and maintain the house.

There are disadvantages as well, chief among which are the costs. Women with low incomes often do not have this option. Retirement centers also have an extremely negative image as places the elderly wish to avoid at all costs. Many are legitimate, healthy environments but the exposure of some as nightmarish places in which to die has stigmatized this option.

Evaluation of Options

Where a woman decides to live during her older years is a personal choice based on criteria specific to her situation. Yet there are certain issues which are important for every older woman to consider, and the shelter options we describe above can be evaluated by how well they address these critical issues. The issues include: affordability, socialization, maintenance, and safety.

Affordability

The least affordable options tend to be retirement centers, condominiums, and owning a home. While the first two clearly require enough personal wealth to cover move-in and other monthly costs, it may seem odd to include owning a home in the least affordable category. By the time they reach the older years many people have managed to pay off the mortgage. However, due to property taxes and the threat of losing one's home if these are not paid, along with maintenance expenses, owning a home can be very costly indeed.

Options which are at the midpoint on the affordability scale include HomeShare and accessory apartments, which bring in extra sources of income to the home owner. Another more affordable option is a mobile home.

The only really affordable solution for an older woman with low income is a subsidized apartment. Unfortunately, in the Washtenaw County area, and throughout much of the nation, the supply of subsidized units fails to meet the great demand and the waiting list is long. This scarcity closes the door on an otherwise reasonable option.

Socialization

Women who seek advice from the Housing Bureau for Seniors typically complain of loneliness, especially in the dark winter months. Many seniors do not drive once night has fallen; therefore socializing ends early during the winter. The option which allows for the least amount of socialization tends to be the single home, although this certainly varies depending on an older woman's neighborhood. If she is surrounded by friendly, concerned neighbors or family who check on her frequently, living in her own home may be a very gratifying experience socially.

All too often this is not the case. For many older women, remaining alone in the family home can cause great isolation, especially if they have been residents of their neighborhoods for a long time and have witnessed many changes in the area's composition. An older person may no longer know or socialize with new, unfamiliar neighbors. Isolation may lead to dangerous situations if an older woman should fall or become ill and remain undiscovered.

Socialization needs are better met in the condominiums and mobile home parks, especially if one becomes close to other residents of these typically social communities. And socialization can actually be enhanced through the HomeShare, accessory apartment, and especially the retirement center. In many accessory apartment situations, an older person does not have to venture outside to visit the neighbor. In most retirement centers at least one meal a day is in a common dining hall, creating opportunities for friendly interaction.

Maintenance

Maintenance problems are most troublesome for a senior citizen living in her own home. A home share situation may also poses maintenance problems, unless the home seeker is skilled in home upkeep and agrees to contribute these skills to the household. Maintenance problems are magnified in the accessory apartment option since an older person must maintain not only her own living space but also the tenant's apartment.

Mobile homes provide a middle ground for ease of maintenance; many parks provide some outside upkeep. Maintenance problems are virtually solved in subsidized apartments (depending, of course, on how responsive the apartment managers are to the tenants), condominiums, and retirement centers.

Safety

Older adults should consider two types of safety issues—indoor and outdoor. Indoor dangers include falling down the stairs, accidental burnings, slipping in the shower, and falling ill suddenly, with no one to realize one's dilemma. Outdoor, or external, dangers include burglaries and other types of neighborhood violence.

Indoor safety tends to be a problem for older home owners, mobile home owners, and condominium owners (unless these living spaces are especially adapted for an older person's needs). This issue is partially resolved for the home sharer and with the accessory apartment choice. Indoor safety is enhanced in subsidized apartments and retirement centers. In some subsidized apartments in Washtenaw County, elderly residents are given paper faces which they hang outside their doors. The smiling face lets neighbors know you are awake and going about your daily routine, and the sleeping face lets them know you have turned in for the night. If they do not see the sleeping face turned over and it is already

well into the day, they know to try and contact you to make sure all is well.

Outdoor safety issues may be unavoidable regardless of the option. Yet they tend to be especially problematic for home owners whose neighborhoods may have become more dangerous as they age. External dangers tend to be less of a threat in a home share situation where the home seeker watches out for the home provider's welfare. Outside safety is also partially addressed by mobile home, accessory apartment, subsidized apartment, and condominium options. External dangers tend to be considerably lessened for an older woman in the controlled environment of a retirement center.

Supporting Women in Their Own Homes

The choice of staying in one's own home gets poor marks when considering the critical issues of affordability, socialization, maintenance, and safety. But although their own homes are unaffordable, cause isolation, are difficult to maintain, and can be dangerous, many older women are determined to stay in them. At the Housing Bureau for Seniors, staff members discuss the dilemmas with older women of remaining in the family home, and while many acknowledge the difficulties, most attempt to remain at home as long as they are physically able to do so.

Given the deep meaning older women attach to their homes and the sense of powerfulness they have from surviving in an environment with which they are familiar, the Housing Bureau for Seniors has programs which can help make this choice more comfortable for an older woman. While some do eventually decide to try other housing options, for those women who choose to remain in their own homes the Home Share Match-Up and the Property Tax Foreclosure Prevention Programs can be of assistance.

HomeShare Match-Up Program

This program allows an older adult (home provider) to stay in her home because another person (home seeker) is located, matched, and moves into the older person's home. The home seeker helps to reduce the isolation of the home provider and provides financial assistance through rent. Agreements can be reached where the home seeker provides chore assistance and even home maintenance work if she has the skills. Of the people who enter the Housing Bureau for Seniors' HomeShare program, 74% are women. Often the match is inter-generational: the average age of the home provider is 72 and of the home seeker, 39. Of the home seekers, 83% are women with low incomes (in Washtenaw County that translates into below $15,000 per year) and 68% of the providers also have low incomes. Thus, this type of living arrangement can fit the financial needs of both parties.

The Housing Bureau for Seniors' program begins with counseling and therefore is very labor-intensive. Before someone moves into a provider's home, a Housing Bureau counselor has met with each party at least twelve times. Extensive reference checks are also carried out. Meeting frequently before a match is made helps to avoid potential personality conflicts between the home owner and home seeker.

When asked what they consider important personality traits for a home sharer to possess, counselors often cite flexibility and fairness. In addition, both parties must be forthcoming in stating their needs and expectations of the partnership. Honesty before a partnership begins reduces misunderstandings in the future. Finally, both provider and seeker should be sincerely interested in the welfare of their house mate. While the HomeShare program is a smart financial move for many women, it will not succeed based solely on financial motivations. Truly caring partnerships can provide viable, enabling living situations for both older and younger women, and can reduce the difficulties and dangers of remaining at home for the elderly.

Property Tax Foreclosure Prevention Program

While retirement incomes are remaining stable through-out Washtenaw County, property taxes are escalating. It is not uncommon for a senior citizen to be paying over $4,000 per year in property taxes, and this from an income that may be no more than $7,000 per year. In Michigan, once one gets behind on these taxes one can completely lose the family home and all its equity, even if the mortgage is already paid. In the worst scenario, an older person will be evicted. In the best scenario, she may continue to live at home but has to pay rent to a new home owner, a crushing financial burden for a woman on a fixed income. The typical client who comes to the Housing Bureau for Seniors with the fear of being evicted is a widow in her late 70's. She has spent all her savings on her husband's illness and then on his funeral. She is likely to have several chronic health problems of her own. Her house will likely have major structural problems due to deferred maintenance.

Michigan does offer programs to assist seniors who are having difficulty in paying their property taxes. How-ever, these are not widely used since they tend to be inaccessible and difficult to understand. The Housing Bureau for Seniors intervenes for senior citizens and links them up with the appropriate and available state programs. In addition to providing this information and advocacy, the organization is working on developing new programs to assist older people with this issue. The Housing Bureau is introducing bills to change state laws so that the process of evicting people of all ages from their homes will be discontinued.

Conclusion

An older woman in Washtenaw County has a variety of shelter options to consider. But some may be inappro-priate, because of personal preferences, finances, or other considerations. While remaining in her own home is not easy and can be costly and dangerous, many women choose this option over the others. At the Housing Bureau for Seniors, the staff is determined to provide all the information older women need to evaluate the range of options available to them. If they choose to remain in their homes, the organization tries to help older women make this option viable by lessening the expense and the dangers of living alone.

While active shelter organizations provide valuable information and alternative solutions to women in search of housing, the scarcity of decent, affordable shelter remains a key problem for older women. One promi-nent consideration by women who choose to remain at home is that they simply cannot afford a more support-ive shelter situation. Out of respect and caring for the older generation, and out of the very practical realization that we shall be in their places in the years to come, it is vitally necessary that women work together to increase and make more accessible the housing choices for those in the capstone years of their lives.

References

Hubbard, Linda, editor. 1984. *Housing Options for Older Americans.* Washington, D.C.: American Association of Retired Persons.

Chapter 48
The Meaning of Home and Ecogenic Housing: A New Concept for Elderly Women[1]

Leon A. Pastalan and Benyamin Schwarz

Leon A. Pastalan is an internationally recognized leader in the area of design for aging, Director of the National Center on Housing and Living Arrangements for Older Americans, and editor of the Journal of Housing for the Elderly. *Over a period of more than thirty years, his research and writing have increased the understanding and appreciation of environment and behavior studies, just as his development of the empathic model has provided a foundation for the study of design for aging populations. Dr. Pastalan is on the faculty of the College of Architecture and Urban Planning at the University of Michigan.*

Benyamin Schwarz is a research architect for the National Council on Housing and Living Arrangements for Older Americans at the University of Michigan. As a practicing architect in Israel, with a special focus on settings for aging populations, he designed numerous projects for the kibbutz society, drawing upon the prevalent orientation of this organization to maintain the aging individual within the familiar surroundings of the kibbutz. His research has addressed the design process for extended care facilities in the United States and abroad.

Males and females have very different mortality rates and life expectancy rates. In nearly all countries of the world, women live longer than men. In the United States, Germany, and Italy, women outlive men by approximately 7 years, while in France the gap is 8.5 years. In the U.S. the ratio of women to men varies dramatically with age. Men slightly outnumbered women in all age groups under 35 in 1989, but in the 65 and over age group, there were 18,300,000 women and only 12,600,000 men. Elderly women now outnumber elderly men by three to two. In 1989, there were 84 men between the ages of 65 to 69 for over 100 women in the same age group. Among those 85 and over there were only 39 men for every 100 women.[2]

The increasing numbers of elderly make it clear that housing-based policies to assist them will be critical in the future. Projections of The Urban Institute show that there will be an increase of low-income renters of housing in the world's future—1.780 million in 1990, 2.365 million in 2010, and 3.075 million in 2030. Perhaps more important are the characteristics of this population. In 2030, for example, more than half of the 3.1 million low-income renters will be at least 80 years old.[3] The greater increase among the very old, combined with the evidence that independent living is preferred by the large majority of older people, suggest that one major challenge over the next several decades will be to figure out how housing units can be adapted to allow for the provision of long-term care services. Substantial numbers of frail elderly—the most likely targets of long-term care services delivered in the home—are living in housing units and communities that either impede the efficient delivery of these services or preclude their delivery altogether. There are different remedies to these problems.

The Concept of Home

"Home is the place where, when you have to go there, They have to take you in." [4]; O'Bryant, 1982, 1983; Rowels, 1987; Rubinstein, 1989). Expectations concerning home appear to be important to old people, and this is generally expressed as the wish to stay put (Wheeler, 1982). This suggests that for older people home has a psychological and metaphysical significance over and above being a shelter in which to conduct everyday life.

Much of the research has suggested that the need for a home is a fundamental human imperative, providing a locus of order and control in a world of chaos. Home imparts a sense of identity, security, and belonging

(Rowels, 1987). It is space differentiated from a world outside that is often viewed as hostile. Crossing the threshold to depart involves a transition from the sacred to the profane (Eliade, 1961). Home is a place of protection, a refuge.

To be at home is to know where you are; it means to inhabit a secure center and to be oriented in space. Home as territory can include a room inside a house, a house within a neighborhood, a neighborhood within a city, and a city within a country. At each level the meaning of home gains in intensity and depth from the interaction between the experience of the place and its context at a large scale. This larger home alludes to hierarchy of places within which we are oriented, and distinguished from the larger and stranger surroundings. Home in the sense of territory is a place where one can be independent, be in charge and take control, even if it is perceived control, which means the extent to which we believe that what happens to us is a matter of fate, luck, or our own powerlessness, versus a belief that we are the masters of our own destinies and usually determine our own actions (Howell, 1985).

Within the privacy of home, an older person can control, and often conceal, declining capacities in the management of daily living. The familiarity of the setting permits what Rowels (1983) called a sense of "physical insideness" where familiarity, at a less than conscious level, can compensate for the progressive sensory loss likely to accompany age. The ability to continue to master the physical environment despite frailty confers power upon the individual, and in turn can enhance personal capacity to interact beyond the locus of home (Willcocks, Peace and Kellaher, 1987).

Home is a kind of origin; we go "back" home even when our arrival is in the future. We inhabit our home day after day until we develop a sense of familiarity with the environment to the degree that it becomes predictable and taken for granted (Dovey, 1985). Home has strong roots in the experiences of childhood. Claire Cooper Marcus (1978) suggested that there are connections between the visual images of childhood home and the environmental attitudes towards homes expressed in adult life. Feuerstein (1965) referred to the materials and the forms of home which reflect our knowledge of how the places in which we dwell came into being. This provides us with a sense of home even when we were not engaged in the construction.

There are infinite variations in the forms of dwellings. Cultural beliefs and social practice represent the

ordering systems that select choices from among these possibilities and shape the broad range of formal manifestations of home within any sociocultural context (Benedict, 1946). Spatial arrangements and environmental settings support patterns of experience and behavior. Patterns of activities like dining, talking, bathing, sleeping, studying, and watching television form much of the programs in housing design. These are patterns that orient us in space, in time, and in sociocultural context. They are not embodied in a house or certain building but in our experience and behavior, and as such they can be transposed from place to place. In this sense the meanings of home may be revoked if the patterns are recreated. Although the particular spatial patterns may be sociocultural, the sense of connectedness may be more personal (Dovey, 1985). For example, lovers can transcend a dependence on place; a small motel room can be perceived by them as home. Their love can elevate any place they happen to be into a home. This is not to say that the physical environment makes no difference. However, the sense of home may be developed in any setting for activities if people elevate the place into *home* space by attributing to it certain characteristics and allowing homelike activities to take place.

Home is a place where our identity is continually evoked through connections with the past. Our experience in the world carries its own meanings, and the places in which these experiences occur become ingrained with those meanings. The physical environment plays a very important role because it enables us to materialize our memory through association with places. The memories reflected in the home environment help to create our experiences of home, and those experiences serve in turn to preserve, evoke, and even revise the memory. This theme of connection is fundamental within the conception of home as a focus of self-identity. Home environment may be repository of memories and provide a link with the past, either through meanings accumulated from the recollection of events that took place within the physical setting or through the memories and sense of self that are evoked through personal possessions and artifacts maintained within the home (Rowels, 1987).

Boschetti (1984) expressed this:

> Our past belongs to us. And personal possessions are tangible parts of that past. The silver, crystal, fine china, linens, odd pieces of furniture—mostly wood because it withstands the rigors of time—scrapbooks, photo albums, family portraits, and other random memorabilia of a person's life on earth, which get passed on, are the tangible

parts of a person's life. During life these items by their daily presence serve to remind the person who she or he is; when handed down they carry with them the giver's tangible presence into the future.[5]

Dovey (1985) summarized the concept of home as a schema of relationships that bring order, integrity, and meaning to experience in place—a series of connections between person and world:

Connectedness with people
Connectedness with the place
Connectedness with the past, and
Connectedness with the future

We may distinguish between:

1. Home as a safe place. A shelter from the elements and from other threats. A familiar and predictable place, where we can perform in safety and security.

2. Home as a place where we expect to have support and help, love and happiness. A place where one can live and not only stay. A place where people love us and care for us. An image of a family that evokes connotations such as affection, support, loyalty, obligations, and responsibilities.

3. Home as a place where we choose our own life style and perform desired activities not as patients, but as residents.

4. Home as a territory that we control. A place which symbolizes our permanent right to be there. In this territory we can make the rules and the regulations. We can personalize the place, control the architectural appearance and the furniture arrangement, control the lighting and the temperature, and we can control our and others' behavior.

5. Home as a place for personal identity. A place that we can personalize with our artifacts which express us. A place that we can design based on our preference to express our values in such a way that the place expresses us and we identify with it.

6. Home as a place that protects our privacy. A place where we have the needs, the rights, and the opportunities for the highest level of privacy. Home is a place where we can shut the door on some stranger who wants to intrude on our privacy. Home enables us to take off our "costumes" and "masks" and be ourselves, to take a rest from society's demands, to relax, and to accumulate energy for our next "performance."

7. Home as a place of continuity. A place that symbolizes our personal and family's history, and maintains the connections to our past. Home as a repository of memories and a provider of links with the past.

8. Home as an expression of a social status. Ownership as symbol of status, success, and achievement. Location,

architectural appearance, and interior design all contribute to this meaning.

9. Home as place where we prefer to die.

All these attributes represent the phenomenon of home which is an intangible relationship between people and the places that they dwell. Several publications of environment geared toward elderly intend to derive the images of home through the intangible qualities of artifacts and environmental components such as soft hues or bright airiness. Other properties are more tangible and refer to qualities of home as a contrast to the institutional environment. Properties like central living rooms, carpeting, comfortable chairs, scale of rooms, arrangements of furniture, windows, ventilation, noise reduction devices, lighting, short corridors, etc., have significance. They all evoke collective memories of the warm, small-scale, cozy, comfortable environment of an ideal home setting. They illustrate the promise of a home experience carefully packaged in the homelike concept for the residents and their families.

Promises assumed in the homelike image are an effort to create the complete opposite of the institutional image. In this view, the institution has over-worked, under-paid staff intent on performing instrumental tasks for pay; in homelike environment we have caregivers caring for beloved residents, almost like children in a family caring for beloved parents at home. In an institution the resident is a "case"; in a homelike setting the old person remains a parent, grandparent, and friend. The institutional facility allows little personal autonomy; in the homelike environment individuals are responsible for setting their own schedule and control of their surroundings. Residents of an institution are isolated from the community; members of a homelike facility are involved in the community. Institutional food can be disgusting; home-cooked food, nourishing. The institutional environment is barren and cold; the homelike setting is cheerful and warm. Within an institution elderly sit apathetically waiting for visitors and social interaction; in a homelike environment people socialize with each other.

Indeed, we have constructed a continuum, with the institution at one end and the home at the other (Figure 1).

The Concept of Ecogenic Housing

Ecogenic Housing is a concept developed to balance the issues of security and autonomy in a home environment.

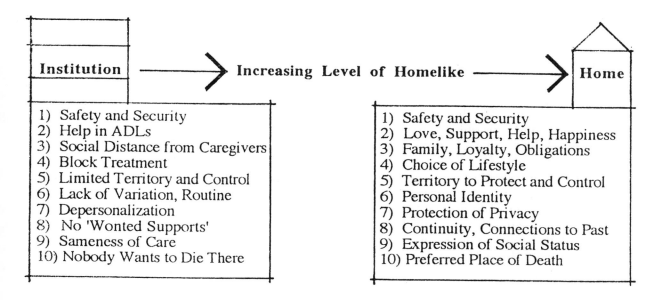

Institution ⟶	Increasing Level of Homelike ⟶	Home

Institution	**Home**
1) Safety and Security	1) Safety and Security
2) Help in ADLs	2) Love, Support, Help, Happiness
3) Social Distance from Caregivers	3) Family, Loyalty, Obligations
4) Block Treatment	4) Choice of Lifestyle
5) Limited Territory and Control	5) Territory to Protect and Control
6) Lack of Variation, Routine	6) Personal Identity
7) Depersonalization	7) Protection of Privacy
8) No 'Wonted Supports'	8) Continuity, Connections to Past
9) Sameness of Care	9) Expression of Social Status
10) Nobody Wants to Die There	10) Preferred Place of Death

Fig. 1: The Home—Institution Continuum.

The purpose of Ecogenic Housing is to provide opportunities for companionship and socialization; safety and protection from crime; enhanced productivity in cooperative efforts regarding activities of daily living; privacy and autonomy; and provision of home health services, all within a family lifestyle at an affordable cost.

Ecogenic Housing for the elderly can be characterized in most instances as a situation in which at least two economically unrelated persons share selected common areas including kitchen and living and dining areas, but have their own private sleeping, social, and sanitation areas. While each individual shares some common areas, each is viewed as independent and constituting a separate household.

Social isolation is very common among the elderly, especially those persons of advanced years who are widowed or unattached. Elderly people living alone comprise close to one-third of all older people. In 1989, 8,900,000 Americans 65 and over lived alone. The economic status of elderly people who live alone is markedly lower than that of those who live with others. For example, 24% of elderly people living alone are poor, compared with 14% of those who live with others.

Companionship and socialization within a family lifestyle can lead to improvement in mental and physical health because activities of daily living (ADL) can be enjoyed and shared by others. Meals, for instance,

would be more enjoyable since one is no longer eating alone and hence better nutrition would positively affect one's level of well-being. The kitchen provides activities for meal preparation and consumption, but does not mandate such activity. The person is free to take meals elsewhere or have meals delivered.

Fear of crime and anxiety regarding safety and security are high among the concerns the elderly express. While perceived threats of crime frequently exceed actual incidences, real as well as perceived security and personal safety are clearly enhanced with numbers as opposed to living alone.

Activities of daily living such as household chores are cooperatively shared and make such tasks easier to deal with. Meal preparation and other household chores demand a continuous involvement and investment of oneself. These demands help to keep the residents active, contrasted with the passivity of persons where such services are provided by others. Cooperative efforts have an important impact on the older person's productivity. Productivity here is viewed broadly and includes anything which produces goods and services. These need not be marketable so long as they reduce the demands on goods and services produced by others. Thus, cooperative efforts with such activities of daily living would be considered productive if the person or persons might otherwise have required someone to provide that care or activity. This, however, does not alter the fact that community agencies and service

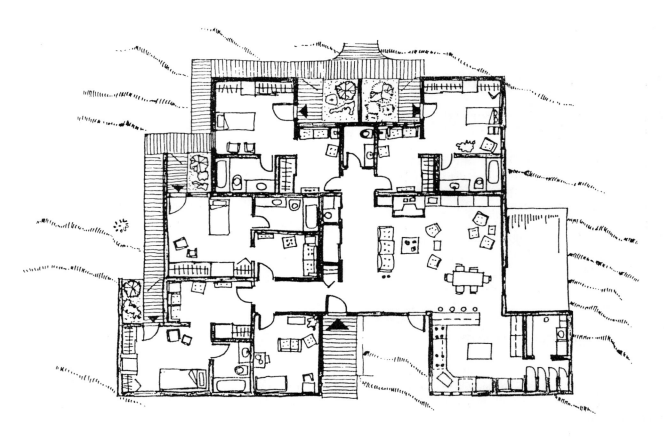

Fig. 2: Ecogenic House. A Floor Plan.

providers could offer various services pertaining to activities of daily living if needed.

Privacy of each individual is assured by the provision of an area for private activity such as sleeping, sanitation, and social as well as other activities of a personal nature. Depending on need and circumstances, the physical arrangement of the unit allows each individual to engage in activities with others or disengage for private activities.

The Ecogenic Housing arrangement can also provide a context for the delivery of home health services in a non-institutionalized, family setting. With a consciously designed supportive environment including flexible physical spaces, products which assist in activities of daily living, as well as appropriately trained service delivery personnel and cooperation from fellow residents, members of such a housing arrangement would require shorter stays in hospitals to recover from an acute illness or, in case of chronic health problems, to avoid premature and costly nursing home care

Affordability is enhanced due to savings in construction costs of the shared spaces such as the kitchen and dining and living areas; and reduced administrative and service costs. In sum, Ecogenic Housing provides decent shelter with many physical, psycho/social, and health care amenities in a non-institutionalized family setting at a price moderate- and low-income elderly persons can afford.

Appearance and Function

The physical appearance of this purpose-built residential unit is that of a four bedroom house with a maximum of four persons (Figure 2).

The style could be made to fit any neighborhood, e.g., from a colonial to a ranch or anything in between. This provides the potential for locating such housing on one lot in a neighborhood or, if it seems called for, a whole subdivision. The important point here is that it is kept in residential context and in a family lifestyle and avoids the negative aspects of an institution.

This approach can serve a whole range of housing needs. For instance, it can respond to the high cost of housing and could serve elderly persons who are physically independent and healthy but have an affordability problem. It could also serve as a non-institutional, family-scale response to congregate housing for the elderly or for assisted living for younger, physically handicapped persons. This would be made possible through the appropriate orchestration of the design of physical spaces and products which assist in activities of daily living and service delivery personnel.

The economic viability of such housing has been demonstrated through a financial analysis and can be viewed as a sound investment. However, perhaps more importantly, an appropriate business organization has an opportunity not only to develop and build such housing but to test and develop a range of supportive products as well.

Research and development in the area of home health care represents a unique opportunity. With the pressure to discharge patients from acute care hospitals in ever shorter periods of time and the prohibitive cost of nursing home care, it is obvious that health care in the home is the wave of the future. The testing and developing of appropriate assistive devices, changing configurations of various residential spaces, more supportive furniture and appliances, etc., in a residential setting are only a few of the necessary things that need to be done. This housing concept promises to meet emerging housing and health care needs of our society through the design and construction of such housing as well as its supportive product environment.

References

AARP. *Aging America (Trends/Projections)*, 1991.

Altman, I. and Werner, C. (Eds.) *Home Environments.* New York: Plenum Press, 1985.

Benedict, R. *Patterns of culture.* New York: Mentor, 1946.

Boschetti, M. A. *The older person's emotional attachment to the physical environment of the residential setting.* Unpublished doctoral dissertation. Ann Arbor: The University of Michigan, 1984.

Dovey, K. "Home and Homelessness." In: *Home Environments.* Eds. I. Altman and C. Werner. New York: Plenum Press, 1985.

Eliade, M. *The sacred and the profane.* New York: Harper & Row, 1961.

Feuerstein, G. "Unpremeditated architecture." *Landscape*, 13 (3), 33–37, 1965.

Howell, S. "Home: A Source of Meaning in Elders' Lives." *Generations*, IX(3): 58–60, 1985.

Marcus, Claire Cooper "Remembrance of landscapes past." *Landscape*, 22 (3), 34–43, 1978.

O'Bryant, S. L. "The value of home to older persons and its relationship to housing satisfaction." *Research on Aging*, 4, 349–363, 1982.

O'Bryant, S. L. "The subjective value of "home" to older homeowners." *Journal of Housing for the Elderly, 1,* 29–43, 1983.

Rowels, G. D. "Place and personal identity in old age: Observations from Appalachia." *Journal of Environmental Psychology*, 3, 299–313, 1983.

Rowels, G. D. "A Place to Call Home." In: *Handbook of Clinical Gerontology.* Ed. L. L. Carstensen and B. A. Edelstein. pp. 335–353. New York: Pergamon Press, 1987.

Rubinstein, R. L. "The Home Environments of Older People: A Description of the Psychosocial Processes Linking Person to Place." *Journal of Gerontology: Social Sciences*, 44 (2), 545–553, 1989.

Seamon, D. "Newcomers, existential outsiders and insiders: Their portrayal in two books by Doris Lessing." In *Humanistic geography and literature.* Ed. D.C. D. Pocock. London: Croon Helm, 1981.

Wheeler, R. "Housing and the Elderly." In *Aging and Social Policy*, C. Philipson and A. Walker (Eds.). Aldershot, Hants: Gower Publishing Co, 1982.

Willcocks, D., Peace, S., and Kellaher, L. *Private Lives in Public Places.* New York: Tavistock Publications, 1987.

Zedlewski, S. R., Barnes, R. O., Burt, M. R., McBride, T. D., and Meyer, J. A. *The Needs of the Elderly in the 21st Century.* Urban Institute Report 90–5. Washington, D.C.: Urban Institute Press, 1990.

Notes

[1] AARP's *Aging America* (Trends/Projections) 1991.

[2] Ibid.

[3] Zedlewski, S.R., *et. al. The Needs of the Elderly in the 21st Century,* 1990.

[4] Robert Frost. *The Death of the Hired Man.*

[5] Boschetti, M.A. (1984). The older person's emotional attachment to the physical environment of the residential setting, p. 39.

[6] AARP's *Aging America* (Trends/Projections) 1991.

Chapter 49
Crossing Oceans: A Cross-Cultural Look at Elderly Immigrant Women in the United States and Elderly Women in India

Rama Sethi

Rama R. Sethi *is a native of New Delhi, India. She did her undergraduate work at the University of California, Berkeley in Political Science and City and Regional Planning and received a Master of Urban Planning in 1993 from the University of Michigan, specializing in International Planning and Development.*

Both the absolute numbers and proportions of elderly persons are rapidly growing throughout the world. Estimates are that the Third World will have 61 percent of the world's 590 million persons age 60 and over by the year 2000. In industrial nations, although social scientists, politicians, and the general public are increasingly aware of the "aging of the population," elderly immigrants are generally not considered a part of this group. Thus the diversity associated with a sizable foreign-born elderly population throws into question general statements regarding "the elderly."

In both cases, the absence of theoretical and empirical data documenting the effects of industrialization and development, specifically housing and support service schemes, is particularly acute with regard to women. The income and housing needs of elderly immigrants in the United States and elderly women in India are only beginning to receive attention and remain little understood. In India the impact of modernization on traditional extended families raises serious questions about continued incentives for and abilities of families to care for elderly women. Similarly, enormous pressures are placed on immigrant families in the United States with limited resources to provide not only financial but also psychological and social support.

The need for increased attention to this area is obvious. Politicians, researchers, and planners must reevaluate assumptions that the needs of elderly women are met within the family network. With increased research must come changes in policy and practice.

Sushila and Toui

Sushila lives in a small village in India with her daughter-in-law and three grandchildren. Everyday, Sushila is awake at 5 a.m. and can already hear her daughter-in-law making *chai* as she awakens the children. Sushila slowly rises to gather her bedding and as she bends over she feels a sharp pain shoot up her right leg. She pauses briefly, shifts her weight, and resumes her work. She has gotten so used to the pain, she hardly notices it any more. Her son took her to the health facility once, but the one-way three-hour bus ride was too much for her to bear and it had taken up a whole day of her son's short visit to the village.

As Sushila goes into the tiny kitchen, she remembers that yesterday's earnings were quite meager, not even sufficient to buy enough milk for today. She makes a mental note to herself to save the milk for the children since they need it more than her old bones. After her cup of tea, Sushila goes out to the fields with Ratni, her daughter-in-law, and her two younger grandchildren, aged 12 and 13. The oldest, 14, has already left to take the bus to town where he will peddle vegetables well into the evening or until he sells out and then make the two-hour commute back to the village.

Toui was 62 years old when she first immigrated to the United States from China to be with her son and daughter who had settled in the States. Today, almost four years later, Toui still feels just as out of place as on her first day in America and the loneliness has just gotten worse. It hadn't been that bad when she lived with her daughter, but Toui's ailing health and her daughter's financial and time constraints required home health care services, but she couldn't qualify for the program as long as she lived with the family. Moreover, the language barrier was also a problem.

Seeing that both Toui and her daughter felt personally responsible for and guilty about the situation, a friend suggested that Toui live alone so she could qualify for home health care. After a long and fruitless search for a health care worker who spoke Chinese, Toui found herself living alone. She rarely left her small efficiency, going out only when she really needed to. Her daughter would come visit and sometimes do her shopping. Other times Toui relied on her neighbors and constantly found herself being torn apart as she reflected on the full and active life she had lived in China. Now, she was acutely aware of her dependency and often remarked that "if you can't drive or afford to drive in the United States, then you're virtually disabled."

Sushila and Toui are two fictional cases that depict the reality of millions of elderly women in India and elderly immigrant women in the United States. Sushila and Toui highlight women's day-to-day struggle to survive and live meaningful life as full, complete, living beings in a world that continually and constantly threatens, if not thwarts, their efforts.

Painting the Picture

Like Sushila, a large majority of elderly women in India live in rural areas. Like Sushila, the problems India's poor elderly women face are compounded by the lack of even the most basic services. Not only do poor elderly women suffer gravely and disproportionately from India's severe lack of decent housing, and health care, but they also lack financial and psychological security at a time when they need it most in their lives. India's full-fledged, open-arm thrust for development has left her poor elderly population in the trenches, while national planners and politicians alongside with bilateral and multilateral organizations rush to create and finance schemes to hasten the process, virtually ignoring their impact on one of society's weakest and most vulnerable groups.

Increasing industrialization and modernization are steadily chipping away at the economic and social base of even the most remote areas of the country. And it is India's elderly women who are the forgotten victims of four decades of development. As cash-cropping, growing monetization, industrialization, and urbanization erode traditional family structures and systems of security, leaving little in their place, social services geared to this group are absolutely imperative.

Elderly immigrant women in the United States face similar problems. While popular culture, epitomized by the sitcom, "The Golden Girls" — which depicts four white active women living in a single-family suburban home — hardly acknowledges the reality of millions of elderly women in the United States, it is completely oblivious to elderly immigrant women. Besides tackling the daily difficulties of a society that offers little diversity in living, traveling, and working conditions, elderly immigrant women are confronted with a host of issues that they are little, if at all, prepared for.

Faced with cultural and language barriers, elderly immigrant women find that even the most basic function becomes an arduous task, requiring continuous help from and dependence on others. America's fascination with freeways coupled with its growing suburbanization make difficult daily activities like shopping and access to health care not only in suburban settings, but in central cities as well.

The cities' shrinking tax base, poor land-use and transportation planning, and America's affinity for the automobile have contributed to the low popularity and minimal maintenance of mass transit. Again, it is the elderly who suffer disproportionately, as their mobility is severely constrained. And in cities where mass transit is well developed, cultural and language barriers combined with inadequate safety and lack of user-friendly facilities create almost insurmountable situations for elderly immigrant women. Like elderly women in India, the lack of control over their environment coupled with their physical isolation usually leads to a life of alienation and disempowerment for elderly immigrant women in the United States.

This paper will examine the situation and needs of poor elderly women in India and low-income elderly immigrant women in the United States, highlighting four areas particularly important to improving the well-being of both groups: information, housing, transportation, and public welfare programs (known as pension programs in the Indian context). In all these areas, accessibility, affordability, and flexibility are the determinants of how and where both groups will live out the last years of their lives.

While the range of social services in the United States is wide and well-developed, these services do not necessarily reach elderly immigrant women. In comparison to the indigenous white population, elderly immigrant women make little or no use of services or programs established to cater to their needs. Ignorance, fear of government agencies, cultural differences, transportation difficulties, language problems, and racism are usually the underlying reasons for the low utilization of such services (Wong).

The U.S.'s housing stock and living arrangements lack diversity as well as flexibility. The diminishing pool of low-income housing in recent years has adversely affected elderly women, as a large majority of them tend to live in urban areas. And while the elderly living in urban areas may have greater resources than their suburban-dwelling counterparts, the urban areas are often unsafe and poorly maintained. Social, economic, and legal barriers discourage, and in some cases, deter, extended and creative family living arrangements.

Recently, growing national attention to "the aging of America" coupled with the drastic cuts in social services, have led to a proliferation of literature calling for more flexible, family-oriented living arrangements. Carefully planned strategies may offer creative alternatives to immigrant families with limited resources to help provide not only financial, but also psychological and social support to elderly immigrant women. Elderly immigrant women's diverse backgrounds and living experiences can serve as an important source of information in developing alternative and imaginative housing and living arrangements. Third World countries like India are also a rich source of information. An exchange of ideas and increased interaction between international and domestic planners and their target groups would do much to facilitate and implement effective programs and policies in their respective countries.

India needs to improve its social services markedly, paying particular attention to the needs of poor elderly women. Pension programs, health care, and transportation are some of the crucial areas requiring considerable attention. Development strategies and government programs aimed at improving India's social services have traditionally aimed at and funneled resources into urban areas, leaving rural areas vastly underserved. Worsening conditions in the villages "push" while the struggle to survive and hopes for a better life "pull" the most able-bodied to the cities (Dandekar). Consequently, as the younger persons migrate to the cities, elderly women are deprived not only of their support base, but are left alone in miserable conditions.

Lack of Information

Empirical and theoretical data on the needs of elderly women in India and elderly immigrant women in the United States are scanty. This lack of information not only impedes programmers and planners, but also presents a major barrier to testing theories devised to explain and predict program and policy development (Nair). The few studies conducted so far show that elderly women in India fare much worse than their male counterparts. Most Indian women live and work in agricultural areas, will probably age there, and, hence, are at considerable risk for living out the last years of their lives in impoverished conditions.

Indian old women in rural areas are more at economic and social risk than men. One major reason is that women tend to live longer and thus face more years of financial and social hardship as widows. Another is that a growing number of women live alone due to the increasing break-up of the extended family. As family support declines, public welfare becomes almost essential. It is important to understand the needs of this group if effective programs and policies catering to them are to be implemented.

Similarly, information on elderly immigrant women in the United States is insufficient, including their particular requirements as they seek to become meaningful members of their new society. For many immigrant groups, certain assumptions have served to cloud their particular needs and to delay effective policy and service development. For example, due to the traditional extended family system of many immigrant cultures, it has been assumed that the needs of elderly immigrant women are met within the family network. Literature on the immigrant family often reinforces this stereotype by basing ideas and information on prior literature rather than on current hard data. However, recent research also shows that generalizing about housing from trends exhibited by native elderly women to elderly immigrant women is a mistake as well; living alone is less characteristic of the foreign-born elderly, especially if they migrate in old age (Martinez). Obviously the need for research is crucial if concrete improvements are to be made.

Information is particularly lacking in the area of housing and transportation needs of this group. Thus, the diversity associated with a sizable foreign-born population throws into question general statements regarding "the elderly." Such general statements consequently lead to programs and policies ill-equipped to address the need of elderly immigrant women. As elderly immigrants age alongside native-born Americans [projections show that by the year 2030, the percentage of the elderly in the total population may increase from 11 to 17 percent (Wong)], increased research on and programs for elderly immigrant women should be devised and implemented if they are to live meaningful lives in their adopted home.

Immigration to the United States generates two types of demographic cohorts: young immigrants, who, like their native-born counterparts, grow old, and elderly people, usually parents, whose immigration is stimulated by the immigration of young adults (Boyd). These varying immigration patterns further diversify the elderly population.

Housing and Transportation

While it is impossible to meet all the various needs of different groups, the need for diverse and affordable housing is shared by almost all sectors of the elderly in the United States. Likewise, the lives of older people, particularly those who are poor, will be improved by increased mobility. Knowledge of and ability to speak English increases the tendency of elderly immigrant women to live alone because such fluency helps to determine the ease or difficulty of obtaining support services by the elderly (Boyd). The tendency to live alone increases with length of stay in the U.S. Also, the loss in purchasing power experienced from moving to this country makes living alone more costly for elderly immigrants.

Flexible zoning, creative land-use and transportation planning, and a diversified and affordable housing stock are the keys to providing decent housing that fits the needs of the consumer, particularly elderly immigrant women. Pedestrian areas which provide a comfortable living environment for a mixed group of people as well as accessibility to shopping and services is one way to improve the situation. Congregate housing, nursing homes sensitive to the needs of elderly immigrant women, and housing projects with reduced rent for extended family living are just some of the ways where a little imagination and flexibility will go a long way to ensure a safe and comfortable environment for elderly immigrant women.

Perhaps one of the greatest difficulties facing elderly immigrant women, particularly recent immigrants, is the virtual loss of mobility they experience. Since automobiles are the "legs" of America, many of the women find themselves "handicapped." One of the major challenges, then, is to encourage barrier-free transportation by expanding mass transit, while decreasing our dependency on the car. Also, existing mass transit must be seriously improved in regard to frequency, timing, and safety. Encouraging and subsidizing mini-van operations that would provide frequent and affordable door-to-door service is another option. A flexible and accessible transportation system will produce results that will benefit the society at large. Countries like India provide rich examples of flexible and accessible transportation, and improved communications between the two countries may generate some significant solutions.

India's housing crisis adversely affects a large majority of poor elderly women. Many of them are landless and have barely enough to survive from day to day. Serious and substantial improvements must be made in India's rural areas, with programs specifically designed for elderly immigrant women. Increased investment is necessary in programs and projects that will lead to tangible and long-term improvements for rural areas (improved utilities services, appropriate economic development, alternative sources of income, etc.). Stop-gap measures like free meal programs to meet the immediate needs of elderly women, coupled with long-term programs that provide sustenance are key to ensuring the survival not only of elderly women, but also of rural India.

Public Welfare

Poor elderly women's lack of income makes them especially vulnerable to destitution. Elderly Indian women are more disadvantaged than men because they usually have accumulated fewer savings due to fewer days of work and lower pay through their working years. Moreover, the nature of the type and scope of work under arduous conditions coupled with women's primary responsibility for housework often leads to chronic health problems in old age, especially for women over 70. And in the rare case when pension programs are provided as part of a social welfare scheme, women are not only less likely than men to receive benefits, but also to receive a lower amount when they do. Moreover, older women are usually treated as marginal workers, are assigned fewer days of work, and are the first to be fired (Nair).

As traditional systems of support have gradually transformed a system of support for the elderly where the landlord assumed a part of the responsibility for housing and medical care and for providing jobs suited to an elderly person's capabilities, the burden has fallen on sons and daughters to assume full responsibility for their parents, even when they themselves are poor and ill-equipped to provide assistance. Even this traditional form of support is being threatened in certain parts of India where there is a growing number of elderly 70 and older, and their children themselves may be 50 or 60 and older, and living in poverty (Nair).

Clearly, the need for pension programs and a well-developed welfare program is great, especially for women. India should make a major effort to channel funds into rural areas, particularly for elderly women. Pension schemes should be well publicized and easily accessible to elderly women. The application process should be thorough, yet simple, since elderly women's applications are prone to be more defective than men's because of higher illiteracy rates and greater difficulties in obtaining necessary documentation. Pension programs should be implemented in rural areas nationwide, since they are probably the only source of income of India's poor elderly women and hence, their only source of survival.

Similarly, public welfare schemes are crucial to low-income immigrant women in the United States, especially when federal and state funds have been drastically cut for such services. And although social services still exist, elderly immigrant women know little, if anything, about them. Likewise, enormous pressures are placed on immigrant families with limited resources to provide not only financial but also psychological and social support. Accessibility and flexibility are important factors to consider in devising programs and policies for elderly immigrant women in the U.S. Because language is often a barrier to women benefiting from social security and medical care programs, offices dealing with these programs should consider employing bilingual staff persons.

Home health care should be strengthened and encouraged rather than nursing homes. Currently, it is much easier for an older person to get into a nursing home than to be cared for at home. This unnecessary institutionalization entails high cost for a quality of care considerably lower than home health care. Moreover, most older people, particularly immigrant women, would prefer to "age in place." Families who would like to look after older relatives themselves should be supported with home health care support services.

Conclusion

In both India and the United States, the growing number of elderly will have a large impact on future social and economic conditions in both countries. In recent years, the "aging of the world," the "new population bomb," has received widespread attention, as researchers, demographers, politicians, and planners, among others, call for careful planning to address the needs of this cohort effectively. This paper has highlighted some of the crucial issues that need to be seriously considered and acted upon if elderly women in India and elderly immigrant women in the U.S. are going to live the last years of their lives in a meaningful manner. As both countries grapple with a burgeoning older population, both countries should tap each other's wealth of experiences to address successfully not only the needs of elderly women, but also of their diverse populations.

References

American Association for International Aging. *Aging Populations in Developing Nations*. Washington, D.C., 1985.

Birdsall, William C. "Who Will Take Care of Mother?" Ann Arbor: University of Michigan, School of Social Work, Working paper, 1990–91.

Boyd, Monica. "Immigration and Living Arrangements: Elderly Women in Canada." *International Migration Review*, Winter, 1990.

Dandekar, Hemalata C. *Men to Bombay, Women at Home*. Ann Arbor: The University of Michigan, Center for South and Southeast Asian Studies, 1986.

Donahue, Wilma T., *et al. Congregate Housing for Older People: An Urgent Need, A Growing Demand*. Washington, D.C.: U.S. Dept. of Health, Education, and Welfare, 1977.

Kane, Sid. "The New Population Bomb." *World Development*, May 1991, United Nations Development Programme.

Kinderknecht, Cheryl H. "What's Out There and How to Get It: A Practical Resource Guide for the Helpers of Older Women." in Dianne Garner, Susan O. Mercer, eds., *Women as They Age: Challenge, Opportunity and Triumph*, New York: Haworth Press, 1989.

Lawton, Powell M. *Planning and Managing Housing for the Elderly.* New York: John Wiley & Sons, 1975.

Mammen, K.J. "Demographic Slide-Back Must be Checked." *The Hindu*, December 29, 1937.

Martinez, Maria Z. "Family Policy for Mexican Americans and their Aged," *Urban-and-Social-Change-Review, 12* (2), pp. 16–19, summer, 1979.

Midgley, J. *Social Security, Inequality, and the Third World.* New York: Wiley & Sons, 1984.

Montrero, D. "The Elderly Japanese Americans: Aging Among the First Generation Immigrants." *Genetic Psychology Monographs, 101*: 99–118, 1980.

Nair, Sobha B., and Martin, Tracy B. "Pensions for Women In The Third World: A Case Study of Kerala, India." *International Journal of Contemporary Sociology, 26*, Nos. 3–4, 1989.

National Policy Center on Housing and Living Arrangements For Older People. *Elderly Housing Guidelines.* The University of Michigan, College of Architecture and Urban Planning, 1981.

Rosenberry, Sara, and Hartmann, Chester. *Housing Issues of The 1990s.* New York: Praeger Publishers, 1989.

Salcido, R.M., *et al.* "The Use of Formal and Informal Health and Welfare Services of The Asian-American Elderly: An Exploratory Study." *California Sociologist 3* (2): 213–219, 1980.

Soldo, Beth J. "America's Elderly in the 1980s." *Population Bulletin*, Vol. 35, No. 4 Washington, D.C.: Population Reference Bureau, Inc., 1980.

Wilner, Mary Ann, et al. *Planning and Financing Facilities for The Elderly.* Washington, D.C.: American Association of Homes for the Aging, 1978.

Wong, Morrison G. "Economic Survival: The Case of Asian-American Elderly." *Sociological Perspectives, 27*(2), April, 1984.

Chapter 50
Housing and the Creation of Security in Old Age by Rural Women of Ghana: A Development Perspective

Barbara R. Stucki

Barbara R. Stucki is a research analyst in the Public Policy Institute at the American Association of Retired Persons. She deals with policy issues concerning long-term care needs of older persons, with special emphasis on minority elders, persons with disabilities, and the family support network. Information for this paper was collected as part of dissertation research conducted in 1990–1991, funded by a Fulbright Scholarship and grants from the Wenner Gren Foundation for Anthropological Research and the Social Science Research Council. She also holds a master's degree from Washington State University and a bachelor's degree from the University of California, Berkeley, in the field of Anthropology. She maintains her focus on international development and aging as a member of the African Gerontological Society, the Society for International Development, and the Society for Cross-Cultural Research.

The desire for adequate housing as the basis for security is shared by aging people throughout the world. This has led to the need for policies and programs that reinforce aspects of the residential environment which contribute to well-being in old age. In the United States, such programs have focused on the provision of community services and increasing residential choices (see, for example, Lawton, 1989; Golant, 1992; deLaski-Smith, 1985). In most African countries, older persons have to rely on their family for support. Concern for older persons has focused on reinforcing the traditional ties that bind the generations (Adadevoh, 1985). As a consequence, in discussing housing and older women in West Africa, development plans must also include the dynamics of old age security and its implications for the design and implementation of housing policies.

The task of building security in old age through traditional ties and strategies is becoming increasingly complex. Numerous studies of aging in Ghana highlight the negative impact of modernization on the rights and privileges of the elderly within the extended family (Apt, 1988; Twumasi, 1987; Caldwell, 1966; Brown, 1984). Even in rural areas, farmers are not isolated from the effects of the introduction of cash crops, changing agricultural policies, and exposure to western values and material goods. In addition, between 1970 and 1980, the real wage of Ghanaian farmers declined by 69% (Wilde, 1980; Ewusi, 1984).

Among the Ashanti of Ghana, high status and security are not attained solely by virtue of age. Instead, they are earned through a lifelong commitment to the welfare of the extended family. The ability to use kin ties as a source of help depends in large part on daily interaction, and keeping up with kinship obligations. For many, this means that comfort and security in old age increasingly depend on the ability to create ties of reciprocal rights and to reinforce filial obligation. Housing, as the context for family interaction, plays an important role in determining the nature of support provided to older persons.

This paper examines housing and development from the perspective of empowerment, that is, women's capacity to create an environment which will provide the support they need in old age. There are strong links between the provision of shelter and women's ability to secure a stable and secure old age. Two main themes have emerged: (1) house ownership as a way in which women acquire wealth and status, and (2) the importance of housing as the social environment in which women create relationships of reciprocal rights and obligation. House ownership and housing as a social environment are becoming increasingly important in the lives of rural Ashanti women. In this paper, I identify the strategies and limitations for house ownership among women, and their consequences for old age security. I also show that the power that women acquire as heads of households can extend their authority into the public realm as village elders.

Research Setting and Methods

The data on which this paper is based are derived from thirteen months of fieldwork among the Ashanti of central Ghana. Most rural Ashanti are engaged in a mix of subsistence and cash crop agriculture. The most important cash crop is cocoa, which is cultivated on small-scale individual or family farms. The sample consists of 211 cocoa farmers aged 50 or older who were living in villages 40 km north of the city of Kumasi. In this study, women accounted for 39% of the cocoa farmers. Methods used included a local census, a survey of the history of housing construction in this area, and participant observation. Interviews were conducted in Twi with the aid of an interpreter. Demographic data were collected by working with local government workers. Age was estimated by correlating the life histories of the farmers with remembered historical events.

Visitors are often struck by the extent to which women in this region are assertive, independent, and powerful. This is largely due to the fact that Ashanti kinship is based upon a matrilineal system, in which the extended family (*abusua*) includes all maternal relatives who trace their descent through the female line (Fortes, 1953). In this system, children belong to the mother's lineage and a wife's property is separate from and independent of that of her husband. The conjugal family is polygamous, in which a man may marry more than one wife. In general, Ashanti regard women as capable as men in undertaking economic and political endeavors.

Continuity and Change in Rural Housing

To understand the changing role of housing in women's strategies for creating and reinforcing support in old age, it is important to understand the courtyard house as the context of daily interaction among members of the extended family. The enclosed courtyard house is the traditional style of building among the Ashanti (Woode, 1969). The design of this house consists of a central square courtyard, enclosed by numerous sleeping rooms and open verandahs. In the past, young families would

start by building a single room which would serve as a place to sleep and store valuables. The open space in front of this room would be used as a general purpose activity and kitchen area (Sutherland, 1981). Additional rooms would be added as the family grew, so that the final shape of the house would eventually conform to the courtyard pattern. For the most part, rural Ashanti still live in traditional courtyard houses. Even modern, multi-story buildings are designed around a central courtyard where most of the cooking is done.

Housing has only recently become a significant concern in the lives of aging farmers in Ghana. In the past, housing was made of readily available local materials, primarily mud with a thatch roof. The technique involved in constructing this type of house was relatively simple, and could be done with the help of family members. Land was plentiful, and new dwellings were usually constructed adjacent to existing family houses. This provided a close spatial framework for the interaction and support among members of the extended family. These days, such mud and thatch houses are rare, though it is still possible to see a few of them in remote farming villages.

It is becoming increasingly difficult to construct a house. Most towns have building codes which require the use of imported materials, such as concrete blocks and corrugated iron roofing sheets. These materials are expensive, and may be difficult to obtain at times. Construction techniques are more complex, and usually require the help of a specialist. In addition, land for building has become scarce in most communities, and must now be purchased from the chief. The process of purchasing land is in itself a complicated and expensive process. Due to all these factors, most people wait to build a house until they have saved sufficient resources to build several rooms, or the entire courtyard house.

Housing and Old Age Support

The ability to contribute to the welfare of the *abusua* and community are regarded as evidence of wisdom and maturity, regardless of age. It takes considerable skill to accumulate the resources needed to build a house, and as a consequence, house ownership is now one of the most important and visible marks of a mature, successful adult. Such individuals who remain physically and intellectually vigorous have traditionally been held in high regard, and are often selected as lineage elders. One of the tasks of the lineage elders is to administer family property, including the allocation of rooms within family-owned (*abusua*) courtyard houses. This is a source of considerable power, because the dramatic increase in the rate of population growth has put a tremendous pressure on the available housing (United Nations, 1980). In this area, I found that housing stock has grown very slowly within the last century, primarily due to fluctuations in the profitability of cocoa. A high proportion of courtyard houses in this area (more than 75% in some communities) were built before 1940, during periods when cocoa profits were high.

Each room in the house is controlled by a different member of the extended family, usually the children and siblings of the head of the household. Rooms in *abusua* houses are allocated according to traditional rules of inheritance, with the old given priority over the young. Men tend to inherit the entire courtyard house while the right to use a specific room is usually passed from a woman to her daughters. Sisters and mothers are also more likely be given space in a house newly built by a member of the family.

In contrast to *abusua* houses, a self-acquired house is not controlled by rules of inheritance. Those individuals who build their own house are generally free to allocate rooms as they choose. Such house owners can become powerful patrons by creating ties of obligation and allegiance with those they shelter.

House ownership, age, and generation determine who is in charge, or "head," of the courtyard house. Both women and men can be selected for this position. Household heads have an important role within the *abusua* and the community. They are responsible for the conduct of all those who reside in the courtyard house. As house owner or the representative of the house owner, the head of the household has considerable authority and is treated with respect. In addition, local custom requires that all visitors greet village elders and the head of the household. Visiting family members often bring gifts, especially for female kin. The custom of greeting family elders also gives older household heads a chance to make their needs known and to ask for assistance. Household heads thus have many opportunities to establish and maintain a large network of support. This is particularly important in a society where assistance is based on personal contact.

Women's Strategies and Problems

Women who are able to build a house are in a position to control their residential environment. They are able to keep their children and grandchildren in the village, and thus surround themselves with willing helpers.

Childless older women can create ties to children and young parents by taking a foster child into their home (Apt, 1988). The ability to control the labor of others also gives women the time to engage in more lucrative business activities. Rent from tenants also provides an important source of regular income. These resources help insure adequate support and leadership roles for women as they grow old.

A serious problem facing aging Ashanti women is that society offers them unequal opportunities to accumulate the resources needed to build houses of their own. The two main source of cash for women farmers are from cocoa cultivation and from trading. It takes considerable time and effort to establish a cocoa farm. This often places a woman at a disadvantage because her labor is in large part controlled by her husband during her child-bearing years. Although women and men work together, cocoa farming is not regarded as a joint venture. Women expect to receive some land or money as compensation for working on their husbands' cocoa farms. However, there is no guarantee that a wife will be compensated, and inheritance by the wife is often challenged by the husband's family (Okali, 1983; Vellenga, 1986). Women who acquire a cocoa farm usually do so late in life. These holdings are usually small, under-developed, and often do not provide sufficient resources for building a house. Women also sell surplus food crops to obtain cash for petty trading. The recent introduction of practices which discriminate against women has eroded many opportunities for more lucrative, large-scale trading by women (Robertson, 1984; Clarke, 1984). As a consequence of these economic limitations, most of the women house owners in this study obtained their houses either from their husband or their son (Stucki, 1992).

For most rural women who cannot build a house, the ability to ensure old age support is influenced by inheritance of a room in an *abusua* house. This is causing hardships for many women, because housing shortages limit the availability of such rooms, and because there are now many potential heirs for each room. The heir to a room is selected primarily based on seniority and demonstrated need. Under these circumstances, younger sisters who remain in the village are particularly disadvantaged. They must usually find their own housing or live in crowded conditions until they are the most senior of the remaining siblings.

The desperate need for housing often requires that older women share a single 8x10' room with up to eight people, including their adult children and grandchildren.

While housing shortages can provide older women with considerable power, such crowding can also lead to considerable friction among family members. Daughters often decide to migrate to urban areas in search of housing and employment. Many leave their children behind in the village to be cared for by their grandmothers. Poor aging women may face considerable hardship and make great sacrifices to support their grandchildren.

Conclusions

Recent studies suggest that traditional authority and status of older Ghanaians are being undermined by the effects of modernization which weaken traditional family ties. However, it appears that recent housing shortages among rural Ashanti are helping successful older farmers maintain traditional roles as elders. In Ghana as throughout the world, control of resources helps reinforce filial obligation (Rubinstein and Johnson, 1982; Gray and Gulliver, 1964). Older farmers who are heads of households can continue to maintain their authority over junior family members, and can establish strong networks of support through ties of patronage and child care.

Since women are able to earn their own income through trading or cash crop farming, one of the most significant recent changes is that now both men and women are in a position to build security in old age through house ownership. However, housing shortages are also resulting in significant problems for the majority of rural Ashanti women. Older women have been disadvantaged in their life chances of accumulating sufficient resources to build houses, due to unequal access to education and economic opportunities.

In developing countries such as Ghana, the lives of women remain embedded in the extended family. The courtyard house provides a framework within which to build and reinforce the social connections which bind the generations. Within this context, the design and implementation of housing policies must address both the special needs and strategies of women to create security for their old age.

References

Adadevoh, B.K. 1985, "The impact of modernization on traditional family support systems for the elderly in Africa;" in: Z. Bankowski and J.H. Bryant, eds., *Health Policy, Ethics and Human Values*, Geneva: Council for International Organizations of Medical Sciences.

Apt, N, 1988, " Aging in Africa," in: E. Gort, ed., *Aging in Cross-Cultural Perspective*, New York: Phelps-Stokes Fund.

Brown, C.K., 1984, *Improving the Social Protection of the Aging Population in Ghana*. Legon: University of Ghana, ISSER Technical Publication Series.

Caldwell, J.C, 1966, "The erosion of the family: A study of the fate of the family in Ghana," *Population Studies,* 20:5–26.

Clarke, G., 1984, *The Position of Asante Women Traders in Kumasi Central Market, Ghana,* Cambridge: Cambridge University, Department of Social Anthropology. Ph.D. thesis.

deLaski-Smith, D.L., 1985, "Housing and the Elderly: Intergenerational Family Settings," *Journal of Housing for the Elderly, 2*(3): 61–70.

Ewusi, K. 1984. The Dimensions and Characteristics of Rural Poverty in Ghana. Legon: University of Ghana, ISSER Technical Publication 43.

Fortes, M., 1953, "Kinship and marriage among the Ashanti," in A.R. Radcliffe-Brown and D. Forde, eds., *African Systems of Kinship and Marriage,* London: Oxford University Press.

Golant, S.M, 1992, *Housing America's Elderly*, Newbury Park: Sage Publications.

Gray, R.F., and P.H. Gulliver, 1964, *The Family Estate in Africa,* London: Routledge and Kegan Paul.

Lawton, M.P., 1989, "Three Functions of the Residential Environment," in *Lifestyles and Housing of Older Adults: The Florida Experience*, L.A. Pastalan, and M.E. Cowart, eds., New York: Haworth Press.

Okali, C., 1983, *Cocoa and Kinship in Ghana*, London: Paul Kegan International.

Robertson, C. 1984. *Sharing the Same Bowl: A Socioeconomic History of Women and Class in Accra, Ghana*, Bloomington: Indiana University Press.

Rubinstein, R.L., and P.T. Johnson, 1982, "Toward a comparative perspective on filial response to aging populations," in J. Sokolovsky, ed., *Aging and the Aged in the Third World, Part 1,* Williamsburg, VA: College of William and Mary, Dept. of Anthropology.

Stucki, B.R., 1992, "The long voyage home: Return migration among aging cocoa farmers of Ghana," *Journal of Cross-Cultural Gerontology,* 7:363–78.

Sutherland, R.D.G., 1981, *The Outdoor Room*, Kumasi, Ghana: University of Science and Technology, Master's thesis.

Twumasi, P.A., 1987, "Aging and problems of old age in Africa: A study in social change and a model for its solution," in L. Lennart, ed., *Society, Stress and Disease,* Volume 5: *Old Age*, Oxford: Oxford University Press.

United Nations, 1980, *Demographic Indicators of Countries: Estimates and Projections as Answered in 1980*, United Nations Publication No. E.82.XIII.5.

Vellenga, D.V., 1986, "Matriliny, Patriliny, and Class Formation
    Among Women Cocoa Farmers in Two Rural Areas of
    Ghana," in C. Robertson and I. Berger, eds., *Women and
    Class in Africa*, New York: Africana Publishing Co.

Wilde, J.C. de, 1980, "Case Studies: Kenya, Tanzania, and Ghana," in
    R.H Bates and M.F. Lofchie, eds., *Agricultural
    Development in Africa*, New York: Praeger, pp. 113–69

Woode, E.B., 1969, *A Study of the Courtyard House (with Reference
    to the Traditional Akan Family House Forms*, Kumasi,
    Ghana: University of science and Technology, Master's
    thesis.

Epilogue

State Senator Lana Pollack is in her third term in the Michigan Senate, having first taken office in 1983. She is a member of the Appropriations Committee, serving on its subcommittees on capital outlay, natural resources, and agriculture. Among her achievements is a law which requires detention of domestic violence offenders until arraignment. She has travelled extensively around the world and has lived and worked in Zambia and the United Kingdom.

In a brief presentation to the Shelter, Women, and Development conference participants at a banquet on Saturday, May 8, 1992, Senator Lana Pollack spoke about the issue of women and empowerment and the processes by which this is achieved. Her words are very germane to the larger objectives of this conference and these proceedings. She struck a sensitive chord in the gathering of highly trained women architects, planners, university professors, activists, and policy makers present in the room, in pointing out that in the U.S., as in many parts of the world,

> Women are deterred from entering certain professions, and if they do enter them are kept from rising to the top of those professions, for example, librarians are women, library directors are primarily men, school teachers are women, principals and superintendents are usually men, hospitals are staffed primarily by females but are managed and run mostly by men. Thus there is both a vertical segregation by field of endeavor and a horizontal segregation by rank along gender lines which results in the appearance of women in certain places as a cause of wonderment

What does this universal truth mandate for women who do achieve such positions in the professions, in academic institutions, in the realm of policy making and regulation? Lana Pollack was elected following only three other women in the State Senate, which was first convened in 1835. Reflecting on her experiences, she recollected an occasion, when she had first gone to Lansing as a new senator, being introduced in a small group of colleagues as "Lana" when all the others, males, in the group were referred to as "Senator." When she corrected her colleague, saying "Senator, that is Senator Pollack," her colleague replied, "I have difficulty in calling you Senator." She answered, "Practice."

Senator Pollack demonstrated that women need to learn ways of consolidating and applying the use of the power that they achieve through very hard work, in fields that are not receptive to their presence or readily respectful of their achievements. As Senator Pollack explained,

> My point is not that I need the formality of my title or any other title. That is not what is significant. My point is that I will demand the respect that is generally associated with somebody who has earned that which I have earned. I know, and I have learned this, that with good humor or otherwise we must demand for ourselves the same respect that comes to men in similar positions. Just achieving the position is not enough, demanding the respect, and asserting the authority that comes with that position is the second job that we women must assume. It does make running the race more difficult. We have the problem of being different both by virtue of our gender and by the fact that that

difference can be trivialized. This adds an extra burden to our task. In a related situation I found, in a collegial, at times heated, conversation between a small group of senators in which adversarial positions were being taken, that one of my colleagues, a male, would apologize only to me for differences in opinion. I responded, "Don't apologize for disagreeing with me, because I won't apologize for disagreeing with you." The fact is that men can find it difficult to deal with women in an adversarial position. This senator and others are confused by my presence in the Senate halls.

Asserting that one is an equal, with equal power, is sometimes required to be able to exercise the power that comes with that authority and that position.

In terms of working specifically on women's issues Senator Pollack described a path that must have seemed very familiar to those who were in the room, having reached in their own work the need to deal with the specific topic of women's relationship to shelter and its implication for their development. She recounted,

> When I first went to the Senate I did not intend to work on women's issues specifically. I did not want to be pigeonholed in that way. But being a woman in a body that has so few women has been an enormous drain on me. I have found that all issues are women's issues, aspects of workplace safety, access to health care, education, virtually everything has a perspective and voice that is female, that is different because our lives are different, and that perspective is usually missing in the discourse. The suggested topic for my talk was "policies for women." The fact is every policy needs a woman's perspective, a reality check to see the fit of policy with our lives and the lives of our sisters. But more important for understanding policy is that women need power. For women there will be no sufficiency of sensitive, realistic, pragmatic policy until there is sufficiency of power. We in our lives must understand that. We must aspire to power, we must have ambition, we must eschew the modesty that in many ways through socialization we were raised to assume. We will always be, I hope, supportive, humane, human beings, but I would hope we would become assertive, even aggressive, human beings on behalf of human justice for all — and that includes women. We will ourselves see the ubiquitous absence of women in positions of power and, once seeing our absence we will make eliminating it a part of our professional obligation.

> I am bringing coals to Newcastle when I talk to this gathering about how it is different for women. You have risen to your positions through efforts that I cannot know or understand. You as women have had to do that much more, the personal responsibility of childbearing, of being pleasing without being too attractive, dealing with sexual harassment from bosses and those with authority over you, just the undefined burden of being different, slightly off the norm. All of these things make your life harder, and you stronger. It is claimed that women don't help each other. That has not been my experience. Women have helped me tremendously. I have had excellent support, from women and men. When they reach positions of authority and power, women are under the microscope, in the spotlight. You represent all women. You are under special scrutiny. Under this special scrutiny, as the first to get there, to be there, you are asked when you are walking this tight rope and hoping you will get to the other side without tripping, falling, and stumbling with everyone watching you, to reach down and pull someone else, your sister, up. That is very hard. But I think that is what we have to do. Women have been enormously supportive of me. I try to spend a certain amount of time, every month if not every week, with young women. I think we owe it to our daughters, we owe it to our sisters, to help them and hope that their burden of being a woman is a little lighter than ours.

In stressing the need for women to seek out and accept the positions that offer managerial and resource allocation responsibilities and to exercise the power that accrues with these positions and to use it with a women's perspective in mind, Senator Pollack reinforced a posture that many contributors to this book have reached over long years in their chosen professions. As has been pointed out in the introduction of this book, the relationship of women and shelter is one that is only on the margins of the discourse in architecture and planning. The relationship of shelter to women's development has only been recently recognized in the discourse on women and development, which itself has been peripheral to the mainstream professional efforts in development planning. The work presented in this book is an initial step in considering the importance of shelter in women's development as not just a First World, or a Third World, but a global concern that demands more attention, thought, and action. This conference, as a venue for discourse on the topic, has heartened many younger women working in this area by building the understanding that this is a legitimate and important area for them to turn their energies to. The work of the conference and this book needs to be continued in the academic, practical and policy realms. Hopefully, this book will stimulate such continued effort and investment.

Hemalata C. Dandekar

CONFERENCE PROGRAM

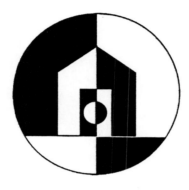

An International Conference and Exhibit

Shelter, Women and Development

First and Third World Perspectives

The College of Architecture and Urban Planning
The University of Michigan, Ann Arbor

May 7 – 9, 1992

Shelter, Women and Development

First and Third World Perspectives

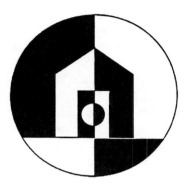

Architects and urban planners have long recognized the importance of housing/shelter to people's sense of well-being and to their social and psychological development. But in national policy deliberations, the provision of housing, especially to lower-income groups, has been viewed as primarily an investment in social welfare. The idea that some component of investment in the housing sector stimulates economic development has only recently gained some currency.

Feminist discourse in architecture and urban planning has quite specifically tried to establish the importance of housing/shelter for the well-being of women and their dependent children. In this they have drawn on the experiences of activists, professionals and service providers and on the opinions of individual beneficiaries of these investments. They have introduced the notion that gender must be considered in the shelter sector, but this emphasis on ways to bring professional service to focus on gender issues has remained marginal despite the fact that there are substantial indications that the international shortage of housing is most importantly a woman's problem.

As the title, *Shelter, Women and Development* indicates, this conference discourse seeks to establish and underscore the linkage of shelter issues with the larger discourse on gender and on development. It brings to focus the idea that a gendered approach to shelter provision can yield development for women. This conference aims to enhance our understanding of the topic and reveal strategies to obtain women's development through shelter provision.

Adopting a general definition of development as meeting basic needs and incorporating intangibles such as self esteem, empowerment, and a capacity to participate and gain from the community, nine themes are to be addressed. Acknowledging that gender-based case studies of shelter often address elements that pertain to several of the nine themes, theme moderators have defined thematic boundaries for operational purposes.

Theme 1
Shelter Policy – Implications for Women's Development
Student Moderators: Vini Aliyar, Sujata Shetty

Two assumptions underlie the formulation of policy related to women-shelter. The first is that difficulties in access to shelter affect men and women equally but are differentiated across income lines. This has served to make income the sole basis for assessing housing needs. The second is the all-pervasive notion that the nuclear family is the norm. However, with the continually increasing trend of non-traditional, single-parent households, past standards have begun to come under increasing scrutiny. This panel will explore the issue from two directions. On the one hand, it will seek to answer questions such as: Is there a strong case for formulating policies geared specifically to the needs of women. If so, what should be the aims of such policies? Who frames such policies and how? What is the time frame under which such policies operate? Do these policies meet strategic and practical gender needs? On the other hand, the panel will look at existing housing policies and critically examine their genesis, evolution and impact. Analysis of housing policies in different countries and the ideas current in the major aid institutions can perhaps shed light on the questions of how far we have come, and how far we have to go, in forging gender-sensitive housing policy.

Theme 2: The Structure of Legal Interventions
Student Moderator: Karen DeGannes

This panel will focus on the historical and existing legacies of the law which perpetuate gender-biased policies. It will examine laws from selected First and Third World nations as they impact the bundle of services associated with women's access to adequate shelter. This examination of legal interventions will necessarily assume two separate units of analysis; (1) the individual woman and (2) the woman with regards to reproductive functions, as care-giver of the family (including non-traditional families) and/or the household. The examination of legal interventions will be divided into three major categories: (1) laws affecting women's reproductive rights, (2) land tenure laws and other laws affecting women's access to resources through the marriage institution, and (3) other laws affecting women's human and social rights which may not on the surface be gender-specific but have latent effects on women's access. The panel will examine how the law itself develops to address women's issues and the contexts in which specific forms of law affecting women are developed. The panel seeks to identify the specific laws which are most in need of gender-sensitive reform and the points at which intervention is most appropriate and feasible.

Theme 3: Shelter and Women in Crisis
Student Moderator: Margrit Bergholz

The absence of appropriate housing options plays a key role in the situation of many women in crisis. Women experiencing spousal abuse, women addicted to drugs or alcohol, women abandoned by their partners, and impoverished women who are physically or mentally ill all may require immediate access to a safe, affordable shelter. Shelter alone, however, is inadequate to assist such women in resolving their crises. The necessity of coordinating affordable shelter with appropriate social services creates a unique challenge to practitioners in both fields. This panel will investigate ways in which organizations from both the First and Third World have met this challenge. The goal is to focus attention on the spectrum of needs of women in crisis and to provide a networking opportunity for practitioners and academics from the First and Third Worlds to exchange ideas and information.

Theme 4: Women's Participation in the Production of Shelter
Student Moderators: Victoria Basolo, Michelle Morlan

This panel will examine examples of women's involvement in the production of shelter with the aim of understanding not only what currently exists in this area but what is possible in the future. Aspects addressed will include: characteristics of the women involved, the organizations they form, and the work that they do. The different contexts from which these successful examples come (socioeconomic, political, and personal) will be examined in an attempt to identify commonalities and differences in contexts and constraints which may limit current efforts and expansion to a larger scale. The objective is to facilitate women's participation in shelter production in other countries which may have similar housing needs. The panel hopes to identify the types of support, technological or planning, which are needed by women active in the production of shelter and the lessons these successes can offer others.

Theme 5: Shelter and Income Opportunities
Student Moderator: Abdi Kusow

Historically, traditional family or kin systems have provided some social security for poor women, thereby reducing their need for cash income. However, current structural economic and social changes, such as the fragmentation of land, technological changes, and migration, have increased the necessity for these women to earn incomes. These changes have also pushed women into the secondary job market which is characterized by low-skill, low-paying jobs. Moreover, cultural restrictions on some Third World women exclude them from participation in the public domain. Therefore an increasing number of third world women have sought to earn income in the informal sector often from work that can take place in the family home. The success of women in such income-generating activities often depends upon their access to proper shelter and property ownership. In light of this, this panel will first look at the perceptual and structural factors that limit women's access to shelter, and how this lack of access hinders women's income-generating opportunities. Second, the panel will examine how some women have skillfully adopted the space within their dwelling in order to carry out income generating activities. Third, the panel will examine some parallel concerns between First and Third World women in relation to shelter and income opportunities. Finally, the panel will address current and future policy implications, and the role of women's organizations in influencing such policies.

Theme 6: Women and Shelter-Related Services and Infrastructure
Student moderator: Moshira El-Rafey

A responsive approach to women's needs in the housing and neighborhood environment must necessarily take into consideration culture and ethnicity as well as responsibility for family life. During the twentieth century, there have been rapid technological and economic changes throughout the world that have greatly impacted women's position in society. Many women now work outside the home, whether by choice or necessity, which affects their needs both inside and outside the home where they access a variety of housing-related services. While their responsibilities for domestic life continue, their integration into the public environment is also needed. In those countries where women can move about freely, their ability to meet family responsibilities is undoubtedly limited by concerns for personal safety, inadequate transportation, travel distances between the home and shelter-related services including shopping, health care, and work. Since women have never been full participants in the decision making process, their voices have been silent or hidden behind male power and control. There is a need therefore, to bring about political and economic reforms in housing and neighborhood design so as to be responsive to women. This panel will identify women's needs for housing-related services. The goal is to strengthen and inform the trend of women's influence on housing policy and to work toward more gender-responsive solutions. The panel will focus on infrastructure in the context of cultural change and continuity, religious and political norms and values, emerging living patterns, and descriptions of physical and social infrastructure redressing women's oppression in their lives.

Theme 7: Non-traditional Living Arrangements: Beyond the Nuclear Family
Student Moderator: Kameshwari Pothukuchi

In the First World and Third World, housing policies have been insensitive to social and demographic changes. This has resulted in a mismatch between the real diversity of family structures and the family as assumed by housing policy. In most cases, across various cultures and regions, women are worse off for not being recognized as heads of families (de facto or de jure) in the planning and design processes, given the contexts of patriarchy and capitalism that impinge on their circumstances. Women have special needs arising out of their roles in production, reproduction and community management. Furthermore, the intangible needs of independence, control, community, security, and opportunities for growth, etc., also are important, given the disadvantaged status of women in general and particularly of women in non-traditional family settings. This panel seeks to raise awareness of the diversity of households that women find themselves in, and the needs that result out of their situations. It addresses the following four broad questions: who are the non-traditional households? what are their shelter needs and problems? why are these not being met? and what are the strategies to address these needs in the context of personal, community and national development?

Theme 8: Design and the Creation of Shelter for Women
Student Moderator: Vassiliki Mangana

Throughout time, cultural and religious requirements concerning the status and position of women have produced distinct typological, functional and even stylistic solutions in domestic architecture of various civilizations. Despite the profound and prolific literature on women's issues, modern western societies have tended to exclude women from the core of architectural theory and practice. Yet, recent social developments have presented actual and urgent problems that call for immediate solutions. The increasing percentages of single women heading households and the issue of homelessness of women often resulting from purely economic reasons but also from domestic violence, alcohol and drug abuse and so forth are some of those problems for which theoretical inquiry and architectural explorations seek to provide answers. A common theme in this panel is the need for transitional and single-female-parent family housing to provide protection, security, safety and home-like appearance. Building for oppressed women, then, should produce spaces that allow them to dwell and subsequently provide the preconditions that will lead to the emergence of their true being. The production of an architecture expressive of such qualities as safety, protection, stability, homeliness that the authors in this panel advocate, will not only contribute to accomplishing a significant social mission, but will also provide the means by which the true nature of women's being, and though it the true nature of humankind in general, can emerge.

Theme 9: Shelter Options for Elderly Women
Student Moderator: Maria M. Yen

As women grow older, shelter which is appropriate to their changing needs is often difficult to locate and secure. Thus, just when issues such as housing affordability, home maintenance, and personal mobility become most challenging, women tend to find themselves alone in their struggle to meet these challenges. In developing countries where elderly women have traditionally remained part of an extended family unit, some face uncertainties as this unit begins to dissolve in the wake of industrialized development. In light of these challenges, consideration of shelter options for elderly women must necessarily be linked to the provision of those services critical to the health and well-being of older women. This panel will focus on the evaluation of shelter options for elderly women across countries and cultures including the particular needs of elderly women who have immigrated to North America and who find their traditional support systems altered or completely erased. The panel will examine various options such as retirement centers, home share programs, ecogenic housing and accessory apartments, and evaluate these options in terms of affordability, access to services, maintenance requirements, safety, and cultural fit. In addition to outlining the opportunities available, the panel will consider the constraints on these opportunities in terms of design, construction costs, zoning regulations and cultural norms. In bringing together the academic and activist communities along with elderly women themselves, it is hoped that this panel will provide a forum and a springboard from which further action can be taken to enhance the shelter choices available to women as they grow older.

LIST OF PARTICIPANTS

Neera Adarkar --- Session 2: Theme 6
    Independent architect and feminist activist, Bombay, India

Faten al-Maddah ------------------------------------- Session 3: Theme 4
    King Faisal University, Dammam, Saudi Arabia

Dr. Meera Bapat ------------------------------------- Session 1: Theme 4
    Architect and planner, SPARC, Bombay, India

Brenda J. Baxter ------------------------------------- Session 2: Theme 8
    Department of Architecture, McGill University, Montreal, Canada.

K.K. Bhatnagar --------------------------------------- Session 5: Theme 1
    Chairman and Managing Director, Housing and Urban Development Corporation, New Delhi, India

Neema Bhatt--- Session 2: Theme 8
    University of Michigan, Ann Arbor, Michigan

Catherine Bishop ------------------------------------- Session 6: Theme 2
    National Housing Law Project, Berkeley, California

Joyce Brown and Diana Capponi ----------------- Session 4: Theme 3
    Nellie's Hostel, Toronto, Canada

Dr. Theresa Cameron -------------------------------- Session 7: Theme 3
    Assistant Professor, University of Colorado, Denver

Dr. Aliye Celik -- Session 3: Theme 4
    Human Settlements Officer, HABITAT, New York

Tasneem Chowdhury --------------------------------- Session 2: Theme 8
    Minimum Cost Housing Group, McGill University, Montreal, Canada

Neela Dabir --- Session 4: Theme 3
    Tata Institute of Social Sciences and Coordinating Officer, Shraddhanand Mahilashram, Bombay, India

Surabhi Dabir --- Session 6: Theme 2
    Senior Reference Specialist, Aspen Systems Corporation, Rockville, Maryland.

Dr. Hemalata Dandekar------------------------------ Session 7: Theme 6
    Professor, College of Architecture and Urban Planing, University of Michigan

Sandra Davis --- Session 8: Theme 4
    Jamaica Construction Collective, Kingston, Jamaica

Valerie Du Plessis ----------------------------------- Session 4: Theme 7
    University School of Rural Planning and Development, University of Guelph, Canada

Dr. Madiha El-Safty --------------------------------- Session 2: Theme 6
    Professor of Sociology, American University, Cairo, Egypt

Dr. Roberta Feldman, Chicago -------------------- Session 2: Theme 6
    Assistant Professor, School of Architecture, University of Illinois, Chicago

Mary J. Follenweider -------------------------------- Session 3: Theme 8
    Shoestring Design, Boulder, Colorado

Patricia Gardiner------------------------------------- Session 2: Theme 1
    San Diego State University, California

Robert Gillette --------------------------------------- Session 7: Theme 3
    Attorney, Legal Services of Southeast Michigan

Carolyn Hastings ------------------------------------ Session 7: Theme 9
    Executive Director, The Housing Bureau for Seniors, Ann Arbor, Michigan

Dr. Frannie Humplick -------------------------------- Session 7: Theme 6
    Infrastructure Systems Analyst Urban Division, The World Bank, Washington, D.C.

Dr. Sharon M. Keigher ----------------------------- Session 6: Theme 9
    Assistant Professor, School Of Social Work, University of Michigan

Dr. Anita Larsson ----------------------------------- Session 3: Theme 2
    The National Swedish Institute for Building Research, Lund, Sweden

Sulakshana Mahajan --------------------------------- Session 6: Theme 5
    Senior Architect, Gherzi Eastern Limited, Bombay, India

Ann H. May -- Session 3: Theme 4
    Assistant Professor, Landscape Architecture, North Dakota StateUniversity, Fargo, North Dakota

David K. May ---Session 3: Theme 4
    Assistant Professor, Landscape Architecture, North Dakota StateUniversity, Fargo, North Dakota

Faranak Miraftab ------------------------------------- Session 6: Theme 5
    University of California, Berkeley, California

Jacqueline M. Mraz ----------------------------------- Session 6: Theme 2
    University of California, Los Angeles

Sylvia Novac--- Session 2: Theme 1
    Ontario Institute for Studies in Education, Toronto, Canada

Yomi Oruwari --- Session 3: Theme 2
    Architect/Lecturer, Dept. of Architecture, River State University, Port Harcourt, Nigeria

Dr. Leon A. Pastalan --------------------------------- Session 7: Theme 9
    Professor, College of Architecture and Urban Planning, University of Michigan

Lynn Peterson -- Session 4: Theme 3
    Project Manager, WINGS and Re-Vision HouseWomen's Institute for Housing and Economic Development, Inc., Boston.

Pamela L. Sayne ------------------------------------- Session 3: Theme 2
    Ontario Institute for Studies in Education, Toronto, Canada

Dr. Norazit Mohd. Selat ----------------------------- Session 6: Theme 5
    Associate Professor, Department of Malay Studies, University of Malaya, Kuala Lumpur, Malaysia

Rama Sethi -- Session 6: Theme 9
    University of Michigan, Ann Arbor, Michigan

Theodore Sevransky --------------------------------- Session 7: Theme 6
    University of Michigan, Ann Arbor, Michigan

Tami Silverman --------------------------------------- Session 3: Theme 8
    Artist and photographer, Fargo, North Dakota

Sara J. Snyder, Jay C. Juergensen --------------- Session 7: Theme 3
    Grateful Home, Inc. Detroit

Joan Forrester Sprague------------------------- Plenary, May 9: Theme 8
    Consulting architect, planner and author Boston, Massachusetts

Dr. Susan J. Stall ----------------------------------- Session 2: Theme 6
    Assistant Professor, Departments of Sociology and Women's Studies, Northeastern Illinois University, Chicago

Barbara R. Stucki ------------------------------------ Session 6: Theme 9
    Public Policy Division, American Association of Retired Persons, Washington D.C.

Kim Tanzer -- Session 3: Theme 8
    Assistant Professor, Department of Architecture, University of Florida, Gainesville, Florida

Chris Taylor --- Session 3: Theme 8
    Department of Architecture and Landscape Architecture, North Dakota State University, Fargo, North Dakota

Carolyn Thompson ----------------------------------- Session 4: Theme 7
    Assistant Professor, Department of Interior Architecture, College of Architecture and Design, Kansas State University, Manhattan, Kansas.

Dr. Irene Tinker -------------------------------------- Session 5: Theme 1
    Professor, Department of City and Regional Planning, University of California, Berkeley, California

Alison Todes -- Session 5: Theme 1
    Lecturer, Department of Town and Regional Planning, University of Natal, Natal, South Africa

Dr. Marta Trejos ------------------------------------- Session 1: Theme 4
    Executive Director, Centro Feminista de Informacion y Accion (CEFEMINA), San Jose, Costa Rica

Dr. Anna Vakil -- Session 2: Theme 1
    Independent planner, Ypsilanti, Michigan

Dr. Ann Varley -- Session 4: Theme 7
    Department of Geography, University College, London

Dr. Gerda Wekerle ----------------------------- Plenary, May 8: Theme 4
    Professor, Faculty of Environmental Studies, York University, Ontario, Canada

Conference and Exhibit Organization

Conference Chair: Dr. Hemalata C. Dandekar
Exhibit Co-Chairs: Professors Melissa Harris and Elizabeth Williams

Student and Faculty Theme Committees:

1 *Shelter Policy: Implications for Women's Development*
   Sujata Shetty, Vinitha Aliyar, Prof. Hemalata C. Dandekar
2 *The Structure of Legal Interventions*
   Karen De Gannes, Prof. Ann Larimore
3 *Shelter and Women in Crisis*
   Margrit Bergholz, Prof. Beth Reed
4 *Women's Participation in the Production of Shelter*
   Victoria Basolo, Michelle Morlan, Prof. Kate Warner
5 *Shelter and Income Opportunities*
   Abdi Kusow, Prof. Gracia Clark
6 *Women and Shelter-related Services and Infrastructure*
   Moshira El-Rafey, Prof. Sharon Sutton
7 *Non-Traditional Living Arrangements: Beyond the Nuclear Family*
   Kameshwari Pothukuchi, Prof. Joanne Leonard
8 *Design and the Creation of Shelter for Women*
   Vassiliki Mangana, Prof. Donna Salzer
9 *Shelter Options for Elderly Women*
   Maria Yen, Prof Sharon Keigher

Book Exhibit: Vinitha Aliyar
Conference Arrangements: Joan Britton, Department of Conferences and Seminars

Conference Sponsors

The United Nations:

   United Nations Centre for Human Settlements (Habitat)
   United Nations Development Fund for Women (UNIFEM)

The University of Michigan:

   The College of Architecture and Urban Planning
   University Council on International Academic Affairs
   Office of Minority Affairs
   Horace H. Rackham School of Graduate Studies
   Office of the Vice President for Research
   Women's Studies Program

PROGRAM AT A GLANCE

DAY 1   **THURSDAY, MAY 7, 1992**

4:00 PM   **Registration**   (Slusser Lobby)
5:30-7:30   **Reception**   (Slusser Gallery)
5:30-6:15   Music by the CAUP Sextet
6:15-6:45   1. Welcome: Hemalata Dandekar
            2. Remarks: Robert Beckley
            3. Gallery Talk: Melissa Harris and Elizabeth Williams
            4. Registration orientation and conference concerns: Joan Britton
6:45-7:30   Music by the CAUP Sextet
7:30 PM   Informal dinners with panelists and moderators (Dutch)

DAY 2   **FRIDAY, MAY 8, 1992**

8:00-8:30   **BREAKFAST***
            (Studio Cafe)

AUDITORIUM	**ROOM 2216-7**	**ROOM 2210**

8:30-10:00 **SESSION 1: PLENARY**
            THEME 4: PRODUCTION (1)
            1. Meera Bapat-SPARC
            2. Marta Trejos-CEFEMINA

10:00-10:30 **Coffee**
            (Art and Architecture Courtyard)

10:30-12:00 **SESSION 2**

THEME 6: INFRASTR. (1)	**THEME 1: POLICY(1)**	**THEME 8: DESIGN (1)**
1. Susan Stall/Roberta Feldman	1. Anna Vakil	1. Brenda Baxter
2. Neera Adarkar	2. Patricia Gardiner	2. Neema Bhatt
3. Madiha El-Safty	3. Sylvia Novac	3. Tasneem Chowdhury

12:00-1:00 **LUNCH***
            (Studio Cafe)

1:00-2:00   **PLENARY**
            THEME 4: PRODUCTION (2)
            1. Gerda Wekerle

2:15-3:45   **SESSION 3**

THEME 2: LEGAL (1)	**THEME 8: DESIGN (2)**	**THEME 4: PRODUCTION (3**
1. Anita Larsson	1. Kim Tanzer	1. Faten al-Maddah
2. Pamela Sayne	2. Mary Follenweider	2. Aliye Celik
3. Yomi Oruwari	3. Chris Taylor/Tami Silverman	3. Ann May/David May

3:45-4:15   **Coffee**
            (Art and Architecture Courtyard)

4:15-5:45   **SESSION 4**

THEME 3: CRISIS (1)	**THEME 7: NON-TRAD. (1)**
1. Joyce Brown/ Diana Capponi	1. Ann Varley
2. Neela Dabir	2. Carolyn Thompson
3. Lynn Peterson	3. Valerie du Plessis

5:45-7:00   The Slusser Gallery will be open for conversation.

7:00-9:00   **DINNER***
            (Michigan Union: Pendleton Room)

DAY 3   SATURDAY, MAY 9, 1992

8:00-8:30   **BREAKFAST***
             (Studio Cafe)

             AUDITORIUM   **ROOM 2216-7**   **ROOM 2210**

8:30-10:00   **SESSION 5: PLENARY**
             THEME 1: POLICY (2)
             1. Alison Todes
             2. K.K. Bhatnagar
             3. Irene Tinker

10:00-10:30 **Coffee**
             (Art and Architecture Courtyard)

10:30-12:00 **SESSION 6**
             THEME 5: INCOME (1)   **THEME 9: ELDERLY (1)**   **THEME 2: LEGAL (2)**
             1. Sulakshana Mahajan   1. Sharon Keigher   1. Surabhi Dabir
             2. Norazit M. Selat   2. Rama Sethi   2. Jacqueline Mraz
             3. Faranak Miraftab   3. Barbara Stucki   3. Cathy Bishop

12:00-1:00   **LUNCH***
             (Studio Cafe)

1:00-2:00   **PLENARY**
             THEME 8: DESIGN (3)
             1. Joan Sprague

2:15-3:45   **SESSION 7**
             THEME 3: CRISIS (2)   **THEME 9: ELDERLY (2)**   **THEME 6: INFRASTR. (2)**
             1. Theresa Cameron   1. Lee Pastalan   1. Frannie Humplick
             2. Sara Snyder/ Jay Juergensen   2. Carolyn Hastings   2. Hemalata Dandekar
             3. Robert Gillette   3. Theodore Sevransky

3:45-4:00   **Coffee**
             (Art and Architecture Courtyard)

4:00-4:30   **THEME 4: PRODUCTION (4)**
             1. Jamaica Construction Collective

4:30-6:00   **PLENARY CLOSING**
             1. Theme Summaries and Future Directions
             2. Closing Remarks: Hemalata Dandekar

6:30- 8:30   **Pizza/ Beer**
             (Studio Cafe - Optional/ Dutch)

             * FOR REGISTERED PARTICIPANTS (NON-STUDENT LEVEL), OR BY INVITATION.

EXHIBIT CONTRIBUTORS

BUILT PROJECTS AND ORGANIZATIONS

Neighborhood Women Renaissance Housing
Katrin Adams

Mad Housers, Chicago

A Conference and Design Charrette For Alternative Housing,
Boston

East Metro Womens Council
Bowers, Bryan and Fiedt, with Mary Vogel

Passage Community Center
Bowers, Bryan and Fiedt, with Mary Vogel

Garfield School Housing
Bowers, Bryan and Fiedt, with Mary Vogel

Cedar Apartments
Bowers, Bryan and Fiedt, with Mary Vogel

Older Womens Network
Oleson/Worland (Heather Taylor)

Tahanan
Oleson/Worland (Heather Taylor)

Addition to Shelter for Battered Women
Kim Tanzer

Riley Center: Brennan House
Laura Riggs

Sparksway Commons
Mui Ho

The Neil Houston House
August Associates

Concord Assabet
Flavin Architects

Women's Development Corporation
Providence RI

CEFIMINA
Guarari, Costa Rica

Dream Weaver Project
Detroit, MI

PHOTOGRAPHY

Two Oakland Homes
Joanne Leonard

Women in Zimbabwe Cooperatives
Anna Vakil

Women's Participation in Housing Construction in Rural Iran
Faroukh Afshar

Women's Access to Sites and Service Housing Project in
Madras
Hemalata Dandekar

Go In and Out the Window...As We Have Done Before
Laverne Wells-Bowie

Homeless Women in the Bay Area
Tom Levy

Women in Public Housing Mural
Harriet Bellerjeau

PAINTINGS AND SCULPTURE

Warli Paintings from a Tribal Group:
Thana District, Maharashtra State, India
Hemalata Dandekar

Sculpture: "Eggs, Nest..., " Know What You Know", "Holding
Back", and "Interruptions"
Abigail Read

One Apron, Three Generations
Carol Ann Carter

VIDEOS

Housing Ideals and Disappointments: Alternative Housing
Options for Single Parent Families
Wendy Garber

The Women's Constructive Collective of Jamaican
Ruth McCleod, Inter America Foundation

Shelter for the Homeless

Women's Power — a Women's Place Is

MISCELLANEOUS

Excerpts from *Lilian Bloom,* Poetry
Judith Steinbergh

PROGRAM

DAY 1 — Thursday, May 7, 1992

Slusser Lobby, Registration, 4:00 – 8:00

Slusser Gallery, Reception, 5:30 – 7:30

WELCOME
Dr. Hemalata Dandekar
Conference Chair

REMARKS
Robert Beckley
Dean, College of Architecture and Urban Planning

GALLERY TALK
Melissa Harris and Elizabeth Williams
Exhibit Co-Chairs

MUSIC
The College of Architecture and Urban Planning, "CAUP" Sextet

DINNER
Informal (Dutch) dinners with panelists and moderators

Day 2 — Friday, May 8, 1992

Session 1 (Plenary) — 8:30 – 10:00

Breakfast, 8:00 – 8:30, Studio Cafe

AUDITORIUM

Theme 4: Women's Participation in the Production of Shelter (1)
Moderator: Michelle Morlan

1. **WOMEN'S PARTICIPATION IN THE DECISION-MAKING PROCESS WITH RESPECT TO SHELTER**
Dr. Meera Bapat
Architect and planner, Society for Promotion of Area Resource Centres (SPARC0, Bombay, India

2. **WOMEN CREATE THEIR HOMES**
Dr. Marta Trejos
Executive Director, Centro Feminista de Informacion y Accion (CEFEMINA), San Jose, Costa Rica

Coffee, 10:00 – 10:30, Art and Architecture Courtyard

ROOM 2216 –7

ROOM 2210

Session 2 — 10:30 – 12:00

Theme 6: Women and Shelter-Related Services and Infrastructure (1)
Moderator: Dr. Sharon Sutton

1. **HOMEPLACE AS SITE OF RESISTANCE IN CHICAGO PUBLIC HOUSING**
Dr. Susan J. Stall
Assistant Professor, Departments of Sociology and Women's Studies, Northeastern Illinois University, Chicago

Dr. Roberta Feldman, Chicago
Assistant Professor, School of Architecture, University of Illinois, Chicago

2. **SHELTER-RELATED SERVICES AND INFRASTRUCTURE: CASE STUDY, BOMBAY**
Neera Adarkar
Independent architect and feminist activist, Bombay, India

3. **WOMEN AND SHELTER-RELATED SERVICES AND INFRASTRUCTURE: THE CASE OF A VULNERABLE GROUP**
Dr. Madiha El Safty
Professor of Sociology, American University, Cairo, Egypt

Lunch, 12:00–1:00, Studio Cafe

Theme 1: Shelter Policy — Implications for Women's Development (1)
Moderator: Sujata Shetty

1. **COMMUNITY-BASED HOUSING ORGANIZATIONS AS A MEANS OF IMPROVING WOMEN'S ACCESS TO SHELTER: SOME PRELIMINARY FINDINGS FROM ZMBABWE**
Dr. Anna Vakil
Independent planner, Ypsilsnti, Michigan

2. **PUBLIC HOUSING, DESIGN AND GENDER: A HISTORICAL PERSPECTIVE**
Patricia Gardiner
San Diego State University, California

3. **BOUNDARY VIOLATIONS: SEXUAL HARASSMENT WITHIN TENANCY RELATIONS**
Sylvia Novac
Ontario Institute for Studies in Education, Toronto, Canada

Discussant: Vinitha Aliyar

Theme 8: Design and the Creation of Shelter for Women (1)
Moderator: Vassiliki Mangana

1. **DESIGN GUIDELINES FOR HOUSING SINGLE PARENT FAMILIES**
Brenda J. Baxter
Department of Architecture, McGill University, Montreal, Canada

2. **THE SOCIO-ECONOMIC IMPACT OF OPEN SPACES ON WOMEN IN A SPONTANEOUS SETTLEMENT : INDIA**
Neema Bhatt, Ann Arbor
University of Michigan, Ann Arbor, Michigan

3. **SEGREGATION OF WOMEN IN ISLAMIC SOCIETIES AND ITS EFFECTS ON RURAL HOUSING DESIGN: BANGLADESH**
Tasneem Chowdhury
Minimum Cost Housing Group, McGill University, Montreal, Canada

Day 2 — Friday, May 8, 1992

Plenary — 1:00 – 2:00

AUDITORIUM

ROOM 2216 – 7

ROOM 2210

Theme 4: Women's Participation in the Production of Shelter (1)

RESPONDING TO WOMEN'S DIVERSITY: HOUSING DEVELOPED FOR AND BY WOMEN
Dr. Gerda Wekerle
Professor, Faculty of Environmental Studies, York University, Ontario, Canada

Session 3 — 2:15 – 3:45

Theme 2: The Structure of Legal Interventions (1)

Moderator: Dr. Ann Larimore

1. WOMEN'S LEGAL ACCESS TO HOUSING AS A REFLECTION OF THE GENDER SYSTEM: BOTSWANA
Dr. Anita Larsson
The National Swedish Institute for Building Research, Lund, Sweden

2. IDEOLOGY AS LAW: IS THERE ROOM FOR DIFFERENCE IN THE RIGHT TO HOUSING?
Pamela L. Sayne
Ontario Institute for Studies in Education, Toronto, Canada

3. THE INVISIBLE CONTRIBUTION OF MARRIED WOMEN IN HOUSING FINANCE AND ITS LEGAL IMPLICATIONS: A CASE STUDY FROM PORT HARCOURT, NIGERIA
Yomi Oruwari
Architect/Lecturer, Dept. of Architecture, River State University, Port Harcourt, Nigeria

Coffee, 3:45–4:15,
Art and Architecture Courtyard

Theme 8: Design and the Creation of Shelter for Women

Moderator: Vassiliki Mangana

1. LANGUAGE, SACRED AND TRANSITIONAL HOUSING
Mary J. Follenweider
Shoestring Design, Boulder, Colorado

2. SHELTER: A PLACE OF THE TELLING
Chris Taylor, Tami Silverman
Department of Architecture and Landscape Architecture, North Dakota State University, Fargo, North Dakota

3. DEFINING STANDARDS
Kim Tanzer
Assistant Professor, Department of Architecture, University of Florida, Gainesville, Florida

Theme 4: Women's Participation in the Production of Shelter (3)

Moderator: Victoria Basolo

1. TOWARDS A PIONEERING ROLE: WOMEN'S PARTICIPATION IN THE DECISION-MAKING PROCESS IN DESIGN IN SAUDI ARABIA
Faten al-Maddah
King Faisal University, Dammam, Saudi Arabia

2. WOMEN'S ROLE IN THE CONSTRUCTION PROCESS
Dr. Aliye Celik, New York
Human Settlements Officer, HABITAT, New York

3. ISSUES ASSOCIATED WITH PROVIDING ADEQUATE HOUSING FOR SINGLE MOTHER HOUSEHOLDS IN THIRD WORLD COUNTRIES
Ann H. May
Assistant Professor, Dept. of Architecture, North Dakota State University, Fargo, North Dakota

David K. May,
Assistant Professor, Landscape Architecture, North Dakota State University, Fargo, North Dakota

Day 2 — Friday, May 8, 1992

Session 4 — 4:15 – 5:45

AUDITORIUM

Theme 3: Shelter and Women in Crisis (1)

Moderator: Dr. Beth Reed

1. SHELTERING HOMELESS WOMEN, THE LESSONS OF EXPERIENCE IN TORONTO
Joyce Brown and Diana Capponi
Nellie's Hostel, Toronto, Canada

2. SHELTER HOMES, BOMBAY
Neela Dabir
Tata Institute of Social Sciences and Coordinating Officer, Shraddhanand Mahilashram, Bombay, India

3. WINGS, KA-FARM AND RE-VISION HOUSE: CASE STUDIES OF TRANSITIONAL HOUSING FOR WOMEN
Lynn Peterson, Boston, Massachusetts.
Project Manager, WINGS and Re-Vision House, Women's Institute for Housing and Economic Development, Inc., Boston.

ROOM 2216 – 7

Theme 7: Non-Traditional Living Arrangements: Beyond the Nuclear Family (1)

Moderator: Kameshwari Pothukuchi

1. GENDER, IDEOLOGY AND PRACTICE IN SELF-HELP HOUSING: THE PROVISION OF RENT-FREE ACCOMMODATION FOR YOUNG ADULTS IN URBAN MEXICO
Dr. Ann Varley, London.
Department of Geography, University College, London

2. CARE FACILITIES IN CENTRAL EUROPE AS A FORM OF SHELTER: IMPLICATIONS FOR WOMEN
Carolyn Thompson
Assistant Professor, Department of Interior Architecture, College of Architecture and Design, Kansas State University, Manhattan, Kansas.

3. YOUNG MOTHERS AND AFFORDABLE HOUSING: INFORMATION AND ORGANIZATION FOR CHANGE
Valerie Du Plessis
University School of Rural Planning and Development, University of Guelph, Canada

Exhibit viewing and conversation, 5:45–7:00, Slusser Gallery

Conference Banquet, 7:00–9:00, Pendleton Room, Michigan Union.

Fully registered conferees and invited guests will participate in the banquet. The Michigan Union is on Central Campus. A schedule showing stops for the free campus shuttle bus is in conference packets.

Day 3 — Saturday, May 9, 1992

Session 5 (Plenary) 8:30 – 10:00

Breakfast, 8:00 – 8:30, Studio Cafe

AUDITORIUM   **ROOM 2216 –7**   **ROOM 2210**

Theme 1: Shelter Policy- Implications for Women's Development (2)
Moderator: Prof. Hemalata Dandekar

1. WOMEN AND HOUSING POLICY IN SOUTH AFRICA
   Dr. Alison Todes
   Lecturer, Department of Town and Regional Planning, University of Natal, Natal, South Africa

2. WOMEN AND HOUSING POLICY IN INDIA
   K.K. Bhatnagar
   Chairman and Managing Director, Housing and Urban Development Corporation, New Delhi, India

3. U.N. HABITAT POLICIES REGARDING WOMEN IN ASIA
   Dr. Irene Tinker
   Professor, Department of City and Regional Planning, University of California, Berkeley, California

*Coffee, 10:00–10:30,
Art and Architecture Auditorium*

Session 6 — 10:30 – 12:00

Theme 5: Shelter and Income Opportunities (1)
Moderator: Abdi Kusow

1. SHELTER AND INCOME OPPORTUNITIES FOR WOMEN IN INDIA
   Sulakshana Mahajan, Bombay, India
   Senior Architect, Gherzi Eastern Limited, Bombay, India

2. MY HOME IS MY WORLD: WOMEN, SHELTER AND WORK IN A MALAYSIAN TOWN
   Dr. Norazit Mohd. Selat
   Associate Professor, Department of Malay Studies, University of Malaya, Kuala Lumpur, Malaysia

3. SHELTER AS SUSTENANCE: EXCLUSIONARY MECHANISMS LIMITING WOMEN'S ACCESS TO HOUSING
   Faranak Miraftab
   University of California, Berkeley, California

   Discussant: Dr. Gracia Clark

Theme 9: Shelter Options for Elderly Women (1)
Moderator: Maria Yen

1. WHY IS AFFORDABLE, ADAPTABLE AND ASSISTED HOUSING FOR OLDER WOMEN SO HARD TO FIND?
   Dr. Sharon M. Keigher
   Assistant Professor, School Of Social Work, University of Michigan

2. ELDERLY WOMEN'S HOUSING NEEDS IN INDIA AND AS IMMIGRANTS IN THE USA
   Rama Sethi
   University of Michigan, Ann Arbor, Michigan

3. WOMEN, HOUSING AND RETIREMENT: ASHANTI WOMEN IN RURAL GHANA
   Barbara R. Stucki
   Public Policy Division, American Association of Retired Persons, Washington D.C.

Theme 2: The Structure of Legal Interventions (2)
Moderator: Karen DeGannes

1. FAIR HOUSING AMENDMENTS ACT OF 1988: CREATING NEW HOUSING OPPORTUNITIES FOR WOMEN
   Surabhi Dabir
   Senior Reference Specialist, Aspen Systems Corporation, Rockville, Maryland.

2. HOUSING DISCRIMINATION ON THE BASIS OF GENDER: WHY WON'T THE LAW RESPOND?
   Jacqueline M. Mraz
   University of California, Los Angeles

3. TENURE SECURITY FOR LOW-INCOME WOMEN
   Catherine Bishop
   National Housing Law Project, Berkeley, California

Lunch, 12:00–1:00, Studio Cafe

Day 3 — Saturday, May 9, 1992

Plenary — 1:00 – 2:00

AUDITORIUM	ROOM 2216 – 7	ROOM 2210

AUDITORIUM

Theme 8: Design and the Creation of Shelter for Women

1. LIFEBOATS: MORE THAN HOUSING
   Joan Forrester Sprague
   Consulting architect, planner and author, Boston, Massachusetts

Theme 3: Shelter and Women in Crisis

Moderator: Margrit Bergholz

1. RESIDENTIAL CARE OPTION FOR WOMEN WITH AIDS
   Dr. Theresa Cameron
   Assistant Professor, University of Colorado, Denver

2. DREAMWEAVER P.O.W.E.R. PROJECT, DETROIT
   Sara J. Snyder
   Executive Director, Grateful Home, Inc. Detroit

   Jay C. Juergensen
   Project management consultant, Grateful Home, Inc. Detroit

3. WOMEN AND HOMELESSNESS: POVERTY AND VIOLENCE
   Robert Gillette
   Attorney, Legal Services of Southeast Michigan

Coffee, 3:45 – 4:00,
Art and Architecture Courtyard

Session 8 (Plenary) — 4:00 — 4:30

Theme 4: Women's Participation in the Production of Shelter

1. WOMEN IN THE HOUSING PRODUCTION PROCESS: THE JAMAICA EXPERIENCE
   Jamaica Construction Collective, Kingston, Jamaica

Optional Dinner, 6:30–8:30, Studio Café. Join participants for pizza, beer, and conversation. Costs will be shared by the group.

ROOM 2216 – 7

Session 7 — 2:15 – 3:45

Theme 9: Shelter Options for Elderly Women (2)

Moderator: Dr. Sharon Keigher

1. ECOGENIC HOUSING: A NEW HOUSING CONCEPT FOR ELDERLY WOMEN
   Dr. Leon A. Pastalan
   Professor, College of Architecture and Urban Planning, University of Michigan

2. HOUSING NEEDS OF ELDERLY WOMEN: THE WASHTENAW COUNTY EXPERIENCE
   Carolyn Hastings
   Executive Director, The Housing Bureau for Seniors, Ann Arbor, Michigan

ROOM 2210

Theme 6: Women and Shelter-Related Services and Infrastructure (2)

Moderator: Moshira El-Rafey

1. WOMEN AND INFRASTRUCTURE SERVICES
   Dr. Frannie Humplick
   Inrastructure Systems Analyst Urban Division, The World Bank, Washington, D.C.

2. WOMEN'S ACCESS TO SHELTER AND INFRASTRUCTURE: CASE STUDIES IN MADRAS AND BOMBAY
   Dr. Hemalata Dandekar
   Professor, College of Architecture and Urban Planing, University of Michigan

3. WOMEN AND SHELTER-RELATED INFRA-STRUCTURE
   Theodore Sevransky
   University of Michigan

Plenary Closing — 4:30 – 6:00
AUDITORIUM
Theme Summaries and Future Directions (5 minutes each)

Theme 1: Sujata Shetty	Theme 6: Dr. Sharon Sutton
Theme 2: Dr. Ann Larimore	Theme 7: Joanne Leonard
Theme 3: Dr. Beth Reed	Theme 8: Vassiliki Mangana
Theme 4: Dr. Kate Warner	Theme 9: Dr. Sharon Keigher
Theme 5: Dr. Gracia Clarke	Closing Remarks
	Dr. Hemalata Dandekar

List of Conference Participants

Neera Adarkar
  Architect, Bombay, India

Vinitha Aliyar
  University of Michigan College of Architecture & Urban
  Planning (U-M CAUP), Ann Arbor, Michigan

Frank Aukeman
  U-M CAUP, Ann Arbor, Michigan

Meera Bapat
  Society for Promotion of Area Resource Centres (SPARC),
  Bombay, India

Vickie Basolo
  U-M CAUP, Ann Arbor, Michigan

Robert M. Beckley
  U-M CAUP, Ann Arbor, Michigan

Margit Bergholz
  U-M CAUP, Ann Arbor, Michigan

K.K. Bhatnagar
  Housing and Development Corporation (HUDCO),
  Government of India, New Delhi, India

Neema Bhatt
  U-M CAUP, Ann Arbor, Michigan

Catherine Bishop
  National Housing Law Project, Oakland, California

Lynn Bjorkman
  U-M CAUP, Ann Arbor, Michigan

Laura Briggs
  U-M CAUP, Ann Arbor, Michigan

Beverly Brockman
  U-M CAUP, Ann Arbor, Michigan

Joyce Brown
  Nellie's Hostel, Toronto, Canada

Theresa Cameron
  University of Colorado at Denver, Colorado

Diana Capponi
  Nellie's Hostel, Toronto, Canada

Robert Carpenter
U-M CAUP, Ann Arbor, Michigan

Francisco Castano
University of Michigan Business Administration, Ann Arbor, Michigan

Aliye Celik
UNCHS - Human Settlement Office, New York, New York

James Chaffers
U-M CAUP, Ann Arbor, Michigan

Dave Chapman
U-M CAUP, Ann Arbor, Michigan

Tasneem Chowdhury
School of Architecture, McGill University, Montreal, Quebec

Susan Christian
Michigan Housing Trust Fund, Lansing, Michigan

Gracia Clark
University of Michigan Anthropology Department and Center for Afro-American and African Studies, Ann Arbor, Michigan

Beckey Conekin
U-M CAUP, Ann Arbor, Michigan

Gerald Crane
U-M CAUP, Ann Arbor, Michigan

Neela Dabir
Shraddhanand Mahila Ashram, Bombay, India

Surabhi Dabir
Aspen Systems Corporation, Rockville, Maryland

Hemalata Dandekar
U-M CAUP, Ann Arbor, Michigan

Eva Darvas
University of Michigan, Ann Arbor, Michigan

Robert Darvas
U-M CAUP, Ann Arbor, Michigan

Karen DeGannes
University of Michigan School of Natural Sciences and Environment, Ann Arbor, Michigan

Margaret Dewar
U-M CAUP, Ann Arbor, Michigan

Lisa Docter
U-M CAUP, Ann Arbor, Michigan

Michael Dorsey
University of Michigan School of Natural Sciences and Environment, Ann Arbor, Michigan

Mary Ann Drew
U-M CAUP, Ann Arbor, Michigan

Valerie Du Plessis
University of Guelph, Ontario, Canada

Allison Dutoit
U-M CAUP, Ann Arbor, Michigan

Moshira El-Rafey
U-M CAUP, Ann Arbor, Michigan

Madiha El-Safty
The American University, Cairo, Egypt

Lisa Erhards
U-M CAUP, Ann Arbor, Michigan

David Ernst
U-M CAUP, Ann Arbor, Michigan

Jeff Etelamaki
U-M CAUP, Ann Arbor, Michigan

Roberta Feldman
University of Illinois School of Architecture, Chicago, Illinois

Allan Feldt
U-M CAUP, Ann Arbor, Michigan

Mary Follenweider
Herndon & Associates, Denver, Colorado

Lynn Forrester
U-M CAUP, Ann Arbor, Michigan

Wendy Garber
University of Wisconsin at Milwaukee, Wisconsin

Patricia Gardiner
San Diego State University, San Diego, California

Robert Gillette
Legal Services of Southeast Michigan

Raoul Goulet
U-M CAUP, Ann Arbor, Michigan

Matthew Greene
U-M CAUP, Ann Arbor, Michigan

Bonnie Greenspoon
U-M CAUP, Ann Arbor, Michigan

Melissa Harris
U-M CAUP, Ann Arbor, Michigan

Helen Hartnett
Ohio State University Center for Women's Studies and
Social Work, Columbus, Ohio

Carolyn Hastings
Housing Bureau for Seniors, Ann Arbor, Michigan

Ana Hinton
U-M CAUP, Ann Arbor, Michigan

Earl Holbrook
U-M CAUP, Ann Arbor, Michigan

Frannie Humplick
Urban Division of the World Bank, Washington, DC

Diego Jordan
University of Cincinnati College of Design, Art,
Architecture and Planning, Cincinnati, Ohio

Michael Kampreth
U-M CAUP, Ann Arbor, Michigan

Sharon Keigher
University of Michigan, Ann Arbor, Michigan

Susan Kevorkian
Ann Arbor, Michigan

Habibullah Khan
Ohaka, Bangladesh

Salma Khan
National Planning Commission, Government of Bangladesh,
Dhaka, Bangladesh

Mark Krecic
U-M CAUP, Ann Arbor, Michigan

Neema Kudva
University of California at Berkeley, California

Abdi Kusow
U-M CAUP, Ann Arbor, Michigan

Ann E. Larimore
University of Michigan Women's Studies, Ann Arbor,
Michigan

Anita Larsson
National Swedish Institute for Building Res., Lund, Sweden

Jerold Lax
U-M CAUP, Ann Arbor, Michigan

Arleen Lee
U-M CAUP, Ann Arbor, Michigan

Joanne Leonard
University of Michigan School of Art, Ann Arbor, Michigan

Janet Lineer
University of Michigan Space Physics Research Laboratory,
Ann Arbor, Michigan

Johanna Looye
University of Cincinnati School of Planning, Cincinnati,
Ohio

Melissa Lucksinger
U-M CAUP, Ann Arbor, Michigan

Sulakshana Mahajan
Gherzi Eastern Limited, Bombay, India

Veena Mandrekar
U-M CAUP, Ann Arbor, Michigan

Vassiliki Mangana
U-M CAUP, Ann Arbor, Michigan

Robert Marans
U-M CAUP, Ann Arbor, Michigan

Ann H. May
North Dakota State University Department of Architecture
and Landscape Architecture, Fargo, North Dakota

David May
North Dakota State University Department of Architecture
and Landscape Architecture, Fargo, North Dakota

Eric McDonald
  U-M CAUP, Ann Arbor, Michigan

Mark Miller
  U-M CAUP, Ann Arbor, Michigan

Faranak Miraftab
  University of California at Berkeley, California

Carla Morelli
  Massachusetts Institute of Technology Architecture and
  Urban Studies, Cambridge, Massachusetts

Michelle Morlan
  U-M CAUP, Ann Arbor, Michigan

Bob Moustakas
  U-M CAUP, Ann Arbor, Michigan

Suki Mwendwa
  University of Nairobi, Kenya

Lisa Newberry
  U-M CAUP, Ann Arbor, Michigan

Sylvia Novac
  Ontario Institute for Studies in Education, Toronto, Ontario,
  Canada

Gerhard Olving
  U-M CAUP, Ann Arbor, Michigan

Yomi Oruwari
  Rivers State University of Science and Technology, and
  Department of Architecture, Port Harcourt, Nigeria

Peter Osler
  U-M CAUP, Ann Arbor, Michigan

Fritz Paper
  U-M CAUP, Ann Arbor, Michigan

David Pate
  Ounce of Prevention, Chicago, Illinois

Sandy Patton
  U-M CAUP, Ann Arbor, Michigan

Lyn Peterson
  Women's Institute for Housing and Economic
  Development, Boston, Massachusetts

Analise Pietras
  U-M CAUP, Ann Arbor, Michigan

Kameshwari Pothukuchi
  U-M CAUP, Ann Arbor, Michigan

Shally Prasad
  University of Michigan Institute of Public Policy Studies,
  Ann Arbor, Michigan

J. Lane Randolph II
  University of Cincinnati College of Design, Art, Architecure
  and Planning, Cincinnati, Ohio

Tracey Robilliard
  Accessing Information for Young Mothers, Burlington,
  Ontario, Canada

Michael Romanowski
  University of Hawaii, Honolulu, Hawaii

Deborah Rosenstein
  University of Michigan School of Natural Resources, Ann
  Arbor, Michigan

Magnus Rothman
  Uppsala, Sweden

Donna Salzer
  University of Michigan, Ann Arbor, Michigan

Pamela Sayne
  University of Toronto Ontario Institute for Studies in
  Education, Toronto, Ontario, Canada

Erik Schultz
  U-M CAUP, Ann Arbor, Michigan

Bernard Schwartz
  U-M CAUP, Ann Arbor, Michigan

Martin Schwartz
  U-M CAUP, Ann Arbor, Michigan

Norazit Selat
  University of Malaya, Kualalumpur, Malaya

Rama Sethi
  U-M CAUP, Ann Arbor, Michigan

Ted Sevransky
  University of Michigan, Ann Arbor, Michigan

Sujata Shetty
U-M CAUP, Ann Arbor, Michigan

Tami Silverman
North Dakota State University, Fargo, North Dakota

Lily Singh
Nellie's Hostel, Toronto, Canada

Sara J. Snyder
Grateful Home, Inc., Detroit, Michigan

Don Sonnta
U-M CAUP, Ann Arbor, Michigan

Daniel Sonntag
U-M CAUP, Ann Arbor, Michigan

Aditya Sood
U-M CAUP, Ann Arbor, Michigan

Carolyn Spatta
California State University at Hayward, California

Joan Sprague
Sprague Consulting, Architecture and Planning, Boston,
Massachusetts

Susan Stall
Northeastern Illinois University Department of Sociology,
Chicago, Illinois

Alan Steiss
U-M CAUP, Ann Arbor, Michigan

Barbara Stucki
Amercan Association of Retired Persons, Silver Spring,
Maryland

Sharon Sutton
U-M CAUP, Ann Arbor, Michigan

Kim Tanzer
University of Florida, Gainesville, Florida

Chris Taylor
North Dakota State University, Fargo, North Dakota

Ken Thomas
U-M CAUP, Ann Arbor, Michigan

Carolyn Thompson
Kansas State University Department of Interior
Architecture, Manattan, Kansas

Irene Tinker
University of California at Berkeley, California

Alison Todes
University of Nabal Department of Regional Planning,
Duban, South Africa

Jim Turner
U-M CAUP, Ann Arbor, Michigan

Anna Vakil
Ypsilanti, Michigan

Ann Varley
Unviersity College London, United Kingdom

Christine Weisblat
Galesburg, Michigan

Gerda Wekerle
York University, North York, Ontario, Canada

Betsy Williams
U-M CAUP, Ann Arbor, Michigan

Crystal Wilson
U-M CAUP, Ann Arbor, Michigan

Regina Winters
Yale School of Architecture, New Haven, Connecticut

Mark Womble
U-M CAUP, Ann Arbor, Michigan

Maria Yen
U-M CAUP, Ann Arbor, Michigan

Carrie Yoon
U-M CAUP, Ann Arbor, Michigan

List of Books Exhibited

Book Exhibit

A Development Primer. 1984. Boston, MA.: Women's Institute for Housing and Economic Development.

A Guide to Your Rights for Women. (n.d.) San Francisco, CA.: Bay Area Women's Center.

Agrest, D. I. 1991. *Architecture From Without: Theoretical Framings for a Critical Practice.* Cambridge, MA.: The MIT Press.

Buroway, M., *et al.* 1991. *Ethnography Unbound: Power and Resistance in the Modern Metropolis.* Berkeley, CA.: Univ. of California Press.

Buvinic, M., and Mehra, R. *Women in Agriculture: What Development Can Do.* Washington, D.C: ICRW

Child Care: An Annotated Bibliography. 1990. Bibliography #5. Geneva: ILO.

Cooper-Marcus, C., and Sarkissian, W. 1986. *Housing As If People Mattered.* Berkeley, CA.: University of California Press.

Dandekar, H. *Beyond Curry: Quick and Easy Indian Cooking.* Ann Arbor, MI.: CSSEAS Press.

Dandekar, H. *Men to Bombay: Women at Home.* Ann Arbor, MI.: CSSEAS Press

Dreaming a Different Reality—Challenge and Change: Creating New Traditions. Minneapolis, MN.: IWRAW.

Everett, J. *The Global Empowerment of Women.* Blacksburg, VA.: VA Tech.

Ferguson, R., Gever, M. *et al.* 1990. *Marginalization and Contemporary Cultures.* Cambridge, MA.: The MIT Press.

Ferrill, L. 1991. *A Far Cry From Home: Life In a Shelter for Homeless Women.* Chicago, IL: The Noble Press.

Finimore, B. 1989. *Houses From the Factory: System Building and the Welfare State.* London, UK.: Rivers Oram Press.

Golden, S. 1992. *The Women Outside: Meanings and Myths of Homelessness.* Berkeley, CA.: University of California Press.

Harris, M. 1991. *Sisters of the Shadow.* Norman, OK.: University of Oklahoma Press.

Hayden, D. 1981. *The Grand Domestic Revolution: A History of Feminist Designs for American Homes, Neighborhoods and Cities.* Cambridge, MA.: The MIT Press.

Hayden, D. 1984. *Redesigning the American Dream: The Future of Housing, Work and Family Life.* New York: WW Norton and Co. Inc.

ICRW Annual Report. 1991. Washington DC.: ICRW.

Kozol, J. 1988. *Rachel and Her Children: Homeless Families in America.* New York: Crown Publishing.

Lycette, M., and Jaramillo, C. *Low-Income Housing: A Women's Perspective*. Washington, DC.: ICRW

Lynch, P. D., and Fahmy, H. 1984. *Craftswomen in Kerdassa, Egypt*. Washington DC.: ILO. (Women, Work and Development #7)

Mies, M. 1986. *Indian Women in Subsistence and Agricultural Labor*. Washington, DC.: ILO. (Women, Work and Development #12)

Moghadam, V. M. 1990. *Gender, Development and Policy: Toward Equity and Empowerment*. Helsinki, Finland: World Institute for Development Economics Research of the U. N. University.

Moghadam, V. M. 1992. *Privatization and Democratization in Central and Eastern Europe and the Soviet Union: The Gender Dimension*. Helsinki, Finland: World Institute for Development Economics Research of the U. N. University.

More Than Shelter: A Manual on Transitional Housing (n.d.). Boston, MA.: Women's Institute for Housing and Economic Development Inc.

Mulroy, E. (ed.). 1988. *Women as Single Parents*. New York: Auburn House.

Planning and Developing Transitional Housing: Sample Administrative Forms for Housing Programs. Boston, MA.: Women's Institute for Housing and Economic Development Inc.

Redburn, S. F., and Buss, T. F. 1986. *Responding to America's Homeless: Public Policy Alternatives*. New York: Praeger Publishers.

Roberts, M. 1991. *Living In a Man-Made World: Gender Assumptions in Modern Housing Design*. New York, NY.: Routledge, Chapman and Hall.

Rosenberry, S., and Hartman, C. (eds.). 1989. *Housing Issues of the 1990s*. New York: Praeger.

Rousseau, A. M. 1981. *Shopping Bag Ladies: Homeless Women Speak About Their Lives*. Cleveland, OH: The Pilgrim Press.

Sprague, J. F. 1988. *Taking Action: A Comprehensive Approach to Housing Women and Children in Massachusetts*. Boston, MA.: Women's Institute for Housing and Economic Development Inc.

Sprague, J. F. 1991. *More Than Housing: Lifeboats for Women and Children*. Boston, MA: Butterworths.

Steinbergh, J. 1980. *Lillian's Bloom: A Separation*. Green Harbor, MA: Wampete Press.

Steinbergh, J. 1983. *Motherwriter*. Green Harbor, MA.: Wampete Press.

Steinbergh, J. 1988. *A Living Anytime*. Green Harbor, MA.: Wampete Press.

The Future of Women in Development: Voices From the South. 1990. Proceedings of the Association for Women in Development Colloquium. The North South Institute

Whitehead, C. M. E., and Cross, D. T. 1991. *Affordable Housing in London*. New York: Pergammon Press.

Wilson, E. 1991. *The Sphinx in the City*. Berkeley, CA.: University of California Press.

Wright, G. 1981. *Building the Dream: A Social History of Housing in America*. New York: Pantheon Books.

Zarembka, A. 1990. *The Urban Housing Crisis: Social and Economic and Legal Issues and Proposal*. New York: Greenwood Press.

Working Papers From WID Michigan State University

Berik, G. 1989. *Born Factories: Women's Labor in Carpet Workshops in Rural Turkey* (#177).

Chaney, E.M., and Lewis, M.W. 1985. *Women, Migration and the Decline of Smallholder Agriculture* (#97).

Chasin, B.H. 1990. *Land Reform and Women's Work in a Kerala Village* (#207).

Christiansen-Ruffman, L. 1987. *Wealth Re-Examined: Toward a Feminist Analysis of Women's Development Projects in Canada and in the Third World* (#140).

Devi, A.K.R. 1989. *Women in Agriculture and Rural Areas—India* (#183).

Engle, P.L., and Kinser, S.L. 1989. *The Intersecting Needs of Working Mothers and Their Young Children: Comparing Theory and Expectations Cross-Culturally* (#196).

Ferree, M.M., and Gugler, J. 1984. *The Participation of Women in the Urban Labor Force and in Rural-Urban Migration in India* (#46).

Gallin, R.S.; Whittier, P.; and Graham, M.A. 1985. *Research and Policy: An Analysis of the Working Papers on Women in International Development* (WID Forum 85-V).

Heath, D. 1990. *Class and Gender: Social Uses of Space in Urban Senegal* (#217).

Joel, S. 1990. *Women Factory Workers in Less Developed Countries* (#214).

Kurwijila, R.V. 1990. *The Role of Appropriate Technology in Reducing Women's Workload in Agricultural Activities in Tanzania* (#208).

Longwe, S.H. 1990. *Toward a Strategy for Increasing Women's Participation in Economic Development* (WID Forum XVIII).

Longwe, S.H. 1990. *From Welfare to Empowerment: The Situation of Women in Development in Africa, a Post UN Women's Decade Update and Future Directions* (#204).

McLellan, S. 1985. *Reciprocity or Exploitation? Mothers and Daughters in the Changing Economy of Rural Malaysia* (#93).

Mencher, J.P. 1989. *South Indian Female Cultivators and Agricultural Laborers: Who Are They and What Do They Do?* (#192).

Morsy, S.A. 1985. *Familial Adaptations to the Internationalization of Egyptian Labor* (#94).

Mueller, A. 1991. *In and Against Development: Feminists Confront Development on Its Own Ground* (#219).

Nelson, C., and Saunders, L.W. 1986. *An Exploratory Analysis of Income-Generating Strategies in Contemporary Rural Egypt* (#122).

Norris, W.P. 1985. *The Social Networks of Impoverished Brazilian Women: Work Patterns and Household Structure in an Urban Squatter Settlement* (#84).

Segal, M.T. 1986. *Land and Labor: A Comparison of Female- and Male-Headed Households in Malawi's Small-Holder Sector* (WID Forum X).

Smith-Sreen, P. 1990. *Women's Cooperatives—A Vehicle for Development* (#201).

Strassmann, W.P. 1985. *Home-Based Restaurants, Snack Bars, and Retail Stores: Their Contribution to Income and Employment in Lima, Peru* (#86).

Viswanath, V. 1989. *Extending Credit to Rural Women: Ngo Models From South India* (#184).

Watson-Franke, M-B. 1986. *The Urbanization and Liberation of Women: A Study of Urban Impact on Guajiro Women in Venezuela* (#121).